MEMOIRS OF MY PEOPLE
THROUGH A THOUSAND YEARS

BOOKS BY

LEO W. SCHWARZ

THE JEWISH CARAVAN
GREAT STORIES OF TWENTY-FIVE CENTURIES

A GOLDEN TREASURY OF JEWISH LITERATURE

WHERE HOPE LIES

MEMOIRS OF MY PEOPLE
THROUGH A THOUSAND YEARS

MEMOIRS OF MY PEOPLE

THROUGH
A THOUSAND YEARS

SELECTED AND EDITED BY

LEO W. SCHWARZ

PHILADELPHIA
THE JEWISH PUBLICATION SOCIETY
OF AMERICA
5705–1945

Gift of Jewish Chautauqua Soc. 1945

CONTENTS

FOREWORD   ix

INTRODUCTION   xiii

BOOK ONE: *FLOOD TIDE OF REMEMBRANCE*

FAMILY ALBUM   3
     Ahimaaz ben Paltiel

LOGBOOK OF A PHYSICIAN   15
     Moses Maimonides

EVERY MAN HIS OWN MESSIAH   21
     Abraham Aboulafia

BY THE WATERS OF THE TAGUS   30
     Judah Asheri

CASTILIAN VIGNETTE   37
     Menahem ben Zerah

ADVENTURE IN THE HOLY LAND   40
     Meshullam ben Menahem

TWILIGHT OF SPANISH GLORY   43
     Don Isaac Abravanel

THE ROAD TO ROME   48
     David Reubeni

POPE, EMPEROR, AND THE INQUISITION   62
     Solomon Molko

THE STORY OF MY IMPRISONMENT   68
     Yomtob Lipmann Heller

LIFE IN LOMBARDY   75
     Leone da Modena

vi CONTENTS

My Double Life and Excommunication   84
Uriel da Costa

Trouble in the Siena Ghetto   95
Joseph da Modena

Memories of an Unhappy Childhood   103
Anonymous

My Joys and Sorrows   115
Glückel of Hameln

Defeat of Satan   128
Jacob Emden

I Was a Slave   139
Abraham Hertz

King for a Night   143
Pinhas Katzenellenbogen

Daybook of an Adventurer   149
Simon von Geldern

Victory for Justice   161
Ber Birkenthal

Pioneer in Sweden   166
Aron Isak

A Kabbalist in Paris   182
Hayyim David Azulai

A Trip With Israel Baalshem   190
Meir Margolis

My Struggle With Amazons   192
Solomon Maimon

Wedded to the Muse   208
Mendele Mocher Seforim

How I Wrote My Songs   221
Eliakum Zunser

Love Found a Way   233
Ezekiel Kotick

Life of a Humorist   243
Sholem Aleichem

CONTENTS

MEMORIES OF CHILDHOOD 248
Ahad Ha'am

BEFORE THIRTY 254
Hayyim Nahman Bialik

CHILDHOOD IN LITHUANIA 269
Rebecca Himber Berg

BOOK TWO: *TANGLED DESTINIES*

WHEN THE BRITISH CAPTURED SAVANNAH 283
Mordecai Sheftall

I PROTECTED OLD GLORY 287
Mordecai Manuel Noah

MENDOZA, THE FAMOUS PUGILIST 292
Daniel Mendoza

A SALONIST REMEMBERS 313
Henriette Herz

SCHOOLDAYS 319
Leopold Zunz

THE STAMP OF MY BEING 325
Heinrich Heine

ROTHSCHILD OF ARTISTS 356
Moritz Oppenheim

VANITIES OF YOUTH 367
Ferdinand Lassalle

MY MOTHER'S MAGIC 376
Berthold Auerbach

MUSICAL RECOLLECTIONS 378
Heymann Steinthal

TORAH IN AMERICA 383
Isaac Mayer Wise

MY SOUL'S TRUE NATIVE LAND 390
Georg Brandes

WELLSPRINGS OF MY FAITH 395
Luigi Luzzatti

A Festival Reverie 404
Israel Abrahams

Preface to Skepticism 412
Fritz Mauthner

The Death and Birth of an Artist 420
Boris Schatz

From Russian Pale to Argentinian Pampas 430
Marcos Alperson

Birth Pangs in Zion 443
Moses Smilanski

Birth of a Zionist 459
Theodor Herzl

The Prophet's Language—and the People's 482
Eliezer ben Yehuda

My Life in San Francisco 489
Rebekah Kohut

The Anarchist Ideal 504
Abraham Frumkin

My Road to Hasidism 514
Martin Buber

In the Wake of the Russian Revolution 523
Jacob Masé

The World Is My Fatherland 529
Ernst Toller

On the Mount of Olives 539
Jessie E. Sampter

Israel, Lost and Regained 544
Edmond Fleg

Sources and Literature 568

Index 591

FOREWORD

SINCE this huge gallery of self-portraits is the first of its kind in any language, I will comment briefly on the literature that has been included. The earliest account in the volume was written in the first half of the eleventh century and the latest within our own memory. Thus a panorama of a thousand years unfolds itself, a dramatic record of the experiences of men and women who form one of the most civilized branches of the human race. Their personal histories, vividly related in diaries, memoirs and letters, are more than the lives of worthies and plain folks; they are the embodiment of a tradition that created an unquenchable hunger for life and an undying faith in its goodness. Enshrined in these *documents humaines* are the despairs, the consolations and the strivings that comprise the immortal saga of modern life.

Scholars have lamented the dearth of memoirs in Jewish literature. While there is just cause for lamentation, more such materials exist than has been suspected. My own research indicates that a large number of journals and reminiscences are rotting away in family trunks and in dust-covered bundles of family papers. It is heart-rending to contemplate the wealth of documents that has been lost in the havoc of recent years, or, like half of Theodor Lessing's masterpiece, *Einmal Und Nie Wieder,* has been deliberately destroyed by the Nazis. Even the published memoirs are largely buried in learned publications or are unavailable in English. The fifty-nine selections chosen for this collection are mostly rendered from foreign tongues (the bulk from Hebrew, Yiddish and German; the remainder from Latin, Italian, French, Danish, and English), and several are printed from manuscript for the first time. For those who enjoy following a stream to its sources, I have noted the relevant literature in appendices which chart the original sources.

The principles I have employed in the organization of the contents are considerably influenced by the desire to make this a book for popular reading. First, I have reduced to a minimum the scholarly paraphernalia which is boring, if not exasperating, to the general reader. This has required the incorporation of explanatory notes into the body of the narrative, leaving only such footnotes as heighten the interest of the story. Secondly, the translations are uniformly free. Where the original is cast in a literary form unpalatable to modern taste, as in the case of the rhymed prose of Ahimaaz ben Paltiel and Don Isaac Abravanel, or where the language is unliterary or debased, as in the tale of Pinhas Katzenellenbogen, I have tried to render them into clear, fluent English. The prose of medieval Hebrew writers is studded with biblical quotations and allusions, and I have followed their example by keeping biblical phrases as an integral part of the text. The counsel of that versatile genius Maimonides seems to me still to be worth following. "Any translator," he wrote to Samuel ibn Tibbon in 1199, "who intends to render a work from one language to another merely by rendering word for word, and slavishly following the order of the chapters and sentences in the original, will come to grief. The product of his labor will be unintelligible and ludicrous. That method is utterly incorrect. The first step is to read the original until the translator is fully at home in it and has complete understanding of what the author has written. Then he should render the contents clearly and idiomatically. However, this can be done only if he grasps syntax by the neck and vigorously shakes it, changing the order of paragraphs and words, substituting many words for one when necessary and vice versa, and altering punctuation until the translation reads clearly, gracefully and meaningfully." Finally, I have limited the selections written after the eighteenth century to pure autobiography. Correspondence and travelers' notebooks, though filled with personal experiences, are vast independent branches of literature. In the Introduction I have made further observations on the scope and spirit of the selections.

How incredibly recent the interest in autobiographical Jewish literature is may be indicated by a few illustrations. I have already noted the lack of an adequate bibliography. Encyclopaedias and library catalogues in the main have passed over the subject as though a literature did not exist. When Letteris, an outstanding bibliophile of the last century, published his memoirs in 1868, he listed less than two dozen predecessors! A few scattered articles on the subject have appeared in scholarly publications, but, however helpful, they hardly intended to make an exhaustive survey. I was myself amazed to discover upon checking my notes that I had accumulated more than six hundred (including manuscript materials) individual references. The Americana items alone, especially from the South and the regions west of the Mississippi, have become so abundant that my publishers have agreed to issue a separate collection.

My good fortune in this regard is largely due to the interest and helpfulness of friends on several continents. It would require pages to name all of them, and I can hardly thank them adequately. I have tried to acknowledge specific obligations in the Notes. But I must record here my indebtedness to Dr. Henry R. Lydenburg, former Librarian of the New York Public Library, for granting me certain privileges in the course of my study, and to the staff of the Jewish Room of the same library for cheerful cooperation; to Professor Gershom Sholem of the Hebrew University in Jerusalem for the use of the memoir of Aboulafia's disciple out of his *Major Trends in Jewish Mysticism,* and to Professor Martin Buber of the same University for permission to include his unique *Mein Weg zum Chassidismus;* to Mrs. Tamara Berkowitz Kahana of Tel Aviv, Palestine, the granddaughter of Sholem Aleichem, for her translation of his brief life; to Dr. Julian Morgenstern, President of the Hebrew Union College in Cincinnati and to Professor Alexander Marx of the Jewish Theological Seminary in New York, for reprinting respectively the anonymous documents I have entitled *Trouble in the Siena Ghetto* and *Memories of an Unhappy Childhood;* to Mrs. Stephen S. Wise for the use of her translation of Fleg's *Pourquoi Je Suis Juif;* to the Trustees of the Jewish Publication Society of America for the Asheri selection from I. Abrahams' *Hebrew Ethical Wills.* Particularly I am indebted to Mr. Marcel Grilli of New York for the translation of the Luzzatti selection, to Mr. Samuel Kreiter and Mr. Maurice T. Galpert for several translations from the Yiddish and Hebrew; and I am under greater obligations than I can express to my fellow-translators, Miss Libby Benedict of New York and Mr. Israel M. Lask of Jerusalem, Palestine. I wish to thank also my friends, Professor Shalom Spiegel of the Jewish Institute of Religion and Henry Hurwitz, editor of *The Menorah Journal,* for reading parts of the typescript and for many helpful criticisms. Finally, I wish to express my deep appreciation to my publishers without whose generous cooperation it would have been impossible to complete the undertaking.

LEO W. SCHWARZ

New York City
May, 1942

INTRODUCTION

I

THE anthologist, like the historian and the novelist, is an autobiographer in disguise. He is driven into the jungles and watering places of literature by instinct as well as by design. The ultimate form in which he exhibits his loot is dictated not only by public taste; it is above all the expression of those fundamental impulses and habits that lead him to the library-cubicle rather than to the market-place. For this reason, and for weightier ones that will soon appear evident, I shall endeavor to explain autobiographically, in part at least, the genesis and character of this book.

II

During my university years I had the good fortune of being guided down the labyrinth of my people's checquered career by one of our most brilliant teachers and scholars. No Harvard student ever left the lecture hall of Professor Harry A. Wolfson without the feeling that he had been in the presence of a towering repository of learning as well as a man of keen wit and imagination. When he elucidated a puzzling historical or philosophical text, perplexities melted away like fog in the sunshine. He revealed the punctures in the universes of Aristotle, of Maimonides, and of Averroes with uncanny diagnostic skill; he was no less adept in cutting through the distortions of centuries and recreating the texture of great minds. His matchless studies of Spinoza and Crescas testify amply to this. Yet, some years after I had left Cambridge, I soon realized that, despite my continuing studies in the same field, my appreciation of the 4,000-year Jewish experience was dangerously one-sided. There were sources, periods, books, personages galore. But what of their taproots—the wonderful vigor, passion and yearning of the people? I had certainly failed to see the emotional glow and color of passing generations, the electric contact between men, women and children linked enduringly by a passionately remembered experience, the nobility and the degradation of the inarticulate common man. In short, I had failed to understand the essential spirit, the hot-burning heart of my people.

Probably, I am typical of my contemporaries. As I write, a clinching illustration has reached me in a letter from a young business man. "The other night you opened up a new field for me", he writes, alluding to a lecture. "I have always felt proud of being a Jew in a sentimental way, but I never had a cultural basis for this feeling. It has always seemed that the knowledge I could possess exists in the Hebrew and Yiddish tongues, neither of which I read. I majored in history and psychology at college, and I once even ventured to write a paper in a history course on 'The Jews in Europe during the Middle Ages'. But I was greatly handicapped by my ignorance of Hebrew. My general impression was that the Jews were a people of the Book and have been persecuted ever since. Could you guide me to some literature that would give me an insight into the living experiences of Jews? Not merely pogroms and pietists, but the pageant of their customs, traditions, thoughts—their day-to-day life with its problems, conflicts, joys, loves. As you indicated, we are witnesses to something more than commentaries and tears."

While the reason for this shortcoming might conceivably be attributed to ignorance—the bewildering haze of four millennia has cowed more informed minds—it is more likely to be found in the rather prevalent scholastic approach to the Jewish humanities. To continue with myself as a guinea pig, I recall the study, during college years, of historical texts in the admirable Hebrew volumes of Abraham Kahana. Imbedded among them were excerpts of experience told in the first person. (Incidentally, many of them appear in this book for the first time in English translation.) These revelations of character passed over my mind almost without making a dent. I was intent only on the light that these passages threw upon the development of legal and religious tradition. It hardly occurred to me then that such personal accounts and piquant details were revelations of central significance or that the manner of life of the narrator might be something more than a chunk of literary archeology. I did not look upon them as expressions of the "life-drive" that gave a peculiar cast to the living tradition and helped to explain the epic of group survival. Nor had I discovered that an intimately personal anecdote, a tactless letter, or a flash of humor, brings us closer to the stuff of life than a papal bull or a rabbinical responsum. I was lacking, in Gamaliel Bradford's fine phrase, in psychographic experience.

That experience came, fortunately. I cannot point to any event or moment when a radical change of attitude was markedly noticeable.

In retrospect, I can detect a number of contributing and connecting causes that operated gradually and simultaneously. First of all, there was a warm association with the Menorah Movement. I first came into contact with it through the channel of the Harvard Menorah Society, then was infected by the wonderful pages of *The Menorah Journal,* and finally developed happy friendships with some of its leading spirits. In that most distinguished of Jewish literary periodicals in English and in Menorah circles, the phrase "Jewish heritage" underwent a vital transformation: it became, implicitly and explicitly, modern and contemporary. The past became a lamp to illuminate the present, and in turn what happened before took on new significance. For example, I recall how upon re-reading the prophet Ezekiel, who had previously appeared to me as a cramped mystic nursing his private apocalypse in Tel Aviv by the River Chebar, I now rediscovered him as an emigré thinker, uprooted from home and culture, agonizing over the fate of his people and of civilization, hoping passionately through the chaos and despair of a world catastrophe, and finally attempting, in a literary work, to reconstruct a picture of the world in which he would like to live. I realized that he was in his day what Thomas Mann and Eduard Beneš are to liberty-loving Germans and Czechs today.

I do not want to give the impression that the Menorah circle was concerned only or chiefly with the rehabilitation of the past. Far from it. It had drawn together scholars, writers, artists, musicians, creative workers in every field of intellectual endeavor in order that they might lend their magic to the stuff of Jewish culture and dreams. How many young writers found their first sympathetic audience and opportunity in this oasis! Irving Fineman, Albert Halper, Meyer Levin, Marvin Lowenthal, Charles Reznikoff, Cecil Roth, to mention but a few. Here, too, the sternest critical standards were maintained; the chaff was separated from the wheat without fear of those who placed interest above truth. The effect was to give vital meaning, for Jew and non-Jew alike, to a much abused and misunderstood stream of culture. That, in any case, was the impact upon my own thinking and thus a strong leaven in altering the perspective of my outlook.

Another influence of paramount importance was derived from my participation in two separate yet not unrelated movements, Zionism and Hasidism. I came upon Zionism first, even though it developed after Hasidism had lost its hold on the mind of the people. My earliest contact with Zionism was made in a club organized by the Intercollegiate Zionist Society in Townsend Harris Hall High School, but it was a dull affair and left little impression upon me. In my later years at college, however, I was electrified by a small group of ardent student Zionists, and found myself swept up in the emotional drive of the movement. Palestine, in our ecstatic vision of it, became the fulcrum of our thoughts and the Hebrew language and literature were the instruments of individual salvation. We met, read, debated, collected funds for Palestinian agencies, and put aside trifling sums in a savings account in the hope of settling ultimately in a Palestinian commune. There was comradeship of a high order, such as one rarely finds in student clubs. I recall vividly a celebration arranged by the group on the evening that the Hebrew University in Jerusalem was inaugurated. The chairman(now a rabbi and Zionist leader) read passages from the Hebrew essays of Ahad Ha'am, a classical scholar read the Latin greeting of Harvard to the newest institution of learning, we sang Hebrew songs, talked animatedly about the new page of history that Palestine would write, and devoured enormous quantities of pretzels and light drinks. I was deeply touched by the significance of the occasion and had a difficult time, during the readings, to sit through with dry eyes. I mention this incident to show the personal emotion and loyalty generated by the ideal inherent in Zionism. Some years later, in the colonies and cities of Palestine, I witnessed the transformation of this spirit into a deeply-felt consciousness of being: it provided its bearers with a habitation and a name. Imperceptibly, each adherent became a tiny stream converging to make a rising Jordan. You will readily understand, then, the shift of interest from past to present, even though the center was fixed in Palestine; and, through the participation in constructive social effort, the natural growth of a spirit of active hopefulness.

Now, it was in the course of these associations that I developed an intense curiosity for the lore of Hasidism. I had acquired from hearsay in my youth and from the standard histories the notion that this religious and social movement of the eighteenth and nineteenth centuries was a relapse of the illiterate masses into a warped mysticism. This view was challenged only when I stumbled upon Martin Buber's graceful essay on Nahman of Brazlaw on a shelf in the rarely-used library of the Semitic Museum in Cambridge. I was further stimulated by the magnificent presentation of Ansky's *Dybbuk* by the famous Moscow Habima Company, following the memorable performances from Boston to Worcester and then to New York. But the impulse to delve into the folklore and literature, and later the psychology, of the movement stemmed from a young European (now a Palestinian writer) who himself was brought up in a hasidic home and community and, as a leader of Hashomer

Hatzair, a Zionist pioneer movement dedicated uncompromisingly to co-operative living, had blended these nationalistic and religious tendencies into a kind of mystical nationalism. In him the élan of Hasidism was vibrant, and with quiet eloquence he transferred it to a sympathetic listener. He introduced me especially to the writings of Nahman of Brazlaw, revealing those unrecorded nuances that are part of the feeling of the initiated. From then on my fascination for the extraordinary array of hasidic personalities (how William James would have delighted, had he known of them, to treat of their experiences in his classic *The Varieties of Religious Experience!*) grew and with it an increasing curiosity in personal experience. One of the first autobiographies that intrigued me was a little work in which Nahman's amanuensis Boswelled him. Without conscious effort I began to search for memoirs, and it was natural that I should come upon the engrossing works of Gamaliel Bradford who had, as no other writer before, mastered the whole field of auto-biographical literature. But this takes us to a later period, and another vital experience was in progress.

The third and last impetus that I shall sketch here came from an unexpected quarter. During the years 1931-1935 I directed a small experimental project in Jewish education in Westchester, New York. A group of forty or more children, largely from cultivated, liberal homes, met in small round-table sessions, and it was my task to provide some knowledge and understanding of the culture group in which they found themselves, in harmony with the progressive spirit of their schools and homes. The experience of the children would be a digression here but at least one parent has written a long account.*

I quickly learned, among other things, the truth of a talmudic sage's epigram: "I have learned much from my teachers, even more from my colleagues, but from my pupils more than from all of them." These intelligent young Americans put a man on his mettle. They take little for granted, they insist upon substance, they will tackle a problem or topic with zest and imagination, if—and only if—they are convinced or feel it is organically related to the throbbing panorama of which they are a part, and they have an irrepressible sense of humor. I recall a lad of thirteen, endowed with an acute intelligence, who for some time remained lukewarm about the class. I failed to win his interest until he felt that he was being challenged. A few weeks before the Purim holiday, hoping to interest him in biblical literature

* "The Westchester Experiment," by Ruth Sapin Hurwitz, *The Menorah Journal*, Vol. XXV, No. 2, pp. 195-207 (1937).

(I made a point always of giving the student, whenever possible, the text rather than a second- or third-rate commentary), I asked him whether he might not like to read the Book of Esther and tell me what he thought of it. He consented without any display of enthusiasm, and the following week I inquired whether he had gotten around to the Esther tale.

"Yes," he replied, and I thought I detected a curious sparkle in his eyes.

"Did you enjoy it?"

"It's a pretty good story, pretty good."

"Do you think you could improve upon it?" I ventured.

"Yes," he shot back, without blinking an eyelash.

I encouraged him to try his hand at it. The following week he quietly placed in my hands a very original product. He had retold the story in the form of a satirical musical comedy which not only kept the group and their parents in stitches, but also provided a motive for the conspirators which is lacking in the biblical account.

I could relate many tales equally revealing, but I must cling to the main point. These youngsters, alive to the furious tempo of the times— they keenly discussed the big issues of the day, the New Deal, Fascism, Nazism, Soviet Russia, antisemitism, War and Peace, etc.—became sensitive indicators of the revolutionary forces that are remaking the world. In their appetite for biographical detail (which for lack of adequate literature in English I could whet but not satisfy) they deepened my own understanding and quickened a desire to prepare reading materials suitable to a highly autobiographic generation. My previous anthologies, *The Jewish Caravan* and *A Golden Treasury of Jewish Literature,* were the immediate products of that happy association. This book, tempered of course by the unsurpassable upheavals of the past decade, as well as the above-mentioned evolution, is another by-product.

III

My preoccupation with autobiography during recent years has convinced me that personal narratives of experience, aside from being a mine of entertainment, are the clearest mirrors of character and culture. Certainly this is true of the stream of experience of which the autobiographers in this book are a part. To be sure, their accounts are slices of history and frequently pages of literature. But the personalities that people these pages and the hundred little dramas they enact are essentially human nature in action with its infinite range of tragedy and joy, of absurdity and nobility. In what other form of expression can one find a deeper consciousness of the community of human beings? Or the meaning of human bondage and human freedom?

If you are in doubt, ponder for a moment the motives that impelled these men and women to record their experiences. With some it is vanity, imitation, profit, discipline, with others the urge for immortality, but with the majority it is the overpowering need to express themselves. A shattering event has broken their lives, inner pain tortures their spirits, an historic upheaval has cast them from their moorings—they must willy-nilly write down their reactions. "These notes of mine," writes Herzl, "are no labor to me but merely relief." Glückel, driven no less inexorably by the pain of bereavement, recounts her tale "in the hope of distracting my soul from the burdens laid upon it" so that she may "live through many wakeful nights." Stranded in Petersburg during the revolution of 1917, the historian Dubnow writes in his diary, "March 22nd. A momentous day. The Provisional Government published a declaration of religious and national matters, i.e. a declaration emancipating the Jews of Russia. The dream of a lifetime, the goal of four decades of struggle and suffering had been realized. I cannot grasp the whole dramatic range of this historic act. Later on when we are somewhat removed from it, when the terrible clouds that stand before the gates like a German Hannibal will have been dissolved in the sunny heaven of history, we will be able to feel the warmth through a new clarity of vision, and splendor will flow down upon us." On November 28th, just as he is mourning the death of the writer Mendele Mocher Seforim, "the bright star of the best days of my life," he makes another jotting: "English troops have marched into Jerusalem. The epoch of Turkish rule over Palestine has come to an end—1517 to 1917—precisely four hundred years. How long will this one last? Our masses, under the influence of Zionist agitation, begin to believe in a free Palestine but they will certainly be cheated out of their hopes. Yet, whatever perspective opens, it is a gleam of light in the midst of Egyptian darkness. . . ." Natural catastrophes also incite the memory. Leone de Modena, one of the most curious autobiographers in the gallery, tells us that when he was seven months old his parents fled Ferrara because of a great earthquake. Another survivor of the disaster, the distinguished Azariah dei Rossi, was impelled to describe the experience:

Friday, the 18th of November, 1571, was a memorable day. At about ten o'clock, when folks were peacefully asleep, the rumbling of a violent earthquake was heard. It lasted about three minutes. Nothing like it has happened in our time nor have our forebears reported anything to match it for centuries. Frightening detonations resounded from the sky whereupon roof-gutters tottered and roofs moved and clashed with such force that anyone who heard the din—and who could have been so deaf as not to have heard it?—felt a tingling in the ears and a pain in the heart. Every moment brought new horrors, forcing upon one the belief that the earth was cracking open and the world was coming to an end.

At first, in the interval between being shocked out of sleep and the sudden destruction, the people thought that the disaster had been caused by fire or that a storm had shook the earth violently. They did not realize what was happening until every bed moved and tossed about like a toy. Then everyone understood that the turbulence was in reality an earthquake, causing the earth to burst and shift. Those who kept their heads praised God whose might fills the world. They waited silently, hoping that God would relent His fury, set the world fast again, and give us peace. Soon, the earth appeared to be at rest. But God had not turned away His anger, as we supposed, for the earth continued to shake at periodic intervals until morning and her bowels were in constant ferment. Many who counted the small tremors during those three hours testified that there were more than eighteen. As a consequence, all the people arose from their beds and waited fearfully to see what would happen to the city. Towers and chimneys, indeed everything that was high, were cast down by the first great tremor. And as soon as it was light enough to recognize a person the people hurried into the city and wandered about the streets, examining the heaps of debris and discussing the remarkable event.

While they were thus engaged and Friday advanced to the nineteenth hour, a quake of medium force occurred. Similarly, in the twenty-second hour and in the first and second hours of Sabbath. All these tremors, even though they were not as vehement as the first, unsettled and terrified the householders. Then, about the third hour of that fearful Sabbath night, there suddenly broke loose upon the country and the people a terrifying tremor which also lasted about three minutes. It cast down buildings, demolished walls, caused clefts in the homes, to an even greater extent than the first quake. In the first, the din was greater than the impact; in the latter, the situation was the reverse. I noted also that these tremors did not follow any one direction but crisscrossed, going first from west to east and then from south to north as though the intention were to wreak destruction everywhere. It was this tremor which caused most of the clefts and destruction here in Ferrara. All the compact buildings, especially the corner structures in the markets and streets that were without the support of nearby buildings, were completely demolished. The whole population of Ferrara, young and old, fled from their homes to open spaces. They left their goods and chattels in ruins and unguarded for they were plagued by the fear that the house might suddenly collapse. That is precisely what happened here and there to more than seventy citizens who did not flee quickly enough so that their homes became their tombs.

Among the generous wardens of Ferrara who should be highly praised are Don Isaac Abravanel (the grandson of the great Spanish noble who bore the same name), Isaac Berachia, Joseph Halevi, and Aaron Danieli. They opened their houses, courtyards, and enclosed gardens to all those, rich and poor, who had been bereft of their homes and possessions. Some of them harbored at least a hundred souls; they fed and clothed the poor, providing for all needs such as fuel.

I, too, must praise the mercies of the Lord Who took me from the jaws of death. During the big quake on the night of the Sabbath the roof of my house fell in, destroying my bedroom and living room. I and my family would have been killed by the falling bricks and beams, but by some miracle we happened to be in my daughter's room which remained intact. Then we were like the other victims, wandering hither and thither. We heard many tales of how other householders were miraculously saved. Certainly God's hand was visible in the fact that, although about a dozen churches and monasteries were wrecked and almost two hundred persons killed, in all the devastation of our homes not a single Jew perished. Thereupon I decided, in the tradition of our sages, to record this awful happening in a book as a testimony to the might of the Lord Whom every living soul will glorify forever.

These recordings are neither naughty gossip nor prying curiosity; they constitute in large measure spiritual exchange of a high order. The quality of the writer's character is refracted in the confession. Autobiography is the product of psychological conditions that express the core of culture as art represents its aspiration.

Those who are concerned with semantics will discover decisive illustrations to their search for the meaning of words in these personal narratives. Recently I heard an intelligent young psychologist comment on the much discussed phenomenon of "self-hatred" among Jews, or "Jewish antisemitism". (The phrase "self-hatred" was coined by the eminent thinker Theodor Lessing and the practice of it elaborated in his unique little book *Der jüdische Selbsthass*.) I was shocked by his flagrant misinterpretation of a psychological condition which Lessing had described and illustrated with precision. This psychologist proposed as examples the novelist Jakob Wassermann and the critic Georg Brandes. As the latter speaks for himself in this book, I continue with Wassermann. Wassermann, the apostle of justice who never, in his own words, fought with the closed visor! Wassermann, the author of *The Jews of Zirndorf, Etzel Andergast* and *Of Service to Life!* The man who declared in his *My Life as a German and a Jew,* "I do not wish to display a martyr's crown or to exult in suffering. Nor am I one who, having broken his ties in both camps, seeks refuge in boastful isolation. Nor one who, with the crushed pride and sullen obstinacy of the rejected, lays plots and sows dissension, suddenly rediscovers and clings to venerable ancient loyalties because his membership in the group of his intellectual choice is disputed!" The psychology of frustration assumes many diverse forms; the one which ultimately can be labeled "antisemitic" must be carefully weighed and tested by every instrument at our command before the label is irrevocably applied. Incidentally, I know of no more precise, compact phrasing of this problem than Disraeli's description of his grandmother: "My grandmother, the beautiful daughter of a family which had suffered much from persecution, had imbibed that dislike for her race which the vain are too apt to adopt when they find that they are born to public contempt. The indignant feeling that should be reserved for the persecutor, in the mortification of their disturbed sensibility, is too often visited on the victim; and the cause of annoyance is recognized, not in the ignorant malevolence of the powerful, but in the consciencious conviction of the innocent sufferer."

It is unfortunate but understandable that the ordeal of modern life has exacted a heavy toll in the case of gifted, sensitive Jews. But wherever there is self-esteem, the intense inner struggle lifts the spirit to the loftiest heights of affirmation and achievement. I will close this section with an account of the great actress Alla Nazimova who is now engaged in completing her memoirs. Her brief, poignant Odyssey will probably strike a familiar chord for many readers.

I am a Jewess, a full-blooded one, too, and I am proud of it. But unfortunately, I am Jewish by birth only, since I was never given my birthright of Jewish knowledge. My parents were Russian intellectuals, atheists, and freethinkers who believed in no religion. As a very small child, I was taken to Switzerland and put in the care of a non-Jewish family, who also were cold intellectuals and determined atheists.

Even my dolls were taken away from me as they felt that there was no room in life for imaginative sentimentality. And those dolls that I loved were sold to an ugly, unkempt old man, with a big pack on his back, who came to our back door every month to buy all the things we no longer needed. They referred to him as the "Jew." When I was naughty these foster-parents threatened to sell me to the old man who would take me away in his sack. That was my first impression and knowledge of a Jew. Naturally, it was far from pleasant!

When I was ten years old, my father came to Switzerland to take me back to my native Russia. We had to pass through Galicia and a group of Jews came on the train. When I saw them and recognized that they were Jews, I became hysterical with fright and screamed with terror, "They're Jews, they're Jews!"

My father, embarrassed and angry, and not understanding the phobia that had been developed in me, slapped me in the face and said, "Sh-h, I am a Jew too. Your mother is a Jewess and you yourself are Jewish."

So, you see, I was "conditioned", as the psychologists would say, against Jews in my early childhood. My parents never again referred to their Jewishness and I was never taught anything positive about Judaism to counterbalance my early impressions. All the people who came to our home were atheists and intellectuals, always excitingly discussing problems, but never a Jewish one. Now that I look back, I realize that almost all our relatives intermarried, many were baptized. I remember only an uncle who was a Jew.

He was the family saint. A gifted surgeon, the government offered him enticing positions if he would become converted to Catholicism, but he chose to live among his people in the ghetto. Up and down the crowded alleys he spent his life, never accepting money for his services, consequently living in poverty. The people idolized him. The family didn't understand him, but we all loved him. He was truly saintlike, and oh, how noble! My other uncle was baptized and became a famous judge. He had money, prestige, power and everything.

I had one Greek Catholic grandmother, under whose care and influence I was. My intense emotional nature was starved in the rationalistic environment of my home, and I became enraptured with the first forms of religion that she taught me. I immediately told my father that I wanted to become a Greek Catholic, but he forbade me to seek baptism until I was seventeen. But at that age, I was attracted to Roman Catholicism, and when I was twenty, I was baptized. Not until it was too late, did I realize that it would never bring me inner happiness!

For I am still a Jewess. No matter how many times I crossed myself in my early youth, I know that by instinct and emotion, I am a Jew. And that the Jews are my people. But I had to learn all that, and that learning was painful. It was punctured by theosophism and other isms, and has left me a barren thing—a religious orphan.

Of Judaism, its philosophy, its spirit or its tradition, I know nothing. My Jewish friends sent me matzos and poppy-seed cakes —food for the Jewish body—but food for the Jewish spirit, no one has ever given me. And yet, I once acted as a Jewess. Doesn't that seem a whim of fate?

The second part of this volume, "Tangled Destinies," presents the whole gamut of modern figures, ranging from pugilist to philosopher, valiantly standing their ground before the storms of our age. In my opinion, they are worth tons of psychoanalysis.

IV

If you are seeking the eternally human element in the main stream of Jewish life and history, you will find it in the torrent of memory overflowing in the pages of the first part of this volume. You will find flesh-and-blood beings—martyrs and merrymakers, rabbis and rapscallions, sages and sinners—with all their virtues as well as faults laid bare. They go through life, as we do, facing every conceivable problem, living tragically and joyfully, forgiving "wrongs darker than death or night" and hoping "till hope creates from its own wreck the thing it contemplates". These men and women are tough with a spiritual fiber that the best histories could hardly portray, and they tell their tales with heartthrob and spirit. Neither honey nor gall is lacking. A medieval poet sums this up in a couplet:

Knowledge held their minds and hearts in thrall,
And God's anointment made them more than kings.

You will note also the strong sense of community feeling and the
prodigious attachment to intellectual effort. I mention these because they
help to explain why I have launched this collection in midstream rather
than at the source. The first tale is by an Italian poet of the eleventh
century, and the dramatis personae move across an Eastern Mediterranean
stage. What of the Biblical epoch, the Greek and Roman epochs? Simply
this: Virtually no autobiographical literature is extant from these times.
It may be and some biblical scholars are convinced that the prophetic
and other luminaries wrote memoirs, but the biblical editors chose to
include only the merest fragments.* From the Roman period we possess
only the imitative *Life* of Josephus, which Lion Feuchtwanger has used
to good advantage in his trilogy devoted to him and his times. Until
the Middle Ages there is a virtual blank, and it is really only in the last
century and a half that memoirs have poured forth in cornucopian
fullness. The gist of the matter is given in the admirable introduction
of Henrietta Szold to the memoirs of Rebekah Kohut: "That Jewish
literature should be deficient in personal material lay in the nature of
Jewish life as it was perforce constituted. In the overwhelming sum of
communal woe and communal aspiration, the individual sank out of
sight. His personal desires, trials, successes were frail straws rapidly
swirled out of sight on the stream of community life." From the Jewish
point of view, the public weal was better served by reticence than by
self-expression. In the moving drama of Israel, the chorus alone was
vocal. Only at critical times it would happen that the recluse scholar
disengaged himself from the background as a speaking character, to
admonish in the face of spiritual backsliding, or encourage in the face
of danger; or the man of affairs was forced into leadership, to save his
brethren by his wealth or his resourceful wit, when expulsion or massacre
threatened. These two outstanding figures are not tempted to self-
revelation. The scholar's word spoke for him; the intercessor's was too
delicate to court publicity. They remained silent, and by their silence
emphasized the relation of the individual to the community and of the
community to the individual. Fortunately, there were exceptions, both
among the leaders and the people, and they have made the first part of
this book possible.

---

* Amos, chaps. VII-IX; Isaiah, VI-VIII; Hosea, III; Ezra, VII; 27 fol., and a solid part
of Nehemiah.

I cannot close without yielding slightly to an irresistible urge to generalize. As I reread these pages, a question posed itself relentlessly: Do these personalities really exhibit only a people of the Book? Does not the life they reveal transcend the Book, and even the Word? I do not pretend to have a ready answer, but an answer must be found if the love of life and joy in wisdom and beauty that is reflected in the highest moments of this millennial experience are to continue. I wonder whether the sovereign achievement of Jews is in their extraordinary religious and intellectual attainments or in the high order of social life they achieved in chronically hostile states and cultures. I am reminded that this pageant of personal history underlines the dangers of black-and-white judgments. The historian, the apologist and the journalist have given us a set of neat labels that for the most part portray Jews as angels or devils. But Jews, like other historical families, like life itself, elude generalization; they are human natural, so to speak, reflecting all the complications and all the contradictions that characterize the struggle for survival and self-expression. Matthew Arnold's classic distinction between Hellenism and Hebraism does not square with experience: there is as much "sweetness and light" in the character of Jews as there is "fire and strength" in the Greek mind. Nor does Israel Zangwill's superlative epigram, when put to the test, fare any better: the sons of Hellas lived in "the beauty of holiness" just as the sons of Jacob felt the "holiness of beauty". Indeed, what does seem to shine out of the literature of personal experience is the fundamental unity of the human spirit.

I
FLOOD TIDE
OF REMEMBRANCE

FAMILY ALBUM

AHIMAAZ BEN PALTIEL (1017-?)

It was with good reason that Ahimaaz, a poet of distinction, fixed his thoughts on the exploits of his illustrious ancestors. He was the scion of an Italian family whose traditions reached back a thousand years and whose great lights had been ministers to the potentates of the Byzantine Empire and the Fatimid Caliphate. Accordingly he collected every scrap of written and oral information to compose this record, extended himself to arrange the material in orderly sequence, and then cast the memory portraits into the literary form then in vogue—rhymed prose. Despite an occasional lapse into the miraculous, characteristic of his times, his story is a saga of valiant men, devoted to the faith of their fathers and respected by the powerful rulers they served. It is a pity that Ahimaaz' wholehearted veneration of his notable forebears prevented him from telling us more about his own experiences. Nevertheless, the tales are welcome flashlight rays in the darkness that veils those distant times.

✳ ✳ ✳

I, AHIMAAZ, the son of Paltiel ben Samuel ben Hananel ben Amittai, sought God's aid and guidance in order to find the lineage of my family and He bountifully granted my request. I concentrated my mind and soul upon this work; I put the family documents and traditions in order, and I narrated the story in rhymed form. I began with the earliest tradition during the time of the destruction of Jerusalem and of the Temple by the Romans; then I traced it through the settlement of the exiles in the city of Oria in Italy (where I am now living) and the arrival of my ancestors in Capua; and finally, I have concluded with my own generation. I have written it all in this book for the use of future generations. I completed it in the month of Sivan and I praise and I honor and thank God for helping me to finish the book in the spirit and form I desired.

Wherefore, I will now carefully relate the traditions of my fore-

3

fathers. Carried upon a vessel with the captives whom Titus took from Jerusalem, they went to the city of Oria. There they established a community, and by deeds of labor and love they grew and prospered. Among their descendants there arose a great light whose name was Rabbi Amittai. He was both scholar and poet, and eminent for his piety and learning. His three sons were no less distinguished, being deeply versed in the Bible and the Talmud, as well as in the mystical and philosophic lore of their times. Worthy disciples of an eminent father were these learned men: Rabbi Shephatiah, seeker after wisdom; Rabbi Hananel, master of Torah; and Eleazar, expert in law.

In the 800th year after the destruction of Jerusalem (868), King Basil I was elevated to the throne of the Byzantine Empire. He seized the kingdom by bloodshed and treachery and, in his zeal for the Christian faith, he was determined to destroy Israel or compel the people to forsake the Law of Moses and adopt the religion of Jesus. He sent cavalrymen to the furthest corners of his empire to compel the Jews to change their religion. They arrived at the port of Otranto, embarked for the province of Apulia, and announced the fearsome report throughout the land. They also came to Oria, bearing an epistle with the Chrysobulla—the royal seal of gold—from the Emperor to Rabbi Shephatiah.

I give herewith the contents of the epistle:

"I, King Basil, request that you, Rabbi Shephatiah, come to visit me. Pray do not refuse to come, for I have heard of your great wisdom and knowledge and I yearn to see you. I swear by my life and my crown that your coming and returning will be in peace. I will receive you with the same honor as my own kith and kin and I will grant in bountiful affection whatsoever you request."

Whereupon Rabbi Shephatiah sailed to Constantinople, the city that was built by Emperor Constantine—may God destroy its glory and power!—and God granted that he win the favor of the King and the people.

Then the King engaged Rabbi Shephatiah in a discussion of religious matters. He questioned him regarding the Temple in Jerusalem and the Church called the Hagia Sophia in Constantinople, inquiring which building had required greater wealth. The King contended that the Church was the greater of the two inasmuch as untold wealth and treasure had been used to build it. Rabbi Shephatiah appropriately asked that a copy of the Scriptures be placed before them.

"There you will find the facts," he said, "by which you can judge which structure consumed more wealth."

The King immediately procured the Scriptures and, by comparing the figures recorded by David and Solomon, he was satisfied that the treasure used in building the Temple was greater by 120 talents of gold and 500 talents of silver. Whereupon the King exclaimed, "The wisdom of Rabbi Shephatiah has prevailed against me."

And the Rabbi graciously replied, "My Lord, it is the Scriptures, not I, that have prevailed against you."

Afterwards the King invited him to a royal banquet. The table was overflowing with delicacies and fruits, and food was served to Rabbi Shephatiah in golden dishes so that he might eat in accordance with the dietary laws. These dishes were lowered on chains of precious silver and the place from which they were lowered was invisible.

Now Basil had a daughter whom he loved as the apple of his eye. She was tormented by a demon and no cure could be found for her.

The King spoke to the Rabbi secretly, imploring his aid. "Help me, Shephatiah; cure my daughter of her sickness."

He replied that he would do so with the help of the Almighty, but he must have a place free of the impurities of idol worship. The King offered the beautiful garden of Bukoleon, the palace on the walls facing the Sea of Marmora. After examining it thoroughly, the Rabbi approved the Bukoleon, which means "Mouth of the Lion." He took the girl there and conjured up the demon in the name of God who dwells on high and who founded the earth in his wisdom.

And the demon cried aloud, "Why are you helping the daughter of a wicked man who wreaks his wickedness upon your people? God has placed her in my power so that I may humble her. Now depart because I will not leave her body."

But the Rabbi replied, "I refuse to listen to your words. Come out, in the name of God, so that the King may know there is a God in Israel."

The demon came forth and attempted to flee but Rabbi Shephatiah seized it, enclosed it in a leaden vessel which he sealed with the name of God, and then threw the vessel to the bottom of the sea. Thereupon the girl became calm and poised and returned to the King and the Queen.

Then Shephatiah sought the King's permission to depart. The King came forth to greet him, put his arm around his shoulders, and led him into his private chambers. There he tried, by offering huge rewards, to induce Shephatiah to abandon his faith. He walked up and down with him, urging him zealously to embrace his heathen faith. He offered him treasures and appointed companions to influence him. Shephatiah, oppressed by the King's zeal and insolence, objected vehemently.

"O Mighty Lord," he cried, "you are subjecting me to violence!"

Whereupon the King descended from his throne, took Rabbi Shephatiah from the midst of the people, and granted him permission to depart. He sent him to the Queen so that she might give him gifts and a blessing. The Queen asked him whether he had any children, and he replied, "Your servant has a son and two daughters."

The Queen offered him her earrings and her girdle and urged him to accept them. "I give them to you as a token of my regard for your wisdom. They are priceless; give them to your daughters." The weight of the earrings was a litra of gold and the girdle was of equal worth.

Before his departure the King summoned him and said, "Shephatiah, ask of me whatsoever you desire. If it is not wealth you wish, you shall have an inheritance of cities and provinces. I wish to fulfill my promise."

"If my Lord wishes to favor Shephatiah," he replied, filled with pain and almost in tears, "allow those engaged in the study of our Law to continue without interference. Do not oppress them and make their lives sorrowful. If my Lord cannot grant me this, then it is my wish that at least my city be free from religious persecution."

The King replied angrily, "If I had not given you my word, I would make an example of you here and now. But I wrote the letter and cannot break faith with you."

Consequently the King issued an edict sealed with a seal of fine gold, and commanded that there should be no religious persecution in the city of Oria. And he sent Rabbi Shephatiah home in peace and honor.

But that wicked King continued to send his representatives throughout the empire in order to compel the people to accept the errors of the pagan faith. For a quarter of a century—until the day of his death—the sun and the moon were darkened. May his end be cursed and may his evil and sin be remembered!

In the days when Basil's son Leo the Wise (886-912) succeeded him to the throne—may his memory be blessed—and the Arabs began to overrun Calabria and Apulia, capturing and plundering many cities, Sudan, their leader, who ruled the country, was in Bari. He sent couriers to Oria to make a covenant of peace, guaranteeing that the land would not be laid waste but only tribute would be exacted. However, this covenant was merely a trick whereby he hoped to plunder and destroy our famous city.

Now the Governor of Bari sent Rabbi Shephatiah as an ambassador to discuss the pact and arrange that the conditions be incorporated in a written document officially sealed. Sudan received him with signal honor and spoke with him in a friendly manner in the presence of his assembled chieftains. He purposely delayed almost until evening so that Shephatiah might not be able to return by reason of the Sabbath and thus inform the Governor of his stratagem.

Shephatiah finally grew aware of his deceit and asked for permission to leave. "You have tricked me," he declared angrily, "let me go."

"Where will you go now?" asked Sudan. "It is almost Sabbath."

But Shephatiah persisted, saying that Sudan need not be anxious about him. At last Sudan let him go. Invoking the aid of God Almighty, Rabbi Shephatiah wrote a formula on the horse's hooves in order to speed the journey. Then he uttered the name of God imploringly and the ground shrank before him.

As soon as he reached the outer sections of the city, he urged the people to flee. "Sudan, leader of the Arabs, and his hosts are coming to loot and destroy," he announced.

The Governor came to meet him at the gates of the city. He told him what the situation was and they held counsel in regard to what steps should be taken. Then Shephatiah entered the city before darkness had fallen, made his ablutions, put on his holiday garments, and, as custom prescribed, welcomed the Sabbath with joy, food, drink and study.

Sudan, puffed up with pride, defiant in his arrogance, reached the city with his hosts by forced marches. He found the country deserted and, infuriated by this disappointment, he summoned Rabbi Shephatiah.

"Hand over that man who desecrated the Sabbath and thus by his own Law is worthy of death," were his ominous words.

But Shephatiah, strong with the power of God, replied, "Why do you make a false accusation? Heaven is my witness, and the whole population of the city too, that I entered the city while it was still day, and before the sun had gone down I had prepared myself for the Sabbath and welcomed the holy day fittingly in accordance with the commandment of my King and Redeemer, the Holy One of Israel."

Rabbi Shephatiah had a daughter of rare beauty named Cassia. He was anxious that the girl should be wedded but her mother stood in the way. Whensoever anyone asked her hand in marriage, her haughtiness acted as a damper. She would say, "She is the daughter of a great man and a girl of exceptional qualities. I will not allow her to leave this house unless a man like him can be found. I will let her marry only a man of equal scholarly accomplishments."

One night, as Rabbi Shephatiah engaged in prayer and study, the girl arose from her bed and in her dressing gown prepared the water for his ablutions. As she stood before him, he noticed that she had a fully developed body and was ripe for marriage. After prayers he returned to his wife and rebuked her for her behavior.

"We have a beautiful dove who is without blemish and ready for marriage, and my brother has asked her hand for his son Hasadiah. By listening to you I have transgressed our laws and interfered with her happiness."

On the way to the synagogue the next morning he met his brother Rabbi Hananel and told him that it was his wish to have Hasadiah become the husband of Cassia. His brother showed his gratitude and esteem by falling upon his knees before him. After the service he invited the congregation to his house and blessed the children in marriage. Rabbi Amittai, brother of the radiant bride, wrote in her honor the poem *O Lord, Who Telleth of the End from the Beginning* . . . to crown the occasion with splendor.

God blessed Shephatiah with long life, deep learning, great wealth, and favored him with a worthy son. Both he and his son were upright and perfect men. Rabbi Shephatiah died in peace, first among the learned, and ever devoted to the just and righteous God.

Rabbi Hananel, the brother of Shephatiah, was no less distinguished and upright. I will now tell of his wonderful deeds.

One day the Archbishop and Hananel were discussing religious subjects and treated of the calculations regarding the appearance of the new moon. It happened that the next day would be the first day of the new moon which is sanctified by Israel. The Archbishop asked him in how many hours the moon would make its appearance and the Rabbi named the exact hour. But he had erred.

The Archbishop, differing with him, said, "If your answer is an example of your calculations, you certainly are not an expert."

Rabbi Hananel had not calculated carefully, but the Archbishop had and would have caught him in his net had not God come to his rescue.

For the Archbishop said, "O wise Hananel, if my calculation is accurate, then you will do my bidding. You must abandon your religion and accept the faith of the Gospel. On the other hand, if your calculation is accurate, then I will do as you bid. I will give you my New Year's gift of a horse valued at three hundred gold coins. If you prefer, you may take the money instead."

They accepted the terms and agreed, before the magistrates and the ruling prince, to abide by the pact.

That night the Archbishop ordered men stationed on the city-wall and the towers to observe the exact time of the moon's appearance and what fraction of it appeared.

When Rabbi Hananel returned to his house, he checked his calculation and discovered that he had made an error. His heart melted within him, his strength left him. However, he found courage and appealed to God to lift him out of the pit. He revealed his plight to his brothers and his family, entreating them to pour out their supplication to God in the hope that He would hear their prayers and perform a miracle as He had done for their ancestors in Egypt. What night came, he went to his roof and kept his eyes fixed on Him to whom great praise is due. As the time of the waxing of the moon approached, he appealed, in pain and tears, to the loving God for succor and, in fervent devotion and prayer, sought His intervention.

God heard his prayers and hid the moon behind the clouds until the following night. When the Rabbi went to hear the decision in the morning, the Archbishop said to him in the presence of all the people, "You know as well as I that I was correct and the moon appeared at the time I stated. But who can punish you? You have won grace from your God even as an erring son escapes punishment by cajoling his father."

Whereupon he paid him the three hundred gold coins which Rabbi Hananel did not keep, but distributed among the needy. Then his brothers and friends assembled and gave praise to God who saves His servants from distress and brings them from darkness to light.

Rabbi Amittai, the beloved son of Shephatiah, became his worthy successor. The day before his death, the father requested his son to maintain the collegium of scholars and administer it wisely so that both teachers and students might continue their studies. Amittai carried out his father's wish, expounding reverently and brilliantly on all branches of religious and legal knowledge in association with the rabbis and scholars. All the days of his life he lamented the destruction of the Temple in Jerusalem and was deeply concerned over the persecution of his people.

Once he had gone to his estate in the suburbs, and it happened that a pious and learned pilgrim died in the city. The elders of the community summoned Rabbi Amittai to participate in the burial services. He informed them he would join the procession when it passed beyond the city and would recite the prayers at the burial place. The whole community was present when Rabbi Amittai intoned the service and recited an elegy which he had composed in honor of the deceased. It opened with the words, "O Soul in Exile! He who knows thee not reviles thee; he who knows thee laments thy fate."

Rabbi Moses, a brother of the deceased, who was a teacher of children, happened to be there and made an offensive pun on the verse. Rabbi Amittai overheard him and the teacher's cut remained fresh in his mind.

Years later a married woman was suspected of committing a transgression and the community, gathered to investigate the evidence and judge her guilt, found that this same Rabbi Moses was the only witness against her.

Rabbi Amittai thereupon asked him, "Have you another witness, as our law requires?"

As another witness could not be produced, Amittai pronounced the sentence prescribed for a false witness: he put Rabbi Moses under a ban and exiled him from Oria. He went first to Capua and then to Pavia.

I will now tell of Rabbi Paltiel who was a master astrologer. He was the son of Cassia, a great-granddaughter of Shephatiah.

In his time an Arab army under Caliph Abu Tamim Mead Al Muizz overran Italy and devastated the province of Calabria. The invader put Oria under siege and, wearing down the resistance of its defenders, took the city by storm, slaughtered most of the inhabitants and took the rest captive. The Caliph summoned the descendants of Rabbi Shephatiah. God let Paltiel win his favor and Al Muizz later made him his astrologer and, later on, his Vizir.

One night the Caliph and Paltiel were observing the stars, and lo and behold! the Caliph's star devoured three stars in succession. He asked Paltiel to interpret the phenomenon.

"First let me hear your interpretation," said Paltiel.

"The three stars that were devoured," the Caliph declared, "symbolize the cities of Tarento, Otranto and Bari which I am destined to vanquish."

"No, my Lord," replied Paltiel, "I see a greater destiny. The three stars symbolize three countries which you will rule: Sicily, Africa and Egypt."

No sooner had he spoken than Al Muizz embraced him, gave him a ring from his finger, and swore that if his prophecy proved true he would appoint him Vizir.

In less than a week emissaries from the princes of Sicily informed Al Muizz that the Emir had died and invited him to become their ruler. Whereupon he sailed to Sicily with his army and became the lord of the country. As a consequence, he had complete faith in Paltiel and appointed him Vizir.

Afterwards the Caliph went to Africa with Paltiel, leaving his brother behind to rule in his stead. Paltiel's influence became second only to that of the Caliph and his renown reached everywhere.

Now at that time there came a deputation from the Emperor of Macedonia, impressively arrayed and bearing gifts in accordance with their custom, to seek an audience with the Caliph. The ambassador inquired for the steward of the royal household, and an Arab attendant replied, "A Jew has authority over the whole realm and he decides who may or may not see the Caliph. You must have his permission to obtain an audience."

"Why, I would rather return to my lord in Constantinople," the ambassador replied contemptuously, "than appeal to a Jew for permission to speak with the Caliph!"

When the report of his remarks reached Paltiel, he issued an order forbidding anyone to approach the ambassador's quarters or to pay the slightest attention to him and his suite.

The thwarted Greek kept to himself, fuming and cursing, for ten days. Then he humbly and penitently returned, pleading that Paltiel forgive his offensive behavior. The Vizir made him cool his heels for three days. When at last he did receive him, it was in a manner befitting a royal envoy: The whole palace, from the gate to the banquet hall, was luxuriously decorated. The walls were hung with scarlet tapestries and precious ornaments; the floors were covered with silk rugs; and all was resplendent with the brilliance of treasures of onyx and opal, and sweetened with the fragrance of rare perfume. In this setting of splendor Paltiel welcomed the ambassador and honored him with rich gifts. As the envoy entered he saw the Vizir reclining upon a couch, and he was given a chair wrought of gold. They conversed amiably about the Jewish religion and about Paltiel's native country and lineage.

After a festive repast, a prearranged incident added another surprise. Paltiel ordered a servant to bring the washing-bowl. The servant appeared with a delicately wrought bowl and plate of onyx and jasper, and, after pouring water over his lord's hand, he suddenly stumbled and fell, in accordance with Paltiel's orders, and broke the costly utensils into bits.

As the envoy jumped up and turned pale, Paltiel simply smiled and said, "Why do you appear so shocked?"

"Because," answered the envoy, "I have just witnessed irreparable damage. To see priceless plates smashed to pieces!"

Paltiel then asked him whether the Emperor used plates of precious stones or merely those of gold. When the envoy replied that the Emperor possessed only plates of gold, Paltiel remarked, "Of course dishes wrought of precious stones are infinitely more valuable than those of gold and cannot be mended if broken. Yet many plates of even rarer gems than the one you have just seen smashed are broken in the palace of my Lord, the Caliph."

After this Paltiel dismissed the ambassador with honor and sent him away with gifts for his lord in Constantinople.

When the Caliph of Egypt died, his subject princes sent a deputation of dignitaries with an epistle to Caliph Al Muizz, inviting him to become the ruler of Egypt.

"We have heard," the letter read, "of your prowess and wisdom which surpasses that of our former ruler, and our princes and nobles are unanimous in their desire to become your loyal subjects."

After consulting with Paltiel, it was decided that the Vizir should depart in advance and set up encampments because of the length of the journey, the starkness of the country, and the scarcity of victuals. Paltiel carried out these orders, establishing way stations where the Caliph's entourage, as well as the warriors, could lodge and eat. As the Caliph bivouacked three miles outside of Cairo, the nobles and the people joyfully marched out to present themselves to the new monarch. They prostrated themselves as they took an oath of allegiance and made the traditional exchange of noble hostages. Then the Caliph, preceded by a body of warriors who were stationed at all the points of vantage and in all public places, marched into the city at the head of his army and ascended the throne. The nation swore fealty to the Caliph, presenting him with the sceptre and crown. Thereupon he ruled Egypt with honor and glory, and Paltiel, now the Vizir of the lands of the East, including Egypt, Syria, Palestine and Babylonia, shared his riches and power.

It befell once on the awesome Day of Atonement that when Paltiel was elected to read a passage from the scrolls of the Torah, the whole congregation rose in unison as a gesture of respect. But, although he appreciated the honor, he was loath to strain their energies and said, "Unless the aged sit down and only the young remain standing, I will not accept the honor of reading from the Torah."

After the reading, he made a pledge before God and his holy congregation to have 5,000 gold dinars be distributed as follows: 1,000 to the President and Faculty of the Academy; 1,000 to those who had dedicated their lives to mourning in the Holy Land; 1,000 to the Academies of Babylonia; 1,000 to the poor; and 1,000 for the purchase of oils to light up the splendor of the Torah. The very next morning, lest anything interfere with his charitable intentions, he hired a number of fully equipped and guarded caravans to deliver the donations to those he had designated.

When Al Muizz was afflicted with the illness that ultimately killed him, he appointed his son Al Azizz as his successor and Paltiel his regent. Al Azizz ruled after his father's death, but the native officials slandered Paltiel and intrigued against him. The young Caliph, furious at their behavior, rebuked them and disclosed their charges to his Vizir. Taking counsel together, they devised a plan to put a stop to these machinations.

Paltiel removed his family and household to a magnificent country estate which he had received from the Caliph as a gift.

Soon thereafter, Al Azizz inquired, "Where is our beloved Rabbi Paltiel?"

The court attendants replied, "He is at his country estate with his kith and kin, seeking rest and relaxation."

Whereupon the Caliph summoned all the nobles and officials and declared, "Our dear friend Paltiel, sage and Vizir of our realm, is at his country estate. Let us all show our admiration and respect for him by visiting him in state."

He immediately set out in the royal chariot, followed by all the lords of the realm. Instead of waiting for Paltiel to make obeisance to him as he approached the palace, Al Azizz ordered the runners not to announce his arrival, stepped down from the chariot, and went to meet the venerable Vizir. He embraced Paltiel affectionately and, in order to show his esteem and love as a shining example to his detractors, he walked off arm and arm to a place apart from the whole assemblage. Then the court musicians and jesters entertained with music, dance, and jesting until evening, when the Caliph returned to Cairo. In this way the tongues of his enemies were silenced once and for all, praise be to God.

One night, as Paltiel and the Caliph were taking a stroll under the canopy of heaven, they watched three brilliant stars disappear simultaneously. Paltiel ventured this interpretation: "The stars that were blacked out symbolize those who will die within the year: King John of Macedonia, the King of Baghdad. . . ."

"And you," added the Caliph, interrupting him, "the king of the East, are the third."

"Oh no, my Lord," said Paltiel, "That cannot be, for I am a Jew. The third star represents the Caliph of Spain."

But the Caliph persisted. "Truly you are the third as I have said."

And in that very year, 976, as the Caliph had predicted, Paltiel died. May his soul repose in Eden. His son Samuel, who succeeded him in greatness and wisdom and benificence, took the remains of his parents as well as those of his grand-uncle Hananel in coffins to Jerusalem. He made gifts totalling 20,000 gold drachmas for religious, educational and charitable purposes. May he be granted a long life and may his name be remembered for a blessing!

Samuel had great influence in the palace of the rulers in Capua (where I was born). He was appointed Minister of Finance, administering the customs of the port and the budgets of all the city departments. He followed Paltiel's illustrious example by dispensing his wealth for educational and religious purposes and he showed reverence for his forefathers by rebuilding his grandfather's synagogue. All his other children died when they were infants, but God was merciful and left him an only son whom he called Ahimaaz. He gave this child every advantage of education so that, like his illustrious ancestors, he might live in the spirit of the teachings of the divine commandments.

And I am that Ahimaaz, the son of Paltiel. I composed this book of my family history in the year 1054, not only by my own wisdom and intelligence, but also by the grace and aid of God. I glorify His majesty and give Him my thanks for helping me to complete the book as I had planned it, from beginning to end.

LOGBOOK OF A PHYSICIAN

MOSES MAIMONIDES (1135-1204)

When his octocentennial was celebrated in 1935, Maimonides was signally honored in Madrid by an official decree of the Government of Spain, the land of his birth. The world, too, recognized one of the very great spirits of medieval times. His philosophy influenced Western as well as Jewish thought, and his voluminous ethical, legal and medical writings are all stamped with genius. Driven from Spain when he was only thirteen, and later fleeing the same fanatical persecution of the Moorish sect of Almohades in Fez, he passed the remainder of his life in Egypt as the mentor of his people and the physician to Saladin's Vizir. Even these brief extracts from his letters bear witness to the deep humanity of a great mind.

✳ ✳ ✳

(1165)

I PUT to sea on Sunday, the fourth day of the second month, and on the following Sabbath we encountered very rough weather. The storm was so fierce that I vowed to observe annually these two days as strict fast days together with my people and the whole household. I also ordered my children always to observe these fasts in our home, and laid upon them the duty of making charitable donations as liberal as their means permitted. As for myself, I vowed solemnly that as on this occasion I was alone with God on the tempestuous sea and succored by Him alone, so every year on this day I will cease all work, withdraw from men, and devote myself completely to study and prayer in His presence.

On Sunday night, the 3rd of Sivan, I landed safe and happy in Acco and thereby escaped enforced apostasy. So at last we arrived in the Land of Israel, and I also vowed to set aside this day of our arrival as an annual family holiday to be celebrated festively with a banquet and the distribution of gifts to the poor. We left Acco on Wednesday, the 4th of

Marheshvan, and reached Jerusalem after a perilous journey. I spent the entire day, as well as the following two days, praying at the remains (the Wailing Wall) of the ancient Temple. On Sunday, the 9th of Marheshvan, I left Jerusalem for Hebron where I prayed at the graves of the Patriarchs in the Cave of Machpelah. These two days, the 6th and 9th of Marheshvan, I appointed as festivals for me and mine, which should be passed in prayer and in feasting. May God help me and bring to fulfillment in me the words of Psalmist, "My vows will I pay unto the Lord."

(1167) When storms threatened in the past, I wandered from place to place, but now, by God's mercy, I have been enabled to find a sanctuary in Cairo. Upon my arrival, I perceived to my great distress that the learned of the city were at loggerheads, unmindful of what was happening in the community. I therefore felt it my duty to undertake the task of guiding the holy flock, of reconciling the hearts of the fathers to their children, and of correcting their false ways. Great is the evil, but I may succeed in curing it; and in accordance with the prophetic prescription, "I will seek the lost one, and that which has been cast out I will bring back, and the broken one I will heal."

(1172) The news that the government ordered all the Jews in Yemen (Southern Arabia) to apostasize in the same manner as the ruling powers in western countries have acted toward us, filled us with terror. A whole community shares your grief; we are bewildered; we feel unable to think calmly, so terrible is the alternative in which Israel has been placed on all sides, in the East and in the West. That, on the one hand, several among our people have become restive and unsettled in their ideas, and on the other hand others continue unshaken in their beliefs is precisely what was predicted by Daniel; namely, that when our captivity would be prolonged and we be made to suffer severely, many would leave our fold because of the oppression. They would sink into a sea of doubts and be lost; while others would entertain no misgiving nor would they be confused. Be assured, however, that our main opponents—oppression, intellectual confusion, and false authority—will vanish away. They may prosper for a limited period, but their supremacy will be fleeting. We have the certain promise of the Almighty that decrees aiming at our apostacy or destruction will be brought to naught.

I am not at all surprised to hear of the conduct of our coreligionist in South Arabia, who proclaims himself the Messiah, nor of the credulity of his followers. The man is beyond doubt demented. His actions are consequently the effect of his disease over which he has no control, and those who have faith in him are misguided and cannot form a right idea of the character of the Messiah. But I am surprised at you who possess learning, who must have read what the rabbis have taught. Are you not aware that the Prince who is to redeem Israel from their suffering must prove himself greater than all prophets, with the exception of Moses? Are you not also aware that one who proclaims himself a prophet and is shown to be false by subsequent circumstances should be put to death? Besides, tradition requires three requisites in the character of the redeemer of the outcasts; namely, wisdom, vigor, and riches. He must be wise in forecasting consequences; vigorous in holding his actions under proper control, and rich in mental resources. But when a person who lacks these attainments declares himself a prophet, we give no heed to his assertions. How much less so if he is an ignoramus! In no way does he who arose in your country show such characteristics as I have just described. Can anyone who is in his right senses even entertain the idea that he is the Messiah? No: you must make a laughingstock of the simpleton. In short, if he were perfectly sane, his conduct would, I think, be deserving of death. But I am fully persuaded that he is mad and his thoughts lack foundation. I will give some good advice, useful to him as well as to yourselves: put the brainless fellow away for a time, and meanwhile take care to circulate the news of his insanity among the gentiles; then, set him at large, and he will not be hurt for having styled himself the Messiah. In that manner you will also have saved the people from the persecution of our religious enemies.

I must add that in the first era of Islam a Jew arose in Syria, who declared himself to be the Messiah. Ten thousand Jews espoused his cause. He offered as evidence of his mission the capacity he possessed to cure himself at will: he could go to bed a leper and rise in the morning as healthy as a newborn child. His ridiculous endeavors failed. He forswore his faith, but his dupes, and unhappily many others, suffered terribly. Again in Africa, in the city of Fez, forty-five years ago another man pretended to be the herald of the Messiah, commissioned to announce that within twelve months the Redeemer would come to Zion. This promise was not fulfilled, and through it our people were exposed to innumerable sorrows. I heard this from an eyewitness. Ten years before that, a Jew of Spain stood forth in Cordova and declared himself the Messiah. Nearly all the Jews of that country ran the risk of being exterminated. The same plan was tried, thirty years previous to that, in

France. The fool performed wonders—as many believed—but he could not save himself from the block; and, what is worse, he could not deliver from persecution and death many of the congregation of Jacob.

(1176)   A few months after I left my friend Japhet ben Elijah, my father, may his memory be blessed, died, and I received letters of consolation from the distant parts of Spain and North Africa. I too suffered great personal misfortunes here in Egypt from illness, loss of money, and the activities of informers who would bring about my death. Then followed the saddest blow that I have suffered to this day: the death of my righteous and beloved brother David. He was drowned on a business voyage in the Indian Ocean, and with him was lost a fortune which belonged to me and him and others. His little daughter and widow were left in my care. From the day that I heard the evil tidings I was stricken in bed with fever. I was plagued with despair and mourned like a child. Almost eight years have passed, yet still I mourn and nothing will console me. He grew up on my knees, he was my brother and my pupil—how shall I be consoled? He engaged in trade, sailing the seas, so that I might devote myself to religious and intellectual pursuits at home without worry. He was learned in biblical and talmudic lore and well-versed as a grammarian. What a joy it was merely to see him! He has gone to his eternal abode and left me bewildered in a strange land. Whenever I look at a page with his handwriting or one of his books, my heart throbs and my grief is reawakened. In short, I should have died of grief, were it not for the Torah which is my delight and the sciences in the study of which I forget my sorrow.

(1191)   Know that in my capacity as a physician I have won high regard among the powers that be in this land. I refer to the Judges, the Emir, and the palace of the Vizir Al Fadhel. Since I am so occupied with the great, the plain folk cannot gain access to me. My official position requires that I devote my entire day to my patients in Cairo, and when I return to Fostat I am too fagged out to spend the remainder of the day or part of the night looking into medical literature. Medicine, as you know, is an unbounded field of study. The lot of one who is faithful and conscientious, who will not pass an opinion unless there is reasonable evidence for its validity, who cannot continue reading if he does not know the author and the method by which he has demonstrated his point, is a particularly hard one. It follows that I can hardly find a moment for my religious studies except on the Sabbath. Nor can I make any progress with the other sciences. This predicament causes me great sorrow.

(1192)   My heart is pained in your pain, dear friend Joseph, but you will please me better by actively propagating to men what is true than by setting yourself as my champion against the untrue. Teach, do not recriminate. Remember that you have injured this man, that his revenues are at stake. Shall such a man, being stricken, not cry? He concerns himself with what the multitude holds highest. Leave him to his trivialities. What does he know of the soul and of philosophy? Remember he is old and occupies a position of dignity, and you are young and owe his age and position respect. You ask me as to your plan of opening a school in Baghdad in which you will teach the Law with my *Code* as the textbook. I have already sanctioned your proposal. Yet I fear two things. You will be constantly embroiled with these men. Or, if you assume the duty of teaching, you will neglect your own business affairs. I counsel you to take nothing from them. Better in my eyes is a single dirhem gained by you as a weaver, a tailor, or a carpenter, than a whole revenue enjoyed under the auspices of the Head of the Captivity.

(1199)   My day is occupied in the following manner: I live in Fostat and the Sultan dwells in Cairo. These two palaces are two Sabbath days' journey (about one mile and a half) distant from each other. My duties to the Sultan are very heavy. I am obliged to visit him every day, early in the morning; and when he or any of his children, or any of the inmates of his harem, are indisposed. I dare not quit Cairo, but must stay during the greater part of the day in the palace. It also frequently happens that one or two of the royal officers fall sick, and I must attend to their healing.

Hence, as a rule, I repair to Cairo very early in the day, and even if nothing very unusual happens, I do not return to Fostat until the afternoon. Then I nearly perish of hunger. I find the antechambers filled with people, both Jews and gentiles, nobles and common people, judges and bailiffs, friends and foes—a mixed multitude, who await the time of my return.

I dismount from my animal, wash my hands, go forth to my patients, entreat them to bear with me while I partake of some slight refreshment, and the only meal I take in twenty-four hours. Then I attend to my patients, write prescriptions and give directions for their various ailments. Patients go in and out until nightfall, and sometimes even later.

I converse with and prescribe for them while lying down from sheer fatigue, and when night falls I am so exhausted that I can scarcely speak.

In consequence of this, no Israelite can have any private interview with me except on the Sabbath. On that day the whole congregation, or at least the majority of the members, come to me after the morning service when I instruct them as to their proceedings during the whole week; we study together a little until noon, when they depart. Some of them return, and read with me after the afternoon service until evening prayers. That is how I spend the Sabbath. I have here related to you only part of what you would see if you were to visit me.

EVERY MAN HIS OWN MESSIAH

ABRAHAM ABOULAFIA (1240-1292)

Some measure of the completeness with which the mystical passion took hold of Aboulafia's spirit is revealed in his serious attempt to convert Pope Nicholas III to Judaism. His family was one of the most distinguished in Spanish Jewry—it is still in existence in Palestine and elsewhere—and his incredible activities aroused the curiosity and animosity of his contemporaries. Especially did he leave his impress on the Kabbalah, creating a whole school of disciples. Aboulafia developed a system which had much in common with Indian Yoga. "His teachings can be put into effect by practically everyone who tries," writes Professor Scholem, the greatest living authority on Kabbalah. "That is probably one of the reasons why the kabbalists refrained from publishing them." He represented himself as the Messiah both to Christians and Jews. As a result of his own spiritual experiences and researches, he gave a new interpretation to the function of the Messiah, which he declared himself prepared to fulfil; but, as the following confessions indicate, it seems to have comprised the propagation of a method of individual spiritual regeneration rather than of political salvation. Aboulafia's account has been combined with that of an anonymous disciple who reflects the immense influence of the master.

❋　❋　❋

IT HAS been my purpose in all that I have written to reach that which I shall reveal to you herein. I was born at Saragossa in the Kingdom of Spain, where I dwelt until I was weaned, with my mother, brothers and sisters. I grew up on the Ebro, which is the river passing between Saragossa and Tudela; and I began to study Scriptures with commentaries and grammar with my father and teacher of blessed memory. In addition I learnt a little Mishna and a little Talmud with him; for most of what I learnt comes from him. But when I was eighteen years old he died.

I remained in Spain for two more years after the death of my father. Then when I was twenty years old, the spirit of the Lord roused me and set me on the move; and I went forth from there to the Land of Israel by land and sea; for it was my purpose to go to the River Sambatyon.* But I could go no further than Acre. So I departed by reason of the strife that increased between the Moslems and the Crusaders, and I returned through the Kingdom of Greece where I was married.

Then the spirit of the Lord roused me and I took my wife with me and set my face to reach my people. My desire was to learn Torah; and when I was in the city of Capua, five days' journey from Rome, I found a worthy man, wise, understanding, a philosopher and experienced physician. His name was Rabbi Hillel of blessed memory; and I made companionship with him, learning from him something of the science of philosophy. Straightway it became exceedingly sweet to me and I endeavored to achieve the knowledge of it with all my strength. I devoted myself to it by day and night; and my desire was not satisfied until I had studied Maimonides' *Guide to the Perplexed* many times. I also taught it in many places; to four students in Capua, but they took to bad courses, for they were young fellows without knowledge. At another place there were ten and not one of them succeeded. At Azriepo there were four, who also did not succeed; for views are very different among men, and all the more so as regards the depths of wisdom and the secrets of the Torah. I found not a single one among them who was worthy of being given even the chapter headings of the actual truth.

In Rome I taught the two elders, Rabbi Zedekiah and Rabbi Isaiah, my friends of blessed memory. They succeeded therein somewhat but passed away, for they were very old. In Barcelona there were two. One was old and went by the name of Rabbi Kalonymos of blessed memory, a great man; and the other was an intelligent and understanding and very worthy youth of good family, whose name was Rabbi Judah, known as Solomon, who succeeded therein very greatly. At Burgos there were two, a rabbi and a student. The rabbi's name was Moses Sianpo of blessed memory, a great, wise and worthy man; that of the student was Rabbi Shem Tob, also a fine and good lad, but his youth made him

---

* A mystical river that plays an important role in Jewish legendry. In an autobiographical letter, Eldad the Danite, a picturesque globe-trotter who flourished in the ninth century, writes, "Now the breadth of the Sambatyon River is two hundred cubits; the waters are glut with large and small stones and the noise they make sounds like a great storm and during the night the sound of it is heard a day's journey away. The river runs and the stones and sand rumble during the six weekdays, but it rests on the seventh day and is quiet until the close of the Sabbath."

unsuitable for the study, so that neither he nor his master learnt more from me than a few external traditions.

At Celi there were two, one of them Rabbi Samuel, the prophet, who received certain kabbalistic traditions from me, and the other Rabbi Joseph Gikitila (one of the leading kabbalists of the thirteenth century), who undoubtedly succeeded to a remarkable degree in what he learnt from me, and who added from his own knowledge and power; and the Lord was with him. And in this town, to be sure, where I am today, namely Messina, I found six men and I was the seventh. From me they learnt for a very short while, and each of them received from me as much as he could absorb, whether little or much. But they all parted from me with the exception of the first; and he is the first cause of all that each of his companions learnt from me. His name is Rabbi Saadiah bar Isaac Sinalmafi of blessed memory; he was followed by Rabbi Abraham ben Shalon, who was followed by his son Jacob, and he in turn by his friend Isaac, who was also followed by a friend of theirs. Three of them were of three grades of initiation, and three of lower grades of initiation. The name of the seventh was Rabbi Natronai, the Frenchman, of blessed memory, and the grades of initiation and revealed knowledge vanished at once, and he diverted it from them. The reasons for this were in the nature of their wills and temperaments; then there were some that were accidental and some that were inevitable.

Now when I was thirty-one years old, the Lord awakened me from my sleep in the city of Barcelona. I studied *The Book of Creation* (one of the earliest kabbalist or possibly pre-kabbalist works in Hebrew literature) with its commentaries; and the hand of the Lord was on me and I wrote a book that was wiser yet than those, and books of strange prophecies. My spirit became quick within me, and the spirit of the Lord reached my mouth and the Holy Spirit worked through me so that I manifested many dread and awful sights with signs and wonders. And on account of them jealous sprites gathered around me and I saw imaginary things and errors; and my ideas were confused because I found no man of my kind to teach me the way to go. Therefore I did grope like a blind man at noon for fifteen years, with Satan at my right hand to lead me astray; and I became crazed at the things my eyes saw, fifteen years ere the Lord, vouchsafed to me knowledge and counsel.

From the year 1281 to 1285 the Lord was with me to deliver me from all troubles. At the beginning of the year 1285 the Lord brought me into the Holy Temple (i.e., I became fully acquainted with the whole of mystic lore) and that was the time when I completed this book which

I wrote here at Messina for my precious, honorable, wise and understanding pupil, who longs to know the incorruptible Torah, namely, Saadiah, who is the first-mentioned of my seven disciples. I wrote the book because I do see that he loves me greatly and in order that it may serve as a memorial of what he learnt with me.

For forgetfulness is always present, and also I know that if he possesses the book, it will be useful to his companions aforementioned, for their understanding; likewise for those resembling them as concerns the greater part of what is written therein. And I know that were it not for the matter of false visions, the aforementioned would not have departed from me; and the false visions which were the cause of their departure were for me myself divine trials to make me aware of my qualities and to try me, in order at last to give light to the eyes of my heart.

For on account of them I guarded my mouth and tongue and restrained them from speech and my heart from purposeless thought. I returned unto the All-Present, who is worthy of such return; and I kept the covenant made, and I recognized and grasped what had been too much for me before this time. Therefore I praise the name of my God and the God of my fathers, who did not forsake His loving kindness and truth at any time, in whose mercies I trust. He set in my heart by His grace that which is too wondrous for me.

For it came into my mind, when I saw the happenings that were coming about in the world, to bring back the heart of the fathers to the sons, and hearts of the sons to the father (i.e. to act as the Messiah). There is no doubt that among the Christians there are certain sages who know this secret. They spoke to me in secret and revealed to me that this was their opinion without any doubt. Thereupon I reckoned them likewise among the pious of the nations of the world. And there is no point in paying attention to the fools of any nation; for the doctrine is given only to those who know.

At thirty-nine, after having studied diligently the secrets of the Kabbalah for nine years, I wrote my first real prophetic book, which I entitled *The Book of the Righteous*. The year—5039 since the Creation, the place—Patras, Greece. A year later, under very trying circumstances, I came to write *The Book of Testimony*. I had been inspired by the Lord to go to Rome and there to convert Pope Nicholas III to Judaism. On the way I passed through Trani where I was beset by a band of ruffians who had been incited by malevolent Jews, and only through the intervention of God did I manage to escape them. Next I passed through Capua where I stayed long enough to compose *The Book of Life*.

Finally, in the month of Ab, ten years after having left Barcelona, I arrived in Rome.

My plans were to look up the Pope the day before Rosh Hashana, 1280. The Pontiff, however, who was then in Suriano, a day's distance from Rome, upon being informed of my coming, arranged for a stake to be erected near the inner gate of the town so as to be spared the inconvenience of an audience with me. When I heard of these solicitous preparations in my behalf, I retired to a lonely chamber where I beheld the most wondrous visions. It was then that I composed *The Book of Testimony,* a sacred confirmation of my constant alacrity to give my life for God's commandments, and of His promptitude in rescuing me from my enemies. I proceeded to Suriano. But just as I was passing through the outer gate a herald came running toward me and announced that the Pope had died suddenly during the preceding night. Returning to Rome two days later, I was seized by some Franciscan friars and imprisoned for twenty-eight days, being finally released on the first day of Heshvan.

Such have been the glorious miracles that the Lord has wrought with me and his faithful servants.

Know, friends, that from the beginning I felt a desire to study Torah and learned a little of it and of the rest of Scripture. But I found no one to guide me in the study of the Talmud, not so much because of the lack of teachers, but rather because of my longing for my home, and my love for father and mother. At last, however, God gave me strength to search for the Torah, and I went out and sought and found, and for several years I stayed abroad studying Talmud. But the flame of the Torah kept glowing within me, though without my realizing it.

I returned to my native land and God brought me together with a Jewish philosopher with whom I studied some of Maimonides' *Guide to the Perplexed* and this only added to my desire. I acquired a little of the science of logic and a little of natural science, and this was very sweet to me for, as you know, "nature attracts nature". And God is my witness: If I had not previously acquired strength of faith by what little I had learned of the Torah and the Talmud, the impulse to keep many of the religious commands would have left me, although the fire of pure intention was ablaze in my heart. But what this teacher communicated to me in the way of philosophy (on the meaning of the commandments) did not suffice me, until the Lord had me meet a godly man, a kabbalist who taught me the general outlines of the Kabbalah. Nevertheless, in consequence of my smattering of natural science, the way of Kabbalah seemed all but impossible to me. It was then that my teacher said to me:

"My son, why do you deny something you have not tried? Much rather would it befit you to make a trial of it. If you then should find that it is nothing to you—and if you are not perfect enough to find the fault with yourself—then you may say that there is nothing to it."

But, in order to make things sweet to me until my reason might accept them and I might penetrate into them with eagerness, he used always to make me grasp in a natural way everything in which he instructed me. I reasoned thus within myself: There can only be gain here and no loss. I shall see; if I find something in all of this that is sheer gain; and if not, that which I have already had will still be mine. So I gave in and he taught me the method of the permutations and combinations of letters and the mysticism of numbers and the other "Paths of the book of *Yetsirah*". In each path he had me wander for two weeks until each form had been engraven in my heart, and so he led me on for four months or so and then ordered me to "efface" everything.

He used to tell me: "My son, it is not the intention that you come to a stop with some finite or given form, even though it be of the highest order. Much rather is this the 'Path of the Names': The less understandable they are, the higher their order, until you arrive at the activity of a force which is no longer in your control, but rather your reason and your thought is in its control."

I replied: "If that be so (that all mental and sense images must be effaced), why then do you, Sir, compose books in which the methods of the natural scientists are coupled with instruction in the holy names?"

He answered: "For you and the likes of you among the followers of philosophy, to allure your human intellect through natural means, so that perhaps this attraction may cause you to arrive at the knowledge of the Holy Name."

And he produced books for me made up of (combinations of) letters and names and mystic numbers (*Gematrioth*), of which nobody will ever be able to understand anything for they are not composed in a way meant to be understood.

He said to me: "This is the (undefiled) 'Path of the Names'."

And indeed, I would see none of it as my reason did not accept it. He said: "It was very stupid of me to have them shown to you."

In short, after two months had elapsed and my thought had disengaged itself (from everything material) and I had become aware of strange phenomena occurring within me, I set myself the task at night of combining letters with one another and of pondering over them in philosophical meditation, a little different from the way I do now, and so I continued for three nights without telling him. The third night, after midnight, I nodded off a little, quill in hand and paper on my knees. Then I noticed that the candle was about to go out. I rose to put it right, as oftentimes happens to a person awake. Then I saw that the light continued. I was greatly astonished, as though, after close examination, I saw that it issued from myself. I said: "I do not believe it." I walked to and fro all through the house and, behold, the light is with me; I lay on a couch and covered myself up, and behold, the light is with me all the while. I said: "This is truly a great sign and a new phenomenon which I have perceived."

The next morning I communicated it to my teacher and I brought him the sheets which I had covered with combinations of letters.

He congratulated me and said: "My son, if you would devote yourself to combining Holy Names, still greater things would happen to you. And now, my son, admit that you are unable to bear not combining. Give half to this and half to that, that is, do combinations half of the night, and permutations half of the night."

I practiced this method for about a week. During the second week the power of meditation became so strong in me that I could not manage to write down the combinations of letters (which automatically spurted out of my pen), and if there had been ten people present they would not have been able to write down so many combinations as came to me during the influx. When I came to the night in which this power was conferred on me, and midnight—when this power especially expands and gains strength whereas the body weakens—had passed, I set out to take up the Great Name of God, consisting of seventy-two names, permuting and combining it. But when I had done this for a little while, behold, the letters took on in my eyes the shape of great mountains, strong trembling seized me and I could summon no strength, my hair stood on end, and it was as if I were not in this world. At once I fell down, for I no longer felt the least strength in any of my limbs. And behold, something resembling speech emerged from my heart and came to my lips and forced them to move. I thought—perhaps this is, God forbid, a spirit of madness that has entered into me? But behold, I saw it uttering wisdom. I said: "This is indeed the spirit of wisdom." After a little while my natural strength returned to me. I rose very much impaired and I still did not believe myself. Once more I took up the Name to do with it as before and, behold, it had exactly the same effect on me. Nevertheless I did not believe it until I had tried it four or five times.

When I got up in the morning I told my teacher about it. He said to me: "And who was it that allowed you to touch the Name? Did I not tell you to permute only letters?" He spoke on: "What happened to you represents indeed a high stage among the prophetic degrees." He wanted to free me of it for he saw that my face had changed.

But I said to him: "In heaven's name, can you perhaps impart to me some power to enable me to bear this force emerging from my heart and to receive influx from it?" For I wanted to draw this force towards me and receive influx from it, for it much resembles a spring filling a great basin with water. If a man (not being properly prepared for it) should open the dam, he would be drowned in its waters and his soul would desert him.

He said to me: "My son, it is the Lord who must bestow such power upon you for such power is not within man's control."

That Sabbath night also the power was active in me in the same way. When, after two sleepless nights, I had passed day and night in meditating on the permutations or on the principles essential to a recognition of this true reality and to the annihilation of all extraneous thought—then I had two signs by which I knew that I was in the right receptive mood. The one sign was the intensification of natural thought on very profound objects of knowledge, a debility of the body and strengthening of the soul until I sat there, my self all soul. The second sign was that imagination grew strong within me and it seemed as though my forehead were going to burst. Then I knew that I was ready to receive the Name. I also that Sabbath night ventured at the great ineffable Name of God (the name JHWH). But immediately that I touched it, it weakened me and a voice issued from me saying: "Thou shalt surely die and not live! Who brought thee to touch the Great Name?" And behold, immediately I fell prone and implored the Lord God saying: "Lord of the universe! I entered into this place only for the sake of heaven, as Thy glory knowest. What is my sin and what my transgression? I entered only to know Thee, for has not David already commanded Solomon: Know the God of thy father and serve Him; and has not our master Moses, peace be upon him, revealed this to us in the Torah saying: Show me now Thy way, that I may know Thee, that I may there find grace in Thy sight?" And behold, I was still speaking and oil like the oil of the anointment anointed me from head to foot and very great joy seized me which for its spirituality and the sweetness of its rapture I cannot describe.

All this happened to your servant in his beginnings. And I do not, God forbid, relate this account from boastfulness in order to be thought great in the eyes of the mob, for I know full well that greatness with the mob is deficiency and inferiority with those searching for the true rank which differs from it in genus and in species as light from darkness.

Now, if some of our own philosophizers, sons of our people who feel themselves attracted towards the naturalistic way of knowledge and whose intellectual power in regard to the mysteries of the Torah is very weak, read this, they will laugh at me and say: See how he tries to attract our reason with windy talk and tales, with fanciful imaginations which have muddled his mind and which he takes at their face value because of his weak mental hold on natural science. Should, however, kabbalists see this, such as have some grasp of this subject or even better such as have had things divulged to them in experiences of their own, they will rejoice and my words will win their favor. But their difficulty will be that I have disclosed all of this in detail. Nevertheless, God is my witness that my intention is in *majorem dei gloriam* and I would wish that every single one of your holy nation were even more excellent herein and purer than I. Perhaps it would then be possible to reveal things of which I do not as yet know. . . . As for me, I cannot bear not to give generously to others what God has bestowed upon me. But since for this science there is no naturalistic evidence, its premises being as spiritual as are its inferences, I was forced to tell this story of the experience that befell me. Indeed, there is no proof in this science except experience itself. . . . That is why I say, to the man who contests this path, that I can give him an experimental proof, namely, my own evidence of the spiritual results of my own experiences in the science of letters according to *The Book of Creation*. I did not, to be sure, experience the corporeal (magic) effects (of such practices); and even granting the possibility of such a form of experience, I for my part want none of it, for it is an inferior form, especially when measured by the perfection which the soul can attain spiritually. Indeed, it seems to me that he who attempts to secure these (magic) effects desecrates God's name, and it is this that our teachers hint at when they say: Since license prevailed, the name of God has been taught only to the most reticent priests.

BY THE WATERS OF THE TAGUS

JUDAH ASHERI (1270-1349)

In this memoir the reader may gain an intimate picture of the personality and times of a luminary whose activities centered in Germany and Spain. His father, Asher ben Yehiel, and brother Jacob left an indelible imprint on talmudic literature and tradition, and he takes enormous pride in the family achievement. Despite his modest appraisal of his abilities, Judah was an ever busy, just, devout leader of his people; when his illustrious father died he was immediately elected in his place as rabbi of the important congregation of Toledo. He bemoans the need of accepting a salary, a measure that became a necessity in that period. This selfportrait is part of a long testament which he left for the guidance and inspiration of his family.

※　※　※

I WILL open with a voice of thanksgiving, I, Judah, to the Rock whose works are awe-inspiring, to whom appertain glory and greatness transcending man's capacity to express them; who, ere ever I was born, remembered me for good. My mother dreamed how she was told that she would bear a son, and was asked whether she wished him to be wise or wealthy? She chose wisdom. And though in reality dreams speak vain things, for I learned not wisdom, yet in a certain deceptive sense the dream was fulfilled. The world imagines that I am a scholar, one who giveth goodly words! Wealth, too, the Lord, blessed be He, hath bestowed upon me beyond the ordinary, in that He hath provided me with the measure of mine allotted bread. I rejoice in my portion.

When I was an infant about three months old, my eyes were affected, and were never completely restored. A certain woman tried to cure me when I was about three years of age, but she added to my blindness, to the extent that I remained for a year confined to the house, being unable to see the road on which to walk. Then a Jewess, a skilled oculist, appeared on the scene; she treated me for about two months, and then died.

30

Had she lived another month, I might have received my sight fully. As it was, but for the two months' attention from her, I might never have been able to see at all. Blessed be the Lord, who exercised marvelous loving-kindness toward me, and opened for me a lattice through which I might behold, with my own eye, the work of His hands.

I left Germany at the age of thirteen, and when fifteen I came to Toledo, in the new moon of Iyar in the year 1305. It is obvious that at my exodus when thirteen I possessed nothing; nor when I married first the daughter of R. Yehiel and later the daughter of R. Solomon, did I receive even enough to pay for the wedding garments and celebrations. From my lord, my father, of blessed memory, I inherited only a trifle as my share of his library. All that he owned at the time of his demise, together with all his household goods, did not suffice to carry out his testamentary bequests. Never in my life did I accept gifts from individuals, except about 1400 gold pieces which were given to me by three men, from whom I sought a loan but who insisted on making a gift. Because of their importance and position, I was unable to refuse their bounty. I used the money for my sister's marriage. I also lost money through those who transacted business for me, although that money was not my own. For 7000 gold pieces of borrowed capital were in the hands of my brother Eliakim, 8500 were deposited with R. Mordecai the Frenchman, who only returned to me 2000, 3000 were entrusted to R. Nissim, and the rest in the hands of others whom it would weary me to mention. I could not have survived till now but for the mercy of God, who put it in the heart of men to lend me capital, from the profits of which I maintained myself. For from the time of the death of my lord, my father, of blessed memory, that is to say for twenty-seven years and three months—I have not taken from the congregation (whom may God preserve!) under contract more than 1290 gold pieces. This I accepted for two years and four months, and I ceased to enter into any contract until the ten years mentioned were completed. Thereafter I received up to August (1340) from them 1500 pieces annually for nine years and ten months, a total of 14,750. Thenceforth they contracted to increase the annual payment to 3000 pieces. They agreed that after my death an annual pension of 1000 pieces should be paid for ten consecutive years to my wife and children or to any of them then living in Toledo. During my lifetime each of my sons was guaranteed 300 pieces a year for ten years, so long as he should pursue his studies and dwell in Toledo. A similar sum was appointed, under similar conditions, to be paid after my death to each of my sons out of the total of 1000 pieces mentioned above. I received from them from the August named to the end of November in this year 1348, for seven years and four months, 22,000 pieces. The total received by me from the congregation till the end of November has been 37,240 gold pieces. Of this sum, my son Solomon received, for two years and two months, 800 pieces in accordance with the arrangement already explained.

The contract which the congregation granted was not entered into because I demanded it of them (for I knew that I was unworthy of such consideration) but it was due to their abundant generosity and their affection for my lord, my father. But in the tenth year of my office, the congregation heard that it was my intention to seek a resting place elsewhere. They then fixed for me the payment of 1500 pieces annually. Had I been willing to accept more, they would have given it, as is expressly stated in their letter (which I still possess) of the year 1341. When the aforesaid Mordecai absconded I lost in his hand more than 6000, and it became known to the heads of the congregation that I designed emigrating to Seville. They besought me to remain, and they increased the sum payable under the contract to 3000 gold pieces a year. I am aware that all this was not due to my own deserts. It was due to the bounty of the Merciful One, the faithful God, and to the merit of my fathers, the repairers of the breach, the holy ones who were in the earth.

He who searcheth hearts knoweth that all my yearning desire for children in this world was solely dictated by my wish to raise up offspring which should fill my father's place in the study of the Law, in good works, and in the service of God. And in this sense I besought Him who is enthroned o'er the Cherubim, entreating God for myself, my children, and all our generations after us, that we may dwell in the house of the Lord all the days of our life, to behold the graciousness of the Lord and to pass our time in the inner shrine of His Law from morn to eve and from eve to morn, in the precious presence of God. I prayed that He would keep us far from men of vanity and frivolity, that we might maintain the example of our fathers, who, as our tradition assures us, were for many generations before us men of learning, of right-doing, and God-fearers—men from whom the Torah went forth unto Israel. And this has been my constant prayer at the graves of the righteous and perfect: "Lord of the Universe, King that sittest on the throne of mercy! It is revealed and known before Thee that all my desire for children was not out of my love for them, nor to gain honor through them, but only to perform that duty of continuing the race which Thou hast ordained. May it be Thy will to order us in all our affairs in good counsel before Thee. O may the fear of Thee be with us that we sin not, and may we live in Thy presence in reverence. Grant unto me sons who may grow into maturity, and may fill my father's place. And may God in His mercy raise up for us the merit of the righteous one buried in this grave. May my prayer be heard here, and may He too pray on our behalf, blessing us continually and at all hours."

One of the good methods which I desired for maintaining the family record was the marriage of my sons to members of my father's house. I had many reasons for this. First, it is a fair and fit thing to join fruit of vine to fruit of vine. It is indeed an important duty, for as our Sages said: "He who loves his relatives, he who marries his sister's daughter, and he who lends to the poor in the hour of his distress—to him applies the text. 'Then shalt thou call, and the Lord will answer; thou shalt cry and He will say, Here I am.'" Furthermore, the women of our family have grown accustomed to the ways of students, and the love of the Torah has entered their hearts, so that they are a help to their husbands in their scholarly pursuits. Moreover, they are not used to extravagant expenditure; they do not demand luxuries, the provision of which disturbs a man from his study. Then again, children for the most part resemble the mother's family. Finally, if with changing times a man see fit to seek his livelihood in another city, there will be none to place obstacles in the way of the wife accompanying her husband.

The second plan is for me to write something of the history of my saintly progenitors, for the edification of those that come after us. Seeing that the Lord, blessed be He, brought us to Toledo, that great and renowned city, and that a little later the Jews were expelled from France, possibly some may think that we were among the exiles, or that we left our country in consequence of some whispered suspicion. Therefore, it seems desirable to me to disabuse everyone of such an imputation. And further, when our posterity regards the upright lives of our ancestors, they will be ashamed if they walk not in the same paths. Rather will they strive in all things to imitate their fathers, thus finding grace and good favor in the sight of God and man. Otherwise, better were it for them never to be born, like infants who never see the light. As I left Germany when about thirteen years of age, I did not acquire exact information as to our fathers' righteous lives, except the little which I heard from my lord, my father of blessed memory, and from his sister and my grandmother, who related to me some of the family history. What little I heard of the doings of our first ancestors I set down here.

My grandfather, R. Yehiel ben Asher, was born in the year 1210.

When he was ten years old he had a firm friend in R. Solomon ha-Kohen. They entered into a pact that each should share the other's rewards, whether religious or secular. They held to this agreement all their days, and were unique in their generation for saintliness and benevolence. Now on the eve of the Day of Atonement in the year 1264, early in the night, the candle of my grandfather went out in the synagogue. For it was customary in Germany to kindle a wax candle for every male in the synagogue, on the eve of the Fast, and the candle was of a size to burn the whole day and night. Later (during the middle days of Tabernacles) my grandfather died and great honor was shown unto him at his death, people from neighboring places attending his funeral. Now it is the practice in Germany to set the coffin on a stone appointed for the purpose near the cemetery, and to open it to see whether the body has been dislocated by the jolting of the coffin. When they did this to him, R. Solomon ha-Kohen approached up to four cubits, and said in the presence of the assembly, "In your presence I call upon him to remember our covenant." Within the coffin a look of joy lit his face, most of those present saw him smile, and I testify on the evidence of my father and grandmother that this happened. A day came when R. Solomon ha-Kohen was studying in his college in the daytime, and lo! my grandfather of blessed memory was seated by his side. Amazed, R. Solomon asked how he fared, and he answered, exceeding well, and that a seat was ready at his side for his friend. "I wonder", said R. Solomon, "that thou art permitted to be visible to mortals." He answered: "I have liberty to go to my house as of aforetime, but I am unwilling that they should say: How this saint prides it over the other righteous men!" Six months after his death, at midnight on the Sabbath night, he appeared to his wife and said: "Haste and rise, take thy sons and daughters, and remove them hence, for tomorrow all the Jews of this place will be slain. So was it decreed against the whole neighborhood, but we prayed and our petition was successful except as regards this place." She rose and obeyed, but returning to save her belongings, she was killed with the congregation. She had previously rescued my lord, my father, R. Asher of blessed memory, and his brother, R. Hayyim, fellow disciple of R. Meir of Rothenburg, teacher of my father. They had another brother, by name R. Eleazar, who died at the age of twenty-seven. He was reported to be as fine a scholar as his brother R. Hayyim. They had six sisters, the whole family saintly—all bearing deservedly high reputations among their contemporaries. The nine of them escaped on the day and under the circumstances narrated above. All of them had large families of sons and daughters, and I have heard that one of the sons of my uncle R. Hayyim, of blessed memory, married in Germany, and that there were at his wedding about five hundred men and women, all relatives, the relationship reaching to that of third cousins.

The cause of my father's departure from Germany was due to the imprisonment of Rabbi Meir of Rothenburg, of blessed memory. Count Meinhard of Goiz, then head of the government, arrested him, and the congregation of Germany ransomed him for a considerable sum. The governor refused to accept as guarantor any other person than my lord, my father, of blessed memory. He was compelled to become security for a large amount. But before the contributions were apportioned to the various congregations, Rabbi Meir died in prison. The Governor unjustly refused to admit my father's plea that as Rabbi Meir died before his release, the guarantee had lapsed. Payment was still demanded from my father and the congregation, and my father escaped to another city; he left Germany altogether because of his fear of the authorities, and settled in the great city of Toledo. In the first year of his residence there, they sent him a written communication from the town council of the place where he formerly lived, inviting him to return home. They would dispatch fifty officers to meet him on the German frontier, and would give him a documentary safe-conduct from the Emperor. For they recognized his wisdom and excellence, and were wont to follow his advice in all matters. But in face of the frequent ill-treatment of the Jews there, he was unwilling to go back. This was the reason of the coming of my lord, my father of blessed memory, to this country. "This was the Lord's doing," to the end that my father might raise up many disciples on Spanish soil. "He executed the righteousness of the Lord, and His ordinances with Israel." For there were not in these lands any thorough commentaries. He also wrote commentaries and decisions to the Talmud. Wherever his commentaries, responsa and decisions reached, they made known the statutes of the Lord and His laws. His sons walked in his ways, and maintained his opinions. "As for Asher, his bread was fat;" his Rock guarded him with every care, because he was faithful to its charge. "And of Asher he said: blessed be Asher because of his sons"—all of them were interpreters of uprightness, who from the least to the greatest of them held fast to the law of God, the Lord of the Universe, and by what they wrought were a shield to their generation. I was by far the most insignificant of all of them; through His grace God raised me up in my father's place, a tendril of his stock, a shooting of his roots and planting, to maintain his School on its site, even better equipped than of yore. And also in what pertained to the affairs and organization of the community, we passed our time together in settlement of causes and judgments. Men of the government also agreed to abide by my decisions, not because of my wisdom or wit, for "I am brutish, unlike a man, and have not a man's understanding," but God filled them with a kindly disposition towards me, so that my words were acceptable to them, in that they deemed me in their thoughts an impartial judge.

As for me, my prayer is made before the Lord of the Universe, that He may requite with a good recompense this holy congregation for their labors, and for all the good which they as a body and as individuals have done unto me in granting all my requests and of their heart's generosity and not for any selfish motive. And so will it ever continue until I part from them in great love, "and my seed shall be established in their sight, and my offspring before their eyes." And may it be their good will to prepare a way for my progeny to settle among them as they did with my father and me, kindness after kindness. For what has passed and for what is to come, unto the Rock tremendous in His doing, Judah shall lead the thanksgiving. And may the bounty of God and the merit of our fathers cause that there never fail from us in Toledo—until the majestic and awful God establish Jerusalem and a Redeemer come unto Zion— one to fill the seat of my lord, my father, R. Asher of beloved memory; (may this be so) for all time until Shiloh cometh and people be gathered unto him, and there arise a priest with Urim and with Thummim.

Ended and completed, praise to the God of the Universe!

CASTILIAN VIGNETTE

MENAHEM BEN ZERAH (?-1385)

Menahem was an eyewitness to epoch-making events in France and Spain during the fourteenth century. Born into a family of scholars, he steadfastly continued his studious life despite the ravages of war, pestilence and want. This brief succinct account of his life, written in a preface to a book to explain its purpose, indicates how talmudic scholarship flourished even in chaotic times. He was typical of many modest, self-sacrificing scholars of the Middle Ages, whose industry and courage made possible the unbroken continuity of religious and social tradition.

❋ ❋ ❋

I MENAHEM BEN AARON BEN ZERAH, the humblest of my family, was born in the land of Navarre. My noble father was among those who were driven from France in the month of Ab in the year 5066 of the Creation (1306).* When I was about sixteen years old, I married a daughter of Rabbi Benjamin Abetz, may his soul rest in Eden. He spread the study of Torah in Etoile, and many of his students were of the house of Askra, a family distinguished for learning and wealth.

Now in the year 1322 the wrath of the Lord was kindled against His people. The King of France (Philip V, 1316-1322) who ruled over Navarre died, and the populace arose and decided to destroy, murder and devastate all the Jews in their realm. In Etoile and in other places of the land, they killed about six thousand Jews. My father, my mother and four younger brothers suffered martyrs' deaths for the sanctification

---

* This happened during the reign of Louis X who issued the decree of expulsion on June 21st. The crown seized both real and personal property of the Jews and permitted them a month to leave the country. Although they were recalled in 1315, this vandalism marked the beginning of the decline of French Jewry. Esthori Pharhi, who was studying at Montpellier at the time, left a brief account of his experience, "They yanked me out of the schoolroom," he wrote, "they stripped me of my very shirt. Naked, I left my father's house and my native land; I wandered as a mere lad from nation to nation without a knowledge of their tongues until I finally found peace in the Holy Land."

of God—may He avenge their blood! I alone, of my father's house, escaped —stricken, smitten of God, and afflicted. For twenty-five mobsters smote me mercilessly; I was thrown among the dead where I lay from evening till midnight on the 23rd of the month of Adar. At midnight, a certain knight who knew my father came and had mercy upon me. He took me from the dead and carried me to his house. When the Healer, may He be blessed, undeservedly healed my wounds, I decided to go to Toledo to study Torah.

Then a new King arose over Navarre (Charles IV, 1322-1328), and the children of those who had been slain complained to him of the oppression, asking that he punish those who had spilt the blood of our fathers. But he did not heed our request.

In those days I studied for about two years with my master, Rabbi Joshua ben Shoab, may he rest in Eden. Afterwards, I came to this land (Spain) in the year 1331. I dwelt in Alcala and studied there with Rabbi Joseph ibn Alayish, may he rest in Eden. He and I used to study continually, day and night: it was our custom to start a treatise of the Talmud from the beginning and read the entire text with the *Supplements* of Rabbi Perez. After his death in 1360, the leaders of the community asked me to teach in his place, and, although I was unworthy of this honor, I did as they requested.

While Rabbi Joseph ibn Alayish was still alive, I also studied in Toledo with my master, Rabbi Judah,* may he rest in Eden. We examined two sections of the Talmud—Seder Zeraim (Seeds) and Seder Toharoth (Purifications) according to the system of the Rosh, and I investigated with him the variant readings of the texts of Seder Moed (Festivals), Seder Nezikim (Damages) and the Gemara of Gittin (Divorce) arranging them in accordance with his interpretation. Between 1350 and 1368 I studied uninterruptedly with my associates and friends in Alcala, our studies being chiefly according to the method of our master, Rabbi Perez.

And it came to pass that the Lord awakened the spirit of Don Henry,** son of King Alfonso. He fought with his brother Don Pedro who ruled after the death of his father. He besieged the fortified cities and captured them. In the month of Iyar, 1368, he besieged Toledo. And it happened that at the end of that year Don Pedro went forth from

---

* Judah Asheri who in 1328 succeeded his father, Asher ben Yehiel (referred to as the "Rosh") as Rabbi of Toledo. See Judah's *vita*, pp. 30-36.

** This paragraph refers to the struggle between Pedro the Cruel (1350-1369) and Henry de Trastamond II (1369-1379).

Seville with his entire army to fight against his brother and to rescue Toledo from the siege; and the King, Don Henry, marched out to meet him and slew him in the city of Montilla. Thereupon the kingdom was secure in the hands of King Henry and his power was greatly strengthened.

Now, during this period of war the whole earth was chaotic and everyone did as he pleased. The populace pillaged and robbed most of the communities of Spain and pauperized Israel. It was a time of distress for Jews who dwelt throughout the kingdom of Castile, without parallel since the time they were exiled there. They died by the sword and were carried away as captive slaves. The holy community of Toledo suffered so severely during the siege that they ate the flesh of their sons and daughters. About eight thousand souls, young and old, died during the siege from hunger and dire want. And so heavily were they taxed by the King that hardly a crumb remained to an inhabitant. I, too, was completely bereft of all that I had; they despoiled, robbed and smote me. They took the clothes off my back and left me nothing of all my labor. Gone my books, my home, my land!

Then, with the aid of the eminent Don Samuel Abarbanel of Seville, may God watch over him, I was revived and enabled to support my old age. He helped me to extricate myself from the destruction, and I went to live in Toledo where some of the notables who survived and knew me before entreated me to remain. So I consented to stay with them, may the Lord of Hosts have mercy upon the remnant of our people. They gave me, as well as my companion scholars, our allotted bread.

All the good which the eminent Don Samuel did for me, I remembered. I found him an intelligent man, fond of learned men whom he fed and to whom he was devoted. Even though the times gave him no peace, he longed to study the works of authors. And I saw that those who served in the courtyard of the King, may his glory be exalted, those who, in accordance with their excellency and station, were the shield and refuge of their people, tended to neglect the observance of the obligatory commandments (prayer, blessings, Sabbath, festivals and the like) because of the great unrest and the lust for privilege. For this reason and on account of my love for Don Samuel, may God watch over him, I followed the footsteps of our teachers and sages: I sharpened my quill, I entered into privacy and composed a book which I called *Provender for the Journey*. And I completed the work in the hope of the coming of the Messiah and of a portion in the World To Come.

ADVENTURE IN THE HOLY LAND

MESHULLAM BEN MENAHEM (FIFTEENTH CENTURY)

The traveler, the merchant and the pilgrim are among the most typical and most interesting of wandering Jews. From the patriarchs, A'braham and Joseph, to modern globe-trotters like Arminius Vambéry and Louis Golding, they have given to Jewish literature a strong aroma of the caravansary. Meshullam was a merchant of Volterra, Italy, who knew his way around in the fifteenth century, and left us a graphic account of a trip to the Levant in 1481. At Palermo he chanced upon Rabbi Obadiah of Bertinoro, a notable whom he accompanied through the Archipelago. But he also met with mishaps and adventures which he describes warmly and in detail. Admirers of Mark Twain's *Innocents Abroad* will recognize the same Holy Land in this tale out of Meshullam's letter, recording the cleverness with which he outwitted both cutthroats and customs.

❊   ❊   ❊

WE LEFT Hebron on Tuesday, the 28th of July, 1481, and traveled in the company of two good and honored mamelukes, inasmuch as caravans of Christian merchants pass only occasionally between Hebron and Jerusalem. Thus we were obliged to accompany these two men and with them there was a bastard whose intention was to kill us. His name is Ali and he was a Moslem. We went with him and took our lives in our hands.

At nightfall we reached a village called Halibi, and Ali went into the village and persuaded three of his companions to rob us on the journey. Then that Ali came to us and spoke deceitfully. He said that we should accompany him and the two mamelukes and he would take us by an indirect road so that we should not have to pay tolls until we reached Jerusalem. The mamelukes believed him and so did we. We journeyed forth at midnight and he led us in a circle to a place ten miles from Hebron, where there was a house in ruins and a cave where Jesse, the father of David, was buried (they say that this cave reaches to the cave of Machpelah). And the cursed fellow led us by ways which nobody had passed before into a great wood on the hills, and when we reached the middle of the woods the cursed Ali said, "I now want the two ducats which you have promised me." My companion, the dragoman, replied, "We promised you only one golden ducat. Anyhow, we shall give you what you want when we reach Jerusalem. Now you may have half a ducat because we have no more." But he wanted to see our money and therefore made excuses.

He had a bow and arrows and was riding on a fine horse, a jennet, and he left us, went into the woods and called aloud. When the mamelukes saw this they went after him and appealed to his heart. And Joseph, the dragoman, into whose mouth God had put the words, said to them, "Know that if this man does any wrong to us or kills us you will not escape for the Jews will know of it. We went with the Niepo, the Lord of Ḥebron, from his city and they will seek us through him and he knows that we went with you. What will you reply when the Niepo seeks us at your hands?" The good mamelukes who did not intend to harm us replied, "By our lives, we will kill him."

Now they also had bows and arrows and they went after the man and brought him back. And Joseph, the dragoman, went after them in stealth in order to listen to their conversation, and I and Raphael, my companion, were left alone in the woods. The dragoman heard Ali say, "Let me do this. I have three companions with whom I spoke last night in Halibi, and we will kill them and take their horses and all their possessions and divide it equally, because they are very rich. Who will seek them at our hands?" Then the mamelukes replied, "Do not think so for it is our duty to protect them. The Lord, the Niepo of Hebron, has entrusted them to us and we must account for them." Then Ali answered, "Tell the Niepo that you left them near Jerusalem or that the Orbanites slew them, and that you fled with their good horses and they pursued you, because they recognized that you were mamelukes, and you were not able to save them and are guiltless." All this Joseph heard when he went behind them in order to find out whether the mamelukes would consent after all the talk. When the mamelukes saw that Ali would not listen to them they said to him, "Choose one of two things: Either die here, for we will slay you, or come with us. We do not wish to call your companions because the responsibility for this rests upon us. If you come with us, we swear by the Life of our King that we will not betray your secret to anybody." And that is why he returned against his will.

Now the mamelukes said to us, "Let us go in front with this cursed fellow and you follow behind, near to us." Then there was much talk between them, and the mamelukes placed him between them so that he could not flee. And in this way we traveled at night by the light of the moon until dawn. When Ali saw that it was dawn he said to the mamelukes, "I wish to leave my horse here in the village." He was afraid to enter Jerusalem for fear that the mamelukes would betray him to the Emir of Jerusalem. So he disappeared.

And we hastened to Bethlehem and from there on the high road we found Rachel's tomb. It is a high monument of stones and the Moslems have erected above her grave an arch resting upon four pillars. They honor her, and both Jews and Moslems pray there. God protected us from the hands of that betrayer and robber, and we gave a ducat to each of the mamelukes instead of the villain; anyhow, we paid no tax because of the roundabout journey we made, for there are seven toll-houses between Hebron and Jerusalem.

On the same day we arrived in Jerusalem, the Holy City, in peace, thanks be to the Lord, who sent us those two mamelukes to save us from death. On the way we found at the Well of the Virgin more than ten thousand men who were proceeding against the Orbanites and none could go out and none could come in. You see, therefore, that if we had delayed a single day we should not have been able to get through and should have been in great danger. Blessed be He and blessed be His Name, Who doeth good to the undeserving.

TWILIGHT OF SPANISH GLORY

DON ISAAC ABRAVANEL (1437-1509)

Born in Lisbon of a distinguished family and the father of the poet Judah Leo Medigo and the scholar-diplomat Samuel Abravanel, Don Isaac played a great role during stirring times. He served as finance minister to the kings of Portugal, Spain, and Naples successively, and in each instance was rewarded with confiscation of his possessions and exile. What he experienced during the tragic destruction of Spanish Jewry and the expulsion of 1492 is touchingly described in his reminiscences. An interesting sidelight is provided in the diary of Columbus who incidentally was assisted by many Jews. "In the same month during which their Majesties decreed that all Jews should be driven out of the Kingdom and its territories," the diary begins, "they gave me the commission to undertake with sufficient men my expedition of discovery to the Indies." Abravanel was a prolific author, composing expansive commentaries on the Bible and eloquent speculations on the messianic salvation of his people.

* * *

I ISAAC ABRAVANEL, am the son of that prince in Israel, Judah the son of Samuel ben Judah ben Joseph ben Judah of the house of Abravanel. All of my forebears, descended from King David, son of Jesse of Bethlehem, were worthy leaders of our people. May their memory be forever blessed.

I lived in the beautiful city of Lisbon, capital of the realm of Portugal, secure in the wealth of my family inheritance. My home was filled with God's blessings. I enjoyed honor, riches, and the joy of my fellow men. I builded myself a spacious home and made it a gathering place for the wise, a hall of justice and learning. How happy I was at the palace of King Alphonso V, who ruled justly over a realm that touched two seas, who prospered in all that he did! His throne was a veritable seat of justice and a wellspring of righteousness, for he trusted in the Almighty,

43

eschewed evil, and ruled his people well. He was wise in his choice of leaders. Richly did he eat of the Tree of Knowledge, but the fullness of the Tree of Life the Lord did not grant him. In his power and prosperity were the safety and freedom of the Jews. Under his shadow I delighted to sit; I was near unto him and he delighted in me; so long as he lived I was in attendance at his palace.

Then came an evil day for all the people and especially Israel—a day of darkness, lamentation and oppression. Death quickly mounted his windows and terror gripped his palace. She filled the halls, grasped the knife to slay her son, and slew him as the divine sentence decreed. Thus a spirit passed and went unto his God even as the chaff blows from the threshing floor. And the Daughter of Zion was left as a booth in the vineyard without a support; her being departed with his soul. The people hungered and mourned, and great was the lamentation in the House of Judah. I too suffered woefully in my mourning; like Job, my soul was poured out within me and I became as dust and ashes.

In his place ruled his son Don Juan II (1481-1495), who knew not the greatness and wisdom of his father. His perverted heart hated the princes and deceived all who served him. He estranged himself from all those who had loved his father, nobles of the highest lineage throughout the realm as well as his own flesh and bone. "All of you are worthy of death," he said deceitfully. "You have conspired to surrender me and my country to the kings of Spain." He seized one of the greatest and most trustworthy nobles, Ferdinand, Duke of Braganza, who was second in rank to the King, and had him executed. (This occurred in 1483.) His brothers, seeing that the pride and glory of their family was dead and fearing for their lives, fled in haste and disappeared. The King confiscated their estates and possessions, and blotted out their whole royal house.

The King was also incensed with me because I would not be a party to deceit and oppression. He vented his wrath against me because in the good old days I had been a bosom friend of the princes who had fled and they had sought my counsel. The nobles of the country also made severe charges against me, accusing me of being one of the conspirators. They declared that the conspirators would certainly not have kept their secret from me. Other wicked men, desiring to overthrow me and seize my possessions, sharpened their tongues like serpents and attributed to me wickedness that could not even enter my mind.

In the midst of the turmoil, evil couriers brought me the following message, "The King commands that you appear before him at once." I obeyed, and innocently proceeded to the appointed place of meeting.

While stopping on the way at an inn, a certain man approached me. "Go not near that place of meeting," he warned. "These are evil times. Save yourself. Fear has gripped the country; ugly rumors are rife; your enemies have made a death-pact against you." I saw that the world was topsyturvy, that truth and kindness were driven underground and the fear of God was no more. I meditated: Whither shall I go? I know how greedy these men are for gain and how ready to plunder and rob. Who will stay the anger of the King and the lust of his henchmen? Who will say to him: What in the world are you doing? Of what use is gold and silver? They will pursue and destroy me. Even if I managed to survive, I would be mercilessly oppressed all the time. Consequently I abandoned my inheritance, my wife and children, and all that I possessed, and I escaped alone. I arose in the night and took to the road; I put on strength in the face of misfortune and fled. Suddenly my fate became as the chaff that the storm stealeth away. I was deprived of my all as a result of a ban and I escaped by the skin of my teeth. When the sun shone forth the next morning, I heard the tumult of Pharaoh's House; couriers pressed forward with the King's command to seize and kill me. At the same time the royal troops and cavalry pursued me all that day and night through the wilderness.

Through God's compassion, they were unable to harm me. At midnight I left that Egypt, the kingdom of Portugal, and entered the kingdom of Castile by way of the border town of Segura della Orden. I went the way the Lord sent me; when the King saw that he could not lay hands on me, he fumed and raged and took all that I possessed—silver, gold, princely treasures and estates. Out of the bowels of the netherworld I cried out: "Save me, O King! What good can come of your oppression? Is not the Judge of the world just? Why do you act evilly toward your servant? Why do you strive against me and persecute me? Why does not my lord test me?" But he was as silent as an adder; his ears were stopped. I look for justice but behold violence; for righteousness, but behold a cry.

So I escaped alone to the Kingdom of Castile from the sword of my oppressor. I came there as a sojourner, and in order to pay my debt to God for saving me, I turned my attention to an investigation of the Scriptures. I made notes on the books of Joshua, Judges, and Samuel. This took place in the year 1484. As I intended to begin a commentary on the books of Kings, I was summoned before Ferdinand, King of Spain, the mightiest of the kings of the earth, who ruled the kingdoms of Castile, Aragon, Catalonia, Sicily, and other Mediterranean islands. I went to the court of the King and the Queen, and for a long time I served them, finding grace in their eyes and in the eyes of the first princes of the realm. I was in their service for eight years, being blessed with wealth and honor. But as a result of my heavy duties to the King, my literary efforts slackened, and I abandoned my inheritance from the Kings of Israel and Judah for the King of Aragon and Castile.

In 1492 the King of Spain seized the great city of Granada,* together with the whole kingdom. His haughtiness brought a change of character; his power led him to sin against his God. He thought to himself: "How can I better show my gratitude to my God, Who gave victory to my army and put this city into my power, than by bringing under His wing the scattered flock of Israel that walks in darkness? How shall I better serve Him than to bring back to His faith the apostate daughter? Or, if they remain stiffnecked, to drive them to another land so that they will not dwell here nor be seen in my presence?" Consequently the King enacted a decree as fixed as the law of the Medes and the Persians. He commanded that the children of Israel could remain in the country only if they submitted to baptism; but if they were unwilling to embrace Christian faith, they must leave the territories of Spain, Sicily, Majorca, and Sardinia. "Within three months," he decreed,** "there must not remain in my kingdoms a single Jew."

I was at court when the decree was proclaimed. I was disconsolate with grief. Thrice I addressed the King, imploring his mercy: "O King, save your loyal subjects. Why do you act so cruelly toward us? We have prospered in this land and we would gladly give all we possess for our country." I begged my noble friends at court to intercede for my people. The King's most trusted counsellors pleaded desperately that he revoke the decree and turn from his design to destroy the Jews. But his ears were closed as though he were stone deaf.*** The Queen, seated at his right, opposed revoking the decree; she pressed him to complete the task he had begun. Our exertions were therefore without effect. Despite the fact that I neither rested nor relaxed, the thunderbolt struck.

When the dreadful news reached the people, they mourned their fate; and wherever the report of the decree spread, Jews wept bitterly.

---

* With the capture of that magnificent city passed the last foothold of Moslem power in Spain. Ferdinand and Isabella erected a large cross in the Alhambra on January 2nd.

** The decree was issued in Granada on March 31, making June 31 the *terminus ad quem*.

*** It is reported that the King, persuaded by a delegation headed by the author promising a payment of 300,000 ducats, was on the point of revoking the decree when Torquemada, the notorious Inquisitor, appeared on the scene and declared, "Judas Iscariot sold his Master for 30 pieces of silver. You want to sell him for 300,000 ducats. Here He is—take Him and sell Him!" The decree became irrevocable.

The terror and lamentation were greater than at any time since the expulsion of our forefathers from their own soil in Judah to foreign strands. However, they bravely encouraged each other: "Let us cling unflinchingly to our faith, holding our heads with pride before the voice of the enemy that taunts and blasphemes. If they let us live, we will live; if they kill us, we will perish. But we will not break our Divine Covenant nor shall we turn back. We will go forth in the name of the Lord our God."

In this spirit the people, old and young, women and children, a multitude of 300,000 from every province, went forth on one day, unarmed and afoot. I was among them. They went whithersoever the wind carried them. Some fled to the kingdom of Portugal, others to the kingdom of Navarre. Many chose the way of the sea and were lost, drowned, burnt to death, and sold into slavery. They suffered the curses written in our Scriptures: "The Lord will cause thee to be smitten before thine enemies; thou shalt flee seven ways before them; thou shalt be a horror to all the kingdoms of the earth." (Deuteronomy 28:25) Of this vast host, only a small number survived. Blessed be the name of the Lord!

I, too, chose the path of my people, departing on a seagoing vessel. I went into exile with my whole family and came to this glorious city of Naples, whose kings are merciful. Thereupon I decided to pay my vow to God by setting upon the task of writing a commentary on the books of Kings. It was a time to recall the destruction of our Holy Temple and the Exile of our people, which are recorded in these books. It was a time to remember our glories and our misfortunes.

THE ROAD TO ROME

DAVID REUBENI (?-1537)

Reubeni was a fabulous figure in a fabulous century. He was called Messiah, kabbalist, prophet and impostor—some modern historians cling to the last—but, in his own words, "I am a sinner and a man of war". He was a combined Herzl and Jabotinsky of the sixteenth century. Claiming that he was the brother, generalissimo and emissary of King Joseph of Habor (north of Medina in Arabia) who commissioned him to interest the Pope and the monarchs of Spain and Portugal in raising an armed force to recapture Palestine from the Turks, he traveled from Arabia via Egypt and the Mediterranean between 1522 and 1525. The following excerpt from his diary describes the journey to the gates of Rome. He was then accorded the status of an ambassador by Pope Clement, King John of Portugal and Charles V, and for a time enjoyed diplomatic triumphs, but in 1537 he was imprisoned by Charles and died there. The last years of his life were closely tied to the activities of a Marrano disciple, Solomon Molko, whose story is told in the next selection.

❋　❋　❋

I AM David, the son of King Solomon (may the memory of the righteous be for a blessing), and my brother is King Joseph, who is older than I, and who sits on the throne of his kingdom in the wilderness of Habor (Khorgbar), and rules over thirty myriads of the tribe of Gad and of the tribe of Reuben and of the half-tribe of Manesseh. I have journeyed from before the King, my brother and his counsellors, the seventy Elders. They charged me to go first to Rome to the presence of the Pope, may his glory be exalted.

I left them by way of the hills, ten days' journey, till I arrived at Jeddah, where I was taken with a great sickness and remained five weeks, until I heard that a ship was going to the land of Ethiopia. I embarked on the ship in the Red Sea and went three days, and on the fourth day we arrived at the city of Suakim, in Ethiopia. I took a house and stayed there two months, but I was ill, and being cupped lost fifty pounds of blood; for in order to get better I had more than one hundred applications of hot nails. Afterwards I met many merchants who were traveling by way of Mecca to the kingdom of Sheba, and I called the chief of them, a descendant of the Prophet of the Ishmaelites named Omar Abu Kamil. I took two camels to journey with them, and they were a great multitude with more than three thousand camels. I improved in health daily, and we passed through great deserts and forests and fields in which there are many good herbs and good pasturage and rivers, a journey of two months, until we arrived at the capital of the kingdom of Sheba in Ethiopia, where resides King Omara, who dwells on the Nile. He is a black king and reigns over black and white, and the name of his city is Lamula, and I stayed with him ten months. The King travels in his countries, every month a different journey. I traveled with the King and had as my servants more than sixty men of the sons of the Prophet riding on horses, and they honored me with great honor.

All the time that I stayed in the country of Ethiopia with the King I fasted daily, when I lay down and when I got up, and I prayed day and night and I stayed not in the company of scoffers nor of merrymakers. On every journey they prepared for me a wooden hut near the King's house. The King has maidservants and menservants and slaves, most of them naked, and the Queen and the concubines and the ladies are dressed in golden bracelets, two on the hands and two on the legs; and they cover their nakedness with a golden chain, hand-embroidered, and a cubit wide round their loins closed before and behind. But their body is quite naked and bare, and they wear a golden wreath in their noses. The males and females eat elephants and wolves, leopards, dogs, and camels, and they eat human flesh. The King called me every day before him and said, "What askest thou of us, thou son of the Prophet; if thou desirest slaves, camels, or horses, take them." And I replied, "I want nothing of thee, but I have heard of the glory of thy kingdom and I have brought thee this gift with love and pleasure, and behold, I give thee a garment of silk and seven hundred ducats, florins of gold. I love thee and I grant thee pardon and forgiveness and a full title to paradise, to thee and to thy sons and daughters, and all thy household, and thou shalt come to us next year to the city of Mecca, the place for the atonement of sins." After these things an Ishmaelite came from the city of Mecca and slandered me before the King and said, "This man in whom thou believest is not of the sons of the Prophet, but from the wilderness of Habor." When the King heard this and sent for Abu Kamil and told him the words and the slander, Abu Kamil answered and said, "I know neither one man nor the other, but I have seen that the first man is honorable and fasts every day and fears God, and does not go after merriment nor after women and does not love money. But the other man loves money and does many evil things and talks a great deal"; and the King said, "Thy words are true," and Abu Kamil left him and told me these matters. After that the King's wife heard the words of the slanderer and sent for me and said to me, "Do not remain in this country for this new man who has come from Mecca has slandered thee to the King in words unfitting, and he is taking counsel with many men to seek from the King to slay thee." And I said to her, "How can I go away without the King's permission?" But the Queen replied, "The King comes tonight to my house and I will send for thee, and thou shalt come before me and before the King and thou shalt ask permission from the King, and I shall help thee and thou shalt go tomorrow on thy way in peace." So when I came before the King I burst forth and said, "What is my transgression, and what is my sin?" Have I not come before thee with gifts and love and kindness, and desired not to receive from thee, either silver or gold or slaves or maidservants or menservants; but this knave who has slandered me to thee loves money and speaks falsehood, and behold, I have been with thee ten months. Call thy servants and thy lords and let them tell thee if they have found in me any sin or transgression or any fault. Therefore, in thy kindness and for God's sake, give me permission to go on my way and I shall pray for thee and bless thee." And the Queen also said, "Give him permission that he may go on his way, for he is honorable and trusty and we have found no blemish in him, but only good report." And the King answered and said to me, "What needest thou, slaves, or camels, or horses? Take them and go in peace;" and I said to the King, "I want nothing but permission from thee that I may go tomorrow at dawn, for I know that I have wicked enemies against me; therefore may it be good in thy sight to send with me one of thy honored servants to the place of the house of Abu Kamil."

Then the King called one of his servants and ordered him to go with him and gave us two horses and we rode to the house of Abu Kamil, and on the way we crossed many rivers and the feeding ground of elephants. There was one river of mud and water in which horses, when crossing it, sank in the mire up to their bellies, and many men and horses had been drowned in this place. But we crossed it on horseback, and thanked God we were safe. We traveled eighteen days until we arrived at Senaar, and next morning I and my servant journeyed on further five days on the River Nile until I reached the city of Sheba, but it is in ruins and desolate, and there are wooden huts in it, and Abu Kamil came to me and said, "How art thou come from the King and he did not give thee slaves? I know that the King loves thee, therefore stay in my house and I will go up to the King and will beg him for thee;" and I said, "I will do so." But that night I dreamt in the house of Abu Kamil, and I saw my father, on whom be peace, and he said to me, "Why has thou come to this far land? Go hence tomorrow in peace and no evil will come upon thee, but if thou waitest until Abu Kamil returns, know that thou wilt die;" and when I woke from my sleep I said to Abu Kamil, "Let me go, I do not wish thee to go to the King for me," and in the morning I journeyed from Sheba, and Abu Kamil sent his brother with me, and we went ten days' journey to the kingdom of Elgel. Elgel is in the kingdom of Sheba and under the rule of Omara, and the name of the King of Elgel is Abu Akrab, and we came before him and Abu Kamil's brother said to him, "The King has ordered us to conduct this our lord, the son of the Prophet, by this way;" and I stayed before that King three days, and afterwards I journeyed on, I and my servant, till we came to Mount Takaki, and I stood before a great lord called Abd Alohab, and he wished me to go by way of a short desert to the land of Dongola, and I stayed in his house six days and gave him twenty ducats and garments. They filled me six water skins and placed them on three camels, and I journeyed on, I and my servant and the servant of Alohab, ten days by the desert way, and we found many men on horses, and I said to the servant of Alohab, "Lead me to Masah, five days' distance from this land, which is at the end of the kingdom of Sheba, on the River Nile;" and he said to me, "I will do according to thy words, and if thou wishest I will go with thee to Egypt." Then I bowed myself down before the King of heaven and earth, when I heard the words of the man, for I feared to remain in the land of Sheba, and I and he went through the beginning of the desert, where there is much sand, and we went on the sand as upon hills and I fasted three days consecutively until I reached the city of al Habor; and afterwards I reached the River Nile and behold, there was an old Ishmaelite of the lords of Egypt in front of me, and he came and kissed my hands, and said, "Come, O blessed of the Lord, O lord the son of our lord, do me kindness and come into my house and I will take thy blessing. I have food and provender and place to lodge," and I went with that man whose name is Osman. He had a wife and children, and prepared the house for me and my servant, and then I sent away the servant of Alohab to his country, and I gave him ten ducats and he went home.

And in that land five young men came to me from the two tribes and gave me two little lions, and I took the lions to bring them to Egypt, and the men returned to their country; and I stayed in the house of the old man with my servant one month, and the honored old man said to me, "Behold thy camels are very weak and cannot travel in this desert; thou wilt have to feed them two or three months until they get fat and then they can travel the three days' journey in the desert, where camels can find neither grass nor food nor anything to eat until you get to Girgeh, on the River Nile near to Egypt." I bought from the old man a she-camel, good and fat, for twenty ducats, and the old man bought for me two strong camels for seventy ducats, and the camels which I had I gave at camel price in exchange, and afterwards the lords of that city and its surroundings came and brought me flour, barley, rye, lambs, and bullocks, by way of tithe to the house of the old man, and they filled his house. But of what they gave me I only took what the camels eat and the remainder I gave to the old man and to the poor as a gift, and I said to the old man, "Come with me to King Mehmel," and I went with him before the King and his servants, and he was drinking date-wine and eating mutton without bread. The King was pleased with me and said, "This day is blessed on which our lord, the son of our lord the Prophet, has come before us, and it is my will that thou shalt remain in my house and, if thou wilt, I will do thee honor and glory," and I said to the King, "Be thou blessed before the Lord, I will pray for thee and I will give thee pardon and atonement for all thy sins."

On the 14th day of the month of Kislev I journeyed with my servant from the house of the old man, with many men by way of the great desert, and I was always fasting and praying to God, when I lay down and when I got up, and when I went forth and when I journeyed; and I determined not to eat or drink, save only once in every three days and nights, and did not eat between one oasis and another, for in this desert even wells three days' distance from each other are reckoned near, and some wells are four days' journey apart, and some wells five days. We could only drink the water which was on our camels until we arrived at the city of Girgeh, after forty-five days, and we had a man with us who knew the way in the desert like a pilot in the sea, by way of the stars by night and through his knowledge by day, for this desert is like the great sea. That wise man said to me, "Come with me to my house until

I find thee a way to go to Egypt"; and the man's name was Shalom, in Arabic Selim. His house was a mile from the end of the desert and I went with him to his house, which is on the Nile, and he gave me a hut and bed, and one of his servants to do for me. My servant and I stayed with the man twenty days, and I sold my camels for one hundred golden florins and I sailed in a small boat on the River Nile until I reached the gates of Egypt. There the Ishmaelite Turks detained me, and wished to examine my stuff and boxes in order to take tithe from me, and they wanted twenty florins for the servants. But when the Turks saw the two lions I had with me, they asked them of me as a present, and they would free me from the customs and the tithe. So I gave them the lions and I had no other expenses, and they honored me with great honor and their joy was very great, for they said they wished to send the lions to the King of Turkey.

I entered Cairo on the New Moon of Adar, 5283 (1523). I had journeyed with a man who had friends in Cairo, who said to me, "Come to my house tonight and stay till morning, and tomorrow I will seek for you a suitable lodging." I went with this man, I and my slave, and all my stuff.

It was a big house with large trees, and they gave me a room and placed before me bread and cheese. I said, "I cannot eat cheese, give me eggs," and I ate and slept till the morning. That morning I took out my pieces of gold and said, "Come with me to sell the gold to the Jews, because they are better versed in business than the ordinary people." He came with me to the Jewish quarter, and I stood in front of the door of a shop in which were Jewish money-changers. I asked them in Hebrew, "Who is the chief among you?" so that the Ishmaelites should not understand. The Jew said, "I will come with thee," and I and he went till we came to the house of R. Abraham (De Castro), Chief of the Mint. He was the most esteemed in Cairo. I said to him, "I am a Jew, and wish to stay with thee three or four days, and I will tell you a secret. Put me on the way to go to Jerusalem. I want neither silver nor gold nor food from you, but only lodging." R. Abraham answered, "I cannot let thee come to my house, because thou hast come disguised as an Ishmaelite, and if thou didst stay in my house it would do me harm." I said to him, "Do me this kindness for the love of God and the love of the Elders, for one good deed leads to another." He answered, "It would be good for me and all the Israelites that live in Egypt if thou dost not come to my house." So I left his house and went with the Ishmaelite and came to the house of an Ishmaelite merchant, whose name in Hebrew was Zachariah and in Arabic Jahia, the son of Abdallah.

Then I sold my Ethiopian slave to the merchant for 200 broad florins, and traveled with several merchants from Cairo to Gaza. We came to a big khan like an encampment, and they gave me one of the upper rooms and in my room a Jewish merchant from Beyrouth was staying, called Abraham Dunaz. I stayed in that room two days and spoke nothing to him; all day I prayed and spoke to nobody. After that I called him and asked his name, and I asked, "What do you pray for at this season, for rain or dew?" He replied, "For rain," and also told me that he had seen many Ishmaelites, and even descendants of the Prophet, but never saw a man as wise as me. I said to him, "I know by calculation that today is a festival of yours, the day of Purim." He replied, "Yes, that is true," and asked me, "Who told you all this?" I replied that in my country there are many Jews and wise men, and their houses are near to my house, and I have friends among them who eat at my table of fruit but not meat, and they love me and I love them. And he said to me that in his country Jews cannot talk with any Ishmaelites nor any descendants of the Prophet, for they hate us and they love dogs more than Israelites. I told the Jew, "Fear not nor be dismayed, for speedily the end will come for you, and the Almighty will humble the wicked to the ground and raise up the lowly upon high, and speedily make you see great matters and much confusion among the kings. Now, Abraham, do me a kindness and seek for me merchants to conduct me to the Temple in Jerusalem, but first to Hebron." He told me that he would do so, and went and found a donkey man and made the bargain between him and me. I did not wish to reveal my secret to him, but when starting on my journey told him the beginning of the matter. The money changer, Joseph, the shopkeeper, came to me with his brother, Jacob, and their old father, who was still living. They were with me about two hours and I told them no more of my business than the barest headings. Through the Jew, Abraham, the Jews sent me meat and bread, and I stayed at Gaza five days.

On the 19th Adar, 5283 (1523), I journeyed from Gaza to Hebron, and traveled day and night until I arrived at Hebron at the site of the cave of Machpelah on the 23rd Adar at noon. The keepers of the cave came to kiss my hands and feet, and said to me, "Come in, O blessed of the Lord, our Lord, the son of our Lord;" and two of the guardians of the Mosque of Abraham, who were wise and great and appointed over all the guardians and Judges in Hebron, took me by the hand and brought me to one grave and said to me, "This is the grave of Abraham, our father", and I prayed at that place; and then they showed me on the left hand a small chapel and therein is the tomb of Sarah, our mother, and between them is the Ishmaelites' praying chapel. Above Abraham's tomb is the tomb of Isaac in the great Mosque, and near to his tomb is Rebecca's, above the tomb of Sarah; and at the foot of Abraham's tomb is a plan of Jacob's tomb in another great Mosque, and near the plan of his grave is Leah's, alongside of Sarah's. I gave them ten florins charity to buy olive oil for the lamps and said to the guardians that this plan is not true, for Abraham, Isaac, and Jacob are in one cave underground, and they are not buried on the surface. They replied, "Thy words are true," and I asked them to show me the cave, and I went with them. They showed me a well with a lamp therein burning day and night, and lowered the lamp into the well by a rope, and I saw, from the mouth of the well, a door of man's height. I believed that this was the real cave and rejoiced in my heart, and sent the Ishmaelites away and prayed by that well until I had finished my prayer. After that I called the oldest of the guardians and said to them, "This is not the door of the well, but there is another door," and they replied, "It is so. In olden days the door of the cave was in the middle of the great Mosque, in which is the plan of Isaac's tomb." I asked them to show me the place of that door and went with them. They removed the carpets from the floor of the Mosque and showed me the place of the door, closed by big stones and leaden weights, and no man can remove that overburden. I told them to cover the ground again with the carpets, and asked them if they knew who built the door of the cave. They took out a book and read out before me that a king, the second after Mahomet, built the gate of the cave after the Ishmaelites had taken the holy place from the Christians. That King sent four men into the cave, each with a candle in his hand, and they stayed an hour in the cave and came out. Three of them died immediately after they came out, but the fourth survived for three days. The King asked what they had seen in the cave and the survivor replied, "I saw these forms; our father Abraham in his coffin in the place of the upper plan, and round Abraham's tomb many lamps and books and a covering of beautiful cloths over it; and near to our father Abraham, our mother Sarah and Isaac and Rebecca above at their head, and our father Jacob and our mother Leah at their feet; and there were lamps round each tomb, and on each was an image, a man on a man's tomb, and a woman on a woman's. The lamps in our hands were extinguished, and in the cave shone a great light like the light of the sun, and in the cave there was a pleasant odor like that of incense. When we passed Rebecca's tomb the man's image on Isaac's tomb called out to us in a great voice, and we remained breathless until we left the cave." The King commanded that the gate should be closed and it remains closed to this very day.

I stayed to pray at the mouth of the well and watched the door of the cave on Sabbath eve until dawn, and in the morning I stayed to pray until the evening, and on the Sunday night I prayed and did not sleep until the morning. The two Elders had told me that on the third day I should find a sign and I remained, wondering what I should see. On the Sunday morning the guardians called me with great joy and said to me, "Our Lord and Prophet, rejoice with us for we have had a great joy. Water has come to the bath of the Mosque, and it is now four years since water came to it"; and I went with them to see the water. It was good and clear and came to the bath from a distant land.

I journeyed from Hebron on the 24th Adar and came to Jerusalem, and there were robbers on the way. My companions said to me, "Our lord, son of the Prophet, there are enemies before us;" and I said to them, "Fear not nor be dismayed, they are afraid and you are safe." I was still speaking when, behold, the Turkish judge had come from Hebron with many servants. The robbers saw him and all of them fled, and I journeyed with him to Jerusalem. I entered it on the 25th Adar, 5283 (1523), and that day I entered the house of the Holy of Holies, and when I came to the sanctuary all the Ishmaelite guardians came to bow before me and to kiss my feet, and said to me, "Enter, Oh blessed of the Lord, our Lord, the son of our Lord," and the two chief among them came and took me to the cavern which is under the *Eben Shethiah,* and said to me, "This is the place of Elijah the Prophet, and this the place of King David, and this King Solomon's place, and this the place of Abraham and Isaac, and this the place of King David, and this King Solomon's place, and this the place of Abraham and Isaac, and this the place of Mahomet." I said to the guardians, "Now that I know all these places go ye on your way, for I wish to pray, and in the morning I will give you charity." They went away and I knew at once that all their words were false and vain. I prayed until all the Ishmaelites came to prayer. They left the Temple court after their prayer two hours after dark. I went below the *Eben Shethiah.* Then the guards extinguished all the lights in the court except four, and before they closed the gates they searched to see if any man were sleeping in the cavern, so as to turn him out. They found me, and said, "Leave this place, for we are the guards and may allow no one to remain to sleep here. We have so sworn to the King, and if thou wilt not go we shall ask the Governor to remove thee against thy will." When I heard these words, I came out of the court and they shut the doors, and I prayed outside the court all night, and fasted, and this was my fourth day. In the morning, when the Ishmaelites came to pray in the court, I entered with them, and when they had finished their prayer, I called out with a loud voice, "Where are the guards? Let them all come before me;" and I said to them, "I am your Lord, and the son of your Lord, the Prophet. I have come from a distant country to this holy house and my soul desireth to remain therein to pray and not to sleep." And after that four of the guards came to expel me, and I said to them, "I am your Lord, the son of your Lord, if you wish peace wish me well and I will bless you; but if not I will be avenged of you and will write to the King of Turkey your evil deeds." They replied, "Forgive us this time for we wish to serve thee and to be thy slaves as long as thou remainest in the holy house, and will do thy will." Then I gave them ten ducats for charity, and stayed in the sanctuary and fasted in the Holy of Holies five weeks. I ate no bread and drank no water except from Sabbath eve to close of Sabbath, and I prayed below the *Eben Shethiah* and above it. Afterwards ten messengers from King Joseph, my brother, and his Elders came before me, and they recognized and stood before me in the sanctuary.

The Ishmaelites have a sign on the top of the cupola of the court, and this sign is like a half-moon turned westward; and on the first day of Pentecost of 5283 (1523), it turned eastward. When the Ishmaelites saw this they cried out with a loud voice, and I said, "Why do you cry?" and they replied, "For our sins, this sign of the half-moon is turned eastwards, and that is an evil sign for the Ishmaelites"; and the Ishmaelite workmen went on the Sunday to restore the sign to its place, and on Monday the sign again turned eastward while I was praying, and the Ishmaelites were crying and weeping, and they sought to turn it round but they could not; and our Elders had already told me, "When thou seest this sign go to Rome," and I saw the gates of mercy and the gates of repentance, and walked in the sanctuary. It is a big structure like the upper buildings, and I did that which the Elders ordered me underneath the sanctuary, out of man's reach, and the turning of the sign took place after I had done what the Elders commanded beneath the sanctuary. I went up the Mount of Olives, and I saw two caves there and returned to Jerusalem and ascended Mount Zion. There are two places of worship there in the town; the upper place is in the hands of the Christians and the lower in that of the Ishmaelites. This the Ishmaelites opened for me and showed me a grave, and told me that it was the grave of King David, on whom be peace, and I prayed there. Then I left and went to the upper place of worship, which the Christians opened for me. I entered it and prayed there and returned to Jerusalem, and went to the house of a Jew called Abraham Hager. He was smelting near the synagogue, and there were women there cleaning the candlesticks of the synagogue. I asked him his name and he said, "Abraham"; and I sent the Ishmaelites away and said to them, "I have work to do with the smelter." They went away and I asked him, "At this season do you pray for rain or dew?" and he said, "Dew," and was astonished, and I spoke a good deal with him but did not tell him I was a Jew. But on the third time that I went to his house before leaving Jerusalem, I said to him, "Make me a model showing Venice, Rome, and Portugal." He made me such a model, being a Sefardi, who had come from there and I said I wished to go to Rome, and he said, "Why?" and I answered, "I am going for a good cause, but it is a secret which I cannot reveal, and I want thee to advise me how I should go"; and I then gave him a letter which I had written to Jerusalem and said to him, "Give this letter into the hand of R. Isaac the Nagid."

I left Jerusalem on the 24th Sivan, 5283, and a number of Ishmaelites came on horseback to accompany me five miles. I went on my way and arrived in Gaza in the month of Tammuz at the place where I stayed on the first occasion. An old Jew, a dealer in spices, called Ephraim, came to me and I said to him, "Go summon unto me Joseph, the money-changer, and let him bring with him weights for gold and silver and pictures of coins, and come together to me in the presence of Ishmaelites." The old man did so, and two of them came to me and I asked Joseph, the money-changer, as to the health of his old father, and his brother, Jacob, and he said, "They are well." Afterwards four old men came before me, and I said to them, "I am a Jew, and my father is King Solomon, and my brother, Joseph, who is my elder, is now King over thirty myriads in the wilderness of Habor." We ate and drank wine that night, though from the day I journeyed from the wilderness of Habor I had drunk no wine till that night. Afterwards I went with old Ephraim that night to the house of a Jew called R. Daniel. He is the richest of the Jews in Gaza and honest and pious, and he told me of all the Turkish governors who had come to Gaza. R. Daniel has a son valiant and handsome, called Solomon, but the Jews hate him because they say he is wild. I summoned him and rebuked him between ourselves and said, "Turn from thy evil ways before Jerusalem is taken; if thou dost not repent, thy blood be on thy head," and he swore that he would repent. Then the Rabbi, R. Samuel, sent me through old Ephraim a thousand greetings and begged me to take the Sabbath meal with him that night. I did so and stayed with him till midnight, and asked them to show me their synagogue, and I went and prayed therein about two hours. I returned to the house of the R. Ishmael and said to him, "If thou wilt do me a favor for the sake of God and thy love of the Elders and the rest of Israel, find me speedily a ship going to Alexandria." They told me that a ship was starting that week for Damietta with Jews from Jerusalem therein and this old man, R. Ephraim, would accompany me. I said to them, "Be blessed of the Lord, remove from you causeless hate and return to the Lord in order that he may speed our redemption and the redemption of the house of Israel, for thus said the Elders." I journeyed from Gaza on the 15th of Tammuz, 5283, and in two days reached Damietta, where I took a house, and then I went to the house of a Jew called R. Mordecai, whose brother, R. Samuel, lives in Cairo. I stayed with him over Sabbath, and on Sunday he took me to the seashore, and we rode on a camel for twenty days along the shore.

I embarked on a ship and reached Alexandria on the 24th Tammuz, and went to the khan, and the learned kabbalist, R. Mordecai, came to me and I said, "I am a Jew, the brother of the King of the wilderness of Habor, and I wish thee to direct me by sea to Rome." R. Mordecai said to me, "Go to the Consul and he will advise thee what to do, for he is an honorable man. Tell me what he tells thee." I went to the Consul and said to him, "I am the brother of the King of the wilderness of Habor, and I have come by the command of my brother, King Joseph, and the advice of the seventy Elders, and I wish to go to the Pope and then to the King of Portugal. Therefore advise me what I shall do and find me the ship in which I shall go." The Consul replied, "There is a ship going to Puglia, but I fear evil will come to me because of thee; therefore, I advise thee to wait till a galley goes to Venice, and the Ishmaelites will direct thee." I returned to my place and went to the house of the said R. Mordecai. A young man called Joseph, whose father and mother were of Naples, and who had a wife from Turkey, came there, and I asked R. Mordecai to let the young man go with me to Rome. He said to me, "Go, this young man will be thy interpreter in Rome." Then I went home and stayed until the eve of the New Year, 5284, and prayed in the little synagogue on New Year's eve. The name of the landlord was Isaac Bucapzi, and he and a Jew called R. Benjamin joined me in prayers. I stayed there the two days New Year, and then went home, and during the feast of Tabernacles I went to the house of R. Mordecai to stay with him the first two days. I remained in Alexandria until I heard the galley was about to start for Venice, and I went to the great Turkish Pasha to get his permission. There were mighty lords with him and I said to him, "I seek a kindness from you because of my love and the love of the Prophet, and I will pray to the Prophet for you that he may give you a right to paradise; speak to the captain of the galley and order him to conduct me in the ship to Venice." They did so, and they sent with me their servants and ordered the captain accordingly, and the captain said, "So will I do."

I and my servant, Joseph, traveled from Alexandria in the middle of Kislev, 5284 (November, 1523), and I fasted all day and prayed day and night, and took with me from Alexandria all kinds of food for Joseph. But it was no use, for all became mixed up with the food of the Christians. He ate from their utensils, and I cried out against him, but he cared not. When I reached Candia I bought many kinds of food, and the Christians and the captain complained to me of Joseph that he stole bread and wine from the people on the ship. I was ashamed of him but could not speak with him, for he regarded not my word.

When I reached Venice I went to the captain's house, where he gave me room, and I fasted in his house six days and six nights, and when I had finished prayers I saw a man behind me, and said in Hebrew, "Who art thou?" He replied, "I am a Jew," and I asked him who told him I was here. He replied, "Thy servant Joseph says that thou art a holy envoy." I asked him his name, and he replied Elchanan. Another time this Elchanan returned with another Jew called R. Moses Castilis, a painter. I said to R. Moses, "I am greatly in need of seven ducats, for my servant Joseph is poor and sick, and I have spent for him and in Alexandria much money." I went with R. Moses to the Ghetto (the place of the Jews) and a respected Jew called R. Mazliah came to me, and I spoke to him as to the expense, and he said he would go to the house of R. Hiyya. We went there and I said to him, "I am a Jew from the wilderness of Habor, a holy envoy sent by the seventy Elders." I was in his eyes as one who mocked, so I said to him, "I require seven ducats; speak with the wardens and find out if they will give this." He replied, "If the rest of the Jews will give, I will give my share." I told him this was the sixth day of my fast and I was only eating at nightfall, and asked him to send me some wine. I returned to my lodging at the captain's house, but he sent me nothing. So I only ate eggs, bread and water, but the respected R. Mazliah had done his best, and R. Simon ben Asher Meshullam came to me and said, "I hear that you are a holy envoy from the seventy Elders and going to Rome; tell me wherefore they have sent you and I will send two Jews with you and pay all the expenses." I said to him, "I am going to the Pope and can say nothing more than that I am going for the good of Israel. If thou wilt send two men with me to Rome, thou wilt have a share in the good deed, and they will bring you back good tidings." Afterwards I and R. Moses, the painter, went to the captain's house and took leave of him, and took all my things and went to the ghetto to the house of R. Moses, the painter; and R. Mazliah came to me and I asked him to find me a ship for Rome. He did so and that night I got into a small boat, and from there into the ship, and I fasted. I and Joseph started on our journey on Friday, the new moon of Adar, 5284 (about March, 1524), and stayed over Sabbath on the ship until I reached Pesaro. Here I stayed in the house of R. Foligno, and said to him, "Do me the kindness to put me on my way to Rome, as I do not wish to sleep here overnight." He went and found me horses, and I and Joseph rode to another city where there were Jews; and so every evening from journey to journey, with many Jews, until we arrived, on the eve of Purim, at midday at Castel Nuovo, near Rome, at the house of a Jew called R. Samuel, and I stayed with him over Purim; and on that day I bought the skipping hoop with which I did what the Elders had ordered me and next day I left and arrived at Rome, thank God!

POPE, EMPEROR, AND THE INQUISITION

SOLOMON MOLKO (?-1534)

Among those Marranos—crypto-Jews—who did not escape the fires of the Inquisition was the romantic figure of Solomon Molko. Born in Portugal of a family of Spanish emigrés, he already held a government post when David Reubeni flashed across his horizon like a messianic comet. He reverted to his ancestral religion, symbolically changed his Christian name (Diego Pires), initiated himself into the lore of Kabbalah, and joined Reubeni in his meteoric career. "I was constantly with him," he writes, "as a servant before a master." They appeared together before Charles V at Ratisbon in 1532, flying a banner with the Hebrew initials of the Maccabaean rallying cry, "Who is like unto Thee, O Lord, among the mighty?" Their appeal that Charles mobilize the Jews against the Turks led to their seizure. Soon afterwards, Molko was condemned to death by the Inquisition. The following account is excerpted from the famous historical work *Vale of Weeping* by a contemporary, Joseph Ha-Cohen. Molko's autobiographical letter is printed in Roman type.

❋   ❋   ❋

*N*OW *there came out of Portugal a noble whose name was Solomon Molko. He was of those who had fled there in the days of the Inquisition. While he was still a youth, he served as one of the secretaries of the king (John III, 1521-1557). But when he saw David Reubeni, the Lord touched his heart and he returned to the Lord, the God of our ancestors, and he was circumcised.*

At that time he knew nothing of the Law or the Scriptures. After he was circumcised, the Lord endowed him with wisdom. Soon he became the wisest of men, arousing much wonder. He went to Italy, and with great daring spoke of the Divine Law in the presence of kings. Thence he went to Turkey, and later returned to Rome. He spoke with Pope Clement (VII, 1523-1534) who, against the desire of his intimates, extended every kindness to him. The Pope gave him a letter of safe-

conduct, signed with his own hand, permitting him to live as he pleased, and without delay Solomon lived openly as a Jew.

Now Solomon became learned in the wisdom of the Kabbalah. From his lips came words of grace, for the spirit of the Lord was upon him and His word was constantly on his tongue. He continually drew forth marvelous words from the deep fountain of the Kabbalah and he wrote them upon tablets. But I have not yet seen them. He preached to large audiences in Bologna and in other places. Many followed him both to hear his wisdom and to test him with riddles, but Solomon answered all their questions. Nothing was hidden from him. When they heard Solomon's words of wisdom they said, "What we heard about you was a true report. You have gained wisdom even exceeding your fame."

Many clothed themselves with envy, but they could inflict no harm upon him in Italy, for he was beloved by the nobles. He united himself with David Reubeni; in those days they were as one.

And Solomon wrote to the sages a letter containing words of peace and truth, saying,

". . . It was rumored that Prince David Reubeni had come to Italy, and he too suffered from the malicious tongues of the slanderers. When we met, it was my design that I should sit at his feet as a disciple, but the contrary happened, for he inquired of me. Notwithstanding, I believed him to be a very learned man, and when he said that he did not know the law and the sciences, it was only to deceive the people and to see how I would behave towards him. In accordance with my intention, I was constantly with him, even as a servant is with his master.

"When I went to Venice to ask a printer to publish for me wonderful and profound things from the mysteries on the Holy Law, so that others might be encouraged to study the Book, I found a physician, a man of true faith, whose name was Jacob Mantino. He was engaged in a controversy with another physician, Elijah Halphon. I tried, without success, to make peace between them. As Dr. Halphon intended to go to Rome, I tried to prevail upon him not to do so. When I told him that the destruction of the city by the waters of the flood was nigh,* he went to another city, saying that he would not remain in the same city with his enemies. Seeing that I was friendly with Dr. Mantino, he too became my enemy. While these things occurred, the flood was upon the city of Rome. . . .

"After an attempt had been made by the enemies to poison me and I was healed, I went to Rome to observe the stars and interpret their

* The flood actually occurred as predicted, on October 8, 1530.

meaning. And before certain events took place I prophesied in a letter to the Pope, and also to some of the cardinals belonging to the court. I also wrote to the King of Portugal through this ambassador, for I had had a private conference with him. And when the earthquake actually came to pass (January 26, 1531), they were all astounded and marveled at my powers. The ambassador said to me, 'If the king had known how wise you are before you left Portugal, he would have given you permission to leave as you wish.'

"And daily he and his servants showed me great honor at his home and in the presence of the Pope. The cardinals held countless meetings and assemblies. When they saw the honors bestowed upon me by the Pope, some said, 'He should be killed. Did he not despise the waters of baptism in Portugal?' But others defended me, 'He should not be killed,' they said, 'for he is a sage. Did he not predict events that have actually occurred?' And with words and deeds they honored me before the people.

"The widespread report of this finally came to the ears of Dr. Jacob Mantino of Venice. He said to the Jews of that community, 'Now I shall go to Rome, and pursue that Solomon until I have injured him. Either he will return to Christianity or he shall be burned at the stake.' When Dr. Mantino came to Rome, he went first to the home of the ambassador of Portugal, and said to him, 'Why are you not zealous in honoring the King, your master? Is it because of that man who stands in the Pope's court, who was a servant and a scribe in the King's palace, before he became a Jew?' The ambassador answered, 'It is not our custom to go about condemning and slandering secretly. And it shall not be done here.'

"And Dr. Mantino left him in anger, and went before the judges, the great men of the city, 'with the voice of Jacob and the hands of Esau.' But the judges said, 'We cannot do anything without witnesses. When you bring witnesses, we will do all you desire.'

"And he went to and fro to seek witnesses among the Portuguese who were then in Rome. And after a diligent search, he found witnesses and brought them into the Court of Justice of the Inquisition. And they wrote out an accusation, condemning me, and called me before them to explain how I justified my claim to being a Jew after having belonged to another religion, and further by what right I preached the Law to the multitude. Then I showed them the security of the Pope, written and sealed, ordering that the permission to live as I pleased be respected. In great anger, they took it from me and brought it to the Pope, saying:

'Why does this come from you? If you pervert judgment, why have you appointed us judges?' And he answered, 'What you say is true. But I ask you to be silent, for we have a secret understanding between us. The times require this to be so.' And when this man saw that he could not prevail against me, he took with him the portion of my book dealing with the First Vision which I had sent to Dr. Joseph Titsak, and he translated it into the Italian language. He showed it to many cardinals so that they might be ashamed and blush at that which the Pope suffered against their own law. Finally, because of their continual urgings and intrigues, the Pope gave the nobles permission to do what the law required. But to me he said, 'Stay here with me lest these men seize you.' And the most high God, for the sake of His mercies and loving kindness which have not ceased, caused them to meet a man of my form and likeness, clothed in garments like mine; and they took him suddenly and burned him alive. And they came to the palace of the Pope, and said, 'The man in whose honor you delight is now a burning fire.' I, however, was hidden in the most secret chambers. And when I appeared, he feigned astonishment at my appearance. And he called to the Chief Justice, and said, 'What have you done? Look! There is Rabbi Solomon with us, and you have burned another in his stead. And now hasten and write in the judgment-place that the victim had reviled and blasphemed, and cursed his God and his King so that it may not be known that he was burned instead of Rabbi Solomon, lest trouble follow.' And they hastened to follow his orders.

"Then I said to the Pope, 'You have already observed the stars with your own eyes, just as I have told you from the beginning, as you know, as these stars show, what will happen to you; that weeping may endure for a night, but joy cometh in the morning. Send me away, now, I beg you, for I may no longer remain here on trial.' And he dismissed me in peace, and I rode away in the night on a fast horse, accompanied by a good escort provided by the Pope.

"You may recognize and know that everything which I have related to you is true, from the contents of the credentials of the heads of the communities of Rome and the Rabbis, which I send to you. And many are the trials I have suffered. I am weary of writing about them, for no book can contain them. And because my enemies say vain things and publish false writings, and quote words which I have never uttered and which I have not commanded, neither came into my heart, therefore do I warn you not to pay any attention to any writings except those which are written by mine own hand, and signed with my name and sealed with my seal. Regard not lies and misrepresentations, but only the words of truth which I utter. Stand fast, all ye who hope in the Lord, and your hearts will be strengthened. Blessed be the Lord forevermore! Amen, Amen!"

Now Solomon was accustomed to discuss the beliefs and faith with the emperor (Charles V). When the emperor was in Ratisbon (in 1532), he went there and talked with him. But the emperor was unresponsive and, because of his ill temper, he would not listen to him. The emperor commanded that he be clapped into prison, he and his friend Prince David and their followers. And they remained there several days.

After the Turks were repulsed there was a period of respite and the emperor left Ratisbon. He returned to Italy, and took all the prisoners, bound in fetters, in wagons, setting a special guard over them. Then, in accordance with his imperial custom, the emperor discussed them with his advisers. . . . They found Solomon guilty and condemned him to death. And they said, "Bring him forth, and let him be burned." In order to prevent him from addressing the people, they put a bridle on his jawbones, and thus he came before them. The whole population surged about him, as he stood facing the crackling flames. And one of the emperor's nobles said, "Take the bridle from between his teeth, for I have a message to him from the King." When this was done, he said to Solomon, "The emperor sent me to you to say this: 'If you repent, your repentance will be accepted and you shall live.' He shall provide for you and you shall be one of his court; but if not—death is your fate." He did not move an eyelash. Even as a saint or an angel of God, he said, "Because I have lived your religion, my heart is bitter and grieved. Now do as you please. My soul, I know, will return to her Father's house where it will be better off than here."

And they were incensed, and cast him upon the burning woodpile. He was as a burnt offering to the Lord, and He smelled the sweet savour, and took to Him his pure soul. Then they brought his servants from the prison and they suffered the same fate. None escaped the destruction, except the noble David Reubeni, his friend; over him they set a guard. Whereupon the emperor went to Bologna, and they brought along Reubeni, bound in fetters, in a wagon, and took him to Spain. There he lived for a long time and died in the prison house.

During these days there were many in Italy who believed that Solomon Molko had, by his wisdom, delivered himself from his enemies, and that the fire did not touch his body. Some even took an oath before the community and the assembly that he was in his home eight days after the auto-da-fé, and that he left there and was never again seen. Almighty God alone knows the truth. Would to God I could write down with certainty whether his words were true or false.

THE STORY OF MY IMPRISONMENT

YOMTOB LIPMANN HELLER (1579-1654)

The dramatic tale of this celebrity's imprisonment in 1629, due to the treachery of his enemies, has as its setting the first phase of the Thirty Years' War (1618-1648). Heller had been elected rabbi of Prague, the metropolis of Bohemia, as a youth two years earlier, and had published a number of notable legal commentaries which contained references to Christians, that were used as a basis of a charge of defamation. It is a tribute to his integrity that he would not compromise with his influential defamers and suffered the loss of his high office as well as exile in Poland, where he ultimately became rabbi and head of a talmudic academy in Cracow. This unusual memoir is the simple, honest story of a noble man.

❊   ❊   ❊

BY REASON of the continued war round the city of Prague between the armies of Emperor Ferdinand II and Duke Frederick von der Pfalz, wealth declined and taxations and levies increased. As a result the members of the community were compelled to raise many loans at high rates of interest. When the time of repayment arrived, disputes became numerous in Israel regarding the share to be paid by each, and hearts were torn asunder; those close together became distant; plots were hatched in secret and some even openly as well. And all my toil as rabbi to bring them together with gentle words and entreaties were of no avail. On account of this bad situation I shall not mention the names of the people who sinned against their souls. May they be blotted out of the Book of Life, and may the Exalted Name atone for them all, and the name of the Lord be blessed for ever.

When I was warned that a plot was being hatched against the leaders and against me as well, I did not believe it, because I knew that I had done no harm to anybody, that I had never twisted judgment and that I had done nobody any ill. Yet as for me, who am a worm and not a man—why, even with regard to King David, we find that he had enemies for no reason and false foes. How much more so should it be the case for me, the lowly and contemptible, who am not worthy to be mentioned in the same breath as our lord King David, may he rest in peace.

On Monday, the 4th of July, 1629, at the time of the afternoon service, a Jew came to tell me that the Imperial Judge had asked him about me, and whether I was at home, as he had a secret matter to discuss with me. This man had told him, "I do not know: maybe he is in the House of Study, or teaching at the school after his fashion." Further he said, "Why should Your Honor go to him? If you so desire, I shall tell him that you wish to talk with him, and then the Rabbi will come to your house." But the Imperial Judge said, "No, I shall go to him myself."

That was as much as this Jew told my sons. When I heard it, I was concerned, but went to the synagogue; and upon my return I brought with me the leaders and outstanding folk, and told them of the incident. While we were talking, the Imperial Judge came in a coach to the house of a Jew just opposite my house, and remained there till about one o'clock in the morning. Then he came to my house and sent to the winter house to ask permission to enter my rooms. The leaders and fine folk who had come with me, and I myself, all invited him in. And when he entered he gave his hand to each of us in friendly fashion. I had already prepared two chairs. He set me on his right hand side and sat to my left, and began chatting about one thing and another. Thereafter the gentleman said to me that he had a private matter to talk over. So I conducted him to an inner chamber, kept for my studies.

Now letters which I had received that day from the Holy Congregation of Vienna had informed me that the Kaiser had ordered his regent in Prague to have me conducted to Vienna in iron chains. And so when the Judge came alone and said that he had a private matter to discuss. I guessed that matter was connected with this, and replied,

"Please say what you have to say in the house of our communal head His Honor Rabbi Jacob Shmilas."

He asked me to go in his coach with him to the house in question, but I requested him to ride while I walked so that we should not be seen together. (The truth was that I feared that he would take me to prison and not to the house of Rabbi Jacob.)

Thereupon he replied, "I shall accompany you afoot in order to do him honor."

So the leaders and fine folk accompanied us, and there too he set me on his right hand and spent a little time chatting. Then he asked

Rabbi Jacob to accompany him into another room, and there the Imperial Judge said: "I am very sorry, I have no words to tell the Rabbi how bad things are, because in my eyes he is a good man. So I shall tell you what the matter is, and you in your wisdom will put it to the Rabbi, so that he should not be upset and overwhelmed."

And this is what he told him: the Kaiser had ordered his regent by letter to take the Rabbi in iron chains and lead him thus to Vienna under close guard; the irons and fourteen guards were already waiting at his house. And the Viceroy had ordered the Imperial Judge to bring the Rabbi that same night.

Thereupon Rabbi Jacob was exceedingly startled and upset and besought him not to hurry.

"I myself," he said, "shall send some of our leaders to the Regent to entreat him about this thing."

"Do so," replied the Judge, "and I shall stay here all night long if necessary until I hear what the Viceroy has to say."

So the communal leaders, namely David Lurie, Reb Hena and Reb Israel Weisels went there. Now the dwelling of the Regent was in a small spot beyond the River Elbe in Prague. When they came there, the palace was closed and locked because it was midnight. They knocked at the door but there was no reply, because the deep slumber of the first watch of the night had fallen upon the watchmen. Nevertheless the emissaries did not return but knocked again on the door with all their force until the chamberlain of the Prince, who was on the watch that night and was on guard at the entrance to the Regent's bedroom, heard the noise of the knocking and looked out at them through the window, asking, "Why are you knocking like this? Can't you see that everybody is asleep and we are not to be awakened?"

Thereupon they asked him to open to them as they were the leaders of the Jews and had been sent to the Lord Viceroy on a very urgent matter. When he opened the door, they requested him to awaken the Prince and tell him that the leaders of the Jews had to speak to him on a matter of life or death. Then he went to the Prince's bedroom with a burning taper, awakened him and told him, claiming that it was a matter of life and death.

"Let them come in," said he.

When they entered, they prostrated themselves on the ground and said, "Your Lordship sent the Imperial Judge to arrest the Rabbi and lead him bound to Vienna under strong guard. But where shall we hide our reproach? Tomorrow people will say that he is the most important

of them, and that the only reason for arresting him is that the Jews have
rebelled against the Kaiser. And in every town where this report will be
spread, they will maltreat the Jews who are subject to our Imperial
Majesty the Kaiser, who himself can only lose as a result. Therefore we
beg and beseech that the Rabbi should be permitted to travel to Vienna
himself in order to appear before whomsoever Your Lordship may command. And we shall be security that he will hasten to carry out Your
Lordship's orders."

The Prince ordered his chamberlain to bring him the Kaiser's letter,
and read them the order. Then he said, "Return to your homes tonight
and come back tomorrow for my answer. Tonight I give you the Rabbi
on your security that he will not flee. And tell the Imperial Judge in my
name to go home and come here with you tomorrow."

On the morrow the leaders returned according to the order of the
Viceroy, together with the Imperial Judge; and he ordered the latter to
accept the security of the leaders that the Rabbi would within six days
be in Vienna and appear before the Chancellor of State; and if the Rabbi
were not there within the appointed time, they would be punished by a
great fine, and their bodies and money were offered in his stead. And all
this was written down. May God remember them for good by reason of
this good deed they did for me. And on Tuesday, the 8th day of Tammuz,
I started out.

On the following Sunday, which was before the appointed sixth day,
I reached Vienna. I was accompanied by the said Reb Hena for the
purpose of intercession. We went the same day to the Palace of the
Chancellor, but he was not there. On the following day I appeared
before him. He spoke harshly to me in the name of the Kaiser with
regard to my two works *Maadenai Melech* (The Sweets of the King)
and *Lehem Hamudoth* (Desirable Bread). For the Kaiser had been told
that in these works I had written against their faith. Of this he spoke at
very great length.

"God forbid," I replied, "that I should do any such thing. All our
books deal with the writing of the Talmud in accordance with the Torah
of Moses which is our faith, and this Talmud is an interpretation of the
written law decreed for us by His Blessed Name. These are foreign to
idolaters and star worshippers, to whom the words of the Talmud apply;
and all the sages and authors since the compilation of the Talmud are
required not to depart from its words."

It is unnecessary to repeat in detail the things said to me by the
Chancellor or the answers I gave him; but they all referred to matters of

religion, not, as I had heard, to the fact that my book was called *The Sweets of the King*. This was not the reason why the Kaiser was wroth with me, but the truth will appear further on.

When he had finished, he said to me, "Stay in your lodging, and do not go out of it under pain of punishment in money and body. For such is the order of the Kaiser."

When I entreated him, he replied that the Kaiser had desired to arrest me and imprison me immediately, but he had recommended that I should not be imprisoned.

"Further," said he to me, "the matter will be brought before a commission of scholars expert in the literature and language of the Jews, and they will report to the Kaiser in accordance with their findings."

On Sunday, the 17th of Tammuz, after the said commission had already held its meeting, the second town judge came to me with two beadles carrying an order from the Chancellor in the name of the Kaiser, to lead me to the prison kept for those sentenced to death. After much entreaty, he dismissed the beadles but accompanied me himself. Many of the honorable and important Jews of the town also accompanied me and endeavored to strengthen and encourage me. I stayed in that prison all the day and night, and no Jew was permitted to talk to me there, not even through the spy hole. Yet His Blessed Name showed me His loving-kindness, because all the prisoners treated me with honor, and each one endeavored to serve me as far as he could. Next day the Chief Judge gave me a special room in the building above, and permitted all the important Jews to visit me there. On the Tuesday the intermediaries succeeded in having me brought out of that building to the prison of the King's prisoners.

There I was comfortable because I had a bed, a table, a chair and a lamp. And the building was in the street of the Jews' warehouses. There was no lack of Jews to sit with me at any time. In addition the Chief Warder treated me well and provided me with anything for which I might ask.

On the 25th day of Tammuz, I was summoned to appear before the commission. To begin with, they asked me why I praised the Talmud in my introduction, despite the fact that it had been burnt by order of the Pope; and the Kaiser was required to go by the Pope's edict.

My reply was, "My praises were intended for my own people, who must hearken to all the words of our sages, that being an essential part of the Torah."

Then they asked me once again why I had written against their faith, in accordance with the questions asked me by the Chancellor. I replied to them as I had replied to him, and they dismissed me to my place in the prison.

On Thursday, the 27th of Tammuz, the judgment of the Kaiser was issued in the following terms: despite the fact that, in accordance with the findings of the commission, I should have been condemned to death, yet since the Kaiser like his forefathers before him was a merciful monarch, therefore he showed me the mercy of permitting me to redeem myself by the payment immediately of 12,000 reichsthalers, without any period of time in which to make the payment. As for the books, they were to be burnt. If I should refuse to give the said sum, no mercy would be shown and I would have to submit to the death penalty.

In my distress I prepared an appeal, saying, "I prostrate myself in gratitude for the favor shown me by His Majesty the Kaiser who permits me to live. Yet be it known unto him that his terms are equivalent to an order to mount aloft to the very heavens or to swallow a tube a hundred ells in length."

But he did not believe me because of the denunciations concerning me, in which much mention had been made of my wealth.

On Sabbath, the 18th of Ab, the Chancellor spoke as follows in the name of the Kaiser to the intercessor: "If he does not pay this sum of money, I shall send him back to the prison where he was at first, and from there he will be led to three squares in the city of Vienna, where he will be stripped naked, beaten on his naked body, and then led to Prague, where he will again be stripped and beaten in three public squares in order that he may be a shame and a reproach to all Israel; for no such thing has been done since the days when Israel was exiled from its land. For what will the onlookers say when they see the great shame done to their great Rabbi in this largest of cities, where there are so many Jews?"

Then the intercessors fell on their faces and said, "But it is impossible for us to pay this great fine demanded by the Kaiser."

To which the Chancellor replied, "But there are Jews who say that he is so rich that this fine is not even a fifth part of his wealth."

Then they entreated him, saying that they knew in all truth and verity that this was falsehood.

"Return to me afterwards," said he at length. "I shall recommend the Kaiser to treat him with even more favor."

So they went away and returned on the Sunday, on the Monday, and on the Tuesday, when he swore to them in anger that the Kaiser had ordered that the punishment of flogging was to be carried out, but he had acted as an intercessor and had won the Kaiser over to lessen the punishment.

"Therefore hearken to me and give 10,000 Rhenish gulden to redeem him. All the Jews are expected to redeem one another, particularly if it is the case of a man who is as great as he is according to your account. And I have heard say that not only the Jews who dwell in the countries and states of the Kaiser but also the Jews who dwell under the Moslem rule are ordered to help ransom and redeem one another."

To which the intercessors replied that our law forbade us to pay more than the actual value of a man as ransom.

He laughed in annoyance, saying, "Can you estimate the value of so great a man? Is he not worth the ten thousand? If you agree to this sum, it is good; I shall go to the Kaiser and may be able to mollify him with this gift. But if you do not listen to me, I shall be unable to raise the matter any more, and his judgment will be carried out."

On Thursday, the 6th of Ab, the Chancellor said that the Kaiser had agreed to this sum. Thereupon I requested that I might be given time for making the payments, for how could I pay at once? Following much entreaty, he gave me time for payment, namely 2,000 Rhenish gulden in ready money, 1,000 gulden six weeks later, while a further thousand reichsthalers of the remainder would be paid off every three months until the full sum had been paid. May God remember the upright Rabbi Jacob Shmilas, who sent me a bill for 2,000 Rhenish gulden in ready money from his own pocket and property. And the leaders of the Vienna congregation, who contributed 700 Rhenish gulden to help me; apart from my honorable and beloved kinsman by marriage Rabbi Enoch Schiff, who gave me 100 reichsthalers; and various other honorable men who stood security on my behalf for half of the balance. The other half had the security of Rabbi Hena, who had come to Vienna with me, and of my son-in-law Rabbi Wolf Slavis.

LIFE IN LOMBARDY

LEONE DA MODENA (1571-1648)

Born in Venice of the family of a physician whom Emperor
Charles V had dubbed a Knight of the Golden Fleece, Leone was a
personality of rare fascination. He showed great promise and versatility in his childhood, but his later development was somewhat
frustrated by the loss of the family fortune and his struggle to eke
out a living. He lists twenty-six occupations, ranging from tutoring to matchmaking, which he pursued during the course of his
checkered existence. He could deal out a hand of cards with the
same expertness as he composed in Italian and Hebrew. His memoirs
afford a glimpse into the curious psychological nature of a mind
that was a battleground for the opposing elements of rationalism and
occultism.

❋ ❋ ❋

IN THE year 1569 Mistress Penina, my father's wife, died; and in the
same year at the Feast of Weeks he took to wife Mistress Rachel,
daughter of Johanan Halevy of blessed memory, who came from
Apulia but was of German stock. At the time she was the widow of
Mordecai, known as Gumpeln Parenzo, the brother of Meir Parenzo,
who is mentioned by name in sundry printed books. She had one son
from the aforesaid Master Mordecai, whose name was Abraham and who
was then about nine years old. Before the marriage my father asked Rabbi
Abraham da Rovigo, who was well versed in many wisdoms, whether
he would succeed if he took this woman, and the Rabbi told him that he
would not succeed with her in property, and if he took her, she should
change her name; so she changed her name to Diana. And the said
Mistress Diana conceived from him in the year 1571.

Now there was a very great and powerful earthquake in the city of
Ferrara, the like of which had not been known in any country, just as is

75

written in the book *Light of the Eyes* by the sage Azariah dei Rossi.*
And my father and his household fled for their very lives to Venice.

While they were there I, the bitter and hasty, was born on Monday
between the eighteenth and nineteenth hour on the 23rd of April, 1571.
Well-nigh like Job and Jeremiah may I curse that day, for wherefore did
I come forth to see toil and wrath, distress and straits and evil alone all
the while?

The birth was extremely hard for my mother, and when I came forth
I was doubled over with my breech facing outwards, even then having to
do with reverses. At the end of eight days I was circumcised with great
joy by the renowned scholar and kabbalist, Rabbi Menahem Azariah of
Fano, and my father and Mistress Sarah, daughter of my uncle Shemaiah,
were my godparents; and my Hebrew name was called Judah Arieh.
May the Lord have mercy on my soul and may the upsets of my life be
an atonement for my sins and transgressions.

They dwelt in Venice for about eight months and then returned to
Ferrara. While they were on the way to Francolino, near Ferrara, they
left the ship and gave me to a gentile porter, who fled and bore me away
in his bosom. As soon as they saw that I had vanished, his honor Master
Samson Meshullam of blessed memory, who was my father's guide,
pursued him about two miles and caught up with him and took me. Then
he thrashed him thoroughly, and brought me back to my parents; and we
came to Ferrara and dwelt there.

I began to learn the alphabet from a certain teacher known as
Hazaneto, afterwards from Rabbi Isaac Supino, and afterwards from the
Rabbi Azriel Basola. And though it is said, "Let a stranger praise thee
but not thine own mouth," I may admit since I am now fully grown and
it is no longer praise that in truth I did well with my studies from the
very beginning. When I was two and a half years old, I said the
Haphtarah in the synagogue, and when I was three I recognized my
Creator and the value of study and knowledge, and I would explain the
portion of the week and understand it. (There appears to have been an
ancient custom of this kind in the Italian Jewish Community, and other
sources also refer to it.) And so I passed from class to class.

One day I was walking about in the garden and fell from a stone
and twisted my hand and was sick for some time, to say nothing of the
worms which troubled me. A certain woman gave me rock oil, and I
fainted, and almost remained in that faint. A little later I became sick
with smallpox; and these were all things that happened to me before I

* Dei Rossi's account is quoted in the Introduction, pp. xx-xxi.

was four, yet are as clear in my mind and memory as if they happened yesterday; for I still know what my thoughts were then.

In 1575 we left Ferrara and went to live in Colonia, a small town belonging to Venice, to conduct a pawnshop. My father went to a great deal of trouble to prepare a ritual bath for the womenfolk in his house and to draw suitable water there. At the end of 1576 it was declared fitting, and at the time I was studying Mishna together with Rabbi Gershon Cohen, who is now the head of a Yeshibah in Poland, and was then a boy like me.

The teacher went somewhere, and both of us went down to the bath to play, as boys do; and I fell in to it when it was full to the brim, and the other boy ran away shouting, and the housefolk heard him and came dashing with my father and mother and looked for me here and there and did not know where I had fallen. And meanwhile an hour passed while I kept hold of a ledge round the bath until the housefolk came. Then a servant girl jumped into the water and took me out; and they carried me to bed as though I had been dead of dread and fear.

There at Colonia my brother Samuel was married to Mistress Giuditta, daughter of Angelo della Faggiani of Pesaro, with feasting and festival, and I spoke Torah at the table as my teacher had instructed me, so that everybody there was astonished. As teacher I had Malachi Gallico of blessed memory, a rabbi, a physician and a kabbalist. In those days a certain gentile named Priamo had been beaten and wounded and people were discussing in the presence of my father and various guests of our house, whether he would die or not. I jumped up and said that he certainly would, making a pun on a Bible verse in this connection which set them all laughing.

In the month of Elul (August-September) 1578, we left Colonia for Montagnana about five miles away, and father made a synagogue in his house, where it can still be found in the home of Master Zerah Halevy, long life to him. For during many years the men of the spot had not prayed in congregation, because of quarrels among themselves. But we put the matter in order.

Rabbi Malachi left us, and for a year my teacher was Rabbi Eliakim da Macerata of blessed memory, a kabbalist and holy. Soon after, Rabbi Malachi was murdered in Piedmont on the way by the servant of a horse-owner for the sake of his money. And since he took his red vest and put it on, the Jew whom he had left understood what had happened and the servant was arrested and executed. May the Lord avenge the blood of Rabbi Malachi. In Nisan, 1580, my father sent me to Ferrara to the house of his grandson, Mordecai de Modena, to study books and wisdom, and there I spent a year. For four months I studied with Rabbi Yehiel Taureolo, and for eight months with Rabbi Hezekiah Finzi. It was his practice that every Sabbath all the pupils who studied *Alfasi* (a talmudic compendium) should prepare a discourse of their own on the portion of the week. And at the house of study on the Sabbath Day he would gather a quorum and the boy would deliver his discourse to him. When it came to my turn it was the portion on heave offerings, and I took as my subject the words "gold and silver and copper," and the saying "Rabbi Simeon ben Gamliel says the world depends on three things: on the Torah, and on the temple service, and on mutual aid." And I compared the first three with the second three, these being the things which the Lord desires of men and wherein He let His Presence rest on Israel.

When I had finished Rabbi Hezekiah said to two old men who were there, "I am convinced that this boy will preach sermons in Israel, for his manner shows that he will succeed with them."

Later, in 1605, 1606, and 1607, when I delivered sermons at the Great Synagogue every Sabbath by order of the community, he would always come to hear me; and when they used to praise my words he would say, "I prophesied twenty-five years ago that he would be a preacher."

I also learnt to play instruments, to sing, to dance, to do fine penmanship, and a little Latin. But on account of two servant women who hated me and embittered my life, I returned home when the year was over. So in the spring of 1581 my father of blessed memory sent me to Padua to the house of Rabbi Samuel Archivolti of blessed memory, to board with him and learn Torah from him. From him I learnt the craft of versifying and how to write prose, and he loved me very much until the day of his death; for he used to say that I was one of the pupils who was his very likeness and image in wisdom.

I was there for a whole year and then my father summoned me home. Now since my parents wanted to keep me there, the Lord provided us in the spring of 1582 with a young man from Italy who, however, came at the time from Safed. His name was Moses, son of Benjamin della Rocca, a grandson of the scholar Rabbi Moses Basola and a knowledgeable and understanding man. And this Moses became my teacher and from him I learnt much. During two years he was with me, after which he left for Cyprus where he married. While still a fine young man, he was summoned to the Upper Assembly. When I heard this sad news, I wrote laments for him and particularly the Hebrew and Italian *ottava rima* which is printed in my volume of sermons *Midbar Yehudah;* at the time

I was thirteen years old. All the poets saw it and praised it, and up to the present it is a wonder for Christian and Jewish sages alike. Thereafter I ceased to study with any regular teacher, but only on my own, though I was not in a large city where comrades might have helped me to maintain my studies. Alas that I dwelt during the best period for study without a teacher and rabbi!

At that time my father began to send me from time to time to Ferrara to supervise business affairs and collect debts. There our affairs were conducted by Samson Meshullam of blessed memory and I would come in and go out and have nothing to do. In the month of Tishri, 1587, when my father Isaac was growing old, his eyes grew dim. For about six months he was blind, groping in the dark. After many treatments everybody said that there was no hope any longer. All the same he did not cease praying day and night unto the Lord, until the Lord heard his voice and set it in the heart of a certain physician to give him an easy water to put in his eyes; and he returned to his strength, and the light came back to his eyes. What was even more miraculous, previously he had been accustomed to read with spectacles (Hebrew literally "eye-houses") and afterwards he read and saw everything without them for the five years that he still lived. But all that time we were growing steadily poorer, eating and doing nothing; for my father was disturbed and affrighted and in dread from the constellations which fought against him; and his heart would not raise him to any decision to leave this unlucky spot and to travel elsewhere, or anything similar.

At that time my brother, my mother's son Abraham Parenzo, who had grown up in father's house in childhood and youth, came into bad company who incited him to gaming, and he lost both his own and father's money, yet father always had for him the father's mercy for his son and always treated him well. But when this said brother saw how badly he had behaved, he went to Ancona, where there were many families that were kin to my mother of blessed memory, and he found favor in their eyes, for he was handsome, good-looking and intelligent. So they gave him a wife and trained him for the right path, while he too repented and went the proper way without going wrong any more. He was beloved and esteemed by all the gentile merchants of the city and by the whole Jewish community, who honored him; and he succeeded and earned very much, gaining more than he had lost. He wrote to my father several times that the time had come to repay him for all the good he had done, and entreated him to remove thither, since he would be doing him a favor. In addition he promised to train me in business because he loved me very much. Despite his entreaties father did not wish to listen until he saw nothing but evil all the time and had lost all hope. Then he sent property there with flax and silk and household goods and synagogue requirements, and agreed to send me in advance.

Now that year there was a great plague at Ancona in which many householders died; and my brother lost two sons, and the two brothers of his wife also died, married men and fathers of children. In the month of Iyar, 1588, I left Montegnano for Ancona; when I reached Venice I heard that my brother's mother-in-law had also died while his wife was very sick. But I went on, made a very stormy passage by water, and reached Ancona on the new moon of Sivan, 1588, where I found that the Lord had held my brother's wife, but he was very bitter in spirit at all the mishaps which had befallen him. Still, when he saw me he rejoiced very much and felt a little better, esteeming me exceedingly, as the townsfolk also did.

But on the day after the Feast of Weeks, his head pained him and he went to bed; and from day to day his sickness grew worse though nobody knew what it was. While from the time that he took to his bed, he said that he was going to die and told dreams he had dreamt. And when flies buzzed round his bed, he used to say that they were death flies. Finally he lost his mind, and after fifteen days, on the eve of Sabbath, the 18th of June, 1588, as the morning star arose, he passed away, at the age of twenty-eight years. And the whole community honored me exceedingly at his death with sermons and laments. And they all bewailed him because he had been acceptable to all his brethren and acquaintances. I wrote a lament for him in rhyme with an echo. It is found among my poems and writings.

Then I remained perplexed and at a loss, for they warred against me from Heaven; and I went on a ship alone without any Jews with me, and I came to Venice and then returned home to Montegnano. Here I cannot describe the pain and grief which my mother suffered, for she had loved him with all her soul and did not forget him till the day of her death. My father of blessed memory also wept for him as a father weeps for his son. And in truth from that time all the well-being of our house vanished and our hope and support came to an end. Since that time the stars have decided that I shall not see anything good.

On the New Moon of Tammuz, 1589, in order that I should not remain idle, I began to teach Torah to the son of Manasseh Levy of blessed memory and to Joseph the son of Zerah Halevy; an employment with which I continued until 1612 in my own despite, for it was not proper in my own eyes.

After this my mother spoke to me every day, saying,

"If only you were to listen to me and comfort me in my grief! Take the daughter of my sister, namely Esther, daughter of Mistress Gioja, wife of Isaac Simha, for she is fitting for you in my opinion; then I shall have found a match for you among my kin, and there will be peace in our home."

And she also begged my father of blessed memory with all her might, and wrote to her sister about it; and her sister also replied suitably, and it came about.

Meanwhile I had undertaken a Query to Heaven by process of dream, by prayer but without conjuration, to see the woman who was intended as my match. And I dreamt: a certain old man took me by the hand and led me to a wall where there was a picture painted with a curtain in front of it. He removed the cover and I saw the likeness of Mistress Esther, daughter of my said aunt, and the very color and fashion of her clothes. Yet while I looked at her, that likeness was changed, and in its place there came another which my eyes could not clearly distinguish. Next morning I told the dream to my father and mother, but they did not believe it.

In the month of Elul, 1589, my mother and I came to Venice to journey to Ancona in order to recover the property and goods which had been in the hands of my brother of blessed memory; for his wife had taken them and we did not see as much as a shoelace. Still, afterwards we decided not to go, and stayed in Venice. While we were there, my mother and her sister and the kinsfolk again took up the matter of the match; and we came to an agreement and gave our hands on it, and I took possession at the betrothal with great joy, and to my mother I pointed out the color of the clothes and ornaments which I had described to her more than a year earlier, when I had seen her in my dream. She was indeed a beautiful woman and wise, and I said that the words of Proverbs would apply about her and not the words of Ecclesiastes. (In Proverbs there is a verse "He who finds a wife finds something good." In Ecclesiastes, however, there is a verse, "A woman more bitter than death I have found.")

When the time of the wedding came, which was on the 13th day of Sivan, 1590, I wrote to my father, who was then in Bologna, and he came. And I summoned all my friends and relations and we went immediately after Shebuoth, all of us rejoicing and merry at heart, to Venice.

When we got there, we found the bride in bed; but everybody said that there was nothing more serious than a little diarrhea, which would soon be cured. But from day to day the sickness grew worse, till she was on the verge of dying; but her heart was as the heart of a lion, and she was not frightened.

On the day of her death she called me and embraced and kissed me, saying, "I know that this is shamelessness. But God knows that during the whole year of our match we have not touched one another, even with the little finger. And now at the hour of death, the right of death is permitted me. I did not merit to be your wife. What shall I do if it is decreed from on high? Let the Lord do His Will."

Then she requested that a sage be called for her to confess; and he came and she said the death confession and requested the blessing of her parents and my mother. And on the eve of Sabbath, the 24th of Sivan, 1590, almost the anniversary of the time my brother died, my bride departed as the bride Sabbath came in, with a life of vanity to a life of eternity; and she passed away to her own place. There was much weeping in and out of the house among all who knew her; and she was laid to rest in all honor.

Immediately after she was buried all the kinsfolk came to my mother and me and said, "The sister who follows her is as good as she is. Why should we not maintain the kinship and give comfort to the father and mother of the girl?"

And they pressed me unceasingly to take her sister Rachel as my wife. So I wrote to my father, who replied to me as he always replied regarding this matter, as follows: "Do what you wish, for you have to make the choice. Today or tomorrow I shall be taken from you, but you and your children will stay with her. Therefore understand what lies before you and do as the hand of the Lord doth show you."

So in order to give satisfaction to my mother and the dead girl after the fashion she had hinted in her words, I agreed and took the aforesaid Mistress Rachel as my wife. And we immediately wrote the contract and made the wedding on Friday, the 5th of Tammuz, 1590, under a good star.

On the 10th of Tishri, 1615, my son Mordecai went away because a godless man troubled us; and he ceased to teach the pupils of the society. In the month of Kislev he returned and began to engage in the art of alchemy, together with the priest Joseph Grillo, a great sage; and he toiled therein exceedingly. He grew so wise in this art that all the followers of it, who had grown gray and aged thereat, were astonished that a lad like him should know so much. Finally in the month of Iyyar he prepared himself a house in the Old Ghetto and himself made all the preparations necessary for the work. Then he repeated a certain experiment which he had learnt and tried at the house of the priest; namely, to take nine onkias of lead and one of silver and transform them into ten onkias of pure silver. This I saw and tested on the two occasions it was done by him. I myself sold this silver for six and a half pounds the onkia. It stood the test of the *coppella* (a small instrument used at the period for testing gold and silver). And I knew that it was really so, although this work involved great labor and toil and took two and a half months each time.

It should finally have brought in about a thousand ducats a year. And this is not all; for I also devoted my life to understanding things like that and was not likely to deceive myself. But thanks to our sins, at the festival of Tabernacles, 1616, much blood suddenly descended from his head to his mouth. After that he ceased to engage in this work, for people said that this might be due to the vapors and smokes of the arsenic and the salts which entered his head and harmed him. So he remained engaged in trifles for two years until he died.

Here I wish to write down for a memorial the number of ways I sought to earn my living; and I tried and did not succeed:

1. Jewish pupils. 2. Gentile pupils. 3. Teaching how to write. 4. Sermons. 5. Sermons written for others. 6. Acting as cantor. 7. Secretary of charitable and other societies. 8. Officiating as rabbi. 9. Decisions in ritual law. 10. Officiating as judge. 11. Daily lessons in the synagogue. 12. Conferring rabbinical diplomas. 13. Letters written in the names of others. 14 Music. 15. Verses for weddings and tombstones. 16. Italian sonnets. 17. Writing comedies. 18. Producing them. 19. Drawing up legal documents. 20. Translation. 21. Printing my own writings. 22. Proofreading. 23. Teaching the writings of charms and talismans. 24. Selling books of charms. 25. Commercial agent. 26. Matchmaker.

MY DOUBLE LIFE AND EXCOMMUNICATION

URIEL DA COSTA (1590-1640)

Of the colorful array of Marrano personalities, there is none more fascinating than Uriel da Costa, the tragic younger contemporary of Spinoza. He was born in Oporto, Portugal, in 1590, escaped to Holland with his family in 1618, and there embraced Judaism. But his uncompromising struggle for religious freedom led to constant persecution and finally public disgrace. His revealing autobiography, written in Latin, is a moving document, and has become a classic in the literature of religious liberty. So tortured was he by the heartless treatment of the community that he is reported—there is no actual verification, however—to have committed suicide in 1640, soon after the writing of this testament.

✻ ✻ ✻

I WAS born in Portugal in a city of the same name but commonly called Oporto. My parents were of the nobility, originally descended from those Jews who were forced to embrace Christianity in that kingdom. My father was a true Christian and a man of unquestioned honor and integrity. I had a good education at home, servants always at my command, and I rode a Spanish jennet to perfect myself in horsemanship, an art in which my father was so skilled and in which I endeavored to follow his steps. At length, being grown up, and as well accomplished in the liberal arts as young gentlemen generally are, I applied myself to the study of law. As to my character and disposition, I was by nature very pious and compassionate. So much so that I could not hear the story of any person's misfortunes without melting into tears. I had so strong an innate sense of modesty that I dreaded nothing so much as to suffer disgrace. Not that I had the least degree of cowardice in my nature. When there was reasonable justification I was not free from resentment. It is for this reason that I always had an aversion to that haughty and insolent tribe of men who are inclined to despise and

84

trample upon others, and I therefore took every opportunity to defend the oppressed and to make their cause my own.

Religion has brought incredible suffering into my life. According to the custom of the country, I was educated in Roman Catholicism. When I was but a youth the dread of eternal damnation made me anxious to observe all its doctrines punctiliously. I employed my leisure time in reading the Gospels, the Breviaries of the Confessors and other religious literature. But the more time I devoted to them, the more perplexed did I become. Little by little this caused me such difficulties, doubts and conflicts that I was overwhelmed with grief and melancholy.

Reflection led me to believe that the obtaining of a plenary absolution by the confession of sins and the fulfillment of all that the Church required was impossible. This consequently made me despair of salvation inasmuch as it was to be obtained only by such special rules. But as it was very difficult to shake off quickly a religion in which I had been educated from my infancy and which by a long unquestioning faith had taken deep root, I began, when I was about twenty years old, to question the teachings concerning the afterlife. I asked myself whether or not they were forgeries and whether belief in them was consistent with reason. My reason perpetually suggested to me conclusions that were just the contrary. Under the shadow of this doubt I continued for some time, and finally I was persuaded that salvation could not be obtained in the prescribed manner.

During this time I continued to apply myself to the study of law. When I was in my twenty-fifth year an opportunity presented itself whereby I obtained an ecclesiastical benefice as treasurer in the church. But I was unable to find the satisfaction I wanted in the Catholic church. I wanted, however, to attach myself to a religion and, aware of the great dispute between the Christians and the Jews, I made a study of the *Books of Moses* and of the *Prophets*. I found some things sharply contradictory to the doctrines of the New Testament. There seemed to be less difficulty in believing those things which were revealed by God Himself. Besides, the Old Testament was assented to by both Jews and Christians whereas the New Testament was believed only by Christians. Hence I decided to become a convert to the Law of Moses. As he declared himself to be only a deliverer of what was revealed by God Himself, being called to that mission or rather constrained to accept it, I thought it my duty to make the Law the rule of my life. Having made this decision and finding it unsafe to profess this religion in Portugal, I began to think of changing my residence and leaving my native home. In order to do this, I immediately resigned from my ecclesiastical benefice in favor of another, uninfluenced either by profit or honor, the two prevailing motives among the people of our country. I also left a beautiful house situated in the best part of the city, which my father had built. When I had concluded all the necessary arrangements, my mother, brothers and myself boarded a ship, not without danger for it is illegal for those who are descended from Jews to depart without a special permit from the King. I must tell the reader that out of natural affection, I had communicated to my family my sentiments on the falsity of our religion even though the discovery of it might have proved fatal to me—so dangerous is it in that country to speak freely on this subject, even to one's dearest friends. At the end of our voyage we arrived at Amsterdam where we found the Jews professing their religion with great freedom, as the Law directs them. We immediately fulfilled the precept concerning circumcision.

I had not been there very long before I observed that the customs and ordinances of the modern Jews were quite different from those commanded by Moses. Now if the Law was to be observed according to the letter, as it expressly declares, the Jewish interpreters are not justified in adding to it interpretations quite contrary to the original text. This provoked me to oppose them openly. Nay, I looked upon the open defense of the Law against such innovations as a service to God. The modern rabbis, like their ancestors, are an obstinate and stiffnecked race of men, vigorous advocates of the teachings and institutions of the Pharisees, not without a view to gain and, as is justly imputed to them, vainly fond of the conspicuous seats in the synagogue and greetings in the market place. Men of this character could not bear my differing with them in the slightest degree. They insisted that I follow unswervingly their prescribed regulations or else suffer exclusion from the synagogue and the full sentence of excommunication. But it would have been unworthy of him who had so recently left his native country and been content to forego many other temporal advantages for liberty of conscience to be overawed and to submit to men who had no right to such power. Besides, I thought it both sinful and beneath a man to be a slave in things pertaining to the conscience. Therefore I resolved to suffer the worst they could inflict rather than recant. Accordingly they excommunicated me from their congregation. Even my own brothers who before had looked upon me as their teacher, dared not take any notice of me as they passed me in the streets, for fear of the rabbis.

This state of affairs led me to write a tract in defense of myself and to prove plainly out of the Law of Moses the vanity and the invalidity of the traditions and ordinances of the Pharisees as well as their conflict with the Law. After I had begun this work (for I consider myself obliged to relate everything clearly and circumstantially), it so happened that I entirely agreed with the opinion of those who confine the rewards and punishments proposed in the Old Testament to this life only and are little concerned with the future life or the immortality of the soul. The following argument, among others, led to this viewpoint: The Law of Moses is completely silent as to the latter problems and proposes only temporal rewards and punishments to observers and transgressors thereof. The discovery that I entertained such opinions was no small triumph to my adversaries who felt that as a result they had the Christians as their allies, who by their faith in the Gospel which expressly mentions eternal rewards and punishments, do believe and preach the immortality of the soul. It was with the idea of rendering me odious to the Christians and of silencing me completely that, even before my tract went to press, they employed a certain scholar * to publish a book entitled *Of the Immortality of the Soul*. In it the scholar inveighed bitterly against me as one who defended the philosophy of Epicurus and who by denying the immortality of the soul disputed the very existence of God. At that very time I had, in reality, an incorrect idea of Epicurus and, prejudiced by my unsavory relations with other persons without even hearing what he had to say for himself, I did not scruple to censure him freely. But now that I have heard from impartial lovers of the truth some estimate of this philosopher and his teaching, I have found reason to change my opinion and to be sorry for the injustice I did him then when I pronounced him a ridiculous madman even though, being an utter stranger to his writings, I was far from being competent to judge his opinions.

The next step they took was to set their children upon me in the streets. They insulted me en masse as I walked along, abusing and railing at me. They cried out, "There goes a heretic, there goes an imposter." At other times they assembled before my doors, flung stones at the windows and did everything they could to disturb and annoy me so that I could not live at peace in my own house. After the above-mentioned book was published, I immediately set about my own defense. I wrote an answer in which I opposed with all the power at my command the doctrine of the immortality of the soul, incidentally dealing with the deviations of the Pharisees from Mosaic institutions. No sooner had this appeared in print than the elders and officials of the Jews agreed to make a complaint against me before the public magistrate. They asserted that

* Samuel da Silva. The book appeared in 1623.

I had published a book to disprove the immortality of the soul in order to subvert, not only the Jewish, but also the Christian religion. As a result, I was apprehended and sent to prison from which, after a confinement of eight or ten days, I was discharged upon giving security. For the magistrate fined me three hundred florins ($120) and confiscated my recently published books.

Let me here declare my mind freely. What should hinder a man from speaking the truth without reservation, who is just about to make his exit and to leave behind him a sad though true example of human misery? Sometime after this (as age and experience are apt to bring new discoveries to the mind of man and consequently to alter his judgment of things) I began to ask myself whether the law of Moses should be considered the law of God inasmuch as there were many arguments which seemed to persuade or rather determine the contrary. At length I came to the conclusion that it was nothing but a human invention, like many other religious and legal systems in the world, and that Moses was not really its author. I noted that it contained many things contrary to the laws of nature; and God, who was the author of those laws, could not contradict Himself, which He must have done had He given to mankind rules and regulations contrary to the laws of nature. Having thus determined this point, I began to reason with myself in the following manner (I wish I had never entertained such a thought!): What can it profit me to spend all my days in this melancholy state, isolated from the society of this people and their elders, especially since I am a stranger in this country without any acquaintance among its inhabitants or even any knowledge of its language? How much better will it be for me to return to their community and conform to their ways in compliance with the proverb which directs us to do in Rome as the Romans do. These considerations led me to return to their society. Accordingly, I made a formal recantation and subscribed to such regulations as they were pleased to impose upon me, after having lived for fifteen years in a state of separation from them. I must note that a certain cousin of mine helped to mediate this reconciliation.

A few days after this I was accused by my nephew, a lad whom I kept in my house, of breaking the dietary laws. New and cruel proceedings were begun against me. My cousin, whom I mentioned before as a kind of mediator between us, thinking that my behavior brought dishonor on his mediation and being a proud, bold fellow and very hasty, declared himself openly my inveterate enemy. He won all my brothers over to his side and left nothing undone that might ruin my reputation and fortune, and deprive me of life itself. He prevented a marriage which I was then just on the point of concluding, for I had lost my wife recently. He was also the cause for one of my brothers withholding my property which was in his possession. He also put a stop to the dealings which existed between us, as a result of which I suffered incredibly in my business affairs. In a word, he was a most implacable enemy to my reputation, fortune and life. Besides this domestic war, if I may so call it, another of a more public nature was carried on against me by the rabbis and the people who began to persecute me with fresh hatred, behaving with such insolence to me that I justly came to abhor and detest them.

About this time a new situation arose. One day I happened to be in the company of two men, one a Spaniard and the other an Italian, who came from London to Amsterdam. Both of them were Christians and not even related to Jews by descent. They revealed to me their present situation and asked my advice concerning the possibility of their becoming converts to Judaism. I dissuaded them from any such intention, advising them rather to bear the inconveniences of their present condition rather than to subject themselves to so burdensome a yoke with which they were unacquainted. At the same time I cautioned them not to make the least mention to the Jews of what had passed between us. This they faithfully promised me. These perfidious wretches, however, induced by the hope of filthy lucre, instead of repaying me with gratitude, went and disclosed everything to my dear friends, the Pharisees. The officers of the synagogue convened, the rabbis were inflamed with resentment and the insolent rabble cried out with one voice, "Crucify him!" In short, I was asked to appear before the rabbinical court where the charges against me were read with as much solemnity and impressiveness as though I had been on trial for life. Then it was decided that if I were really a Jew, I ought to submit to their sentence; otherwise I must be excommunicated again.

O just and equitable judges who take upon yourselves the power of condemnation and punishment! But when I appealed to your authority for protection against oppression and wrong then indeed you pretend that you have not the authority to interfere in such matters and are only servants of civil power. Of what validity, then, is your judgment that I should obey it? Then my sentence was read out of a little book. It declared that I must enter the synagogue dressed in the clothes of mourning, holding a black wax taper in my hand and there to read distinctly before the whole congregation a form of recantation in which they described in the blackest colors the magnitude of my crimes. Then I was to submit to a public whipping with a scourge made of leather thongs. After that I was to prostrate myself at the entrance of the synagogue that they might all pass over me. Moreover, I was to fast a certain number of days.

No sooner had I heard my sentence than I was fired with indignation and resentment. However, withholding my anger as well as I could, I answered only that I could not consent to undergo such a severe sentence. They consulted together and proceeded to excommunicate a second time. But not content with this, many of them spit upon me as they passed me in the streets and encouraged their children to do likewise. The only reason why they did not stone me was because they wanted power. This persecution lasted for a period of seven years, and should I relate all that I suffered it would seem incredible. For two parties violently persecuted me—the whole Jewish community and my family who sought their revenge in my disgrace. Nor would they be satisfied until they got me into their own power and jurisdiction, saying among themselves: "He is stubborn. He will do nothing until he is forced to, and therefore ought to be compelled." When I was sick nobody would attend me. If I suffered any other misfortune, it became a triumph and joy to them; if I proposed any one of them to act as judge between us the proposal was rejected. When I attempted to lay the whole case before a public magistrate, I found it very tedious and difficult, for judicial proceedings are at best both expensive and dilatory.

During these troubles they would often exhort me to submit, saying, "We are all your fathers and therefore you need not fear that we shall act unfairly or unkindly toward you. Only say that you are ready to perform whatever we ask of you, leave the rest to us and all shall be made easy." This was the very point in dispute, and I understood how disgraceful it would be to surrender out of discretion and depend upon their mercy. Yet I wanted to put an end to this long affair and after much reluctance I prevailed upon myself to submit to their terms and to test their honor. For I argued with myself thus: If they deal dishonorably with me they will stand convicted by their own behavior and exhibit their implacable enmity toward me and how little they are to be trusted. At length this execrable and detested people did plainly show what their religion and principles are by treating men of honor and character as though they had been the vilest slaves. In a word, I said to them, "I depend upon your mercy and I am ready to undergo whatsoever you are pleased to impose upon me." Now let every man of truth and humanity observe my situation and judge the sentence which a particular set of people, under foreign jurisdiction, passed upon an innocent man.

I entered the synagogue which was filled with curious spectators of both sexes. At the appointed time I walked up to the reading desk which was in the center and with a clear voice read aloud the form of confession which they had drawn up for me, namely, that I deserved to die a thousand deaths for the crimes I had committed such as the profanation of the Sabbath, the breach of my religious vows, etc., which I had carried so far as to dissuade others from being converts to Judaism. To atone for these violations I submitted to their sentence and was ready to undergo whatever they wished to lay upon me, promising not to be guilty of similar crimes in the future. When I had finished the reading I stepped down from the desk. The chief elder came up to me and, whispering in my ear, bid me go to a certain corner of the synagogue. When I had done this, the doorkeeper asked me to strip. Accordingly I stripped myself down to the waist, tied a kerchief about my head, pulled off my shoes and, holding up my arms above my head, clasped a kind of pillar in my hands, to which the doorkeeper tied them with a rope. Having thus prepared myself for my punishment, the verger stepped forward and with a scourge of leather thongs gave me nine and thirty stripes, according to the Jewish custom (it was a legal commandment that the number of stripes shall not exceed forty) for these very scrupulous and pious gentlemen take due care not to offend by overstepping their bounds. During the period of my whipping they sang a psalm. Then I was ordered to sit down on the ground whereupon an elder came forward and absolved me from my excommunication. So now the gates of heaven which were doubly locked and barred against me were suddenly flung wide open. O the ridiculous ideas and conceits of mortals! After this I dressed and went to the entrance of the synagogue where I prostrated myself. The doorkeeper held up my head while everyone, both young and old, passed over me, stepping with one foot on the lower part of my legs and making ridiculous gestures, more like monkeys than human beings. After they had all done this I got up and, being washed and made clean by a man who stood near me for that purpose, I went home.

Now let nobody say that they did not do me honor, for if they scourged me yet they lamented over me and stroked my head. O shameless race of men! O detested fathers! You from whom I had nothing dishonorable to fear! You who said, far be it from us to abuse you indecently! Now let anyone who has heard my story judge how decent a spectacle it was to see an old man, a person of no mean rank, and one who was by nature exceedingly modest, strip naked before a large assemblage of men, women and children and scourged by order of his judges and those who deserved rather to be called abject slaves. Let him imagine the confusion and anguish such a one must suffer by being obliged to lie at the feet of his bitterest enemies and to be trampled upon by those who had already loaded him with injuries and insults. Think of him seeing his own brothers (O monstrous, inhuman and shameful treatment) who were educated in the same house, joining in an unnatural confederacy with his persecutors and unmindful of that great affection with which I always loved them; and all this, regardless of the many good deeds I had done them, requiting all my kindness and tenderness with shameful injuries and disgrace.

My detestable persecutors said in their own defense that they only made me a public example in order to deter others of their faith from open violation of religious ordinances and from writing books against their rabbis. O wicked wretches and fathers of untruth! With how much more justice could I have made you a public example of punishment in order to deter you from practicing similar abuses on men who are sincere lovers of truth, haters of deceit and invariably the friends of all mankind. Of such men you are the common enemies, esteeming all others but as the beasts of the field and scum of the earth while you arrogantly extol yourselves with vain praises as the only favorites of Heaven. In reality, you really have nothing to boast of unless you regard it as praiseworthy to live as outcasts, isolated from the society of men, despised and hated by all for your absurd customs by means of which you distinguish yourselves from the rest of the world. . . .

Permit me at this point to propound the following question: If the groundless fears which you instill into the minds of men are contrived on purpose to restrain the natural evil which is inherent in them and thus to keep within the bounds of their duty those who would otherwise lead immoral lives, must you not at the same time reflect that you yourselves are men of similar passions, naturally averse to good, prone to evil, without compassion or mercy? But I can see every one of you filled with rage at so insolent a question and cleverly justifying his own conduct. "What, are we not all pious and merciful and followers of truth and justice?" My answer is that what you so boastingly say of yourselves is patently false. Your accusation of all other men whose natural inclination to evil you pretend to correct with your terrors is outrageously unjust. How impiously you reflect upon the majesty and goodness of God whom you represent as a tyrant and destroyer. How you distort human

nature in supposing it to be subjected to so deplorable a fate, just as if
the ordinary calamities of life were not a sufficient portion of misery
for human beings. Granting that the natural corruption of man is great,
which I readily allow (you yourselves are sufficient proof of it for otherwise you could not be capable of such scandalous falsities) you ought to
search for a more effective remedy to heal this general disorder without
introducing a worse one in its place, and to put aside those impositions
which are likely to frighten only children and simple folk. On the other
hand, if the disorder is incurable then cease from your vain, delusive
pretenses and do not act like impudent quacks in promising men health
which you are unable to give them. Be content with establishing among
yourselves just and reasonable laws which provide rewards for the good
and suitable punishments for the bad. Defend the cause of the down-
trodden against the violence of the oppressor so that there be no complaint
that justice is not executed in the earth and that there is none to deliver
the weak from the hands of the strong. In sum, if men would follow the
dictates of reason and live according to the laws of nature they would
all mutually love one another. Everyone would then contribute his utmost
to the relief of his neighbor or at least no man would injure another for
that would be acting contrary to human nature. Indeed many of the
evils in life arise out of the fact that men have invented laws directly
contrary to those of nature and thereby create the cause for one man
injuring and persecuting another. Then, too, many men easily deceive
the unsuspecting by their extraordinary pretense to piety. They use
religion as a cloak in order to prey upon those who are superstitious.
These may aptly be compared to a thief in the night, who treacherously
attacks us when we are off our guard and do not suspect any danger.
Yet these are the men who continually vaunt their honesty and patriotism:
"I am a Jew, or I am a Christian. You do not doubt my integrity? Rely
upon me, I will not deceive you." Infamous wretches! He who pretends
to be neither of these and only calls himself a man is far preferable to
you. If you do not believe him you may at least stand upon your guard.
But who can defend himself against you, hypocrites, who under the
mask of sanctity, like a thief in the night, come in by stealth and murder
us in our sleep?

There is one thing beyond many others that puzzles and surprises
me. How is it that the Pharisees, living in a Christian country, enjoy so
great a degree of liberty as to exercise judicial power and authority? I
may safely declare that if Jesus of Nazareth, whom the Christians worship,
were to preach today in Amsterdam and the Pharisees, like their fore-

fathers, decided to scourge him for opposing and condemning their tradition and hypocrisy, they might do it with impunity. Such freedom is a matter of reproach and ought not to be tolerated in a free city which professes to protect men in the peaceable enjoyment of their liberty. Where a man is not permitted an advocate to defend his cause or a judge to punish the injuries inflicted upon him, it should not be a cause of wonder if, as a result, he takes every opportunity to defend and revenge himself.

I have here given a true account of my life. I have laid before you fairly the part that I acted on the vain stage of this world during the course of a checkered and unsettled life. Now, readers, judge impartially and render your opinion on what I have written with freedom and truth, like brave and honest men. If there is anything in my story which arouses your compassion let it teach you to pity me and to lament the miserable state of mankind in which you yourselves have an equal share. In order that it may be known who the author of this account was, let me note that while I lived as a Christian in Portugal, I was called Gabriel da Costa; but when I joined the Jewish fold (would that I never had done it!) my name was changed to Uriel.

TROUBLE IN THE SIENA GHETTO

JOSEPH DA MODENA (SEVENTEENTH CENTURY)

Because personal records of simple folk are almost unknown until modern times, this diary of a secondhand clothes dealer of the ghetto of Siena is a document of rare curiosity and significance. He jotted down his doings and feelings in Italian on the blank pages of the ledger of the business house of Jacob ben Eleazar Modena, and, although he tells us only his first name, it is probable that he belonged to the same family. Joseph did not get on well with his relatives, neighbors and competitors. The following graphic account of a squabble with his sister-in-law bares the reasons for his unsociability. From the social point of view, it portrays vividly the elements of popular democracy characteristic of community life in the ghetto.

❊ ❊ ❊

I RECORD herewith, how, in the year 1633, Donna Stella, widow of Solomon Toscano, intended to marry Salvador, son of Isaac Gallichi. This match was treated by Donna Angela, wife of Moses Rieti. In the same year died my wife Anna, sister of Stella who died in childbed, after bearing a male child. The Donna Stella was godmother, and her father (my father-in-law) was godfather. I gave the child to nurse to my aunt Dianora, who lives over against Donna Stella. By reason of this, she took care of my son, and kept him in her house all day, for the great affection which she bore for me and for my son, her nephew, wherefore she declared many times that before she married, she would leave a hundred scudi out of her dowry on interest for my son. Besides this, I went freely into her house and into her chamber with all familiarity and liberty; she shewing me great affection and friendliness. One day, I was called by Messer Angelo Semilini, and he took me outside the ghetto, and said to me:

"You know, that your sister-in-law is in treaty to be married to Salvador Gallichi. I therefore advise you, if she has anything of yours in her hands, to have it restored, because, if she comes to an understanding with Salvador, you will have great trouble to get it out of his hands."

I replied, as was true, that she had all my wife's furniture, with the brassware and copperware of my house. I, on the other hand, had some of her household goods which she had given me to look after when she was left a widow, for fear that her husband's brothers would come to make an inventory of his property and would take it away from her; wherefore she gave it to me to look after: which property was worth about twenty scudi. Moreover, I had certain pawn tickets for apparel and coats of hers, which she had lent me to use, and the said tickets were left in my hand in order that I should redeem them. All this I communicated to Messer Angelo, telling him that if she returned my property, I would return hers. But, if I thought that the match with Salvador would really come about, as he said, I would do anything to impede it, and though I did not desire to do her annoyance, after receiving my property I desired to send hers to the dead man's brothers, to prevent it from coming into the hands of the said Salvador. Whereat Messer Angelo was very content that I should act thus and hinder the match, because he hated and wished no good to Salvador, although he still spoke to him, and treated him like a friend.

Now the reason for the hatred which Messer Angelo bore for Salvador was as follows. In the year 1632 Messer Angelo had gone to Acquabona with all his household, and left no one at home. Whereat Salvador enticed Angelo, son of Donato Semilini, to enter his uncle's house by some means, while he was away, and urged Angelo to rob him of a certain sum of money. Angelo did this; he broke open a chest belonging to his uncle, and, finding there a bag containing a thousand piastri, took thereof one hundred. When Salvador was apprised of this, he threatened to play the spy, and, to prevent this, Angelo, gave him twenty piastri, in return for which Salvador promised to keep the secret. With these ill-gotten moneys, Salvador went with the wenches: whence it happened that one Saturday night at eleven o'clock he was caught in a wench's house with the money in a purse. Whereupon he was given the strappado, and the wench as well, but they both remained firm and were released without being condemned, by reason of the great bribe which his father gave.

The theft of Angelo Semilini was discovered on a certain occasion when Angelo was in conversation with a certain Abraham Cohen, husband of Fiore, a Levantine, and they were in dispute about the division of the money; and on that occasion the affair was made known. It was for this reason that Messer Angelo hated Salvador. And so Messer Angelo acted as go-between, carrying messages between the Donna Stella and myself, and always shewed himself to be on my side. He did tell me that Stella desired to give me seventy scudi in order to settle our accounts, and she commissioned Abraham Meniati to inform me thereof in the presence of the Messer Angelo. Whereupon this Abraham gave me the message, and then he informed me that Salvador would not have it, nor yet do anything else, and he summoned me before the Captain of Justice. I appeared with my attorney, Doctor Marzocchi, and the Captain of Justice made a serious charge against us, telling me that he had been informed about my affairs, how I was only occupied with stolen goods and villainies, and if I did not give up all that the woman asked, he threatened that he would have me flogged, and send me to the galleys. I answered, that he was ill-informed about my affairs, and that they were persons who wished me ill, and that the said woman had all of my worldly property, which I had given her to keep (she being my sister-in-law) in order that my brother should not squander it.

Whereat the Captain, increasing his abuse of me, forbade me to answer him on that point lest he should clap me into a dungeon, and commanded that I should give up all of the property of the woman, particularly the pawn tickets. I answered him a second time: "Master Captain, if you will not have me tell you my reasons, I cannot justify my innocence. As for the pawn tickets which she says she gave me, see, here is this box of pawn tickets she gave me which I had given her to keep no more than a fortnight ago, as I gave her other things." Whereat the Captain took the box from my hand, and said: "Since you confess that you received them from her, you must prove that you gave them to her, and that they are yours, and if you do not, I will punish you, as I said." Then the tickets were read before Stella, and she said that they were hers. The Captain then gave me a fortnight to prove that the tickets were mine, and we were thus dismissed.

Turning to my attorney, I said he should advise me in the matter, should tell me how to defend myself; for it would be difficult to prove sixteen or eighteen tickets to be mine, since the greater number of the articles specified were old household articles. He replied that it was difficult for him to defend me, since I could not prove my case, and the Captain was against me; he advised me to consult some other person besides himself. I replied, that all the Jews wished one another ill, and no one would desire to interfere. He answered that he would endeavor to settle it himself with the attorney of the opposing side, so as to prevent my bearing resentment of the Captain. His advice pleased me. I told him that I would leave it all and in every respect to him. Similarly, Stella consented to leave the matter in the hands of her attorney. Whereupon, an accommodation was made before the officials of the Mercanzia.

While they were on the point of coming to a decision, Donna Stella obtained a ban of excommunication from Rome. When this was known, there were many who would not have desired it to be proclaimed, but who, seeing my disaster within their reach, procured that it should be, amongst these being Clement and Abraham Pesar. At this time Clement was Warden; so, to demonstrate underhand that they did not wish the ban to be proclaimed, they summoned me to attend a meeting of the Council before Messer Prospero Semilini, Messer Isaac del Borgo, Messer Clement Pesaro, Messer Reuben Frosolone, Messer Samuel Nissim, Messer Isaac Gallichi, Messer Solomon Milano, father of Stella, and others of the community.

They said to me: "You know full well that Donna Stella, having no proof to shew in support of her claim against you, has procured a ban of excommunication from Rome, so that any one who has any information should be forced to reveal it. We are sure that all will tell that which they know, and you as well, in order not to fall in so grave a sin. Nevertheless, we have thought fit to call you here before these gentlemen in order to inform you of the great danger involved if your conduct should be such that the said ban be proclaimed. For in this blessed community such a thing has never happened before, and moreover (God forbid!) the whole congregation may suffer, and, as the saying goes, 'the innocent man suffers with the guilty.'" Whereupon they addressed to me a sermon composed of these and other yet better chosen words, and each one gave his opinion, to which I gave an attentive ear. Then when all had finished, I said: "I thank you all, who have had the goodness to summon me to this holy place on this account. In reply, I tell you that I do not desire aught of the property of any other person. It is true that I have in my possession some wares belonging to Donna Stella, but she has more of mine in her hands. In any case, I desire to give full satisfaction to the whole community as well as to Donna Stella, so that it should not be said that through my love any disorder arose in the community. Moreover, though I have every right on my side, one who wishes to remain a good Jew must obey Jewish law. Therefore, I am ready to submit the whole dispute to two persons, one chosen by each of us, or else to a Bet-Din appointed by the community, with respect to what she claims from me as well as to what I claim from her. In this, I do not think that anybody can oppose me." Whereupon those who wished me ill and desired that the ban should be proclaimed were dumbfounded at my reply, and all responded with one accord: "Bless you! you speak most wisely!" Then they turned to Messer Solomon Milano and said: "You can tell your daughter that Joseph here desires to abide by the Jewish law." He replied: "And I accept in the name of my daughter."

Thus we all parted, and Solomon went to tell his daughter how matters had been left in the Council. She consented to what her father had done, and gave her word to that effect in the presence of Messer Prospero, Messer Isaac del Borgo, and Messer Clement, one of the Wardens. But when Salvador knew of it, he sent word to Stella that, now the ban was arrived, she should no longer abide by the Jewish law; for, in order to avoid falling into excommunication, I would have to give up everything I had of hers, not she what she had of mine. She sent therefore to tell the Council that she was not inclined to proceed further. Whereupon the Council waited upon Solomon Milano and his daughter, and rebuked them, saying that whosoever wants to remain a good Jew must abide by Jewish law in any matter whatsoever, all the more so since her father had given his word to that effect before the whole congregation. She made answer, that in this she had nothing to do with her father, being a widow, and able to manage her affairs by herself, and that she did not wish to proceed further in the matter. They replied that, if she insisted on having the ban published, it would have reciprocal consequences, applying equally to what I had to give her as well as to what she had to give me. She answered, that nonetheless she did not wish to abide by Jewish law, since the ban was in her favor. Upon this, the entire congregation took leave of her in great indignation for having failed to do that which she had promised, and they were displeased also that the said ban should be proclaimed, because such a thing had never happened before. For these reasons they waxed resentful against her.

And thus it happened three days after, during the morning service, that Solomon Milano and Salvador Gallichi came with all the constabulary and with an order from the Governor that no one should prevent the ban from being proclaimed. Even as they were approaching they were sighted by Abraham Pesaro, who hastened into the synagogue to tell the congregation to leave, so that it might not hear the recital of the ban. And so the reading of the prayers was interrupted (the Amidah being then in the course of repetition), and the whole congregation tried to leave the synagogue. Even as they were halfway down the stairs, they were met by the constables, who made them turn back by force of blows with the flat of the sword, and locked the gate from outside. Clement Pesaro tried desperately to escape, and received many blows from the constables with the flats of their swords and the pommels of their daggers. Likewise, Solomon received many blows from them. At the same time the Bargello came up, and laid about many more with the naked sword, while others prevented people from going out by the windows. At this point, Bonaventura Gallichi, who was officiating as Hazzan that morning, took the ban of excommunication in his hand and set about reading it from the window of the synagogue, because everybody had gone out. As he stood reading it, his nephew Salvador held the black candle in his hand, and it all dripped down on the head of Bonaventura while he was reading.

Inside, there were remaining only Solomon Milano and Salvador and Bonaventura and Abraham da Bologna, and a certain Abraham the hermit, and Sforzo Nissim, and three or four more whose names I have forgotten. These were banging on the benches, while the others were outside the synagogue, and all the women were on their knees crying: "May it recoil on the head of him who is reading it and the person who has procured it!" Meanwhile, the boys were throwing cabbage stalks and stones at the said Bonaventura as he stood reading at the window. Thus on that day there was caused a great outcry and an uproar. No sooner Milano and Salvador and Bonaventura issued from the synagogue, than everyone cried after them: "On your own head," adding all manner of opprobrious insults. And everyone with one voice said of the aforementioned Stella: "It is through that shameless hussy that this disturbance has come about." In consequence of the great insults which were addressed to her by all the congregation, she did not dare to show herself either at her doors or windows: and to remedy this, she had to procure five or six injunctions from the Captain of Justice that no one should molest her, one of which was sent to me. Thus the people were quieted down.

After this, the congregation refused for some time to speak to Solomon Milano or to Salvador Gallichi or to Bonaventura Gallichi, who had read the ban. Only Prospero Semilini continued to speak to them, because Isaac Gallichi was his relative, besides having exerted himself to bring him to Siena when he failed, and sending his sons to him to study. For this reason, he made every effort in the matter, and it was to him that they had delivered the denunciations made as a result of the said ban. He excused himself by saying that he did not like to meddle in such an affair, but because he received commands from the Rabbi, he could not do less than carry out whatsoever he was commanded. Under his pretext, he imposed upon everybody as a point of conscience to report to him in minute detail everything they knew about the matter, in order not to fall into misdoing. He told the people, however, that they should write details only of those, whether myself or any other, whom they knew to have in their possession property belonging to Stella; but if they knew that Stella had some of my property, or anybody else's, they should not write about that, as he would not accept their information. Aware that Prospero was acting partially in this matter, for the discharge of my conscience, I went to my uncle Ephriam, and begged him to tell me what he knew about it, since I did not wish to prejudice my soul thereby, even though I should indubitably lose all that I had in the world. He told me that he would study the matter, and requested me to bring him a legal compendium entitled "Caro". When he had studied it, he told me to banish my fears, of which he made light, since, for a variety of reasons, he did not think that the ban was valid. Firstly, they had not given the requisite warnings, which are usually given. Secondly, the whole congregation was not in agreement. Thirdly, it was not heard by the whole congregation. Fourthly, there was not even a *minyan* (quorum) present; and even if there had been, they were all relatives and interested persons. Moreover, he gave other reasons which I have forgotten. I replied, imploring him not to prejudice my spiritual welfare, to which he answered that I should rely upon him. Therefore, I did so, and refused to make any denunciation. Three days later, all the denunciations were presented by all the men, women and boys to Messer Prospero Semilini, and he presented them to the arbitrators whom we had appointed according to the compromise, to whom were presented also the pawn tickets which I had left in the hands of the Captain of Justice. All these were returned to me with the exception of two, one for towels and other articles, and the other for bracelets: with respect to which they ordered me to prove within ten days that they had been given me on account of the dowry. I summoned as witnesses Messer Angelo Semilini and Messer Reuben Frosolone, who had valued the said articles. Messer Reuben said that he did not remember anything at all about it, and he refused to come to make an inspection; for he was uncle of Salvador, and did not wish to act against his own nephew. Madonna Fiore, widow of the late Laudadio Galletti, offered to give evidence in my favor in this matter, because she had been present when my property had been valued and could recognize it in all good conscience, for Solomon Milano was living at that time there in her house.

She told me, therefore, that I might summon her, and that she would testify truthfully. The reason for this was that Salvador had told her to go to empty her purse, besides which he gave her a blow. For this reason, hatred grew up between them. And so I had her summoned as witness, and Messer Angelo Semilini as well. After I had them summoned, both of them changed their minds about doing me this service, although they would have been doing what was both right and just. After my prayers, they consented to give evidence; but they had delayed so long that the time fixed by the arbitrators had passed. So, for love of the opposite party, the officials passed sentence against me, saying that the time allowed me by the award had elapsed. These two pledged together amounted to more than eighty scudi.

I have put this on record, wishing to show, that there are to be found in this world none but hypocrites and traitors. I also place on record how, in the same year that the ban was proclaimed, there died the wife of Messer Prospero Semilini; Messer Amadeo Betarbo, a young man of thirty-five years of age; Messer Aaron Emilio, a youth of eighteen, who was affianced to the daughter of the said Bonaventura Gallichi; the mother of Salvador died eight days after giving birth to a male child; a male child of my own died, aged eight months; the wife of Reuben Frosolone miscarried of a male child; and the wife of Clement Pesaro likewise miscarried of a male child; there died also Abraham Pesaro, at that time President, who sickened on the morrow following his departure from office, and died eighteen days later. Wherefore, shall I pray to God, who has left good life to me and to all Israel, to save us from traitors: Amen, and thus be His will!

MEMORIES OF AN UNHAPPY CHILDHOOD

ANONYMOUS (1668-?)

Here is the story of a simple, modest, perplexed man. The author—he records his family tree for four generations * but fails to mention his own name—was the victim of a "hot-tempered and quarrelsome" father, who placed his own ambitions above the care and education of his son. This intimate record of his childhood and youth in Central Europe during the years 1668-1685 reveals strikingly those psychological drives that made for bachelorhood (and still do) in an age when marriage among Jews was considered as essential as food and shelter. The detailed recollections of family life in seventeenth century Bohemia and of the author's survival of a plague make absorbing reading.

❈ ❈ ❈

MY father devoted himself to the study of Torah in his youth, being an only son, and he showed acumen and skill in talmudic debates which brought him recognition from prominent men and scholars. They married him to a girl of a very prominent family, Gnendel, the daughter of R. Ezekiel of Chelm, in Little Poland. The latter, my grandfather, died in Poland before the times of the terrible persecutions under Chmielnicki, and my grandmother, Nuhah, remained a widow with three sons and two little daughters. I was told that she was a good, energetic, shrewd woman, who supported her family com-

* "I can trace my family tree for only four generations. I learned from my grandfather Jacob that his father Abraham Halevi had come to Bohemia from Poland as a young man possessed of considerable scholarly attainments. He married in Kolin, Bohemia, and died soon after the birth of his son Jacob, my grandfather. As the latter was left an orphan in childhood, he did not know from which city his father had come or to what family he belonged. My grandfather married Lieble, the daughter of Kalman of Bisenz, who was the son-in-law of Eliezer Perels, the author of the book *Damesek Eliezer,* a commentary on the *Sefer ha-Kanah,* as well as other works. His son was Moses Kuskes. This whole family lived in Prague. My grandfather had many sons, but they all died early, and only my father, Abraham Halevi, and two daughters, Rebekah and Pessel, were spared."

103

fortably up to the time of the great uprising throughout Poland, when she fled with them to Nikolsburg, Moravia, to her brother, the famous R. Menahem Mendel Krochmal, the author of the responsa *Semah Zaddik*, then rabbi of that community and of the whole of Moravia. My mother was brought up in his house. He arranged a splendid wedding, and my father then brought her to his house. At the time he lived in Meseritsch, Moravia. My grandfather, Jacob Halevi, was then rich and prosperous. My grandmother, his wife, was very pious and charitable, and visited the synagogue every morning and evening. This was true of my mother Gnendel in an even higher degree; she was, moreover, a very intelligent woman. My father continued to study the Torah.

Three or four years after the winter wedding, the Mohammedans and Tartars swept over Moravia to destroy it, and all fled in confusion and terror to Bohemia. My grandfather, a rich man, lost nearly all his property, so that but very little of their fortune remained in his hands. My grandfather, his wife, two daughters, and my father and mother with the rest of the family remained in Bohemia. They finally came to Lichtenstadt, where my father secured a post as an elementary Hebrew teacher. After some years he returned and found his house entirely empty. My mother showed her ability in supporting the family by her own efforts, and started to manufacture brandy out of oats in a copper alembic, as was the custom in those parts. This was difficult work, but she succeeded. In the meantime, my father pursued his studies.

One day a holy man, Loeb, the Rabbi of Trebitsch, whose authority extended over Meseritsch, where my father lived, came to our town and stayed in our house. When he saw the troubles of my mother, his cousin, he had pity on her, and gave my father some gold and silver merchandise, such as rings, to get him used to trade in an honest and intelligent way. My father was successful and did a good business.

Incidentally, this brought him the acquaintance of the Count who owned the city. The Count liked him, and turned over to him the "Branntweinhaus" (distillery), in which they were working with seven great kettles, and he gave him servants to do the work and grain to prepare brandy. For this my father paid him at the end of the year a specified amount, in addition to disbursing a certain percentage of the income in taxes, as was customary. Thenceforth he became prominent. My mother bore him first a daughter who died, then three sons, my rich and prominent brother Kalman, my poor self, and a son Moses, who died during the year following his mother's death.

When my mother was at last able to rest from her exertions, she fell sick in consequence of the heat and the fumes of the brandy, and she died at the age of thirty-four. There was no one in our town or outside of it who was like her in wisdom, piety, and charity. She died on a Sabbath, May 21, 1672. I was then four years old, and my older brother seven. In the course of the next year my father married again a great lady, Freidel, the daughter of R. Meir, from Vienna. At the same time he gave his sister Pessel to his brother-in-law Samuel for a wife, so that they made an exchange. The wife of my father was herself still a young child who did not know how to bring us up in cleanliness as is necessary with little boys, nor could she properly care for us when we were sick. We have to thank God and the help of our grandmother Lieble, and her good daughters, that we grew up at all. Even so, little Moses, who was only one year old, died.

After my mother's death my father began to strive for prominence and power, for as long as my mother lived, she kept him back and reproved him in the manner that a mother reproves her son. His father, also, may God forgive him, was all his life hot-tempered and quarrelsome, and from him my father, if I may be forgiven for saying so, had partly inherited the same temperament, for he was still young and had not gone as an exile to foreign countries as I had. But he found his match, who paid him back in his own coin. For there arose against him wicked men with whom my father had quarreled for years, and who had fallen under his power through his influence with the Count. Now the Count sold his property after three years and went to war against the enemies in foreign lands. He left my father in the hands of another Count who had bought the town. This new Count was not so favorable to my father as the first had been. My father thought otherwise, and he relied on a broken reed to combat his enemies. These, however, were numerous and more cunning and deliberate, for my father at that time was hasty in all his actions, and sometimes transacted his business without taking proper counsel and consideration, and he planned great undertakings to increase his wealth and honor, but it turned out otherwise. His enemies ruined the esteem he had enjoyed in the eyes of the Count. The latter made charges against him in connection with the "Branntweinhaus" and other business matters, and put him in prison for two months. Since the first Count was far away, nothing could be done to save my father, and he had to give up half his wealth in order to be released. On this occasion his enemies wreaked their revenge on his saying, "When the ox has fallen, sharpen the knife" (Shabbat 32); and they urged the Count to expel my father, together with his old father

Jacob, from his property. The Count did so. He expelled my father in Tammuz 1675, while my grandfather fled in secret, for he owed money to many gentiles and was unable to pay them. I was seven years old at the time. My father found a temporary shelter in the town of Humpoletz, a town of wool-weavers, and he traded there for a year, while I was cut off from study and good deeds and left to my own devices. He then went to a village Wostrow, for the Count had in the meantime returned from the military expedition and bought this village, and my father followed him there.

As for myself, I was constantly going back in my studies as well as in manners and conduct. After a while my father decided to send me to Prague, which was a day's journey. My elder brother was also there; it was winter then, and I was nine years old. There, too, I did nothing, for my father did not know how to arrange matters properly, and in his endeavor to save money he placed me for a small sum in charge of a teacher who took little care of me, while I needed great attention if I were to be taught with any success. At that time my power of comprehension and my memory were weak as a result of illness. I was full of ulcers, and the meals I ate were very unwholesome, for it is the custom in Prague to eat at the midday meal peas and millet with a little butter, which proved very injurious. But nobody thought to give me medical treatment. Although my father came several times to Prague, he did not observe my need.

I gratefully remember R. Loeb Fleckeles, who gave me meals in his house and kept me for about six months for a small sum, my father paying him about six gulden a month. He wished me to be a companion to his son Simon, who was then five years old, and I helped him by taking him to school and going over his lessons with him. I was very humble at the time and ready to be a slave to everybody, and to do anything I was ordered. If my father only had left me in this house, I would have become used to good manners and learned a little more than in the village of Wostrow among the country people. My father, however, wished to save money and took me home; my older brother was there at the time also. He thought that he himself would teach us, and my brother, who was thirteen or fourteen years old, actually learned from him haggadic literature, such as Rashi and Midrashim, as well as the laws of Shehitah; but I needed a special teacher. My father started to teach me Gemara Sotah once or twice, though I had never before studied Talmud or even Mishna.

Thus a long time passed by without my learning anything, until

I became a thorn in my own eyes and even more so in the eyes of my father, because, for the lack of a mother, I was a boor, brought up in dirt without any cleanliness; and I remember that at the age of eleven I ran around barefooted and without trousers, and no one cared. My father then had many little children, for his wife bore him a son or a daughter almost every year. I am sure that if anybody had announced my death to him at that time, he would have thought this good news, for he considered me ignorant and good for nothing, so that my existence was a burden to him. My brother was a strong boy who did hard work in the slaughter-house and made himself otherwise useful, while I was oppressed by all the members of the house; everyone ordered me around. This continued for the years, 1678-1679.

In 1680 a plague broke out in Bohemia, and especially in Prague. From that city the Rabbi, Jacob Backofen (Reischer), the author of *Minhat Jacob,* came with his wife Jettel and her sister Freidel, the daughters of Rabbi Wolf ben Simon Spira; and they stayed with us in our house in the village. I still remember the great modesty of that scholar who was willing to take the trouble to teach me like a common schoolmaster. But his wife, a domineering woman, did not permit him to carry out his good intention. In the course of Tammuz I fell sick, and the symptoms of the plague became apparent. For three days and nights I had high fever, and was near to death. Then a swelling broke out behind my ear on the neck, which burned like fire, and all the members of the family became frightened. The Rabbi and his wife noticed it, and fled from our house to the house of his uncle in Wotitz.

The plague was raging in the neighborhood of our village, and the Count established a "lazaretto" (a small wooden house of two rooms) in the midst of a big forest about a mile away from his castle. If some one fell sick in one of the villages he was driven out of his house with all his belongings and forced to go into that forest. The Count had set aside an open space some yards wide all around his castle, which only those living in the castle were permitted to approach. He only kept very few people in his castle, and shut himself up there, and never left it with his people. He admitted no outsider except my father, who was clever, and with whom he liked to talk, and he wanted him to appear before him and stay with him most of the day. He had ordered my father to act in the same way, and to forbid his family to leave the house or to admit strangers. He also told him that if, God forbid, a member of his own family should fall sick, he should not conceal it, but of his own accord should leave the house and go with everything into the forest. He warned my father that if he were to find out that he had concealed such a thing he would permit the gentiles to burn the house down with all the inmates in it.

When my father now realized that he had the plague in his house, he was very much upset, and did not know what to do. To carry out the order of the Count and to go with his family into the forest would involve grave danger, for the fact would become known to the inhabitants of the villages, mostly wicked men, thieves and murderers, lying in wait for the blood and property of Jews. Even in the cities they loved to oppress and rob them in their houses; how much greater, then, was the danger of their coming to murder us in the forest. Hence, he decided to hide me in the garret, asking his father Jacob Halevi to take care of me, which he did, although he was an old man himself. He tended me so carefully that no other member of the household needed to come to the room in which I stayed. It was hoped thus to prevent the plague from attacking others. In this way he stayed with me about six days.

But one day, slanderers came to the Count and reported they had seen my grandfather with another Jew, a certain Saul Pollack, who lived in our house with his wife, go together to trade in other villages in which the plague was raging. At once the Court decreed the expulsion of both from his territory at the risk of jeopardizing their lives if they should be seen there again. Then my grandfather was compelled to leave me alone on my sickbed, for it was dangerous to hide, as they would have searched for him in all the rooms, and if I had been discovered it would have involved danger for all. Therefore, both had to leave the territory under the eyes of the Count. But God took pity on my suffering, seeing that there was no one to attend to me, and sent me full recovery, and what was particularly fortunate, the abscess did not open again when in the absence of any one to take care of me, but it went down daily by the grace of God. For there happened to come to us the brother of my father's wife, R. Samson of Kamnitz, who told my father how to prepare a plaster from the white of an egg with a little alum, about the size of a nut. Both of these had to be stirred quickly and carefully in a little kettle until they turned solid. He followed this advice. The plaster was handed to me from a distance and I put it on, although I was only a boy of twelve and sick, for I had been compelled to devise ways of how to take proper care of myself. Similarly they brought my meals to the top of the staircase, which they closed at once. I had to get up from my bed to take them. I lay there alone day and night, and at that time I saw apparitions and dreamed dreams. That I remained alive was against the laws of nature. God in his mercy gave me strength so that I improved from day to day, the fever left me, and only the place of a swelling was burning like fire, and my whole face was red.

One day, however, our gentile neighbors, who noticed my absence, began to say to one another: "See what these Jews did; one of their children evidently died of the plague, and they have concealed it. As trusty servants of the Count, we ought to go and tell him, and take our revenge of the Jews."

When this rumor reached the ears of our family, my father cleverly ordered me to dress, to fold a linen cloth around my neck, and put it on in such a way that the redness could not be seen. He urged me to be courageous, and asked me to go though the garden, over the fields, and to return along the river, passing the houses of the gentiles and the castle. If somebody were to ask me whence I came, I should answer that I was coming from school, that I had stayed with a teacher in the village of Memain two miles away, and had felt the desire to come home. I did so, and, thank God, I ran and jumped like a young deer, passed the castle and the village, and was seen by many Christians, who were thus put to shame, and their scheme failed. Many of our neighbors came to the store to tell my father: "Your son whom we thought dead has returned."

He answered them, "You are dead, but we live forever."

They almost revealed to him what had been in their minds.

My father further showed his ingenuity by telling my older brother to put a ladder to our fruit tree in the garden and ordered me to ascend the tree nearest the street of the village so that all passers-by could see that I was well. He also ordered me to be playful with the village children, to throw fruits into their faces, and to call at them and jest with them. I obeyed and laughed while my heart felt bitter. Thus it was through God's counsel that the rumors stopped. I repeated this several times, but I could not appear before them often, lest they should notice the change in my appearance, for I never used to go with a neckcloth before, and now it was already some days since I had returned from my journey. Once I saw a gentile going before me with his hand on his cheeks, for he suffered from toothache, and his face looked drawn. I jestingly remarked, "Woe unto you. I am afraid you suffer from the plague." I said this to show how healthy and merry I was, following my father's order. But he answered back, "You have the plague yourself; remove that cloth from your neck, and the swelling will be seen underneath." I was frightened and hid myself, but God made the gentiles blind and forgetful.

After a month I came down to the house and mingled with my brothers and sisters as before, participating in the common meals, and no one paid attention to it. I grew stouter and stronger after this.

In the year 1680, in the beginning of the month of Tishri, the plague stopped in Prague, but in the rest of Bohemia it spread to such an extent that people grew tired of keeping away from one another. In our village many even among the people of the castle fell sick and died. My sister Leah, who was then six years old, got the swelling characteristic of the plague, but it was not so dangerous, even though it became public, since the Count had become weary of taking precautions, and my father did not come to him. At the end of Kislev the plague stopped, but in Heshvan the plague had ranged around our neighborhood, and many Jews died from it. In some villages all the male population died out, and only a few women were left. No one was there to take charge of the dead, who remained unburied, for it was winter and the earth was as hard as marble, and there was a heavy snowfall in those parts; so the corpses were only covered with snow, and often wolves came and consumed them, and sometimes the dogs scratched the snow off the bodies. May God have pity on their souls, and may they be bound up in the bundle of life with the other righteous. In our house, thank God, no one died. Only the aforementioned Saul died from the plague two months after the Count had expelled him, so that even this turned out to our good, for in this way he did not die in our house.

In the winter of 1680-81, in the month of Kislev, a great column was seen in the sky towards the east, which was very high, and remained for a month. Some claimed that it was a natural phenomenon called "comet," which sometimes appears in a very cold winter, but the astronomers explained it in various ways, and so it happened that in this year a new great world war (the Turkish war) started, which did not end till 1698.

During this winter my father made great profits, and was successful in all his transactions with various kinds of merchandise. My own impulse led me to the resolve to go to some Jewish community to study Torah. For I was ignorant, and God had shown his great mercy to us. My father promised, but did not keep his word; I often saw guests come (with whom my father went away) and he had promised to take me with him to Moravia, but he changed his mind. This happened several times; the obstacle was that the necessary clothing for me was not ready, as no one looked upon me with kindness. My father's wife had her hands full with her own little ones.

One night before my father was to leave, I was awake the whole night sewing for myself sheepskins which are called "Pelz", and I made a kind of long gown for underwear, and something for my feet. I took secretly some shirts so that my father would not notice anything, and before daybreak I went to the place where the sleigh was prepared for my father, and stayed there. When he came, day had not yet broken, and when he noticed me he thought the house dog was there, and he wanted to kick him away. I then said, "Father, this is thy son, who is ready to serve thee on the way which I take in order to study."

There were many strangers present, business men, who had come to buy wool. They saw my good resolve, though I was very young, and urged my father to take me along; they were sure I would become a great scholar and a good man. My father answered that it was impossible to take me along, for I had no proper clothing and it was very cold. I then exhibited the results of my ingenuity, the things I had myself prepared for the journey. He finally agreed and took me along; but the cold was so severe that several times I thought I was going to die; the snow was falling and the wind blew it into our faces, and it caused my father great pain; it was literally like the sacrifice of Isaac when they (he and Abraham) were on the way, and as the Midrash tells us, Satan brought them into the water up to their throat, etc. But those who are travelling for the fulfilment of a *mizwah* suffer no harm, and we reached Herschmanik. I was left there in the house of a teacher, R. Jacob from Gaja, and he began to teach me Rashi, Midrash, other haggadic texts, and the *Sayings of the Fathers*. He noticed that I could not read properly through the fault of my first teacher, who had not instructed me well. The little I had known I had forgotten, and I was in great trouble, for the new teacher was of an irritable temper, and had neither composure nor common sense. He struck me and put me to shame, but did not make good my deficiency, and only taught me the melodies for the readings from the Torah and the Prophets and a little *Haggada* and the *Sayings of the Fathers*. I asked questions and searched in the haggadic passages, but as he often laughed at me, I stopped. This was surely a grave mistake, but the teachers are foolish, and do not realize the harm they do.

I remained with him from Adar 1, 1681 till the middle of Tammuz, boarding in his house. During the first two months, when he had to slaughter calves, he gave me good meals, the spleen and part of the liver, but when the time of slaughtering calves had passed, my meals became worse and worse, for poor though he was, he was rather fastidious, and he and his wife ate the good things themselves and gave me coarse village bread, which caused me severe headaches and stomach trouble. I was there all alone with no relative near; all the townspeople observed my appearance and questioned me; if I had told them, it might have helped a little, but I was very modest and humble and God-fearing, and I thought it would be a sin to rebel against my teacher.

In the middle of Tammuz, while the teacher was away from home, my father came in company with his brother-in-law, Samson, and stayed for some time in the town. His brother-in-law had a son Sender, who studied together with me and knew all my troubles. He told my father everything, and although I contradicted him, my father believed Sender and took me away from Herschmanik and brought me to Meseritsch, my birthplace, where all my family on my father's side lived; here my two aunts were married, and I had my meals in the house of my aunt Pessel and her husband Samuel, the brother of my stepmother. There was also a good and intelligent teacher, Mordecai from Brod. I went to minyan (became Bar-Miswah) on Sabbath Nahamu; they furnished me with new clothes, and boys of the same age who knew more than I did were jealous of me. They could follow the teacher in the study of Talmud with Tosafot, which I did not know before, and only began for the first time to study here. They were younger and went in torn clothes and rags, as was usual in those parts. Therefore they annoyed me and tried to disgrace and humiliate me, so that I became almost weary of my life. The women of the community all praised me because I was modest and treated them with respect; that was another cause of jealousy. Their parents also were jealous of my father and of me; some of them were really bad. One Aaron, the son of Berl Pollack, I am sure, is still hated by the people for his wicked deeds, which I had occasion to observe: the other, Jonathan ben Lipman ben David, a big lunatic, is now, I believe, a scholarly man. Sometimes he was friendly with me. My intentions were to devote myself exclusively to study and good deeds, but there were many obstacles; I suffered various ailments. I had boils on my whole body, and headaches. My schoolmates were wild and ill-mannered, and our teacher flattered us and showed no inclination to exert himself; what I needed was a regular tutor, but he never employed assistants, nor did he take pains himself. He taught me a little part of Kiddushin.

At the end of the summer he left the place, and the community engaged in his place the pious R. Lazar of Cracow, who was married to a pious, sensible, intelligent woman, and gifted with all good qualities. He taught us Talmud and Tosafot, she taught us the fear of God and a virtuous life. He took great pains to teach me. May he be praised and rewarded for it. Of all my teachers he alone was the one who gave me the key and taught me more than all those I had before or after, except what I studied by myself. Still the whole situation was far from satisfactory, for he too failed to employ an assistant, and sometimes he fell sick; he was also very irascible, while I suffered from headaches during the whole winter.

In the summer 1682 the old teacher returned with his wife Blümele; they had no children, and flattered the pupils and their parents. We learned with a little of Hullin and small treatises of Moed without Tosafot; moreover, I already began to study a little Talmud for myself.

Altogether I stayed in Meseritsch two years and two months. At that time many Jews from Moravia came to Meseritsch, Trebitsch, and Polna on account of the war, for the Turks came to besiege Vienna. I then returned to our house at Wostrow, and stayed there the whole winter in greater discomfort than ever. Everybody, including my older brother, ill-treated me; I was still sick and looked bad till the winter had passed.

Then, at the age of fifteen, I went to Prague, with no knowledge of life in a large community. In spite of this, I found maintenance in the house of a rich man, Moses Ginzburg, who had two little boys. They really needed a tutor better fitted than I was to guide them in study and understanding. I had never tried this before, and could only stay with them a short time. Then God sent me a happy chance, for the scholarly, acute, and pious R. Mordecai, the son-in-law of the Dayyan R. Perez of Nikolsburg, who taught me without pay, had another pupil, Sinai ben Isaiah Wagenmacher, a boy ten years of age, the only son of rich parents, fondled and spoiled, who knew better how to behave than I did. By the help of God, he acted amiably towards me. I had only to go over his studies with him. His parents were charitable people; their house was outside of the street (ghetto), on a large pleasant place; there I gained in strength and health. I lived with them about two years; I felt as if I dwelt amid roses, and never in my life did I feel as happy as in those two years.

Unfortunately no one looked after me, and I fell into bad company. They constantly talked to me about women, and led me in their evil ways. We were a misguided set of young men, of different ages, wasting our time with useless things and fooling with girls, as was their habit. I finally came to think that this is the whole aim of life, since during the entire time we never spoke of anything but of following the inclinations of the heart. The greater part of my days I spent with my young friends who lived an immoral life. Among them were some who were over twenty-three years old, and had more talmudic knowledge and better manners than I. Therefore, with the consent of my father, I joined them and followed in their footsteps, like the blind in the dark, thinking in my simplicity that the purpose of good manners was to find favor in the eyes of women, and that this is human happiness in one's youth. Even in the house where I lived, the young working men who were employed in building carriages for the noblemen were a bad sort; their ringleader was a certain Abraham Bass, who was boisterous and wild, so that I was under evil influences from all sides. I was more passionate at that time than ever again in my life. How happy should I be now if my father had then given me a wife. I would have raised a large family, no doubt, in my early life, and would now have been in a position to retire from all worldly affairs.

Now, unfortunately, I am devoid of wisdom and intelligence, without sons and spouse. I wish to retire from the affairs of this world, but I do not know whether, after all, it would not be better for me to marry; possibly I might have pious children and a capable wife who would be a help to me. I wait for an answer from God, hoping that he might notify me by a sign or a dream or a verse, of which I might think when I wake up, or which a child might answer when I ask for its lesson. May I be successful according to the wish of God. Amen.

MY JOYS AND SORROWS

GLÜCKEL OF HAMELN (1646-1724)

Glückel was a woman of immense resourcefulness and talent who composed a fascinating full-length autobiography. Born in the busy port of Hamburg two years before the close of the Thirty Years War, she spent a good part of her eventful life there as the wife of Hayyim Hameln, a successful merchant. Though engaged in her husband's business enterprises, she managed to raise and guide a dozen children. After his death, she carried on heroically; but the effort was too great, and she wed the banker Cerf Levi of Metz, only to be left the widow of a bankrupt in 1712. She died in Metz in 1724. Written for her children "upon the death of your good father, in the hope of distracting my soul from the burdens laid upon it," this memoir is unique. In its graphic account of intimate experiences, its lively sketches of character, its warm humor and frank self-revelation, it not only throws a flood of light on the period but also introduces a plucky, intelligent, independent woman whom it would have been a joy to know.

❄ ❄ ❄

I BEGIN this fifth book, dear children, with a heavy heart, for I mean to tell, from the beginning to end, of the sickness and death of your beloved father.

The evening of the 19th of Tebet, 1689, your father went into town to arrange certain business with a merchant. When he was close to the merchant's house, he stumbled and fell over a sharp stone, and hurt himself so badly we were all alarmed.

He came home in great agony. I chanced to be visiting my mother, and I was called back at once. I found my husband groaning by the fire, and badly frightened I asked him what had happened. He told me he had fallen, and feared there was much for me to do. He was unable to stir, and I had to empty his pockets myself. For when he set forth he had laden them with jewelry.

We did not at once, God help us! know the real nature of his injury. He had long suffered from a rupture, and in stumbling he had fallen on the ruptured spot and badly twisted his bowels.

A bed stood always ready in the lower room, but he did not wish to use it, and we had to bring him upstairs to the bedchamber. It was a bitter cold night, as though the skies would freeze together, and we remained by his side through the cold hours, doing our best for him. But we could stand it no longer, neither did it do him good to lie there in the cold, and at last he saw the harm of it, and we brought him downstairs once more.

We worried along in this way until past midnight, and still he grew no better. I saw my sorrowful fate staring me in the face, and I begged him, in Heaven's name, to let us call a doctor and attendants. Whereat he said, "I would rather die than let the world know of it." I stood before him and wept and screamed, "What talk is this?" I said, "Why shouldn't people know? It has come through no shame or sin."

But my talk proved all of no avail. He clung to the foolish fancy that it might do his children harm; people would say that the weakness was in the blood. For he never had thought of else than his children. And so we had to contend with him the livelong night, and applying every manner of poultice.

When day broke, I said to him, "Praise God the night is over, now I will send for a doctor and a rupture-cutter." But he would not listen to it, and bade me send for the Sephardi Abraham Lopez, a physician and chirurgeon barber. I had him fetched at once.

When he came and saw the injury, he said, "Have no fear. I will lay on something that will heal him forthwith. I have dealt with hundreds like him, and it has never failed me."

This was early Wednesday morning. Dr. Lopez applied his remedy, thinking it would shortly heal him. But, God have mercy! when noon-time came, he said, "My cure, I see, is not enough—I will go and bring a rupture-cutter whom I know to have a clever hand." The rupture-cutter came and worked the entire day in the hope of easing the injury. But the longer he labored, the worse it became.

Thursday I brought in another rupture-cutter and two more physicians, one of them Dr. Fonseca. When I talked with him and related all the circumstances, he told me, "There is little I can say—or do. Alas, the bowels are so badly twisted he will not be able to evacuate." And what should have gone off naturally broke, God help us! through the open wound. Every aid failed him, and still he refused to have strangers about him and begged us all to keep it a secret. As for me, I knew and saw my fate before my eyes.

So Thursday passed, day and night, in bitter distress. Friday Dr. Lopez brought us a Berlin doctor, for many years physician to the Elector. He too gave him something to take and laid on a bandage, alas, to no purpose.

It was Saturday morning when my brother-in-law Joseph first learned that something was wrong with my blessed husband. He came running to our house and begged to be let into the sickroom. When my husband heard him, he said, let him enter.

As soon as Joseph saw him, *nebbich,* he knew what it meant. He struck his head against the wall and tore his hair and with bitter tears he cried aloud, "Woe unto me that I must lose a brother-in-law like him!" And he cast himself on my husband's bed, and with streaming eyes begged forgiveness for aught he had done.

My husband answered him from the bottom of his heart. "My beloved brother-in-law," he said, "I forgive you and all living men, and give me, I pray, your forgiveness too." Whereat my brother-in-law sought to calm him and bade him be patient, God would yet come to his aid. And my husband replied, he was content to be in God's hands.

As for myself, he did not tell me a half of his illness, but he kept ever at his side my son Loeb, then a lad of sixteen. When I was out of the room, he called the lad to him and told him how matters stood, and the boy wept sorely. But as soon as my husband marked I had returned, he quickly said to the boy, "Silence for the mercy of God! Your mother comes—let her not see your tears!" Even at death's door he thought of nothing but to spare me pain.

Saturday morning, after mealtime, my mother came and flung herself upon him, and kissing him between her tears, she said, "My son, must you now abandon us? Is there naught I may do for you?" Whereat he answered, "You know I have loved you like a mother—I have naught to ask or say—only comfort my poor Glüchelchen." That was the last word he spoke to her.

But who is now my comforter? To whom shall I pour out my soul? Whither shall I turn? All his life my beloved companion hearkened to my troubles, and they were many, and comforted me so that somehow they would quickly vanish. But now, alas, I am left to flounder in my woe.

Later, more doctors and rupture-cutters came, but they could do nothing. By the close of the Sabbath, no one remained but Dr. Lopez and myself.

Towards midnight Dr. Lopez sent for a chirurgeon, in the hope that the wound was fit; but he came and saw at a glance that nothing could be done, and he departed.

Whereat I said to my husband, "Dearest heart, shall I embrace you —I am unclean?" For I was then at a time I dared not touch him. And he said, "God forbid, my child—it will not be long before you take your cleansing." But, alas, it was then too late.

Upon the advice of Dr. Lopez I now summoned Feibisch Levi who knew how to be with a man in his dying hour. He arrived towards two in the morning, when I also called in our teacher, a most trustworthy man.

Feibisch Levi went at once to my husband. "Reb Hayyim," he said, "have you any last wishes to give us?" Whereat my husband answered. "None. My wife knows everything. She shall do as she has always done." And then he asked Reb Feibisch to bring him the works of the learned Rabbi Isaiah Hurwitz.

After he had read in them for about half an hour, he turned to Reb Feibisch and our teacher. "Don't you see," he said, "how near I am? Let my wife and children leave. It is high time." Whereupon Reb Feibisch thrust us by main force from the room.

Reb Feibisch now sought to engage him in further talk. He gave no answer, but began speaking to himself. They could only see his lips moving. So it was for nearly another half hour, and then Reb Feibisch said to Dr. Lopez, "Abraham my friend, lay your ear to his mouth, perchance you can hear what he is saying." Dr. Lopez did so, and after a space he heard him say, "Hear, O Israel, the Lord our God, the Lord is One!" With that, his breath ceased and he had breathed away his pure soul.

Thus he died in purity and holiness, and they saw from his end the man that he was.

What shall I write, dear children, of all our bitter grief? I had always stood so high in his eyes, and now I was abandoned with eight of my twelve forlorn children—and one of them, my daughter Esther, betrothed! May God have mercy on us and be the Father of my children, for He is the Father of the fatherless! I truly believe I shall never cease from mourning my dear friend.

Sunday, the 24th of Tebet, 5449 (January 16, 1689), he was buried with all honor. The entire community was struck with horror and grief at the sudden blow of it.

With my children gathered around me, I sat upon the ground for the seven days of mourning, and a sad sight it must have been to see me sitting thus, with my twelve fatherless children by my side.

We immediately secured our ten men for the daily prayers in the house of mourning, and we engaged scholars to "learn" Torah day and night through the whole year—be it not to my reproach! And the children diligently said kaddish for their departed father. And there was not a man or woman who did not come, daily, to comfort the bereaved among us.

My son Joseph was then a youngster of fourteen, a fine lad and exceedingly apt to "learn" Talmud. It liked me, therefore, to send him forth to "learn" as he should, but I hardly knew where.

At that time Isaac Polack had a teacher in his house, a solid young man from Lissa (Poland) and a mighty Talmud scholar. This teacher heard that I wished to place my son out for his studies, and proposed I should give my boy in his care. He asked not a penny for board or teaching fees until the end of two years, at which time he promised to return me my son fit to expound the Law.

I made inquiries after him, and everyone advised me to accept his offer. Whereat I drew up a contract with him, and sent my son in God's name with his teacher on to Lissa.

My son lost no time in writing me, first of his safe arrival, and then, in truth weekly, of his great content with his teacher and of how earnestly he "learned". And more of him I did not ask.

About two weeks later, my son Joseph wrote me, begging me to send on a half-year's payment for his board and teacher's fee. I was not, to be sure, obliged to do it—so he wrote me—but life had grown very dear in Lissa, so that his teacher was beset with the need of raising money, naturally a hindrance to the progress of the studies. But were his teacher relieved of these cares, he could the more rapidly advance in his learning. The teacher had other children from Hamburg—the letter continued—and their parents had all sent money, so he prayed me not to remain behind the others.

It really mattered little to me whether I paid the fees sooner or later, and I sent him the money for the half year. So all went well, and I learned from passing travelers that my son worked hard at his studies.

But when the six months were nearly over, I received a letter from

my son Joseph—it was on the eve of Sabbath as we made ready to go
to synagogue—that read as follows:

> "My dear mother, you know that I have always been a good boy
> and never done anything against your wishes. So now I hope you
> will not withhold from me your mother's love, nor let me fall
> into the hands of the gentiles.
> "For I must tell you, mother dear, that the Jewish community
> of Lissa is greatly in debt to the church powers and cannot pay
> either capital or interest. The community sees no other way out,
> save to hand the children of the German Jews over to the church
> powers by way of a pledge. And then their German parents
> may ransom them as they can.
> "The administrator of the community secretly revealed the plan
> to all the teachers with German pupils, and a Talmud student
> who is my good friend whispered it in my ears. I dare not write
> you of it myself, for my teacher watches me too closely and
> reads every one of my letters, so I have asked the young man to
> write in my stead.
> "For the love of God, mother dear, write to Tockel's son-in-law
> to give me fifty or sixty Reichsthalers that I may pay my teacher
> and that he send me home in secrecy, and I escape from their
> hands.
> "I beg you, in God's name, hasten! For if you delay I shall fall
> into the power, God forbid, of the Poles, and should that happen
> and it come to a question of ransom it will cost us tenfold. So I
> beg you, for a bit of money do not forsake your child, and let
> me not fall into hands from which it will be hard to get free."

When I read this my strength left me. I summoned my son Mordecai
and showed him the letter. He, too, was stricken with alarm. Sabbath
had just begun. At its close we decided to send my son Mordecai to Lissa
forthwith, and have him bring home my son Joseph.

Mordecai set out at once for Berlin, and thence to Frankfort on the
Oder. As he left the gate of Frankfort, my son Joseph came riding
towards him in a little Polish cart. My son Mordecai saw him, bade
him descend, and asked him by what strange hap he was riding to
Frankfort and what he meant by such a letter to his mother. And he
showed him the letter.

My son Joseph read it, and said, "What does it mean? Really, I
haven't the slightest notion. My teacher—may his name be blotted out!—
must have written it himself, and thought to pump another bit of money

out of me, as he has already squeezed all he could and pleased. He has taken all my belongings, cut the silver buttons from my coat, and made off with everything.

"When I wanted to leave him, he charged me with all manner of false debts, I had eaten like a pig, devoured his house, and despoiled him. I saw that nothing good could come of it, so I asked Tockel's son-in-law to make terms with him. He paid thirty reichsthalers and took me away, and sent me on here. Thank God I am free of that scoundrel! What is more, he taught me nothing."

My son Mordecai was only too happy to have chanced on him, and they returned at once in their coach to Hamburg. I rejoiced mightily and thereat took me an honest teacher and had my son "learn" at home.

About this time, something terrible happened in Hamburg.

There lived in Altona one Abraham Metz, whose wife was my kinswoman: Sarah the daughter of Elias Cohen. Before coming to Hamburg he had dwelt in Herford and married the daughter of Loeb Herford. Two years after marriage, his wife died, whereat he moved to Hamburg and took to himself the aforesaid Sarah.

He came a man of means, with some 3000 reichsthalers or more; but strange to Hamburg, he knew nothing of its way or manners of business. He kept losing ground steadily, and within a few years he had nearly reached the end. Thereafter he moved to Altona and became a money-changer.

One morning his wife comes to Hamburg and asks of all the houses where he was known, if he had not passed the night beneath their roof. But despite all her inquiries she found no trace of him. The woman now sank into despair. Many said she had quarreled with her husband and he had taken to flight.

So the matter stood for three years, and everyone wagged their tongues as they pleased. There were those who spoke great evil of him— God revenge his blood!—things that for the sake of a martyred saint I dare not repeat. But, alas for human frailty, our mouths often speak what our eyes have never seen.

Thus, for more than three years, our Sarah lived as a widow and sat with her fatherless children about her, suffering people to say and judge what they liked of her husband.

Then there was Aaron ben Moses, another householder in Hamburg —a money-changer too, an honest man and by no means rich, yet a decent provider of his wife and children.

Now, money-changers must run about the whole day long in search of business, and towards afternoon prayers they return home and go to synagogue. Or they have every one his *chevra* (society) where they study Talmud and then betake themselves home.

One evening the wife of Reb Aaron waited till long after dark for her husband to return, that they might sup together. But she waited in vain. Then she ran out searching among all their friends, and found no sign of him. And he, too, remained lost.

The next day a cry went up everywhere. One man said he had seen him here, and another there.

When noon came, people gathered on the Bourse and talked of nothing else. Samuel, the son of Meir Heckscher, said, "Yesterday a wench came to me, who had a little money. She asked me whether I had six or seven hundred thalers, and if so I should come home with her, where there was a well-to-do stranger who had quantities of gold and precious stones to sell. But I lacked the money and did not go with her."

When he had finished his story, a man named Lipmann, who was standing by, asked him what kind of a person the wench might be, and how she was dressed. Whereat Samuel Heckscher told him. And Reb Lipmann said, "I know who she is, and where she works. And I have no reason to think good of her master."

After this talk and more like it, everyone left the Bourse and went home.

When Reb Lipmann reached his house, he said to his wife, "What think you of this? The wench who works for the son of the keeper of the Navigators Tavern went up to Samuel Heckscher and wanted him, if he had six or seven hundred thalers about him, to go home with her. I fear me that the little fellow who is lost did as much, and it cost him his life."

Then his wife struck her head and said, "By my sins! I remember now this wench once came to me, and wanted either you or me to go off with her. You know right well the wicked head that tavern keeper's son carries on his neck. He is no one else but the murderer, and the little man, I say, was killed in his house."

An energetic soul, the wife of Reb Lipmann swore she would give herself neither rest nor peace till she brought the matter to light. But her husband answered her, "Foolish woman, even if it were true, what could be done? This is Hamburg, and we dare not breathe a syllable about it."

Several days passed. Then the Town Council was induced to send forth a crier with a drum: whoso knew aught of the missing Jew, whether he be dead or alive, let him tell what he knew and he should receive a hundred ducats reward and his name would never be said.

But no one came with anything to tell.

So time went on, and the affair was nigh forgotten, as is the way of the world. No matter how urgent or important be a thing, if it leads nowhere, it soon vanishes from the mind of man. But not so the anguish of the grass widow and her fatherless children.

Then, early of one Sabbath morning the wife of Reb Lipmann found she could not go to sleep.

Thus it was with the King of Spain who asked a learned Jew the meaning of the Hebrew words, *Hiné lo yonum ve-lo yishon shomer Yisroél*. Whereat the learned Jew gave him the plain meaning, "Behold, He that keepeth Israel shall neither slumber nor sleep." But the King said, "Nay, it means otherwise. Methinks it means 'God, the keeper of Israel, lets one neither slumber nor sleep.' For had I slept this night as it my wont, the slanders laid to the door of the Jews would have brought them to their ruin. But God who is their keeper would not let me sleep, and I rose and saw the murdered child cast into the Jew's house. Had I seen it not, it would have cost the life of all the Jews."

So, too, the wife of Reb Lipmann could not sleep. And early mornings she sat by her window, for she lived in the top story on the Alter Steinweg which leads to Altona, and everyone going to and from Altona must pass her door.

That Friday night the poor woman never slept a wink and she drove everyone mad in the house. Her husband groaned, what a life—she will drive herself crazy! But she said, there was no help for it, as long as the crime goes unavenged she could give herself no peace, for well she knew and her heart told her who had done the deed.

Meanwhile day broke, and she stood again at the window and looked in the street. There she saw the very man passing by with his wife, and a servant went with them carrying a large chest.

When the woman saw them, she began to scream, "God be with me now! And I'll have peace at last!" And she snatched her apron and her shawl and ran down from the room.

Her husband sprang from the bed and sought to withhold her. But she shook herself loose and ran after the people.

They made their way to Altona and laid their chest by the bank of the Elbe. Rebecca—that was the name of Reb Lipmann's wife—was persuaded the chest held the body of the victim.

She flew to people in Altona and begged them, for God's sake, help her, for she knew she had the murderer before her eyes. But no one wanted to hearken to her, and they said, it is easy to begin something but who knows how it will end? However, she kept on crying, Only take me to the President!

Finally, two householders went with her to the President, and told him everything. Whereat the President said to them, "Beware of what you begin. If you do not prove what you say, all you have and hold is forfeit."

But Frau Rebecca refused to be daunted, and said she would stake her very life upon it. "For the love of God," she said, "send, my lord, and fetch the man and all he has with him."

Then the President dispatched watchmen and soldiers to the Elbe. The suspects had on the instant boarded ship heading for Hamburg, about an hour away from Altona. Once they reached Hamburg, they were free, for Hamburg lay in another jurisdiction.

But the watch arrived in the nick of time, and brought the man, his wife and their chest back to the President. He ordered the chest opened. And naught was found save clothes that belonged to the man and his wife.

You can readily picture the alarm of the poor Jews. The man was questioned in every way, but he would own to nothing. On the contrary, he delivered himself of such threats that the Jews trembled with fear. For the man came of a very high family. And, finally, the Jews ran off in terror.

But Frau Rebecca never ceased saying, "Good folk, I beg you, do not despair—you will see how God shall help us!"

As she came running, all distraught, across the fields lying between Altona and Hamburg she met upon the wench who worked for the man. She knew the wench well, the same it was who had gone among the Jews to bring whosoever had six or seven hundred thalers to her master's house.

Frau Rebecca at once said to her, "Lucky for you and lucky for your master and mistress that we are met. Both of them are now imprisoned in Altona for the murder they have done. They have confessed to everything, and there lacks only your own confession, and once you have given it, the boat stands ready to carry you off to safety with your master and his wife. For all that the Jews want of you is to know that Reb Aaron be really dead, so his wife may be allowed to marry again. Apart from that we Jews want nothing from you."

Frau Rebecca kept on talking to the wench in this strain. She was a clever and glib woman, and through her chatter she won the wench over into talking herself; and pell-mell the wench told everything: how she had met Reb Aaron on the Bourse, and later Reb Lipmann and other Jews, how none, for a lucky lack of money, went with her, save the poor Reb Aaron, cursed as he was with a full purse, and how she showed him a gold chain and told him that an officer in her master's house had gold and diamonds for sale.

"So this Aaron," she continued, "went with me. But before he ever entered the house, the slaughter block was set for him. My master led him down to his chamber, and we did away with him, and buried him under the threshold."

And then she said, "Frau Rebecca, I have told you this in all confidence—you will not use it against me?" Whereat Frau Rebecca answered her, "Are you a fool? Don't you know my honest heart? I am thinking of naught but the safety of your master and mistress, that they go free from Altona. Once you come and tell our people what you have said, all will be well."

So the maidservant went with Frau Rebecca to the President's house. The President listened to the maid, and though she began to stammer and regret she had opened her mouth, still all was out, and not least the place where the victim lay buried.

Thereat the President summoned the murderer and his wife, each apart, and they both denied the deed, and said, "Everything our maid has told you is false, she lies like a strumpet."

Once again this put a bad face on things, and the President said to the Jews, "I can help you no further. If I put the man to torture on the word of his maid, and he persists in his denials, 'twould be pretty work. It is for you to seek justice now in Hamburg, and quickly as you can. Secure leave from the authorities to search the house for the body, and should you find it as the maid has said, I shall see to the rest."

The administrators ran at once and arranged to bring twenty soldiers to the spot the maid had mentioned, and began digging. They also received leave, if the body were found, to carry it to Altona for a Jewish burial. But they were likewise warned, "Take you heed, if the body be not found, you are all of you done for. You know right well what sort the Hamburg rabble are—we could never hold them back."

We one and all lay in grave danger. But Frau Rebecca was everywhere, at each man's elbow, and she kept repeating, "Do not weaken, I know in sooth the body will be found." For the maidservant had talked away her life and given her no end of proof.

Ten stout-hearted fellows and a number of seamen known to be loyal and bold were gathered together, along with certain watchmen. And they went in God's name to the murderer's house, which lay not far from the Alten Schrangen, hard by the house of the jailer.

Meanwhile a cry arose throughout the city, and a mob of working men and general rout of *canaille,* countless numbers, swarmed before the door of the murderer's house.

With one will they said to themselves, "If the Jews find the body, well and good; but if they don't, there'll not be hide or hair left of them."

But the good Lord did not keep us long in suspense. As soon as our people entered the house, they dug up the spot by the doorsill and found what they sought—at once with tears in their eyes and joy in their hearts.

They wept to find the youth of twenty-four in such a pitiable state, and rejoiced that the community was saved and justice at hand.

They summoned the entire Council, and showed them the body and the place where the maid said it would be found. The Council drew up a sworn statement of their findings and put their seal to the affidavit.

Then the body was placed on a cart and taken to Altona. Throngs of seamen and apprentices looked on, I can't tell you how many, perhaps a hundred thousand; but not one of them let slip an evil word. Wicked folk though they were and even in peaceful times forever hounding the Jews, now they were silent, and each man returned quietly to his place.

The next day our administrators took the affidavit and brought it to the President of Altona, who had the murderer and justice in his hands. And the Jews were better pleased to have the trial held in Altona.

The President again summoned the murderer and told him all that had passed. Whereat he confessed to everything. The widow received what share of the money still remained, and they sent the man back to prison for trial.

I will now resume from where I left off.

Several matches were proposed for my son Joseph, but none found favor with God save the daughter of Meir Stadthagen, who dwelt in Hamburg. We, therefore, blessed the match and celebrated the betrothals in Hamburg. The wedding was set for a year later.

When time drew near for the wedding, which was to be held in Copenhagen, I planned to journey there with my son Nathan.

Nathan was now heavily engaged in business with the rich Samuel

Oppenheimer of Vienna and his son Mendel. He held their notes to the amount of 20,000 reichsthalers, and they were on the point of falling due. But my son received neither remittances whereby the notes might be met without default, nor even a letter explaining their delay. For this reason he found himself unable to go to Copenhagen. Instead, he must keep watch for his own honor and the honor of his correspondents.

You may readily conceive our worry and heartache. I set forth alone with my son Joseph, and God knows with what anxiety and bitterness of soul. For I knew naught of how things stood with the rich Viennese.

I left Hamburg together with the bridegroom and Moses, the son of Meir Stadthagen and the son-in-law of Hayyim Cleve. And we arrived safe in Copenhagen.

There I awaited letters from my son Nathan, hoping to hear that he had received word and remittances from the wealthy Viennese. And in truth he wrote me, the good son he was, that though he had no news from Vienna I should not worry or rejoice any the less at the wedding.

Though my heart was not in it, still I left all in God's hands and dismissed my cares. We exchanged our dowries and the wedding was prepared for the following week.

From one post to another I awaited good news from my son Nathan. Praise be God, the tidings came the day before the wedding. Nathan wrote me that Mendel Oppenheimer had sent him remittances to several thousands more than we were owing him or needed, together with apologies for the delay, due to his absence from Vienna. And the wedding was celebrated in high spirits and to our mutual content.

After the festivities I was anxious to speed my way home, but I had no other traveling companion than Moses, the son of Meir Stadthagen, and he was in no haste to leave his folks. So, against my will I remained two weeks in Copenhagen. Yet despite all the honors and courtesies they bestowed on me, I longed to be home with my little ones. At length I pressed Moses Stadthagen so hard, he consented to depart. Thereupon we set forth, and praise God, arrived safe and sound in Hamburg.

I went into accounting with my son Loeb for the wares I had left in his hands, and he gave me a clean bill for everything, so I was mighty content.

DEFEAT OF SATAN

JACOB EMDEN (1697-1776)

Emden was one of the most controversial figures of his time,
and the following narrative out of his full-length autobiography will
introduce the reader to an issue that split Jewish communities everywhere into warring factions. It was the teaching and practices of the
Sabbaitians, the followers of the picturesque false messiah, Sabbatai
Zevi, who had stirred the imagination of the Jews in a period of
vast upheavals. The movement had broken up into splinter factions
under the leadership of extraordinary personalities like Abraham
Cardozo whom Emden regarded as agents of Satan and whom he
fought with satanic passion. But Emden's vehemence makes him
suspect. It was not only a matter of venting spleen, but, as his unre-
lenting attack on Rabbi Eybeschütz reveals, there was something that
weighed like a cloud upon his tormented spirit. It was not merely
an opponent's job he envied, as has been suggested, but more likely
the intensity of his physical and psychical ailments. Thus his autobiography is a psychological document of immense significance.

※ ※ ※

BEFORE I begin the story of what befell me, I faithfully declare
that I am not doing so in order to describe my name and fame;
for I myself know that there is nothing worth while in me, neither
Torah nor wisdom. I did not inherit greatness wherewith to preen myself.
Please God that I do not write on these sheets what will reveal my
deficiencies. But my people know that I have chosen humility, that ever
since I have been able to think I have known my small value and defects.
For this reason itself it does not matter to me and I shall inform everybody of my lowliness because I love only truth. . . .

During the period of my gestation my father suffered from melancholy because of the loss of his money. The sickness was so bad that
they almost despaired of curing him had it not been for the mercies
of heaven which returned him to his strength. A few days before I was

born he came home from the baths at Ems. There he had taken the medicinal baths and returned to Altona after my mother of blessed memory had borne me, on the 15th of Sivan, 1697. And he circumcised me after he had already despaired of doing so and the honor of fulfilling this commandment had been entrusted to another *mohel;* and he inducted me into the Covenant with doubly great joy because he had returned to his former health and now had a son after giving up all hope. For until that time he had only had daughters; and I was the fourth child and first son and very delicate, so my parents trembled for me exceedingly, and I grew up on their knees as a plaything amid much pleasure and tenderness. My father of blessed memory, withal, hastened to put me to school after I was three years old, so that in my fifth year I was already learning the tractate *Berakot* of the Talmud. I was so devoted to my books while others of my age could not even read their prayers. But afterwards he refrained from sending my brothers who were born after me to the teacher while yet they were so small, saying that he had weakened me thereby.

When I became a little understanding I felt father's suffering, his pain and shame because of the people who wished to deprive him of his livelihood and degrade him from his honor. After this he became very sick with pleurisy on account of an excess of bile caused on account of the dispute at Altona. The doctors had already given him up but my sisters and I fasted on his account on the Monday and Thursday of one week when I was only twelve years old. When my father was appointed Rabbi of the Ashkenazic congregation at Amsterdam the time of my wanderings and exile began.

Father's household started out at the end of the winter in the year 1710, at the time of the melting of the snows, which had fallen in exceeding great plenty during that powerful and mighty winter. We were in great danger on the way. The cart in which the women and children were sitting all but broke, and fell into the water which rose vastly high. Our outcry went up aloft and if the Lord had not delivered us the waters would have carried us away. But we came alive and well to another land, Holland, which we had not known yesterday or previously; new air and new customs. How many changes we underwent until we grew accustomed to the nature of the country, particularly as the food and drink were not those to which we had been accustomed and most of all the quiet did not last long, nor did they permit my weary father to rest; for immediately there commenced quarrels and persecutions of two powerful groups. Each side strove to swallow the other alive. My father was crushed between them, for as he could not bring them to agreement and could not justify either of them but prevented the weaker side from being trodden underfoot, they waged war against him and embittered his life, thinking to bring his honor down to earth as already described. But the Lord aided him and protected him, and at that time the Sephardic community supported him. Nevertheless this was a time of trouble to Jacob, and perplexity because of father's suffering. In addition, this dispute wasted much time which should have been devoted to the study of Torah. At that point I was confirmed, but the times did not permit me to devote myself to books, nor to acquire complete knowledge on account of the absence of teacher and comrade, leader and director with whom I might prosper. Nor was there any cure for this absence of restfulness for the sins of that place led to the coming of the hypocritical serpent, the abominable Nehemiah Hayun who confused everybody and everything. And my righteous father of blessed memory was compelled to engage in a heavy war, standing out against the prideful Sephardic magnates who broke their former covenant of love with him and became his foes, after intervening in a quarrel that was not theirs, in order to hide the shame of their Rabbi Solomon Ayllon who was responsible for all this. So that my father of blessed memory was compelled to remove his dwelling from thence and to wander once again in order to find a refuge for himself and his household.

Now this is what happened. The sins of the community led to the coming of Satan to make the world chaotic; namely the evil spirit and poisonous serpent, the abominable hypocrite Hayun who bemused the holy congregation of Sephardim and Ashkenazim alike. The heart of all the people was divided into two, those who went to the right and those who went to the left. Yet at the beginning the entire congregation of Sephardim to a man were true to their Father in Heaven, and it was they who awakened and roused love against which the whole wealth of a man is esteemed with contempt, as is written in Writ. They came to my father of blessed memory to consider the case of this hypocrite and man of violence, to investigate his impure and worthless book; wishing to depend primarily on the authority of my father, knowing him to be an absolutely reliable person possessed of wisdom and understanding.

To begin with they refused to accept their own Rabbi Solomon Ayllon, who was already suspect in their eyes on account of a certain unsatisfactory incident, resembling this but preceding it, in connection with the sectarian writings of the heretic Abraham Michael Cardozo, which had been brought to Amsterdam a year before Hayun had arrived. These writings had been written in the Spanish tongue and so were understandable to the ordinary Sephardic Jew. Reading them would be enough to make their hair stand on end by reason of the vast heresy they revealed; yet this Rabbi of the Sephardim had passed them, saying that they were good, holy and pure. But that did not help at the time since the members of the Mahamad (presiding committee of the Sephardic community) burnt them in his presence because they were written clearly in their own Spanish language. From that time forward the said teacher of falsehood was under suspicion of being affected by the filth of the false faith of Sabbatai Zevi. As is mentioned in the books *The War of the Lord* and *The Reward of the Wicked,* it was made clear that he had previously been one of the followers of that false Messiah, and although he had already departed from them and reverted to the Jewish faith, nevertheless the old weakness had remained.

Now like had found like. Therefore when this bad matter of Hayun developed they did not want to depend on him at all to begin with, not trusting him as regards this very grave and rare matter of faith. Therefore they all agreed unanimously to send to my father of blessed memory and hear his opinion and do as he counseled; for his name and fame were very widespread among them as being unique for striving to maintain and strengthen the faith. So they gave him the book of Hayun for a certain time to examine, since it had reached them only for a little while by dint of great stratagems, as is told in the two pamphlets above-mentioned. And they placed the sword in father's hands to execute justice against that enemy of the Lord who had thought to replace Judaism by his imaginary new faith; and who set out to remove Israel from the traditions of their fathers, as was finally proved in all the courts of Israel from East to West. They all thanked my father and teacher of blessed memory for being zealous on behalf of the Lord, and issuing a stern verdict against that troubler of Israel, to remove him from the boundaries of Israel. Afterwards many more of his abominations were revealed. For he did the deeds of Balaam and polluted the Holy Land; the very world cannot contain all that he has done, as has already been set out in print in sundry pamphlets and broadsheets.

Yet at that time Satan was advancing among the members of the holy congregation of Sephardim, and all but in their very sight. After they came back and took the book of abomination from my father of blessed memory, they accepted his words and accordingly undertook to drive the disgusting Hayun out of their synagogue; but then they reconsidered and set out to destroy all that they had built; their hearts turned to hatred of father, they turned their backs upon him and did not wish to hearken unto him any more about executing justice upon that man. And after they had already done as my father of blessed memory counseled and very shamefully thrust Hayun forth from their synagogue, they changed their minds and admitted him to their congregation, entreating him with great honor.

The chief reason was because their said spiritual teacher, who was bound up with Hayun, went about his dark plots. He went to the house of each of the members of the Mahamad and fell at their feet and wept and entreated them, saying: Despite the fact that he is a sinner and a transgressor, still they must take pity on his honor which is their own, seeing whither would they bear their shame and reproach in confirming the suspicion and shameful report that he belonged to the followers of Sabbatai Zevi, thereby increasing the rank of the Ashkenazic Rabbi over that of the Sephardic Haham; particularly as they claimed that they had more power and esteem than the Ashkenazim.

Ever since the community had been established, said he, the Ashkenazim had been abject and submissive before the Sephardic congregation of Amsterdam, because of the leading position of the latter with their wealth, their pedigree and greatness; while they also had precedence in time, since scarcely had Holland become a free kingdom on its own than the forced-convert Sephardim fled from Spain and established themselves in Amsterdam. For the Hollanders had broken off the yoke of the king of Spain, and all the inhabitants were liberated, and they gave permission to men of all faiths and religions to dwell in their midst. Hence the forced-converts of Spain had found a resting place there to begin with, through a Jew of Emden who had brought them to Amsterdam and circumcised them and instructed them in Judaism; and only after them had Ashkenazic Jews been attracted to settle in the town. Hence it befitted their honor to precede them in everything, particularly in view of the wealth of the first Sephardim who came to dwell in Holland; for these had been great men in Spain and brought their gold and silver with them, wealth vast indeed; and therefore they were important and honored by the government authorities.

But the Ashkenazim who had come thither were mean creatures compared to them, since they were unimportant as regards wealth and greatness in those days; and now what nightmare was this wherein the lower ones were on top and the upper ones below!

The man spoke after this fashion and stole their hearts which had been whole with the Lord to begin with, by reason of his smooth foreign tongue and flattery; so that their minds turned to follow him when he said: Although the law may not be so, the time requires this so that you may protect the honor of yourselves and our chief congregation by not accepting the decision of the Ashkenazic Rabbi, but by repenting of all that you have already done. By weeping and entreaty and supplication and prostration and chicanery, by smooth words and deceitful lips he succeeded in leading them astray to destroy what they had first set about doing, to repent of the good; so they sank their feet in mire and a smooth tongue broke the well-built flight of stairs; and they agreed to do that which had never been done in Israel. By deceit and wily false conduct of the kind called politics he led them astray to withdraw and be false to their faith; he caught them in the net of error to destroy them. All this chapter and the stratagems and instruments and strange and bitter falsehoods which came about at that time have already been made known to those who are still alive and well remember this evil mishap, which is not yet as far back as fifty years. Also many works and pamphlets were written and published at the time of this grave war which lasted a full year. . . . Actually it was this incident which led me to write this book in order to proclaim the wonders and loving kindness of His blessed Name; for the new is as the old, the father reveals his truth unto his children and all that happened to the fathers befell the sons; a thing which cannot be written in full detail. Therefore I shall not deal further with this incident which occurred more than forty years ago. . . . For that which befell my father of blessed memory befell me in the case of Rabbi Jonathan Eybeschütz, an absolute parallel, so that which befell the father also befell the son.

In Summer, 1722, half a year before I left the rabbinical office at Emden there came to the town a sending of evil angels, who declared that they had been sent by the community of Minsk in Lithuania because of an ill hap that they said had befallen there. These emissaries invented this in order to mislead Israel and steal the money of the charitable, declaring that the folk of the holy congregation of Minsk were in great distress. With them they brought false documents which purported to be written by the rabbi of that community to the congregations of Israel, to make their distress known to all and sundry and beseech aid; further, that he had appointed those persons named by him in the document to go about through the length and breadth of the land and gather money everywhere to bring for those who were in peril of death. And throughout the communities of Germany it is notorious what these robbers did, how they emptied the charity chests of the poor and misled many German communities, likewise the Sephardim of London and Amsterdam. The latter in particular treated them with great honor, and generously donated for them more than ever all the honest and reputable causes had received from them since time untold. For they had banned all granting of their charity funds to German-Jewish poor, no matter who they might be. I remember that once soon after my father and teacher of blessed memory settled in Amsterdam the emissaries of the holy congregation of Lublin arrived there, worthy men and faithful to those who sent them; and father did all he could on their behalf, also recommending the Sephardic congregation to be with them in time of trouble; and by pressure and energetic intercession, since they could not send him empty away, particularly at that time when they esteemed him like a veritable angel of the Lord, they acceded and handed over to him the donation they thought fit to give the Lublin emissaries; in order that it might seem as though they gave him a gift, because they regarded him as being like a Sephardi too; but they did it that way because they did not wish to transgress against their resolution to give nothing to the Ashkenazim.

That was the strict way they kept this prohibition. But still they took a liking to these forgers and swindlers and gave them donations in plenty, disregarding their oath on this occasion. This shows that they and many of the magnates of Germany came under the curse of Jeremiah the Prophet of being misled by a people who are not worthy. At the last these men came to me at Emden. I felt that all they were doing was deceit and forgery but nevertheless I treated them in friendly fashion to begin with; particularly as one of them was a kinsman on my father's side, Reb H. Wilner, one of the scholars of the house of study of Mannheim who belonged to the sect of Rabbi Yehuda Hasid. I have no reason to be proud of the kinship, although he was a pleasant fellow, handsome and something of a scholar, and I esteemed him and liked him before the forgery became apparent.

One of the others was an exponent of practical Kabbalah and could use the Holy Names for his works. I sounded his cask and found him to be worthless, a man of blood and deceit and an ignoramus. In my opinion they certainly belonged to the followers of Sabbatai Zevi, and went about with a fellow from Minsk, who was likewise a young man of good understanding, knowing something about the insides of books, the Gemarah with commentaries and other knowledges, besides belonging to one of the proudest families of Lithuania. He had separated from the wife to whom his kinsfolk had wed him when he was still small, and dwelt in Germany. This was the fellow they took with them to bear witness to their trustworthiness and faithfulness, for he was known in Germany as an outstanding scholar about whom nothing bad was known except his separation from his wife. Maybe he had some satisfactory reason for this and did not wish to leave her a living widow, God forbid, being prepared to give her a bill of divorcement and pay what was provided in the wedding agreement; but to that she objected and did not wish to be divorced. I also liked him because I saw signs of wisdom in him; though he was still young, I said, "this little one will grow big in the course of time."

After these false emissaries had been staying with us a while in Emden I was visited by my uncle, the brother of my mother, who came from Lithuania from the town of Grodno, and whose name was Rabbi Benjamin. I had never expected to see him, but although he was at the other end of the world the Holy and Blest One made him travel and brought him to us; and when he ate at my table we began to talk of the two emissaries who were in the city at the time, and who were traveling about on account of an unfortunate incident which had happened in the congregation of Minsk. Now this uncle of mine was a simple man who spoke without ulterior motives, and when he heard this he stood gaping and could not believe his ears, saying to us, "What are you talking about? What mishap has there been at Minsk that I know nothing about? How long have I been away? The town is quite close to me and yet nothing is known about this. In our parts nothing is known of any mishap, great or small." Now the supposed mishap had already happened a year earlier according to the liars, while he had just come from there.

I therefore decided that this tale was a falsehood and a vast lie; and I brought these men to examination, and took a legal document signed by the leaders of the Minsk community which I had with me. "If you are honest men," said I to them, "I shall help you with all my power, for I am even more anxious than you to have the merit of fulfilling an injunction like the redemption of captives, as you request. But in order to put you to the test and confound the rumors circulating, I suggest that you should entrust us with the monies which you collected from the communities in Germany, Holland and England, so that we should send it to Breslau; and we shall arrange that the money should reach your Community in a safe and direct manner, to whatever worthy leader you choose. And we shall give you a properly attested quittance to deliver you from ill report and libels. Further, whatever gifts you have received for yourselves will remain your own and we shall add to them; but we shall take steps to ensure that the poor of your Community should receive the sums donated specially for them. If you agree it will be all the better for you and double merit. And in any case why should you take the responsibility of the road upon you? For this is the custom of all faithful emissaries since time immemorial in order to be clear before the Lord and before Israel."

But I could not make those deaf ears hearken or understand this straightforward matter. No matter how much I spoke, whether hard or soft, calling upon them not to refuse, it all proved in vain. For these two men were cunning as serpents to mislead everybody with seductive words and smooth tongues; and even a great friend of mine with whom one of these scapegoats was staying was trapped in the net of their deceit. From beginning to end he was a friend closer than a brother to me; but this time even he opposed me and supported the evildoers, swearing in the Synagogue that these were upright and worthy men and that I had no reason to give them a bad name. Then I knew that an ignoramus cannot be truly God-fearing, and that there was no dwelling near him, because he swore in vain after hearing the falsehoods and smooth words of the suspect. In any case most of the communal leaders of our times are fools believing all the flattering deceivers and erring with unsuitable people who stay in their houses and steal their minds and their money, thereby misleading others as well through the recommendations they give to aid such transgressors. I still grieve exceedingly for this faithful friend whose end by reason of our many sins was bitter; he lost his wealth, and what was more the very gifted wife of his youth passed away sometime after I left the place; and he took a different wife who lost him all his wealth. And in a little while he also died; and his new wife took what she could and went to another husband, and what she brought him when he married was lost because she also died; and his children were left poor orphans, alas and alack. For this my heart bleeds when I think of the goodness of their mother, may she rest in peace. And who knows whether that false oath did not destroy him and his household? Let the leaders hearken and take heed, and not trust too much in their wealth; which is enough of this matter.

Now the end of the business of the said false emissaries, who were skilled in smiting fools with the fist of flattery and of trapping men with their mouths, was that they fled from under my hands at Emden and I could not get anything out of them; but they received large donations there as well; and I had to laugh at the fools who threw away their money on unworthy people. But in any case I did not rest until I found out what the truth of the matter was. What did I do, I took their attestation from Minsk with regard to their mission to deliver people who were sentenced to be slain, and to bring money to annul this evil decree. This document was signed by the leaders of the congregation of Minsk. I sent it by post to Altona to my then faithful friend Haham Hagiz, may he rest in peace, and requested him to investigate the matter and find a Lithuanian who could identify the signatures and say whether they were true, or whether anything was known there of this mishap in the said community.

And now hearken to the wonder; for the sage of blessed memory at once found a warden from Minsk whose name was also signed on the said attestation and who had just come to Altona. Now this was a worthy and aged man who had never previously been in Germany, but had lost his possessions in his old age and so had to go wandering. He arrived there the same week as the forged letter of the swindling emissaries. The Haham summoned him to his house and showed him the document with his signature, and said, can you recognize whose signature it is? Thereupon the old man stood astounded and said, what man has dared to do such a thing, to forge a handwriting and signature and to invent an evil happening which never really existed?

When I received the answer from the Haham telling me of the wonderful happening how the Lord had sent him one of those mentioned by name in the false document, and how the Lord had brought this worthy man from the ends of the world at the right time in order to prove the falsehood and forgery, thereby showing the truth of my words, I showed this letter to my friends. But not only did it make no impression, not only did they not take back what was stolen from the poor, but on the contrary they gave them gifts and sent them honorably away.

To be sure, I at least warned those men who were going to make the rounds of the world and empty the charity coffers. I adjured them for their own sakes not to go to Altona where they would fall into a trap. But they would not listen to my counsel, relying on the success they had had until then. They thought that the Three Congregations (Hamburg, Altona and Wansbeck) were the same fools as those they had found it Emden, whose eyes could be blinded and whose hearts could be stolen by smooth words; so they went there.

But if nobody was prepared to listen to me in Emden, my net was set for them in the congregation of Altona; and what I foretold them came about. For as soon as they arrived they were arrested by order of the wardens and leaders of the community, who had them imprisoned and expended the charges of arrest and imprisonment on them; but they could not succeed in delivering the money of the poor which was in their hands, nor to make them give up what they had stolen. Still, they were driven out of there with mockery and much contumely.

As for this Reb Wolf whom they had taken with them as a false witness, he parted from them and repented and confessed without being ashamed as mentioned in my volume of *Responsa;* for he confessed his sin and recognized his transgression in the query he sent me on a matter of Torah. I shall mention the subject in brief before making an end of the things that happened to me in Emden; since it was another very worthy and pious deed which His Blessed Name brought my way while I was there. The Lord sent me a certain man who came to me to be shown his way of repentance; and he already despaired of marrying because he was already old. And as a proper means of readjustment and repentance I enjoined upon him that he must wed a wife within a year; and he did so and succeeded and merited to have children ere he died.

I did not wish to have any benefit on this account from the considerable sums of money he brought with him. Afterwards he wrote me that he had merited to have a son when I was already in Altona; and he summoned me then and I remembered the incident.

I WAS A SLAVE

ABRAHAM HERTZ (1706-1776)

Autobiographical accounts of those sold into slavery are rare. This curious record is unique in Jewish literature. Hertz's recollections naturally center about an experience which ultimately led to his conversion to Christianity, and the sincerity and candor of the narrative leave little question that the conversion was a genuine religious experience. He changed his name to John C. Leberecht, and passed his later years as the principal of a small children's school in Königsberg, Germany. "The narration," says an anonymous preface, "was taken from the deceased's own lips, and his own phrase has, as much as possible, been preserved throughout."

❋ ❋ ❋

I WAS born in 1706, according to the Christian era, at Glogau in Silesia. My father Moses Levi Hertz was a man of learning. On being circumcised on the eighth day, I was called Abraham. I was brought up in my father's house till I was eighteen years old, at which time both my father and mother died, within one month of each other. Thereupon my grandfather, and other relations, sent me to the famous Jewish university at Prague in Bohemia. Here I pursued my studies for five years, till 1728, when the Rabbi procured me a place at Nikolsburg in Moravia, as tutor of the children of Moses Cohen, a wealthy Jew, in whose family I continued three years. My term in this family having expired, I went in the same capacity to Pressburg in Hungary, and entered as tutor into the family of Jacob Rachmetz, with whom I likewise remained three years. Then, with his consent, I went to his brother in Belgrade, on the border of Turkey, and was employed in the same occupation for about six years, till the year 1739.

At this period, the city of Belgrade was ceded to the Turks. About eight thousand of the inhabitants, Christians and Jews, were made slaves; and I, with the whole family in which I lived, sharing the same fate, we were all carried to the Turkish fortress Niffa. Here I was sold to a Turk, Temershe Ali, who had already purchased another of the unhappy captives, a young man, and a Christian of the Lutheran persuasion. We were both chained together, and taken by our master to Serras in Greece.

The name of this young Christian was Neuman. The Turk, our master, required this unfortunate man to submit to a very heinous sin; but not being able to persuade him to it, he ordered him to be whipped in so cruel a manner that the poor fellow had not a sound spot left on his whole body, but was covered all over with wounds and sores; and I, his fellow slave, had to wash his wounds, the stench of which was intolerable. I therefore took great care not to come too near him in my sleep, lest I should touch him, and thereby increase the anguish of his pains.

Soon afterwards, the Turk made me his interpreter, compelling me to convey his abominable desires to Neuman. And as once, in the folly and ignorance of my heart, I advised him to submit rather than expose himself to the barbarous treatment of the Turk, he remained not only adamant in his refusal, but declared that he could by no means bear the thought of thus offending his Lord Jesus, and that he would rather die than commit a sin. He then reproved me, saying: "Are you one of God's people, of the Jews, who boast of their being a peculiar people of God, and dare you advise me to commit sin?" These words went to my very heart, nor could I, from that hour, be easy in mind, but became deeply concerned for my salvation. Add to this that my poor, wounded fellow captive continually called upon the name of Jesus, which used formerly to be odious to me as a Jew, and prayed to him so fervently, that my inmost soul was often moved at it, and I, by degree, got a hearty love for this Christian.

One day, as he was speaking to me very feelingly of Redemption, I was persuaded to acknowledge his religion to be the true one, giving him my hand upon it, and promising to embrace the Christian faith and to be baptized as soon as I should again come into a Christian country. Before very long poor Neuman died of his sufferings, still bound with his chains. Notwithstanding the barbarous treatment the deceased had suffered, there was something uncommonly striking in the aspect of his lifeless body: far from filling me with the horror the sight of a corpse is apt to excite, there appeared something so lovely and pleasing in this corpse, that I could not behold it without pleasure; nor could I ever afterwards think of him without tender sensibility or forget his image.

It was as if the form of this happy man were constantly present and hovering before my eyes.

My late friend had told me, that he was the undutiful son of a Lutheran clergyman in Saxony; that he had learned the business of a stocking-weaver, or framework-knitter; but that, disregarding the admonitions of his parents, which he since often lamented, he left them. He went into Silesia, where, being taken by the Imperial troops, he entered into the army and was sent as a soldier to Belgrade, where he was taken and made a slave by the Turks.

According to a promise I had given him, I now attempted to have his body decently buried; a business which the Christians here, as well as the Turks, were afraid to undertake. But before I could do it, the Turk, my master, hearing of the unexpected death of his slave, which happened in the night, fell into such a fury that he ordered me to receive an hundred and fifty lashes on the bare soles of my feet, on the pretext that I had killed Neuman in the night. I complained of this outrage to the cadi, a Turkish magistrate, who, upon examination, found that the deceased had died of his wounds and the barbarous usage of his master. Thus was I acquitted, and the judge obliged the merciless Temershe Ali to dispose of me to another Turk, called Hadshi Mustapha. He took me from Serras in Greece to Constantinople, and thence to a place in the neighborhood of Smyrna, where he was settled. This Turk was a very good-natured man, and showed me much kindness during the two years (till 1741) I was with him. But all his mild treatment was not sufficient to lessen the unhappiness and distress of my mind. The demise of the late Neuman and the memory of all his discourses with me, presented themselves unceasingly to my spirit. I now resolved to write to a Jew at Smyrna, requesting that I might be ransomed by my nation and delivered from slavery. This letter had the wished-for effect. I was immediately ransomed, though my new master was very reluctant to part with me, and when at length he consented to it, he had the goodness to make me a present of sixteen zechins (about seven guineas) towards my traveling expenses, and kindly entreated me to call at his house, if ever I should come again into those parts.

From Smyrna certain charitable Jews sent me to Constantinople, where they endeavored to persuade me to settle. But, such was my uneasiness that I could not think of staying there. Declining therefore every proposal, I expressed a desire to travel farther in order to visit the graves of my relations in Silesia, which is agreeable to custom among the Jews. Upon this I obtained the necessary testimonials from the Haham, the Chief Rabbi, and was forwarded, by sea, to Bender, thence, by way of Jassy, to Hungary, and next to Mohilew in Poland. But being desirous to go to Silesia, the Jews were obliged to conduct me thither. We traveled to Kamenietz through the confines of Hungary, by way of Osen and Pressburg, into Moravia, and at last to Breslau and Glogau in Silesia, where, being arrived at the graves of my parents, my conductors left me.

In consequence of what I promised the late Neuman, I was determined to go in quest of his worthy father in order to acquaint him, if he should be living, how his son had died. I traveled on foot to Saxony, where I heard that the Reverend Mr. Neuman was deceased; but learned at the same time, that his widow lived at Naumburg. I went thither, and, having found Mrs. Neuman, gave her an account of the painful, and yet happy, departure of her late son, which the good woman heard with all the emotions and tears a tender parent feels on such occasions.

KING FOR A NIGHT

PINHAS KATZENELLENBOGEN (1691-1760)

The family tradition of an ancestor who reigned as king of Poland for a night has persisted with unbroken continuity. The author of the account here given was the great-grandson of Saul Wahl and the Rabbi of Anspach, Leitnik and several other communities. Historians tend to identify Saul with the prominent business agent of the Lithuanian Prince Radzivill, who had considerable influence at court as well as the unique privilege of bearing a saber, and was known in contemporary records as Saul Yuditch. The event occurred in the interregnum between the reigns of Stephen Bathori and Sigismund III which would place the event in 1586. Pinhas accepted his father's deathbed story uncritically, he is unaware of certain historical inaccuracies, but family and national pride rarely differentiate between legend and history.

✳ ✳ ✳

MY grandfather, Rabbi Samuel Judah of Padua, had a son who was the illustrious Saul Wahl of blessed memory. The surname Wahl, according to those versed in history, was conferred upon him because he was chosen (Wahl means "choice" in the vernacular) King of Poland by the unanimous vote of the nobles of the country. I heard from my father and teacher of blessed memory that this extraordinary event happened in the following manner.

Saul was beloved by the great princes of Poland and esteemed for his remarkable ability. While he was at the peak of his influence, the king of Poland died. It was the custom of the great nobles to assemble for the election of a new ruler on a specified day on which it was prescribed that a decision must be reached. When that day came, the nobles, disagreeing among themselves, were unable to decide who should be king. They debated until evening when it appeared that it would be impossible to elect a new king on the day prescribed by law. In order not to permit the day to pass without appointing a ruler and thus transgress their own enactments, all the nobles agreed to make the illustrious Saul Wahl king for the remainder of the day and the following night, thereby conforming to the letter of the law. Immediately they crowned Saul, shouting in their own tongue "Long live our Lord, the King." They loaded him with royal honors, and he reigned all that night.

My father told me that they placed at his disposal all the documents of the royal archives, for it is the custom of every ruler to add enactments according to his wisdom. The eminent Saul Wahl inscribed on the rolls many enactments and decrees for the welfare of the Jews. I have forgotten those that my father told me of, excepting one: a decree ordering that any one who murders a Jew should suffer the death penalty just like the murderer of a prince. No ransom was to be allowed—a life for a life. This law had applied up to that time only to Christians of noble rank.

The following day the nobles agreed upon a candidate and elected a king.

Now in order that these events may be remembered by future generations, I shall record how it came about that Saul won the esteem of the nobles of Poland, particularly as his father, Samuel Judah, was Rabbi in Padua and Venice in Italy. This is the account my father gave me. In his youth while his father was still alive, Saul was seized by an irresistible urge to travel to foreign countries. He left his paternal home in Padua and journeyed from country to country, and from city to city, until he came to Brisk in Lithuania. There he married the daughter of Rabbi David Drucker and lived in straitened circumstances.

About that time it happened that Prince Radziwill, who was second in rank to the King and one of the richest nobles of the realm, desired intensely to travel abroad. It was the custom of princes to travel far and wide in order to observe the character and customs of foreign peoples. So Prince Radziwill journeyed from country to country until his purse was empty. As he did not wish to reveal his plight to the princes of the land, he was in a quandry. He was in Padua at that time, and decided at length to reveal his identity to the Rabbi and make a substantial loan so that he might continue on his way. (That is the way of the Polish nobles. They befriend wise Jews, especially rabbis, in order that they may borrow from them; as a consequence, influential Jews in those days were held in high esteem by the princes.) So Prince Radziwill visited Rabbi Samuel Judah and told him his story. The Rabbi gladly provided him with money and equipment. Whereupon the Prince said to him, "Quite apart from my financial obligation to you, how can I recompense you? How can I return good for good?" The Rabbi replied, "First, I request that you act kindly and justly toward the Jews who dwell in your power. I have another request. A son of mine named Saul lives in Brisk. The good which you desire to grant me, I beg that you grant my son." The Prince immediately took the name and address of the son so that he might carry out the Rabbi's wishes.

After he had returned safely and settled himself in his home, he immediately made inquiries about Saul and summoned him. It did not take him long to discover that Saul was a man of uncommon ability. Whereupon he granted him many favors, showering him with gifts and appointments and praising him to the skies to the other nobles. They took a great fancy to him and he prospered in their circle. It was then that the incident I have related above occurred. He was chosen king for that night, and consequently they called him—Saul Wahl. I heard this whole story from the lips of my pious and learned father.

I will digress now to give an account that came to me from another source. When Prince Radziwill left his native land to see the world, he followed the custom of taking with him a large retinue of servants. As his means diminished in the course of his travels, he gradually disposed of the servants so that when he reached Padua, not only did he lack money, but only one servant remained with him. The Prince sent him to Rabbi Judah to arrange an interview. The Rabbi inquired about the Prince's background, and the servant told him the whole story of how he had lost both servants and money. Immediately the Rabbi ordered his household to prepare a banquet in honor of the Prince, and invited him to attend as the honored guest.

He came and feasted at the table of the Rabbi. Then, in the midst of festivities, the Rabbi said to his servant, "Go to the market place and fetch me one of the captive slaves." (It was the custom then, as it still is in Turkey, for every citizen to take one slave from the market, and the owner had the right to do with him as he pleased, even to kill him if he so fancied.) The servant followed his instructions and brought a slave to the Rabbi in the presence of the guests. The Rabbi, pretending to be serious, said to the servant, "Take this slave to the proper chamber and kill him." Taking the slave away, the servant waited a while in order to give the impression that he had carried out the order. Then he returned and said, "I have done as you commanded, my lord." Thereupon the Rabbi said to him, "Return to the market and fetch another slave, bigger and comelier than the first." Again the servant appeared with a slave. "Well done", said the Rabbi, "take him and do with him as you did with the first slave." The servant put the slave in the same chamber with the first and gave them food and drink. Then he returned and told the Rabbi that he had carried out his command. Then the Rabbi repeated the performance a third, a fourth and a fifth time, the servant in each instance placing the slave with his fellows and providing him with victuals.

The Prince was bewildered by the performance. He could not restrain himself. He asked, finally, "What is the meaning of this? Why in the world do you spend your money purchasing five slaves and then killing them off for no reason?" Rabbi Judah responded enigmatically, "Aren't we Jews required to spill blood? Is not my lord aware of this?" The Prince was amazed at the explanation. He scrutinized the Rabbi's face closely. At length the Rabbi broke his silence, explaining his mystifying conduct. "I have done what you have seen," he said, "in order that you may know that the accusation against us regarding the use of blood is utterly evil and false. Our religion forbids us to spill blood. Yet, as a result of this false charge, many innocent souls have suffered and many have been martyred. Now I know, my lord, that you are a great prince and second only to the King in Poland. Why have I done all this? To show you that even though it was in my power to slay five souls without hurt or murmur or responsibility, I had no such intention. Isn't this proof that the blood accusation is false? Even if we assume that the charge were true—Heaven forbid—why should the Jews of Poland endanger their lives by killing a Christian when it would be possible for us to send them casks filled with the blood of slaves? You can see that this accusation is contrary to fact and reason, and I solemnly hope that in the future you will do all in your power to serve the glory of God by correcting the injustice. Verily, we are innocent just as I am today. For I bought those five slaves, not to slay them, but to provide your excellency with the servants your station requires; and I wish to provide for your other needs."

The Prince recognized the truth of the Rabbi's acts and the wisdom of his words, and assured him that he would guard the welfare of the Jews and protect them from this sinful slander. He would like, he continued, to reward the Rabbi's generosity. "Is there anything else I can do," he asked, "to repay you for rescuing me from my plight?" Thereupon the Rabbi told him that he had a son named Saul who lived in Brisk, as I have related above. The Prince assured him that he would interest himself in his son upon his return. The rest of the story you already know.

To return to my narrative, I heard more of Saul's history from my learned and pious father in 1733. He lay mortally ill in Fürth, a city where many physicians reside. I went there from Markbreit, and I stayed with him for three weeks. When I was alone with him, he dictated his will, which I wrote down word for word. Then, speaking almost inaudibly, he told me the following in order that I might know, he said, what happened to our noted ancestor, Saul Wahl:

"The King who was elected by the nobles the day following Saul's brief reign placed him in a high position, and he was revered as a leader among the Jews. His success went to his head, however, and he became very haughty. This brought him great misfortune. He had a daughter by the name, I believe, of Händele, a girl of rare beauty and intellect who was famous throughout Poland. Many suitors sought her hand. Among them was a brilliant young scholar, the son of a noted rabbi. (My father did not reveal his name, either because he did not know it or preferred not to mention it.) To make a long story short, the Rabbi brought his celebrated son to Brisk, and, staying as a guest at the home of one of the community elders, broached the match. But our ancestor, puffed up with pride, considered himself high and mighty and thought that his beautiful daughter was worthy of a more distinguished suitor. This match he would not even consider, thus humiliating both father and son. The whole community was outraged. They murmured against Saul Wahl. They sought to assuage the wounded feelings of the distinguished guests, and one of the most prominent citizens gave his daughter in marriage to the young scholar. But from that time our ancestor suffered the hatred of the whole community. They sought eagerly to bring about his downfall.

"An opportunity came. It happened at that time that the Queen died. Some of the men of Brisk, intent upon revenging Saul's insult, went to the nobles with whom they were in favor and spoke to them of Händele. They described her exquisite beauty and remarkable intellect, as excellences worthy of a queen. As a matter of fact, was she not a queen? Had not her father sat upon the throne? They filled the ears of the nobles with such talk, suggesting that they in turn repeat it to the King and inflame his passion. Of course, they perpetrated their evil plot most subtly, lest Saul get wind of it and frustrate them. They cautioned the nobles to act quietly so that the King might seize the girl before her father became aware of it. The nobles followed the counsel of these slanderers, secretly winning the ear of the King. He had the girl brought to the palace secretly by the royal guard.

"But God, who watches over Israel and dispenses His everlasting mercies, willed otherwise. He had mercy upon Händele and granted Saul the wisdom and power to prevent the consummation of the plot. With the help of the Almighty, he acted speedily and wisely. And whoever knew what had happened and saw the outcome wondered greatly."

DAYBOOK OF AN ADVENTURER

SIMON VON GELDERN (1720-1788)

Von Geldern was described by Heinrich Heine, upon whom this grand-uncle of his made an indelible impression, as "conspicuous by his personal beauty and imposing appearance and also by the splendor of his oriental dress which exercised, especially upon the women, a magic influence. . . . He was on the one side somewhat of a dreamer, who made propaganda for cosmopolitan and Utopian ideas, and on the other side one of those adventurers who, confiding in their individual superiority, either break down the rotten boundaries of a rotten society or else disregard them. At any rate, he was a genuine man." Certainly Heine leaned heavily upon the tales related to him by his aunts about his grand-uncle's wanderings and adventures, not to mention his own vivid imagination. Von Geldern might have become a successful banker or rabbi, but he succumbed to the lure of a life of adventure. The asceticism of his later life failed to pull him out of the world of fantasy which he had fashioned to compensate for his deep frustrations. While he is not as expansive as we should like him to be in these notebook jottings, his enigmatic personality is nevertheless stamped upon the pages. The reader will find Heine's portrait of von Geldern on pages 334-335.

❋ ❋ ❋

HE WHO takes these things to heart will exult and tremble, since each moment brings him nearer to the terrible bitterness of the day of great and fearful judgment, in the presence of Him before Whom he must offer his explanations and submit his record. He will rue all his sins, errors and misdeeds; he will confess them—for "he who confesses and recants, merits forgiveness"—and remove himself from all those allurements which might lead him to sin again; he will control his lust for food and drink, since they are the source of all other evil desires (God save us!); he will make the Torah his everlasting absorption, and business only his passing interest, and he will bear in mind the verse: "I always have God before me," as well as the other scriptural passages which purify thought.

Behold, I now regret all my errors, sins and misdeeds; once more I resolve—though I have often done so before—never to sin again; with tears I beg my Creator, the King of Kings, to forgive the sins, misdeeds and errors that I have committed and to accept my good resolution as if I had submitted to every punishment prescribed for every sin. I haven't the strength to impose them on myself; God knows that as a result of one of the mortifications which I did undertake, I became mortally ill, and though I am finally recovered, I am still very weak. Our prophets said: "Return the day before your death." Perhaps that day is already at hand, and I am in a strange country, far from my family and my father's house—God protect them! Therefore I write all this down, as a testament, for whatever may occur, and to recapitulate my own recollection of the forces which have driven me onward from the days of my youth until now.

My venerable father, who was the respected and renowned leader of his community, and intercessor for the province of Julich and Berg (near Holland), was Elieser, the son of my venerable grandfather, the respected and famous leader of the community, Herr Juspa, of sacred memory, of Düsseldorf. My father was called Josef von Geldern; he married my venerable mother, the chaste and pious Leah Sarah, of sacred memory, the daughter of my venerable grandfather, the intercessor Simeon Pressburg of sacred memory, who lived in Vienna, the residential city of the Emperor, and who will be known and respected among his kind for generations to come. The marriage took place in Düsseldorf. Later my parents moved to Vienna, and in Vienna I was born, for good fortune, on Tuesday, the 11th of Marheshvan, 1720. Certainly, if I were to say, "It is better not to have been born," it would not seem to have been for good fortune; but I take into consideration the words, "My beginning was small, but at the end I shall become great." My godfather was my uncle Henoch Pressburg, and the circumciser was the distinguished and renowned Mordecai Pösing of Vienna, who now lives in Pressburg.

When I was about a year old, my parents took me to Düsseldorf, and I thank them for the agony they had to suffer on my account, when I fell from the wagon and a wheel passed over me. But when they lifted me off the ground, they found me safe and unharmed. From what I have been told of this period, only trivial things happened to me.

When I was four years old, I was already studying section *Beza* of the Talmud. At the age of eight I delivered an address at the consecration of a Torah scroll which my honored father had donated to the sacred vestments of the synagogue. The scroll was worth more than 1,000 gulden. Of my teachers I remember the wise Baruch of Posen (Poland) of sacred memory, and the distinguished Elia Helm of Lemberg, as well as my kinsman, Abraham Frank, son-in-law of the Chief Rabbi of Koblenz, near Düsseldorf.

When I was ten years old I accompanied Reb Abraham to Mannheim, in order to engage in the study of the Talmud at the higher academy, under the great teacher Reb Samuel Helman. I lived there two years, after which I returned to my father's home in Düsseldorf and studied another year.

In Heshvan of 1733 I was confirmed, and my parents arranged a festive dinner on that Sabbath. Then I went to Frankfort-on-the-Main and studied for about a year at the Talmudical Academy of the great Gaon, alone among his kind, Jacob Cohen, of sacred memory. I studied Talmud with Rabbi Lasi Heller of Halberstadt. I lived in a small room, though I paid a great deal of money for it. Therefore I resolved to move away, but I did not want to embarrass my landlord by moving into other quarters, though there were many people who offered me a room free of charge. So I gave my landlord more than three groschen every week and he let me have a larger room. I took leave of my teacher, who introduced me to a traveling companion, and gave me his blessing for the journey.

Invoking the Rabbi's efforts, I hope that God, glory be to Him, will save me from every sin and protect me, so that I may serve my Creator according to His will, and if such is His design, that I may receive death for the sanctity of His great Name. Behold, I confess and repent all the wicked desires which the evil instigator planted in my heart, for they are futile and temporal, and all against my will. I turn ruefully back and tearfully seek forgiveness for the sins, the missteps and misdeeds which I committed before the King of Kings.

I arranged a banquet on the Sabbath for the young people, the students at the Academy, and on Sunday I gave a banquet for the youth of the whole city. Then, in the company of Reb Jekel Nobel, the son-in-law of the Rabbi of Rappeswir (he was still a bachelor then), I went to Darmstadt, where I stayed about two weeks at the home of the distinguished Reb Israel Wiener. Then I journeyed to Mannheim, where I found my grandmother, of sacred memory, sick in bed. She had fallen and broken a limb. She arose from the illness forever freed and released of the burden of this life, on the 19th of Elul, 1735. On the same day my venerable father came to Mannheim. At this time a great war was raging between the Kaiser and the King of France, over the kingdom of Poland. Ten thousand soldiers came out of Moscow to help the Kaiser, and the whole war treasury was in the hands of my venerable uncle, Samuel Pressburg of Vienna, who brought it to Heilbronn.

When my father heard of his arrival, he went to Heilbronn to meet him, and took me along. My uncle accompanied our whole party—my uncle Reb Yehiel Pressburg, his son Isaac Berlin and others—to Frank-fort-on-the-Main and then to Düsseldorf, to see his sister, my venerable and chaste mother (peace be to her).

We arrived in Frankfort in Tebeth of 1736. The distinguished Elia Wohl wished to give me his daughter in marriage, together with a dowry of 10,000 gulden. But my father did not want it, nor did I, being too tender of years, since I was only fourteen.

When we returned to Düsseldorf, my father and my uncles, Reb Samuel and Reb Yehiel Pressburg, arranged a marriage between my sister Hannah and my cousin Loeb. I found my teacher Elia Chelm in my home, and with him I studied the sections of *Yoma* and the commentary *Sifte Cohen to Yoreh Deah*. At the same time a respected citizen of Düsseldorf wished to give me his daughter in marriage, together with a dowry of 10,000 gulden. I carried on with her very zealously, since she was a kinswoman as well, and today I remember my sins sorrowfully, and regret having squandered so much time and neglected my duties. But my mother was against it, since the girl was much over thirty.

Then I wanted to marry the daughter of my uncle Reb Mendel Düsseldorf, of sacred memory. She possessed incalculable wealth, but my parents were against it. During 1737 I was ill with the four-day fever, which held me in its grip from the Day of Atonement until the month of Nisan. That same year a miracle-worker, Reb Ephraim, came to our city and laid amulets on me. I fell into a delirium and saw ghosts and spirits until the amulets were removed. The miracle-worker fled. In the month of Nissan the fever left me, but I remained weak. May God, in the fulness of His generosity, send me full health soon, may He send health of body and health of soul, to me and to all the sufferers of Israel.

In that year my father took on a business assignment from the Elector for a period of three years. In 1739 there was a great famine, so that my father lost more than 50,000 gulden. My mother decided to go to Mannheim despite the severe winter (1740), and because of her genius for negotiation and her great wisdom, she was fortunate in her trip and brought an order from the sovereign stating that she be given more than 10,000 groschen, so that a small portion of her loss might be made good. There was great joy among us, that my mother had returned safely home. I was all the more happy when she wanted to marry me to a maiden from Mannheim, the daughter of a respected resident. The marriage was very suitable, since she was the daughter of a scholar and also because the father offered a dowry of 10,000 gulden. But because of my many sins, our joy was suddenly turned to sorrow and affliction, and from that time on we suffered blow after blow, misfortune after misfortune. One day, after my venerable mother had returned home, about a week before Passover in the year 1741, the spell of an evil eye struck the abundance of our happiness. My mother took to her bed, and on the 8th day of Iyar our crown and glory fell, and the world around was darkened. I weep that my mother was wrested away from us, my venerable and chaste mother, peace be to her. She went to her rest, leaving us behind in trouble, sorrow and misery, and from that day on our distress was great.

We still had not received what the sovereign had promised, not to speak of the other losses my father had suffered. And finally, to fill my cup of misery to overflowing, conditions became such that marriage could no longer be thought of. In 1742, my father took over another business order from the Elector. I devoted all my energies to purveying and was under a great strain. These years passed; the work that I accomplished during them is not worthy of note. Once more I confess and regret, out of the bottom of my heart, every violation of the Torah and the other misdeeds I committed, and all the evil desires to which I succumbed and felt during that period. I recant in full contrition and resolve never to sin again.

At this time I was also engaged in the sale of lottery tickets, but I made no profit at all. I used to receive letters from many distinguished people in Holland, who wanted to enter into correspondence with me. Just before the Feast of Weeks, in the year 1745, I went to Aachen where warm baths, like those in Tiberias, are to be found, in order to treat the weakness in my foot, which was the result of my illness. I can still feel a residue of the sickness, because my bad foot has not been cured, and I was then in great distress. From there I journeyed to Brabant, via Maastricht, and saw some beautiful scenery. I visited Brussels and Antwerp and from there went to Rotterdam and saw all of Holland. I stopped in Amsterdam several weeks and purchased books to the value of seventy gold pieces from my kinsman, the scholarly and wise *Dayyan* of Amsterdam, Josef, of sacred memory. At this time I also had an opportunity to get married, to a young widow with a fortune of more than 10,000 gulden. But in my misery I was well aware of my impossible predicament, and knew I could not, under my present circumstances, remain in Amsterdam any longer. Besides, a wedding would entail a great deal of expense, so I went back to Nynwegen and Cleve. Here Baer Cleve-Gomperz, a most esteemed man, offered me his daughter in marriage, but I really had neither ears for listening nor eyes for seeing, because my heart was overflowing with grief. Yet no one knew this. During all the days of my misery I found no man sincere enough and worthy of my friendship so that I might bare my secrets to him and ask him for advice.

Before the 9th of Ab I arrived in Düsseldorf, and remained there about a year. After Passover of the year 1747, my father became provoked at me and suspicious without reason. (But I was in no condition to tolerate an unjust accusation, and still less to have a hand laid on me.) The matter upset me so that I left my father's house for the second time, intending to go to my native city, Vienna, to stay with my uncle Reb Samuel Pressburg. Accordingly, I went to Deutz, then to Bonn, then to Koblenz, then to Mainz, where I found a kinsman, the distinguished Mordecai Jaffe, and stayed with him about two weeks. On the 7th of Iyar, 1747, I traveled with him and his brother-in-law, Reb Seligmann, to the fair at Frankfort. I bought a winter outfit for Mordecai and a large fur for women, and rested only two days. In the company of the venerable and chaste Frau Breindel I traveled by boat to Mildenburg, and over land to Bischisa, where we spent the Sabbath. At the expiration of the Sabbath, we started out and took the road toward Rotenburg.

I arrived in Düsseldorf, spent one night in my father's house, then traveled by coach through Rheinberg to Cleve and spent the night in the house of the worthy Reb Feiwelmann, son of Reb Benedict Nynwegen (Philip, son of Benedict Gomperz). Reb Feiwelmann's sister, Frau Simelie, lived with her brother. From there I went to Nynwegen, and did not want to disclose my disagreeable predicament to anyone except to the son of Reb Benedict Nynwegen, of sacred memory. I went to Amsterdam again, stopped at an inn, and did not want to expose my circumstances to anyone. My idea was to go to England, but I lacked money for carrying the plan through. Therefore I took a boat for Hamburg and went to Altona, to my kinsman, the distinguished Josef Cohen-Düren, to whom I told my story. He accompanied me to my kinswoman, Frau Hanna of sacred memory, the wife of the Reb Wolf Scheier. Her sister Esther, of Vienna, also my kinswoman, since they were both daughters of my uncle, Reb Samuel, was stopping with her. They understood me, were much concerned about me, and helped me, so that I was able to go to England.

I spent more than twenty days on the boat from Hamburg to London and observed the New Year of 1748 on the sea. Many dangers surrounded us. There were terrible storms, and I arrived at Gravesend after the New Year. The boat had begun to leak. I left it and went ashore. A day or two before the Day of Atonement I reached London, where I spent several weeks at the home of the respected Wolf Berlin (he had been in Petersburg). He wanted to send me to Holland, but Reb Nata London, the son-in-law of my uncle Reb Liebmann Berlin (peace be to him) was also visiting there, and said to me:

"Why devote yourself to fruitless affairs? Stay here and I will find a good connection for you."

And he did so. I moved to the home of the genteel Frau Röschen, wife of the esteemed Reb Moses Cleve-Gomperz, who was in India, to tutor her son Meir. I lived there, reading the talmudic tractate *Yoma* with the boy, and more than fifty pages of *Baba Kamma*. I was very penitent, and it was God's will to accept my repentance with favor. But I lived in sorrow the whole time, and told myself that these surroundings were not commensurate with my honor or the honor of my family. I related the whole story to Wolf Berlin. He spent more than fifty gold pieces on my behalf and transferred a series of commissions to me, so that I might have earned a good deal of money if luck had been with me. But time went fast. I was born to misery and trouble, sorrow and torment. On the 7th of Adar, 5509 (February 25, 1745), I left London for Harwich and took a boat for Helfavoedsfluid in Holland. To carry out a commission for the patrician mentioned above I left on Monday, the 1st of Tammuz (June 17, 1749), for Freising, Landeshut, Dindolfing, Landau. Wednesday, the 2nd of Tammuz, I arrived at Leidling, Passau; Thursday, the 3rd, at Oberhausen, Engelhartszell, Klosterneuberg, Linz; Friday, Krems and Ibbs; Saturday, the 5th of Tammuz (June 21, 1749), I arrived in Vienna, my native city. After the Sabbath was over I moved to the home of my uncle, Reb Samuel Pressburg. Sunday, the 6th of Tammuz, before dawn, I left the house to arrange for my baggage, which was still on board the boat, and paid for its transport and release. Though I gave several esteemed gentlemen instruction in English, I left Vienna without a heller to my name on the 11th of Heshvan, 5511 (November 10, 1750), with Reb Moses Cholschin of Modena, who lived with the Reb Abraham Sinzheim. We left by coach for Steiermark and arrived in Görz the 20th of Heshvan. On Friday, midnight, I arrived in Trieste, where Reb Amschel Marburg lived with his wife Hannah, my kinswoman. I stayed with Reb Manasseh Marburg until Friday, the 13th of Kislev, when I embarked for Venice, where I stayed with the venerable Isaac Berlin, taking my Sabbath meals for two weeks with Reb Abraham Jessurun, and left the first night of Hanukkah.

I bought provisions for the trip across the sea to Alexandria. I found a good English boat, Captain Cotton's *Sitbehind*. We left Livorno Thursday, the 16th of Shevat, 5511 (February 11, 1751). On Friday the 17th, Haham Moreno came on board, with his servant Abraham Castilia, and we sailed for Alexandria in the name of the God of Israel. We were on the water twenty-five days. On Sunday, the 10th of Adar, 5511 (March 7, 1751), I arrived safely in Alexandria, bringing letters of recommendation to Señor Blanes and Señor Salomon Cohen. The latter, however, was visiting Cairo, and I spent the night at the home of the head of the community, the Haham Kunarti, who received me very hospitably. I stayed with him until Purim, at which time his wife bore him a daughter. I wanted to leave for Damiette before Passover, but I was unable to do so because of my ailment, and I spent the holiday at his home. Since I had no money at all, I wanted to sell my clothing and buy raiment according to the custom of the land.

On Friday, the 12th of Iyar, we came to Cyprus, and left it on Monday. On the Sabbath day, Haham Nissim quit the boat, and on Wednesday, the 24th of Iyar (May 19th), we reached Acre, where I spent the night at the home of a non-Jew, a French merchant named Monsieur Martin Blanc à Acre.

On Friday, the 27th of Iyar, I went to Meron to visit the graves of our worthies of old, of Rabbi Simon ben Yohai, his son Elieser and Isaac Luria, and the sepulchres of Johanan Ha-Sandelar, Shammai and Hillel, and that of the daughter-in-law of Shammai. On Monday I returned to Safed and received a gift from the community, in the form of wine and meat—the best of the land. I lived in the house of the Haham Isaac Sagura. On Sunday, the 25th of Tammuz (July 18th), I became very ill and was at the door of death, but the Eternal, praise be to His Name, in the abundance of His grace and compassion, sent recovery to me from Heaven. But I remained weak. God grant full recovery to me and to all the ailing of Israel. Amen!

On Wednesday, the 8th of Marcheshvan, I left Safed in the company of Aaron, the horse-trader, intending to return almost at once. On Friday, the 10th, just before sundown, we reached Zidon. Thursday, the 22nd, at supper time, I set out on a French boat for Damiette, which I reached on Thursday, the day before the first of Kislev. The following Thursday, the 7th of Kislev, I left Damiette and, with God's help, reached Bulak safely on Thursday, the 14th. I rested there one hour and then traveled in peace, with two donkeys, to Cairo. With God's help my departure and my arrival were unmarked by sin. I stopped with a poor man, Reb Israel, who came from Brest-Litovsk. I was ill, and the doctor put me on a diet of chicken and rice.

On Wednesday, the 16th of Tammuz, I arrived safely in Rosetta, where I lived at the home of a wealthy and influential man, Reb Moses Sakim. Then, with two mules, I set out in good company for Alexandria. Thursday, the fast day, turned into a day of rejoicing. I arrived in Alexandria for the second time, and put up in the home of the wise Reb Isaac Kunarti-Provencal.

On the 15th of Ab, I received a letter from Loppard, from Reb Liebman Jost Berlin, may he rest in peace, containing a message from my father and my brother Reb Juspa, bringing me the good tidings that my sister Yente had married the worthy Reb Liebermann of Bonn.

5513 (1753): Friday, the 25th of Tummuz, the boat set sail very early and I had to undertake its pursuit in a small boat. My life was in danger, but God saved me. From Friday until Monday I was seasick. On Tuesday, the day before the first of Ab, we arrived in Cyprus, where I visited the English consul, with whom I stayed three days. On Friday, the 2d of Ab, the captain set sail without giving me notice, and I was left in Cyprus without my belongings.

5514 (1754): A terrible storm has been raging all this time—Monday, Tuesday, Wednesday and Thursday. I could neither eat nor drink. Only on Friday, the 7th of Adar, did I recover, with God's help, and the sea grew quiet. Yet I was uncomfortable all the time. On the holy Sabbath, however, I had quite recovered. We saw Rhodes that day. On the 9th and 10th of Adar, a dreadful storm raged again. Only on Tuesday, the 11th of Adar, did the fury of the sea subside, and we saw Rhodes again, as we had on the Sabbath. May God send us fortunate winds! Amen!

On Tuesday evening, the 11th of Adar, clouds darkened the sky; there was a terrible storm and heavy rain. During that night we passed Rhodes and on Wednesday we passed Capo Stanzio (Chios). The following night and Thursday we spent in a dreadful storm, in a haven in an unpopulated part of the Calabrian coast. Thursday night and Friday

I read the *Megillah* (Book of Esther) and observed Purim. Before dawn, on the holy Sabbath, we quit our haven and on Sunday, the 16th, we passed Capo Samos, where we met a French boat under Captain Chiraud. Reb Moses del Medigo was a passenger on the boat. On Sunday night we passed through the Straits of Chios; on the 17th we reached the island of Duracco. But we had to turn back to the harbor of Voghera, because of the great storm which arose. There we met Captain André's boat from Ragusa, which had left Alexandria fourteen days before us. On Tuesday, the 18th of Adar, we were still in port. I had a fight with a Turk, who almost killed me. Wednesday, the 19th, was again stormy and rainy, as was Thursday. The wind subsided on Friday, and we left port that night, in completely calm weather. Saturday afternoon such a terrible storm arose that we were forced to anchor in the open sea. It stormed so during the whole night that we lost our anchor. Praise be to the Lord, who saved us from this danger. Sunday, the 23rd of Adar, the storm and rain continued. On Monday, the 24th, I set off in a small boat and arrived safely in Ismir (Smyrna).

5515 (1755): Sunday, the 27th of Tishri, I left Semlin on the way to Pancsova and Weisskirchen, to see a widow. On the 28th, I left for Merschetz, to see Reb Moses. On Thursday, the first of Heshvan, I left for Temesvar, to Reb Meir Amigo. On Sunday, the 11th, I arrived in Bodin (Ofen) at Reb Shemaya Pressburg's, where I met my kinswoman Chaya and remained for the marriage of her daughter.

5516 (1756): On Wednesday, the 5th of Tishri, I left Nancy for Luneville and Phalsbourg. On Wednesday, the first day of the Feast of Tabernacles mid-week, I left Rosheim for Oberrehnheim. I went to visit the Rabbi of Niederrehnheim, Josef Steinhard. He had married the venerable Kröndel, the widow of Yehiel Pressburg, my esteemed uncle, of sacred memory. And behold, my sins confused my thoughts. Though I held to my intention of spending the winter in the northern countries, going as far as Denmark and Königsberg, I was so oppressed by the vanity of the world, that I was unable to make a decision. May God, praise to his Name, grant me support. I was forced to spend almost three weeks in Berlin, during which time the entire community was at the Frankfort fair. During this period I quarreled with Reb Hirsch Präger, the silk manufacturer. On Tuesday, the 21st, I was summoned to the prime minister, Prince Heinrich von Podewill. I spent some time with him and presented him with my coins. On Friday, the 24th, I visited his daughter, Madame de Marschall, and I shall never forget the graciousness with which she received me. I also talked with the Margrave Karl von Ausbach and saw his palace. On Tuesday, the 28th, I went to Potsdam. The next day I went through Sans Souci, the palace of the King, and talked with a son of the Prince of Prussia. An officer invited me to visit Prince Heinrich in the evening, but I did not know whether he meant it seriously or not. I went to the synagogue of Potsdam on Thursday, and talked with Reb Simeon Alik, who graced the position of cantor. He had once been a teacher in the home of my venerable father. On Monday, the 5th of Nisan, I went to take my leave of Madame Marschall. She told me to visit the Princess Amalia, though my baggage was already gone. While I waited in her court, one of her ladies came to tell me she had gone to the Queen.

I arrived safely in Breslau on Friday, the 9th of Nisan, at the home of my kinswoman, Hannah Spitz. On Sunday I had a quarrel with Reb Abraham ben Eleasar and his son, who had slandered me to the police inspector. I went to see the Minister, to whom I had been recommended by the esteemed Reb Daniel Halfon, and the Governor. But the police inspector had denounced me and I did not want to start a tedious suit. On Saturday, the 8th of Iyar, I had a quarrel with Reb Jakob Neufeld, the teacher at Reb Löw Wertheim's and son-in-law of Reb Saul Kempner, and with the brothers Wolf and Moses Zirels, who hurled the vilest insults at me but did not beat me. All this baseless hatred, however, arose from their envy of me, because of the praise and the commendation with which I am received. I had always dreaded this. On Monday, the first of Tammuz, I left Vienna by stagecoach and arrived in Larbach on Friday, the 5th of Tammuz. I was forced to spend the Sabbath there and received much consideration from the Count of Auersperg and Baron Roset. I went through the castle of the Count of Lamberg and made the acquaintance of a certain Captain Brown, an Irishman, captain of a regiment. Before dawn on Sunday, the 7th of Tammuz, I left for Trieste again. Near the village of Pilanje, I met Baron Roset and his wife. They and other travelers urged me to break my journey, since robbers were in the vicinity. Praise be to God that I stopped there, because just at this time three traveling merchants were gruesomely murdered. On the evening of the same day I came uninjured to Trieste, for the second time, and stopped with the esteemed Reb Manasseh Marburg.

Tuesday evening, the 15th of Tammuz, I arrived safely in Venice, and though I had letters of recommendation to Mordecai Padua, Abraham Cracovia and Isaac Delama, I was forced to live in very poor quarters, in the house of an inn keeper. On Tuesday, the 29th of Tammuz, I arrived in Padua, a large city, but full of fools and of poverty. Here I lived in a miserable house, whose mistress was very surly. Dr. Cantarini, the treasurer of the Palestinian Charities, was not at home, but away at a health resort. Dr. Fortis was quite unfriendly. Friday I arrived safely in Verona, with recommendations to Senor Virlingo and Dr. Navarro. On Monday, the 6th of Ab, they gave me fare and recommendation to the rabbi of Mantua and to Dr. Cazes. In Venice I was cheated by a scholar named Jekuthiel, who gave me an *En Jacob* for a *Zohar,* the *Tikkunim* included, *Hesed Abraham* and a Gemara *Berakoth.* I lost more than six florins thereby. All the rabbis in Italy are either Sabbatians or cheats. I found fasting on the 9th of Ab very difficult. On the 10th I was in Guastalla, on the 12th in Reggio, on the 13th in Modena. Tuesday, the 14th, I was in Bologna, where I met a woman from Zirndorf, in Germany. On the 15th, Signor Sulami and Signor Sanguinetti arrived from Modena with a sick girl. The same evening I set out for Florence by sedan-chair.

I had to leave Livorno because it was not easy to find a safe boat, since there was war between England and France. Jewish merchants frequently sent out boats, on which I could have traveled practically free of charge. Yet I was afraid I would have to spend the winter in Livorno. May God soon send me suitable surcease for my needs. I haven't the patience to be docile any longer, and to listen to a daily lecture from my dear Swedish captain, who, like a Polish scholar, believes himself to be the most cultured man in the world. In addition to his other attributes, he is also deaf. . . .

VICTORY FOR JUSTICE

BER BIRKENTHAL (1723-1805)

Wine not only gladdened the heart of man, but constituted an old and honorable trade among Jews since biblical times. Ber was a successful wine merchant, blessed with intelligence and great energy. His business took him to all parts of Eastern Europe, and as a consequence he developed a more worldly outlook than most of his coreligionists in Poland. Recorded in his memoirs are day-to-day business experiences, sketches of persons humble and great as well as events of historical importance in which he was involved. For Ber was a leader of communal affairs, serving as President of the Provincial Jewish Assembly which was dissolved in his time and taking an active role in the Frankist Disputation in Lemberg in 1759. Toward the end of his long life, he wrote, in addition to his memoirs, a book on Jewish sectarian movements.

✻ ✻ ✻

I WILL now tell how my knowledge of the Polish tongue proved of great advantage to the children of Israel, and how the esteemed Chief Rabbi and President of the Rabbinical Court of the holy community of Lemberg heard of me.

It happened that the respected and wealthy Reb Aaron died in 1753 in the town of Komarno, which is in the neighborhood of Lemberg, and willed his fortune to his sons. But his son-in-law, Reb Samuel, the son of Reb Jacob, the son of Reb Fischel, who lived in Kalusz, a small town in Eastern Galicia, appeared before the court and presented a deed in which the deceased father settled upon his daughter half of the amount willed to the sons. The deed, attested to by trustworthy witnesses and properly sealed, stated that the late Reb Aaron had promised him 40,000 gulden.

The case was brought before the great Rabbinical Court of Lemberg and the Provinces and the eminent jurist, Rabbi Hayyim Cohen Zedek Rapaport, heard the case. Reb Samuel presented the deed and placed it on the examination table of the court so that the rabbis might test the genuineness of the seal and thoroughly investigate the claim. The heirs of the deceased presented a counter claim against their brother-in-law, charging that the deed was a forgery. Their late father, they declared, could not have made a deed for so large a sum because the total value of his property was less than 40,000 gulden and because their father's whole fortune, even during his lifetime, probably was never so large.

The judges, presided over by the esteemed Rabbi Rapaport, requested that they be furnished with corroborative letters signed by all persons who had acted as witnesses. When these letters were presented, the judges scrutinized them and compared the signatures with those on the deed, written at Komarno, and found that they did not differ in any detail. The claim of the dependents the heirs, was therefore without proof and the deed was found valid.

The arguments of the defendants, however, were considered sincere and weighty. In order to prevent injustice and to pacify the defendants, the judge and the members of the court ruled that the plaintiff, Reb Samuel, should take a solemn oath and should swear publicly as to the truth and justice of his claim by the oath of the Torah; in addition, his wife was ordered to be present in the synagogue to listen to the oath and to verify it with the response "Amen." After these instructions had been carried out, the defendants were to pay the whole sum mentioned in the deed out of the choicest property left by their father. This verdict was signed and sealed by the presiding judge and given to Reb Samuel.

Reb Samuel's wife, however, refused to be present in the synagogue in order to listen to and corroborate the oath, for she felt that such action would wrong her brothers. Her husband was thus obliged to arbitrate and to accept a compromise settlement. Both parties chose two judges each and the President of the Rabbinical Court of Lemberg was selected by both parties to be the fifth judge or what is known in Latin as the "superarbiter." All of them appeared before their chosen judges and declared that they were acting voluntarily and they would agree to whatever decision was made and abide by it. They signed and sealed the declaration, and, in accordance with established custom, withdrew their claims and handed over the documents to the court. The judges agreed upon the following verdict: the heirs must desist from their demand on oath of the Torah, and they should give to Reb Samuel, in exchange for the deed, 10,000 gulden. The first verdict was declared null and void.

When Reb Samuel reported the whole affair to his father, Reb Jacob, who lived in Kalusz, he made the verdict the beginning instead of the end of a story by slandering the President of the court. He said that the

Rabbi had accepted a bribe of forty ducats from him for the first verdict and for the second verdict his brother-in-law had paid him ten ducats. Reb Jacob was incensed because his son had lost 30,000 gulden through the bribery of the President of the court.

Soon afterwards there arrived in Kalusz, Cieszkowski, Chief Steward of the estates of Prince Czartoryski, the Regent of the province of Red Ruthenia and Governor of the district of Lemberg. Red Jacob laid before the Steward a serious charge against the President of the court. He accused him of perverting justice by accepting bribes from both parties concerned. Reb Jacob explained to the Steward the Rabbi had first given a verdict in accordance with Jewish law, whereby his son was to receive 40,000 gulden, and that the Rabbi had accepted a bribe of forty ducats. Later he had given another verdict whereby his son received only 10,000 gulden; the Rabbi had accepted a bribe of ten ducats from the defendants. "Has it ever happened," he declared, "that a Rabbi and President of a court committed so great a wrong and that on his account my son should lose the huge sum of 30,000 gulden?" He strengthened his accusation by heaping more slanders against both the Rabbi and the court until the Steward became very angry and declared that such a travesty of justice was unheard-of in all of the courts of the world.

He immediately summoned the Rabbi's grandson, Rabbi Judah Loeb, who, although a young man, was President of the talmudic Academy of Lemberg. After pouring abuse on his grandfather, he said excitedly: "Has it ever happened anywhere that in one lawsuit two contradictory verdicts should be given?

"After accepting a bribe of forty ducats from one side, your grandfather took ten ducats from the other side to make his first decision null and void. Neither God nor man can tolerate such a wrong, and you may tell your grandfather this: Until now I have been his friend. Since he was made a rabbi I trusted everything he said and did. I presented him to the Prince, the Voyevoda, and I succeeded in obtaining for him a letter of appointment. I have used whatever influence I commanded to keep him in his position for twenty years. Charges were made against him by several Jews, yet I regarded them as groundless calumnies cooked up by his envious enemies. I kept him in his position because I considered him an elderly man of upright character, respected and loved by his fellow-Jews. But now that his real worthlessness has come to light, I realize that he has had committed many injustices while he was in office and that all the charges made against him are true. I see no other alternative for him therefore but to quit Lemberg before I arrive there, if he wishes to escape the severe punishment which I shall be compelled to inflict upon him. Do not regard my warning as an idle threat. Since you are his grandson, write to him immediately and say that should I find him in Lemberg, he will regret it because I will judge him as befits a rabbi who perverts justice."

It happened at that very time that a Jew from Skole, Rabbi Jacob, the son of Rabbi Loeb Klimster, appeared before the Steward to request his seal to confirm a verdict passed by the President of the Jewish court of Lemberg against another Jew of Skole. When he observed with what contempt the Steward spoke of the President of the court of Lemberg, he decided not to present the verdict lest the nobleman tear it up in his rage. As he left, he advised the Rabbi of Kalusz not to stay any longer with the Steward. "If you wish to write a letter," he said, "and send it to your venerable grandfather, I will wait until the letter is written and deliver it to him directly." The Rabbi wrote a letter in which he told his grandfather that the Steward was incensed because it was alleged that he had taken bribes from the two parties to a suit and had given two contradictory verdicts in one case.

When Rabbi Jacob arrived in Lemberg, he immediately delivered the letter to the President of the Court. Visibly perturbed, this venerable Rabbi said, "If I could only find some one who writes Polish well, then I would be able to explain the whole affair to the Steward. He would understand that I surely did what was right in this case, and how greatly I really benefited the son of the man who now denounces me." Rabbi Jacob came to his aid. "I know a man," he said, "who is a Jew and writes an incomparable Polish. All the nobles are surprised by the excellence of his prose and praise him for his fluency in the Polish tongue. Only it is a pity that I cannot bring him here, for he is engaged all day selling wine in his shop and cannot leave his business for even an hour. I refer to young Ber, the brother of the well-known Rabbi Aryeh Loeb of Bolechow." The Rabbi answered: "I myself know Polish but not sufficiently well so that when a gentile writes for me he never expresses precisely what I want to say. The only course left for me is to write what I want to say in Polish on a fresh sheet of paper, and if you will be good enough to take it to Ber and request him to rewrite the substance of it, then I will examine both copies and send to the Steward the one which pleases me better." The Rabbi sent immediately for Rabbi Isaac, the *shtadlan* (public Advocate) of the Council of Four Lands in Poland (governing body of the Jews) and ordered him to copy from his minutes both verdicts, that is to say, the first sentence passed in accordance with Jewish law, which prescribed that if the plaintiff took the oath he would receive 40,000 gulden, and the second based upon the decision of the judges chosen by both parties to the effect that he should receive 10,000 gulden if he did not take an oath. The Rabbi then finished the letter and gave it to Rabbi Jacob who, after he had said his afternoon prayers, brought it to me, before dark and requested me on behalf of the Rabbi, to read it and write it anew. He gave me several sheets of fine, heavy foolscap paper on which to rewrite the better, relying on my thorough knowledge of the Polish tongue. After reading the whole document I understood that the Rabbi had a perfectly good case and that the accusations of his detractor were the insensate calumnies of an ignoramus who had no conception of legal procedure.

In the middle of the night I took my pen and composed a letter in scholarly Polish, such as is used in legal affairs, stating the Rabbi's case. I explained precisely how two verdicts came to be rendered, and because they were written in a style unintelligible in the Polish tongue I rewrote the two verdicts. Then I placed the three documents in an envelope and wrote upon it all the titles of the Steward. In the morning Rabbi Jacob came to get the letter for the Rabbi who, after reading it through, said to his wife, "Blessed be the Lord whose loving-kindness has not left me. I trust to the compassion of Heaven that when the Steward sees this letter he will surely acknowledge that my action in this case was just and that those who libel me are liars, ignorant of legal procedure." An expert Jewish horseman was fetched at once. The Rabbi wrapped the letter together with the copies of the verdicts in one envelope and gave it to the messenger. It was placed into the Steward's hands in the town of Brzezan (in Eastern Galicia); after reading it, he quickly understood that the Rabbi's decisions were just and that the charges of his defamers were malicious lies and repudiations of God and His holy law.

PIONEER IN SWEDEN

ARON ISAK (1730-1817)

Something of the strength and individuality of Isak is reflected in an oil portrait of him which is reproduced as a frontispiece of his autobiography. His father, a wealthy merchant, was the only Jew in Treuenbrietzen (a small city in the Duchy of Mecklenburg) who had the right of residence. Beginning his career as a peddler, Aron succumbed to a strong inclination to become an artist. He taught himself the craft of seal-engraving and enjoyed a modest success until the Seven Years War, when he turned to trade. Learning from Swedish soldiers that there were no practitioners of his craft in Sweden, during the period that followed, he resolved, even though he knew that Jews had no right of residence there, to make a place for himself and his people. His sobriety and persistence won the favor of the king, and he thereby became the founder of the Jewish community of Stockholm. He composed his autobiography at the age of 71, when he recalled with satisfaction the eventful life that had made him the most respected burgher and elder of an established community. Among his descendants is Sven Heden, the great Swedish explorer.

❊ ❊ ❊

WHEN the Seven Years War broke out in 1756, I was the father of four children, and the cost of living was high. I had tried to make my way in the world like an honorable man. When the enemy Prussians seized Mecklenburg, I did a brisk business with them, selling mostly fancy goods. The following year the Swedes entered Mecklenburg as friends. They gave me a lot of work and I sold them huge quantities of fancy goods. Indeed, within a short time I earned 500 reichsthalers, which I used to purchase more of the same stock at the fair in Frankfort-on-the-Oder. That is how I suddenly became a fancy goods dealer, a trade that was much more profitable than seal-engraving. So I packed my tools away in a trunk, and as a prosperous merchant bought a house and garden. Within five years I had a fortune of several thousand reichsthalers and a fine establishment filled with good furniture and beautiful silverware.

At the end of the war it was difficult to sell fancy goods to the officers. I consequently thought of going into another business. I invested a few thousand reichsthalers in dry goods which the farmers needed, and choosing four lads who used to sell to the army for me, I sent them to the country in pairs in order to sell the goods to the farmers and at the ducal castles. They were to return every three or four weeks. The sales, however, were slim, bringing little profit for me or my salesmen. Yet I held out for about two years. Then two of the men vanished with considerable merchandise and cash collections amounting to more than 1,000 reichsthalers. I was also cheated out of a large sum by a business associate in Bützow. At the same time my sister was married in Malchin. My brother had promised the groom a dowry of a 1,000 reichsthalers and asked me to make it good. My brother Moses, who had married well, contributed 200 thaler, my brother Mordecai 100 thaler, and I took care of the rest. I arranged the wedding, made a gift of furniture, and attended with my wife. Altogether my expenses exceeded 500 thaler.

Well, my affairs were not in good shape. Fortunately, I was not indebted to anybody. I was a free man. Then I recalled that the Swedish officers had given me a good deal of seal-engraving to do and had suggested that I should go to Sweden, as there was no practitioner of my craft in the entire realm. Conditions took a bad turn in the whole of Mecklenburg. A plague spread among the cattle herds, killing them off like flies. Milk was scarce. Of 500 cows in Bützow barely thirty survived. My whole household, my wife and five children, the manservant and maid, were afflicted with dysentery and were confined to bed for three months. You can readily understand that under these circumstances business was at a standstill and everyone sustained losses. One had to seek a new occupation if disaster were to be averted.

I decided to take a trip to Schwerin before departing for Sweden, for the court-medalist, Herr Abraham Pach, who was the most expert diamond-cutter and seal-engraver in Germany, lived there. I had worked with him in his brother Lipmann's workshop. During the reign of the former duke he had been court-medalist and had had an annual stipend of 500 reichsthalers. However, when the duke died the mint was closed and he was dismissed. Then this Abraham had himself appointed court-medalist without salary; he earned a mite—barely 100 reichsthalers a year—from the waste of the mint. On the eve of his marriage his capital amounted to 1,000 reichsthalers, and he received 1,500 reichsthalers as a dowry. But I knew that he had already used up his money.

We took a stroll. I felt towards him like a brother. When I inquired about the state of his affairs, he complained bitterly.

"It serves you right," I observed. "It is incredible that an artist of your talent should remain in Mecklenburg where you can't make a living. Come to Sweden with me. We shall be the only practitioners of our craft there, and we shall have more work than we can handle. Why, you admitted that you haven't earned ten reichsthalers in ten weeks!"

I impressed upon him that I knew the fancy goods business, but he was hesitant.

"I have never been away from home," he replied. "How can I leave my wife and children? Besides, how can we succeed when Jews are not permitted to live there? You say that because there are no craftsmen of our kind in Sweden, it will be possible to secure the right of residence. Very well, then. Suppose you make the trip. I will share the traveling expenses with you, and as soon as you secure permission to live and work there, I will join you."

I replied, "Brother, I agree. Keep this a secret. Tell it to nobody, not even your wife."

He likewise asked me not to mention our plan, even to my brother.

"Brother," I continued, "I will give you my answer tomorrow."

Then I went to the house of my brother Abraham, who was the richest Jew in Schwerin and was said to be worth 100,000 thalers. He knew nothing of my difficult circumstances. I owned some serviceable silver worth about 200 thalers, and on the next morning I sold it to him. After lunch I returned to Herr Abraham and said, "I accept your proposition. But we must put it into writing and have it notarized."

He agreed wholeheartedly. As we did not want any one to learn of our plan, we were at a loss as to where we could have the agreement drawn up.

At length Herr Abraham said, "I have a very good friend who works at the grinding-mill less than a quarter of a mile outside the city where we will not easily be seen. I also know a notary who will accompany us."

We returned to his house and drank coffee.

"I must go out for a while," he said. "Please stay here in the company of my wife. I'll be back soon and we shall take a stroll by the City Gate."

He left and arranged with the notary to go to an inn outside the Gate, order a bottle of wine and await us. He returned home, we left together, met the notary, paid for the wine, and walked further. We found a room where we enjoyed privacy and wrote down our agreement in the form of a contract, taking a sacred oath to observe it faithfully. It could be broken only by mutual agreement; all profits, whether from work or trade, were to be shared equally.

Hours passed; it was evening. I wanted to go to my brother's house; but Herr Abraham had arranged, without my knowledge, that his wife prepare a special dinner and insisted that I join him and a group of friends. To be sure, the dinner was excellent, the wine superb, and the evening gay. It was eleven o'clock before I could tear myself away.

When I reached hime I found that the table was set. My sister-in-law grumbled.

"We delayed supper and waited for you so long," she scolded, "that the children fell asleep. They refused to eat without their Uncle Aron and went to bed hungry."

My brother chimed in, "Of course, he could hardly be spared from his beloved card game!"

Well, the wine had gone to my head. I retorted, "Where is the maid? I want to go to sleep. I visit you so seldom and now you fuss as though you want to get rid of me. Very well, I'll leave tomorrow."

She begged me to have a bite, explaining that she had meant no harm. I replied that I did not wish to eat. As there was no maid in the house, I took one of the three lamps on the table, said good night, and went towards my room. My sister-in-law followed closely.

"I never would have believed," she said meekly, "that you could become so enraged."

But her grumbling impelled me to increase her aggravation. "I certainly will not visit you again. Good night, dear sister-in-law," were my last words. But I knew in my heart that I was quite tipsy.

The next morning when I came downstairs, pipe in mouth, she was there to greet me. Immediately she asked whether I was still in bad humor.

"What do you mean? Are you as angry as you were last night? Heavens, I have been good to you always and you must believe that I really was not angry last night."

Thus I apologized and kissed her hand. She kissed mine and said, "You are indeed my dear brother-in-law."

Then she asked me whether I wanted my coffee as usual, for I always arose earlier than they did. I said that I would wait for the whole family. Finally my brother joined us and coffee was served.

As we were drinking, he addressed me as follows: "Tell me, brother, why didn't you eat with us last night? You are always as welcome here as you were at home in Treuenbrietzen. Perhaps you need something? We have never quarreled. Must you leave today?"

I replied that I must depart. He paid me for the silver, and after posting the money to Bützow I took leave of my good friends and journeyed home.

As soon as I reached home, I said to my wife, "You know that about a fortnight ago I received a letter from Count Janke of Stralsund (in Swedish Pomerania), asking me to visit there. He and his brother, the Lieutenant-Colonel, have been decorated, and I have been recommended to engrave their coat-of-arms on their medals. As you know, I promised to be there in three weeks, and since a fair will be held the following week, I will leave on Sunday. I will be the only engraver there, so that I may be detained for several months."

Not knowing what I was up to, she readily consented. I gave her 120 reichsthalers and left her and my five children.

I arrived safely with my tools in Stralsund, and went immediately to Count Janke. He and his brother gave me stones to engrave. Then I reported to Count Fredrik Carl Sinclair, the Governor, and to Count Anders von Höpkin, the Commandant. Work was abundant. I sent the orders requiring delicate craftsmanship to Herr Abraham in Schwerin, requesting that he take special pains as I was depending upon these folks to recommend me to the King of Sweden. I was flooded with work —already more than 200 reichsthalers—from all the élite. I was much esteemed by Count Höpkin, who recommended me to his brother, the Imperial Councillor, and to the Governor-General Karl Sparre. In fact, he made it a point of speaking of me in all his circles in Stralsund with the result that the whole government gave me letters of approbation to the king. When Herr Abraham's engravings arrived and were delivered, everyone was amazed by their exquisite craftsmanship. And whatever I desired was freely and respectfully given.

In the meantime one of the Stralsunders must have written to Schwerin reporting that the aristocracy held me in high esteem and the government had granted me a passport to journey to Sweden. My brother heard the news, but nobody knew of my agreement with Abraham Pach. My brother immediately wrote to my wife urging her not to allow me to go to Sweden. At the same time he sent me an insolent letter to Stralsund, accusing me of abandoning my wife and children.

"It is unthinkable that you are in such miserable circumstances. You have done many stupid things in your life, but this beats them all. To think of going to a country where a Jew has never lived, which does not welcome Jews, and whose language you do not know! You must be mad. Think twice about the step you are taking. I have often warned you not to put your confidence in bad people, but you would never listen. Now take my advice. Return home. There is a large Jewish community there, and I never heard of anyone who went away and left a wife and children to fend for themselves. I will give you whatever help you require."

However, I had made my decision and refused to be deterred. I made no reply to my brother's letter. A few days before my departure, my eldest daughter came to Stralsund with a piteous letter from my wife pleading that I should not sail. My daughter was more precious to me than anything.

"Dear father," she pleaded tearfully, "if you leave us now, we will never see you again."

I was aware that this had unfortunately happened in other instances. Nevertheless, I explained the state of my affairs to her and how this was an opportunity to make my fortune again. Then I gave her some gifts and set her mind at peace. The next day she went home on the mail-coach.

I had made a reservation on a packet-boat and paid my passage to Ystadt. All the Stralsund Jews came and reproached me and urged me not to sail. But I never was a poltroon. I always stuck to my decisions. As I went down to the bridge to embark, the householders, including some of the women, accompanied me. They continued to discourage me even when I was on the ship. The women lamented as though I were leaving for America. But I was determined to carry out my plan. When they saw that the anchor was about to be lifted, they left the ship, shouting and waving their blessings as long as the ship was in sight.

We sailed from Stralsund at three o'clock in the afternoon and arrived in Ystadt at eleven o'clock the next morning. The captain of the ship found lodgings for me at the home of a modest couple. The man, a native of Germany, spoke German fluently. I intended to remain in Ystadt for a month in order to acquire a smattering of the language and to see what sort of relations might be established with the people. As I had my tools with me, I might also find work. My host advised me to report my presence and my plans to the burgomaster. So I did. The burgomaster spoke a little German, and I showed him my passport and fourteen letters of recommendation to the King. He proved his cordiality by ordering a signet from me. I did not receive a great deal of work, but I netted a good profit from the sale of pearls and jewels. When there was no work, my host tried to teach me Swedish. The words came difficult to my tongue.

Four weeks passed and I was about to continue onward with my journey. My host warned me that it would be disadvantageous to travel in Sweden without a knowledge of the language. He suggested that I first spend a month in Malmö, a port on the southwestern tip of Sweden. He said it was a lovely city where I could undoubtedly secure work and at the same time learn more of the language. He gave me a letter to a good friend, an organ-builder who had traveled widely in Germany and spoke German. Furthermore, he had his apprentice accompany me as a guide and helper.

I followed his advice and all turned out well. I reached Malmö safely. My host, an upright and wealthy man, provided me with beautiful lodgings. Then I went to the burgomaster. I presented my passport and letters of recommendation and related my desires. He knew no German and I knew no Swedish; but he signed my passport, returned it to me, and only said, "Good." I bowed politely in appreciation and bid him adieu.

On my way home I encountered a Jew who had been converted to Christianity. Shaking my hand, he said, "How do you do, Herr Aron!"

I was puzzled. I asked him where we had met.

"When I was an itinerant Talmud student, I once spent a week end in Bützow accompanied by a fellow-student. That was about four years ago and I was then called Abraham Brody, but I have since joined the Church and my name is B——. I recall that I had arrived in Bützow on Thursday and spent the Sabbath with Rabbi David who lived near the castle. On Sunday I followed the custom of the Talmud students, making the round of the homes in order to gather some money for living and travel expenses. I also went to your home, knocked at the door, and entered. Nobody was in sight. I noticed a pair of black silk stockings on a chair, and as I was desperately in need of them I quickly concealed them under my cloak and left. Outside the door I met your wife. I greeted her and asked for a contribution to enable me to continue with my journey. She gave me four shillings and some bread and butter. My companion and I traveled on but we were unable to find suitable employment. Finally I came to this city, found happiness and married. Now, dear Herr Aron, I should like to repay you for the stockings. I am now a grain merchant and I should be pleased to have you accept the hospitality of my spacious house. Please don't think that on account of my conversion I am not to be trusted; on the contrary, my heart is filled with joy whenever I meet a Jew."

I thanked him for his offer of hospitality, and explained that my stay in Malmö would be brief for I had to attend to some legal matters in Stockholm; also that my portmanteau was already at my quarters. But he was so persistent (he pleaded too that his wife had never seen any other Jew) that I could not shake him off. I accompanied him to his house. It was large and beautiful, and his wife was genteel. They had an infant about a month old.

The way he had won his wife makes an odd tale. This B——appeared one day at the church in the German colony in Malmö and informed the pastor that he wished to be converted. The pastor taught him the elements of Christianity and took him into his own home. He was a noble old man, and as he had neither wife nor child, a niece served as his housekeeper. B—— became intimate with the girl and she found herself in a family way. Her sister, who was the wife of a prominent Malmö merchant, told her to get rid of B—— and seek an upright man, else she would have nothing more to do with her. But the girl insisted that since B—— had deprived her of her honor, he must restore it. Meanwhile the good, old pastor died, quite unaware of the affair. During his illness B—— took good care of him. While the pastor was considered a man of means, no money was found among his possessions. Then B—— married the girl and led a merry existence. He bought a big house and told tall tales. He bought a share in a trading company, paid little attention to business, and entertained lavishly. With his money, it was easy come, easy go. This is the gist of the story that my host told me.

Having spent a month in Malmö quite profitably—I did especially well in trading pearls and jewelry—I thought of continuing my journey. When B—— heard that I was going, he hastened to me and said, "Dear friend, if you remain here another week, I will accompany you to Stockholm. I have 6,000 thaler in the bank, and I will gladly lend it to you at five per cent. interest. I am very well known in Stockholm and can help you with legal matters by recommending you to my friend Duke Karl. You will prosper in trading pearls and jewelry. Besides, you will require two horses and it will be more economical if both of us use them."

I let him talk me into it only because my knowledge of the language was so meager. His wife begged me to speak to him about his impetuousness. She had thought that all Jews were like that until she saw how calm I was.

We journeyed to Kristianstadt, where I spent a month. On the way

B—— behaved himself, but in the city he came home tipsy every night with a bunch of drunkards. I warned him that he would either have to change his ways or seek other quarters. This had some effect on him, but I made up my mind to get rid of him as soon as we arrived in Stockholm. He tried to get me to go to Gothenburg. He said it was a large city where much business could be gotten, and proposed that he would hawk for a third of the income. But he was a toper and a brawler. I was not personally concerned, but such company embarrassed me exceedingly where I had taken lodgings. Finally we left Kristianstadt. I did not want to be delayed by any more stopovers. I gave him no indication of what my real object in Stockholm was.

We arrived in Stockholm at nine o'clock in the morning on a hot day in July, 1774. For two hours he left me alone on the street where I was waiting in the carriage. Passers-by stared at me. When he returned, I asked him where he had been all that time.

"Lodgings cannot be found here as quickly as in other cities," he replied. "Of course there are places that can be rented, but a stranger is in great danger."

Assuring me that he would have definite word in half an hour, he left me again. Then a brewer who lived nearby and who understood German passed by the carriage and heard the driver grumble about waiting and threatening to dump the portmanteaux. The brewer noticed that I had been waiting there a long time and inquired if anything was wrong. I told him that my companion had said he would return in half an hour from his search for lodgings, but that he was an hour late.

"There are plenty of vacant rooms here," he commented genially. "There is no reason for keeping the horses and porter while you wait, you are being charged for this time."

I paid the driver a sum suggested by the brewer so that he would wait until my companion returned. At two o'clock, I was still standing there. I was incensed. At that time the brewer reappeared and asked whether my companion had succeeded in locating quarters. He offered to direct me to suitable quarters in the neighborhood, at the home of a man who spoke German fluently. I thanked him and he accompanied me to the house of an upright man, where I rented two rooms.

Late in the afternoon B—— turned up, indignant and drunk. Why, he had searched the whole city for me and thought that I had already been murdered. Even on the journey he had filled my head with tales about the dangers that beset a stranger in Stockholm. His favorite warning was that one risked one's life if one merely ventured to drink a glass of brandy or a bottle of wine. It was his purpose to inspire me with fear so that I would be sure to keep him with me.

I arose early as usual the next morning, and smoked my pipe. My host was already up. I told him that I had a letter to the Lord Mayor and would like to present it to him. This fine man offered to take me to the Mayor's residence at ten o'clock. I asked him not to say anything of this to B——, of whose bad habits I disapproved. At the appointed time he accompanied me to the Lord Mayor's residence, directed me to the proper hall, and told an attendant that I wished an audience with His Excellency, for whom I had a letter. Of course I had taken along my passport and all my letters.

The room was full of people. An hour passed before I was called.

I entered holding the letters in my hand, and stammered in Swedish, "Your Excellency, I regret that I am unable to speak Swedish."

"You are a Hebrew," he began without hesitation. "You may speak German. I spent five years as a volunteer cadet in the service of the King of Prussia."

I quickly told him my wish and showed him my letters of recommendation from the government officials and notables of Stralsund.

"Dear friend," he commented, "this is an extremely difficult matter. A Jew has never lived in Sweden. My good friends have recommended you very highly, but it is not in my power to grant your wish. I will gladly give you whatever aid I can. Suppose you return in a few days and I shall let you know what you may expect. I must ask you in the meanwhile not to trade in gold or silver, for if anyone complains I will not be able to help you. But you may do as much seal-engraving as you can secure."

He asked me to leave all my documents with him and to set his own coat-of-arms in carnelian stone. He was most gracious with his time, permitting me to tell him about Abraham Pach and my brother Marcus.

On my way home I met B——. He was angry.

"You won't get out of Stockholm alive," he ranted. "You are taking too many chances in running about the city so freely."

I did not want to be in his company, as he might insist upon breaking my promise not to trade. I simply said that I would not lock myself in my room. After all, no one would murder me on the streets.

I immediately sent the Lord Mayor's coat-of-arms to Abraham Pach at Schwerin. I also write to my brother Mordecai, suggesting that he join me as soon as possible via Wismar, whence ships frequently sailed to Stockholm in three days. A few days later I saw the Lord Mayor again.

This time I brought my Mecklenburg certificate of residence. I pointed out that I had lived in Bützow for nineteen years and showed him a certificate from the local university attesting to my good character and reputation. He advised me to consult a German-speaking attorney whom he recommended, and sketched the contents of the application for the right of residence that should be drawn up. I was to bring the application to him and he promised to deliver it to the King in person.

I followed his advice and engaged the attorney. He asked me to return in two days and he would have the application ready. During this time I visited several councillors to whom I had letters of recommendation. All of them said that they would help me.

When the document was completed I took it to the Lord Mayor and asked him to forgive me for putting him to so much trouble.

"You may come as often as you like," he said, "and if I have the time I shall be glad to talk with you. I enjoy conversing in German. Come to see me again in a few days."

When I returned he was most gracious. He reported that he had given my application to the King and was glad to inform me that the King was not averse to aiding me to secure the right of residence. He promised to have more definite word in eight days.

Two days later Duke Karl sent a lackey to my house to escort me to the palace. As he already knew that I could not speak Swedish, there was a courtier present to act as interpreter. He asked whether I was the man who had petitioned for the King's aid in order to engage in seal-engraving and stone-cutting. Duke Karl looked on as the interpreter told me that the Duke wished his coat-of-arms (he held an impression of it in his hand) cut in precious stones. We agreed upon a price of forty ducats. I could not help feeling that the Duke was acting for the King, who wanted to see a specimen of our work. I immediately sent the impression to Abraham Pach and wrote a letter stressing the importance of doing his best. It was a sample for His Majesty and our fate hung thereon.

One morning my host hailed me. "My dear Herr Aron," he remarked, "I threw that low rascal out of my house during your absence. He has already taken his portmanteau. His impudence and insults drove my wife to tears. Of course you may remain here as long as you wish, but I cannot tolerate that scoundrel. He deserved a sound drubbing, but I restrained myself because I didn't want to aggravate you."

I told the good man that I still had some business accounts to settle so that I could not let him go. This was the truth. I remained over night, and on the morrow B—— met me outside the house. He said that he had taken other quarters in the neighborhood, with better rooms and more light for my work. I went with him and found that the owner of the house was a modest widow. I moved in and set up my workshop.

I had lived there hardly a week when this hostess complained that B—— was a mean wretch and that he gave her no peace. She said that she would be delighted to have me remain, but he must go. Well, that was the last straw: I settled our accounts and told him that if he wanted me to handle any of his business he could visit me, but I could not live in the same house. He took about 100 reichsthalers, which was due him, and never turned up again. He carried on in the city until his money gave out and then returned home.

The very same day that I broke off with B—— (it was September 2, 1774), my brother Mordecai arrived on the Wismar ship. We accepted the hospitality of one of the Queen's footmen, who was a fellow-townsman from Mecklenburg. Then I took my brother to the Lord Mayor in order that he might learn of his arrival. He was pleased.

"I must tell you that the King has sent your application and recommendations to the Council, where a decision will be reached. You may give this information to your attorney. He will know what to do."

My attorney accompanied me to the Council, where he inquired whether the petition that I had given to the King had been acted upon. They requested that we return in a month for the decision.

When we reappeared at the end of the month, they again refused to act on the petition and asked that we come again in two weeks. My attorney now told me that he would not accompany me again, but inasmuch as I knew where to go I should go alone. I was to let him know of the decision when it was made. A month must have passed before the Council acted. Their decision was laconic:

"We cannot permit you to practice your religion in this country, much less to engage in business."

It was signed by Karl Sparre.

I was shocked. I went directly to the Lord Mayor. "You promised to aid me," I complained, "and now see the sort of decision you approved."

"Let me explain," he replied. "In my capacity of president of the tribunals I must affix my signature to all decrees and decisions. However, you need not let the matter rest there. You must ask your attorney to appeal the Council's decision."

We followed his advice, but another month passed before we received the very same decision. I complained again to the Lord Mayor, declaring that if he simply signed whatever action the Council took, I had better save his time and my money and return home. He laughed, and told me that I was much too impatient, that I must again make an appeal before the magistrates.

I consulted my attorney. When I mentioned the suggestion of the Lord Mayor, he was skeptical. He thought that the magistrates would act just as the members of the Council had done. I went to see all the councillors who had promised to help me. They pointed out that the Lord Mayor, who was president of the judges, could do much, but that their own hands were tied. However, they repeated that they would be glad to help when the appeal came before them. Their friendlinss heartened me. A week later I again went before the magistrates. I waited two hours. Finally one of them took down my name and address and said that they would send for me at the proper time. I returned home. I was much esteemed by all these notables. They lavished praise on my work and I got a reputation as the greatest artist in the world.

I saw a good deal of the jewellers, especially those gallant gentlemen, Herr Suter and Herr Wilhelmson. They were my good friends and knew how great was my desire to remain here. At long last I was summoned to the town hall by the magistrates. One of them, by the name of Flodin, a gentleman and a scholar, came forward and spoke to me in German.

"My dear Herr Aron," he said, "you have petitioned the King for the right to live here. All of us have seen your recommendations. You have been praised as a man of character as well as an expert craftsman, and we know that these testimonials are justified. The King himself wishes you to remain, especially since there is no other such craftsman in the realm. But your adherence to the Jewish religion is an insurmountable obstacle. Let me show you what the statutes say in this regard." He translated freely into German from an old tome: "'If a Jew comes to our shores on a ship that requires repairs, the said ship shall have precedence over all others in order that the Jew may leave the realm. If a Jew becomes ill while his ship is in port, a physician shall be sent to cure him that he may quickly leave the realm. A Jew may neither buy nor sell in the realm.' Such is our law and our franchise."

"So this is your franchise!" I replied. "O how miserable a franchise! How contrary to human life!"

He replied quietly but firmly, "A Jew has not lived in our kingdom since the beginning of time. Nevertheless we have decided, because it is the King's wish, to make it possible for you to remain here. You cannot do so as a Jew, since that is contrary to our laws; but if you embrace Christianity, you may have your citizenship immediately, together with exemption from all taxes for a period of ten years. Such an offer has never been made to anyone else. Think it over and let us have your decision within a week."

I replied without hesitation, "My dear man, I do not need to think it over. I would not change my religion for all the gold in the world. I did not come here to trade in religion. How could I deny a faith through which I hope to gain salvation?"

He listened very patiently and remarked, "We are ignorant of the Jewish religion and its doctrine of salvation."

"I am not a learned man," I continued, "and certainly this is not the place to expound religious doctrine. This much, however, I can tell you: the fundamental principle of Judaism is to fear God and to love one's neighbors. I intend to hold this sacred as long as I live."

"We hold the same beliefs," he responded, "but man cannot attain salvation without the Savior whom Jews call the Messiah."

I repeated that that was not the place for a religious disputation, and in any case no good end could be served. The upshot was that I would be informed of their decision. I bowed and went my way.

A few days later I met Councillor Flodin on the street. He asked me to visit his home, which was nearby, and examine an exquisite carnelian that he would like to have cut into a seal. I accompanied him to his house and agreed to make the seal. Then I asked him whether he would help me to remain in the country. He told me that neither he nor all the magistrates could grant my petition. Only the King could make it possible, if he wished to exercise his authority. He was inclined to think, however, that the King would not be in favor of granting me these rights since there was no precedent for this act. He was sure that I would have the decision of the magistrates by the end of the week.

Again I received the same answer, again the signature of Karl Sparre! My hopes were crushed. I hurried to the Lord Mayor.

"Well," he inquired cheerfully, "what is the good news?"

"There is only bad news. Here is the decision to which you affixed your signature. You know well its contents. Is this the last word?"

"Yes," he replied, "that is the final decision from the Town Hall."

"Your Excellency might have told me long ago that I might as well return home," I replied, expressing my disappointment, "and I could have saved a large sum of money."

He said that I surely had had no experience in legal proceedings. "If you wish to take issue with me, why don't you institute a suit?"

I bowed humbly, asked his forgiveness, and requested him to tell me when I should leave.

"No, no," he protested, "you misunderstand me. I am quite serious. You must make a legal protest against my decision to the King. Ask your attorney to draw it up and take it to Johan von Heland, the Secretary of State, who will present it to the King. I will do all that I can to help."

My attorney drew up a brief and I took it to von Heland. He was at home in the German language. I handed him the brief, requesting that he bring it to the King's attention. He read it from beginning to end. When he had finished, he cried angrily, "Who in the world do you think you are? How dare you bring this sort of protest against the Lord Mayor? Would you like to be horsewhipped? You had better leave the country at once or I'll drive you out. What stupid arrogance! Out! Out!"

I shook with fear. "Gracious Sir!" I explained, "the Lord Mayor himself asked me to do this." He stood motionless for a while, summed up my appearance, and exclaimed, "Hear him now! A liar to boot!" I repeated anxiously that the Lord Mayor had instructed me to make the protest. "I cannot accept your word alone," he said finally, "I shall call on him this afternoon. Meanwhile I will keep this document, and you may return in the morning."

As I left I suddenly realized that I had blundered. I had given my word to the Lord Mayor that I would not divulge our understanding, and now the cat was out of the bag. I ran to his office as fast as my legs could carry me. Still panting, I exclaimed, "Your Excellency sent me to a horrible person!" "What happened?" he asked with concern. "What did he do to you?" "He read the protest and told me that I should be whipped for bringing an action against you, that I should leave the city or he would throw me out. He was so angry that I expected him to thrash me then and there. I was so terrified that I told him you had sent me. I hardly knew what I was saying. He kept the document and said that he would speak to you this afternoon." The Lord Mayor assured me that I had acted properly, and I went home relieved and overjoyed that he was not angry with me.

The Secretary of State was most cordial when I saw him again the following morning. He told me that he had had a satisfactory conversation about me with the Lord Mayor. The protest, however, required some revision. He volunteered to attend to this and suggested that I return the following day to sign the new document. After I had done this, he asked whether I had spoken to the councillors. I told him that I had seen some of them. He suggested that I intensify my efforts. "Tomorrow the

King will hold council in Ulrichsdal and four councillors [he named them] will be present. If you know any of them, go to see them immediately and ask their assistance." He added that he would be away for four or five days but would be glad to see me upon his return.

It so happened that two of these councillors were among those to whom I had letters of recommendation. I had seen them often and won their favor. I went to them once more, and to the other two as well, and told them the story. All of them promised to do everything in their power and assured me that I need have no fears about the outcome.

At the appointed time I again went to see Secretary of State Heland. As I entered his office, he congratulated me. He told me that my request had been granted and I would find the papers at the Lord Mayor's. I thanked him more than a thousand times and said that I hoped I would have the privilege of repaying this great obligation. Then I hurried to the Lord Mayor's. He instructed me to go to the Chancery at the royal castle and ask for the royal secretary, von Sieverts. Off I went to the castle. The secretary gave me the privilege papers and I paid the required fee.

When I visited the Lord Mayor with the intention of expressing my deep appreciation, he spoke to me abruptly. "I've done the Devil's work and prefer not to hear of it. If you must thank some one, thank the King. But be sure to go to the Town Hall tomorrow with your attorney and have the papers officially recorded."

The councillor there requested that I leave the papers and return for them in a week. I hesitated to let them out of my hands, but as my attorney assured me, in German, that there was no reason for worrying about their return, I left them. The papers were certified in Ulrichsdal on May 2, 1775. They granted me, my brother Mordecai, and Herr Abraham Pach the right of residence with our wives and children provided we paid the regular levies.

A week later I returned to the councillor and received my papers. I wrote forthwith to Herr Pach asking him to join me, and to my wife, whom I told to sell the house and garden and to bring the children.

A KABBALIST IN PARIS

HAYYIM DAVID AZULAI (1726-1807)

Azulai's diary bears witness to the cosmopolitan character of the numerous itinerant rabbi-scholars who appeared in the capitals of Europe and America in the eighteenth century. They were lionized by learned men and aristocratic ladies whose journals contain many colorful references to their picturesque dress and esoteric wisdom. Ezra Stiles, the first president of Yale, recorded the topics of learned conversation with Rabbi Hayyim Isaac Karrigal and even wrote a memoir of his life. Azulai was born in Jerusalem, traveled considerably in behalf of the Hebron Rabbinical Seminary and was the premier bibliophile of his generation. Despite his devotion to kabbalistic lore and practices, these jottings of his observations and experiences in Paris on the eve of the Revolution reveal keen intelligence and a vivid personality. The time is December, 1777.

❄ ❄ ❄

THIS city, the capital of France, is of great size, it is said to be fifteen miles round. Its streets and squares are wide enough for two coaches to pass each other with ease, even though foot passengers are walking along the sides of the roads. The city is served by its river, the Seine, over which there is a great bridge, long and wide, called the "Pont Neuf," that is to say, the "New Bridge." All day long, and all through the night, without ceasing, pedestrians are wending their way over it. Here stands the clock "la Samaritaine," which is surrounded by water. There is a saying that never in the twenty-four hours is there an instant without a white horse, a monk and a prostitute at this spot. The city is of great beauty and everything is to be found in it, but all at a very high price, except prostitution, which is very cheap and openly displayed; there are said to be thirty thousand public prostitutes inscribed on the registers, without counting the thousands who are not public and offered to all comers. There are academies in great numbers, and every kind of manufacture is carried on. The Jews enjoy tranquillity, there are many Germans, many Portuguese from Bordeaux and Bayonne, and many who hail from Avignon. People pray together every Saturday, but there is no fixed community, birds of passage for the most part resorting hither for trading purposes. The synagogues are without "privilege," and exist only by a miracle.

On Tuesday evening M. Israel Bernal de Valabrègue came. He enjoys a salary from the King, twelve hundred livres a year, and the title of the King's Interpreter, because he pretends to know all the Oriental languages. He thinks he is a rabbi, a casuist, a poet, and versed in the sciences: he knows the kabbalistic names. He boasts that all the world writes letters to him. He came to see me three evenings in succession. The first time he sang his own praises as a scientist, the second time as having journeyed to Amsterdam; the third on account of the ladies who correspond with him, he says, and the academies which consult him. One evening his boasting of himself was to the tune of making a mock of M. Mordecai Ravel; the latter has roundly insulted him and lavished praise on him too. But enough.

In the course of the day M. Fabre came to visit me, a learned Christian of the Academy of Science. He plied me with questions about science and kabbalist practices, which I answered.

On Friday I paid a visit to him and stayed with him a couple of hours. He showed me a book in French in which were written the names of the angels, their features, and their letters, as well as consultations in regard to dreams by means of adjurations, all in the French language. This Christian gave me a cordial welcome; I went to him in the company of M. Mordecai Venture, a grammarian and linguist, who took a great deal of trouble on my behalf. May God reward him!

The evening before I had gone to dine at the house of the eminent David Naquet. There were present the *parnassim* (administrators) of the synagogue and a certain number of private individuals. It was a great affair. Much honor was paid to me. Then we dined with M. Venture and M. Mordecai Ashkenazi, of the town of Hâvre-de-Grace in France. The master of the house treated me with much distinction, as did also his worthy wife. On Saturday we went to the synagogue. There was singing in honor of the confraternity "Gemilot Hasadim" just founded. My name was placed at the head, and they brought me the honor of opening the ark and of carrying the sefer-Torah (Scroll). Much oil was offered to the synagogue in my honor. I took lunch with M. David Naquet. M. Elie Perpignan, brother of the mistress of the house, and his wife, were fellow guests. Great disputes between this couple had ended in a quarrel, and I had been asked at Bordeaux to make peace. After our meal we went to the synagogue and I preached on morality and the praise of the brotherhood "G. H.," after which they made me an offering without being asked to do so. May God reward them for it!

On Sunday, the 28th of Kislev, came M. Elie Perpignan and his wife. I gave her a "Shema Israel" to swallow, according to the formula of R. Menahem Azariah, because it was feared she contemplated being converted, and I invited them to make peace once and for all.

After that came MM. Mardochée Ashkenazi and David Naquet, and I visited a rich German Jew who told me he would come to see me in order to give me an offering.

On Sunday night MM. Abraham Vidal and Moses Perpignan came and gave an offering for Hebron with many tokens of respect. I thank God that I have a great name and am held a hundred times higher in esteem than I deserve. It is useless my telling them that I am an ignorant man; they think that is all modesty. My renown has even spread among Christian savants, who question the Jews about me—it is extraordinary! When I speak to them they hold my words more precious than pearls. These, indeed, are the wonders of Him who "raiseth the poor out of the dust and lifteth up the beggar from the dunghill to set them up among princes." But what rare goodness have I met with from the man of Avignon! Wherever they are to be found, even if it is only one, I have reaped honors and profit. Thus it has been in the seven cities of France where I have come across them and they have been my guiding light; they live in the Four Communities, Nimes, Montpellier, Pézénas, Narbonne, Bordeaux, Paris. To them I owe every care for my comfort and much honor; their persons and their money have been at my service, and they have never ceased to cherish and respect me—it is extraordinary! "And David blesses them," them and their houses. May God repay them, and may their reward be riches and honor, a long life and worthy posterity; may God deliver them from all evil and may the virtue of the Holy Land protect them and their descendants so that they may be prosperous and flourishing, with abundance of all things! Amen!

That evening there came to me the very wealthy M. Peixotto to discuss with me the question of his wife and induce me to get her to accept the act of repudiation. He undertook to give a thousand "crowns" for Hebron if I would move in the matter. I answered: "If you wish to make peace, I will interest myself in your affair with a good grace, for everyone knows that your wife is a virtuous woman; lay down what conditions you will, I will strive to obtain them. But as to a separation, that would be sacrilege." I added that the Law forbids him to repudiate his virtuous wife as long as she is a mother and his first wife. I have told him, moreover, many other things of this kind. A man even offered me four "louis d'or" to countersign a decision written by a celebrated rabbi concerning the marriage of Israel Vidal to his second wife, and I replied that though the decision may be just in principle in the eyes of the people, it was a sacrilege, and that I would not see the decision and still less would I countersign it. May God help me, for the glory of His name, and may all our actions be done in the sight of Heaven, that I may act according to His will! Amen!

On Rosh-Hodesh Tebet I went to see Monsieur Fabre, the Christian savant mentioned before. He showed me an abridgement of the Kabbalah in French, which began with the name of seventy-two letters, by whose help Moses was said to have brought about the plagues of Egypt and which confounded these things with the constellations. I told him: "You must know that that is a branch of the practical Kabbalah, the ten plagues have not been the work of this name; moreover, it has nothing to do with the constellations." This Christian paid me great honor, and had us served with chocolate and "pain d'Espagne." Snow was falling; he took us in a coach to the "Bibliothèque." But as it was the end of the civil year, none of the conservators were there, and we came back again. I went with M. Mordecai Venture to Elie Perpignan. To his wife I addressed remonstrances of a general nature, and, on her husband's arrival, I got him to concede that he would give her all that was necessary for their expenses, so that she might be the mistress. In short, I strove to do all that was in my power to make peace between them.

On Thursday evening I was speaking in praise of the science, when a young Portuguese, Jacob Laguna, got up to speak in a contrary sense; he told me he knew he was not orthodox. I was much pained, and afterwards made inquiries about him. I was told extraordinary things; my informants said definitely they had had it from himself, from his own mouth, that he had studied the books of Voltaire and believed in nothing, etc. What is more, a man of standing told me that here in Paris, at the table of the master of the house, he did not drink wine prepared by gentiles, but that he would go forthwith and drink with him in a Christian "auberge," and had done so many times. In truth, I was much troubled about him for many reasons. If this is all true, may God bring him back to the way of perfection. Amen!

In the daytime, we went to pay a visit to M. Peixotto. It was a considerable distance to go, for as we wrote above, this is a very large city, said to have nine hundred and fifty streets, five thousand coaches, and more than a million inhabitants; they say a day is not long enough to go round all the town on foot, if one wants to go everywhere. And at the end of it all he was not at home. In the evening, I went with Hananel de Milhaud and his son in a coach to visit M. Liefmann Calmer. He is a German Jew who in his youth was in the service of the rich Suasso de la Haye in Holland; then he entered commerce and has elevated himself to the position of Baron of Picquigny, that is to say, lord of the town of Picquigny (which he has bought from the heirs of its lord for the sum of a million and a half francs) and "vidame of Amiens," that is to say, he is a "defender" of the "church," for that is what the lord of Picquigny must be. He has a great privilege from the Government. In fact, the late King Louis XV had a mistress whom he had served, and she procured him this elevation. We went to see him; he gave us a cordial welcome and an offering of two "louis." I recommended to him, and to his son also, M. Benjamin Abraham of Bordeaux, because he is related to him, and grows poorer and poorer. They said they would send him an offering.

On Friday we went with the Christian, M. Fabre, to the "Bibliothéque" of manuscripts, and such is the consideration in which he is held, although it was not the day for it to be open, he received the necessary authority, and it was opened for us. There are thousands of manuscripts there dealing with all the sciences. I saw a Bible on parchment which was written in 1061 of the ordinary reckoning, about seven hundred and seventeen years old now, and which seems quite new, hundreds of our (i.e., Hebrew) books in manuscript, among them David Kimchi on the Psalms, with additions to the edition (on Psalm II, verse 12, we noticed nearly a whole column demi-folio), many works on natural science, on philosophy, on mathematics, on the calendar, the ancient Kabbalah, the works of R. Joseph ibn Caspi, and of Isaac Israeli, who composed the *Yesod Olam* for Rabbi Asher; many copies of *Semak* and of other printed works, the *Shibbole ha-Leket* (1st part), and the *Sefer Yereim* complete (and it contains 464 precepts and the author says he has followed in his reckoning of the precepts the order of Rab Jehudái Gaon, the author of the *Halakhot Gedolot,* except that he has sometimes put two precepts together into one), and the notes of Rabbi Isaiah the Elder, on the Pentateuch (in these he sometimes criticises Rashi).

I took my three Sabbath repasts in the house of the rich David Naquet, where I was a much honored guest; on Friday evening and on the day itself M. Abraham Vidal and M. Mordecai Venture partook of these meals.

On Sunday I went to see the decision (about Vidal), but read the question only. I saw that the facts were not correctly stated, so it is possible the decision may differ . . . treats him as a man who has been deceived but with overabundance of epithets; probably the copyist's contribution . . . to make a big sum of money out of it . . . I was promised a certain sum if I would countersign, but I avoided "what is ugly and what looks like it," and may God bring them to penitence! Enough.

Monday. I took chocolate with Solomon Ravel. Then I went, with David Naquet, to Jacob Goldschmidt, a rich and eminent Ashkenazi. It was a miserable day; the snow was falling, the distance was great, and we could not find a coach. When we got there he behaved as all the Ashkenazim do, they are full of doubts and arguments; the end of it was he gave us twelve francs. After that we went to M. Jacob Péreire, who had been twice to see me, he is a notable held in great consideration. I found at his house a letter from my son, written with modesty and respect, etc.

The evening before, Tuesday, the Marquis de Thomé, a Christian savant, came to see me with great demonstrations of respect, as well as another Christian of mark and an "Italian abbé." They stayed nearly two hours, and I answered their questions. At the end the Marquis asked me to bless him. I blessed him, as well as the other Christian—it is strange!

Next morning M. Fabre sent a fine coach for us to go to Versailles. We went there with M. Venture. . . . I put on a handsome coat, and went to the sign of the "Cheval Rouge" in the "rue du Vieux-Versailles" at Versailles, where M. Fabre was in the house of a relation of his, a lady. We had a cordial reception and drank chocolate.

Then we went to Court. The Christian entered and we followed. We came first into a beautiful room, adorned with numerous gilded columns arranged in two rows and supporting great candlesticks. This is the gallery, and courtiers were standing about. We went through numerous royal apartments to reach the Council Chamber. At the upper end there is a canopy royally gilt and painted. There the King sits on his throne, while the courtiers take their places lower down the room. We next went through into the inner apartments, and stopped at the further end of the chief room. After a little while some great lords began to pass us, and among them the King's brother, "Monsieur le Comte de Provence", called "Monsieur" and nothing more, and his younger brother, "Monsieur le Comte d'Artois". They stayed beside me nearly five minutes. Then it was the King who passed, accompanied by great lords, and I pronounced the benediction for the King. He was dressed in red, wearing the "ordre d'azur", on which were arms. Hardly had he passed, when a lord came to say to M. Fabre, who was by my side, that the King was asking from what country I was ambassador. He answered him that I was not an ambassador, but that I came from Egypt out of "curiosity" to see what I could. Then we took our leave, saluted by all the company. Some of the "ladies" who were passing even made a curtsey to us, as their manner is.

We returned to the house of M. Fabre's relation, where great honor was done to me. He gave me a cup with its dish, in "porcelain", which "Madame la Comtesse d'Artois" had presented to M. Fabre's relation; the cup bore the arms of King Louis. He gave me also at the same time a little chest for taking papers, such as a newspaper; this box was made of crystal and the shape of a coat-of-mail. The mistress of the house asked me what I should like to eat. I replied, some eggs cooked by my servant. They laid the table, we sat down, and I ate some bread with two boiled eggs. I then recited grace and afternoon prayer.

We took our places in the coach again; everything was covered with snow. The Christian told me there was a collection here of great animals, but that on account of the snow they were shut up under cover, and could not be seen. The "garden" is twenty-one miles round, but in winter, when there is snow, nothing is to be seen. We got back without more ado. The Christian wanted to pay for the coach. It is wonderful to see with what kindly feelings of regard God had filled him for me. I give Him thanks and homage. . . . The relative of this M. Fabre and her daughter asked me to give them my blessing; I went a little nearer to them and did bless them, but would not place my hand on their heads —it is extraordinary! Praised be God, who has elevated me, unworthy as I am of so many favors, lacking everything, in such wise; it is His mercy which has been granted to me; may He be forever blessed and exalted!

In the evening, the eve of Thursday, the Marquis de Thomé came, with the Marquise de Croix. She took a seat near me and asked me to pray for her. Then she told me that she was studying the Bible, and that she saw angels and spirits who talked with her, but that, when they were evil, she repulsed them. She made offering of a "louis" for Hebron, and mentioned the Baal-Shem of London. She told me that a Jew had given her a book of kabbalistic lore, and other matters she imparted to me, too. How strange it all is! As for myself, I answered her with such remarks as were suitable to her. Then she informed me that she was a lady held in much consideration and that at Avignon she had saved many Jews from the hands of the Inquisitor, that she was the daughter of a Marquis and her husband was a Marquis—so many tales of this Christian lady. But how many Christians have been led away by the man called Baal-Shem who, in his pride and presumption, has revealed the practices of the Kabbalah and the adjurations to so many nobles and ladies out of vanity. I have been plied with many questions about him, which I have answered.

On the morrow I went to the "Bibliothèque" and copied a part of the *Notes* of Rabbi Isaiah on the Pentateuch. I went over the whole building; it holds many rooms filled with manuscripts in all languages dealing with all the sciences and all the religions. Among the Chinese manuscripts there is a book, with a beautiful, upright clear handwriting. There are said to be nearly fifty-thousand manuscript volumes here. The "Bibliothèque" of printed books I have not, however, seen this time, but I did see all over it twenty-two years ago: it is marvelous and worthy of a King. This "Bibliothèque" of Paris is said to be the largest and most remarkable in the world.

On Friday I went to collect some of the offerings written down below for the Yeshiba "Keneset Israel" of Hebron.

On the Sabbath—the day itself and the evening of the day before—I was at the house of M. David Naquet, where I was received with much honor; M. Abraham and M. Venture shared our meals. May God reward them!

On Sunday we departed in peace from Paris, accompanied, until we reached the outskirts of Paris, by M. Solomon Ravel, M. David Naquet and M. Hananel, who made the start with us in our coach.

A TRIP WITH ISRAEL BAALSHEM

MEIR MARGOLIS (?-1790)

The extraordinary figure of Israel Baalshem Tob, the founder of Hasidism, is obscured in legends that parallel in many ways the gospels of the New Testament. His opinions were recorded by a host of disciples but his life was transfigured into miraculous performances by the naiveté and mysticism of the masses. The following brief reminiscence, not entirely untouched by legendry, is a unique portrait by a contemporary. Meir is said to have been a pupil of the Baalshem. He was rabbi of the community of Lemberg, the center of Poland then ruled by Austria-Hungary, and the author of a number of works dealing with ethics and mysticism.

✻ ✻ ✻

ONCE Israel Baalshem Tob was journeying to the holy city of Brody by way of Horodenka, and he stopped in front of my house and sent for me to come out. He said, "Meir, come, join me on the wagon and accompany me to Brody." I took my bag with prayer shawl, phylacteries and long coat and made the trip. When we reached the city, he took quarters at an inn in the manner of the merchants. There he was visited only by two honorable men, one who was rich and a second who was not. They spent a good deal of time with him and brought him peace.

Now, I noticed that the Baalshem Tob did not carry a cent, and I was worried. Why didn't I take some money from my house? I thought. Then I heard him say to the wagoner, "Make ready for travel." I went and informed those two men that the Baalshem Tob was leaving. They came. Finding that his departure was delayed, they said, "We are going to the Beth Hamidrash. Do you let us know when he is ready to leave and we shall come."

And so it was. I let them know and they came.

Now, during the first visit the rich man had given the Baalshem

Tob a gold ducat. But when they returned to bid him adieu, the Baalshem Tob returned the ducat to this man, saying, "Take the money and give half of it to the members of the *Klaus*.* (The members were much beloved by Baalshem Tob. He said that the Shekinah—the Presence of God—rested upon the Klaus.) And divide the other half among the poor." Then we left the city.

When I saw him squander the gold ducat, my heart melted within me, for I knew he was without a penny. I inquired: "Why did you do it? Does it add to your stature to be without a penny for living expenses?" He simply answered, "O faithful guardian, know that so long as the blessed Lord lives we have nothing to worry about."

And so it was. When we arrived in Radwill, the people came to him to be healed. The same happened everywhere until in the end his home did not lack the wherewithal to live.

* Hasidic conclave for prayer and discussion.

MY STRUGGLE WITH AMAZONS

SOLOMON MAIMON (1754-1800)

Maimon's self-portrait was characterized by George Eliot as "that wonderful piece of Autobiography." He is, indeed, the autobiographer *par excellence*. Born into the medieval climate of Lithuanian rural culture, he fought his way to the enlightened circle of the *Judengasse* of Berlin, which was then dominated by the personality of Moses Mendelssohn. He was soon recognized as one of the keenest minds among the Berlin intellectuals—Immanuel Kant paid him high tribute—but he never completely succeeded in divesting himself of the impress of his early background. Maimon is an extraordinary example of the "marginal mind," in which two streams of culture were in constant conflict. So utterly frank and revealing is the narrative of his life—even the following chapter hardly suggests how fascinating it is—that the book has always had, and probably will have, a warm circle of fans.

❋   ❋   ❋

IN my youth I was very lively, and had in my nature a good deal that was agreeable. In my passions I was violent and impatient. Till about my eleventh year, as I had the benefit of a very strict education and was kept from all contact with women, I never traced any special inclination towards the fair sex. But an incident produced a great change in this respect.

A poor but very pretty girl about my own age was taken into our house as a servant. She charmed me uncommonly. Desires began to stir in me, which till this time I had never known. But in accordance with the strict rabbinical morals, I was obliged to keep on my guard against looking on the girl with attentive gaze, and still more against speaking with her, so that I was able only now and then to throw her a stolen glance.

It happened once, however, that the women of the house were going to bathe, which by the usage of the country they are accustomed to do two or three times a week. By chance my instinct drove me without reflection towards the place where they bathed; and there I suddenly perceived this beautiful girl, as she stepped out of the steam bath and plunged into the river flowing by. At that sight I fell into a sort of rapture. After my feelings had calmed down again, being mindful of the strict talmudic laws, I wished to flee. But I could not; I remained standing, as if rooted to the spot. As I dreaded, however, lest I might be surprised here, I was obliged to return with a heavy heart. From that time I became restless, was sometimes beside myself; and this state continued till my marriage.

Our neighbor, the arendator, had two sons and three daughters. The eldest daughter, Deborah, was already married. The second, Pessel, was about my age; the peasantry of the place professed to find even a certain resemblance in our features, and therefore, in accordance with all the laws of probability, conjectured that there would be a match between us. We formed also a mutual affection. But by ill luck the youngest daughter, Rachel, had to fall into a cellar and dislocate one of her legs. She herself, indeed, completely recovered, but the leg remained somewhat crooked. The arendator then started a hunt after me; he was absolutely determined to have me for a son-in-law. My father was quite agreeable, but he wished to have for his daughter-in-law the straight-legged Pessel rather than Rachel of the crooked leg. The arendator, however, declared that this was impracticable, inasmuch as he had fixed on a rich husband for the elder, while the youngest was destined for me; and as my father was unable to give me anything, he was willing to provide for her richly out of his own fortune. Besides a considerable sum which he agreed to give as a dowry, he was willing in addition to make me a joint-heir of his fortune, and to provide me with all necessaries the whole of my life. Moreover, he promised to pay my father a fixed sum immediately after the betrothal, and not only to leave him undisturbed in his rights, but also to try and promote his domestic happiness in every possible way. The feuds between the two families were to cease from this time, and a league of friendship was to unite them for the future into one family.

Had my father lent an ear to these representations, he would without doubt have established the fortune of his house, and I should have lived with a spouse, who, it is true, had a crooked leg, but (as I found out some time afterwards when I was a tutor in her family) was in other respects an amiable woman. I should thus have been freed from all cares in the midst of good fortune, and I should have been able to apply myself without hindrance to my studies. But unhappily my father rejected this proposal with scorn. He was absolutely determined to have Pessel for his daughter-in-law; and since this, as already mentioned, was impracticable, the feuds between the two families broke out afresh. But as the arendator was rich, and my father was a poor man, the latter was necessarily always the loser.

Some time afterwards another matrimonial proposal for me turned up. Mr. L. of Schmilowitz, a learned and at the same time a rich man, who had an only daughter, was so enchanted with my fame that he chose me for his son-in-law without having seen me. He began by entering into correspondence with my father on the subject, and left it to him to prescribe the conditions of the union. My father answered his letter in lofty style, made up of Biblical verses and passages from the Talmud, in which he expressed the conditions briefly by means of the following verses from the Canticles, "The thousand gulden are for thee, O Solomon, and the two hundred for those who keep his fruits.*" Consent was given to everything.

My father accordingly made a journey to Schmilowitz, saw his future daughter-in-law, and had the marriage-contract drawn in accordance with the terms agreed upon. Two hundred gulden were paid to him on the spot. With this, however, he was not content, but insisted that in his letter he had been obliged to limit himself to two hundred gulden merely for the sake of the beautiful verse which he did not wish to spoil; but he would not enter into the transaction at all unless he received for himself twice two hundred gulden (fifty thalers in Polish money). They had, therefore, to pay him two hundred gulden more, and to hand over to him the so-called little presents for me, namely, a cap of black velvet trimmed with gold lace, a Bible bound in green velvet with silver clasps, etc. With these things he came home full of joy, gave me the presents, and told me that I was to prepare myself for a disputation to be held on my marriage day, which would be in two months' time.

Already my mother had begun to bake the cakes she was expected to take with her to the wedding, and to prepare all sorts of preserves. I began also to think about the disputation I was to hold, when suddenly the mournful news arrived that my bride had died of smallpox. My father could easily reconcile himself to this loss, because he thought to himself that he had made fifty thalers by his son in an honorable way,

* Evidently VIII, 12, rendered in the Authorized Version, "Thou, O Solomon, must have a thousand (pieces of silver), and those that keep the fruit thereof two hundred." Maimon translates apparently from memory, "Die tausend Gulden sind für dich, Salomo, und die Zweihundert für die, die seine Früchte bewahren." In this rendering of this, the pronoun "his" must be understood in its old English latitude as either neuter or masculine.

and that now he could get fifty thalers for him again. I, too, who had never seen my bride, could not particularly mourn her loss. I thought to myself, "The cap and the silver-clasped Bible are already mine, and a bride will also not be awanting long, while my disputation can serve me again." My mother alone was inconsolable about this loss. Cakes and preserves are of a perishable nature and will not keep long. The labor which my mother had expended was therefore rendered fruitless by this fatal accident; and to this must be added, that she could find no place to keep the delicious cakes from my secret attacks.

Meanwhile the domestic circumstances of my father became every day worse. He saw himself, therefore, compelled to make a journey to the town of Nesvij, and apply for a position as teacher there, whither I also had to follow him. Here he opened under favorable conditions a school of his own, in which he employed me as assistant.

A widow, celebrated for her superior talents, as well as for her Xanthippe-like character, kept a public house at the extremity of one of the suburbs. She had a daughter who yielded to her in none of the above-mentioned qualities, and who was indispensable to her in the management of the house. Madam Rissia (this was the widow's name), excited by my constantly increasing reputation as a talmudic scholar, fixed on me as a husband for her daughter Sarah. Her family represented to her the impossibility of carrying out this plan; first, my father's pride and the demands which he would therefore make and which she could never satisfy; then my fame, which had already excited the attention of the most prominent and wealthy people of the town; and finally, the moderate character of her own fortune, which was far from sufficient to carry out such a proposal. All these representations, however, were of no avail with her. She had once for all taken it into her head to have me for a son-in-law, cost her what it might; and, she thought, the devil would needs be in it, if she could not get the young man.

She sent a proposal to my father, let him have no rest the whole time he was in the town, discussed the matter with him herself on various occasions, and promised to satisfy all his demands. My father, however, sought to gain time for deliberation, and to put off the decision for a while. But the time came when we were to return home. My father went with me to the widow's house, which was the last on our road, in order to wait for a conveyance which started from that place. Madam Rissia made use of the opportunity, began to caress me, introduced my bride, and asked me how I was pleased with her. At last she pressed for a decisive answer from my father. He was still holding back, however, and sought in every possible way to represent the difficulties connected with the subject.

While they were thus treating with one another, suddenly there burst into the room the chief rabbi, the preacher, and the elders of the place, with many of the most respectable people. This sudden appearance was brought about without any magic in the following way. These gentlemen had been invited to a circumcision at the house of a prominent man in this very suburb. Madam Rissia, who knew this very well, sent her son at once to the house with an invitation to the whole company to come, immediately after rising from table, to a betrothal at her house. They came therefore half tipsy, and as they believed nothing was wanting but to write out and subscribe the contract, they sat down to table, set my father in the midst, and the chief rabbi began to dictate the contract to the scribe of the community.

My father assured them that on the main point nothing had yet been decided, and that still less had the preliminary articles been settled. The chief rabbi fell into a passion at this, for he supposed that it was only a quibble, and that his sacred person and the whole honorable company were being made sport of. He turned therefore to the company, and said with a haughty air, "Who is this Rabbi Joshua, who makes himself of so much consequence?" My father replied, "The Rabbi is here super- fluous. I am, 'tis true, a common man; but I believe no man can dispute my right to care for the welfare of my son, and to place his future happiness on a firm footing."

The chief rabbi was greatly offended with the ambiguity of the expression, "The Rabbi is here superfluous." He saw clearly that he had no right to lay down the law to my father in the matter, and that it was rash of Madam Rissia to invite a company to a betrothal before the parties were agreed on the preliminary articles. He began therefore to strike a lower tone. He represented to my father the advantages of this match, the high ancestry of the bride (her grandfather, father, and uncle having been learned men and chief rabbis), her personal attractions, and the willingness and ability of Madam Rissia to satisfy all his demands.

My father, who in fact had nothing to say against all this, was com- pelled to yield. The marriage contract was made out, and in it Madam Rissia made over to her daughter her public-house with all its belong- ings as a bridal portion, and came under an obligation also to board and clothe the newly-married couple for six years. Besides I received as a present a complete edition of the Talmud with its commentaries, together worth two or three hundred thalers, and a number of other gifts. My father came under no obligation at all, and in addition received fifty thalers in cash. Very wisely he had refused to accept a note for this sum; it had to be paid to him before the betrothal.

After all this had been arranged, there was a capital entertainment, and the brandy bottle was vigorously plied. The very next day my father and I went home. My mother-in-law promised to send after us as soon as possible the so-called little presents and the articles of clothing for me, which in the haste she had not been able to get ready. Many weeks, however, passed without our hearing or seeing anything of these. My father was perplexed about this; and as the character of my mother-in-law had long been suspicious to him, he could think nothing else than that this intriguing woman was seeking some subterfuge to escape from her burdensome contract. He resolved therefore to repay like with like.

The following circumstances strengthened him in this resolve. A rich arendator who used to bring spirits to Nesvij for sale, and to lodge in our house on his journey through Mohilna, likewise cast his eye upon me. He had an only daughter, for whom he had decided on me as a husband. He knew, however, what difficulties he would have to overcome, if he were to treat of the subject directly with my father. He chose, therefore, an indirect way. His plan was to make my father his debtor; and as his critical circumstances would make it impossible for him to clear off the debt, he expected to force him, as it were, to consent to this union with the view of wiping out the debt by means of the amount stipulated for the son. He offered my father some barrels of spirits on credit, and the offer was accepted with delight.

As the date of payment approached, Hersch Dukor (this was the name of the arendator) came and reminded my father. The latter assured him that at the moment he was not in a position to clear off the debt, and begged him to have patience with him for some time yet. "Herr Joshua," said the arendator, "I will speak with you quite frankly on this matter. Your circumstances are growing daily worse; and if no fortunate accident occurs, I do not see any possibility of your being able to clear off your debt. The best thing for us both, therefore, is this. You have a son, and I have a daughter who is the sole heiress of all my property. Let us enter into an alliance. By this means not only will your debt be wiped out, but a sum to be fixed by yourself will be paid in addition, and I shall exert myself to improve your circumstances."

No one could be more joyous over this proposal than my father. Immediately a contract was closed, in which the bride's dowry, as well as the required presents, was decided in accordance with my father's suggestion. The bill for the debt, which amounted to fifty thalers in Polish money, was returned to my father, and torn on the spot, while fifty thalers in addition were paid to him.

Thereupon my new father-in-law went on to Nesvij to collect some debts there. Unfortunately he had to lodge at my former mother-in-law's. She, being a great prattler, told him of her own accord about the good match which her daughter had made. "The father of the bridegroom," said she, "is himself a great scholar, and the bridegroom is a young man of eleven years, who has scarcely his equal."

"I also," replied the arendator, "have, thank God, made a good choice for my daughter. You have perhaps heard of the celebrated scholar, Rabbi Joshua, in Mohilna, and of his young son, Solomon. He is my daughter's bridegroom."

Scarcely had these words been spoken, when she cried out, "That is a confounded lie. Solomon is my daughter's bridegroom; and here, sir, is the marriage contract."

The arendator then showed her his contract too; and they fell into a dispute, the result of which was that Madam Rissia had my father summoned before the court to give a categorical explanation. My father, however, did not put in an appearance, although she had him summoned twice.

Meanwhile my mother died, and was brought to Nesvij for burial. My mother-in-law obtained from the court an attachment on the dead body, by which its interment was interdicted till the termination of the suit. My father, therefore, saw himself compelled to appear in court; my mother-in-law endeavored to satisfy all his demands in accordance with her promise, clothed me from head to toe, and even paid my father for my board from the date of the betrothal to the marriage. My mother also was now buried, and we returned home again.

My second father-in-law came too, and called upon my father for the ratification of his contract. He, however, pointed out that it was null and void, as it contravened a previous contract, and had been made by him merely in the supposition that my mother-in-law had no intention of fulfilling hers. The arendator seemed to give an ear to these representations and reconcile himself to his loss; but in reality he was thinking of some means to get me into his hands. Accordingly he rose by night, yoked his horses, took me in silence from the table on which I was sleeping, packed me with all despatch into his carriage, and made off with his booty out of the gate. But as this could not be accomplished without some noise, the people in the house awoke, discovered the theft, pursued the kidnaper, and snatched me out of his hand. To me the whole incident appeared at the time like a dream.

In this way my father was released from his debt, and got fifty thalers besides as a gratuity; but I was immediately afterwards carried off by my legal mother-in-law, and made the husband of my legal bride. I must, of course, confess that this transaction of my father's cannot be justified from a moral viewpoint. Only his great need at the time can in some measure serve as an excuse.

On the first evening of my marriage my father was not present. As he told me at my departure that he had still to settle some articles on my account, and therefore I was to wait for his arrival, I refused, in spite of all the efforts that were made, to appear that evening. Nevertheless the marriage festivities went on. We waited the next day for my father, but still he did not come. They then threatened to bring a party of soldiers to drag me to the marriage ceremony; but I gave them for an answer that, if this were done, it would help them little, for the ceremony would not be lawful except as a voluntary act. At last, to the joy of all interested, my father arrived towards evening, the articles referred to were amended, and the marriage ceremony was performed.

Here I must mention a little anecdote. I had read in a Hebrew book of an approved plan for a husband to secure lordship over his better half for life. He was to tread on her foot at the marriage ceremony; and if both hit on the stratagem, the first to succeed would retain the upper hand. Accordingly, when my bride and I were placed side by side at the ceremony, this trick occurred to me, and I said to myself, "Now you must not let the opportunity pass of securing for your whole lifetime lordship over your wife." I was just going to tread on her foot, but a certain *Je ne sais quoi,* whether fear, shame, or love, held me back. While I was in this irresolute state, all at once I felt the slipper of my wife on my foot with such an impression that I should almost have screamed aloud if I had not been checked by shame. I took this for a bad omen and thought to myself, "Providence has destined you to be the slave of your wife; you must not try to slip out of her fetters." From my faint-heartedness and the heroic mettle of my wife, the reader may easily conceive why this prophecy had to be actually realized.

I stood, however, not only under the slipper of my wife, but—what was very much worse—under the lash of my mother-in-law. Nothing of all that she had promised was fulfilled. Her house, which she had settled on her daughter as a dowry, was burdened with debt. Of the six years' board which she had promised me I enjoyed scarcely half a year's, and this amid constant brawls and squabbles. She even, trusting to my youth and want of spirit, ventured now and then to lay hands on me, but this I repaid not infrequently with compound interest. Scarcely a meal passed during which we did not fling at each other's heads bowls, plates, spoons, and similar articles.

Once I came home from the academy quite famished. As my mother-in-law and wife were occupied with the business of the public house, I went myself into the room where the milk was kept; and as I found a dish of curds and cream, I fell upon it, and began to eat. My mother-in-law came as I was thus occupied, and screamed in rage, "You are not going to devour the milk with the cream!" The more cream the better, thought I, and went on eating, without disturbing myself by her cry. She wrested the dish forcibly from my hands, beat me with her fists, and let me feel all her ill will. Exasperated by such treatment, I pushed her from me, seized the dish, and smashed it on her head. That was a sight! The curds ran down all over her. She seized in rage a piece of wood, and if I had not cleared out in all haste, she would certainly have beat me to death.

Scenes like this occurred very often. At such skirmishes of course my wife had to remain neutral, and whichever party gained the upper hand, it came home to her very closely. "Oh!" she often complained, "if only the one or the other of you had a little more patience!"

Tired of ceaseless open war, I once hit upon a stratagem which had a good effect for a short time at least. I rose about midnight, took a large vessel of earthenware, crept with it under my mother-in-law's bed, and began to speak aloud into the vessel after the following fashion— "O Rissia, Rissia, you ungodly woman, why do you treat my beloved son so ill? If you do not mend your ways, your end is near, and you will be damned to all eternity." Then I crept out again, and began to pinch her cruelly, and after a while I slipped silently back into bed.

The following morning she got up in consternation and told my wife that my mother had appeared to her in a dream and had threatened and pinched her on my account. In confirmation she showed the blue marks on her arm. When I came from the synagogue, I did not find my mother-in-law at home but found my wife in tears. I asked the reason, but she would tell me nothing. My mother-in-law returned with dejected look, and eyes red with weeping. She had gone, as I afterwards learned, to the Jewish place of burial, thrown herself on my mother's grave, and begged for forgiveness of her fault. She then had the burial place measured, and ordered a wax-light as long as its circumference, for burning in the synagogue. She also fasted the whole day, and towards me showed herself extremely amiable.

I knew of course what was the cause of all this, but acted as if I did not observe it, and rejoiced in secret over the success of my stratagem. In this manner I had peace for some time, but unfortunately it did not last long. The whole was soon forgotten again, and on the slightest occasion the dance went on as before. In short, I was soon afterwards obliged to leave the house altogether and accept a position as a private tutor. Only on the great feast days I used to come home.

In my fourteenth year I had my eldest son, David. At my marriage I was only eleven years old, and owing to the retired life common among our people in those regions, as well as the want of mutual intercourse between the two sexes, I had no idea of the essential duties of marriage, but looked on a pretty girl as on any other work of nature or art, somewhat as on the pretty medicine box that I stole. It was therefore natural that for a considerable time after marriage I could not have any thought about the fulfillment of its duties. I used to approach my wife with trembling as a mysterious object. It was therefore supposed that I had been bewitched at the time of the wedding; and under this supposition I was brought to a witch to be cured. She performed all sorts of operations, which of course had a good effect, although indirectly through the help of the imagination.

My life in Poland from my marriage to my emigration, which period embraces the springtime of my existence, was a series of miseries with a want of all means for the promotion of culture; and, necessarily connected with that, an aimless application of my powers, in the description of which the pen drops from my hands, and the painful memories of which I try to stifle.

Once Prince Radzivil, one of the greatest Polish magnates, sent for a respectable Jewish barber, who, suspecting nothing but that he was wanted for some surgical operation, brought his instruments with him and appeared before the Prince.

"Have you brought your instruments with you?" he was asked.

"Yes, Serene Highness," he replied.

"Then," said the Prince, "give me a lancet, and I will open one of your veins."

The poor barber had to submit. The Prince seized the lancet; and as he did not know how to go about the operation, and besides his hand trembled as a result of his hard drinking, of course he wounded the barber in a pitiable manner. But his courtiers smiled their applause, and praised his great skill in surgery.

He went one day into a church, and being so drunk that he did not know where he was, he stood against the altar and acted like a beast. All who were present became horrified. Next morning when he was sober, the clergy brought to his mind the misdeed he had committed the day before. "Eh!" said the Prince, "we will soon make that good." Thereupon he issued a command to the Jews of the place, to provide at their own expense fifty stone of wax for burning in the church. The poor Jews were therefore obliged to bring a sin offering for the desecration of a Christian Church by an orthodox Catholic Christian.

He once took it into his head to drive on the wall round the town. But as the wall was too narrow for a coach with six horses—and he never drove in any other—his hussars were obliged, with much labor and peril of their lives, to carry the coach with their hands till he had driven round the town in this way.

Once he drove with the whole pomp of his court to a synagogue and, without any one to this day knowing the reason, committed the greatest havoc: he smashed windows and stoves, broke all the vessels, threw on the ground the copies of the Holy Scriptures kept in the ark, and so forth. A learned, pious Jew, who was present, ventured to lift one of these copies from the ground, and had the honor of being struck with a musket-ball by His Serene Highness' own hand. From here the train went to a second synagogue, where the same performance was repeated, and from there they proceeded to the Jewish burial place, where the buildings were demolished and the monuments cast into the fire.

Can it be conceived that a Prince could show himself so malicious towards his own poor subjects, whom he was in a position to punish legally whenever they really did anything wrong? Yet this is what happened here.

On one occasion he took it into his head to make a trip to Mohilna, a hamlet belonging to him, which lay four short miles from his palace. This had to be done with his usual suite and all the pomp of his court. On the morning of the appointed day the train went forth. First marched the army in order according to its usual regimental divisions—infantry, artillery, cavalry, and so on. Then followed his bodyguard, Strelitzi, consisting of volunteers from the poor nobility. After them came his kitchen-wagons, in which Hungarian wine had not been forgotten. These were followed by the music of his janissaries, and other bands. Then came his coach, and last of all his satraps. I give them this name, because I can compare this train with no other than that of Darius in the war against Alexander. Towards evening His Serene Highness arrived at our public house in the suburb of the town which was His Serene Highness' residence, Nesvij. I cannot say that he arrived in his own high person, for the Hungarian wine had robbed him of all consciousness, in which alone, of course, personality rests. He was carried into the house and thrown with all his clothes, booted and spurred, on to my mother-in-law's dirty bed, without giving it a supply of clean linen.

As usual, I had taken to flight. My amazons, however, I mean my mother-in-law and my wife, trusted to their heroic mettle and remained at home alone. Riot went on the whole night. In the very room where His Serene Highness slept, wood was chopped, cooking and baking were done. It was well known that when His Serene Highness slept, nothing could waken his high person except perhaps the trumpets of the Judgment Day. The next morning, when he wakened and looked around, he scarcely knew whether to trust his eyes when he found himself in a wretched public house, thrown on to a dirty bed swarming with bugs. His valets, pages, and Negroes waited on his commands. He asked how he had come there and was answered that His Serene Highness had yesterday commenced a journey to Mohilna, but had halted here to take rest, that his whole train had meanwhile gone on, and had undoubtedly arrived in Mohilna by this time.

The journey to Mohilna was for the present given up, and the whole train ordered back. They returned accordingly to the Palace in the usual order and pomp. But the Prince was pleased to hold a great banquet in our public house. All the foreign gentlemen who happened to be in the palace at the time were invited. The service used on the occasion was of gold, and it is impossible adequately to realize the contrast which reigned here in one house, between Asiatic splendor and Lappish poverty. In a miserable public house, whose walls were black as coal with smoke and soot, whose rafters were supported by undressed round stems of trees, whose windows consisted of some fragments of broken panes of bad glass and small strips of pine covered with paper,—in this house sat princes on dirty benches at a still dirtier table and had the choicest dishes and the finest wines served to them on gold plate.

Before the banquet the Prince took a stroll with the other gentlemen in front of the house and by chance observed my wife. She was then in the bloom of her youth; and although I am now separated from her, still I must do her the justice to allow that—leaving, of course, out of account all that taste and art contribute to the heightening of a person's charms, inasmuch as these had had no influence on her—she was a beauty of the first rank. It was therefore natural that she should please the Prince. He turned to his companions and said, "Really a pretty young woman! Only she ought to get a white chemise." This was a common signal with him and meant as much as the throwing of a handkerchief by the Grand Sultan. When these gentlemen heard it, they became solicitous for the honor of my wife and gave her a hint to clear out as fast as possible. She took the hint, slipped silently out, and was soon over the hills and far away.

After the banquet His Serene Highness proceeded again with the other gentlemen into town amid trumpets, kettledrums, and the music of his janissaries. Then the usual order of the day was followed; that is, a carousal was carried on the whole afternoon and evening, and then the party went to a pleasure house at the entrance to the Prince's zoological garden, where fireworks were set off at great expense, but usually with accidents. As every goblet was drained, cannons were fired; but the poor cannoneers, who knew better how to handle the plough than the cannon, were not seldom injured. "Vivat Kschondsie Radzivil," that is, "Long live Prince Radzivil," shouted the guests. The palm in this bacchanalian sport was of course awarded to the Prince; and those who awarded it were loaded by him with presents, not in perishable corn or golden snuffboxes or anything of that sort, but in real estate with many hundred peasants. At the close a concert was given, during which His Serene Highness fell gently asleep and was carried to the castle.

The expenses of such extravagance were of course extorted from the poor tenantry. If this was not sufficient, debts were contracted and estates sold to wipe them out. Not even the twelve golden statues in life-size—whether they represented the twelve apostles or the twelve giants, I do not know—nor the golden table which had been made for himself, were spared on such emergencies. And thus the noble estates of this great prince were diminished, his treasures which had accumulated during many generations were exhausted, and his tenants . . . But I must break off.

The Prince died not long ago without heirs. His brother's sons inherited the estates.

The place where I first occupied the position of family tutor was at the distance of a league from my residence. The family was that of a miserable farmer in a still more miserable village, and my salary was five thalers in Polish money. The poverty, ignorance, and rudeness in the manner of life which prevailed in this house were indescribable. The farmer himself was a man of about fifty years, the whole of whose face was overgrown with hair, ending in a dirty, thick beard as black as pitch. His language was a sort of muttering, intelligible only to the boors with whom he held intercourse daily. Not only was he ignorant of Hebrew, but he could not speak of a word of Yiddish; his only language was Russian, the common patois of the peasantry. His wife and children were of the same stamp. Moreover, the apartment in which they lived was a hovel of smoke, black as coal inside and out, without a chimney, but with merely a small opening in the roof for the exit of the smoke, an opening which was carefully closed as soon as the fire was allowed to go out, so that the heat might not escape.

The windows were narrow strips of pine laid crosswise over each other, and covered with paper. This apartment served at once for sitting, drinking, eating, study, and sleep. Think of this room intensely heated, and the smoke, as is generally the case in winter, driven back by wind and rain till the whole place is filled with it to suffocation. Here hung a foul washing and other dirty bits of clothing on poles laid across the room in order to kill the vermin with the smoke. There hang sausages to dry, while their fat keeps constantly trickling down on the heads of people below. Yonder stand tubs with sour cabbage and red beets, which form the principal food of the Lithuanians. In a corner the water is kept for daily use, with the dirty water alongside. In the room the bread is kneaded, cooking and baking are done, the cow is milked, and all sorts of operations are carried on.

In this magnificent dwelling the peasants sit on the bare ground: you dare not sit higher if you do not wish to be suffocated with the smoke. Here they guzzle their whisky and make an uproar, while the people of the house sit in a corner. I usually took my place behind the stove with my dirty halfnaked pupils, and expounded to them out of an old tattered Bible from Hebrew into Russian Yiddish. All this together made such a splendid group as deserved to be sketched only by a Hogarth, and to be sung only by a Butler.

It may be easily imagined how pitiable my condition must have been. Whisky had to form my sole comfort; it made me forget all my misery. This was increased by the fact that a regiment of Russians, who were rioting at that time with every conceivable cruelty on the estates of Prince Radzivil, was stationed in the village and its neighborhood. The house was constantly full of drunken Russians, who committed all sorts of excesses, hewed to pieces tables and benches, threw glasses and bottles into the faces of the people of the house, and so on. To give merely one example, a Russian, who was stationed in this house as guard, and whose charge it was to secure the house against all violence, came home once drunk, and demanded something to eat. A dish of millet with butter was placed before him cooked. He shoved the dish away, and shouted an order for more butter. A whole small tub of butter was brought, when he shouted again an order for another dish. This was brought immediately, whereupon he threw all the butter into it, and called for spirits. A whole bottle was brought, and he poured it likewise into the dish. Thereafter milk, pepper, salt, and tobacco, in large quantities had to be brought to him, the whole being put in, and the mixture devoured. After he had taken some spoonfuls, he began to strike about him, pulled the host by the beard, struck him in the face with his fist, so that the blood flowed out of his mouth, poured some of his glorious broth down his throat, and went on in this riotous manner till he became so drunk that he could no longer support himself and fell to the ground.

Such scenes were at that time very common everywhere in Poland. If a Russian army passed a place, they took with them a *prowodnik,* or guide, to the next place. But instead of seeking to be supplied by the mayor or the village magistrate, they used to seize the first person whom they met on the road. He might be young or old, male or female, healthy or sick; it mattered nothing to them; for they knew the road well enough from special charts, and only sought an opportunity for outrage. If it happened that the person seized did not know the way at all, and did not show them the right road, they did not allow themselves to be sent astray on this account; they selected the road all right, but they cudgeled the poor *prowodnik* till he was half-dead, for not knowing the way!

I was once seized as a *prowodnik* myself. I did not indeed know the way, but luckily I hit upon it by chance. Fortunately, therefore, I reached the proper place, and the only violence I suffered, besides a good many blows and kicks from the Russian soldiers, was the threat that, if I ever led them astray, I should certainly be flayed alive—a threat which they might be trusted with carrying into execution.

The other places which I filled as tutor were more or less similar to this. An incident of psychological interest, which happened to another person and of which I was simply eyewitness, must be mentioned here.

A tutor in the next village, who was a somnambulist, rose one night from his bed and went to the village churchyard with a volume of the Jewish ceremonial laws in his hand. After remaining some time there he returned to his bed. In the morning he rose up, without remembering the least of what had happened during the night, and went to the chest where his copy of the ceremonial laws was usually kept, in order to take out the first part, *Orach Hayyim* or the *Way of Life,* which he was accustomed to read every morning. The code consists of four parts, each of which was bound separately, and all the four had certainly been locked up in the chest. He was therefore astonished to find only three of the parts, *Yoreh Deah* or the *Teacher of Wisdom,* being wanting. As he knew about his sleepwalking, he searched everywhere, till at last he came to the churchyard, where he found the *Yoreh Deah* lying open at the chapter, *Hilkhoth Abheloth* or the *Laws of Mourning.* He took this for a bad omen and came home much disquieted. On being asked the cause of his disquietude, he related the incident which had occurred, finishing with the remark, "Ah! God knows how my poor mother is!" He begged of his master the loan of a horse and permission to ride to the nearest town, where his mother lived, in order to inquire after her welfare. As he had to pass the place where I was tutor, and I saw him riding in great excitement without being willing to dismount even for a little while, I asked him the cause of his excitement. He related to me the above-mentioned incident.

I was astonished, not so much about the particular circumstances of this incident as about somnambulism in general, of which till then I had known nothing. My friend, on the other hand, assured me that somnambulism was a common occurrence with him, and that it meant nothing, but that the circumstance of the *Hilkhoth Abheloth* made him forebode some misfortune. Thereupon he rode off, arrived at his mother's house, and found her seated at her frame for needlework. She asked him the reason for his coming, when he replied that he had come merely to pay her a visit, as he had not seen her for a long time. After he had rested for a good while, he rode back; but his disquietude was by no means wholly removed, and the thought of the *Hilkhoth Abheloth* he could not get out of his head. The third day after, a fire broke out in the town where his mother lived, and the poor woman perished in the flames. Scarcely had the son heard of the conflagration, when he began to lament that his mother had so miserably perished. He rode off in all haste to the town, and found what he had foreboded.

WEDDED TO THE MUSE

MENDELE MOCHER SEFORIM (1836-1917)

Writing under the pseudonym Mendele the Bookseller, Sholom
Jacob Abramowitz was pre-eminent in Yiddish and Hebrew Letters
of the nineteenth century. Mendele was a born writer with a gift
for easy flowing narrative and an imaginative grasp of plot and incident. He loved life and nature, but hated the social system which
degraded his people. His novels depict with warm sympathy and a
strong dash of satire the butcher, the baker and the candlestick
maker of the ghetto and pale of Tzarist Russia; with due reservation
he may be considered the Dickens of the nineteenth century Jewish
literature. He also wrote a library of books designed to enlighten and
enhearten the oppressed masses. This account of how he wedded the
Muse reveals as much of his character as of his personal history.

❀ ❀ ❀

M Y birthplace was Kapuli, a tiny country town in the Sutsk
District of the Minsk Governmental region, which God had
forgotten to supply with property and wealth and to which He
has distributed neither commerce nor trade; instead He had given it the
glories of Nature, magnificent forests and the splendor of Life, with
valleys and delightful fields all around. The day of my birth was not
recorded in any document, for in former times that was something which
our people did not bother about, particularly the small townsfolk. But
I was told that I was born in 1836, and my family fixed my birthday
as December 20th. Hayyim Moses, my father of blessed memory, was
held in high respect in our town and the neighborhood, on account of
his extensive scholarship, his large-heartedness, and his knowledge of the
way of the world. Half of his life was devoted to the Lord, that is, to
study by himself and with others gratuitously; and half to himself,
to his own requirements and those of the community to which he devoted
himself. The Lord had given my father a good tongue with which he

would at times deliver sermons, and he had a good and fluent style in our holy language. His sermons and letters are still preserved among the few people left who honored and esteemed him. He was particularly fond of me, choosing me of all his children in order to educate me in a fashion which was then entirely new to our parts. When I was six years old and already knew how to read, he engaged an excellent teacher to teach me Scripture and make me familiar with both Holy Writ and its Aramaic renderings, the Targumim. This teacher, Joseph Hareubenei (further details of whom can be found in Binstock's biography of me) used to engage in his duties faithfully for about twelve hours a day; so that within three years I knew the entire twenty-four books of the Bible by heart and had the Lord's Torah within my very bowels.

While I still delighted in the sweet words of those who saw God and my soul itself visioned forth the Almighty, my teacher led me to the marches of the Talmud, that primeval giant and veritable Og, King of Bashan, among all the literatures of the world. When I came there I was like a person arriving for the first time at a great fair and market, astonished and wondering at the sight of so many kinds of goods and wares and all the many strange and desirable things, and half-dazed at hearing the tumult and noise and shouting from every corner and quarter. There they are, buyers and sellers, agents and merchants, hasting about with much hullabaloo, possessed with the desire of and longing for trafficking, dashing urgent and breathless, one with his pitcher and the other with his barrel, each man thrusting his brother out of the way, these asking questions of those and those shouting answers to these, winking and blinking their eyes, shuffling their feet, chaffering and conferring, weighing and measuring, to the sound of a mighty noise in the camp. By virtue of the power of visualization that is implanted within me I gave shape to all things and form to all that entered the gate of this Talmud. The "former Tannaite" who appeared and reappeared in the arguments, and "the one who said so-and-so", seemed to me a mighty man, meticulous, pernickety and swift to anger, with flaming face; the first, close and middle of the discussion were women all jealous of one another, each pounding at the other, one declaring this and that and the other dissenting, nay indeed, spitefully arguing, with nothing easygoing between them. Then there were the nubile female, the barren woman and the maiden who had been seduced; the deaf and dumb, the idiot and the miner; the man or woman with an issue; the two holding the shawl; the ox that gored the cow; the vicious and the innocent ox; all of these stood as clear as though they were alive in my imagination, each one in its special form and its own strange shape. To be sure, I knew the language of all of these as soon as I met them, for from my childhood I had been familiar with the Aramaic of the Targumim; but much of their actual conversation was beyond me. All this, however, was the case only at the beginning, when first I entered the gate of the Talmud. In the course of time I grew accustomed to it and loved it at heart. I would lodge in the deeps of the Law with the flocks of my comrades, seeing signs and wonders in castles that flew in the air and mountains hanging by a hair, and wonders even greater than these in the field of Sharp and Peppery Debate. I loved to stroll at my ease in the wondrous orchard of the Agada. That orchard is no carefully designed garden with fence and gates and trees set out in orderly rows each according to its own kind, matching one another, growing absolutely level, nature being bound with the bands of a cunning artificer; no, it is like the boundless and endless wildwood, unfenced and unordered, with its plants all one great medley. Flowers innumerable you will find there, all kinds of strange plants growing in profusion like the wild flowers of the field. Yet the lily is the Lily of Sharon, the rose is the rose of the valleys set about with greenery and grass and herbage of all kinds in thousands and myriads. There is a wealth of color before you, a tapestry lovely to see. Imagination wanders free and far in such a garden, and achieves great things. Sometimes it even reaches to the skies and brings down the mighty chariot of God; and sometimes it raises the earth to the heavens, so that angels and mortals do kiss.

At the age of eleven I left my teacher's class. And at the time the following was my manner of study: following the morning prayers my father and teacher taught me a passage of the Mishna at the House of Study, and for the rest of the day I sat there and studied my own. When I returned home in the evening and my father was disengaged from most of his activities he would explain and clarify for me a leaf of Gemara with all the commentaries. If he had many other matters engaging him in the evenings he would rise before dawn, awaken me from my sleep, and we would go off together to our House of Study to engage in the study of Torah there. Truth to tell, it was very hard for a little boy who wanted to go on sleeping, particularly in winter; but once I was actually up and doing and went off to my day's work, I was pleased at heart; while as for my remuneration, the compensations of getting up and studying before dawn were plentiful indeed. There was an absolute silence in all the streets of the town, which was still sunk deep in slumber; and the moon and stars in their set places in the sky wakened

my imagination and I listened, listening hard. Then in vision I could see
the Man Gabriel crowing like a cock and announcing the hours of night
in the highest heavens. Hosts of angels would speedily follow, and open
their mouths in pleasant song. In yet a little while the gates of Paradise
will swing noisily open for the God of Glory to enter. When the sons
of God see the coming of my God and King in all holiness, they are
silent and stand trembling each in his troop and each beside his banner,
never a wing quivering, not one opening his mouth to whisper. And then
suddenly the Lord thunders with a mighty thundering, and the Most
High bursts forth in bitter weeping. It is for His desolate Temple that
He weeps by night, for Jerusalem the forsaken that was once the city
of His glory; for His people, the beloved sons of Zion, wandering wide
amid the gentiles and for the humiliated Shehinah, that Divine Presence
which goes wandering with them in their exile, and which suffers in
their sufferings. His eyes, His eyes do weep—and that is the dew on the
ground and the drops of night upon my curls. . . . And at the voice
of God the saints of the world do quiver, and bitterly they weep with
the angels of peace. And with all these imaginings within me I rouse
myself to study with all my heart and soul. Sweetly I chant as I study,
moving my argumentative thumb. My soul desired for the Lord's Torah
knowledge of all the suggestive hints of the Talmud, that furrowed
my forehead and took all my attention.

This method of study had a double effect on me; on the one hand
it sharpened my intelligence with regard to analysis and acute hypotheses
and gave my scholarship a fine edge, so that I examined and tested
everything in order to arrive at the plain truth; and on the other hand
it awakened my emotions and my imagination with very exalted vision,
preparing me for the influence of fine writing and its holy spirit. In
those days I knew nothing save the four ells of Law, nothing apart
from the Talmud. I had neither seen nor heard of profane books, and
as yet knew nothing about literature, theatre or any artistic activity, for
my birthplace was a lonely nest in a forgotten corner where no strange
feet passed. And in my innocence, like a chick within its egg, I thought
that I saw the whole world before my eyes, and that beyond Kapuli's
horizon lay nothing but a desolate wilderness, the place of the "Mountains
of Darkness" and Sambatyon River, with all kinds of strange and weird
creatures. The earthen houses of my town seemed like beautiful palaces
to me, while the synagogue and the close did not have their like upon
earth, seeing that here Wisdom had builded her house and the townsfolk were the choicest and wisest of mortal kind; particularly those with

long beards and fine appearance. For in those days it was my belief that where there was age there was Torah and wisdom. If anybody was blessed by the Lord with a cow or a goat he seemed to me as wealthy as Korah had been in his own times, and blest with a fat portion here upon earth. The trumpet, even the hurdy-gurdy which found its way to us in some mysterious fashion, and the simple musical instruments heard at local weddings, made up the totality of orchestras and there were none besides them. And happy the trumpeter who could win people's heart and soul by the blast of his trumpet.

I knew the Scriptures, but had not yet attempted to write myself. But when the spirit of the Lord began to move within me I did not pour it forth in verse and fine writing, but stayed solitary and silent, the waves of my emotions coursing and racing; while my soul wept in secret at my heart's belief that this must be the work of Satan, that my evil inclination was moving me to waste my time with evil thoughts and diverting me from the study of Torah; and in order to save myself from this I found no method better than prayer and entreaty to the God of the winds and spirits. There were days when I would suddenly awaken with a sense of energy, telling myself, "Let my soul bless the Lord." And I would promptly be praying. To such prayers I gave up my spirit, and they brought me the pleasures and delights of Eden; and I was satisfied. Then afterwards, if that abominable one came my way I dragged him to forests, to hills and mountains afar, where I spent my time thinking and gazing at the plenitude and magnificence of Nature which, in the course of time, put heart into me with her radiance and glory. I was drawn to her by the cables of love and delighted in her as the bridegroom finds joy in his bride. Day by day I went out to the fields to visit my beloved and take my delight in this most gracious and charming of all that exists. I sought my love in the deeps of the forests and in the shady groves, in green pastures and beside the still waters; and she let all her goodness pass before me, playing before me everywhere. I pursued her leaping upon the hills, clinging to the trees and seated among the sheepfields listening to the bleating of the flocks. The nightingale sang me its songs and the voice of the turtledove was heard in the choir of the winged singers. All of them sang me their best, love songs to my divine beauty, daughter of God who fashions all things. And the love which was then like a bursting flame in my heart was a love of the spirit, not of the flesh, a holy love which bears no corporeal form, a secret hidden love of all that is good, beautiful and exalted, that makes a man rejoice while garbing him in humility and training him to be upright and faithful, loving all creatures and raising him above all happenings. The secret of this love and this outpouring of the soul in prayer and entreaty is known to all poets and men of spirit. They are the musical notes of the Almighty, the signs which the God of Song has set in the heart of his chosen ones. . . .

I remained quietly in my nest thus until I was thirteen years old, thinking that I would stay in my birthplace until the end of my days. But things did not come about as I imagined them. My father suddenly died at the age of forty-one, leaving his wife and children destitute. On account of my poverty I was exiled from my birthplace and went wandering to the Yeshiboth (Rabbinical Colleges) of the towns of Lithuania, near and far. I shall not relate here all that happened to me there, for the happenings were very numerous and I propose to devote a special book to them as a memorial to the Children of Israel regarding the Yeshiboth in those days. Here I merely wish to say that I lived according to the way of the Torah, the suffering life of a disciple of the wise with the "eating days" (eating each day's meals with a different kindhearted householder if the student was lucky, and going without food if he was unlucky) down to the last detail. At the Slutsk Yeshiba I studied with the renowned Rabbi Abraham Baruch in the first class, from which I passed up to the top class and became one of the pupils of the Head of the Yeshiba, the keen and tried Rabbi Michel Mass. Afterwards I fixed my place of study in the House of Study of the wealthy Reb Yonah, and sought Torah from the great Rabbi Abremele. In Vilna I studied with the far-famed Rabbi Reb Senderel at the Rum Mealeh (Lofty Height) Yeshiba and also in the House of Study of the Vilna Gaon Rabbi Elijah of blessed memory. There I meditated on the Lord's Torah by day and night, studying at my post all night long. I came to Vilna at the advice of my kinsman the honored and wealthy Nahum Hayyim Broida, who promised to be a father to me and supply all my requirements. My stay there did not last long, however, and I returned to my birthplace.

At about that time my mother married a man who held the lease of a mill at Melniki about ten miles away from Kapulie; and my mother went to his home together with her smaller children, leaving me forsaken in the town without any support. Suffering at heart and abased in spirit I felt sick of life. For I was a boy, my experience of life very brief and my troubles very great indeed. While I was in this gloomy state my stepfather summoned me to him; and in order not to eat the bread of idleness I taught his children for a few hours a day. My stepfather's house was surrounded by forests, vast ancient woods inhabited by all the forest animals; at night the wolves would howl there for their food and from time to time bears would make their home there. Within its deeps the birds would nest, and give voice from its boughs. The wild goose and every kind of waterfowl were to be found there, sounding their cries from the marshes and swamps. And a great river curled and twined its way between the trees all the way down to the mill, where it dashed down a slope and in so doing thunderously turned the clattering wheels; and the noise of the mill and the crashing of the waters together made one's ears ring.

It was in this lonely and forsaken dwelling that my muse, my first love, appeared to me again, after having forsaken me while I went from Yeshiba to Yeshiba with the puny students; I had no longer hoped to see her again. She appeared to me in all glory and her gracious lips persuaded me to follow her into the woods; there she made a covenant between me and the trees of the field and the birds of heaven and the creeping things of earth, and taught me to understand their tongue and to consider their manners of living. My soul thirsted for these friends, who told me ancient tales and much that was adoing in their world, and the glory of God who fashioned them and His great goodness toward them. I in turn told them of what was in my heart; for the first time I took pen in hand to pour forth my soul, singing them a new Hallelujah that I had written down. The river clapped its hands in applause and all the trees of the fields responded in chorus.

I still have these first poems with me in manuscript but they will never be published, as they are unripe and taste like crab-apples, but, wonderful to relate, no sooner did I begin to sing and devote the first fruits of my pen to the praises of the Lord, than my Satan arrived; that angel of jest and mockery who now rules over me in the guise of Mendele Mocher Seforim, and he incited me to mock at mankind and twitch aside the mysterious masks they wore. And I wrote a drama in rhymes after the fashion of *Praise to the Upright* of Rabbi Moses Hayyim Luzzatto, though I did not know what a drama was and had never read any books of the kind. This work too was childish and full of innumerable errors. This mocking childish Satan of mine babbled a lot of nonsense and gave birth to its first words without knowledge. And if I sometimes mock at my Satan and laugh at him on account of my youthful effusions, he mocks at me and firmly responds: Haven't you learnt yet that the Ancient of Days has never passed anything absolutely perfect out of His hands, and that all He created in His world calls for shaping and reworking? That is the evolution which is a Law of the world and all that is therein, and which applies here too; as you ought to know.

This period of rest did not last long. It seems that Heaven had decreed ere I left my mother's womb that I must be a writer among my people, a nation impoverished and weak; so the Lord wished me to learn something about the ways of my people and consider their behavior; and therefore He said to my soul, wander O bird through my world, misfortunate amid the misfortunate and Jew among Jews shalt thou be upon earth. So the wind raised me and flung me up and down the ladder of life, up and down, up and down; and the Angel of the Lord thrust me ever on. He lowered me down to those of my brethren dwelt at the lowest of levels, at the very bottom, to live their life of suffering with them and feel all their pains; and of the distresses of their souls I received a double portion. At times he elevated me to the very peak of our life where I came and went among our calm and settled wealthy, who rule the House of Israel, in order that I might know their works and see their sitting and their standing, their walking and their lying down, and their dealings—to see all this without being delighted in their goodness. From the time that God took me out of the house of my step-father a new chapter began in the book of my life; a chapter of wanderings, vicissitudes and countless troubles, followed by other chapters of my life all woven together in a tapestry that covers the whole life of the House of Israel, which will be told in separate stories and will serve as a memorial in the history and literature of our people. And the few of them hinted at in Bienstock's biography of me can be taken from there.

I wish to turn over those pages and disregard the happenings of those years of my life in order to describe how I became a writer in Israel and the aim I set before me, for the sake of which I prepared my heart and pen; also the books and essays I have written.

Hebrew literature was something precious and rare in my youth; there were no books or journals published at regular intervals of days, weeks, months or years as at present, to rouse the sons of Judah and set the love of our holy tongue in their hearts. In the absence of any awakener or competition between writers there were few to write, and the daughters of song were abased. When I was at Kamenetz-Podolsk, at the home of my honored and wealthy father-in-law, and later, after I had divorced my wife and become a teacher at the government school (which the Russian Government introduced here and there for Jews as an experimental measuretrans), I devoted myself to study in order to acquire by dint of toil all the knowledge that I lacked; and if anyone had suggested to me that I would ever become a writer among my people, I would have reckoned that he was joking. In my simplicity I thought writers all belonged to some higher sphere; and who was I to come thither?

Chance alone made an author of me, and it happened all of a sudden. One winter night, a dark, cloudy, misty and stormy night, I sat alone in my room, my soul dripping away veritably in unhappiness. In order to drive this away from me by doing some work, I took pen in hand to write a reply to a certain teacher. And all at once I found I had covered both sides of a large sheet with my ideas on education. Next morning I copied a few remarks from this sheet for my correspondent, throwing the sheet itself aside into a corner as something unimportant. It lay there in its corner for a long time till it fell into other hands, and then shifted from place to place in the house, while I had long forgotten about it.

Then one day the postman brought me a packet from abroad. I opened it in surprise, anxious to know who was writing to me from a foreign country where I had no acquaintance; it was No. 31 of the journal *Ha-Maggid,* first year of issue. The lines of the leading article seemed to contain familiar things; its title was *A Letter on Education* in large square Hebrew characters. I turned over the first page in astonishment, and found my name at the end. Further, a note after the essay praised it highly, and ended with a request to those suitably gifted to translate it into other languages. For several minutes I was astonished and all but stupefied; and the letter of the late A. L. Silbermann, editor of *Ha-Maggid,* written in the highest terms and asking me to continue to write for him and enter into relations with him and his journal, only added to my astonishment and wonder. Naturally I soon found out what had happened; my friend M. Levin, secretary of the noble Ginsburg (Baron Ginsburg) had come across the sheet in question at my house, and had liked it so much that he had secretly sent it to the poet Abraham Ber Gottlober for his opinion on it; and in this way it had reached the editor of *Ha-Maggid* and had seen the light. The hands of those two sages planted this first essay of mine in Hebrew literature in those days; and it had proved the foundation stone of all I have done there since.

I then began to examine the state of Hebrew literature in our country, its habits and customs and what was going on in it. I sought worthwhile things, knowledge and intelligence, good taste and beauty; but very little of all these did I find. At that time the literature was a field that lay waste, a garden forsaken in the winter; there was no yield of plants, there were no sweet blossoms; the leaves had withered and the trees had let their leaves fall; here and there could be seen a straggling aftergrowth, but the state of desolation was the thing most noticeable. And the writers? Those keepers of the vineyard were engaged in their eternal rest, calm, quiet and secure, playing like innocent children and babbling nonsense; in their rest they hallowed one another's names and everybody was satisfied.

Indeed, at that particular time somebody had expressed this thought: "There were many days for the writers of Israel, days of peace and contentedness, days of light and goodness, of ineffectuality on the part of the critics, when man's understanding lay concealed and did not disturb and upset their rest or steal their honor and glory from them. Every book and its sanctity were twin; the name of the writer and of his work were as father and son together." He, however, was referring to the distant past and in his simplicity found all this to be highly satisfactory; whereas I found that his remarks suited our own days and our own contemporary Jewish writers, and was highly dissatisfied. For times when men's understanding remains concealed are not good days of light. And a literature in which the critics are ineffectual and every book and its sanctity are twin, is a park without owners; calves graze there and destroy what is planted; swine chew whatever there is and little foxes damage its rows of plants. And if people come into such a vineyard and destroy as much as they like wantonly and then fill their baskets as well, the feeling is that there is no harm done; for license reigns and anarchy, and ye shall know that ye are in the midst of Israel, there are none to see, there are no witnesses, judge and justice are equally absent except for the Lord your God, and therefore my people need never more be ashamed. . . .

All these things I saw and took to heart, and the fruit of my thoughts was my book: *Mishpat Shalom* (A Peaceful Judgment) printed at Vilna in 1860. This book, which passes strictures on the author of *Minim Veugav* (Musical Instruments and Harp) in particular and aims at a number of other authors as well, was like an arrow suddenly shot into the calm and peaceful camp of the writers, who were resting at their posts. To them I seemed like a cruel, hardhearted man come to disturb their rest, to steal their honor and glory; and there was a great outcry in their congregation. There were quarrels and writers' conflicts in the columns of the journals *Ha-Melitz* and *Ha-Carmel,* which were just beginning to appear at that time. But I went on with the good work and from time to time shot my barbed essays among them, finding many holding with me in my conflict. Whether I judged well or always hit the target is something for others to judge; but I knew that I had caused things to move in our literature. Fresh young critics followed me in judging the works of the writers; many of the latter profited and improved their ways; and the discussion between the writers was a living spirit in the literature, the force of which attracted many new readers.

In my eyes the three aims of the writers ought to be: to teach our people good taste and understanding; to bring the daily life of their world and their actions into the sphere of literature in order to make the public fonder of the latter; to instruct and prove beneficial. I wished with all my heart that our poets and writers should not look up to the lofty heavens, nor take as their themes subjects such as the daughters of Lot or the wife of Potiphar and the like trifles which have long come to an end. It is no use questing after life among the dead. Instead let them walk the earth, watch the life of the people and all that is being done in their homes and communities, and offer it to the eyes of the public. Let them try to improve the taste of the latter by writing in good fashion in accordance with the principles of beauty and logic; further, let them instruct their readers in wisdom and knowledge, so that they may gain understanding.

I then thought things over and said to myself: I examine the ways of our people and wish to provide them with tales from Jewish sources in the holy tongue; yet most of them do not know this language and speak only Jewish-German (Yiddish); and what is the use of all the writer's toil and all his fine ideas if he does not benefit his people? This question, for whom do I toil? would not let me rest and put me into great perplexity. For at that time Yiddish was an empty vessel, containing nothing good but only a lot of nonsense written by stuttering fools, nameless folk; and these things were read by the womenfolk and poor folk without any understanding. As for other people, even if they did not know any other language or literature, they felt ashamed to read such stuff for fear other people got to know about it. If anybody did pick up a Yiddish pamphlet and begin reading it, he would laugh at himself, saying, fancy me casually reading a "woman's book". These silly, lightheaded women, how this makes me laugh! While as for our own writers and stylists who wished to increase the influence and prestige of Hebrew and felt no contact with the ordinary people, they proudly looked down on Yiddish and held it in very low esteem. And if one in a town and two in a country occasionally remembered this accursed one and wrote a few lines, they did so secretly and covered themselves over with their works, so that their immodesty might not be revealed nor their good name be lost. How great then was my perplexity when I realized that if I entered this arena I would find my good name replaced by reproach. But my desire to be of use overcame my sense of honor; I told myself, whate'er befall I shall take pity on Yiddish, that unloved and unpetted daughter, for it is time to do things for our people. Certain of my friends also joined me, and together we decided to induce the owner of Hemelitz to issue a periodical in the vernacular of our people. May God remember in his favor that he came to aid his people with the journal *Kol Mevasser* (The Proclaiming Voice) and did much good. And the spirit rested upon me and I wrote *Zemiroth Israel* (Hymns of Israel) for the Sabbath Eve, Sabbath Day and Outgoing of Sabbath, translated into verse and well explained, so that each individual Jew may know how much is to be gained, how lovely they are, a very wonder of God. (Jitomir 1875.) What induced me to translate the hymns was that I saw the translation of prayers for Jewish women in the *Korban Minha* (Gift Offering) Prayerbook and found them to be tasteless, badly expressed, abominable and unsatisfactory. I therefore decided that something must be done for our sisters the daughters of Israel and the plain folk in our midst, who should be supplied with a pure gift in clear language, seeing that they have souls like the rest of us and long to view the sweetness of the Lord; and we have no right to deprive them of this and let their souls do without that goodness, knowledge and wise counsel, keeping true wisdom only for the few chosen. If our forefathers translated the Torah into the common language, and our rabbis, may they rest in peace, appointed special translators so that the ordinary people might understand the living words of God, why should not we too instruct them, providing wisdom and counsel to the seed of the Holy People in the language they understand; and why should we not feel for our daughters and all the multitudes of Israel and give them an opportunity of enjoying the great gifts and wealth concealed in our prayers and faith, instead of leaving them to walk the ways of darkness, going astray with void things and silly tales, while we merely turn our eyes to the few? Are not all the congregation holy, and is not the Lord among them? I began this holy work with the Sabbath Hymns as a specimen; then I translated the Psalms into rhymed verse and still have the manuscript. Then I prepared the work, *A Chapter of Song* (a long hymn of praise which gives the biblical verse that expresses the praises of each kind of creature in the Universe for the Lord) translated into Yiddish rhymed verse with an introduction written in the holy tongue and a commentary *Tub Taam* (Good Taste) which explains each utterance of those who praise, in accordance with natural history and the words of our sages of blessed memory. Let the righteous see and rejoice, and those who honor our rabbis of blessed memory find the key I have given them, wherewith to enter this locked garden; and let them rejoice to see how great were the works of our sages, and how deep indeed were their thoughts.

HOW I WROTE MY SONGS

ELIAKUM ZUNSER (1840-1913)

Zunser was the first popular troubadour of the Russian ghetto. His numerous ballads and lyrics embody the vicissitudes of the old world culture that has almost vanished. Fortunately he recorded his experiences toward the end of his long career, telling of "the times in which I first saw the light, in which I passed my early childhood, and which have moulded my development." Zunzer is a frank, spontaneous, natural autobiographer, as the following lively pages indicate. In 1889 he came to America, where his fame had preceded him, and he continued to compose popular folk melodies and give concerts.

❊   ❊   ❊

ON THE first day of Elul in the year 5613 (1853), after long wanderings, I came to the city of Bobruisk, in the Province of Minsk. As might have been expected, I found no embroiderer there with whom I might work and thus earn my bread. For several days I wandered through the streets of Bobruisk, seeking I know not what. And, to be sure, I found it, in the image of the hazzan, Reb Joel I. Humener (famous in those days), who used to come to Bobruisk annually to chant the services during the holy days. If I cannot work at an embroiderer's, why not earn something as a chorist? thought I, and off I went to Reb Joel Humener. He tested me and found that I had a good voice and a fine ear. He engaged me as a singer at a salary of two rubles (what a fortune!) for all the holy days. He provided me with board at the house of the president of the synagogue, including permission to sleep regularly on a bench in the synagogue.

At that time I composed my song *The Light,* and immediately afterwards a second song, *Reb Tahanun.* This latter song had immense popular success. It was sung everywhere.

We spent a holiday evening very enjoyably in the house of the president of the synagogue, and later in the synagogue. *Reb Tahanun*

was sung by the choir, and all the hassidim were delighted with me—
the young composer. The joy all around affected me but little; nor
could the honors shown me that evening comfort me much. Like a
dark cloud, the question "What will become of me after the holidays?"
was continually before me.

After the holidays the hazzan gave me two rubles, and told me to
go. Whither? The world is large enough, and Jews, bless the Lord,
are plentiful. What matters it, then, where a Jew goes?

It had become very cold, however, and I had nothing but my light
summer clothes. Since I had plenty of money—two rubles—I went to
the market and bought a fur coat. Readers with delicate nerves might
be seriously shocked at the words "fur coat"; but let me hasten to
reassure them a coat was called a "fur coat" solely because it had a
fur collar. There were also in those days "fur coats" which did not
have even a fur collar, but a "future-collar", that is, a collar which might
some day, with the help of a kind Providence, hope to be covered with
some cat or fox fur.

A few days later, as I was proudly parading the streets of Bobruisk
in my "fur", I met a farmer who lived four versts' distance from the
city. He was seeking a Hebrew tutor for his children. I offered myself
for the position, and we readily came to an understanding. My salary
was to be twenty-five rubles for the term (six months), with the privilege
of sleeping on the warm oven. (The Russian "oven" is a house fixture,
built as an extension of one of the walls, allowing the top to be used as
a bed.)

It is generally admitted the world over that a Jew eats that he may
live; whereas, it is the opposite with the Christian—he lives that he
may eat. My new employer devised a novel theory of his own, to wit:
neither to eat nor live, but just to "pass away" the few years of our
earthly existence. And for mere "passing away" purposes, a bit of bread,
baked from oats and barley, with a little *groipen,* to which a few drops
of oil were added, was quite ample. Throughout the week not a morsel
of meat came into the house, and the week days were "passed away"
with this bread-of-misery and with the "soup" in which even the Jewish
impressors could not find one groip.

For the Sabbath, however, the farmer would bring from town a
sheep's head, and I would often refresh myself with a bone. The same
oil with which the hard foods were softened was also used for lighting
the house. And before such light I would sit for six hours daily and talk
myself hoarse in teaching my "scholars", who mentally were not a whit

superior to the children of the village peasants. After this exhausting labor, even such foods tasted royally to me.

Meanwhile, my clothes were wearing down rapidly. Because zero weather was quite frequent, I almost fell ill of exposure. I asked of my employer some part of my salary so that I might clothe myself somewhat decently. At first he gave me empty excuses, but towards the Feast of Passover, he informed me that he would employ me for another term and then he would give me all the money I would want. As I had no choice, I remained with him. All this time I was clad in rags, and my shoes were torn. At the end of Passover, I wrote my song *The Eye,* in which I sang of my own misery.

At Shabuoth he again put me off with some excuse, and, after the holiday, when I began to demand my money, he hit upon a "clever scheme". He went to Bobruisk, approached the leaders of the commune, and offered, if well-paid, to give them a "nefesh" (soul). He received twenty-five rubles, and took along with him an impressor and two Cossacks, who were to bring me to the *isborschik.*

Not knowing my danger, I had sought my bunk and went to sleep. Suddenly I felt a heavy hand fall upon my young body and shake me violently. I awoke and opened my eyes. Three strange men stood before me. One of them held a lantern, which he placed close to my eyes.

"What do you want?" I asked.

"Nothing, sonny—get up," the impressor answered.

"Get up? Why?"

"You'll have to go with us to town."

"Why? What business have I in town?"

"Well, you'll see! Dress yourself, boy, and be quick."

"I don't want to. I won't go!"

A blow in the face dazed me. I was wrapped in my torn clothes, thrown into a wagon, and brought to Bobruisk.

There I was locked up in the barracks.

In order to get rid of the "hidden Jews" (that is, the Jews who were not regularly entered on the public records), Czar Nicholas I issued an ukase which permitted every "hidden Jew" to be sent off as a soldier; a "hidden man" was one who had no passport, and obviously a man whose birth was not recorded could get no passport. This gave anyone the right to seize any young man or boy who had no passport and hand him over to the community as a soldier in lieu of some member of his own or some other family.

For the communal leaders of those dark days, who constantly

sought to thrive on Jewish misery, this ukase opened a new traffic. Each Jewish commune sent out its impressors on all roads and highways; they hid in village inns and watched for prey. Into their hands fell all unfortunate Jewish youths who could not show passports. Nor could all who had passports escape them. Passports were often torn before the very eyes of the victims, who were seized as "hidden" ones.

Those who were seized were bound like sheep, brought to town and locked up in the barracks. There they would be kept for weeks until the recruiting (*priom*) would begin. The authorities were not over-scrupulous with these unfortunates. Were they weak, sick, or defective? No matter—they were taken, dressed in military clothes, and packed off to serve the Czar. These "bodies" were sent in place of men whose families could pay a satisfactory price; the deputies and the *isborschik* divided the money. Many private individuals took part in this traffic. They would seize young children and sell them to the community "bosses". Those times were known among the Russian Jews as the dreaded days of the "impressment" (*Piomanes*). Hundreds of "sales of Josephs" occurred daily. The lesser rabbis of the smaller towns gave supine assent to such outrages, with the argument that it was "more pious" to protect the children of their own towns. The more important wept in silence at these open outrages, but they dared not protest for three reasons. First, these proceedings were in accordance with the Czar's ukase; secondly, they feared the *isborschik* and the deputies at whose pleasure they held their positions; and thirdly, they feared denunciation to the government officials. The result of such denunciation would inevitably have been exile to Siberia. These were times when men devoured men openly and with the consent of the government.

And so at the age of fourteen, I was one of the victims.

I stayed in the barracks for five long weeks. The community was waiting for the recruiting; and as for chances of redemption, it seemed, I had none. How could I? Whence could help come to me? Through what miracle? Can poor sheep bound in the slaughter house hope to escape the slaughterer? Legally or illegally, I would remain a soldier. I would have many years to serve among the cantonists. I would be sent to some peasant in a village many thousands of miles away, perhaps to faraway Siberia, there to tend swine, chop wood, make clumsy peasant shoes, and for every trifling offense suffer cruel beating. Should I emerge safe from this dreadful ordeal, the real Gehenna, with all its horrors, would only have just begun—the "elder" soldier, the Russian barracks, the drills, the marches under a load of three hundred pounds—the lash, the beatings, and other "diversions" of this sort. More than all else, the thought of my unhappy, widowed mother, helpless and miserable, tormented me. For twenty-one dark years she lived with her husband, and when an evil chance deprived her of her supporter, she was left with two orphans. With them she could share only her sorrows—for joys she never had. Her sole comfort were the two orphans, and now she is robbed of both. "A cruel beast hath devoured them!" Nay, no wild beasts of the forest were these, but human beings with hearts of wolves!

Such thoughts occupied me the entire time that I spent in the barracks together with other Jewish victims. Those thoughts stirred my emotions and then, in the barracks, I wrote my poem of 108 stanzas, *The Piomanes*. The theme for the poem I took from the prophet Haggai.

Haggai came to the priests and inquired of them: "Does a man or a garment become holy when this man or this garment touches the holy meat of the sacrifice?"

"No, he does not become holy," the priests replied.

"And does a man or a garment become unclean when either of them comes into contact with the unclean?" the prophet further inquired.

"Yes, verily, they become unclean," answered the priests.

"Such is the entire people," Haggai sorrowfully exclaimed. "No good, clean or holy thing adheres to them; only unholy things cling to them. That is, while living among strange nations, they do not learn good deeds or fine customs; from them they learn only the bad, the impure."

The horrible ukase of the impressment was a severe test for the Jews of that generation, and many stood that test poorly. In thus seizing and bartering their own brothers into conversion and suffering, they revealed to the world a bad element among them. Alas, that this bad element should have gained so strong an ascendancy!

The above is, in brief, the burden of my song, *Tried at the Bar of Justice and Convicted*. I wrote this not with my own blood alone, but with the blood of all my unhappy peoples. Not alone my sorrows resound through my verse, but the despairing wail of all Israel.

And how heartrending was the sight within the barracks! Eighty miserable, pale, emaciated, hungry, half-naked little beings, lying on the floor on a pile of dirty straw! The greater part were small children, who had been snatched from their mothers by tyrannical hands, and who could not realize the great misfortune awaiting them. Even here in the barracks, not comprehending the dark fate awaiting them, they laughed, frolicked, and played with one another; the older ones, regarding them, forgot their own sorrows and shed bitter tears. Twice daily the iron doors opened, and the hideous lackey of the community bosses entered and brought some loaves of bread and a few pots of soup, too dirty even for dogs. If any one dared to complain or make a request, he was seized by the hair and thrust to the wall with such a violence that his young bones cracked.

"I want to go back to my mother," some child broke out with a sob.

"You'll see her, indeed, in the other world! Only be patient!" the Jewish Antiochus replied with a leer.

"Let me go home! I want to go back home!" wailed another little one.

"Wait a few more days!" roars the human tiger. "You will then have a large home! It extends from Bobruisk to Archangel!"

Night is coming on. All lie on the floor and say their prayers; others, the older ones, recite the Psalms by heart, and thus lull themselves to sleep. A flock of sheep awaiting slaughter! They lie on each other in the dirty straw. Misfortune and misery have united these strangers into one body. Here and there a heavy sigh breaks forth from the breast of some older one. The very young ones sleep peacefully, a serene smile on their wan features. Of what are they dreaming? Very likely they are dreaming that they are slumbering on their mother's lap, and she is stroking their pretty curls.

Among the eighty who were in the barracks with me, there were some who possessed good voices for singing. From among them I selected a choir of ten and drilled them in my song, *The Piomanes*. Several times each day we used to sing it, and when the sad strain of the music would resound through the barracks, tears would steel into every eye and not a heart remained unmoved. Even our hideous jailers wept with us, those men with hearts of stone and nerves of iron, who watched us day and night.

The month of Ab passed, and finally came the night preceding the day on which we were to be led to slaughter—to the recruiting.

But help was nearer than any of us suspected. On Purim of 1855 (that is, about a half year before I was seized and locked up in the barracks at Bobruisk), Emperor Nicholas I suddenly died. Alexander II ascended the Russian throne, and the treaty of Paris was signed. The Crimean War was at an end. One of the very first edicts issued by Alexander the II was for the release of the *poimaniks*.

At about one o'clock in the morning, while we were all asleep in the barracks, we were awakened by a great commotion in the street. The noise came nearer and nearer, and soon we heard vigorous knocks on the iron doors and shutters.

"Get up, children! A deliverance! You are free!" some one shouted.

"An ukase from the Czar to release you!" shouted another.

"Praise God, children! Say 'Hallel!'" several voices called out together.

This news sounded to us like the blast of the Great Shofar which will awaken the dead on the day of Resurrection. With a cry of joy we sprang up from our wretched straw heaps, washed and fell to saying *Hallel*. I was the hazzan, and my choir accompanied me. After *Hallel*, we all joined hands and danced a Jewish Karehod (folk dance). I wrote my song *The Deliverance* (Die Yeshuah), and arranged a beautiful melody for it.

It was decided to release us from the barracks at ten o'clock in the morning. The rich Reb Isaac Rabinovitz of Bobruisk donated forty rubles to the synagogue for the privilege of opening the door of the barracks. Long before the appointed hour a great crowd of men and women, young and old, had gathered about the doors of the barracks and waited impatiently for the moment when the doors would open and we would emerge—free. Each and every one praised and blessed the good Emperor Alexander II, who had issued this edict and who had also revoked many of the cruel edicts of his father.

The happy moment came. With the benediction, "Blessed be He who releaseth them that are bound," the rich Reb Isaac Rabinovitz unlocked the door and the crowd surged into the barracks. The town hazzan recited a prayer of blessing for the Emperor, and sang the 45th Psalm. ("I waited patiently for the Lord; He inclined unto me and heard my cry", etc.)

Then my choir and myself were placed upon a large table, and we sang my song, "Placed before the Bar of Justice and Convicted." Many of the people wept. The song also had another effect; the people became so enraged at the community bosses that they were ready to tear them to pieces. But they had already gone into hiding.

Upon the request of some well-known citizens, I sang two additional songs, *The Deliverance* and *Better to Take than to Give,* which described my employer, the farmer, who sold me to the community for twenty-five rubles instead of paying me my hard-earned salary. This song evoked a storm of indignation. Many were ready to proceed to that village and wreck dire vengeance upon him, but Reb Isaac Rabinowitz quieted them and promised to deal with that monster himself. Then the door was opened, and the eighty of us came forth singing from the barracks. Reb Rabinowitz took me to his home in his carriage.

In this rich man's home, I too became somewhat of a personage. I decked myself out in fine clothes, and had in addition a capital of one hundred rubles in cash. My wealth, like my misery, came to me in an unusual manner. To begin with, Reb Rabinowitz sent for the farmer at whose house I slaved with my three scholars. Slapping him soundly across the face several times, he ordered him to pay not only the fifty rubles he owed me for the two terms but also the twenty-five rubles he had received from the community for my "body". This excellent gentleman pleaded that he was poor and could not pay, but this did him little good. My benefactor sent several Cossacks after him, and they seized all that they could find in his house. A few days later the farmer came with the seventy-five rubles and redeemed his chattels. Thus, I suddenly became a wealthy man.

At that time I believed myself to be almost a Rothschild. I had from time to time also received, in addition, some small sums of money from the guests who would visit my host and for whom I would sing the three songs I had composed in the barracks.

When I was first seized as a *poimanik*, the news of my capture had reached a Vilna woman who happened to be in Bobruisk at that time. She immediately wrote of it to my mother in Vilna. One morning, when I had been living at my host's house for some time, the servant informed me that a strange couple—a Jewish man and a woman— wished to see me, and that they were waiting outside. My joy was indeed great when I came out into the street and there to confront my mother and my uncle Abraham-Leb. With a cry of joy my mother threw herself upon me, weeping, and for a long time clasped me in her arms. Just as soon as she had received the letter from Vilna telling her of my capture, she had obtained a passport for me from the Vilna community and walked fifty Russian miles to Bobruisk to free me. My good uncle Abraham-Leb would not hear of letting her walk this long distance alone; he therefore accompanied her the entire way. We spent eight days at my host's house and then left Bobruisk.

I returned to my mother's home in Vilna, and the very first to greet me was again Old Poverty, who still reigned there as a gaunt, grim monarch. It became once more evident that I had no one to provide for me, that I must myself earn my daily bread. The only way to do this was to seek work again at some embroiderer's; but this I could not do in Vilna, for my contract with my first master-embroiderer still hung over me like the sword of Damocles. I had no choice but to leave my mother; I therefore started off to seek work in Kovno, fourteen Russian miles from Vilna.

In Kovno I went to work at an embroiderer's, but at night I used to study at the *Musor-stubel* of Reb Israel Salanter in Yatke-Gass.

Young as I was during the liberal era of Emperor Alexander II, the changes stirred me greatly. Seeing how the Jewish people blossomed forth like a beautiful flower and spread its tender leaves in the sunshine of enlightenment, and with a truly youthful ardor, I wrote my song *Die Blume* (The Flower), in Yiddish and in Hebrew, with the words beginning "Neglected, on the Mother of Highways, lies a beauteous rose."

In that song I represented the Emperor Alexander II as an angel who found in the dust a flower which had been torn from the garden of Zion; and beholding how all trample her under foot, he mercifully rescues her, revives her with living waters, and places her in his garden, among his other flowers.

During the time I spent in Kovno, I wrote many other songs in addition to this one, such as *The Clock, The Inn, The Ferry, Summer and Winter, The Farmer and the City Man.* They were sung everywhere. All Kovno spoke of the young embroiderer, who composed such pleasing songs, and almost every evening I was invited to some social gathering. Crowds of people would assemble around the house in which I sang my songs, and would listen until they learned them by heart. Very soon I discovered that the singing of my songs yielded me better returns than my embroidery, from which I could never hope to have more than three rubles a week. So I decided to abandon that trade.

I will not sing my own praises, and I will not say that my success as the people's bard came solely from the excellence of the songs themselves. Of that only the people must be the judge. But it is certain that I owe my success to the circumstance that at that time I was the only Jewish bard in Russia. That is, I was the first one who composed songs together with appropriate melodies. There lived at that time in Galicia Velvil Zbarser (Ehrenkranz) and Beril Broder; but their songs had not reached Russia, least of all, Lithuania. Russia had as yet not a single railway, and intercourse with Galicia was almost nil. Michael Gordon, too, had written some Yiddish songs, but he lived in Poltava, and Poltava was then to all purposes as distant from Lithuania as

America is from Europe today. In those days the Russian Jews had no songs outside of my own. It is therefore to this fact that my success was largely due.

I spent one year in Kovno, and so great was my success that I could well get along without doing any manual labor.

I returned to Vilna where my songs had made my name known, and I began to officiate as a *badhan* (jester) at weddings. This was in 1861. In that year I published my first volume, *Shirim Hadashim* (New Songs). That same year the building of a railway from St. Petersburg to Warsaw via Vilna was begun, and for the occasion I wrote *Die Eisenbahn* (The Railway). Sixteen years later in Minsk I wrote another song with the same title.

At the outset my new profession yielded me a very small income. I can adduce two reasons for this. First, only the poor invited me to weddings, and my compensation was naturally small; secondly, the recital of my songs necessitated instrumental accompaniment. The musicians who furnished the accompaniment took away the greater share of my earnings. If they did not succeed in getting a very comfortable share on the spot at the wedding they frequently attacked me in the street on my way home, and forcibly took away the money. But later my fortunes improved. The rich begin to invite me to their weddings, and then I was well-paid. Each band of musicians in those days had its own *badhan;* and the rich families used to engage only those musicians who engaged me.

Before my songs had become known, Moses Warshaver alone shone like a bright star among the *badhanim*. He used to be invited to the weddings of the wealthy, and therefore easily earned both glory and money. With my advent in the same profession, I became a serious competitor. He tried to suppress me by various means, but without success until he conceived a plan by which he trapped me. .

Through some friends of his he induced me to enter into partnership with him. I let myself be persuaded, and signed a contract with him. Just what was in the contract I did not exactly know. I discovered only later that he had inserted a clause in the contract stipulating that I was to be in his employ for a term of three years at eight gulden a week. Of course I immediately left him. This was exactly what he wished me to do. He at once sued me for breach of contract, declaring that all the money I should be ordered to pay as fine he would present to the wounded soldiers. (This was during the Polish Rebellion). Then began the most troublesome time of my early years. If I would attend a wedding, Moses Warshaver would be sure to come with the police and take me away. This reached such a stage that people ceased to invite me to weddings because the joy of the occasion was sure to be disturbed by the descent of Moses Warshaver with an escort of police. Thus I remained without means of livelihood; what little I did earn went to my lawyer. Each day I was dragged like a criminal to the police, and daily my troubles increased.

It is curious how help often comes to us in life at the very time when need and despair are greatest, and when we have long abandoned all hope. At the time when I struggled in Moses Warshaver's iron grip and had not the least prospect to escape from his clutches, something happened which led me from slavery to freedom.

Some time before this the Polish Rebellion had broken out, and Count Mouravieff became Governor-General of the four provinces of Vilna, Kovno, Grodno, and Minsk. He resided at Vilna, and from there all orders and ukases dealing with the Polish Rebellion went forth. The war with the Poles began, and blood flowed freely.

I was so young then that I could not judge which side was right in the bloody controversy. My childish instincts inclined me to the side of the stronger. I sympathized with Russia, and inspired by that sympathy, I composed a song entitled *The Polish Rebellion*. I sang this song at the Jewish weddings to which I was invited, and my audiences enjoyed it greatly.

Now it came to pass that I sang this song at a "rich" wedding in Vilna at which a Russian colonel was a guest. He requested that my song be translated to him into Russian, and when the translation was given him, he found it worthy of being presented to the Governor-General, Count Mouravieff. This song greatly pleased the Governor-General, and in recognition he sent me a gift of twenty-five rubles through the colonel. Later, when the wealthy Reb Judah Apatov of Vilna came to visit the Governor-General, with whom he was on terms of friendship, Count Mouravieff praised me to him.

Immediately afterwards an opportunity came which made me acquainted with Reb Judah Apatov, of blessed memory, whose great influence made him a very powerful personage in Vilna. He invited me to the wedding of his daughter to Reb Abrehmele Parness. My songs and my sermon pleased him so much that he engaged me into friendly conversation. I disclosed my sad condition to him, and told him of the bitter persecutions I had to endure from Moses Warshaver because of a false contract. Reb Judah Apatov promised to help me; and he kept his word. A short time later the contract was declared worthless and Moses Warshaver was obliged to leave Vilna.

I now began to breathe freely and to earn comfortable returns. But, day by day, the time set for my wedding was fast approaching. My father-in-law thought it necessary to introduce me to the Rabbi of Kaidanov, and he took me to spend one Sabbath at the Rabbi's. He probably wanted to show the Zaddik what a "find" he had been blessed with for a son-in-law. The impression which the Rabbi of Kaidanov made upon me I described in my humorous song, *The Rabbi's Little Key.* From this song, my father-in-law became only too fully aware of the "treasure" he had gotten, and did not bring me to his Zaddik any more. Two months after my marriage I again returned to Vilna.

At this time I set to work seriously to compose songs. Of the songs that I composed during this period the following attracted most attention: *The Ruble, The Iron Safe, Childbirth,* and *Yekele Bass.*

As a result, my name became widely known, and I was called to weddings in Grodno, Warsaw, Dinanburg, Vitebsk, Kovno, Minsk, and ever further. The Libavo-Romayn Railway had just been built, and it was possible for me to attend weddings in distant places, and hence my earnings increased considerably. I must note here that the melodies to my first songs had never quite satisfied me, because I had drawn mainly upon the motifs of the hazzanim in the Vilna synagogues, and they were by no means musical. During my childhood the hazzan in the Vilna synagogues was Ortschig the Hazzan. He was indeed a brother of the famous hazzan of the Slutzk, known as the Fiedele Hazzan. But he had not the latter's talent. Before becoming hazzan, Ortschig had been a military drummer. Since I had no better source to choose from, I adapted his melodies to my songs; hence my first songs lacked sufficient melody. Later my songs became much more melodious. For this I owe gratitude to the great hazzan, Reb Waserzweig, or Reb Hayyim Lomzer, who became the hazzan of Vilna. He was a good composer, and his book, *Shir Mikdash* (Holy Song), enjoyed a great success among those who loved Jewish music. It was under this new influence that the melodies to my later songs were written.

LOVE FOUND A WAY

EZEKIEL KOTICK (1847-1921)

The engrossing fascination of Kotick's two stout volumes of
Memoirs is due not only to his fine gift of storytelling but above all
to the exotic life of the Jewish villages and ghettos of Eastern
Europe in the second half of the nineteenth century, that he describes.
He wandered most of his life without purpose "like a fish in water",
as he says. But he kept his eyes and ears open so that the swarming
humanity of which he was a part takes on robust flesh and blood in
these remarkable recollections. He gives us fascinating glimpses of
all the typical characters—matchmakers, wagoners, musicians, pan-
handlers, cemetery wardens, synagogue habitués and the like—of a
world that is now virtually non-existent. The tragedy, the gaiety,
and the tenderness of that world are vividly illustrated in the following tale of the vicissitudes of his marriage. It shows how
Hasidism, which began as a protest against the rigors of the talmudic
Judaism in the eighteenth century and afforded an escape for the
masses during a time of great insecurity, degenerated into a system
of rabbi-worship. Communities and families, as this account indicates, were split into warring factions, the *hasidim* (literally
"the pious," the adherents) versus *mithnagedim* (the opponents).
But the poetic side of Hasidism, arising out of its doctrine of worship through joyousness and a return to Nature, should not be overlooked. You will find an account of that aspect of the movement
in Martin Buber's memoir on pages 514-522.

❊ ❊ ❊

IN 1865 my father decided that it was high time for me to marry.
I was then seventeen years old, and he was afraid that I would be
considered an old bachelor and looked upon as a public disgrace.
Accordingly the marriage was set for August. It was to take place at
our house because the bride was an orphan. My father ordered white
socks, slippers and a satin caftan for my wedding clothes. He refused

to hire the musicians from the town of Kobrin because Todrus the Bard, was not a convinced hasid. He preferred the musicians from Brisk because their fiddler and bard were hasidim.

I, on the other hand, declined to make a spectacle of myself at my own wedding by wearing socks and slippers, and wished to have Shebsel's band. In the end I won out. I was to be married in boots, and Shebsel's entourage arrived the day before the wedding.

On that day, too, the bride and her party arrived. They stopped at my uncle's house, where the marriage ceremony was to be performed. It was the custom that on the wedding day women and girls would gather at the bride's quarters at noon and stage a preliminary dance that lasted for several hours. At twilight the men folk would give a similar send-off to the bridegroom, who climaxed the event with a speech, then treated his guests to honeycake with jam, and liquor. Afterwards he was led with music through the streets to the ceremonial veiling of the bride, and thence to the synagogue for the marriage ritual. After the wedding, the principals and guests repaired to the bridal quarters for supper and all-night festivities.

If the wedding took place on a Friday, the couple was paraded home from the synagogue, and the guests left for the services. Only a small party returned to celebrate. Sabbath morning relatives and intimate friends came for the bridegroom and led him to the synagogue, where he was called upon to read from the Holy Scroll. In the evening there was the usual supper and hoopla.

My father, who was a strict hasid, did not think it advisable to introduce me to my bride before marriage. When she arrived, everybody in town went to see her except me. They brought back glowing reports of her beauty. Naturally I felt curious, and resolved to see her for myself. With my trusted friend, Arieh-Leib, I made off secretly to my uncle's home. Indeed she was beautiful! Though I felt shy in her presence, I managed to wish her "good luck". I wanted to prolong the pleasure of her company, but Arieh-Leib said I must not stay; it was forbidden. Wearily I left for my "station"—grandfather's home.

Under the wedding canopy my bride stepped on my foot. I thought it was accidental. Immediately after the ceremony, her relatives whisked her away towards the house so that she might be the first to enter it. This was done in accordance with the then current belief that the one of a newly-wedded couple who first stepped into their home would dominate the other for the rest of their conjugal life. But my friend, Arieh-Leib, was not to be outsmarted. He led us over a shortcut so that

I might get there first. That started a race. I was encumbered by the traditional white gown I was wearing over my satin caftan, and a coat on top. To make running easier for me, Judah-Leib, the tailor, rolled up my overcoat, and the white gown showed, much to my embarrassment.

When we arrived, the bridal party was already perched on the balcony. Sensing failure, Arieh-Leib decreed that the bride must step down, and enter the house with me shoulder to shoulder. She did, and members on both sides were watching carefully that we keep in step while crossing the threshold. In the process, voices kept up a continuous din:

"Keep in line! Keep in line!"

They might have been drilling soldiers.

In my heart I laughed at the whole procedure, and deliberately allowed her to enter first. Let her have the pleasure. This incensed Arieh-Leib, who ordered us to my grandfather's house. If she again attempted to run ahead of me, he threatened to have us do it all over again even if it took us a whole night. They led the way with music. When we reached the house, her group felt tired and disinclined to wrangle with Arieh-Leib. Nevertheless, they watched our feet, and this time we entered the house together.

The "golden" wedding soup was brought over from uncle's to grandfather's house. The musicians, too, were divided between the two domiciles. Sabbath eve descended upon us. Candles were lighted and blessed. The guests departed for the synagogue. We remained home for the prayer.

Grandfather was at odds with father because he refused to have hasidim at the wedding. So they agreed between them to set aside Friday night, Saturday morning and evening for hasidim only. They made merry, and discussed topics of special interest to their kind. I listened to their confabulations. They did not know me for the opponent that I was, nor suspect that I regarded their ways as strange. Throughout the week we made parties for different sections of the town population, according to a long-standing custom.

On the eve of the New Year my father was going to Slonim for a visit with the Rabbi. After the wedding he treated me as a grownup. He did not tell me what or what not to do. I usually divined from his eyes what to do or say. He took it for granted now that I was a married man, that I would join him in the visit to the Rabbi. Newly married hasidic young men usually followed that custom. He thought that since he was going, I would grasp at the opportunity and say,

"Father, I want to go along!" My silence therefore wounded his heart, and he went off alone.

My father felt ill at ease before the Rabbi. The venerable man knew I had been married. Once he had prophesied that I would up to be a handsome hasid. Now my father came to him without me! The situation for him was difficult indeed.

I made up my mind to talk things over with him, and deliver him and me from our common torment. I could stand my ground in argument. He should know that I never was, nor ever could be a hasid. Let him get used to the idea.

That, I soon learned, was not an easy task. My father was a man with an angelic temperament who had brought me up with his eyes, his glances, and mere hints. How could I hurt such a father by proving to him that his ideas were fallacious? To die was much easier. Yet I looked for an opportunity, and prayed for courage.

Unfortunately, my wife was also a fanatical hasid. She was reared in Karlin, at the home of her brother-in-law, an ardent hasid himself. She was fond of relating how Rabbi Aaron, that town's spiritual leader, visited them and how she served him boiled fish especially prepared for him (Pinsker Jews were famous for their fish cooking). As the Rabbi ate, and he was no small eater, he smacked his lips and confessed he had never tasted anything like it.

"Who cooked it?" he wanted to know.

They told him it had been cooked by a young orphan girl who could do everything well. Thereupon he blessed her and predicted that she would one day marry a great hasid. You can imagine my wife's predicament when she found her husband was no hasid at all, and declined to pay the Rabbi homage.

She played a great part in my family's life. They loved her for her beauty, her efficiency, and her tact. My father hoped she would convert me to Hasidism.

On the Sabbath and holidays my wife and I were dinner guests at my grandfather's. On the way we met and joined father, who was on his way home from the prolonged services. With her he talked about Hasidism; for me he had only stinging remarks.

In his desire to have her sway me, my good father went any length to humiliate me, and at the same time he praised her to the skies. He did not understand that such tactics were bound to create friction between us. It would appear that he was determined to wreck my married life if he could not succeed in making me a disciple of his rabbi.

On the Festival of the Joy of the Torah we dined at grandfather's as usual. Leaving at about one o'clock, we saw father leading a number of hasidim home for lunch. Yankel Essigmacher and Shebsel, the scribe, had collected the foodstuff from all the available ovens in town for the occasion.

As they caught sight of us, we crossed over to the other side of the road. Yankel was drunk and bent on insulting me. He yelled at me: "For what does a man desert his father and his mother. . ." and again: "'Hund-Tate' dog-father), 'Hund-Mame' (dog-mother), may a devil enter the soul of your wife!" and so on till we reached home.

I demanded of my father why he allowed Yankel to abuse me in public. Here Yankel broke in apologetically:

"What? When did I abuse you? I merely explained to him a portion of the Pentateuch in the style of the Desser heretic. . ." (He meant the commentary written by Moses Mendelssohn, who was called Rabbi Moishe Desser.) He also added slyly that he said, "Und (and) -Tate" and "Und-Mame."

Then and there I decided to make an end to all this. I would get drunk and start a discussion. In drunkenness one sometimes finds strength.

On the evening of the Festival, following a long-standing custom, the preacher arranged a feast in his home for the town's married young men at public expense. He served roast duck, fruit, wine and liquor. Everyone enjoyed it hugely.

The preacher's son and son-in-law arranged similar dinners at their own homes in honor of the students. I decided to go there and be among my own friends in defiance of my father and his hasidic clique. That day was one of the best in my life. We were twelve in all—the town's prize students. We danced, kissed and sang, and felt a warm comradeship. Later in the evening we joined our elders.

I remember seizing Shmerel, the father of a friend. I was a strong fellow, and the man nearly choked in my embrace. It took the combined efforts of several people to pry him loose from my arms. Then I fell asleep, and was carried off into another room. About one in the morning Moses Aaron, the preacher's son, woke me up and sent me home.

At home the hasidic revelers were still in high gear. Yankel was drunk as Lot. He immediately got hold of me and shouted:

"Hatzkele, you've come from Moses Aaron? May evil spirit seize his father!"

Impulsively I rejoined: "A curse on your rabbi's father!"

Were it not for the presence of my grandfather the enraged hasidim would have pounced upon me and beaten me within an inch of my life. As it was, they gnashed their teeth in silence.

When I went to my room, I found my wife on the bed, crying bitterly. She sobbed that I had ruined the hasidim's fun. It was terrible! Moses Leizer's son had cursed the father of the rabbi! Woe to one's ears for hearing such a thing!

I took her out for some air. We walked along a side street that led to the Polish church. On the way she cried with renewed passion. I could not endure her sobs.

"I love you, Hatzkel," she moaned through her tears, "only now I wish I were dead and not your wife. Don't think I want a divorce, God forbid! But if you could find it in your heart to curse the father of Yankel's rabbi, I am afraid to live under the same roof."

She started weeping all over again. I said nothing, but her whimpering sent shivers through me. Returning home, we heard the men leaving. They seemed to mutter something about "our misfortune", and failed to sing their way home as they were wont to do. My outburst apparently had disrupted their festive mood.

As I was going to my room, my father stopped me. He asked me to take a seat, and directed my wife to the bedroom.

"What is the matter with you, Hatzkel? What possessed you?" he asked in a quiet, trembling voice.

His face frightened me. It was deathly pale; his eyes were bloodshot. I had never seen him so agitated. It was not anger. Anger was not in his nature. It was rather a feeling of profound sorrow. It was the sorrow he showed when a child died, when his sister passed away. Yet not even then was he so moved.

I had an impulse to kiss him, to ask him to forgive me. I was ready to sacrifice my life for him, and wished that somebody would drive a spear through me if that would spare him further agony. I truly loved my father. I have idealized and worshipped him to this very day. I knew what my rebelliousness cost him. He was not to blame.

I confess that whenever I am about to do something wrong, the vision of my father quickly dissipates that urge. Unfortunately, his vision does not come to my mind too often.

I would gladly have given him every drop of my blood. But what to do with my soul? How could I believe in something which I did not believe? Why should I want to destroy my father and my wife whom I both dearly loved?

"Why do you keep quiet?" he finally demanded. "Why don't you speak up? Once and for all I want you to tell me everything that is in your heart. It is all my fault. I should have spoken with you more about Hasidism. I didn't because I thought you needed but few words. Only now I realize my mistake. I should have guided you from the beginning."

It was past midnight. The shutters were closed. Only a single candle light was burning. I spoke for a long time. Whenever his lips moved, I quickly silenced him by telling him what he was going to say. I was in a frenzy. My father sat motionless, listening to me intently without interrupting. When I had finished, morning was already upon us. The clock on the wall struck seven.

I was like a new man to him. He wondered how it had happened. He thought it was sufficient to study under Isaac Asher, without acquiring different ideas in the process. He had an idea that I would naturally become an active hasid, not a tenacious opponent. The glaring error of judgment made him feel faint, and he fell on the bed sighing.

My heart was breaking as I left his room, and tears ran down my face. I composed myself before entering my own room. Opening the door, I realized that my wife had not slept a wink, and had been crying all night. The pillows were drenched with her tears. At the sight of me she became hysterical. Father and mother hurried to our room in great alarm. Father took in the scene with one glance and left.

I did not know how to soothe her. The die was cast. For eighteen months I had accomplished nothing. I explained to my father that I wanted to resume my studies. Father loved my wife as his own, and would certainly take care of her. I was eager to prepare myself for the rabbinate. Upon ordination it would not be difficult for me to find a congregation. In my time the grandchildren of the Wolozhin Rabbi played a prominent part in Jewish life. Any principal of the talmudic seminaries would gladly recommend me to a desirable community. My beautiful young spouse would yet be a rabbi's wife!

My mind was set, even though her crying nearly drove me mad. With the thought that she would eventually calm herself, I reluctantly left for the synagogue. That night's experience imbedded itself permanently in my consciousness.

Friday night, Simche, my cousin, invited me to debate the hasidim at his home. I accepted the challenge. About thirty, with Mr. Orele at their head, were present. Their aim was to win me over to their way of thinking. They regarded me as a spirited, energetic young man. If they could succeed in converting me, they felt I would help them to transform the newly married men into fervent hasidim. They were also afraid of me. If I remained their opponent, they knew it would be the end of Hasidism among the youth of Kamenietz, which they wanted to avoid at any cost.

I won the debate. I answered all their questions; they dodged mine. "The Rabbi will answer that," Simche said repeatedly.

I countered: "What need have I to follow Hasidism? This blind faith in a rabbi does not appeal to me. I shall adhere to my own way of thinking, and be spared the doubts."

"What is wrong with asking questions?" interposed Simche.

"Traveling to the Rabbi for the answer," I replied.

"I'll give you fifty rubles for expenses," persisted Simche. "Ride over to Karlin and see Rabbi Aaron. He will settle everything to your satisfaction."

He religiously pledged the money the moment I was ready to leave for the rabbinic audience. That ended the debate, and my triumph was assured. From then on they showed me great deference, and regarded me as a precocious fellow.

Sabbath morning I said my prayers among the hasidim in their own little chapel, and on weekdays at the new synagogue. After the services I held forth on Hasidism. My victory over the hasidim was widely known, and as time went on, more and more young men flocked to hear my discourses. I was invited to speak at the old synagogue, and for the next few decades not a single young man in Kamenietz was converted. That town has been unhasidic to this very day.

However, I made a mistake in arguing with my father. I hoped he would reconcile himself to my dissenting conviction. Instead, he started to plague me with biting allusions, and to turn my wife against me. He appeared unconcerned over the possible consequences to my married life.

As things were going from bad to worse, I decided to go to Wolozhin and resume my studies for the rabbinate. That would put an end to the friction. The truth was I did not want to leave my beloved wife. I was married only a few months. On the other hand, to continue under those circumstances was impossible.

I wanted to secure a passport. I also wanted a visa, although it was then not necessary for traveling. But no visa could be issued to me without my father's consent. Yet I felt confident that Jacob, the tax-collector, would give it to me. Indeed, he promised that he would. Secretly, however, he sent word to my father, which made me see the folly of exaggerated self-confidence.

"Hatzkel, why do you need a passport?" my father inquired.

"To travel to Wolozhin," I replied, looking at my toes.

Suddenly his patience snapped, and in the presence of my wife, he struck me twice in the face. "Only a few months after marriage," he screamed, beside himself, "and you are planning to desert your wife! Do you want to be a hermit?"

At that moment he was perhaps not so much concerned about my wife as he was intent on antagonizing her against me. He went on at the top of his voice:

"Do you want to desert your orphan-wife? Whoever heard of such a thing? It's criminal! What right have you to plan such a thing without first consulting me? If not your father, why not talk it over with your wife? You are pious, you say. Well, then, don't you know it is written in the Torah that you should stay at home with your wife at least one year even in time of war! So you want to go off to study? I don't believe you want it that much. You could study at home, too, you know. There must be something else. Maybe you don't love your wife any more?" he wound up with a quizzical grin.

His words incensed me. He knew how much I loved my wife, and how gladly I would have given my life for her. He didn't have to pour salt on my wounds. He went on abusing me in her presence and picturing me as the worst possible person in the world.

As usual, my wife reacted with a deluge of tears. Father, who really loved her and could not bear to see her in anguish, kept on raking the fire. Finally, when she became hysterical, he stopped in his tracks, frightened. He immediately sent for Yashke, the healer. Pandemonium broke loose in the house. The family put her to bed. At that moment I realized how cruel my father could be to those who opposed him.

At that time they caught Isaac Beer, an employee of my father, who had been looting his safe with a passkey for God knows how long. Yet the discovery left my father unperturbed. He did not say an unkind word to the thief.

"Tell me, Isaac Beer, did you steal at least with restraint?" And he merely paid him off.

When Isaac Beer whined that he was left without means to support his family and that he had no money for the fare home, which was at Brusk, my father handed him a hundred rubles and wished him luck as if the fellow were a saint, not a crook.

But upon sober deliberation, I could not blame him too much. I concluded it was easier for one to turn hasid than for a hasid to change into an opponent. An ordinary opponent was simply a religious, law-abiding Jew; a hasid believed that God, heaven and paradise were created exclusively for his pleasure. As intensely as hasidim loved their cult, just so intensely they hated disagreements. Moreover, father feared that I might win over my four younger brothers. In this he was right; they took sides with me.

Unfortunately, my wife was on his side, and he sought to fight me through her. Had she not been so lovely, he probably would have gritted his teeth and resigned himself to the situation. But he knew how much I loved her. In that sense she constituted a power for him against me. My intention to leave her and home therefore disturbed him. If I stayed, I might yet, with her aid, be converted. If I didn't, all was lost.

As always in such conflicts between father and son, he gained nothing by his tactics. Instead of my bending under his efforts, I became increasingly obstinate. He failed to comprehend that I would not change my conviction just as he would not yield his. It was not in my nature to falsify, deceive, lie, or pretend. Others, dressed as hasidim, haunted the Rabbi for the sake of a wife, a father, a father-in-law. On the sly they cheated, and even smoked cigars on the Sabbath. I could not be guilty of such duplicity.

The day on which I wanted to procure a visa was the saddest in my life. My wife became bedridden. My father did everything to restore her to health. She refused to speak with me. Her condition affected me badly. My father refused to permit me into her presence. The whole family puttered around her; everybody assisted in one way or another; I alone did nothing!

When she recovered, her attitude changed. She seemed to be sorry for me, to sympathize with my groping. I explained to her that my father had no right to persecute me. He would never make a hasid out of me so long as my heart was not in it. "He insults me in your presence, and humiliates me. No my darling, I would do anything except believe in what I can't. . . . About my going to Wolozhin and leaving you alone," I continued, "you know that my heart belongs to you. I want to go away because our capital is small, and there is not a business here which I could consider with a sense of security. One thing is left: to attain ordination. If not for my father, I might have been a rabbi by now. But I am still young, only eighteen, and it isn't too late. You will be taken care of here in my absence. In four or five years, if God wills it, you will be the beautiful wife of a rabbi."

Fundamentally a practical woman, my wife agreed with me at once. Never for a moment did she doubt my loyalty and devotion. Sensing that we had reached an understanding, my father ceased to torment me.

LIFE OF A HUMORIST

SHOLEM ALEICHEM (1859-1916)

No writer has won greater esteem and popularity among the masses of his people than Sholom Rabinovitch, who adopted as his *nom de plume* the time-honored greeting "Peace be with you". The son of a hasidic squire in a small Russian village, his strong imagination drank in both the beauty and the degradation of the common folk, and it is easy to understand why the gently humorous manner in which he treated their foibles and sentiments endeared him and his numerous writings. He found, like Emerson, that something always sings in the mud and scum of things, and he laughed infectiously when he recorded the music. "To see the comic side of everything and everyone was almost second nature with me." It is a pity that he never composed *The Story of Sholem Aleichem's Life Written by Himself* * which he planned, but we may be grateful for this blithe thumbnail self-portrait.

❋   ❋   ❋

IN THE little town of Voronko, no larger than an olive, a little distance away from the city of Pereyaslav (where I was born in 1859), I spent the golden years of my life, the first lovely, innocent days of my childhood. In this little Voronko, my father was one of the pillars

* "You ask me to give you a few notes for my biography," wrote the author to his friend, V. H. Ravnitski, noted critic. "I am afraid my biography may be superfluous. Isn't it a bit too early? That is point one. Secondly, I myself should very much like to write the story of my life—a whole book of it.. (I actually started to write this book in Italy, entitling it, *The Story of Sholem Aleichem's Life Written by Himself*. Sholem Aleichem's note, 1913.) And thirdly, I am—I hope you may be spared the same—very, very busy— actually with literature. Ever since I started to write, never have I been so productive and fruitful as now. Good or bad, but I do write a lot. And, as you know well enough, I can write sitting on a pinhead, on the blade of a knife. The trouble is that the times are bad; the clouds have been gathering over our people. It's hard to laugh, and if a laugh burst through, there is a note of bitterness in it. . . . And then my correspondence with our elite—the Jews and the gentiles—takes a good slice of my time. And here a good hour of my time has been stolen for you—thief that you are!—in order to let you have a few memoirs. Perhaps they'll be useful in your work. May God help you!"

of the town, the "squire," the chief trustee of all societies—he was "Reb Nahum Vevik's." And we, Reb Nahum Vevik's children, were also of some account. Every Sabbath night the whole town would attend the *melaveh malka* (hasidic communal feast to speed the departing Sabbath Queen) at our house; on every holiday the townspeople would pay their respects to us; all news was brought to our house and carried away from our house; a glassful of wine was drunk at our table; at our house stories were told about hasidic rabbis, and politics were discussed—all at our house. And we, Reb Nahum Vevik's children, were considered of great importance—we were guided in the straight path, given into the tutorship of the best teacher, Reb Zorah, and we really were God-fearing and pious.

To this day I remember the taste of the tears we shed at our teacher's homilies. Every day our teacher, Reb Zorah, would have a new homily for us, and afterwards at prayer time we would beat our breasts, crying "We have trespassed!" in repentance of our sins; for side by side with our piety, we were preys to temptation and were great transgressors; we were liars and gluttons; we disobeyed father, cheated at prayer, stole money from the charity box . . . and what of the strange thoughts and desires! Afterwards, came the teacher with his homilies, and we would weep again. We would again shed copious tears; we again prayed devotedly, without cheating, and beat our breasts crying "We have trespassed," weeping, weeping and repenting.

From very childhood my flaming imagination was remarkably developed. Houses seemed to be transformed into cities; courtyards into empires, trees into people, girls into princesses, rich men's sons into princes. Haystacks became warriors, thorns and thistles were Philistines, Edom and Moab, and upon them I would make battle.

To see the comic side of everything and everyone was almost second nature with me. Quite unwittingly I would imitate people and their actions, beginning with the teacher and his wife, including all my comrades and their parents, down to Baruch Baer, the drunkard, and Oniska, the bowlegged watchman. I got plenty of blows for my aping. In school I was the "constant nuisance"—the comic. Everyone would laugh himself sick, except myself. However, when my mother got wind of my pranks, she started to wean me out of them.

There was only one equal to me in mimicking, "acting," "dressing up," and singing pretty songs. This was Meyer'l, the Rabbi's son, or Meyer'l Medvedeff, afterwards the famous singer. He showed signs of talent when he was still running about barefoot, singing pretty songs for a penny, sometimes for half an apple. The two of us used to play *Robbers,* a drama of our own composition. Medvedeff was the robber, I a pauper Jew. The rest of our comrades were the trees of the forest—the "supers." I, the pauper, would kneel in front of the robber pleading, "What do you want of me? I am only a poor, poor Jew, a pauper! Mercy on my wife and little children!" And he, the robber, with a kitchen knife in hand, would stand over me, singing a song to the effect that he must, he absolutely must, slaughter all Jews. . . .

As spoiled and naughty as we were, compassion for all living creatures was so strong in me that I felt pangs of suffering at the sight of a sick horse; a lame dog would bring tears into my eyes. Even cats—the lowest of the low—aroused tenderness in me, to say nothing of poor sick children.

Remarkably enough, Reb Zorah was responsible for my first urge to write. It was due to his extraordinarily beautiful calligraphy. For a nice "hand" father would present us with a penny (the first "royalty"); and in order to cultivate a nice "hand," I fashioned a notebook and in beautiful characters wrote an entire composition on the Bible and Hebrew grammar. When I showed it to father, he was much amazed at my "creation," and for a long time carried it in his pocket to show everyone how beautifully his son wrote (I must have been ten years old), how well he knew the Bible, and how great was his knowledge of grammar. On this occasion a neighbor of ours, a hasid with a goatee, Reb Isaac by name, whose prayers sounded like the squeal of a kitten, commented, "Grammar-yammer—the real thing is the hand—a golden hand!" (My first "critic.")

In those days I was drawn into the world of the spirit and of dreams. I was drawn to singing and to the world of music; and after bar mizwah I secretly tried playing the fiddle—and got a good dose of it from father.

Then we lost everything; we moved from Voronko back to Pereyaslav. There we were for the first time dressed up in "modern" suits with slit coattails. And after mother died of the cholera, father placed us in a government school, where I distinguished myself. There, at the age of fifteen, I read my first modern book, *Robinson Crusoe,* and at once composed a Robinson Crusoe of my own, entitled *The Jewish Robinson Crusoe.* I showed it to father, who in turn showed it to his customers (at that time we kept a wayside inn), and everyone thought it marvelous!

From that time on, father started to treat me like a precious object. He took me out of stepmother's power, would not permit her to punish me, forbade me to mind the babies, crush raisins (we kept a wine-cellar called "South Shore"), polish the customers' boots, prepare the samovar, run errands or perform similar tasks which in those days used to be mine.

In that epoch, between the ages of seventeen and twenty-one, wanting to become a government rabbi, I started studying seriously. I therefore read a good deal, and wrote even more. I wrote . . . everything that I had read in books: songs, poems, novels, dramas without end, and "articles" about everything under the sun. I used to send my "works" to all the Jewish and non-Jewish editors (I wrote both in Hebrew and Russian), and the editors must have blessed me for providing them with fuel for their stoves. The *Ha-Melitz* alone printed a couple of my "articles," adding a footnote in tiny type: "Sfatcha itcha (thy tongue is with thee) . . . Shlah dvoreyha veklibdanum (Send thy words, and we shall honor them)." Thereupon I started writing Hebrew articles by the ton; I sent wagonloads of articles—but why they were not honored, I do not know.

In those days (1883) there appeared a Yiddish periodical, the first periodical in that language—the *Folksblatt* of Alexander Zederbaum— and since the gentiles would not print my "novels" nor my "dramas," and since the Hebrew "articles" were also languishing unhonored, I tried my hand at writing in the spoken tongue—the tongue of Mendele Mocher Seforim, whose books at that time first came to my notice. And picture my amazement when the *Folksblatt* grabbed it up, and Zederbaum, the editor himself, in his own hand, wrote me a letter requesting me (do you understand—*requesting* me!) to write more. From that time on, I started writing articles in the *Folksblatt,* and the more I gave, the more was demanded of me. Moreover, there appeared one Mordecai Spector, of the *Folksblatt* staff, who never ceased to egg me on to write—and hasn't ceased doing so until this very day. Yet in those days, this was merely a pastime for me, until the affair with a certain penknife which created an upheaval in my writing and in my entire life.

That epoch was for me one of commerce, money, the Bourse, stocks and bonds, and similar things that have nothing to do with literature. I had, as the saying goes, scaled the ladder. I handled thousands and tens of thousands, and it is possible that I might have chosen quite a different path—in the opinion and aspirations of some, the "strait" path. One day, some important business affairs took me to the great city of Kiev. There, during the day, I wore myself out, but when at night I lay down on the bed, I could not fall asleep. Then I rose, sat down at the desk and started to write. I did not really write—rather, I poured out on paper some of the memories of my childhood and gave them the name of the *Penknife*. This I sent to the editor and promptly forgot about it.

And there came a day when I picked up the *Voshod* and suddenly in a literary survey of all kinds of trash by "Criticus" (S. M. Dubnow), I found my *Penknife*. My heart beating furiously, I read his warm lines. He praised the story and prophesied that the author of the *Penknife*, who gave promise of talent, might some day give more good things to our impoverished Yiddish literature.

With tears of joy and gratitude I reread the words by the benevolent "Criticus," and then swore that I would continue writing in the same vein. Until this very day, I see those kind, warm words before my eyes, and sometimes after finishing a new story, I ask myself, "What would 'Criticus' say to this?" Afterwards I lost my money, but I was left with courage, and I have been clutching the pen in my hand with all my might. Do I owe "Criticus" thanks, or otherwise? That is not for me to judge. My writing-sickness has become so bad that I no longer belong either to myself nor to my family, but rather to our literature and to that greater family, called the public.

MEMORIES OF CHILDHOOD

AHAD HA'AM (1856-1926)

Under the pseudonym Ahad Ha'am, "One of the people," Asher Ginzberg won preeminence as an advocate of modern Hebrew nationalism. Vigorously opposed to Herzlian political Zionism, he employed his wide culture (he was in private life a tea merchant) and mastery of the Hebrew tongue to promote self-understanding and advocate a cultural renaissance. During the latter part of his life, he withdrew from literary activity and made his home in Tel Aviv in Palestine where he was regarded with high veneration. The combination of humility and intellectual forthrightness which characterized his later life are noticeable in this chapter of his youth. While he rejected the external expression of his inherited Judaism, the warm and vital core of it remained with him always.

✻ ✻ ✻

I RECEIVED the beginnings of my education from hasidim on the knees of which I was born and within which I spent my early years. My father was one of the chief Sadagore hasidim in the town where I was born, and naturally educated me along similar lines. I used to pray with him in the chapel of the Sadagore hasidim, and learnt to honor the wonder-rabbi of Sadagore, Reb Abraham Jacob, son of Rabbi Israel of Ruzhin. My leisure time, when I was not at school, was spent in the class where I read hasidic books and any others that might be there.

At the beginning of Autumn, 1868, when I was twelve years old, my father took me with him on his visit to the Rabbi for the Tabernacles festival; for he desired that the Rabbi should bless me before my bar mizwah (confirmation) and should put his hand in mine, besides telling me some worthwhile things. We spent the whole of the festival at Sadagore in the company of the Rabbi and his children. One evening (as far as I remember the eve of the Festival of Drawing the Water, which hasidim have revived after it had fallen into desuetude following the

248

destruction of the Temple in Jerusalem) there was no feast at the house of the Rabbi, so father went to the feast of the children and took me with him. We came to the succah (booth), which was full of people. One old man, a Galician, stood beside the table and diverted the children (namely, the Rabbi's eldest son and his better-known brother-in-law) with his gross stories which were full of coarse language. The stories were so gross that even I, a child of twelve, understood practically everything. All those present laughed to their heart's content. Suddenly one of the children closed his eyes tight with great fervor and exclaimed, "Where's Yoshke" (a famous cantor and Sadagore hasid who had also come for the festival). When they found Yoshke he said to him: "Sing 'Let the Rock command His Loving-kindness'." The cantor began to sing and the young "saint" listened with closed eyes to the song, his fervor increasing meanwhile until he seized the saltcellar, which stood not far from me, and began to beat time with it on the table, while the salt shot far and wide across the entire succah; and so it went on until the cantor had finished his song. This scene, particularly the sudden transition from dirty stories to such fervor, made a very bad impression on me; and that impression made a great breach in my Hasidism.

When I arrived at Sadagore my father and I went to "give peace" (a hasidic expression for calling on the Rabbi, who at such times stood at the door of his study with outstretched hand, while all the new guests came and shook hands with him). When father's turn came we both approached the Rabbi and shook his hand like all the other guests; and because my father was one of the important hasidim the Rabbi spoke to him for a few minutes. Many years later, when I was already "outside the camp," certain of the hasidim who had been present on that occasion swore that after I had shaken hands with the Rabbi he had wiped his hand on his girdle.

I could relate a great deal of the days we spent at the Rabbi's, but that is not my purpose here. The outcome of it all was that I left my Hasidism behind me at Sadagore and returned home a complete mitnaged (opponent). I had already begun to study the Talmud and Scriptures and medieval Hebrew literature; and when I returned from Sadagore my devotion to all of these increased and I began to be particular about commandments with which hasidim do not usually concern themselves (such as praying precisely at the duly appointed time). My father, a shrewd man, a scholar and also somewhat advanced, greatly regretted this change which had come about in my manner of life and would bring home the lions of the company of hasidim, in the hope that they might bring me back to the right path. But he did not succeed.

That was the first and last time that I saw a famous saint. He himself, it is true, made a deep impression upon me, both on account of his remarkable appearance, his behavior and his manner of speech; but that did not suffice to close the breach made in my hasidic faith by the behavior of his children and the whole assembly of his hasidim there. Little by little the entire bundle fell apart, as they say in Hebrew. Although I continued to live in that hasidic environment for many years to come, I separated from them and there was no link between us. They went about their own business, while I devoted myself to my studies with all my heart and paid no attention to them.

From my early boyhood, when we still lived in the town and I was about ten or eleven, I had grown accustomed to being examined in my studies. For matchmakers already abounded who took the provision for my future upon themselves and proposed all kinds of matches for me, after my name and fame had spread abroad through the entire district as an infant prodigy. Since there were no *yeshiboth* (higher schools for the study of talmudic literature) in our parts and it was not the custom thereabouts, as it was in Lithuania, for the wealthy folk to choose bridegrooms for their daughters from the yeshibah lads, cases like mine were in great demand. When there were boys in different places for whom great futures were foretold on the strength of their studies, the wealthy folk would compete with each other to get them as sons-in-law. I was one of the boys whose name and fame as a desirable bridegroom went ahead of him. The rich folk who wished to make a match would send "understanding" scholars to our town in order to examine me in my studies in order to learn whether the rumors as to my prodigious attainments were true or not.

As a result strangers came to the school where I studied almost every week, folk I had never seen before, in order to examine my knowledge of Talmud and the great rabbinical authorities. During the final years before I actually became a bridegroom there were two competitors. One was a wealthy man, but an ignoramus, while the other belonged to a pedigreed family into which I did actually marry. The girl in question had been orphaned of her father, the Rabbi of Zhitomir, who died while still a young man. Naturally she had no dowry. The former was famous in our parts at that time as a very wealthy man who was prepared to give his daughter quite a considerable dowry. My father wished to do everything as was most fitting and proper, and resolved that I must be questioned as to which I preferred. The matter was entrusted to my then teacher; he was told to talk to me and did so. I was very perplexed and did not know what to answer. At bottom I preferred the match with the wealthy man, for I feared the excessive sanctity and Hasidism which characterized the pedigreed family. But I was ashamed to admit this openly to my teacher, and instead of a direct answer I reminded him of a saying in the Talmud, "Let a man sell all he possesses and so on," without finishing the quotation, for I thought my teacher would understand what I was driving at. I had wished to indicate that the sages of the Talmud had not thought it of vital importance to marry the daughters of scholars, since one version of the proverb beginning as above ends "and marry the daughter of a scholar," while another, which commenced in precisely the same way, ends, "and buy shoes for his feet." My teacher, however, did not grasp this but thought simply that I was referring to the former of the two sayings. In this way my fate was determined, and before very long my father went to the place of residence of the head of the pedigreed family and arranged the match. The bride was not there, for she was staying with her maternal grandfather some distance away. However, the wife of the head of the family produced her own daughter, who was indeed a pretty girl, and said to him, "Do you see this daughter of mine? I assure you that the bride is no worse than she is." That was sufficient evidence for my father to arrange the match.

But it was about the examinations that I started this section, and I want to finish about them too.

Apart from the examiners who visited my school from time to time, it was the custom of father to examine me himself every Sabbath, after arising from his noonday sleep. In accordance with his system of education he would always end his examination by slapping my face whether I deserved it or not. The same moment my mother would open the door of her room and would say to him: "Hitting him again! May the thunder hit you!" That was the almost invariable end of the examinations, after which I would be free to go out and play with my friends until the time of the afternoon prayers.

Naturally, that was when we still lived in the town, before moving to the village; for in the latter I had no friends and did not take part in any children's games.

While referring to my father's educational system, I should mention another incident. It was the habit in our house that when sitting down to a meal at table each one would bring a book to read between courses. My father himself usually brought the *Midrash Rabbah,* while I would choose various books from father's library. Once father came to see what my book was. After inspecting it, he said to me, "Do you know that the author wrote this book when he was eighteen?" "I know," I answered. "As for you," my father went on, "when you're eighteen years old you won't even be able to understand what he's written in it." This annoyed me exceedingly for I had understood everything perfectly well, despite all its finespun dialectic, although I was no more than eleven at the time. But that was one of the foundations of education according to my father; to lower me in my own eyes. Though I do not know what the purpose was in doing so.

As already mentioned, I married, or rather was married off, before my seventeenth birthday. My wife belonged to a very good hasidic family indeed. On her father's side she was the granddaughter of the then famous Wonder-Rabbi Jacob Israel of Tcherkossi. The latter was then very old and could not come to the wedding which was conducted at Ovrutch in the Wolhynia Government. Some time later the family demanded that my wife and I should go to Tcherkossi in order to be seen by the Old Man. I finally agreed for politeness' sake. At the end of the summer in the same year or the one following—I do not quite remember which—we went there. On account of his age the "Saint" could not take his place at the head of the public table on the Sabbath day, as was the custom. So his place was taken for the purpose by one or other of his many grandsons who used to visit him at frequent intervals. For the Sabbath when we were there, there came one such grandson who was afterwards a "Saint" in his own right; and when I arrived, I went to visit him as well. Among the other things of which we spoke we talked of the day when we would return home. I said that I would be leaving on the Tuesday, to which he replied that in that case he would leave earlier because he wished to go on the Sunday. For some reason or other, which I do not know, I told him: "No, I shall be leaving here first." He laughed, and we made no further reference to the matter.

This happened in the middle of the week. On Friday he went to the bathhouse and a nail ran into his leg and wounded him. The doctor ordered him to stay in bed. And so that Sabbath there was nobody to sit at the head of the table. Thereupon the choice fell upon me to replace the "Saint"; with the result that I was suddenly transformed into a "Saint" conducting the table for his believers, at a time when deep in my heart hasidim was considered a very defective system and institution.

Though this was already practically common knowledge among the hasidim, they nevertheless did not refrain from grabbing what was left on the plate just as they did with the Rabbi himself when he was there (for it is believed that the Rabbi's holy touch imparts some special virtue to the food). On the Tuesday when as I arranged I was to leave, I paid a visit to the grandson with whom I had spoken and who had injured his leg, in order to bid him farewell. I found him still lying in bed. In this way my prophecy was fulfilled and I went first, thus becoming an unintentional wonder-worker.

BEFORE THIRTY

HAYYIM NAHMAN BIALIK (1873-1934)

Bialik was a distinguished Hebrew poet, and in recognition of his attainments an annual "Bialik Prize for Hebrew Literature" has been established in Palestine. His versatility was quite remarkable, for in addition to verse he wrote stories, essays, criticism; he edited anthologies, managed a publishing house, spoke in behalf of his cherished causes and acted as spiritual guide to writers, pioneers and educators. The impulse to creative activity was intensified by the agony of his early life, which he so revealingly recounts in the following fragments out of his posthumous works. (Despite slight overlapping, they interconnect and round off each other.) Here he reminisces less cautiously than in his more formal autobiography, *Aftergrowth,* and thus allows us a few steps closer to the inner spirit of the man.

❀ ❀ ❀

YOU ask me to do you the trifling favor of writing the chapter headings of my life, but I stand and find it very hard indeed. I think to myself: before asking me to write the chapter headings of my life's history, first ask me whether I have any "history" at all? Upon your life: my dear, if there is any man in the world who has no "history," I am that man. My history is so simple, and so resembles the histories of all men like me, that there is nothing to learn from it and willy-nilly it requires no study.

A brief introduction: in the events of my life do not look for order, evolution or connection, cause or effect. There is nothing of that kind or similar to it. I am a passive man by nature, "feminine" in the sense of being subject to influences, and never participated actively in those things that exerted a creative effect upon me. All my powers are sustained, like those of any plant, from what is set prepared round me and nearby, without taking anything of their own; and all the vicissitudes of my life are only in the nature of separate broken notes played by a variety of musical instruments, each being played independently without thought of the rest; and if by chance all those nevertheless combine into one complete tune it is a true heavenly miracle.

Just think: I was born in a village and grew up there until I was six years old. The glory of Nature, the lovely world, fields and forests and all the rest. And in the midst of this lovely world, where my heart and I all but choked, there already sat an usher nipping me in the neck and giving me the command: "Listen, you little bastard, do you see this yoke and two pails?—Call it Aleph!" And then all of a sudden there I was in town, Hebrew classes, thrashings, a muckheap, an inn (my father kept an inn and studied Mishna while serving). Then a year later I am out of the town again.

And once again there are fields, forests, a river and all the rest. . . . And at the same time my heder (Hebrew class) is gloomy as the shadow of death, and the teachers are thoroughly abominable and disgusting, or not thoroughly abominable and disgusting, as the case may be.

And then all of a sudden I am an orphan aged seven and am transferred to the house of an old man of over seventy. My childhood was seething within me, but he threw the ice of his old age over my infancy. My movements, my face, my sitting and my standing were an abomination for him. I showed him my childish actions; and he would respond by producing the *Shebet Musar* (Rod of Reproof) and the *Reshith Hokmah* (Beginning of Wisdom). Then once again the heder and teachers, teachers and heder. The man weds (this was one of my first lessons in Gemara at the age of seven), he who brings a divorce from overseas. Teacher, what's overseas? And what's a divorce? You little ignoramus! A divorce is a divorce. When a woman bears seed (I do not remember which I first began to study—Pentateuch or Talmud); there was the *Or Ha-Hayyim* (The Light of Life, a mystical commentary on the Pentateuch held in high favor by the hasidim), the laws of every oddment and trifle.

And then all of a sudden I found myself in the heder of a strange and lazy teacher with a fondness for legend. We used to study at twilight when the flocks were returning home, for he slept all day long. He taught us Agada (the non-legal portion of the talmudic literature) and Bible, and my heart was attracted to both, and skipped and danced like a lamb on a verdant pasture. And my grandfather had a bookcase full of yellow-leaved old books, large and small, of every kind, and I read them and read them, at first only half understanding, but finally understanding everything. And everything was to be found there: Agada (Legend),

Halakah (Law), Ethics, Kabbalah, Research. There I found how one merits the Holy Spirit.

And in the heart lay hidden some Holy of Holies, something hidden and concealed, all kinds of yearnings the nature of which I do not know but which give me no rest. In my neighborhood I got the reputation of a fine young rascal. I am unique in my suburb as regards both rascality and sharp-mindedness. And so all of a sudden I find people to act as "fathers" to me; uncles and cousins, relations and neighbors, all prepared to teach me how to behave as is fitting for an orphan. One cousin, a big lad, hauls me off without anybody's knowledge to the lavatory, lets down my breeches, turns back my shirt, beats me and laughs, beats me and goes on laughing. I am ashamed to tell anybody about this shameful thing, so come out feeling as though I were full of filth; and in my state of nervous excitement I take open revenge upon old men for the shame done me in private. Sometimes I hid in an attic or in some secret corner, sat daydreaming and staring out of my hiding-place at the outer world, daydreaming all the time. Seen through a crack, the world is much nicer. And sometimes I begin weeping in secret for an hour or two hours; a weeping the taste of which is difficult for me to explain or transmit to you.

Between one teacher and another I was sent to a village and remained there about a year. And once more, and in between whiles, I enter another heder. The teacher was a complicated young fellow, a sort of mixture of Hasidism with a spark of the Enlightenment. Rabbi Meir Leibush Heilprin, the "Malbim," was the end of all wisdom for him, while Hartwig Wessely's *Songs of Glory* was the ultimate peak of poesy; and both of them together were no more than a sandal for the feet of some starched and pressed Hasidism that also had a fine delicate fragrance of scholarship about it, very slightly spiced with it as it were. He knew a little about grammar, bookkeeping, algebra; he could play the violin and chess as well. He was well-versed in the *Or Ha-Hayyim* (a kabbalistic commentary on the Pentateuch by Rabbi Hayyim ibn Atar, and almost a vade mecum for many hasidim and Jewish mystical thinkers) and in ibn Ezra's biblical commentaries. The *Biur* ("Interpretation" or commentary on the Bible prepared by Mendelssohn and his disciples) was not so dangerous; it might be kept on the bottom shelf of the bookcase for reference in case of need. It must be held to the merit of Isaac Bär Levinson that he had written the *Efes Damim* (a book refuting the Blood Libel), and so on and so forth. This teacher opened my heart a little with his talk of hasidim and of the disciples of the sages; he taught us with genuine enjoyment. But in the last resort his zeal spoilt things and he turned very disapproving eyes on my one companion and myself because meanwhile we had advanced considerably in Talmud and he knew less than us.

I was born in the village of Radi (Volhynia Government). In this village I received my first impressions of the world and Nature. It was a place of forests and vast plains. Quiet low white peasant houses lay there in amplitude, lost in a sea of green during the summer and in a sea of snow during the winter. Through the windows of our house I could every day see the magnificent forest standing facing me in its black loftiness, mighty, mysterious and full of hidden things, standing there silent and beckoning, come and search me out!

In summer noons and evenings I would set out, usually alone but sometimes with a little gang of children my own age, to this shady wood and would pass through and through it, leaving my companions for some hidden corner where I would sit alone, meditating silently, with some vast "hidden" one whose breathing I could hear behind me but whose name I did not know.

The rustle of leaves, a light cloud, a strip of sky, the melancholy note of a cuckoo at the top of a tree, the shadow of a plant falling across its own branches, a tiny pool concealed in the deeps of the forest, simple and modest forest flowers, the croaking of frogs, splashes of light falling between the branches to spangle the ground—these were the letters which combined to create my childhood universe, bringing me vague dumb feelings and thoughts the nature and meaning of which I did not know. The world surrounding me and standing over me was not explained to me but remained as sealed as ever, sealed yet calling to my heart. While as for what was explained to me out of the prayerbook—it did not attract me nor did I wish to know it.

And the sunsets? I remember one twilight. A broad plain spread out to the ends of earth. It was all swathed in lush fresh herbage and embroidered with wild blossoms of every kind; white, yellow, blue and pink. The plain and the fringes of the firmament and the whole vast space of the universe were all of them at that hour one sea of radiance, one awesome glorious crimson sea of radiance wherever my eyes might rest. The skies were red, the plain was red, the wild blossoms grew red. And I, together with two little girls dressed in white, stood among the grasses picking "birds' milk"; and the white juice of their cups squirted onto our fingers. Then suddenly I lifted my eyes to the ends of heaven—

and there was the vast light decked with flame hanging great and radiant between the lips of the firmament and the earth, and a sea of fire coursing from thence across the world.

"Yonder! Yonder!" I cried in wonder to my two little companions, and began dashing towards where the sun was, dragging my two pale little friends after me. It seemed to me that nothing more than a small stretch of country lay between me and it; and that finally I must reach it.

Then there is another summer sight which my heart preserves from those days. I understand that it is impossible for such a vision really to have existed, yet my heart and I knew that we actually saw it and very concretely; nor has my heart ever doubted the fact. It is a moonlit night. I stand alone outside the gate of our courtyard; there is a wood to right of me and a plain to left. Over my head is sky and again sky, and in front of me is a small sloping hill covered with dewy green grass, glistening with its myriad tiny drops, gently and quietly in the moonlight. The little hill sloped all the way aloft till it ended where there was a small white house on its top. Everything drowses, sliding into unconsciousness and congealing under a faint dusting of pale bluish light. And suddenly there are two files of child-dwarves, clear of face and black of garb, crossing the hill, proceeding towards the forest. And there was a kind of unutterably sweet song, a silent, interior song, flowing voicelessly from the heart, which came from them to my heart. To my heart. For it was not with my ears I heard their song but with my heart. They passed their way without observing me; but I gazed after them till they had passed out of sight. I remember that when I entered the house the power of speech had left me. I caught at my mother's apron and wished to say "Mamma!" but could not. The word mamma stuck in my throat and is there to this day. (See my poem *Night Dwarves*.)

When I began to grow up and became a heretic and began to disbelieve such things, I invented all kinds of explanations for the vision; at some time or other I must have had some kind of very vivid dream of this kind, and it had stuck in my memory; or else I must assuredly have heard some tale of the kind when I was a child, and it had remained fixed in my imagination. Maybe that is the explanation, and indeed it almost certainly is so; yet all the same that vision will never cease to seem to me a real thing which I saw with my waking eyes in every detail. I can even remember the sight of the fence of our courtyard at the time, the sight of the post next to the gateway, the sight of the little house and its roof on top of the hill and the sight of the byre facing it there. From the roof of the house to the roof of the byre was stretched a rope on which a white shirt hung drying.

All in all, at that time my heart and head were an overflowing treasury of imaginings and dreams both clear and incomprehensible, such as the mouth cannot tell nor the ear hear; but I never told my mother and father what was in my heart. Some kind of silence was enforced upon my heart and everything concealed itself and grew dumb therein, writhing and striving to come out and find expression but unable to do so.

Any kind of stain on the wall, flyspecks on the lamp, beads of moisture on glass, the images of the household utensils in the mirror— all of these were the raw material for my imagination. In particular I used to shape forms for myself and create whole universes during rainy days from the stains of damp on the inner walls of our house. I would gaze and lose myself within those green pale sunken patches, would combine them with each other so that they became mountains and valleys, strange animals and all manner of creatures. . . . All in absolute silence. I would raise my eyes to the world, wonder—and remain silent.

Many more memories of this kind remain from this period of my childhood but even now I feel that despite all the explanations it is absolutely impossible to give you the flavor of those visions. Such things derive from the heart and even the person experiencing them within him as on the day when they were first received; and only at a few rare happy moments will they gleam within him, flashing like lightning just as they had been and with their own original flavor—and in the same instant they grow dim and faint; and they are no longer there.

When I was five or six years old my father moved to Zhitomir. (In the ms. there is another version of this incident: "When I was five or six I left the village with my father's household for Zhitomir in order to dwell there. I remember that when we left the boundaries of the village and the forest, and the trees grew fewer and gradually thinner and poorer, our cow which was tied by the horns behind the cart with a long rope kept on turning her head from time to time as far as the rope would permit her, towards the village behind her, and lowed loud and long, moooooo!") There father built a house outside the town, near a broad sandy track on the flanks of a forest; and there he opened an inn, for selling food and liquor to the peasants passing that way on market days from the villages near the town. Father used to sit behind the bar, reading a book studying a passage of Mishna and incidentally filling a glass for a peasant. I was sent to the Hebrew class; first to a beginners' class and later to a mixed one. It was a place of hills and valleys, with springs rising between the hills, bubbling their song along as they dashed down to the River Titirev.

These were good times for me, particularly the free days, those of the twilights, the Sabbath eves, the Sabbaths themselves, the festivals, the times between terms. The hills led me away, and the valleys hid me in their shade. On this side of the river were lofty rounded hills of clay and sand, spreading with bare flanks like vast monsters that have taken the skin of their bones, so that the piles of living flesh on these flanks gleam red and pink. Beyond the River Titirev there gazed at me a nut wood which called at me. One lofty tree standing above its fellows with what seemed like head and shoulders would peer at me through the twilight like a robber at arms, planting a sweet dread in my heart. I knew' that it was a tree and not a robber, yet all the same I enjoyed being afraid of it. . . . Then there was the bathing in the river, and the little sandy islands in its midst where the naked children would do battle like the savages in the South Sea Islands. And ever so many things more.

The teacher who taught me my letters was a rough bear. The fare which he set before his pupils consisted of curses, blows and beating. Yet I got plenty that was precious out of him. I remember holy and dread moments and holy and sweet moments. It suddenly became dark at noon and there was gloom everywhere. It was very dark outside and twice as dark in the heder. There was a storm coming. The fear of God fell upon the teacher and upon us, his little pupils. We all let fall our Pentateuchs and rose frightened from the benches. The teacher also stood up and gave an order with his eyes. We stood ready. . . . Lightning flashed. And forty mouths suddenly recited the blessing at the top of their voices. The heavens began to thunder and growl from the depths of their belly, and suddenly there came a crash and a reduplicated crash. The heavens split and the earth was cleft in twain; and the children cried out: *Blessed art Thou, O Lord, Whose might and power fill the universe.* And the thunder grew louder and crumbled away and rolled afar, and the children became partners of it and of all the works of creation, in voice, in heart and in fear. . . . While as for the teacher, upon your soul, he was a fine fellow just then; for he was our shield and guardian.

While as for the Thirty-third day of the Omer! And the walks through the forest! These, however, had nothing to do with the teacher, but came direct from the Holy and Blest One. The Thirty-third day of the Omer was His and the forest was His, and the wild apples and wild nuts and "Kol Nidre!" pears were all His; and so were the birds' nests and the wild grapes, together with the Fridays and the Sabbaths; and we just picked it all up where it lay for the taking! Oh, how sweet was one hour of that irresponsible freedom!

There was a big branchy, shady berry tree just opposite the entrance to my father's place at the wayside, with a hollow trunk within which there was a beehive and honey. And every evening we would warily help ourselves to a little of the honey. While behind our house there was a curly birch with long hair standing and dripping with resin in the springtime: and we would catch it in some broken dish and drink it; and the resin was very sweet and clear indeed. Oh friend, friend! Why must a man grow up?

The "mixed" teacher was a pleasant fellow with a good deal of nobility about him, pure of eye and a poet by nature. He and his son were talented and could draw beautiful pictures for the *mizrah* (stylized representation of the Wailing Wall in Jerusalem which were hung on the eastern walls of living rooms in memory of the verse in Psalms "If I forget Thee O Jerusalem, let my right hand forget its cunning"), the plan of the Tabernacle and its vessels, the Candelabrum, all kinds of queer outlandish creatures. The teacher's son used to cut out the shapes from paper with a pair of scissors and would paste them on the window-panes so that folk outside might enjoy them as well. His tiny house with the little booth beside it stood on the slope of the hill leaning over as though about to fall at any moment into the abyss yawning below. . . . And there down in the valley bed, there was a spring flowing and darting and chattering and helping us to chant the Psalms which our teacher taught us in summer under the open sky or under the foliage that covered the booth. In this heder I first began to understand the things I was repeating, and the teacher was very fond of me and loved me. I remember that when I once asked him a knotty point which arose in my mind out of Rashi's commentary, he was as pleased with me as though he had discovered a great treasure, for the point was one that had struck one of the other ancient commentators (at the time I was seven years old). He praised me to my face and showed me to my fellow pupils as a prodigy, though they were much older than I.

This teacher would interpret the simpler Sabbath hymns to us, and at his order we would learn them by heart.

Before two years had passed in this delightful little suburb my father died of poverty and need after a prolonged illness which consumed our household as might the moth. My mother remained a desolate widow with three small children on her hands.

Days of darkness and gloomy oppression came upon us. That period has realized itself in my imagination in the form of a vision which, like that of the dwarves, I actually saw with my eyes, and which will never vanish from my sight. It is a wintry twilight. Outside everything is gloom and darkness, and a furious raging snowstorm. But in the house it is doubly gloomy, doubly dark, with desolation too heavy to bear in all the corners. The two rooms of the tavern stand poor, mournful and empty; and this emptiness seems to have doubled their size. There is far too much space about them. . . . All that day not a single peasant had come there. My mother sat behind the little kegs of spirits, which were empty, her hands on her heart, silent but shaking her head. My little sister and brother sat barefoot on a bench, silent as well. On the floor of the house were little hollows filled with mud and dirty water; I sat kneeling near the stove, shivering and goose-fleshed with cold, my eyes fixed on the stove and the bits of wet wood on which the fire was just beginning to take hold, quivering and starting with weak little tongues that timidly licked at the ragged bark all around. We were all hungry and all half-dazed with cold. The tongues of fire did their best, twist, lick, take on all kinds of colors, yellow, white, red, blue. . . . Tiny snakes. . . . Bits of wood seethe and snap and burst, snap, snap. And everytime there would exude from the crack an ugly drop of green dirt which would spurt and squirt furiously into the fire. I am cold, it is dark, I am hungry. I try to make myself still smaller at the mouth of the stove in the hope that I may feel warmer. Suddenly a tiny, very thin woman, as broad and tall as my finger, appeared from the well of the stove against which I was crouching, came out of there dressed in filthy garments, with a filthy three-pointed kerchief round her head. She went walking along the wall until she entered the mouth of the stove and seated herself on the end of the piece of wood sticking out from there. Suddenly she catches hold of the two ends of the cotton shawl, worn and tattered, which is round my neck and begins dragging, dragging, dragging me down into the stove. . . . I was all but choked. "Mother!" I wished to cry, but the power of speech had departed from me.

My mother could not maintain all her orphans, so brought me to the home of my father's father at the other end of the same town. And here began the second chapter of my life, a chapter of orphaned and foolish education—education that sundered body and soul.

My grandfather was comfortably off and very old, well over seventy, and for the past fifty years had bade adieu to the foolishness of the world and its affairs, remaining closed in his house and engaging solely in Torah for its own sake. By nature he was stern, ascetic and no easy taskmaster, and like most old people had forgotten the spirit and needs of childhood; he disapproved of childhood and its happiness. He felt the burden of looking after me in his old age as something too heavy to bear but which could not be avoided; as at best a commandment which demanded fulfillment at something other than its proper season but which he had of necessity to fulfil according to all the rules and regulations of the codes even though he might not wish to do so. So the old man educated me after *his* fashion, giving me a training in the Fear of God according to the *Reshith Hokmah* and *Shobet Musar* and *Sefer Hasidim*. All my self-reliant movements of behavior were abominable to him. Everything had to be done according to the book and fashioned according to the taste of the ancients, even the clothes I wore; and they were cut after his own.

My grandfather placed me in the usual schools. My first teachers were bears who performed the work of the Lord with fist and strap. Since I was an orphan, hot-tempered and a scamp, I naturally came in for more beatings and blows than all the rest. Incidentally, uncles and cousins took a hand in the good work of teaching me how to behave, together with kinsfolk and neighbors. Many of my aunts and uncles were jealous of me because my talents and knowledge were greater than those of their own children; and they always endeavored to make the old man disapprove of me for all he was worth.

"Just have a look what Isaac Yosi (my father's name) has left behind him," they would say to the old man whenever they saw me entering or leaving his house. "Today that grandson of yours smashed a window at so-and-so's house. That jewel of yours swore at so and so today." And many more such silly charges, whether false or true. Sometimes they would gather together at my grandfather's house to take counsel as to what was to be done with the ruffian. And the end of the discussion would be a thrashing. I would be thrashed by them all jointly. One would let down my breeches, another lift me over his knees, one held me by the legs, another by the arms and another would do the thrashing, proper. Sometimes they would shame me in public at the House of Study and make me bitterly angry and empty filth on my spirit. Such hours of shame degraded me and made me feel contemptible. Hatred and vengeance would heat my soul and sear my little heart. I'll pay them out when I grow up; that was what I was always thinking.

And sure enough this teaching yielded fruit. I became excitable, bad-tempered and malicious and used to work off my hot spirits with all kinds of mischief, in which I achieved for more than the normal run of scamps; and my orphan state served to draw all eyes upon me so that I became notorious throughout the neighborhood, notorious and famous simultaneously.

And my grandfather, who had become a widower, now married a new grandmother, who was excitable and noisy and shouted a great deal when angry, and good-hearted and talkative when in a good mood. When things were all right she would sit knitting socks and telling me fine tales of the good old times and all the marvels performed by her ancestor the Baal Shem Tob, from whom she claimed to be descended, "may his merits protect us. Amen." And I would hang my eyes on her lips, prick my ears up, open my mouth wide, and listen with vast devotion and swallow it all. Listen and swallow. . . .

In my grandfather's house there was a bookcase full of all kinds of outlandish books covering every range of Jewish literature. Legend, law, homilies, ethics, wonder tales and hasidic legends, Kabbalah and a few early research studies and so on and so forth. When I was finished with my studies at the heder I would start looking at these volumes, passing from easy to difficult. The wish to read took possession of me from childhood and every book that came my way, no matter what it might be, I held fast to until I had some detailed or vague idea of its contents. This reading possessed my heart and brain and turned me into a daydreamer. Fragments of ancient ideas and slivers of thought and imaginings with many useless things went coursing in a muddle through my mind; and out of them I would fashion myself all kinds of queer universes.

Somehow or other books of the Enlightenment came my way. Deuce knows where they came to me from but they came. Gradually these books began to attract me and divert me from Torah and from faith. They came my way at a time when my piety and hasidic spirit had risen within me to their absolute peak. And by that time I was already awaiting the Holy Spirit on the basis of Rabbi Hayyim Vital's book Shaar Ha-Kedusha (the Gates of Holiness), which teaches how the Holy Spirit can be attained. I hallowed and purified myself with Torah, prayer, immersions and holy concentrations of thought and so on and so forth; and there the secular literature was all of a sudden. . . .

When I was thirteen years old I left the schools to study. Absolutely by myself, far apart from the dayan (judge, the title of an assistant rabbi in a large town, who would remain in the House of Study until midday) there was not a soul to be found there. Those who dwelt in the suburb were mostly those middle-class people so common of late, who had nothing that interested them in their world except business and money. The dayan, who was a worthy and straightforward man, joined me of his own free will and like comrades we studied Gemara and rabbinical authorities several hours a day. Before a year had passed I had reached the point where I could instruct regarding that which is prohibited and that which is permissible. For even before that my chief studies had been Gemara and Authorities; and when the dayan was not at home I would decide ritual questions in his place.

For the rest of the day I would read much in secular books and write poems on the things I was thinking of. The desire to write had been in me from childhood and I remember that even when I was small and did not yet know how to write my letters properly I used to spoil any amount of paper writing down the conversation of the children and the tales I heard them tell at heder.

After many misadventures which it is difficult for me to touch upon now, I made the journey to Wolozhin at the age of fifteen on the strength of rumors current among the boys in town that at Wolozhin, together with the Talmud, they also taught either openly or secretly the seven wisdoms and the seventy tongues; and that there was barely more than a single step from Wolozhin to Berlin itself. In brief, however, I learned at Wolozhin neither the seven wisdoms nor the seventy tongues, but only how to read Russian. In place of this, however, I devoted myself for the last few months to the study of the Talmud and made great progress. "It can't be anything else but that you are the descendant of a Litvak," said the head of the yeshiba to me during the examination three months after I had come. "This is the first time that I find a boy from Volhynia who knows Talmud as you do." I had almost despaired of the Enlightenment, and the diadem of the rabbinate once more began to gleam before me; were it not that "all those who have come thither do not return."

Day by day my first enthusiasm for the Talmud declined. I would stand at my lectern for hours on end, my mouth repeating "Abaya says" but my heart in quite different words. During the early days of spring I would vanish from the yeshibah and dash as though crazy through the entries and the alleys of the town, my spirit beating frantically like a captive bird.

Those were the days when the first essays of Ahad Ha'am had begun to appear. The best and most enlightened of the Wolozhin lads formed a single group and took oath to devote their lives and abilities to work for their nation. The idea underlying the society they formed was really fine. They argued thus: The Wolozhin yeshibah is the center of the best forces and a refuge for the best talents, which must ultimately be scattered afresh through the Jewish people, to enter into it and take the lead, some as rabbis, some as doctors and scholars, some as presidents and as leaders of the community and some as writers in Israel. For this reason we ought to establish a permanent "nursery garden" of lovers of Zion among the Wolozhin lads and these would afterwards turn everybody into lovers of Zion, and the like. The society was founded and consisted of the best and finest and most disinterested of the yeshibah. Before a member was accepted he was examined sevenfold from every side, and only those were chosen who showed reason for hoping that they would be a blessing to the community in future. I, too, as a future writer (which was already my reputation) was one of those accepted. In a little while two tendencies began to mark themselves in this society: that of Ahad Ha'am and that of Yabetz. I was one of the former. The very name of Ahad Ha'am brought a sort of sacred affection to my heart. Until Ahad Ha'am, I had loved but had not honored the new Hebrew literature, but that sense of honor suddenly started within me immediately after I had read his first essays. The day I read an essay by Ahad Ha'am was a festival for me. Every word which came forth from his pen seemed to be directed to the very center of my heart and to express the quintessence of my thought. My heart prophesied to me that with him a new lustrum was coming in our literary world. At this very time I wrote my first literary attempt at the request of the fellow members of the Society. It was entitled *On the Idea of the Yishub* and was printed in *Ha-Melitz*. This essay was to have served as a sort of manifesto of our society and an expression of its views. I neither knew nor remember the value of this essay, but do remember that it was written in the spirit of both Ahad Ha'am and Yabetz. But at that time there was a new spirit abroad in the yeshibah and its pillars grew weak. Everybody saw that its time had come and its end was approaching. So I told myself, let me got away from here in good time to some other place where I can study in my own fashion. And at the advice and with the assistance of a few of my companions and confidants I went to Odessa in order to prepare myself for Berlin. This departure was made without the knowledge of my grandfather and family.

Wild and dumb, speechless and without manners, I came to Odessa and suffered there for about six months without anybody taking notice of me. An Odessa rabbi who took me into his house found me lessons to a value of twelve rubles a month and a German teacher (an agriculturist) who translated Schiller and Lessing for me into Russian. My pupils did not understand a word of Yiddish and I understood Russian only with difficulty; and now you may imagine the sort of things I taught and learnt. Whenever the time for my lesson came I would have liked to die. Shame, contempt, spiritual suffering. Never have I suffered so painfully as in those lessons. But thank the Lord, the lessons came to an end of themselves within a month. My teacher married and I was left without anything. In Odessa I began to read a little classical Russian literature such as Gogol and Dostoyevsky, and my eyes were opened to a new world. Nevertheless I was careful not to devote myself to Russian too much. I was to get most of my knowledge in Germany, so why waste time to no purpose on Russian.

Meanwhile, however, everything had come to a finish. There was nothing to eat, the Wolozhin yeshibah had been closed and I received a letter from my grandfather (through Wolozhin, sent on by my companions who had remained there) that he was about to die. And my friends wrote me from Zhitomir: "Return home. If your grandfather learns that you are in Odessa it will hasten his end." I wandered like a lost sheep through the streets of Odessa and decided to return home; and let my end be as that of all other Jewish lads.

I forgot to tell you that in Odessa a small collection of my poems came into the hands of the famous writer, Moses L. Lilienblum who chose one of them (*To the Bird*) for publication in a miscellany to be known as *Ha-Pardes;* and he sent it to Ahad Ha'am, who sent me on to Ravnitsky. The latter accepted the poem for *Ha-Pardes,* paid a little attention to me and did something to make me feel at home; but he too could not help me. I would come and visit him at his house on occasion, and the two of us would sit and remain silent together.

I finished off like the other young men in Israel. At the age of eighteen I came under the bridal canopy and from the bridal canopy to commerce; and full stop.

All the time after Odessa, both before and after my wedding, I devoted myself to reading and read much Russian. Afterwards, when I engaged in the forest trade, I spent a number of years alone in the woods. A couple of years ago I lost the little money I had and became a teacher. Now I am thirty years old.

Thus for the open part of my history; but the secret part—which in my opinion constitutes the essential history of every man—that remains deep in the heart and is not talked about.

Finally I shall tell you one thing: all the events of my life are no more than separate fragmentary notes of different instruments each playing for itself, which have all come together to the same place by chance. And if they nevertheless all combine to make some sort of tune it is nothing other than a miracle.

And something else: all my powers have drawn and been maintained, like any wild plant, from what is ready, from what is close at hand and what falls upon it from heaven. And if they are not a barren tree, it is nothing but the bounty of God.

Alone, alone, in a dark corner I grow all my life. I bore and buried seven dreams a day and no man knew I spread my hands like a fearful mother over the tender and modest blossoms of my heart concealing them from the mocking eyes of the gross crowd round about who scorned and laughed at all things wherein my spirit lived.

And when I returned from Odessa to my family, desperate and defeated, the same people received me with secret vengeance and open mockery. "Ha, ha, ha, Hayyim Nahman," one of my uncles slapped on the shoulder, "You've come back to us at last." As much as to say, "and now you'll be one of us."

My instinct of self-preservation taught me to conceal my holy of holies in the deepest places of the heart, and on the surface I became like one of them. My content, soft and tender, since my creation became surrounded with a hard shell on which anybody trying to injure it would break its teeth. In this way it was preserved from their polluting breath, from the gaze of their evil eyes and the fumbling dirty hands of those among whom I lived.

CHILDHOOD IN LITHUANIA

REBECCA HIMBER BERG (1878-)

The author of this memoir was sixty when she began to compose. She is a born storyteller, and her experiences as a child in Lithuania, as a mother struggling for survival in the squalor of the London ghetto, as the wife of a mechanic of the Seaboard Airline Railroad in Portsmouth, Virginia, and finally as the happy matriarch of three children of high intellectual attainments, is rich material for her pen. "It was in these circumstances—highly favorable to a review of her whole life—," writes her son in a letter, "that she decided to write her memoirs. I think my praise of a small sketch (for my diversion and at my insistence, of an episode which she had described to me with great spirit and fine humor) had a good deal to do with the larger undertaking, despite her insistence that she was writing her autobiography entirely for the benefit of her children— so that they might understand her and her times. In brief, I suspect that she always had literary aspirations—and talent." Mrs. Berg rarely misses a class in English for foreigners—the memoirs are written in Yiddish—where she is reported to be the star pupil.

❊　❊　❊

PROPERLY, I ought to begin this account by telling when I was born. But—I am ashamed to admit it—I do not know. You see, I was only a Jewish girl, and in my day and time, in the place where I was born, female births were not recorded.

With a boy it was different. The Jewish community and the Russian Government collaborated in observing his birthdays. The Jewish community had to know when he would be thirteen, so that he could then be confirmed in the faith of his fathers; while the Russian Government wanted to know when he was twenty-one, and a year or two later would not do at all—because they wanted him for the army. But a girl! It was enough if one reckoned that she was born some time before the "big fire," and after that one could begin checking off the places where she

had lived—at Sarah Rifke's one year; at Yankel Hirsh's five years; at
Sarah Nachman's three years—and if one happened to miss a place or
two, what did it matter? Could it hurt a girl to be a few years younger?

Therefore I must begin my autobiography, and count my years as
pleases me. I was born more than sixty years ago, and the world into
which I was born was—then as now—bad for the Jews. My birthplace
was Yanesok, in Lithuania.

My father was a poor man, a petty merchant. He had a reputation
as a scholar, which meant that he spent most of his time in the synagogue
when he should have been earning a living. I was the youngest child of
many, and therefore I know nothing of my parents when they were
young. An older sister of mine once told me that they were formerly
well off, but when I remember them they were desperately poor, and for
the rest of their lives they remained so.

My mother was, I think, an interesting woman. In those days she
was slightly in ill-repute as a modern. She spoke a number of languages
quite well—German, Russian, Polish, Lithuanian, Latvian—and she was
well-read, but in her day, especially in the villages, it was better for a
woman if she concealed her knowledge. When I began to grow up she
told me something of her past. She was born in Jacobstadt, which is a
town in Courland, near the German border. Her mother died in childbirth, and she was reared by a stepmother. Her father was a dayan,
which is to say he used to assist the rabbi in judgments involving Jews,
and these judgments were accepted as legally binding by the Russian
law courts. He was a shrewd man in drawing truth from reluctant witnesses, and a fair man in rendering decisions. His second wife, my
mother's stepmother, ran a tavern that was patronized by both Jews
and gentiles. Jacobstadt at that time was a fine and handsome town,
and a large military garrison was stationed there. My mother's beauty
attracted a number of young officers to the place, and they used to chat
with her and pay her many compliments. On that account her father
was in great haste to get her married off, and married off she was
when she was only fourteen.

Each year, as the custom was, my mother used to give birth to a
child, but by the time I was grown, there were few of them left. Some
had immigrated, far overseas, and some had died, and my mother was
old and sick with grief over them before her time.

At the time I begin my story, I was the only child left at home.
A married sister, many years older than myself, lived elsewhere in the
village. So that my mother and I were drawn closely together, and she

would sit and talk to me for hours, not as to a child, but as if she had found in me a good friend, who could understand her, in whom she could confide. And I did in fact understand her, and the words she used to speak to me are still engraved in my heart. I remember even the German and Russian songs she used to sing for me, in a low voice, because it was forbidden a woman to sing aloud. But even when she sang under her breath, it was sweet and sorrowful, as if a lost soul was weeping that could not find its place of peace. Tears would come to her eyes, and then I would throw my arms around her and say: "Mother, you will see. When I get married I will take you with me, against everybody in the world."

And my mother would kiss me and laugh bitterly. Now I understand her bitter laughter. Time serves no one's convenience.

As a child I suppose I was as other children. I played, I cried. Life was bitter around me and I knew nothing about it. Therefore I prefer to begin my story with the time when I began to notice and to understand things. Five years at Gershon Kremer's, a year at Sarah Rifke's—I must have been about fourteen years old, and we were living at Yankel Hirsh's.

Yankel Hirsh was a shoemaker, but he had done well for himself in this world. He owned a house with nine rooms, and also a wife, eight children, and a cow. The milk from the cow was sold in the village, and six of the nine rooms were rented out to tenants. In one of the rooms we used to live. It was regarded as the best room because one of the walls was built adjoining the back of a huge oven, and it was warm in winter. And in summer as well.

In the second room lived a melamed, a Hebrew teacher. He was an undersized Jew, with a fat little belly that seemed to stick out almost to a point, a pockmarked face, and two tiny eyes, like splinters. In the center of his face a nose was planted, but you saw no more than the tip of it, for his face was puffed up around it like a cake that had risen too high in the oven. He carried a whip with him constantly, as a policeman over here carries a club. He had no children of his own—may it never be said of a Jew—so he used to give vent to his temper on the poor children, his pupils. Every few minutes you could hear through the walls the stifled sobbing of a child. They were whipped double for crying aloud.

In a third room lived a widow with three children. She used to make her living selling meat, which she made kosher at home, and then peddled from door to door. She was my father's customer, my father being, you might say, in the meat business.

After the evening prayer, whenever the spirit moved him, my father would rush around to the market, and if there were a few peasants still around, he would buy up their produce—at a cheap rate because it was usually their last. Sometimes it was a sack of corn, sometimes a bundle of flax. In the course of a month or so he would have a wagon load. And then he would hire a horse and wagon, and drive with the load over the border to Latvia.

In those days Jews used to have to pay a heavy tax on kosher meat. But my father would trade his load for meat, and smuggle the meat home—fisnogis, which is calves' feet for jelly, to be distributed among neighbors, and a side of calf for the widow. But one had to be careful as with a theft. If a Jew were caught with as much as one contraband calf's foot, he would be fined three rubles, and the calf's foot would be taken away from him. A fine business! To pay three rubles when the whole value of the fisnogis was no more than a few kopecks. It was a terrific risk. But my father was a bold man in such matters.

Once, however, he was nearly caught. The neighbors said afterwards that only because Reb Velvel, my father, was such a pious man did God save him from the hands of the gentiles. It happened in this manner:

In every town the Czar stationed a Jewish official, a dershednik, whose business it was to collect the tax, and you can well imagine what sort of a Jew that would be. It was an important post for a Jew in Russia; like here a policeman, but one had also to be like a policeman —a villain, a murderer—to rise so high. One had to be able to tear the flesh from living human beings. And such a one there was among us, a renegade, whom the government had covered with medals. He had the keenest nose to smell out an innocent fisnogis, or maybe it would be a liver, or a side of goat meat. And when Baer Shepps, for that was his kosher name, was to be seen running through the streets in circles like a poisoned rat, then it was known that he had detected somewhere some contraband. And soon, for a fact, there was Baer Shepps coming out of a house with a sack of smuggled veal over his shoulder, and behind him, like a lamb being led to slaughter, the poor Jew who had been caught.

Unhappy Jew. Full well he knew what was in store for him. One did not escape lightly from Baer Shepps' hands. An hour later Baer Shepps would visit the home again, and this time emerge with pillows and a pair of copper candlesticks, in lieu of the fine. For when in his whole life did the little Jew, "the arch criminal," possess three rubles? His whole wealth lay in those same copper candlesticks and the pillows which Baer was now carrying off in triumph. How many nights had his wife sat up with the children, picking the feathers for the pillows! The mother would say to the little ones: "Children, if you finish all the feathers tonight, there will be a *beigel* for each one of you in the morning." And when the children would hear: "A beigel for breakfast!" then their tiny fingers would fly until they would drop asleep from sheer weariness, and it would be impossible to distinguish the sleeping children from the basket of feathers.

In just such houses would Baer Shepps seek out his prey. And it happened at one time that my father smuggled in a load of meat—a whole half-dozen calves' feet, a lung and liver, and a side of meat for the widow. And Baer Shepps somehow got wind of it.

My father had left the pack with the smuggled goods close to a window, and had gone off to the synagogue to give thanks. And I, as it happened, found no vacant chair, and so I spread a white cloth over the bundle, and seating myself upon it, I began to knit a shawl for a neighbor. Because this was to be the very first money I had ever earned, I was happy, and I hummed to myself as I worked. The bundles of wool were on the floor nearby, and my mother was busy unraveling them for me. Just then two women rushed in with faces pale as death, and scarcely able to talk for fright.

"Grandmother," they cried. "God be with you! Baer Shepps is coming!"

My mother trembled with fear, and I sat paralyzed, unable to move. And the smuggled goods were under me. Hastily my mother and the women piled a few things around me, partly concealing the bundle, and I sat with beating heart and resumed my knitting. In marched Baer Shepps like a grenadier, and began to throw things around in his search. He looked under the bed, under the table, in all the corners, everywhere but the right place. Afterwards he went outside to search in the woodshed, and when he returned his eyes were blazing like those of a wild beast in the forest. This time he noticed me, as if the first time. He threw several piercing glances in my direction, but he did not disturb the bundle on which I sat. Finally, he approached and picked up a German book that lay near me. He turned a few pages, and then he pinched my cheek.

"Do you know," he said, "you are a pretty girl. And you read

German? Does that idiot, your father, who has his back bent all day long over a Gemara—does he permit it?"

I did not answer.

"Do you know what," he said. "One kiss from you, and your father could bring in all the stinking calves' feet he pleased."

With this he stroked my hair, pinched my cheek again, made a few obscene Russian gestures, spat on the floor, and left.

No sooner was he gone than all the neighbors came rushing in, and they fairly wept with joy. The widow danced like a little girl. And all agreed that we had been saved by a miracle. God had made Baer Shepps blind at just this particular time, and we prayed that he might remain so forever.

Two rooms of the house in which we lived were occupied by Yankel Hirsh and his wife and eight children. There was really only one room, partitioned off with rude boards into a sleeping chamber and a workshop. In the rear compartment, which held the oven, stood a huge sleeping bench, which served during the day as a dining table and workbench, and at night returned to its original purpose. It was large enough to hold all eight children, packed in a row across the width. And if one child wetted itself during its sleep, the others would dry it.

Yankel Hirsh, our landlord, the shoemaker, was a tall thin Jew, with a bad stomach, who went about continually belching. His first wife had died, leaving him with two children. The second Mrs. Hirsh was a short, fat woman, everlastingly big with child. She had already delivered six children into the world, and was, of course, on her way to the seventh.

I have never made up my mind whether the women in those days were heroines or animals. When the time came to give birth to a child, an old woman was called in, a midwife. She made small ceremony about the affair. The prospective mother was ordered to lie down in bed, and soon after there was a cry of pain and the wailing of a child. Mazeltov! And the very next day you could see the mother sitting up in bed, supping of a huge bowl of groats, and looking smugly innocent of the whole business, as if not she were intended. Nor was there much trouble taken with the new arrival. An old dress would be torn into strips and bound tightly around the baby's body, hindering all movement. It would then be placed into its cradle, and one of the other children, hardly much older, would be assigned the task of rocking it, and of tending to it thereafter. And if the newborn child cried excessively, the mother would take a little bread and sugar, chew it into a pap, and stick it into the infant's mouth. And all would be peaceful again. As for the other children, they wallowed about undisturbed on the floor, smeared with dirt, and with other things as well. Children were cheap in those days. Therefore people could afford to have them often.

And now, into Yankel Hirsh's already crowded establishment, a father brought another darling, his ten-year old son, to learn the cobbler's trade. The boy pleased Hirsh, and a contract was made for three years, for which the father had to pay only ten rubles. Before he left, the father called his son aside, and said to him sternly:

"Listen well, Meishke! From this day, and for time and time to come, this is your new home. Obey your master and your mistress."

And he went away with a light heart. With the help of God, and only ten rubles, he had provided for his son's future, and also rid himself of one of his burdens. It had not been easy to raise ten rubles, but now that it was done, he was pleased. Yankel Hirsh was well thought of as a master. He was hot-tempered, but he kept a good table, and most important of all, he set the apprentice immediately to work learning the trade.

Room was made for Meishke, the apprentice, on the bench where the eight children slept. Close by, hanging by four ropes from the ceiling, was a wooden box that served as the cradle for the youngest child. When the child cried during the night, it was Meishke's job to rouse himself and begin rocking. The job never bothered Meishke. He used to sleep with one hand resting on the cradle. And if the baby so much as whimpered, the boy's hand would automatically begin rocking, without his waking from sleep. Apparently he had had practice at home.

His mistress was, therefore, highly pleased with him. Every morning she gave him a glass of tea with milk, and stroked his hair. And Meishke for a glass of tea and a kind word was willing to go through fire and water. He loved his mistress more than he did his own mother, and followed her about like a faithful dog. When he was through with his own work, he would run to help his mistress.

Once, when he was helping her milk the cows, he noticed that the pails were partly filled with water. He said nothing until she began milking, and then suddenly he began to laugh immoderately. "See, mistress," he said, choking with laughter, "you have forgotten to pour out the water."

His mistress smiled. "I'll tell you, child. You must not question what older people do. Pure milk is unhealthy; it leads to constipation. Therefore we have to add water."

Meishke was satisfied with the explanation. He was a simple-minded child. Nevertheless, he was an apt apprentice, who learned the trade quickly, and soon was doing the work of a full-grown man. Even his master, who was enabled thereby to sleep through most of the day, had to acknowledge himself pleased.

At five in the morning Meishke would rise, and he and the master's oldest son, a boy of eleven, would work at the bench, while the mistress cooked breakfast, and the master scratched himself. Soon the pungent odor of roast herring would fill the room. Over the herring the mistress would pour boiling water, and in a moment a rich steaming herring soup was ready. . . . The herring was for the master; the soup for the apprentice, and for the children. In addition, a large pot of potatoes would be prepared for the whole household. And the master would call out: "Children, wake up! The potatoes will grow cold!"

The children would scramble out of bed, wet and bedraggled in their night clothes, and crowd around the table. The chickens, kept in a coop under the oven, would begin to cackle, the rooster to crow. The cow, in the yard outside, would low. And the neighbors, as if attracted by the noise, would begin to stream into the kitchen for their hot water, which the mistress prepared for all the tenants.

And the children would grab the scalding potatoes with the corners of their nightclothes and seating themselves on the floor, they would begin to eat breakfast, all together. The peelings would be fed to the chickens. The cat, too, would draw close and rub itself purring against the legs of the children. The cat, the chickens, the children, all partners. A lively world!

Breakfast over, Meishke and the master's son would return to their work. And as he tapped with his hammer, Meishke sang. His eyes were still heavy with sleep, his hair thick with feathers, but he sang light-heartedly. He liked it here. Home had never been so good.

But a tragedy was due which was to mar all of Meishke's childish happiness, and to sour the remaining days of his youth and apprentice-ship. It happened on an occasion of great joy—when the sister of his mistress was, with the help of God, finally married.

Our landlady's sister was no longer young—past thirty, and to make matters worse, she had no great dowry. Moreover, she had to take care of her old blind mother. She had, therefore, been long given up as hopeless. But, as the old women used to say, even before a girl is born, the name of her betrothed is called out in heaven. True as gold! For heaven assuredly had a hand in the betrothal of Rosa-Leah, the sister.

Among us Jews, in the old country, Purim was quite a holiday. No small matter, indeed, to have gotten rid of Haman, the evil one. It certainly called for a schnapps or two. True, Haman had given birth to a breed worse than himself—in place of the one Haman there were now thousands! But a Jew lives in hope. The God of Israel had permitter him to suffer so long on this earth; he would permit him to suffer a little longer. Accordingly on Purim he drank until he was merry, and then ran joyfully to the synagogue, where he beat his hands and stamped on the floor, and each beat was a blow to Haman dead and buried these thousands of years. Returning home he was joyful. He had reckoned for once with his enemy!

At Yankel Hirsh's it was the custom to invite many of the towns-people to a Purim celebration. Chia Feige, his wife, would make *teiglich,* syrup cakes, and the men would eat the teiglich and play cards with sticky fingers. At one of these celebrations a stranger appeared, an elderly man who came in the company of his brother, a townsman. All marveled to look at him. So old a man, with so well combed a beard, and such a clean white shirt, like a banker. It was observed that every few minutes this elderly Jew would turn to steal a glance at the landlady's sister, who was busy serving the guests. And sure enough, the very next day, the marriage broker of the town paid a visit.

Chia Fegie saw him, and wondered. She called him aside. "What have you good to tell me!"

And the marriage broker answered: "Such good as I could wish upon all Jews. I have a husband for your sister."

And he went on to explain: "You observed, did you not, a fine, well-dressed Jew at the celebration, with a neatly combed beard?"

"I saw him," Chia Feige said, "and I wondered. Why should so old a man dress up like a youth to his wedding."

"Wait! Wait! He is not so old. Not even past sixty. I assure you. And wealthy. I could wish to have twelve daughters of my own if I thought I could find for them such fine bridegrooms. And he wants to marry your sister. Just so! Without a dowry. Could you believe such a thing! Would you dare to hope for better!"

Naturally, Chia Feige was not content with this. She asked questions.

"He had a wife," the marriage broker answered. "She died last year. He has, it is true, four daughters, all married, but he has—may it never be said of a Jew—no son. He owns his own house, left to him by a grandfather, and he has made improvements—a new straw roof, and a barn where he keeps his own cow. In his youth he was a tailor, one of the best, but now he has given up working in the city. But he still does work for the peasants in the country, and they pay him well, even better than he was paid in the city. True, the peasants have no money to pay him with, but they bring him sacks of flour, beans, barley, eggs, and sometimes even a chicken. His house is stocked from top to bottom with good things to eat, so what does he want with money? And who said there is no money? There is even money. His own brother told me that when the man's wife died, there was found under her pillow a ruble and twenty kopecks. But he would not touch a penny of it. Gave it to the old men to say prayers for her soul, you understand me. Money has no value for him. And if his wife should still need a few groschen, for a bath, let us suppose—why, she can take in washing, and earn enough for a bath, and other luxuries besides. You understand me? A man in the prime of his life—not yet seventy. And generous. His daughters fight to have him with them, but he wants to marry again. Why not? God has helped him, his first wife is dead. Why shouldn't he marry again? And he has no son—God forbid it should remain so. And this fine Jew has seen your sister, and—would you believe me?— he is enamored of her. He says a mother-in-law who is blind is better than one who sees everything. Ha! ha! A lively youth! I tell you, it is a stroke of good fortune such as comes only once in a lifetime!"

And Chia Feige had to agree. She kindled with enthusiasm. In short, the wedding was arranged, and all mothers with elderly daughters were genuinely envious. The wedding was such as no one had dreamed of. Apparently, the marriage broker had not lied. The bridegroom sent in geese, chickens, eggs, flour—enough to feed the village. Chia Feige prepared her famous syrup cakes, and permitted the children afterwards to lick up the syrup in the pans, so that they went around all day with smeared faces.

And the day after the wedding was still a holiday. Chia Feiga still wore her white apron, and wasted half the day receiving the congratulations of her neighbors and extolling the virtues of the bridegroom. And Yankel Hirsh slept.

In the afternoon, a man came in to inquire for his shoes which he had left to be patched. He was in a hurry. In a few hours he was going away on a journey. No one could find his shoes. The house was topsy-

turvy from the wedding feast. The shoes had been crammed away somewhere in a corner, and no one could remember where. They had to
wake up the master. Yankel Hirsh swore, and hunted everywhere for
the shoes, and when he found them at last and saw that they were not
mended, he turned white with rage. His own son, who was in his way,
received such a slap that two teeth were loosened. But with Meishke
he went about the business more deliberately. He grabbed the boy by
the collar and began to beat him over the head with one of the shoes,
until the blood flowed as from a slaughtered animal. In addition, he
kicked him brutally and with method, and at last threw him out of the
house.

He himself then sat down to the bench, and went to work repairing
the shoes that had caused all the trouble. And as he worked he grumbled
to himself, "Such an ingrate. I cram him with the best food . . . the
lazy brat."

Meanwhile my mother and I had happened into the house, and had
witnessed the whole scene, but we were paralyzed with fear. Now, however, we ran out into the street, and found Meishke trembling in front
of the door, half dead with pain and fright. We took him into our room,
and washed his wounds. We put cobwebs over the open cuts to check
the flow of blood, and afterwards bound up his head with a white
cloth. And we gave him bread and butter and tea. He munched the
bread apathetically, and watered the tea with his tears.

When he had somewhat recovered I said to him: "Go straight home
to your father and tell him how cruelly you have been treated."

The child dragged himself home, and hardly ten minutes had
passed when we saw him returning with his father. The man had a
look on his face that boded ill for someone. Now, I thought, there will
be a real scene. Even Yankel Hirsh, who was no coward, turned pale.

Without a word, the father brushed past us, straight into the room
of Shmuel, the Hebrew teacher. When he came out he was carrying
the whip that Shmuel used on his pupils. And then, as the shohet grasps
the chicken he is about to slaughter, he took hold of his son, Meishke,
placed him across the bench, and began to whip him until the boy
quivered with pain like an epileptic. And with every stroke of the whip,
the father yelled:

"Take that, you bandit, and that! Now you will know how to obey
your master. I work myself to the bone to get the ten rubles for your
apprenticeship. I try to make a bit of a man out of you. And this is my

reward. Remember this in the future, you worthless rascal. You are not to come back to me! Remember that!"

And before he left he asked Hirsh's pardon. "Do not hold it against us, Red Hirsh. If it happens again you have my permission to break every bone in his body."

With these words he left, without even another glance at his child. Hirsh said and did nothing. But my mother and I, innocent cause of the child's further misfortune, took Meishke into our room again, and began to stroke his hair and to soothe him. Meishke no longer wept. He seemed to feel and hear nothing.

The next morning he was back to his place at the bench, at work patching up a pair of old shoes. But he no longer sang. It was not the same Meishke. Overnight he had matured, had grown old.

And this was the same Meishke who in later years was hunted by the Czar's police, and who was known in our village as Meishke, the revolutionist.

II
TANGLED DESTINIES

WHEN THE BRITISH CAPTURED SAVANNAH

MORDECAI SHEFTALL (1735-1797)

Certainly Sheftall was, as his captor thought, "a very great rebel". He was every inch an American, being the son of Benjamin Sheftall, one of the forty settlers who arrived in Savannah in 1733, and among the first white children born in Georgia. As a prominent merchant, he assumed a leading role in the American Revolution: he served as chairman of the Rebel Parochial Committee, Commissary-General of the Georgia troops and a staff officer. The following excerpt from his diary describes his conduct during the British attack on and capture of Savannah in 1778. It is easy to understand why he was a respected member of the aristocratic Union Society which is still active and which still counts among its members several living descendants of this great patriot. He always maintained a warm interest in the Jewish congregation of Savannah.

❋ ❋ ❋

THIS day the British troops, consisting of about 3,500 men, including two battalions of Hessians, under the command of Lieutenant-Colonel Archibald Campbell, of the 71st regiment of Highlanders, landed early in the morning at Brewton Hill, two miles below the town of Savannah, where they met with very little opposition before they gained the height. At about three o'clock in the afternoon they entered, and took possession of the town of Savannah, when I endeavored, with my son Sheftall, to make our escape across Musgrove Creek, having first premised that an intrenchment had been thrown up there in order to cover a retreat, and upon seeing Colonel Samuel Elbert and Major James Habersham trying to make their escape that way. But on our arrival at the creek, after having sustained a very heavy fire of musketry from the light infantry under the command of Sir James Baird, during the time we were crossing the Common, without any injury to either of us, we found it high water; and my son, not knowing how to swim, and we, with about one hundred and eighty-six officers and privates, being

283

caught, as it were, in a pen, and the Highlanders keeping up a constant fire on us, it was thought advisable to surrender ourselves prisoners. We accordingly did, and which was no sooner done than the Highlanders plundered every one amongst us, except Major Low, myself and son, who, being foremost, had an opportunity to surrender ourselves to the British officer, namely, Lieutenant Peter Campbell. He disarmed us as we came into the yard formerly occupied by Mr. Moses Nunes. During this business Sir James Baird was missing; but, on his coming into the yard, he mounted himself on the stepladder which was erected at the end of the house, and sounded his brass bugle horn, which the Highlanders no sooner heard than they all got about him, and he addressed himself to them in Highland language when they all dispersed, and finished plundering such of the officers and men as had been fortunate enough to escape their first search. This over we were marched in file, guarded by the Highlanders and York Volunteers, who had come up before we marched, when we were paraded before Mrs. Goffe's door, on the Bay, where we saw the greatest part of the army drawn up. From there, after some time we were all marched through the town to the courthouse, which was very much crowded, the greatest part of the officers they had taken being here collected, and indiscriminately put together. I had been here about two hours, when an officer, who I afterwards learned to be Major Crystie, called for me by name, and ordered me to follow him, which I did, with my blanket and shirt under my arm, my clothing and my son's which were in my saddlebags having been taken from my horse, so that my wardrobe consisted of what I had on my back.

On our way to the white guardhouse we met with Colonel Campbell, who inquired of the major who he had got there. On his naming me to him, he desired that I might be well guarded, as I was a very great rebel. The Major obeyed his orders, for, on lodging me in the guardhouse, he ordered the sentry to guard me with a drawn bayonet, and not to suffer me to go without the reach of it; which orders were strictly complied with, until a Mr. Gild Busler, their Commissary-General, called for me, and ordered me to go with him to my stores, that he might get some provisions for our people, who, he said, were starving, not having eaten anything for three days, which I contradicted, as I had victualled them that morning for the day. On our way to the office where I used to issue the provisions, he ordered me to give him information of what stores I had in town, and what I had sent out of town, and where. This I declined doing, which made him angry. He asked me if I knew that

Charlestown was taken. I told him no. He then called us poor, deluded wretches, and said "Good God! how you are deluded by your leaders!" When I inquired of him who had taken it and when he said General Grant, with ten thousand men, and that it had been taken eight or ten days ago, I smiled, and told him it was not so, as I had a letter in my pocket that was written in Charlestown but three days ago by my brother. He replied we had been misinformed. I then retorted that I found they could be misinformed by their leaders as well as we could be deluded by ours. This made him so angry, that when he returned me to the guardhouse, he ordered me to be confined amongst the drunken soldiers and Negroes, where I suffered a great deal of abuse, and was threatened to be run through the body, or as they termed it, "skivered" by one of the York Volunteers; which threat he attempted to put into execution three times during the night, but was prevented by one Sergeant Campbell.

In this situation I remained two days without a morsel to eat, when a Hessian officer named Zaltman, finding that I could talk his language, removed me to his room, and sympathized with me on my situation. He permitted me to send to Mrs. Minis who sent me some victuals. He also permitted me to go and see my son, and to let him come and stay with me. He introduced me to Captain Kappel, also a Hessian, who treated me very politely. In this situation I remained until Saturday morning, the 2nd of January, 1779, when the Commander, Colonel Innis, sent his orderly for me and my son to bring us to his quarters, which was James Habersham's house, where on the top of the steps I met with Captain Stanhope, of the Raven sloop of war, who treated me with the most illiberal abuse; and, after charging me with having refused the supplying of the King's ships with provisions, and of having shut the church door, together with many ill-natured things, ordered me on board the prison ship, together with my son. I made a point of giving Mr. Stanhope suitable answers to his impertinent treatment, and then turned from him, and inquired for Colonel Innis. I got his leave to go to Mrs. Minis for a shirt she had taken to wash for me as it was the only one I had left, except the one on my back, and that was given me by Captain Kappel, as the British soldiers had plundered both mine and my son's clothes. This favor he granted me under guard; after which I was conducted on board one of the flat boats, and put on board the prison ship *Nancy,* commanded by Captain Samuel Tait, when the first thing that presented itself to my view was one of our poor continental soldiers lying on the ship's main deck in the agonies of death, and who expired in a few hours. After being presented to the Captain with mine and the rest of the prisoners' names, I gave him in charge what paper money I had, and my watch. My son also gave him his money, to take care of. He appeared to be a little more civil after this confidence placed in him, and permitted us to sleep in a stateroom—that is, the Rev. Moses Allen, myself and son. In the evening we were served with what was called our allowance, which consisted of two pints and a half, and a half gill of rice, and about seven ounces of boiled beef per man. We were permitted to choose our mess mates and I accordingly made choice of Capt. Thomas Fineley, Rev. Mr. Allen, Mr. Moses Valentonge, Mr. Daniel Flaherty, myself and son, Sheftall Sheftall.

I PROTECTED OLD GLORY

MORDECAI MANUEL NOAH (1785-1851)

No child of the American Revolution excelled Noah in his passionate attachment to the early Republic. His father served with Washington's forces, and on his mother's side he was a descendant of one of the first Portuguese-Jewish settlers of Savannah, Georgia, who had escaped the Inquisition. As a boy in Philadelphia, he witnessed unforgettable scenes like the opening of Congress, and Benjamin Franklin became his guiding star. Endowed with an alert mind and an exceedingly attractive appearance, he played a prominent role in journalism, theater and politics. During the War of 1812 he was appointed United States Consul to the Barbary States, an appointment that put him on his mettle. A burning love of country and liberty, as well as a flair for drama, are evident in the following vivid description of how he protected the honor of Old Glory. After his return to the United States, Noah made an unsuccessful attempt to found a haven for the persecuted Jews of Europe and Asia, near Buffalo, New York, a fiasco which Zangwill good-humoredly fictionized in *Noah's Ark*.

❋ ❋ ❋

I FOUND only one American gentleman besides the Charge d'Affaires residing in this wretched country (Tunis), and he had been robbed of a fortune by the complicated intrigues of these barbarians. For six years he was compelled to continue there, not having the means to liquidate some paltry debts. My arrival was hailed by him as auspicious. He recounted to me the wrongs which Americans had suffered for nine years past, and I determined to seize the first occasion to satisfy the Bey that such treatment must not be repeated. An opportunity soon presented itself.

A very much respected Italian merchant by the name of Curadi came one day into the American Consulate and informed me that bills of exchange which he had drawn on Leghorn for twenty thousand piasters were returned protested, and that the holders were about to seize upon him and all his property, amounting to double that sum, to sacrifice his merchandise, and ruin his prospects for ever; that his Consul, Mr. Nyssen, the Dutch Agent, being so completely in the power of the Bey, could not protect him, and in this extremity he had ventured to implore the benevolent protection of the United States to enable him to sell his propery with credit to himself and pay his debts honorably. I informed Mr. Curadi that it was not customary to take the subjects of another power under American protection, but if he entered the Consulate and claimed the protection of the flag, he should have it. He then declared that he would not leave the house, as he considered it a sanctuary afforded to the unfortunate, and respected by the Tunisian authorities. I ordered an apartment to be prepared for him and patiently awaited the approaching storm. The Mamelukes who were sent in pursuit of Curadi traced him to the American house, which they dared not to enter, but proceeded to the palace to give information.

The next morning a Janizary arrived with the compliments of the Bey, requesting me to give up the Christian merchant, who, he said, was a debtor endeavoring to defraud his creditors. I desired him to convey my respects to his Highness and inform him that he was aware that no person was ever given up who had taken sanctuary in the American Consulate. The following day the Janizary returned with the same message, to which the same answer was given. These visits continued for several days, with no better effect. Each day augmented something insulting to the message.

Contrary to the usual custom observed among the Consuls, I seldom visited the palace, excepting on business of importance; my visits not being frequent, the Bey heard what I had to say and replied promptly. I had occasion to send the elder dragoman, Abdallah, an honest old Persian, to the palace for a permit to land a barrel of wine, which I was privileged by treaty to land without paying duty. In a short time Abdallah returned in great trepidation.

"Oh, my lord," said he, "such a piece of business, such an unfortunate affair!"

He looked much alarmed, and spoke half *lingua franca,* and partly Arabic and Persian. I could with difficulty understand him; but through the assistance of Ambrosio, the chancellor, I learned that in crossing the patio at the palace, the Bey had perceived him, and calling him, addressed him as follows:

"Abdallah, I have sent for several days past to the Consul with orders to give up that Christian. I had a good opinion of the Consul, and did think him a good man; but he knows that he has not a right to protect a debtor (I knew to the contrary), and finding him indifferent to my orders, you may now tell him that tomorrow I will send twenty Mamelukes into his house and cut the Christian to pieces!"

Curadi heard the message and trembled like an aspen leaf. I lost all patience and temper at this insult. The creditors of Mr. Curadi could have settled honorably with him at my house. I was security for his person, but according to custom they determined to seize him and all his property, sell it for what they pleased, and if they could bring him in debt, to throw him into prison for the balance. They had bribed the Bey to get him from my house, and his highness, flattering himself that I was ignorant of my rights, ventured to experiment by threats. I determined to resist them. We had arms and ammunition, and I resolved to shut all the gates and doors, hoist the flag, and beat off the Mamelukes if they should decide upon an attack. Curadi, "whose head's assurance was but frail," protested against resistance, and solicited me to accompany him to where he would state to the Bey the nature of his concerns.

The next morning I carried him to the palace, accompanied by both dragoman and Ambrosio. His creditors were anxiously waiting for their prey, sure of possessing him. I entered the Hall of Justice where the Bey was seated surrounded by his ministers. After the accustomed salutation, he asked very calmly what my business was.

"Your Excellency is aware," said I, "that any person who takes refuge in the house of a Consul is protected. This Christian entered my house as a sanctuary, and you have endeavored to destroy my rights by attempting to take him from my protection; failing in that, you had recourse to threats, and yesterday you sent me a message by Abdallah, stating that if I did not instantly give him up, you would send twenty Mamelukes and cut him to pieces. Now, sir, that the sanctuary of the American house may not be violated, I have, at his request, brought him to you, finding that you are about to deprive the American flag of a privilege accorded to all civilized powers, and which, I assure you, we shall not relinquish without a struggle."

"I never said such a thing," said the Bey, rising. "The slave is mad. Did I say so, Abdallah?" asked he, with a furious look.

The poor trembling dragoman replied, "No, sir, I was mistaken."

"There, Consul," said the Bey, seating himself, "how could you believe such a thing, such a preposterous thing? Abdallah is an old fool."

I knew the Bey lied and Abdallah had spoken the truth, which, had he insisted upon, his head would have answered for.

"Well, what is all this about?" said the Bey.

Curadi told his story, and asked only sixty days to sell his goods and pay his debts honorably.

"Why, this is fair and just," said the Bey, "and if you will be his security, he shall have that time."

I pledged myself for his safekeeping. His creditors looked disappointed, and Hassan and Mustapha, the two sons of the Bey, who had been the cause of this trouble, darted a furious look at me and left the hall, which look I returned with perfect indifference. Having confirmed the rights and privileges due to the American Consulate, and defeated the intrigues of these rogues, I returned to Tunis triumphant.

Curadi commenced the sale of his property and the payment of his debts. A few days after, Hassan Bey, determined to carry his point, sent a Janizary, with a polite message to Mr. Curadi, requesting him to come to the palace. Not suspecting any treachery, he dressed himself for the purpose and was accompanied by the dragoman. But he had scarcely entered when he was seized and hurried to a dungeon. Abdallah returned and informed me of the event.

It was then near one o'clock. The business for the day had terminated. The Bey, as usual, had retired to his harem, or to take his afternoon nap; notwithstanding which, provoked at the perfidy of the act and determined to put an end at once to these insults, I mounted my horse, and returned to Bardo. The Janizaries at the gate looked at me with astonishment as I passed through the arched way. There were many stretched on their mats asleep, with their arms at their sides. I entered the patio, but saw no person; the palace was silent as death, but I soon roused the guards and slaves, and demanded the release of Curadi, in tones loud and peremptory. The Christian secretary, a very clever and civil Italian, remonstrated against the demand, assured me it was impossible to obtain his release that day, that the Bey was among his women, that his head would be the forfeit of disturbing him, and he entreated me to come tomorrow. I had come with determination to release the Christian instantly, or to go into prison with him. I accordingly unbuckled my sword, divested myself of uniform and epaulettes, and ordered the guards to show me to the prison, which they went about doing cheerfully. The slave, much alarmed, interfered. He solicited me to wait until he could see Sidi Hassan, and left me for the purpose of acquainting him with the object of my visit.

In a short time Hassan, having collected a few persons around him, asked me in a rude and insulting manner what I wanted. I was in a humor to meet him with equal promptness and severity, and demanded the instant release of Curadi. He refused to give him his liberty and censured me for presuming to protect a debtor and interfering with the concerns of the government. He was loud and insolent. I was excessively provoked and irritated, yet listened calmly to him.

"Well, why don't you reply," said he, "what have you to say?"

I told him I had nothing to say to him, that I did not know him, I came to see the Bey of Tunis, and I would know who was Bey; that the sovereign of this country, as I had supposed him to be, had promised the merchant sixty days privilege to see his goods; that he was taken from under the protection of my dragoman and hurried to a dungeon, where, if he was not instantly released, I would bear him company, order my flag to be struck, and terminate at once the pacific relations between the two countries. The tone of Hassan Bey lowered in an instant. He said his father had approved the measure, which I denied. He entreated me to come tomorrow, which I refused. At length he sprung furiously from his seat and left the room.

"Take him then," said he, as he departed. "You shall answer for his debts."

An order was given to release him. I followed the messenger, and in a dark and dismal dungeon, suffocating and filled with vermin, was poor Curadi, dressed in cassimere small-clothes and silk stockings, for his audience. He was as rejoiced and grateful at his deliverance as I was that I had triumphed over the iniquity and bad faith of these wretches, and once more preserved inviolate the rights of the American flag. The Consuls soon heard and rejoiced that such a victory, for the first time, in such a case, was obtained at Bardo.

MENDOZA, THE FAMOUS PUGILIST

DANIEL MENDOZA (1763-1836)

Mendoza is perhaps the first of his profession who may be called a "boxer", for he introduced the scientific strategy of modern boxing in the ring, and by initiating a school and making sparring tours, made the manly art the sport of gentlemen. Born of a poor family in London's Whitechapel, he began his career by exhibiting a masterly prowess over all challengers; his great victories, especially over the outstanding contender Humphreys, made him a byword wherever sports were talked of and they were celebrated in popular songs. He was plagued by economic difficulties from time to time, attempting to retrieve himself by engaging in occupations ranging from actor to sheriff. However, pride of the successful rise from Whitechapel to his acceptance among aristocrats, is unmistakable in his lively memoirs which he wrote "to trace the means by which I acquired a degree of public esteem and fame, which perhaps few men of my rank in life ever attained."

❅   ❅   ❅

I WAS born on the fifth day of July, 1764, in the parish of Aldgate, London. My parents, who were of the Jewish persuasion, were by no means in affluent circumstances; they might however be considered as in the middling class of society: and though their family was large, they contrived to bestow a tolerable education on all their children. They justly conceived this to be an object of the highest importance, as it concerned their future welfare in life, and therefore used every effort in their power to accomplish it.

I was accordingly sent at a very early age to a Jewish school, where I remained some years, and was instructed in English grammar, writing, arithmetic, and those branches of education which are usually taught in schools; I was also instructed in the Hebrew language, in which, before I quitted school, I made considerable progress.

Being blessed with a robust and vigorous constitution, and enjoying excellent health and spirits, I engaged at this early period of my life in several contests with boys considerably older than myself, till I at length attained such a reputation for courage, activity and strength, that none would venture to contend with me, and I was acknowledged by all of them to be their master.

Whenever I returned home with a black eye, or any external mark of violence, my father never failed to inquire strictly into the cause, and would reprove me severely when it appeared I had involved myself wantonly in a quarrel; but on the other hand, if he found I had acted only in self-defense, or from any justifiable motive, he would freely forgive me, and declare he would never exert his paternal authority to prevent me from standing in my own defence, when unjustly assailed, being well aware that courage is not only useful, but almost indispensably necessary to carry us through life.

In justice to the memory of my father, I must have mention that perhaps no man had a clearer notion of the difference between true and false courage than himself; he would often declare how gratified he felt in seeing resolution and fortitude displayed upon proper occasions; thought at the same time no one could hold the character of a bravado, or quarrelsome man, in greater abhorrence. His observations on this subject I have often reflected on, and I trust they will never be effaced from my memory.

As our family was large, my father was accustomed to place his children in different situations and employments very early in life. Accordingly before I had attained the age of thirteen I went to live with a glass-cutter, to whom it was intended I should be bound apprentice if it should appear after passing a few weeks together that we were mutually satisfied.

My master was an honest good-natured man, but too much of an ale-house politician to attend properly to his own affairs. His family consisted only of his wife and son, and the latter was the cause of my quitting my situation. This young man was of a very haughty disposition and would generally, when he had occasion to speak to me on matters relating to business, assume a great deal of unnecessary consequence and be, for the slightest offense, very abusive and scurrilous. Having one day taken the liberty of remonstrating with him on the subject, hoping thereby to induce him to amend his conduct, I found that, so far from such being the effect, he became highly exasperated at my presumption as he was pleased to term it, and made use of such insolent threats that I determined no longer to submit and therefore gave him a severe thrashing (though in his father's house); and having done so thought it prudent to imitate the manners of the great—I resigned my situation to avoid being turned out.

Feeling the utmost aversion to a life of idleness, and unwilling to become an incumbrance on my father, I gladly availed myself of the first opportunity of employment that offered and therefore entered into the service of a fruiterer and greengrocer in our neighborhood, from whom and whose family I experienced, during my stay with them, very kind and liberal treatment. I was here frequently drawn into contests with the butcher and others in the neighborhood, who, on account of my mistress' being of the Jewish religion, were frequently disposed to insult her. In a short time, however, I became the terror of these gentry, and when they found that young as I was, I was always ready to come forward in her defense, they forbore to molest her.

My next situation in life was with a tea dealer, in whose service I fought the first pitched battle that attracted the attention of the public. This was in the year 1780; I was then only sixteen years of age, and the occasion of my fighting arose from the following circumstance.

A porter who had been sent to our house with a load, upon my offering him the price of a pint of porter as a gratuity for himself, rejected the offer in a contemptuous manner, and made a demand of double the money. At this moment my master entered the shop and, remonstrating with him on the impropriety of his behavior, the fellow became still more abusive and challenged him to fight. Upon which I turned him into the street and told him that since he was so desirous of fighting I was at his service, and that I felt myself fully competent to punish him for his insolence, and was willing to give him instant proof of it if he pleased. He accepted my challenge with great eagerness, and most probably flattered himself with the hopes of gaining an easy victory over a youth, (being himself a stout athletic man in the prime of life).

A ring being consequently formed in the street, we immediately set to and, after a severe contest of about three quarters of an hour, my antagonist confessed himself unable to stand longer against me, and gave in. Upon this occasion Mr. Richard Humphreys, whom I shall frequently have occasion to mention in the course of these memoirs, was my second.

This battle which first brought me into public notice, laid the foundation of the fame I afterwards enjoyed; the spirit and resolution I displayed throughout a contest with an antagonist of such superior strength excited the general applause of the spectators (many of whom were intimately acquainted with me) and became the general subject of conversation in the neighborhood for some time after.

Shortly after this one of my friends called upon me and informed me that, having witnessed such uncommon exertion on my part in the last contest, he had matched me to fight a man in the Mile End Road, on the ensuing Saturday (being a leisure day with us); I had never before fought for money, and felt some reluctance to a battle of that sort on the present occasion; however, as my friend had made the match, I was unwilling to disappoint him, and therefore resolved to use my utmost exertions in his favor.

Accordingly, at the time appointed, I met my opponent, and here again had to contend against superior strength; but, after a contest which lasted near an hour, had the satisfaction once more to come off victorious.

Mr. Humphreys was likewise my second on this occasion; and when some of the spectators called out to him to direct me where to strike, I well recollect hearing him reply, "There is no need of it, the lad knows more than us all."

Though the success of these two battles had gained me great repute for courage, as well as for skill and activity, I had not then any intention of devoting my future life to the practice of pugilism, nor of quitting the situation in which I was engaged; but, on my return to my master on the Monday following, he expressed great displeasure at my having fought the last battle, and immediately discharged me from his service.

Shortly after I was dismissed from the service of the tea dealer, I was invited to join some friends in celebrating a Jewish festival and we accordingly agreed, by way of frolic, to disguise ourselves and represent a party of sailors, in which I was to bear the part of the lieutenant. This frolic, however, which seemed likely to produce a great deal of merriment and diversion, had a very unpleasant termination; for, happening to meet with a press gang, I and two of my friends were actually made prisoners by them, and it was not without considerable difficulty that we procured our release; this however we effected after two days confinement.

Highly gratified at regaining our liberty, we resolved to be present at a dramatic performance, taken from scripture history, which was to be acted by some of our acquaintance (it being a common practice with the Jews to perform pieces of this kind during the festival). We accordingly went, and found them preparing for the performance of a drama founded on the History of Esther. On our relating the incident that had occurred, we were strongly urged by them to perform in an interlude, in which a party of sailors were to be introduced, for which our present dress was of course suitable and proper; and as the piece seemed to be exceedingly short, and we had between two and three hours to prepare ourselves, we felt no difficulty in acceding to their solicitations.

Accordingly, after the performance of the drama of Esther, which went off with tolerable success, we were introduced, and the piece opened with a song which was unfortunately assigned to me; unfortunately for I had at this time a hoarseness which had considerably increased from my having sat up the whole of the two preceding nights, and I was scarcely audible when I came on the stage; and this circumstance, together with the awkward and embarrassed behavior of my companions at the time, so excited the disgust of the audience, that they would not suffer us to proceed, and we were finally hissed and hooted off the stage.

This, however, was not the worst of the affair, for when it is considered the performers were all of the Jewish persuasion, it will be readily supposed the entertainment was not to be furnished gratuitously. The steady attachment of my brethren to the "main chance" is too well-known for such an idea to be entertained. Judge then what must have been our disappointment and chagrin, at being not only driven from the stage with disgrace, but at being also deprived of the pecuniary reward of our exertions; for a considerable uproar and tumult having been excited by the ridiculous manner in which we attempted to play the interlude, some persons availed themselves of this circumstance, and found means to purloin the box containing the money that had been paid for admission. I was however more fortunate in this instance than my companions, for having been furnished by the manager of the company, with a valuable epaulette to adorn my uniform coat, I refused to restore it to him till I had obtained a remuneration for my services.

Soon after this I entered into the service of a tobacconist, who resided in the neighborhood of Whitechapel. I was engaged by him chiefly for the purpose of traveling with samples of the various articles he sold, and to procure orders for him, etc., and having been sent into Kent on some business of this sort, was drawn into a pugilistic contest from the following circumstance.

Walking on the road near Chatham Barracks, part of a regiment of soldiers happened to pass, (I believe the 25th, but am not certain) when one of the sergeants accosted me in a very rude manner, and ordered me in a peremptory tone to get out of the way, and upon my remonstrating with him on his uncivil behavior, struck me a severe blow with his halbert; feeling my indignation roused to the highest pitch at this treatment, I could not refrain from offering to fight him on the spot, and he readily accepted my challenge. At this moment a party of sailors happened to come up who, having inquired into the cause of this contest, assured me of their determination of seeing fair play.

We accordingly stripped and set to, and after fighting for nearly an hour, I had the satisfaction of coming off completely victorious, and of inflicting a severe and deserved punishment on my antagonist, in revenge for the ill treatment I had borne from him.

One of the officers of the regiment who, in the first instance, seemed rather inclined to take the part of my opponent, was so much gratified at witnessing what he was pleased to term an uncommon instance of spirit and resolution in a youth, that he immediately presented me with five guineas, and afterwards exerted his influence, with effect, in procuring orders for my employer.

As for the behavior of the sailors, it was so truly noble and generous and made so deep an impression on my mind, that I cannot forbear relating it. These gallant sons of Neptune watched every turn of the battle with the most anxious solicitude, and when it terminated in my favor, expressed their congratulations at my success in the most friendly manner, and cheered me with loud and repeated acclamations. They afterwards carried me with them in triumph to Gravesend, a distance of eight miles. And as the bags which I had out with me containing the different samples of merchandise were, in the course of the affray, thrown down and trampled on, it became necessary for me to return to town for a fresh supply, and I accordingly came up with them on the same boat.

On my return, my master expressed his surprise at seeing me again so soon, but on my relating the cause, and giving him an account of the battle, he expressed the greatest satisfaction at my conduct, and told me that so far from being inclined to blame me for my behavior, he thought I deserved the highest commendation for having acted as I had done.

I returned almost immediately afterwards to Chatham, and transacted the business on which I was sent before, and was prevented in the manner I have just related.

On my return to town, I was induced, at the request of some of my acquaintance, to engage in a pugilistic contest for five guineas, with a man who had signalized himself in many instances, and who the most sanguine of my friends expected would prove a formidable opponent.

Having mentioned the subject to my master, and requested his permission to fight, he very readily granted it, and was afterwards present at the battle.

On this occasion the friends of my opponent were so confident of his success, on account of the evident superiority he possessed in size and strength, and the reputation he had already acquired, that they offered bets of five to one in his favor. Notwithstanding which, however, when I engaged with him, I had the satisfaction of having my exertions crowned with success, after a hard contest of an hour and a quarter.

I was about this time induced to quit the service of the tobacconist upon the prospect of a situation of more emolument; the remuneration I received from him was very trifling and inadequate to procure me many little enjoyments I wished for; I therefore eagerly embraced an offer that was made me of a situation in which I was to receive a guinea per week and my board, which I at that time could not fail of considering a most liberal remuneration for my services, more especially upon being given to understand that my employment would be to assist in conveying different sorts of merchandise from the coast to various places to be disposed of, and that I was to be furnished with an excellent horse for that purpose.

As the application was made to me from a quarter that I had always considered as respectable, I had not the least suspicion of there being anything illegal or improper in the concern; but immediately upon my engaging in it, I was informed that I was hired for the purpose of escorting smuggled property, and was likewise told that I should be expected to guard and protect (even at the hazard of my life) whatever might happen to be entrusted to my care, against any seizures that might be attempted to be made thereon.

This certainly was most unwelcome intelligence to me. I am not aware of ever having wanted resolution and courage upon proper occasions, but was not desperate enough to disregard entirely the consequences of such a dangerous profession, and having learnt that one of our party had, but a few weeks previous to this, lost his life in an affray with some revenue officers, I quitted my employment in disgust, having remained therein only four or five days.

Shortly after my return to town, I was induced to engage in another pugilistic contest; for being present one day in company with a young man at a fight at Kentish Town, my friend happened to be grossly insulted by a man, whom I challenged in consequence, and we accordingly set to, when after a contest of about half an hour, he was forced to give in, being so severely beaten as to be scarcely able to stand and, indeed, he was obliged to be carried off the field.

Being at this time out of employment, and having gained some slight knowledge of the confectionary business, being used to make passover cakes and things of that sort, I was glad to avail myself of an opportunity that offered of accompanying a cousin of mine to Northampton, where there was a likelihood of my obtaining a situation, in which I might in a short time perfect myself in this business. In order to render our journey at as little expense as possible, we determined to travel the whole way on foot, and accordingly, having set out one morning at four o'clock, we reached Northampton the following morning at six. Having taken refreshment and rested ourselves for some time at a public house, we walked out to view the town, and happened in the course of our perambulation, to meet with a young man who was considered as the bully of the place who, observing two Jew lads, strangers to him, walking about and conversing together on different matters, thought proper to show a little consequence on the occasion, and therefore accosted us, observing that he supposed "we were after no good", that "he hated to see such fellows strolling about the place", that "it was a pity we were not sent to Jerusalem", and using many other expressions equally absurd and insolent. I replied with some warmth, which provoked him still further, and he threatened to kick me out of the town. This last menace however had an effect quite the reverse of what he probably expected, for instead of causing me to become more submissive, my indignation was now roused to the highest pitch, and I told him in very plain terms the opinion I held of him, which was that he was both a scoundrel and a coward for insulting those who had not given him the slightest offense, that I knew he placed great reliance upon his superior strength and size, and flattered himself with the idea of behaving as he pleased without meeting with resistance, but that for my own part, I so little feared him or his threats that, boy that I was, I would fight him on the spot, if he chose, for a guinea.

This offer was very readily accepted, and we accordingly returned to the house which we had just left to place the money in the landlord's hands, but when I mentioned the affair to him, he endeavored to dissuade me from engaging in a contest which was so very unlikely to terminate in my favor, assuring me at the same time that my antagonist possessed such repute as a pugilist that he knew not any one in the place who would venture to stand against him. My cousin now (knowing the slender state of our finances, for indeed we had at this time but two guineas between us) joined our landlord in dissuading me from my purpose—but, being unwilling to shrink from my own challenge, I resolved to try the effects of my utmost exertions, and was determined not to give in while I had the power to strike a blow.

We accordingly came out into the street and, a ring having been formed, my opponent and myself set to and fought exceedingly hard for the space of an hour and a half, when he was unable to continue the contest any longer, and acknowledged me to be the victor. So severely was he beaten that he could not walk home without assistance, and was afterwards confined to his room for upwards of three weeks.

This battle excited considerable attention and was for a long time the subject of conversation at Northampton. It was agreed on all hands that my adversary's conduct had drawn on him a proper punishment, and many were gratified at the mortifying repulse he had met with.

I had now so completely established my reputation for a thorough knowledge of the theory and practice of the art of pugilism, that my friends as well as myself were desirous that, instead of seeking fresh contests, I should avail myself of the fame I had already acquired, and make such a use of my skill as would enable me to derive from thence a regular and liberal income; and being now applied to by several gentlemen to teach the art of self-defense, I was induced, in consequence of the number of such applications, to open a school for that purpose in Chapel Court, behind the Royal Exchange, shortly after which a circumstance occurred, which though trivial in itself yet when connected with what had previously happened, tended greatly to widen the breach then existing between Mr. Humphreys and me.

A Mr. R., a great patron and friend of his, had been pleased to venture some money on me, in my contest with Martin, and immediately after I had obtained the victory, was so liberal as to present me with what he had won, being twenty guineas, declaring at the same time that my behavior on the occasion was so much to his satisfaction, that had he won double the money he would with the greatest pleasure have made me a present of the whole. I therefore thanked him for his liberality, and of course expected to hear no more of the matter.

Some time after this, however, I was arrested for twenty guineas, a circumstance at which I was greatly surprised, and still more so, on learning that it was at the suit of this gentleman, who now pretended he had *lent* me the money.

As I never before had the honor of having my name coupled with that of one of those phantoms of the law, John Doe or Richard Roe,

I felt my situation very unpleasant, and therefore was glad to obtain my liberation, by paying the pretended debt and costs.

I confess I felt very much irritated at this ungenerous transaction, which I was inclined to attribute in some measure to Mr. Humphreys' intimacy with his patron.

On my mentioning the affair however to Mr. G., a gentleman to whose liberal patronage and friendship I had frequently been indebted, and by whose persuasion I was chiefly induced to open my academy, he expressed great indignation at the transaction and afterwards, when he went to Lloyd's, made the matter public among his friends there, to most of whom I was well known and who, in order to compensate me for my loss, immediately entered into a subscription for me which, in the course of two hours, amounted to one hundred and forty-five guineas.

About this time, I entered into the married state with my present wife; this match was with the perfect concurrence of our mutual friends; and years of experience in which we have had to encounter, as well the deceitful smiles of prosperity as the terrific frowns of adversity, have never given me reason to repent my choice.

On my marriage, I promised my wife to seek no further contests, and even to decline all challenges for the future that might be offered, except from Mr. Humphreys; but I really conceived myself so ill-treated by him in several instances, that I determined whenever a proper opportunity occurred, to requite him (if I could) for his unhandsome conduct.

Soon after this I agreed one day to meet a few friends at Epping, and to accompany them from thence to Harlow, to see the annual fair which is held there; our object was merely amusement, and I had not the slightest expectation of engaging in any contest; but on my arrival at an Inn at Epping, I met Mr. Humphreys there who, as I afterwards learnt, had been apprized of my excursion, and was determined to meet me, accompanied by some of his friends and, if possible provoke me to fight him. We had frequently met of late at public places and on such occasions had spoken our minds to each other pretty freely; but he now accosted me with more violence than ever, and having accused me of having taken improper liberties with his name, threatened to thrash me. Upon which I told him that if I had made free with his name, he had made equally free with mine, and consequently we were so far even: and I assured him that he mistook greatly if he thought his menaces would avail with me and that, to show what my sentiments were with regard to him, I would fight him that instant, though surrounded by his friends, if any one present would second me.

At this moment an inn-keeper who was in the room, with whom I was slightly acquainted, declared he would see justice done to me; and it was accordingly settled that Mr. Humphreys and myself should adjourn into the inn yard, and there decide our dispute.

A ring being therefore instantly formed, we set to, and after exchanging a few blows, I succeeded in closing one of my opponent's eyes, and almost immediately afterwards gave him a severe bruise over the other, when we were interrupted by a party consisting of peace officers and others, who interposed, and prevented our deciding the contest.

This encounter however, lessened the opinion I had previously formed of Mr. Humphreys' powers, and I now felt confident that, though he was my superior in strength and size, I was fully equal to him in activity and knowledge of the art of pugilism. I afterwards learnt that the peace officers had interfered at the request of his friends, who were apprehensive that he would very soon be beaten, and would thereby suffer considerably in the public estimation.

In the evening of the same day however, I met Mr. Humphreys again at Harlow, when he professed his willingness to renew the contest; but this I declined, telling him I wished not to take the advantage, which was in my power of accepting his offer, and fighting him when he was deprived of an eye; and advising him to take more care of the other, assured him of my readiness to afford him satisfaction at any future opportunity.

About a month after this I went to see a fight on Epping Forest, between two pugilists of the names of Kellyhorne and Savage, and then happened to meet Mr. Humphreys again, when I challenged him to fight me for fifty guineas, and it was settled that we should meet in the evening at the Spread Eagle, Gracechurch Street, to settle the conditions of the battle, and make the deposit. I accordingly went there, on my way to town, accompanied by two friends, and met my opponent who was with a large party. Soon after our arrival there one of my friends, happening to have a dispute with one of Mr. Humphreys' party, on a sudden received a violent blow from him with the handle of a whip loaded with lead and fell down, to appearance lifeless—upon which I immediately seized the fellow who had committed this outrage, and having pulled him into the middle of the room, gave him a severe thrashing in the presence of the whole company, none of whom offered to interfere—and my friend having in some measure recovered, I declared aloud that we would fight any three present instantly, if they chose, in the inn yard; that I would engage with Mr. Humphreys, and my friend with any two of his companions; but this offer was not accepted.

It was settled however at this meeting that Mr. Humphreys and myself should decide our contest on the 9th of January following, at Odiham in Hampshire; and it being probable that this battle would excite considerable interest among the amateurs and patrons of the pugilistic art, it was agreed that we should fight in an inclosed space in an inn yard, that half a guinea should be the price of admission for spectators, and that the money should be divided between us.

About this time I was near falling the victim of a conspiracy, for my adversaries now finding that I feared not any of them in a fair contest, were resolved to try the effect of secret and midnight machinations against me—this was apparent from the following circumstance.

One evening being at Vauxhall Gardens with my wife, my brother-in-law, and another friend, on our preparing to return, we were on a sudden surrounded by a party of about twenty men, among whom I recognized my old antagonist Tyne; they immediately began to insult us, pushing against us in a rude and violent manner, and as their ill behavior was particularly directed against my wife, who was at that time in a state of pregnancy, I became greatly alarmed on her account, and entreated them to suffer me to conduct her to some place of safety; assuring them, at the same time, that if any of them felt the least cause of complaint against me, I was ready and willing to answer it in any manner they pleased. All I could say, however, had no avail with them, and I was actually compelled to fight my way through them, which having effected with the assistance of my two friends, my brother-in-law conveyed my wife away from this scene of riot, and returned as soon as he had placed her in safety, to my assistance. I now singled out one who seemed the stoutest man of the party, and having told him he should give me satisfaction for the conduct of himself and his companions, we set to and fought for about ten minutes, when he had evidently the worst of the contest, but I was now assailed by sticks in all directions, but my friends and myself made such a desperate resistance, that we were on the point of gaining the victory, notwithstanding the superiority of numbers opposed to us, when I was, on a sudden, seized forcibly by the arm, surrounded by several men, carried away from my friends to the servants' hall and locked up in a room over there; from hence however I contrived to escape, by dropping from a window, and with no small surprise, beheld my wife, at a short distance, sitting very disconsolate on a bench, from whom I learnt that my two friends were in custody on the charge of our antagonists, who accused us of being the aggressors. Highly indignant at this false and infamous accusation, but at the same time being aware that my attempting to interfere at that time would serve no purpose, we walked to the water side, and took a boat with the intention of returning home, and on our way, happened to meet our adversaries upon the water, who it appeared had been to take some refreshment, and were on their return, for the purpose of making good their charge against my friend. Having accosted them, considerable altercation ensued between us, and on their evincing a disposition to insult me further, I felt so much irritated, that seizing a staff which lay in the boat I aimed a blow at them with such force that had I not fortunately missed my aim by striking too high, the consequence would probably have been fatal to some of them. I believe they now regretted they had molested me, for some of them had suffered severely in the course of the conflict in the gardens, and conscious of having acted very wrong, proposed to settle the affair amicably, and professed great regret for what had happened, and their willingness to compensate myself and my friends, in consequence of which I consented to let the matter drop. I was dreadfully cut in the head in the course of the affray, the ill effects of which remained for a long time after.

About this time I accepted the invitation of some friends to pass a few weeks with them at Oxford, and was there invited by them to partake of such diversion as the neighborhood afforded.

I was never much attached to the sports of the field—indeed, having been brought up and accustomed to the ways of a town life, it can scarcely be expected that I should have formed an idea of them: it was therefore more in compliance with the solicitations of my friends than from any particular inclination on my own part, that I engaged with a party in the diversion of fox-hunting.

One day however I happened to follow this sport in a way that gave great displeasure to a gentleman who rode up to me, and accusing me of riding among the hounds, and of other improper conduct, threatened to horsewhip me unless I altered my behavior. I felt greatly irritated at this language, for though I perhaps deserved reproof, it might, I thought, have been given in a milder way, and therefore warned him in a resolute manner not to attempt any thing of the sort, and declared that if he even raised his whip for such a purpose, I would certainly strike him off his horse, be the consequence what it would. After some further altercation however, we each continued to follow the sport as it suited our inclination; but my surprise was greatly excited at learning, almost immediately afterwards, that the person I had offended was no other than his Grace himself.

When the hunt was over, the Duke rode up to me again, and asked me how I liked the sport, upon which I told him I had enjoyed it much, and was happy that our previous altercation had terminated as it had; for that had his Grace offered to raise his whip for the purpose of putting his threat into execution, I should undoubtedly have kept my word and have knocked him off his horse, not knowing at the time who he was. His Grace laughed at the circumstance, and observed that the impetuosity of his temper often drew him into an intemperance of behavior by no means becoming.

Having remained at Oxford some weeks, I returned to London, the time now drawing near, when the contest between Mr. Humphreys and myself was to be decided.

Notwithstanding my most ardent expectations were fixed on the event of this battle, I paid no more regard to training on this than on any former occasion, having sufficient confidence in my natural activity and the excellence of my constitution, and therefore passed the interval without varying in any way from my usual mode of living.

On the 9th of January, 1788, this contest took place, according to appointment, at Odiham, a stage having been erected for that purpose in an inn yard, which was speedily filled with spectators, who paid half a guinea each for admission. On this occasion Johnson and Tring were my opponent's second and bottleholder; and two men of the names of Jacobs and Isaacs were mine: Mr. Ford and Mr. Moravia were umpires; the former chosen by my opponent, and the latter by myself.

At the commencement of the contest, the bets were three to two against me; but after a few rounds, there was a material variation, as I evidently then possessed the superiority; and at the end of twenty minutes, the odds were five to two in my favor; notwithstanding which however, Mr. Humphreys had the good fortune to come off victorious, the reasons for which I shall now explain.

It was expressly agreed between my opponent and myself, previous to the contest taking place, that there should be only half a minute allowed between each round, notwithstanding which, at one time, when nearly exhausted, he complained of the tightness of his shoes, and was forty seconds beyond his time in changing them for a pair of socks, yet no advantage was taken or attempted to be taken on my part of this circumstance. Afterwards, at a very critical period of the battle, I aimed a blow which, in all probability, would have proved decisive, had not

Johnson unfairly caught the same, and thereby deprived me of a very favorable chance of gaining the victory: this caused some little altercation at the moment, but passed on, as my umpire yielded to the opinion of my opponent's friends, who offered some frivolous excuse in vindication.*

Notwithstanding these disadvantages however, I felt in high spirits, and was highly gratified with the idea of surmounting every difficulty, and thereby gaining greater honor, and therefore set to again with ardor, when in endeavoring to throw my opponent, he seized the rails surrounding the stage and maintained his hold, with such firmness, that I could not effect my purpose; and being off my balance, he was easily enabled to pitch me on my head, which nearly decided the battle against me. I fought however two more rounds, but in the last, received a fall that completely terminated the contest, for the excruciating pain I now felt in my loins rendered me unable to stand; consequently Mr. Humphreys was declared the victor, after a severe contest of forty-five minutes.

Having, for the reasons stated in the preceding chapter, formed the determination of relinquishing the profession of a teacher of the pugilistic art, I endeavored to procure, through the medium of some of my friends, an employment of a less precarious nature, but, in consequence of my affairs being at this time in a very deranged state, and the different tradesmen to whom I was indebted becoming every day more importunate and clamorous, all the efforts of myself and my friends to bring about any satisfactory arrangement with my creditors were utterly unavailing; and as proceedings at law were, in some instances, commenced against me, the greater part of my creditors evincing the most hostile disposition towards me, and being determined, instead of affording me such reasonable accommodation as my situation required, to insist upon an immediate settlement of their demands, which it was then out of my power to comply with, the most prudent step for me to take, appeared to be to surrender to prison, while any property remained in my possession, and wait there until an arrangement could be made with the whole of my creditors, my intention being to yield up my property without preference to any one of them, but among the whole proportionate to their respective demands.

With the view therefore of doing justice, as far as was in my power, to all my creditors, and to free myself, at once, from the different

---

* The conduct of my umpire appeared very extraordinary at the time; but I afterwards learnt he had laid money against me, consequently he could not be expected to be very willing to decide against himself!

encumbrances that prevented my engaging in any pursuit with comfort or safety, I became, in the year 1793, a prisoner within the rules of the King's Bench.

Having for some time previous to this determined to avoid engaging in any pugilistic contests, except in my own defense, in case of being assaulted, it is obvious that the situation in which I was now unfortunately placed, rendered this resolution more necessary to be adhered to than ever, since any violation of the peace, on my part, except in self-defense, subjected me to the hazard of being deprived even of the privilege of the rules which I then enjoyed, and made me liable to be called within the walls of the prison.

There are circumstances and situations however, which would make any man not devoid of the feelings of human nature, lose sight of prudence at the moment, and at all risks stand forward to punish barbarity, and protect, if he were able, the infirm and defenseless against the attacks they are sometimes compelled to suffer from those who, on account of their superior strength, seem to imagine they have a right to conduct themselves with as much brutality as they please.

A circumstance of this kind occurred during my confinement within the rules of the King's Bench, that caused me to forego every other consideration for the purpose of punishing a fellow who was the general terror of the neighborhood.

This man whose name was Hadlam (a sergeant of the 82nd Regiment) had some time previous to this fought with Bryant (better known by the name of Big Ben) and indeed as far as an athletic form and a savage and brutal disposition qualified a man for the profession of a pugilist, he was fit to engage with any one. In consequence of his superior strength and size, this fellow was in the constant practice of conducting himself in the most insolent manner. One day while I was sitting on a bench at the door of a public house (rulers being prohibited by an order of the court of King's Bench, from entering such houses), an old and infirm man, who was passing that way, stopped to take some refreshment, and entering into conversation with me, happened to mention the circumstance of his having a son in the army, in a regiment that was stationed abroad, and inquired whether I could put him in the way of obtaining any intelligence concerning him, expressing himself to be particularly desirous of ascertaining whether he was living or dead; upon which I referred him to Hadlam, who was sitting near me at the time, whom I described as a person that could probably point out to him the proper channel through which the information he desired might be obtained; consequently the old man accosted him and began to relate his story, but the other, in the most brutal manner, pushed him away and abused him in the most infamous language and, on the old man's remonstrating, this inhuman wretch struck him a violent blow on the face. Highly incensed at this infamous conduct, I could not forbear reproving Hadlam with some degree of asperity, and in consequence of his making use of very insolent threats towards me for interfering, I became so exasperated as to offer to fight him on the spot; to this proposal he readily assented, and we immediately set to. Our contest was not of long duration; my opponent, at the end of fifteen minutes, gave in, being severely beaten and scarcely able to stand.

As there appeared no immediate prospect of my being able to obtain my liberation, I determined, during my residence within the rules, to enter into some sort of business, and flattered myself that by so doing, I should add considerably to the property I then possessed. Having mentioned the subject to my friends, the plan was highly approved of by them, and many of them liberally contributed their assistance on the occasion, by means of which I was enabled to take a house in the London Road and to open a shop in the oil trade, but met with no success in the concern; and soon found that no good could be expected to result from this scheme, for my house being large, was consequently high-rented, my customers were very few, and their orders so small that the money I received was insufficient even to defray the expense of keeping open my shop—ere a few months had elapsed I found myself in a worse condition than when I commenced business. My stock of ready money was entirely exhausted, and for want of a fresh supply, and being unable to obtain credit to a sufficient extent (wholesale dealers having unfortunately some unaccountable prejudices against the neighborhood of Saint George's Fields), I was frequently without many of the most necessary articles in my trade, and obliged to put off my customers with the best excuses in my power: for instance, if sweet oil was wanted and I happened to be without it (no unusual case with me) my answer, perhaps was, "I had just returned the last that was sent me, not being quite of the prime sort, and expected some of the most excellent kind in a day or two, and in the meantime had plenty of rape oil, if that would serve the purpose." If mould candles were asked for, my answer was probably, "I had none left, having just completed an extensive order that was given to me only a few hours before, but had common candles, if they would do." In short, nine times out of ten, I had not the most common articles that were asked for, and my shop, though denominated an oil shop, was, in reality, little better than a repository for empty jars and boxes.

At length, I obtained my liberation, and quitted my shop for the purpose of embarking in some more profitable concern. Having experienced the precarious nature of trade, I determined, instead of setting up again in any way of business that would require money to carry it on, to engage in a pursuit of a very different nature, and therefore procured employment as a sergeant on the recruiting service, in the Fifeshire regiment of fencibles, with whom I remained till the regiment was completed. On quitting them, I obtained the situation of sergeant-major in the Aberdeenshire fencibles. During my engagement in the latter regiment, in the year 1795, notwithstanding the determination I had previously formed of engaging in no more pitched battles, I was induced, in consequence of circumstances which it would at this time be useless to relate, to consent once more to engage in a contest with a professed pugilist, and was matched to fight Mr. Jackson.

A few days previous to the contest between Mr. Jackson and me, I was induced to fight a battle with a man who was at that time the turnpike-keeper at Bilstone in Staffordshire, and who was renowned throughout that part of the country for his pugilistic powers. The occasion of our fighting arose from the following circumstance.

Traveling with a friend on the road from Birmingham to Woolverhampton, in pursuit of some deserters, we had occasion to pass through the turnpike at Cockheath, where, having paid the toll we ought to have been exempted from any further payment at Bilstone, which is at a short distance further on the road but, on arriving at the latter place, the turnpike-keeper, on our apprising him that we had paid at the preceding gate, and were consequently entitled to pass through without further expense, replied in a very insolent manner and, seizing the bridle of my horse, insisted upon my immediately producing the ticket or paying the money; upon which I professed my willingness to pay him (not having taken any ticket at the first gate) but desired him to leave go my horse and, being provoked at his behavior, threatened to knock him down, if he persisted in detaining me. This threat however he treated with great contempt, and, being an uncommonly athletic man, and the terror of the surrounding country, apprehended little danger from the menaces of one so inferior to him in size as myself. To convince me of the confidence he had in his superior strength and size, he immediately, before I was aware of his intention, gave me a violent blow, and knocked me off my horse. My foot remained in the stirrup, and had I not instantly contrived to disengage myself, my situation must have been perilous in the extreme. I lost no time in attacking my antagonist, and had the satisfaction of inflicting a most severe and deserved punishment on him. Our contest lasted scarcely a quarter of an hour, and terminated much to the satisfaction of the spectators, all of whom were his neighbors, and many of them having at different times received very ill treatment from him, and were consequently highly gratified at beholding him at last vanquished and his pride and haughtiness completely humbled.

The contest between Mr. Jackson and myself took place at Hornchurch in Essex, the following week, and after lasting seventeen minutes terminated in his favor.

It was the wish of several of my friends at the time that I should try the event of a second contest with Mr. Jackson at a future opportunity, but the acts of friendship I have since received from him, have caused me to feel desirous of burying in oblivion all our former contentions; and as we are at present friends, I hope and trust we shall ever continue such.

This is the only instance of my losing a battle where I did not *afterwards* defeat my antagonist; and my being vanquished on this occasion cannot, surely, be regarded as a circumstance reflecting disgrace on me, when it is considered that I had to contend with an antagonist who was not only far my superior in strength and size, but who has likewise always ranked as a first-rate pugilist, and is at this time looked upon by many as superior to any man of the present day.

My creditors having now discovered that I had arrived in London, seemed resolved to harass and persecute me. A few mornings after my arrival I was arrested for an old debt, which it was not then in my power to discharge, and was consequently obliged to give bail to the action which I was at length, with considerable difficulty, enabled to settle. In numerous other instances I was subjected to great expense and inconvenience, but in consequence of a great many gentlemen taking lessons of me, and paying me liberally for my trouble, I contrived to settle many of their demands.

About this time I was introduced to the late Lord Camelford, whose impetuosity of temper is well-known to have led him into many difficulties, and finally to have proved fatal to him. When I attended his lordship, he requested me to spar with him, which I accordingly did, and he professed to feel highly gratified at my exertions, and intimated that he would show me an original attitude of his own, in which he had attained a degree of perfection that would counteract any assault that could be made on him. At his request, therefore, I aimed several blows at him, one of which took place, and in consequence of his lordship's throwing back his head with great violence, he thrust it through the glazed door of a bookcase. This accident irritated him greatly, and as soon as he was extricated, which was not done without great difficulty, he asked whether I had ever played at the game of single-stick? On my answering I was not entirely unacquainted with the sport, he insisted on my engaging with him; and having procured a pair of weapons from an adjoining room, we set to. At this game I found his lordship a better proficient than myself; he struck with great force as well as skill, and I speedily received a violent blow over the ear, which caused great pain at the time; however, I was resolved not to yield, and therefore continued till he was tired, when he again proposed to change the amusement to fencing and, though I candidly told him I knew nothing of this art, he insisted on my engaging with him, to which I was with reluctance induced to consent. On one of the foils happening to break, he very coolly observed we might as well change them for a pair of small swords with which, he said, if we took proper care, we could not possibly injure each other. To this proposal I at first strongly objected, and declared my determination not to engage with weapons of such a dangerous nature; upon which my noble antagonist appeared highly irritated, and I began to apprehend the violent effects of his anger; therefore, with the view of appeasing his wrath, I pretended to assent to his proposal, merely expressing a wish that he would take care of my family, in case of any accident happening to me: this he promised to do, and left me for the purpose of fetching the swords. As soon as the coast was clear I rushed out of the room, and flew downstairs with all the rapidity in my power; such was my impatience to depart that I never stopped till I had reached the bottom of the staircase, when I found I had descended too low and had got to the cellar door; consequently I was obliged to return, and having at last reached the street door, departed abruptly from the house, and, as may readily be imagined, never felt the least inclination to re-enter it.

Soon after this I once more availed myself of an opportunity of entering into business, and obtained possession of a public house in the Whitechapel road, the license to which had been forfeited by the last tenant: this, however, by means of great exertion and perseverance, I regained, and soon after taking possession of my house, was enabled to open it for general accommodation. Having obtained the patronage of the magistrates and some of the most respectable inhabitants, besides possessing an extensive connection of my own, and being well-supplied with wines and liquors of the best kind, my house became much resorted to, and I had the flattering prospect of being enabled to relieve myself from all my pecuniary difficulties, and such would undoubtedly have been the case if my creditors would have given me time, and consented to wait till an arrangement could be formed for the settlement of the whole of their demands. It is obvious that their own interest, as well as mine, would have been promoted by such a measure, and had they been disposed to accommodate me, they would, in the end, have received the whole of their respective demands. However, as if they were determined on my ruin, they would not listen to any proposals. On applying to my principal creditor, an eminent brewer, and acquainting him candidly with my situation, his answer was, "He must consult his junior partner": on returning home, he immediately put in force a bond of mine, which he held. Finding it therefore in vain to attempt continuing in business, I surrendered upon one of the actions brought against me, and once more became an inmate of the King's Bench prison, where I remained till October, 1805, when I was discharged by means of the act of parliament then passed for relief of insolvent debtors.

My chief creditor seemed determined to persecute me to the last! He employed counsel to oppose my discharge, who, among other absurd questions, asked what had become of the fifty pounds I had received for the lease of my house? My answer to this inquiry was, he must ask my wife and children. The attempts of my persecutor, however, were unavailing, and in defiance of him and his counsel, I was enabled to take the benefit of the act.

Most of my readers have probably been present at the representation of Shakespeare's *The Merchant of Venice,* have execrated the hard-hearted Shylock, and commiserated the unfortunate Antonio, but here the scene was reversed; the Christian was the unfeeling persecutor— the Jew the unfortunate debtor.

A few months afterwards, notwithstanding my resolution of fighting no more pitched battles, I was once more induced to forego that determination, and to close my career as a professional boxer by engaging in a pugilistic contest with Mr. Lee.

This contest took place on Friday, the 21st day of March, 1806, at Grindsted Green, and after lasting one hour and forty-seven minutes, during which time we fought fifty-two rounds, terminated in my favor.

A SALONIST REMEMBERS

HENRIETTE HERZ (1764-1847)

Among the host of fine spirits who blazed the trail of the Enlightenment in Germany were a group of extraordinary women. Henriette Herz, the daughter of a physician (de Lemos) of Portuguese descent, was not the least of them. Blessed with singular beauty and a remarkable mind, her marriage to Hofrat Markus Herz afforded her the opportunity of establishing a salon which became the hearth of a number of great intellectual lights. She counted among her friends, in addition to those she refers to in these memoirs, Alexander von Humboldt, Börne, Fanny von Arnstein, Maimon, Mirabeau, and the philosopher Schleiermacher, whom she married after her mother's death in 1817, permitting herself to become baptized. She mastered a dozen ancient and modern languages and wrote several novels which, together with her letters, she destroyed before her death. These reminiscences of her youth and friends reflect warmly her intellectual and romantic cast of mind.

❋　❋　❋

THE first dramatic performance I ever saw was the presentation of a tragedy in a private home. Since the actors were amateurs, an unconquerable desire rose in me to act, too. My request to my parents that I be allowed to take part in the frequent dramatic productions was granted with more love than discernment. The actors took me cordially into their company, although I was only eight years old, because I was very large for my age. My first part was to be that of a peasant girl in an operetta.

I was elated, and a superlatively happy time began for me. The monotony of our home life was pleasantly broken by the frequent rehearsals, and the contact with adults flattered my vanity. A very musical young man who had a live interest in our gay undertaking had volunteered to coach us in the songs. I never stopped thinking of the visits he was due to make at my home for this purpose, and whenever the time for a visit approached, I stood impatiently peering through the door to see whether he and his violin were not yet in sight. In the end I combined my interest for the project which the young man was promoting with an exceedingly keen interest in his person.

Finally everything was handsomely prepared, studied and rehearsed. Even the costumes were ready, and I liked myself in mine so much that I can visualize it even today. It had a white silk skirt circled with red bands and a red bodice—both were adorned with sparkling silver spangles—and there was a white silk hat with elaborate porcelain flower decorations. Can anything more beautiful be imagined? The day of the performance approached and the stage was already put up in the home of a rich Jewess—all the participants were Jewish—when suddenly a devastating blow fell on our excited group in the form of a ban from the elders.

The elders consisted of the wealthiest and most distinguished, but also most pious, members of the Jewish community; they ruled the community almost without interference, and our worldly amusement offended them deeply. Opposition to the ban or disregard of it was unthinkable. We were terribly unhappy. There was much scurrying back and forth; respectable members of the community, whose points of view were not so strict as that of the elders, took up for us. Some were seen privately, but all to no avail.

Then I resolved that on the following Sunday, when the elders met, I would appear before them and ask a permit for our innocent entertainment. I informed no one of my intention, neither the other members of the group nor my parents. On the designated day I made my way alone to the meeting place, and suddenly an impudent little girl stood before the grating behind which the worthy elders of the community were in session. They looked in amazement, first at me, then at each other. The plaintiff spoke once. My words seemed ineffectual. My ego was hurt, and in a raised voice I explained to them that it was not seemly for such old and wise men to bother about child's play. Whether the argument or my whole appearance was the reason—I got what I wanted.

In my youth much more group reading was done than today. Partly this was because fewer belletristic books were bought, and partly because we tried to exchange our points of view about what we read. In general, the methods used to educate oneself and the manner in which knowledge was transmitted in company were different then. In those days one could

say, without restraint, that he wanted to acquire culture—a word which
has now become almost ludicrous. Because the intention and the desire
were so openly expressed, very able men did not consider it below their
dignity to share the best they had to offer with these ambitious people.
Later, when pedantry was more widespread, famous scholars also participated. Frequently mixed social groups were treated to discussions
that today would be considered suitable only for advanced students.
Scholars representing all branches of learning—philologists, philosophers,
theologists and jurists—mingled with men and women far below them
in learning and judgment in order to share the beauties of the literature
which, as I have said, was read aloud for this purpose.

One of the first reading groups I remember met every week at the
Under such circumstances everyone naturally wanted to be a good
reader. My husband esteemed the ability greatly, and shortly after our
engagement he asked me whether I knew how to read. Since he treated
me as if I were a child—which I really was, being hardly thirteen years
old, so that as a bride I was still called a child at home—I interpreted
the question to mean the mechanics of reading, and was all the more
hurt because not only had I read the entire lending library through
almost twice, but on one occasion, with a terrible novel in my hand, I
had slipped and fallen just outside the very window at which he stood.
He should have forgotten this instance least of all because my shame
had been only too apparent. Now tears rolled down my cheeks and I
barely managed a weak, "Yes." He asked me to read something for him.
But after the first few sentences he said, smiling, yet with his own kind
of trenchant wit, "I call that reciting." Then he read to me, and he read
quite beautifully. Now I realized what he meant and I had to confess
that I did not know how to read. "I will teach you," he said, and I had
to be pleased with the useful instruction, much as it hurt my vanity.

One of the first reading groups I remember met every week at the
home of a friend of mine who had been married a year before me—
Mendelssohn's daughter, Dorothea Veit, later the wife of Friedrich
Schlegel. Besides the two of us, some other members of our group were
my husband, Moritz and David Friedländer and another one of Mendelssohn's daughters. Mendelssohn was a regular and attentive listener.
How slyly we tried to extract an opinion from him! And how happy
we were when it turned out to be favorable! This wise man was so
good and gentle in his wisdom. He also loved a joke, but it was never
biting. He knew how to clothe his censure in agreeable, even helpful
form. I was spoiled because I was flattered, and developed the tendency
to be sensitive about even harmless criticism. Once, when this occurred,

Mendelssohn reproached me earnestly, but finished by saying: "You should be able to stand something like that without getting upset."

The daughters of well-to-do Jews had once taken up French superficially. Their parents had nothing against it for practical reasons. French was a language with which one could make oneself understood in all civilized countries. The daughters usually had different motives. They wanted mostly to be able to converse freely in this fashionable language with the court cavaliers and handsome young officers, who frequently paid off the money they borrowed from the fathers only with the attention they bestowed on the daughters. Now, however, French was energetically studied for other purposes: we wanted to read the old and new French writers in their original language.

Lessing had illumined French dramatic poetry with his glowing critical insight and at the same time turned our attention to Shakespeare. The translations of Shakespeare's dramas which preceded the Schlegel edition were less fit to satisfy than to direct the reader to the source. In order to follow through this direction, we tried to learn English. The way was opened to many contemporary novels, which brought no little nourishment to the amorous reveries of young females. And I admit that we all dreamed of being heroines in novels. Not one of us but attached herself to some hero or heroine from a contemporary book. At the head of this coterie stood the clever, magnificently imaginative Dorothea, Mendelssohn's daughter. But she led us also in learning and intellectuality.

Even familiarity with Italian literature in the original was possible to some of our group, which by degrees acquired more young married women, because Jewish girls married very early. Since some of the young married people opened their homes to the acquaintances of both husband and wife, wider circles soon came under the influence of the mode marked by the preoccupation of women with literature, the discussion of it and the ideas which were generated in them by both activities. The spirit of the day was really peculiar. It had emerged from the literature of new nations, but the seed had fallen on primitive and original ground. Every idea passed through a tradition and a culture transplanted from generation to generation and kept abreast of the knowledge of the time, but it also encountered the prejudices grown out of this culture. A characteristic of this spirit and the awareness of it was luxury, or wantonness. The departure from traditional forms of expression is also to be ascribed to it, but all this was undeniably original, powerful, piquant, stimulating and often, in addition to being amazingly stirring, very profound. The spirit came to full blossom eventually in Rahel Levin. She was about six years younger than I and most of my friends, but the intensity of her mind and her heart combined with tragedy to mature her early. I knew her from her childhood on, and remember how soon she aroused those great expectations that she was later to fulfill.

It can be said of only one scholar in Berlin that he maintained a house—if for purposes of identification one calls it that—in which friends and their guests, even if uninvited, were certain of a pleasant reception. And he was a merchant by occupation. I refer to Moses Mendelssohn. This splendid man, whose income from the silk business diminished as his literary work increased, and who had six children to support, nevertheless kept open house. Visiting scholars almost invariably sought an introduction to his home. His friends and the friends of his family came unasked, including the lively young women who constituted his daughters' circle. Nor was there a lack of old Orthodox Jews, the most intellectual of our city, toward whom Mendelssohn behaved like a sympathetic fellow-believer. Mendelssohn practised this generous hospitality although his family had to impose limitations on itself because of it. And yet the material pleasures which his house offered to his guests were not allowed to go beyond strict moderation. As a close friend of the daughters, I knew that the mistress of the house had to count out the raisins and almonds—an essential delicacy of the time—in proportion to the number of guests. But Mendelssohn's home was always the only one of its kind and could not satisfy the intellectual needs of many.

There was no trace of a Christian middle class whose inherent intellectual interests were other than those produced by the occupational environment. When Alexander von Humboldt wrote letters to me and to a friend of mine from his family seat Tegel, he usually headed the letters "Castle Boredom." Of course he did this mostly in letters written in Hebrew script, which I had started to teach him and his brother Wilhelm and which someone else had continued to teach successfully, so that they wrote admirably. A young nobleman could not unhesitatingly, in letters anyone might read, commit himself to the opinion that one could derive more pleasure from the company of Jewish young women than in his father's castle.

It is no wonder, then, that as in the midst of such complicated social relations intellectually gratifying contact was created, it was seized on by those who sought intellectual advancement through the oral exchange of ideas and that this was done despite contemporary prejudice against the Jews. Nor was it less understandable that young men were the first to approach our circle. For the spirit that ruled them was that of a new era, and besides, its paladins, by good chance, frequently happened to be attractive young girls and women. So it came about that the progressive young representatives of the nobility were the first to attach themselves to us, because the nobility was socially too remote from Jewish circles to seem part of them even when it permitted itself to move among them.

SCHOOLDAYS

LEOPOLD ZUNZ (1794-1886)

Zunz was one of the great monarchs of the mind in the nineteenth century. Quietly and heroically, he established the foundations of modern Jewish knowledge and to this day his influence is preeminent among the explorers and interpreters of the history and literature of his people. "It is the science of Judaism," he confessed, "in which I find my only comfort and stay." The philistines drove him from the pulpit; his affirmation of the revolution of 1848 lost the official recognition he brilliantly deserved; his refusal to compromise the truth as his keen intellect perceived it deprived him of public approbation until he was a septuagenarian. A strong note of humanity touched with humor runs through these turgid recollections of his childhood and schooldays. Too, they provide a glimpse into the inner life of this scholar who once remarked to a friend that those who read his works "do not know me at all".

❋   ❋   ❋

MY FIRST memories are connected with my fourth year. When I was five, I knew part of the Bible by heart and began to study the Talmud. My father taught me Hebrew grammar, Pentateuch and the Jewish script. Among the first melodies to impress itself on me was the "Marseillaise". The first pictures I remember are those of Bonaparte, Nelson and Surarov, which hung in our home. I was in my fifth year when I entered a school run by a barber named Löwe, and attended by children of both sexes. Toward the end of 1801 I started to go to the school run by our neighbor Moses. For a week a Pole taught me the Talmud. For about eighteen months, or until the spring of 1803, I went to the school of Reb Pelta. Following this, I was with Joseph Tiktin for a semester. Here I studied the talmudic tractate Kiddushin. For a short time, in 1802 and 1803, I took writing lessons with Wolf of Poland, who was later converted, adopted the name of Berendson, and lived in Hamburg as a bookdealer.

My birthday in 1800 I remember clearly. My father presented me
with a crescent cake (it was the day after Büsch's death). On my birthday in 1801, I got a small brass cannon. Wednesday evening, October 14,
1801, my grandfather and Aunt Hannchen came to see us; I remember
it clearly. In the spring of 1802 my father took me out of school; he
was already ailing. On Saturday afternoon, July 3, my father died.
I was spending the day at Moses Frankel's, playing with his sons. One
of them was my age and died long ago; the other, two years older, has
gone to North America. In the summer of 1802 I was introduced to
reading and writing German, and addition and subtraction. My teacher
was my Aunt Hannchen, then about eighteen years old.

Late in the summer of 1806 I studied the Regula Casus in the large
Hemeling. I believe that this book belonged to Jost's grandfather. In
January, 1807, I got several necessary articles of new clothing. In February
we were looking forward eagerly to the new order. Beginning with
April, 1807, I started to study religion, French, history and geography,
and practised translation into German. During the summer of 1808 I
learned Latin declensions. My regular study of Latin began in October.
On April 10, 1809, I entered the upper class of the high school. No Jew
had attended this institution previously. From 1809 to 1812 I studied
under Ehrenberg, taking up the history of the Assyrians, Persians,
Romans and Greeks, also that of Egypt, Sicily and Carthage. In addition, I made various other supplementary translations into Hebrew
of studies on aesthetics and natural history. My notebooks were destroyed
in 1849, with the exception of two, which I retain. In 1808 I also began
to be a tutor—reviewing Hebrew grammar and arithmetic with the
young students and giving them reading assignments. Though I was not
yet fifteen years old, I earned my own livelihood from that time on.
I had been forced to leave the free school in April. On November 9,
1809, my mother died, in Hamburg, at the age of thirty-six. It was
my sister's birthday. During 1810 I gave lessons in the free school, studied
the elements of algebra and attended lectures on optics. That same year
I began to write poetry and to keep a record of my little expenses.
In October I was appointed a teacher by the Jewish consistorium of
Westphalia. During 1810 and 1811 I saw the model of a telegraph and
heard a ventriloquist.

During the summer of 1811 I first saw Wolf's *Bibliotheka Hebraica*
and copied out excerpts from it. I intended to work on a book on
Palestine and Greece, in the style of Anarchi's *Voyages*. In January, 1812,
I began to take books out of a lending library; the free-thinking dialogues

and opinions of Albrecht were not without influence on me. More recent German authors did not come to my attention until later. I never had any lessons in German literature. In April, 1812, I took my first drawing lesson. The following winter, when I was almost eighteen and a half years old, I heard my first concert. On July 24, 1812, my grandparents celebrated their golden wedding anniversary. On the afternoon before Yom Kippur, the entry into Moscow (Napoleon entered Moscow).

At the beginning of 1813 I thought of going ahead with my studies. With this end in view I bought a lottery ticket for the first time and lost five thaler on No. 19367. In May I began to study the flute. In November I started to give lessons in religion to the daughters of L. G. Samson for six dreier an hour.

Only in 1814 did I start to go out with people outside my own home. On January 23, 1814, I was called up for service; on the 24th I was released. On February 3, I bought music for the first time; on March 2, I broke my first compass. On June 20, I had my first tooth pulled, after which I suffered no more toothache until 1864. On September 16, a reply from my English uncle destroyed my hopes for future study. From June until November I had several piano lessons.

In 1815 I began to study the double-bass with Lüdde. At the same time I began to spend an evening now and then playing cards with Ehrenberg's mother; it was my first acquaintance with card games. I was looking for friends, and joined a Langer tour. On February 17, I bought a coat. On February 21, Professor Leiste died; I am grateful to him for my first knowledge of geometry. At times I was the only member of his class. On August 10, I was called to Berlin. On September 3, I played dice for the first time. On September 12, I began to shave.

In 1803, at noon, on Sunday June 5, I arrived at the beth ha-midrash in the carpenter's courtyard, accompanied by my uncle and a soldier from the gate of the city. The soldier left us when Polli took us in charge (Polli was my grandmother's first cousin) and brought us to the home of Herr Samson. There I was given some vegetables to eat. Herr Samson examined me and at about two o'clock we marched over to the old synagogue on the Harzstrasse. Herr Kalman (born, I think, in 1733), stood at the door, a gray cap on his white head. The next day the study of the Talmud began; since I was not yet nine years old, I was spared the strap. In the afternoon we studied until five, during the winter until four. The Bible was taught only on Friday mornings, Herr Kalman keeping the Mendelssohn Bible translations before him. Four or five hours a week we studied the writing of Jewish and German, reading and arithmetic.

The superior rabbi, who lived one floor above, was Reb Lik of Burg Ebrach (near Bamberg), who had studied in Poland and had Polish manners—a gentle man, but married to a devil named Miriam. He was a kabbalist, stayed in the synagogue after the others had gone, and wore his tallith and tfillim to the morning sessions in Talmud. There were no school regulations and records; to a certain extent there was even no pedagogy. We were left to our own games and feuds, except that occasionally the Rabbi went with us to Hartmann's Park. There was no reading or anything like it, no one paid any attention to us; we were obliged to go to school, to attend funerals and to help with baking matzoth. There or four times a year we each received half a thaler from the Samson Free Schools. Herr Samson himself distributed them when he came out of the synagogue. At those times those of us who needed a new shirt or new trousers would get hold of him. I wore short leather trousers and buckled shoes. Except for Bertram, the only one who sat bareheaded, and a woman who combed me, I did not know any Christians. The older boys frequently tyrannized over us smaller ones.

Twice, during the winter of 1803-04, good luck saved me from a flogging; once the Rabbi knocked the lamp over with the stick, so that the oil ran out on the tractate Gittin, the second time our good supervisor, E. S. Ehrenberg, came into the room. Even before he had instituted the reforms of 1806-07 this appearance had given him a secure hold on my affection. Yet Kalman was a kind-hearted and sincere man. During the summer of 1804 he was even more kind-hearted than usual and often brought us cherries. His wife was not bad, either; she was by far the best of the rabbis' wives. During Days of Penitence we had to get up at four, the New Years' eves and the Days of Atonement at three. The sum total of my possessions at the time was an old valise containing a few items of clothing and a small sefirat Omer (table for counting the Omer) which I threw out when I cleared my pockets of hometz. The schoolrooms were not heated during the winter, the sleeping quarters, which had cement floors, were icy. We and Kalman therefore had one room in which we lived, studied and ate. We spent hours in bed. Occasionally I went to Polli's on Saturday, where I was given fruit and now and then a groschen. During the summer of 1804 I had the ague for several weeks—meat, fish, eggs, cheese and fresh bread were forbidden me. Even without this injunction I never had them. The first evening of Passover we always had parsnips or chopped lung; on Saturdays the pudding was often so badly burned that I put it in my pocket and threw it out. We got tea with milk every morning and coffee on Friday noon. During the summer months we went out to look for certain herbs out of which Kalman brewed tea. On the first evening of the Feast of Tabernacles, 1804, there was such a mob wanting to look at the sukkah that Kalman ran to the chief of police for protection. The aggravation, the excitement and the running had a bad effect on his rupture. He went to bed the next day and died during the holiday week, as did also Reb Lik, who had been ill for several weeks with a lung infection. The following winter we attended the Beers' Talmud classes. Philip Samson died in December.

After Passover, 1805, a new rabbi came to the synagogue—Michel, from Burg Ebrach, whose son Leon is an instructor of Göttingen and I believe a convert. He carried a knapsack and looked like a goatherd. He was lazy and preferred to stare out of the window when soldiers were lined up in front of it for a drubbing, so we had it very easy. He lived on the upper floor; on the lower one Kalman's widow ran the household. I was so wild that year that finally I actually had no trousers or stockings to wear. But arithmetic began to clothe me. On Friday afternoons during the summer we went to a park—the gardener was an old man with blond hair and white teeth, we ate gooseberries and took some home. Reuben P. used to accompany us occasionally when we went bathing in the river. During Sefiro, 1806, Michel left us; that same summer our synagogue was remodeled. For a time, while the doors were out, we took turns in staying there overnight. Then we studied at Beers' again, and slept there for a while. At this time I began to keep a rhymed Hebrew diary and to learn the rudiments of algebra from the large *Hemeling*—five years after Gauss, no more than a mile away from me, had written his *Disquisitions*. During 1805 the Rabbi of the Zimmerhof, David Schwersenz, died.

The first steps toward reform were taken in 1806. At the end of 1806, or early in 1807, Inspector Ehrenberg paid us a visit. We were given clothing. When I again had good stockings and trousers I felt like a castaway who had at last reached solid land. I still remember the arrival of the first French soldiers—the period that followed seemed to be one of salvation. During those days, I came to know a little more about the ill-treatment accorded to the pupils who had been turned over to the bears on the Zimmerhof. I shall not forget the day when we knew that we were no longer to sleep on the Zimmerhof, and that the next day would find us back in our renovated dwelling with the rule of the bears at an end. On Tuesday the inspector came and the following day my mother arrived, quite exhausted by the trip (April 1, 1807). In one day, literally, we had passed from the middle ages into a new era, simultaneously with our passing from Jewish helotry to civic liberty. I think of all that I missed—parents, love, instruction, the wherewithal for an education. I was more advanced than others only in arithmetic and Hebrew grammar. I had started to study grammar as a child, with my sainted father. But of the world and its contents, of the many courses that a boy of thirteen today has already taken for three or four years, I knew nothing, nor of human beings and social life.

Every day at noon we studied several paragraphs from the *Shulhan Arukh;* in the interval between Passover and Shebuoth we said maariv in the evening. Previously we had studied Misna, during the winter we sang zimroth at the Sabbath table. On Friday afternoons we prepared Bible interpretations from small books. These had to be said by heart Saturday at noon, for memory practice. Only on Saturday afternoons were we allowed to rest. With the exception of Hemeling's small arithmetic I did not read a German book until the end of 1805, when I read Philadelphia's *Art.* That same year, during the Days of Penitence, I read *A Thousand and One Nights* in Jewish print.

THE STAMP OF MY BEING

HEINRICH HEINE (1797-1856)

Heine remains one of the great poets and writers of modern times, and his enemies, from the Philistines in his family to the Nazi barbarians, have been unable to dim his luster. His struggle for the fresh air of liberty in Germany, his life as an exile in Paris, and the agonizing years of a paralyzing illness on a "mattress bed" are too well known to require elaboration. But the inner life of this genius whom one reads with inexhaustible delight has puzzled his critics and biographers. These memoirs give us a key to Heine's complex and fascinating personality. "You will find," he writes in the prologue to these pages, "in rich abundance those biographical notes which may be interesting to you, all that is important and characteristic is honestly communicated here, and the combined effect of exterior events and of occurrences in the inner life of my soul will reveal to you the stamp of my being and myself. The veil has fallen from my soul, and you may look at it in all its beautiful nakedness. There are no blemishes, only wounds. And alas! wounds made not by the hands of my enemies but by those of my friends." This penetrating self-analysis reveals a person of utter candor, a being full of love and human understanding. After the poet's death, the manuscript of these memoirs was mutilated by his brother Maximilian who could not swallow remarks on members of the family.

❅ ❅ ❅

IT IS certainly remarkable that as early as my thirteenth year, I was made acquainted with all the systems of "Freethinking," by a venerable clergyman, who did not in the least neglect the sacerdotal duties of his office, thus enabling me to learn, while still young, how religion and doubt may walk side by side without hypocrisy, the result of which was, for me, not only infidelity, but the most tolerant indifference.

Time and place are also important considerations. I was born at the end of the skeptical eighteenth century, in a city where, during my childhood, not only the French, but also the French intellect was reigning.

The Frenchmen whose acquaintance I made gave me, I must confess, books which were rather unclean, and created in me a prejudice against the whole French literature.

I therefore never liked it afterwards as much as it deserves.

But I remained the most unjust as regards French poetry, which from my youth was disagreeable to me. The chief cause of this was, perhaps, that confounded Abbé Daunoi, who taught French at the Lyceum of Düsseldorf, and who absolutely wanted to force me to make French verses. It needed but little more, and not only French poetry, but all poetry, would have been completely spoiled for me.

The Abbé Daunoi, an exiled priest, was a little old man, with very elastic features, and a brown wig, which, whenever he became angry, was sure to get awry.

He had written for his different classes several French grammars as well as some *chrestomathies,* in which there were extracts from German and French classics for translation; for the highest class, he had also published *Art Oratoire* and *Art Poëtique,* two little books, of which the former contained receipts for eloquence from Quintilian, that were applied to examples taken from the sermons of Fléchier, Massillon, Bourdaloue, and Bossuet, and which were not altogether tedious to me.

But, when I think of the other book that contained the definitions of poetry: "L'art de peindre par les images"—the flat trash of the school of Batteux—and also of French prosody, and the meter of the French in general, what a fearful nightmare!

I know nothing more absurd than the metrical system of French poetry, that "Art de peindre par les images," as the French definition of it is, which distorted conception is, perhaps, one of the reasons of their continual aberration into pictorial paraphrase.

Their meter must surely have been invented by Procrustes; it is a perfect strait-jacket for thoughts, which, considering their tameness, surely do not need it. That the beauty of a poem consists in overcoming metrical difficulties, is another ridiculous maxim which is of like origin. The French hexameter, that belching in rhymes, is a real horror to me. The French have, themselves, always felt this disgusting deformity, which is more sinful than all the crimes of Sodom and Gomorrah, and their good actors are taught to speak the verses "saccadé" as if they were prose; but why, then, the superfluous trouble of versification?

Thus I think at present, and thus I felt even as a boy, and you may easily imagine that an open war broke out between me and the old Brown Wig, when I declared to him that it was perfectly impossible for me to make French verses. He announced that I had not the least talent for poetry, and called me a barbarian of the Teutoburg Forest.

I still think with horror of the time when I had to translate out of the *Chrestomathie* of the professor, the address of Caiaphas to the Sanhedrin from the hexameters of Klopstock's *Messiah* into French alexandrines! It was a studied cruelty. God pardon me! I cursed the world, and the foreign oppressors who wanted to impose their versification upon us, and I could almost have become a Frenchman-eater.

I might have been willing to die for France, but to make French verses—never!

The difficulty was settled by the rector and my mother. The latter was in fact not satisfied that I should learn to make verses, even if they were only French ones. She at that time had the greatest fear that I might become a poet; that would be the worst, she used to say, that could happen to me.

The ideas which were then associated with the word poet were not very honorable ones, and the poet was regarded as a poor, ragged devil who, for a few thalers, made rhymes on certain occasions, and finally died in a hospital.

Within ourselves are the stars of our fortune.

But my mother had very high-flown ideas with regard to me, and all her educational plans had reference to them. She played the chief part in the history of my development. She made the program of all my studies; and even before my birth began her plans for my education. I followed obediently her outspoken wishes; but I must acknowledge that it was her fault that all my trials and efforts in ordinary pursuits turned out fruitless, for they never responded to my nature.

At first it was the splendor of the Empire which dazzled my mother; and when the daughter of a hardware merchant who lived in our part of the country, with whom she was very intimate, had become a Duchess, and had announced to her that her husband had won many battles and would soon advance to the position of king—ah, then my mother dreamt of seeing me in the most gilded epaulets, or the most embroidered uniform of a courtier of the Emperor, to whose service she wanted to dedicate me entirely.

In consequence of this, I had now to study chiefly those things which are useful to such a course of life, and although there had been already sufficient provision made in the Lyceum for mathematical studies, and

I had been abundantly stuffed by the amiable Professor Brewer with geometry, statics, hydrostatics, hydraulics, etc., and although I was swimming in logarithms and algebra, nevertheless, I had still to take private lessons in these branches of learning, which were to enable me to become a strategist, or, if necessary, the administrator of conquered provinces.

With the fall of the Empire my mother had also to renounce the splendid career for me of which she had dreamt. The studies necessary to it came to an end, and, curiously enough, they left no traces in my mind, so foreign were they to it. It had been a mechanical acquirement which I threw off as useless rubbish.

My mother now began to dream of a splendid future for me in another direction.

The house of Rothschild, with the head of which my father was on intimate terms, had already commenced its fabulous epoch of success. Other princes of finance and of industry had likewise arisen in our neighborhood, and my mother maintained that the time had now come when a clever head could do the most wonderful things in the mercantile branches and could rise to the highest position. She consequently decided that I should become a financial power, and now I had to study foreign languages—especially English, geography, bookkeeping; in short, all the sciences referring to commerce by land or sea, and to industry.

In order to become acquainted with the business of the Exchange and with the colonial products, I had later to enter the counting-house of one of my father's bankers and the warehouse of a wholesale grocer; in the former my instruction lasted at the most three weeks, in the latter four weeks, but I had thus an opportunity of learning how one writes a promissory note, and how a nutmeg looks.

A renowned merchant in whose office I was to become an *apprenti millionnaire,* was of the opinion that I had no talent for gain, and I laughingly acknowledged to him that he might be correct.

When, soon afterwards, a great financial crisis arrived and my father, as many of our friends, lost his fortune, the mercantile soap-bubble burst more quickly and more pitifully than the imperial one, and my mother had now to dream of some other career for me.

This time, she was of the opinion that I would absolutely have to study law. She had remarked that in England long ago, and also in France, and in Constitutional Germany, the profession of law was all-powerful, and that the lawyers especially, on account of their habit of speaking in public, played the chief parts, i.e., the talking parts, and thus rose to the highest offices of state.

As the University of Bonn had just been founded, where the chairs of the legal faculty were occupied by the most renowned professors, my mother sent me immediately to Bonn, where I was soon sitting at the feet of Mackeldey and Welker, sipping the manna of their science.

Of the seven years that I spent in German universities, I wasted three beautiful flourishing years of life in the study of the Roman jurists.

What a horrible book is that *Corpus Juris,* the Bible of Egotism!

Just as the Romans themselves have always been hateful to me, so has been their Code of Laws. These robbers wanted to secure their spoils, and what they had gained by the sword they tried to protect by law; therefore the Roman was at the same time a soldier and a lawyer. Indeed, to those Roman thieves we are indebted for the high-praised Roman Law, which stands in the most flagrant contradiction to Religion, Morals, Humanity, and Reason.

I brought those studies to an end, but I could never make up my mind to utilize such acquirements; and it was, perhaps, because I also felt that others would easily excel me in advocates' tricks and pettifogging, that I hung up my doctor's cap on a nail.

My mother made a still more sober face than usual. But I had now grown to manhood, and had reached the age when one must shake off maternal protection.

The good woman had also grown older, and after so many fiascos in her administration of my life, she repented that she had not dedicated me to a religious calling.

She is now a matron of eighty-seven years * and her mind has not suffered from her age. She has never pretended to direct my manner of thinking, and she has always been tenderness and love itself to me.

Her belief was a severe Deism, which was well adapted to the prevailing drift of her reasoning. She was a disciple of Rousseau, had read his *Emile,* nursed her children herself, and the science of education was her hobby. She herself had enjoyed a scientific education and had shared the studies of a brother, who became an excellent physician, but who died early. When yet a young girl she was obliged to read Latin dissertations and other learned publications aloud to her father, and often astonished the old man by her questions.

* This remark is either the consequence of a slip of the pen or of the misconception in regard to the real age of his mother; for Heine's mother, Betty Heine, was born on the 27th of November, 1771. She therefore was not eighty-seven years of age until 1858, while Heine died in 1856. The long absence from his mother's house—he had been in Hamburg for the last time in 1844—explains his error in regard to the actual age of his mother. She died in 1859, three years after the death of her renowned son.

Her reason and her sentiment were thoroughly healthy, and it was not from her that I inherited fanciful and romantic inclinations. As I have mentioned already, she had a perfect dread of poetry, took from me any romance that she might find in my hands, did not permit me to visit the theater, forbade me to take part in popular amusements, watched over my acquaintances, scolded the maidservants when they told ghost stories in my presence—in short, she did everything to guard me against superstition and poetical fancies.

She was penurious, but only as regarded her own person. In order to give pleasure to others she could be even extravagant, and as she only valued money and did not love it, she gave it with open hand and often astonished me by her charity and liberality.

How great was her self-sacrifice toward her son, whom, under trying circumstances, she furnished not only with the program, but also with the means for his studies! When I went to the University, my father's business was in a very sad condition, and my mother sold her jewelry, necklace, and earrings of considerable value, in order to secure for me a living during the first four years of my University studies.

I was, however, not the first one of our family who, in the University, ate gems and swallowed pearls. The father of my mother, as she herself told me, had tried the same experiment. The jewels, which ornamented the prayer book of his deceased mother, had served to defray his expenses during his sojourn at the University, when his father, old Lazarus de Geldern, on account of a lawsuit with a married sister regarding a question of entailment, was reduced to great poverty—he who had inherited from his father a fortune about which an old great-aunt of mine used to relate wonders to me.

It always sounded to the boy like a tale of the *A Thousand and One Nights* when the old woman told of the great palaces, and the Persian carpets, and the massive gold and silver vessels which the good man, who enjoyed great honors at the court of the Prince Elector (Carl Theodor, Prince Elector of the Palatinate, founder of the Academy of Painting at Düsseldorf) and his consort, had so pitifully lost.

Next to my mother, it was her brother, my uncle Simon de Geldern, who especially occupied himself with my education. He has been dead for twenty years. He was a peculiar man, of unimposing—nay, of an odd appearance; a small, goodlooking figure, with a pale, severe face, and a nose straight as a Greek nose, but surely longer by a third than those noses which were worn by the Greeks.

It was said that during his youth his nose had been of normal proportions, and that it only had attained such a remarkable length from the bad habit of continually pulling it. When we children asked our uncle if this was true, he very emphatically reprimanded us for our disrespectful speech, and then he again pulled his nose.

He was always dressed in an old-fashioned manner, wore short breeches, white silk stockings, buckles on his shoes, and according to the old custom a pigtail of considerable length, which, when the little man was tripping through the streets, flew from one shoulder to the other, cut all kinds of capers, and seemed to mock his master behind his back.

Often, when my good uncle was sitting absorbed in thought or reading his paper, the wicked desire seized me to take hold of his pigtail and to pull it as if it were a bell rope. This exasperated my uncle very much, and he began wringing his hands over the young generation, which has no longer respect for anything, which could be kept in bounds neither by divine nor human authority, and which would finally lay its hands even upon the holiest.

But although the exterior of the man was not made to command respect, his interior, his heart, was the more estimable, and it was the most honest and the most noble heart that I have met with on this earth. There was an honesty in the man which reminded one of the rigor in matters of honor described in the old Spanish dramas, and as regards his fidelity he recalled also their heroes. He never had an occasion to become the "Physician of His Own Honor," but he had always been a "Steadfast Prince" (titles of Spanish dramas) in all knightly grandeur, nor in the least lingered for the palms of death, and although he wore, instead of the brilliant cloak of a knight, a threadbare little swallow-tailed coat.

He was not by any means an ascetic enemy of worldly enjoyment; he liked country fairs, and also that room in Mr. Rasia's tavern which was reserved for the friends of wine, and where he liked to eat fieldfares with juniper berries; but all the pleasures of life he would willingly forego with proud firmness, whenever there was a principle to be defended which he had recognized to be true and good.

From a worldly point of view his life had been a failure. Simon de Geldern had gone through a course of so-called "humanistic studies," or "humaniora," in a Jesuit college. But when the death of his parents left him free to choose any calling whatever, he chose none, gave up the idea of preparing for professional study at one of the foreign universities, and remained at home in Düsseldorf, in the "Ark of Noah," as the little house was named, which his father had left him, and over the door of which could be seen a representation of the "Ark of Noah," nicely carved and painted in bright colors.

With unwavering diligence he abandoned himself to all his learned hobbies and queer fancies, to his bibliomania, and especially to his rage for writing, to which he gave vent chiefly in political journals and obscure periodicals.

By the way, not only writing but thinking also was an extremely difficult task for him.

Was his love for authorship, therefore, only a consequence of the desire to do something useful for the world? He took part in all the leading questions of the day, and the reading of newspapers and pamphlets had become with him a madness. The neighbors called him the "Doctor"; not that he was himself very learned, but because his father and his brother had been Doctors of Medicine.

The old women could not be persuaded that the son of the old physician, who had cured them so often, had not also inherited the remedies of his father, and when they fell sick they came running to him, requesting him to tell them what was the matter. When my poor uncle happened to be thus interrupted in his studies, he would grow very angry, and send the old shrews away wishing them all at the devil.

It was this uncle who had a great influence upon my mental development, and to whom I owe infinitely much in this respect. However different our views, and however poor his literary effort may have been, the latter may nevertheless have awakened in me the desire of making some trials in literature.

My uncle wrote a stiff court style, such as is taught in the Jesuit colleges, where Latin is considered the chief thing. He never learned to like my manner of expressing myself, which seemed to him too easy, too trifling, too irreverent. But his zeal in furnishing me with the means for mental progress was to me extremely useful.

He made a present to me, while I was still a boy, of the most beautiful and most precious books. He placed at my disposal his own library which was very rich in classic works and also in pamphlets on the leading questions of the day, and he even permitted me to rummage in the garret of the "Ark of Noah" amongst the boxes, in which the old books and manuscripts of my deceased grandfather were to be found.

With what mysterious delight throbbed the heart of the boy, when he could spend entire days in that garret, which in reality might have been called a large attic.

It was not exactly an attractive abode, the only creature living there being a fat Angora cat that was not especially given to cleanliness, and that only rarely, with her tail, wiped the dust and cobwebs partially away from the old rubbish that was stored there.

But my heart was still in the bloom of youth, and the sun shone so merrily through the little dormer window, that everything appeared to me in a fantastic light, and the old cat herself seemed to me like a bewitched princess, who might perhaps suddenly be set free from her animal shape, and show herself in her former beauty and splendor, while at the same time the garret might be changed into a magnificent palace, just as it happens in all the fairy tales.

But the good old fairy times are over; cats remain cats; and the garret of the "Ark of Noah" remained a dusty lumber-room, a hospital for incurable household articles, a Salpêtrière (a hospital in Paris) for old furniture that had reached the last degree of decrepitude, while at the same time a sentimental attachment and regard for the pious remembrances which were associated with it prevented one from throwing it out of doors.

There stood a dilapidated old cradle, in which once my mother had been rocked; the gala wig of my grandfather, which was perfectly rotten, and seemed to have become childish from age, was now lying in it.

The rusty gala sword of my grandfather, a pair of fire tongs, of which only one arm was left, and other invalid ironware were hanging on the wall. Near them, upon a shaky board, was standing the stuffed parrot of my grandmother, now without feathers and no longer green but ash-gray, and which, with the single glass eye that remained to him, had a very ghastly look.

A great green pug-dog of porcelain also stood there; it was hollow inside, the back part was partially broken off, and the cat seemed to have a great respect for this Chinese or Japanese work of art; she made before it all kinds of devout contortions, taking it perhaps for a divine being—cats are so superstitious.

In one corner an old flute was lying that had once belonged to my mother, who used to play upon it when she was a young girl; and it was this very attic which she had chosen for her concert hall, either not to disturb the old gentleman, her father, with her music, or to prevent him from getting cross on account of the time which his daughter lost over her sentimental amusement. The cat had now chosen this flute for her favorite toy, drawing it, by the faded pink ribbon which was attached to it, hither and thither upon the floor.

Amongst the antiquities of the attic there were also globes, very curious pictures of planets, stills and retorts, recalling astronomical and alchemistic studies.

In the boxes, among the books of my grandfather, there were also many treatises referring to the secret sciences. Most of these books, however, were old, worthless works on medicine. There was no lack of works on philosophy; but, side by side with the thoroughly reasonable Cartesius, were to be found fantastic authors like Paracelsus, van Helmont—nay, even Agrippa von Nettesheim, whose *Philosophia Occulta* I saw there for the first time.

Even the boy was amused by the dedicatory epistle to the Abbot Trithem, that was accompanied by the answer in which this *compère* pays back, with interest, the bombastic compliments of the other charlatan.

The best and most valuable thing, however, that I found in the dusty boxes, was a notebook containing notes in the handwriting of one of the brothers of my grandfather, who was called the "Chevalier," or the "Oriental," and about whom my old aunts always had much to say and to relate.

This granduncle, who was also named Simon de Geldern, must have been a queer saint. The cognomen of the "Oriental" was given to him because he had undertaken long journeys in oriental countries, and because after his return he always wore oriental costumes.

The most of his time he seems to have spent in the maritime cities of the north of Africa, and especially in the states belonging to Morocco, where from a Portuguese he learned the trade of an armorer, which he carried on with success.

He made a pilgrimage to Jerusalem, and upon Mount Moriah he had a vision during an ecstasy of prayer. What did he see? He never revealed it.

An independent tribe of Bedouins, that did not profess Islam but a kind of Mosaism, and which had their resting place, so to say, in one of the unknown oases of the north African desert, chose him for their leader or sheik. This warlike little nation lived in continual feuds with all the neighboring tribes, and was the terror of the caravans. To speak in plain terms, my deceased granduncle, the pious visionary of the holy Mount Moriah, became the captain of a band of robbers in Africa. In that beautiful country he also acquired his knowledge of horse-breeding, and those equestrian accomplishments on account of which, after his return to Europe, he was so much admired.

At the different courts, where he stopped for a long period, he was conspicuous by his personal beauty and imposing appearance, and also by the splendor of his oriental dress, which, especially upon the women, exercised a magic influence. Perhaps the greatest impression was that which he made with his pretended secret knowledge, and nobody dared to depreciate the mighty necromancer to his high patrons. The spirits of intrigue were afraid of the spirits of the Kabbalah.

Naught but his own recklessness was able to ruin him, and my old aunts used to shake their little gray heads in a peculiarly mysterious manner, when they were speaking in whispers about the gallant relations which the "Oriental" held with a very highborn lady, and the discovery of which forced him to leave in great haste the court and the country. Only by taking to flight and leaving behind him all his possessions, was he able to avoid certain death, and to his tried horsemanship he owed his safety.

After this adventure he seems to have found in England a secure but rather poor place of refuge. I draw this conclusion from a pamphlet of my granduncle, which was printed in London, and which I once by accident discovered when I had climbed up to the highest bookshelves of the Düsseldorf library. It was an oratoria in French verse, entitled *Moses upon Mount Horeb,* and referring perhaps to the above-mentioned vision. The preface, however, was written in English, and dated from London; the verses, like all French verses, were mere lukewarm water in rhymes; but, in the English prose of the preface, the ill-humor of a proud man who is placed in a condition of want could be recognized.

From the notebook of my granduncle I could not obtain much reliable information; it was mostly written, perhaps out of precaution, in Arabic, Syriac and Coptic characters, intermingled curiously enough with French quotations. I also was struck by many other remarks, written likewise in the French language. This seems to have been the language usually employed by the writer.

An enigma difficult to comprehend was this granduncle of mine. He led one of those odd existences which were only possible at the commencement and during the middle of the eighteenth century. He was on the one side somewhat of a dreamer, who made a propaganda for cosmopolitan and Utopian ideas for the benefit of the world; and, on the other side, one of those adventurers who, confiding in their individual superiority, either break down the rotten boundaries of a rotten society or else disregard them. At any rate, he was a genuine man.

His charlatanry, which we do not wish to deny, was not of a common kind. He was not one of those ordinary charlatans who pull the teeth of peasants at fairs, but he courageously entered the palaces of the great, for whom he pulled the strongest molars, just as of yore Knight Huon of Bordeaux did for the Sultan of Babylon. Advertising is necessary for business; and life is a business like any other.

And what remarkable man is not somewhat of a charlatan? The charlatans of modesty with their conceitedness, under the form of meekness, are the worst ones.

The end sanctifies the means. Even the Lord Himself, when from Mount Sinai He promulgated His law, did not disdain on that occasion to produce a sufficient quantity of lightning and thunder, although the law itself was so excellent, so divinely good, that it justly might have remained without any addition of burning colophony and thundering kettledrum music. But the Lord knew His public, which with its oxen and sheep and open mouths, stood at the foot of the mountain, and which he could inspire with greater admiration by some physical trick than by all the miracles of the eternal thought.

However that may be, my granduncle occupied the imagination of the boy to an extraordinary degree. All that was told about him made an ineffaceable impression upon my young mind, and I entered so deeply into his wanderings and fortunes, that often, in clear daylight, an uncomfortable feeling seized me, and it seemed to me as if I were myself the deceased granduncle who had died long ago, and that my life was only the continuation of his.

During the night it was reproduced retrospectively in my dreams. My life resembled at that time a great journal, the upper part of which has the contemporary events, the day with its daily news and the debates on daily questions, while in the lower part the poetical past is fantastically revealed in a series of night dreams resembling the feuilletons of a romance.

In these dreams I identified myself entirely with my granduncle, and at the same time it horrified me that I was, so to say, somebody else, and belonged to another period. There were localities which I had never seen before; there were situations of which hitherto I had had no idea, and nevertheless I moved in them not only without hesitation but with ease.

There I met persons clad in brightly-colored and singular costumes, with peculiarly wild physiognomies, whose hands, nevertheless, I pressed like those of old acquaintances; I not only understood their strange language, which I had never heard before, but I answered them even in the same language, gesticulating at the same time with a vivacity to which I was unaccustomed, and, still more, saying things which disagreeably jarred with my ordinary manner of thinking.

This curious condition lasted about a year, and although I regained the unity of my self-consciousness, there nevertheless remained some faint traces of that state of mind in my soul. Many an idiosyncrasy, many fatal sympathies and antipathies which are foreign to my nature, even actions which are contradictory to my way of thinking, I take to be the aftereffect of the time when I was my own granduncle.

When I commit mistakes, the origin of which seems incomprehensible to me, I like to put them to the account of my oriental double. My father, to whom I once proposed such a hypothesis as an excuse for a little oversight, jestingly remarked that he hoped my granduncle had signed no checks that might some day be presented to me for payment.

No such oriental checks have been shown to me; besides, I have had sufficient trouble with my own occidental checks.

There are, however, worse debts than money debts. Each generation is a continuation of another generation, and is responsible for its acts. The Holy Writ says: "The fathers have eaten green grapes and their grandchildren's teeth are set on edge in consequence of it."

There exists a common responsibility among the generations which succeed each other; even nations, which one after the other enter into the arena, take upon themselves such a joint responsibility, and the whole of humanity will liquidate finally the great inherited debt of the past. In the valley of Jehoshaphat the big account book will be destroyed, or perhaps even before that time a general bankruptcy will take place.

The lawgiver of the Jews thoroughly understood this common responsibility, and gave a special sanction to it in his law of inheritance; for him there probably existed no continuation of individual life after death, and he believed only in the immortality of the family; all goods were family property, and nobody was able to alienate them so completely that they should not return after a certain period to the members of the family.*

* Compare with this the following extract of the *Confessions of Heinrich Heine:* "Moses strove towards the moralization of property, he sought to bring it into harmony with equity, with morality, with the true law of reason, and this he effected by establishing the 'Year of Jubilee', when every alienated heritage (which amongst an agricultural people always consists of land) was restored into the possession of its original proprietor, no matter by what means it had passed into alien hands. This institution forms a most striking contract with the 'prescription' of the Romans, according to which after a lapse of a certain period, the actual possessor of a property could not be compelled to restore it to his legitimate owner, so long as the latter was unable to show that he, during that period, had demanded restitution in due form. This last condition left ample scope for

In striking contrast with this humane idea of the Mosaic law is the Roman legislation, which also in its laws of inheritance shows the egotism of the Roman character.

I will not enter at this time upon an investigation of this question, but returning to my personal confessions, I will utilize the opportunity, which is there offered to me, to show by an example how upon the most innocent acts my enemies have based the most malicious insinuations.

They pretend to have discovered that, in my biographical notes, I speak very much about the relatives of my mother, while I say nothing at all about my father's kith and kin,** declaring this silence and praise to be intentional on my part, and accusing me of having the same concealed motive of which my deceased colleague, Wolfgang Goethe, was suspected.

It is indeed true that in his memoirs he very often speaks with great satisfaction of his grandfather on his father's side, who, as his worship the mayor, presided in the City Council at the "Roemer" of Frankfort, while not a syllable is said of his grandfather on his mother's side, who, in Bockenheim street, as an honest jobbing tailor, sat with crossed legs upon the table, mending the old trousers of the Republic.

It is not my business, however, to defend Goethe for ignoring this fact; but as regards myself, I wish to put an end to these malicious interpretations and insinuations—which have furnished material that has been used against me—by declaring that it is not my fault if I have never spoken in my writings of my grandfather on my father's side. The reason is a very simple one—I never knew much of him to speak about. My deceased father had come to Düsseldorf, my native place, as a perfect stranger, and had no relations there—none of those old aunts and cousins who are the female bards that daily recite to the young folks the old family legends with epic monotony, squeaking through the nose, as a substitute for the bagpipe accompaniment customary amongst the Scots.

It was only in regard to the great heroes of my mother's clan that my young mind received early impressions from that quarter, and attentively I listened when old "Bräunle" or Brunhildis told her stories about them.

My father was a very taciturn man, who disliked talking; and once,

chicanery, particularly in a State in which Despotism and Jurisprudence flourished, and where an unlawful possessor had at his disposition every means of intimidation, especially against the poor who could not afford the means for a lawsuit."

** The expression used in the German original is "Sippen und Magen." This expression occurs several times in Heine's writings, and he always uses it in a manner which shows that he meant to indicate by it a certain contempt for his relatives.

when, as a little boy—at the time I used to spend my workdays in the gloomy school of the Franciscan monastery, while on Sundays I remained at home—I happened to ask my father who my grandfather was, he answered half-laughingly and half-crossly: "Your grandfather was a little Jew with a big beard."

The next day, when I entered the schoolroom where my little comrades had already assembled, I hastened to tell them the important news, that my grandfather was a little Jew with a big beard.

Scarcely had I made this communication when it went from mouth to mouth, was repeated in all tones, and accompanied by imitations of the voices of animals. The little fellows jumped upon tables and benches, tore from the walls the blackboards, which, together with the inkstands, tumbled down upon the floor; and at the same time they kept laughing, bleating, grunting, barking, crowing—making an infernal noise, with the ever-repeated refrain that my grandfather was a little Jew and had a big beard.

The teacher of our class heard the hubbub, and entered the hall, his face red with anger, and asked immediately who had been the cause of the misdemeanor. As it always happens in such cases, everyone tried meekly to exculpate himself, and at the end of the investigation, I, poor fellow, turned out to be the person who by his communication in regard to his grandfather had originated the whole mischief, and I had to pay for it by being soundly whipped.

It was the first whipping which I ever received upon this earth, and on that occasion, for the first time, I made the philosophical observation that our Lord, who ordained the whipping, by His kind providence had also made the arrangement that the person who administers it finally gets tired, as otherwise the punishment might become unendurable.

The stick with which I was whipped was of a yellowish color, but the stripes which it produced upon my back were deep blue. I have never forgotten them.

The name of the teacher who so cruelly beat me has also been remembered by me—it was Father Dickerscheit; he was soon removed from the school for reasons which I have not forgotten either, but which I will not mention.

The Liberals have so often unjustly slandered the clergy that at present one ought to be a little indulgent towards them when an unworthy member commits a crime, which after all is only the outgrowth of the natural, or rather of the unnatural inclinations of man.

Just as the man who whipped me, so also the reason for the whipping never escaped from my memory, viz., that unlucky genealogical communication; and the aftereffect of those early impressions of my youth was so great, that whenever little Jews with big beards were mentioned, I felt an uncomfortable recollection running down my back like a shudder. "A burnt kitten is afraid of a hot kettle," says the proverb, and it is easy to comprehend that since that time I have never felt very much inclined to find out something more positive in regard to that redoubtable grandfather and his pedigree, or to communicate it to the great public, as I did formerly to the little public.

Nevertheless I shall not be silent in regard to my grandmother * on my father's side, although of her also I know but little. She was an extraordinarily beautiful woman, the only daughter of a Hamburg banker, who was known everywhere on account of his wealth. From these circumstances I draw the conclusion that the little Jew who took the beautiful person from the house of her rich parents and led her to his own home in Hanover, must have possessed very remarkable qualities besides a long beard, and must have been quite respectable.

He died early, leaving behind him his young widow and six children, all boys of the most tender age. She returned to Hamburg and died there, though not very old. In the sleeping room of my uncle Salomon Heine, at Hamburg, I once saw the portrait of my grandmother. The painter who, in the manner of Rembrandt, had sought aftereffects of light and shadows, had given to the picture a black headdress like that worn by nuns, a dark robe of similarly severe appearance, and a background black as night itself, so that the full-cheeked face, with its double chin, looked like the moon shining out from the dark clouds.

Her features still bore the traces of great beauty; they were earnest but at the same time mild, and especially the "Morbidezza" of the color of the skin gave to the whole face a peculiarly aristocratic appearance. Had the painter painted the lady with a great cross of diamonds upon her breast, one would surely have taken her to be one of those abbesses who preside over the Protestant refuges for noble ladies, and who have been raised to the rank of princesses.

Of the children of my grandmother, only two, as far as I am aware, have inherited her extraordinary beauty, viz., my father, and my uncle, Salomon Heine, the deceased chief of the Hamburg banking house of that name.

The beauty of my father was of a nature rather too mild, without characteristic outlines, almost feminine. His brother's beauty was of a

* Mathe Eva Popert, who died as Mrs. Heine, in 1799.

much more manly sort, and he was decidedly a man whose strength of character revealed itself in an imposing and sometimes even startling manner in his features, which were of noble and regular proportions.

All of his children, without exception, grew up to be exceedingly beautiful, but death took them away in the bloom of youth; and of that beautiful wreath composed of human flowers, two only are living at the present moment, viz., the present chief of the banking house and his sister, a person of rare . . .*

I loved all these children very much indeed, and I also loved their mother, who herself was really beautiful, and died very early; all of them have made me shed many a tear. I truly shall have at this moment to shake my fool's cap, in order to drown by the noise of its bells my tearful thoughts.

I have said above that my father's beauty had something feminine about it. By this I had not the slightest intention to indicate a want of manliness. The latter he has, especially during his youth, shown on many occasions, and I myself am, after all, a living proof of it. I did not want to injure him by what I have said. I was only referring to the form of his exterior appearance, which was not firm and compact, but rather full and softly rounded. The outlines of his features lacked a marked expression, and had something indefinite about them. In his later years he grew fat, but even in his youth he seems not to have been exactly lean.

This idea which I have of him was confirmed by a portrait, which has since been destroyed during a fire in my mother's house, and which represented my father as a young fellow of eighteen or nineteen years of age, in a red uniform, with powdered hair, done up in a cue.

Fortunately this portrait was painted with pastel colors. I say fortunately, because by the latter that flower pollen, which we observe upon the faces of persons who powder themselves, can be much better indicated than by oil colors with their varnish. The painter, by setting the rosy face in a frame of chalk-white powdered hair and a white necktie, gave it by means of this contrast a more decided color and made it stand out more strongly.

Even the scarlet color of the coat, which in oil pictures grins at us so horribly, had here, on the contrary, a favorable effect, because it softened somewhat the pink color of the face.

The type of beauty which was found in the features reminded one

---

* Three lines of the original manuscript have been cut out, probably by Mr. Maximilian Heine, or by another of the tender relatives who objected to some phrase referring to the children of Salomon Heine.

neither of the severe and chaste ideal expression of Greek works of art, nor of the style of the Renaissance, which spiritualistic and sentimental, at the same time, breathes the heathen fullness of health. On the contrary, the portrait in question bore exactly the character of a time which had no character, and which loved not the beautiful, but rather the pretty, the nice, the coquettishly dainty; the character of a time the flatness of which almost approached the poetical, of that sweetish rococo period, with its queer flourishes and ornaments, which is also called the pigtail time, and which bore as a sign, not upon the forehead but on the back of the head, a cue. Had the picture of my father in that portrait been somewhat more of a miniature in size, one might have believed that it was painted by the excellent Watteau for the purpose of parading it upon a fan of Madame de Pompadour, ornamented with fantastical arabesques, framed with many-colored gems and gold tinsel.

It is, perhaps, worth mentioning that my father, even in later years, remained faithful to the old-fashioned habit of powdering, and had himself powdered every day up to his very death, although he possessed the most beautiful hair imaginable. It was blond, almost golden, and of a softness which I never have found except in Chinese floss.

He surely would have liked to keep the cue also; the progressive spirit of the time, however, was inexorable. In his distress my father struck upon an idea which was a kind of compromise. He sacrificed only the little black pad (*sachet*), the bag, but he now wore his long locks in a broad-braided *chignon,* fastened upon the head by means of a little comb. The braid, because of the softness of the hair, and on account of the powder, was scarcely perceptible, and for this device my father could not actually be called an apostate; like many a person who would disguise his orthodoxy he had submitted to the cruel spirit of the times only as regards appearance.

The red uniform, in which my father was painted in the above-mentioned portrait, indicated his services under the House of Hanover. At the commencement of the French Revolution my father took part in the campaign against Flanders and Brabant in the suite of Prince Ernest of Cumberland, as "provision master" or commissary, *officier de bouche,* as the French, or "meal-worm" as the Prussians, call it.

The real office of the very young man was, however, that of a favorite of the Prince, or that of a "Brummel" * *au petit pied,* minus the striped necktie; and he also shared the fate of those persons who are the

---

* "Brummel" was the name of a renowned lion of fashion and a favorite of the Prince Regent of England, who afterwards became King George IV of England.

playthings of princely favor. My father, it is true, was all his life long of the persuasion that the Prince, who later became King of Hanover, had never forgotten him, but he could not find an explanation why the Prince never sent for him, nor asked about him, as he certainly could not be sure that his former favorite might not live in a condition where he required help.

From that campaign period dated also a good many rather dangerous habits of my father, of which my mother was only gradually able to break him. Thus, for instance, he was easily induced to take part in high gambling, he protected the theater or rather its priestesses, and had even a passion for horses and dogs. When he came to Düsseldorf, where to please my mother he established himself as a merchant, he brought with him twelve very fine horses. But he parted with them at the special wish of his young wife, who represented to him that his four-footed capital consumed too much oats and brought no profit.

More difficult was it for my mother to remove the groom, a big, burly fellow, who would lie all day long in the stable and play cards with some vagabond or other whom he had fished up in the street. Finally, he went of his own accord, accompanied by a gold repeating watch belonging to my father and some other valuable trinkets.

When my mother was rid of that good-for-nothing she also dismissed the hunting dogs of my father, with the exception of one, which was named "Joli," although he was very ugly. He found grace in her eyes, because there was absolutely nothing of the hunting dog about him, and there was a possibility of his becoming a faithful, virtuous house dog. He inhabited the old *calèche* of my father in the empty stable, and when they met there, they used to throw very meaning glances at each other. "Ah, yes, Joli!" sighed then my father, and Joli wagged mournfully his tail.

I believe the dog was a hypocrite, and once in a bad humor, when his favorite whimpered too pitifully from the effects of a kick, my father acknowledged that the scoundrel was playing off. Finally, Joli grew very mangy, and at last became a walking barrack for fleas, and he had to be drowned, which my father permitted without interfering. Other men sacrifice their four-footed favorites with the same indifference as princes their two-footed ones.

From the campaign period of my father's life originated also his extraordinary predilection for the military vocation, or rather for playing soldier, the love for that merry, lazy life, in which gold tinsel and scarlet rags cover the interior hollowness, and intoxicated vanity can behave like courage.

Amongst his noble associates there existed neither military earnestness nor real desire for glory. Heroism was entirely out of the question. The chief thing for him was the parade of the guard-mount, the clanking of the sword, and the closely-fitting uniform so becoming to *beautiful* men.

How happy, therefore, was my father, when the militia was established at Düsseldorf, and when he, as an officer, wearing the beautiful dark-blue uniform with sky-blue velvet facings, could defile before our house at the head of his column! He then saluted, with charming courtesy, my mother, who stood at the window blushing—the plumes upon his three-cornered hat fluttered so proudly, and so gaily glittered his epaulettes in the sunlight.

Still more happy was my father when it was his turn to mount guard as commanding officer, and to watch over the safety of the city. On such days, nothing but wine of Rüdesheim and Assmannshausen, and of the best growth, was flowing in the guardhouse, and all at the expense of the commanding officer, whose liberality his militiamen, his "Creti" and "Pleti," could not too highly praise.

My father also enjoyed among them a popularity that was quite as great as the enthusiasm which the Old Guard had for the Emperor Napoleon.

The latter, it is true, knew how to intoxicate his men in quite a different manner. My father's guards did not lack a certain bravery, even if there was the question of facing barrels of the greatest caliber, that is to say, if these barrels contained wine. Nevertheless, their heroism was of a different kind from that which we find among the Emperor's guards. The latter died without surrendering, while the guardsmen of my father remained alive and surrendered often—what they had drunk.

As regards the safety of the city of Düsseldorf, it was probably greatly endangered during the nights when my father had to command in the guardhouse. He, however, took care to dispatch patrols, who singing and with clanking swords went in different directions through the city. It once happened that two such patrols, when meeting, wanted each to arrest the other as drunkards for disturbing the peace. Fortunately my countrymen are harmless, merry people; they are good-natured when they are drunk; consequently there was no harm done, for *"Ils ont le vin bon,"* and they mutually surrendered—it.

A limitless desire to enjoy life was the chief trait of my father's character; he longed for amusement, and was always gay and in rosy humor. In his mind there was a continual festival, and although boisterous dancing music did not always fill it, at least the tuning of the violins never stopped. Always sky-blue gaiety, always frivolous fanfares— a carelessness which quickly forgot the day past and never thought of the coming morning.

This natural disposition was in curious contradiction with the gravity which was spread out over his serious, quiet face, and was shown in his whole attitude and in every movement of his body. Anyone who did not know him, and saw for the first time this earnest powdered figure, and those grave features, surely might have believed that he looked upon one of the seven wise men of Greece. But on becoming better acquainted with him it was easy to recognize that he was neither a Thales nor a Lampsacus * who bothered himself with the problems of cosmogony. Not that his gravity was borrowed, but it reminded one of those ancient bas-reliefs, in which we see a merry child holding a great tragic mask before its face.

He was really a great child, with a childlike naïveté which certain virtuosos of reason might take for simplicity; but often, by some remark of the deepest meaning, he betrayed a remarkable power of observation (intuition).

He recognized quickly, by his spiritual feelers, what a thinking person understands only after long reflection. He thought more with his heart than with his head, and he had the most amiable heart imaginable. The graceful smile which sometimes played around his lips, and which contrasted amusingly with the abovementioned gravity, was the sweet reflection of his kindness of heart.

Even his voice, although manly and sonorous, had something childlike about it, I might almost say something that reminded one of the voices of the forest—for instance, of that of the redbreast; when he spoke, his voice went direct to the heart, just as if it had not to make its way through the ears.

He spoke the dialect of Hanover, in which city, just as in the neighboring country south of it, German is pronounced in the best manner. It was a great advantage for me that during my childhood, through my father, my ear became early accustomed to a good pronunciation of German; for in our city itself that hateful jargon of the Lower Rhine is spoken, which, although in Düsseldorf it is still some-

* Stands evidently for Pittacus, and whether an intentional or an unintentional mistake is not clear.

what supportable, in the neighboring city of Cologne becomes actually disgusting. Cologne is the Tuscany of a classically bad pronunciation of the German, and Kobes speaks with Marizzebill in a sing-song, which sounds, or almost smells, like stale eggs.

In the language of the Düsseldorf people, a transition to the frog-croaking of the Dutch swamps begins to be perceptible. Be it far from me to depreciate the peculiar beauties of the Dutch language; only I must say that I have no ear for them. It may even be true that our own German language, as patriotic linguists of the Netherlands have maintained, is only a kind of corrupted Dutch. Possibly this is so; but it reminds me of the assertion of a cosmopolitan zoologist, who declares the monkey to be the ancestor of the human race; men, according to his opinion, are only developed, or rather overdeveloped, monkeys. If the monkeys could speak, they would probably make the assertion that men are only degenerated monkeys, and that mankind is a sort of spoiled monkeydom, just as, in the opinion of the Hollanders, the German language is spoiled Dutch.

I say: if monkeys could speak, although I am not at all persuaded of their incapability of speaking. The Negroes of the Senegal maintain firmly that the monkeys are men just like ourselves, only smarter, because they refrain from speaking in order not to be recognized as men, and not to be forced to work; their scurrilous monkey tricks are said by them to be nothing but a clever dissimulation, by which they wish to appear to the potentates of this earth as unfit to be used in the same manner as the rest of us.

Such absence of all vanity would give me a very high idea of that face which guards a silent incognito, and perhaps makes fun of our simplicity. They remain free in their forests, never giving up their natural condition; and they would have a right to say that man is a degenerated monkey.

Perhaps our ancestors of the eighteenth century were already aware of this; and instinctively feeling that our polished overcivilization was only a kind of varnished rottenness, and how necessary it was to return to nature, tried to approach again to our original type, to the natural monkeydom. They did all that could be done; and finally, when there was nothing lacking to them in order to be monkeys except the tail, they adopted instead of it a pigtail. Thus the pigtail is an important symptom of a serious necessity, and not simply a frivolous invention. But it is in vain that I try, by shaking the bells of my fool's cap, to drown with their noise the melancholy which comes over me when I think of my deceased father.

He was of all human beings the one whom upon earth I have loved most; he has been dead now more * than twenty-five years. I never thought I should lose him, and even now I can hardly realize that I have actually lost him. It is so difficult to persuade oneself that those whom we have loved so very much are really dead; but, in fact they are not dead; they continue to live in our hearts.

Not a single night has passed in which I have not thought of my deceased father; and when I awake in the morning, I still often imagine that I hear the sound of his voice, like the echo of a dream. Then it seems to me as if I had to dress myself hastily, and go down to the great room, as I used to do when a boy.

My father was always accustomed to rise and to go to his business very early, in winter as well as in summer; and, when I got up, I usually found him already at his writing desk, where he, without raising his eyes, held out his hand for me to kiss it—a beautiful, finely-cut, aristocratic hand, which he used to wash in bran of almonds. I still see it before me, I still see every little blue vein which ran across this marble-white hand. It is as if the odor of almonds were still tickling my nostrils, and my eyes become moist.

Sometimes the kissing of the hand was not all, and my father took me between his knees and kissed me upon my forehead. One morning he embraced me with unusual tenderness and said: "I have dreamt something beautiful of you, and I am very much satisfied with you, my dear Harry." While he spoke these naïve words a smile played around his lips which seemed to say: "Let Harry be ever so naughty in reality, I will nevertheless dream something beautiful of him, so that nothing may prevent me from loving him."

Harry is, among the English, the familiar name of those who are called Henry, and it corresponds exactly to my German name Heinrich, which I received when I was baptized. The pet names for Heinrich in the dialect of my native country, are anything but euphonious, and sound almost scurrilous; for instance, Heinz, Heinzchen, Hinz. Heinzchen is also the name given to little domestic goblins, and to puss-in-boots in the puppet play, just as puss in the popular fable is called Hinze.

Not on account of this inconvenience, but in honor of one of his best friends in England, my father anglicized my name. Mr. Harry was

* As Heine's father died the 2nd of December, 1828, we may conclude that he commenced these Memoirs in 1854.

my father's correspondent in Liverpool. He knew the best manufacturers of velveteen in that city, an article which had become very dear to my father's heart, more in consequence of his ambition than of his desire for gain; for although he maintained that much money could be made with it, this always remained problematical, and my father would even have been willing to lose money, had there been a question of selling a better quality and a greater quantity of velveteen than his competitors. My father possessed, in fact, no real calculating commercial mind, although he was always calculating; and commerce to him was a sort of amusement, just as playing soldiers or cooking is to children.

His activity was, in fact, nothing else but a continually being busy. Velveteen was his special hobby, and he was perfectly happy when the great carloads were unloaded, and when, during the unloading, all the trading Jews of the neighborhood filled the hall of the house; these were his best customers, and with them his velveteen was not only in great demand, but also met with honorable praise.

As you, my dear reader, perhaps do not know what "velveteen" is, I take the liberty to tell you that it is an English word, meaning velvet-like, and this name is given to a kind of cotton-velvet, of which very beautiful trousers, vests, and even jackets are manufactured. This material is also called "Manchester," after the city of that name, where it was first manufactured.

Because the name of a friend of my father who best understood the buying of velveteen was Harry, I was also named thus, and I was called Harry in our family, among our friends, and among our neighbors.

Even at the present day I like to be called by that name, although it has caused me much annoyance, perhaps the most bitter annoyance of my childhood. Only now, when I no longer live amongst the living, and consequently all social vanity has become extinct in my soul, I can speak about it without embarrassment.

Here in France my German name, "Heinrich," was, immediately after my arrival in Paris, translated into "Henri"; and I had to submit to it, and was finally obliged to call myself so, because the word "Heinrich" does not suit the French ear, and because the French make everything as comfortable to themselves as possible. Even the name "Henri Heine" can never be pronounced quite correctly; most of them call me M. Enri Enn; many contract this into "Enrienne," and some even give me the appellation "M. Un Rien."

This hurts me in many ways, especially with regard to my literary occupation; it is, however, in another way of benefit to me. For instance, among my fine countrymen who come to Paris, there are some who would like to calumniate me; but as they always pronounce my name in the German language, the French never even imagine that the wicked fellow and poisoner of the fountains of innocence, about whom these gentlemen are fearfully raving, is identical with their friend, Monsieur Enrienne. These noble souls give vent to their virtuous zeal all in vain; the French do not know that it is I of whom they speak, and trans-rhenanic virtue thus spends its arrows of calumny without hitting the mark.

It is somewhat awkward if one's name is badly pronounced. There are people who, in such cases, show great sensitiveness. I once indulged in the joke of asking old Cherubini whether it was true that the Emperor Napoleon always pronounced his name Sherubini instead of Kerubini, although the Emperor knew Italian well enough to know, that in it *ch* is pronounced like *que* or like *k*. This question put the old maestro into a most comical rage.

I have never felt like that.

Heinrich, Harry, Henri—all these names sound well when they are falling from beautiful lips. Best, of course, it sounds to be called Signor Enrico. This was my name under the clear blue sky, with its embroidery of great silver stars, peculiar to the summer nights of that noble and unfortunate country which is the home of beauty, and which has given birth to Rafael Sanzio, of Urbino, to Joachim Rossini, and to the Princi-pessa Christina Belgiojoso.

As my bodily condition leaves me no hope of ever being again in society, and as the latter does not really exist any more for me, I have also stripped off all those chains of personal vanity, which everyone wears who must waste his time among men, and in the so-called world.

Consequently I am at present free to speak about the mishap that was connected with my name of "Harry," and which embittered and poisoned the most beautiful years of the springtime of my life.

The case was as follows: In my native city there lived a man who was called Dirty Michael, because every morning he went with his cart, drawn by a donkey, through the streets of the city, stopping before each house in order to collect the rubbish which the servant girls had swept together in nice little heaps, and to transport it to the field outside of the city, where the offal was deposited. The man looked like his business, and the donkey, again, looked like his master; and he stopped before the houses or went off in a trot according to the different modulations in which Michael called out to him the word "Haaryh!"

Was this really his name, or was it only an exclamation for inciting the donkey to go? I do not know; but one thing is certain, that on account of the resemblance of that name to my name Harry, I had to suffer very much from my schoolmates and the neighbors' children. In order to tease me, they pronounced it exactly in the manner in which Dirty Michael called his donkey; and when I became angry about it, the rogues assumed the most innocent air, and asked me to teach them precisely how my name and that of the donkey ought to be pronounced, so that they might avoid mistakes. At the same time, however, they appeared very unteachable, and maintained that Michael on some occasions drew out the first syllable very long, and cut the second syllable very short, while on other occasions just the opposite happened, which made his call sound exactly like my name; and the boys, in the most crazy manner, mixing up all conceptions referring to me with those referring to the donkey, and vice versa, produced such a queer *coq-à-l'âne* that everybody laughed, while I cried.

When I complained about this to my mother, she said that if I would only try to learn a great deal, and become very clever, then nobody would mistake me for a donkey. Nevertheless, my homonym with those long ears remained my nightmare. The big boys, when passing me, saluted me with a "Haa-ryh!" The little ones gave me the same greeting, but from a certain distance. At school the same theme was harped upon with the most studied cruelty. Whenever there was a question about some donkey or other, they threw side glances at me, which always made me blush; and it is really incredible what a faculty schoolboys have for discovering or inventing something disagreeable.

Thus, for instance, one would ask the other: "What is the difference between a zebra and the ass of Balaam?"

The answer was: "The one speaks Zebrew, and the other spoke Hebrew." Then came the question: "What is the difference between the ass of Dirty Michael and his namesake?" And the impertinent answer was: "We do not know any." Then I wanted to throw myself amongst them and to beat them, but they soon quieted me again; and my friend Dietrich, who understood how to manufacture extraordinarily beautiful little pictures of saints, and who later became a renowned painter, on one occasion consoled me by promising me a picture. He painted for me a Saint-Michael—but the wicked fellow had horribly mocked me. The archangel had the features of Dirty Michael, his horse looked exactly like the donkey of that fellow, and instead of a dragon he pierced with his spear the carcass of a dead cat.

Even the gentle effeminate Franz * with his golden hair, whom I loved so much, once betrayed me. He embraced me, leaning his cheek tenderly upon mine, remained a long while sentimentally resting upon my breast, when all at once he cried into my ear, laughing loudly, "Haa-ryh!" and then he ran away, modulating the hateful word in all possible manners, so that it resounded far and wide through the corridors of the cloister.

Still worse was I treated by the children of our neighbors, little blackguards of the lowest kind, whom in Düsseldorf we used to call "Haluten," a word which those whose hobby is etymological studies surely would derive from the "Helots" of Sparta.

Such a "Helot" was little "Jupp," which means Joseph; but I will also give his family name, so that nobody can possibly mistake him for Jupp Rörsch, who was a very good little neighbor, and who at present is a post-official in Bonn. Jupp Flader, on the contrary, when he met me, always used to strike me with a fishing rod, which he was accustomed to carry. He also liked very much to throw horse-dung at my head, which he gathered from the street warm as it came from the oven of Nature, and on such occasions he never forgot to cry out his hateful "Haa-ryh!" in all possible modulations.

The wicked boy was the grandchild of the old woman Flader, who was one of the clients of my father. This poor grandmother was just as good-natured as the boy was wicked; a picture of poverty and misery, not disgusting, however, but rather heart-rending. She was surely over eighty years old, a great lank, slovenly figure, a white leather face, with pale sunken eyes, a low rattling, whining voice, and begging without the slightest ceremony, which is ever terrible.

My father always offered her a chair when she came to get her monthly allowance, on the day when he, as the almoner, distributed money to the poor.

On these occasions, when my father was officiating as an almoner, I only remember those winter days, when he discharged his duty very early in the morning while it was still dark. My father used to sit before a large table, which was covered with paper cornets of all sizes, filled with money; instead of the silver candlesticks generally used, and of which he wished not to boast before the poor—he whose heart possessed so much tact—there were standing now upon the table two copper

---

* Franz von Zuccalmaglio, to whom Heine's first poem is addressed, which commences with the words: "Es zieht mich nach Nordland ein gold'ner Stern."

candlesticks with tallow candles, that, with their thick blackburned wicks and their red flame, threw a kind of sad light upon the people present.

Poor persons of every age were standing in a line extending as far as the hall, and one after the other came to get his paper cornet. Many of them received two—a big one, which contained the private alms of my father, and a small one, which contained the money of the poor-fund.

I was sitting upon a high chair near my father, and I handed him the paper cornets, for my father wished that I should learn how one ought to give, and in this line a great deal could be learned from my father*.

There are many people who have their hearts in the right spot, but they do not understand how to give, and it takes a long time before the wish of the heart finds its way to their pocket; between the good intention and the execution a long time elapses, for their intention travels at the rate of an old mail-coach. Between the heart of my father and his pocket, there already existed, so to say, a railroad. That he did not become rich by that railroad is a matter of course. With the Chemin de fer du Nord and the Chemin de fer de Lyons more money has been made.

Most of my father's clients were women—old ones, however; and even at a later period, when his circumstances began to be anything but splendid, he had a clientelage of aged womenfolk to whom he gave small pensions. They were lying in ambush for him at every place where they knew that he had to pass, and so it happened that he had a kind of secret bodyguard of old women, like the late Robespierre.

In this old guard there was many a hag who ran after him not because of her poverty, but because she liked him personally, and was glad to see his kind and always amiable face.

He was politeness personified, not only toward the younger but also toward the older persons of the female sex. Those old women who prove very cruel antagonists when they are offended are the most grateful people when you have paid them some attention and done them some kindness; and whoever likes to be paid with flattery finds in

---

* Alfred Meissner relates, in his *Reminiscences of Heinrich Heine,* the following in regard to the poet himself: "Many refugees have become acquainted with his benevolence without ever being asked by him to what party they belonged, even though they came from a camp, the flag of which he was ridiculing, and where his antagonists had gathered. He contributed to all collections of money for a noble cause, or for an undeserved misfortune, even more than his means permitted him to do, and as an excuse he used to say; 'I like to leave from time to time my *carte-de-visite* with our Lord.' "

them persons who are not stingy, while the pert young things on whom we waste all kinds of attention, scarcely deign us worthy of a bow.

Considering, therefore, the fact that for those *beautiful,* flattery is a great need, and that it is indifferent to them whether the incense comes from a rosy or from a withered mouth, provided it is furnished strongly and in sufficient quantity, it will be easily understood that my father, without having exactly speculated upon it, in his intercourse with those old ladies, did a good business.

It would be difficult to believe how great was the dose of incense with which they often smoked him, and how well he was able to bear even the strongest portion. This was owing to his happy temperament, it was not by any means simplicity. He knew very well that they flattered him, but he knew also that flattery is sweet like sugar, and he was just like a child which says to its mother: "Flatter me a little, even if a little bit too much."

The relation, however, which my father kept up with those women had still another, more serious reason, for he was their adviser; and it is remarkable that this man, who was so little able to advise himself, was the personified wisdom of the world, when there was a necessity for giving good counsel in trouble. He took in at a glance the whole position; and when the afflicted client had explained to him that in her business everything was growing worse and worse, he brought her complaints to an end with a remark, which, when everything was going badly, I have very often heard him make, viz.: "In this case we must tap another cask." By this he meant to say that one ought not stubbornly to cling to a lost cause, but to commence something new and enter upon another course. It is better to push out the bottom of the old barrel, from which there flows only sour wine, and that only sparingly, and "to tap a new cask!" But instead of this, people lay themselves down with open mouth under the dry bung-hole, and hope that sweet wine will flow from it abundantly.

When old "Hanne" (Johanna) complained to my father that the number of her customers was decreasing, and that there was scarcely a bite, or what was still more disagreeable to her, hardly a drink left in her house, he gave her first a thaler and then he meditated for a while.

Old Hanne had formerly been one of the most fashionable midwives, but in later years she took to drinking and also to snuffing tobacco; and as her nose during that period was continually thawing, and the drops descending from it made brown spots upon the white linen of the lying-in ladies, she everywhere lost her custom.

After my father had carefully considered the matter, he finally said: "Well, we must tap another cask, and this time it ought to be a cask of brandy; I advise you to open a bar, a kind of little brandy shop, in a good-looking street near the harbor, which is frequented by sailors."

The ex-midwife followed this advice, established a drinking-shop near the port, where she did a good business, and would certainly have become rich, had she not been, unfortunately, her own best customer. She also sold tobacco, and I often saw her standing in front of her shop with her red swollen tobacco-nose, a living advertisement which attracted many a sailor.

Among the best qualities of my father was his great politeness, which, as a real gentleman, he showed just as much toward the poor as toward the rich. I especially noticed this on the days above-mentioned, when he handed to the poor their paper cornets filled with money, on which occasions he always added a few polite words.

I there had a chance to really learn something; and many of those charitable men, who are accustomed to throw their money right at the heads of the poor, so that every thaler produces a wound, might also have profited much by this lesson. My father kindly asked most of the poor women how they were faring, and he had become so accustomed to using the phrase, "I have the honor," that he even employed it, when he had to show the door to some old crone who was dissatisfied and behaved impudently. Towards old Flader he was especially polite, and, as above mentioned, he always offered her a chair, for she was really weak in her legs, and was hardly able to hobble away even with her cane.

The last time she came to my father to ask for her monthly allowance, she was so feeble, that Jupp, her grandchild, had to lead her. The latter threw a curious glance at me when he saw me sitting at the table near my father. The old woman, beside the small paper cornet, received from him a large private paper cornet, at which she burst into a torrent of blessings and tears.

It is a fearful sight to see an old grandmother cry so hard. I was tempted to cry myself, and I believe the old woman felt it. She did not cease praising me, saying what a pretty child I was, and she added she would pray to the Mother of God, that He would never let me suffer hunger, and that I would never have to beg money from other people.

My father was not very well pleased with these words, but the old woman meant them well. In her eyes there was something ghostly, but at the same time pious and kind, and at last she said to her grandchild: "Go, Jupp, and kiss the hand of the dear child." Jupp made a sour grimace, but he obeyed the order of his grandmother. I felt his burning lips upon my hand like the sting of a viper. Hardly would I be able to tell why I did it, but I took out of my pocket all my "greasy mannikins" and gave them to Jupp who, with his rude, idiotic face, counted them piece after piece and then composedly put them into the pocket of his breeches.

For the instruction of the reader let it be said that a "greasy mannikin" is the name of a greasy thick copper coin worth about a cent.

The old woman, Flader, died soon afterwards, but Jupp is still alive if he has not been hung. The wicked boy remained unaltered. The very next day, after I had seen him at my father's, I met him in the street. He carried his well-known fishing rod. He again struck me with it, threw horse dung again at me, called again his hateful "Haa-ryh!" so loudly, and imitated the voice of "Dirty Michael" so faithfully, that the donkey of the latter, which with its cart happened to be in a neighboring street, thought it heard the voice of its master and answered with a gay "Ee-ah!"

ROTHSCHILD OF ARTISTS

MORITZ OPPENHEIM (1801-1882)

Oppenheim fortunately matured in a period when his talent could be developed without restriction and he became the first popular Jewish painter of modern times. He studied first at the Munich Academy of Arts, then in Rome and Paris. He first followed the masters and painted biblical subjects which won him a considerable circle of admirers. Notable also are his series of paintings of Jewish ghetto scenes and ceremonies. Of his popularity as a portrait painter he tells in these delightful memoirs.

❋ ❋ ❋

AT the end of the last century, or at the beginning of this one, I first entered this world in a house on the Hanau Judengasse. Jews had not yet come under the jurisdiction of the registrar, so that I am unable to give my exact birth date according to the Christian reckoning. But I have been informed that my good, pious and revered mother fasted the entire day of the 10th of Tebeth, which happens to be a Jewish fast day, and gave birth to me the following night.

From my earliest years I have retained memories of parental prosperity. On holidays, when she went to the synagogue, my mother wore a smart silk gown and a wrap of red velvet, trimmed with soft fur. Our table, particularly on Seder nights, was adorned with a brocaded tablecloth embroidered in silver; on it stood silver goblets, silver candlesticks and even silver rechauds for the food. How very magnificent this evening seemed to me! And how majestic my dear parents were! At the upper end of the table was my father's wicker chair, on which we children—including the grown ones—never dared to sit, out of respect. On this evening the chair was transformed into a throne, covered by a red silk cushion, heavily brocaded in gold and silver. Seated on this throne, my dear father, who was in unusually good humor, looked quite regal. My dear mother, conscious of having successfully completed the

burdensome Passover preparations, gazed lovingly at her table companions, and was a queen for the ceremony, at the side of her husband.
Just as the Seder evening, the festival of joy, showed me a mood of
unrestrained cheer in both of them, so did the serious New Year festival
and the solemnity of the Atonement Day present a picture of pious,
conjugal communion. Here was faith, love, fear, desire and hope. A
sacred light glowed around my dear parents on these festive days.

Even during my boyhood I realized that our prosperity was diminishing. Only three goblets, kept because they were used by my grandparents, remain, and are in my possession. My good father tried hard
to maintain the household in a respectable and moderately elegant fashion, and to give his children an up-to-date education. We were five
brothers and one sister; the trousseau and a dowry of several thousand
gulden for my sister involved great sacrifice. Despite all the strain
that a household run with limited means imposed, my good, pious and
truly God-fearing parents continued to practice philanthropy. Twice a
year, before Easter and before the high holidays in the autumn, the
poor people of the street were sent alms, wrapped separately; the Rabbi
invariably got a big, hard Brabantentaler. Nor were those needy who
were reticent about asking forgotten. Besides, I know that my pious
mother often deprived herself of essentials, and kept secret savings in
her room, to be distributed as alms to certain chosen women.

My first visit to school, where I was taken by my oldest brother
Simon, is also a part of my earliest memories. The school was located
in a small courtyard, in a little narrow house, so low that—I remember—
my brother had to stoop to enter. Along the wall, on a bench no higher
than our shoetops, sat the boys and girls, the children of the entire Judengasse. One by one, according to their places, they were called up to the
teacher, who sat enthroned on an old chair. Before him, on a table,
lay a Hebrew alphabet in large letters. In order to see it, we had to
clamber up on a block. The little old stammering teacher was called
Fälkelchen, evidently Falk subjected to a double diminutive. I was the
youngest, somewhat pampered pupil, and the most sensible thing I know
of myself is that, even then, I considered the years of childhood the
happiest of a lifetime. As I grew into adolescence, I began to concentrate on *tachlith* (advancement). After every semester I asked myself:
"What have you learned during this interval?" Despite his diminishing
income, my father kept a tutor for us at home. His name was Horwitz.
He was succeeded by Solomon Weinheim and others; the two I have

named later attained recognition and significance because of their scholarship.

The Talmud Torah school I attended was in one room, rented from a poor woman for whom every child, during the winter, had to bring a log of wood every day and a tallow candle once a week. Only a few families carried the burden of supporting this school. The teacher was Rebbe Reckendorf of Furth, a very upright, pious man, a good Talmudist, witty, quite ugly and near-sighted. He had the peculiar habit of carrying on conversations with himself or with imaginary people during the lessons; in so doing he often grinned in secret pleasure. Evidently he thought of a joke. As far as I remember, he was the subject of my first portrait. I drew him on the inner cover of a Talmud, as he carried on an amusing conversation with himself, quite forgetful of his surroundings. In the meantime he opened the buckles of his gaiters, let down his black socks a bit and scratched himself comfortably.

In addition to studying the Talmud, I had to study penmanship in the city, where I had to endure a great deal from my Christian fellow students. The penmanship hour was on Wednesday, from ten to eleven; even today, after so many years, this hour of the morning seems longer to me than any other hour of the day, just as—on the contrary—the hour between twelve and one, which was mealtime in my parents' house, still seems the shortest to me. More than once I played truant from that penmanship class, hiding myself in some doorway for its duration. Outside of this I had no contact with Christian children; we Jewish children always carried on a feud with them at the ghetto gates. Nevertheless, I sometimes yearned to leave the ghetto street, but my father forbade it sternly. I went no farther than to poke my head through the gateway, carefully keeping my body within—so respectfully was a parental injunction kept.

My good mother, for all her Jewish piety, liked to read German books —for instance, *Hermann und Dorothea*. Occasionally she also indulged in a visit to the theatre, taking me along. The first performance I saw was *The Devil's Mill*. It impressed me so that I volunteered to decorate the settings of a children's theatre which we ghetto children built in a warehouse. I drew so many diabolical designs on it that the people who saw it said: "This child must go to the Academy and learn to draw."

At this time the Rabbi's grandchild, the son of a rich man, and himself a very handsome boy from Karlsruhe, visited Hanau. (He later became the attorney Ettlinger.) He roused my jealousy, not only because of his get-up, which was different from that of us Jewish children, but with a large drawing portfolio which he got at the Academy and showed off in the Judengasse. My revered father was ready to go even to this expense, though it was looked on as a luxury. My older brother Hirsch had to go to the Academy with me, but whereas he made only inconsequential progress, I displayed more and more desire and love for drawing. Strangely enough, I also wanted to become a doctor, though I now have a great antipathy for that profession. I was therefore sent to the Gymnasium, where I studied Greek and Latin, learning only enough, however, to entrust my secrets and childhood love affairs to my pocket diary in Greek letters.

But the excellent Gymnasium was irksome for me, with its pedantic regularity and well-ordered system, since I was accustomed to the laxity of the Talmud School. I was able to prevail upon my parents to allow me to devote more time to the Academy. The Academy was under the direction of Counselor Professor Westermayer; the assistant instructor was Professor Lotter, who impressed me because of his black suit and white scarf. The basis for the elementary studies was Preisler's drawing copies; later we did mannered, copper engravings. My progress was such that I was soon able to correct the other pupils and became a substitute teacher. The day that I began to paint in oils, under the direction of the Counselor's wife, I perpetuated in large letters on a freshly-plastered building in our courtyard.

I copied a great deal, but had no deep conception of the real meaning of art. My pictures decorated our Feast of Tabernacles hut; in a self-portrait I painted I put Westermayer into the background, holding a drawing pen, and my father handing me a writing pen—an allusion to his esteem for penmanship.

I had often been told that a painter must go to Rome; it was not love of art itself that sent me in that direction. Moreover, I knew only one person in that large city—Christian Haag, a school companion and fellow-painter, no genius, but a dear friend and comrade. I would be glad to see him there. On the way, my fantasy played with imagining his surprise at my arrival; I foresaw our mutual joy. When we were close to Rome, a coach passed us. In it was someone who recognized our courier and ordered it to stop. He was not a little surprised to see me also embraced by one of its passengers—it was no other than Haag. "Where are you bound for, my dear Haag?" "Germany." "Why?" "Because I haven't the money to stay on in Rome." I offered to share my money with him, but could not persuade him to turn back, mostly because a farewell party had been given in his honor the previous night.

My entry into Rome was therefore somewhat melancholy: I was quite alone in this strange city. It was natural, with the Jewish high holidays approaching, that I had a more intense longing for the ghetto and for the old religious customs of my parents' home than for the Vatican with all its art treasures.

I visited the ghetto for the first time on a Friday evening. The people had just left the synagogue and stood chatting on the square in front of it. A distinguished and cultured Parisian Jew had given me a letter of introduction to one of our wealthiest and most scholarly co-religionists in Rome—Signor Uzielli. I asked one of the Jews on the square where this man lived. Instead of receiving the desired instructions, I was asked: "What do you want of Signor Uzielli?" When I replied that this was really none of his affair, he shrugged his shoulders and turned away. I put the same question to another man, and as in the first instance, was met with a query as to my reasons for wanting to see the gentleman. The scene was repeated each time I made inquiry about Signor Uzielli until I grew angry and said: "Am I then in Sodom?" The last word must have sounded like Hebrew to them, for suddenly I was asked: "Are you a Jew?" When I replied: "Of course I'm a Jew!" I found myself at once—not with one guide, but with a crowd to accompany me to the home of Signor Uzielli. On the way they explained their previous behavior. Signor Uzielli naturally did no business on Friday night. A Christian who asked after him could only have something evil in mind, such as, for instance, insisting that during the visit he had baptized one of the children. If anyone made such a claim, the child would be taken away. A similar circumstance had occurred to a Jewish family not long before, and parents preferred to kill their child with brandy rather than to hand it over to the Pope. I saw the possible truth of these stories, and many doubts besieged me as I approached the home of this rich Roman Jew—a home which on the outside was poor and dilapidated. As soon as I opened the door the wife (her husband was not at home) gathered all the children quickly into an adjoining room until she was reassured by my companions, who said "é un jehudi". This first encounter with my Roman co-religionists was not very encouraging and left me with little hope of having either many friends or much pleasure in the ghetto during my projected long stay in the city.

The Café Greco, on the Via Condotti, was and still is the rendezvous for artists of all nationalities. Later, after half a century had passed, I myself found old friends who had for fifty years taken their morning coffee there. Just across the way from the café was the then popular

Restaurant Lepré, where wealthy and penniless alike took their midday meal. The food pleased me; moreover, I became acquainted with many artists and other interesting people. Nevertheless, as the New Year and the Day of Atonement approached—festivals which stirred reverent memories of my parents' home—I grew sad at not dining at a Jewish table. There was then not a single Jewish restaurant in the ghetto. I beseeched Signor Uzielli to find a respectable, if not necessarily well-to-do Jewish family with whom I might make arrangements to take kosher meals during the holidays. Frequently, particularly on the Sabbath, I visited the ghetto and asked Signor Uzielli whether he had accomplished anything in connection with this request. Each time he told me that he had tried hard, but still without success. On the Sabbath before the holiday I pointed out to him again how distressed I would be if I had to spend New Year's Eve alone in a Christian tavern. He reassured me and promised again to try his best.

New Year's Eve came. I went to the synagogue. Signor Uzielli was kind enough to invite me—not to dinner, but to stand with him in the synagogue where he informed me that despite all his efforts he had found no one to provide me with kosher food. I was very much depressed and missed my home terribly. I did not conceal my distress from Signor Uzielli, wanting to see how far his inhospitality would go. It was in vain. He left with reiterations of his sincere regret.

That evening I spent in no tavern; a cup of chocolate constituted my entire supper. I thought of the pleasant, cheerful atmosphere in my parents' home and of the rudeness of the co-religionists I had found in this strange city and who thrust me off so inexplicably.

The next morning I was again beside Signor Uzielli at the synagogue. After the services I wanted to leave, but he restrained me with the invitation to accompany him home and—who can describe my consternation!—to breakfast and dine with him until someone would be found to provide me with meals. After such unexpected kindness I ventured to ask him why he had not invited me the previous evening, which I had spent alone and so sadly. He told me that he had wanted to, but that his wife had not consented; one of her main courses had not gone right in the kitchen.

Eventually a family named Rocas, who it seemed to me had once been well-to-do, consented to give me a skimpy dinner for good pay (half a scudo). Even apart from the fact that I lived far from the ghetto, the non-Jewish food in pleasant company and in friendly cafés pleased me more, and—in the bargain—cost less than one-fourth as much.

Nevertheless, twice a week—Friday night and Saturday noon—usually found me at the Rocas, partly because I realized that the small additional income helped them.

On Friday evenings I used to meet a man named Sabbatino at the Rocas. He was no longer young, and whether out of piety or out of pleasure, he used to sing zmiroth (Sabbath songs). He was single and earned his living, like so many Jews in Rome, by wandering through the streets with a sack on his back and crying "Old clothes!" One evening he did not show up, and when I asked about him I was told, to my amazement, that he had been arrested for some offense and locked up in the Catacumene. This was an institution in which Jews and heathens were given instruction in Christianity until they were ready for baptism. It was around Christmas time; poor Sabbatino studied, was instructed and fussed over until Easter, when custom required that a convert be baptized in the Constantine chapel. I was present at the ceremony; Sabbatino, who had sung zmiroth a short while back, appeared in a cowl and shaved head and was baptized. His offense had consisted of having illicit relations with his Christian laundress and—according to her story—promising to marry her. He never appeared in the ghetto again, and I never found out what became of him.

Otherwise I was quite comfortable at the Rocas, and these good people gave me many proofs of their friendship, as did other Jewish acquaintances, particularly Signor de Castro-Martignani, a brother-in-law of Uzielli, who was very helpful to me. I needed his sympathy most when the Rabbi of Rome informed me of the death of my unforgettable, good mother; this shocking news was transmitted to me as gently as possible by my friends. I told my Christian landlady that I was going to the country for a rest; actually I went to the ghetto to stay at the Rocas. My presence in Rome became known to my landlady, however. Her *cavaliere servente* discovered me at a Jewish funeral which I attended because it was an important one and I was interested in the unusual ceremony. The procession took place at night, in the light of torches; the common people of Rome believe that if a Christian passes under the coffin containing a Jewish corpse, the procession must return home. They are afraid of disorder, and make many turnings.

My distance from the ghetto prevented me from carrying out the religious duty of continuing to say the mourner's prayers daily, but I did it for the first seven days after I was told of the death of my good mother. I slept at the Rocas, and all the other tenants of the house displayed the warmest sympathy for me. It was a low pot-house, but according to Signora Rocas it had been very imposing at the time of her marriage.

I loved my mother infinitely in the true sense of the word. Even now, after half a century, there are moments when the memory of her makes tears almost uncontrollable. When she was dead, Rome and the world became a wilderness. I wanted to perpetuate her dear features and to present her as the fervently loving mother in my painting "Departure of the young Tobias". But I wept so while drawing that the execution of the design went awry.

While in this miserable mood I had a visit from the famous painter Koch, who had been a schoolmate of Schiller's in the Stuttgart Karlsschule. Whenever Koch came to see me he announced himself by banging his heavy cane on my door. He was a powerful man of nature; he could not understand my tears, but he tried, in his own way, to comfort me.

My longing for Germany and for my dear ones finally made me leave Rome at the end of March, 1825. But I was sad at the thought that the jewel of my parents' home—my kind and beloved mother— was no longer there.

Because of this, I did not hurry. I stopped over in Bologna and spent Easter, which I would otherwise have wanted to spend at home, in Venice. A childhood friend of mine from Munich lived there. He had married a wealthy and beautiful Venetian woman. Both he and his parents-in-law, who lived in a magnificent palace on the Grand Canal, were very hospitable to me. I made several sketches of the young woman and after a stay of more than a week I left—slightly enamored— for Munich, where I saw old friends. I paid my respects to King Ludwig who had frequently honored my studio in Rome with his visits. The content of his conversation with me was always that the Rothschilds ought to support me and art. I also spent several days in Stuttgart, where I found a friendly reception in the Kaullasch home. Finally, on the 19th or 20th of May, 1825, I arrived safely in Frankfort, where pleasant lodgings had been arranged for me at the home of the widow of Aaron May, the banker, by my brother Simon, who was on friendly terms with the family. Immediately after my arrival in Frankfort the case of paintings which had been packed and forwarded from Rome, also came. In it was my painting "Susannah in the Bath" which its owner, Baron von Rothschild, had commissioned me to deliver to his home here. How glad I was to be able to exhibit this small picture, which had won so much commendation in Rome and been spoken of so highly in the local newspapers! I envisaged the praise it would evoke here, and what pleasure my family and my friends would derive from seeing my work admired by the public and glorified in the press. I believed I could expect this, because at that time good painters were scarce in the country. Of my genre there was no one at all, and my painting was really good, with firmly delineated features and rich, strong coloring: the Van Eyck school had hovered before me. But how terrified I was when, opening the case, I saw the painting—which had been made on an old, heavy board—entirely out of its frame. In taking it out I saw also that en route it had slipped about on nails, the most important part was torn and damaged. I was in great distress. My brother Simon was also disturbed at the sight. He sent for Dr. Goldschmidt, a doctor of laws, who was considered an art authority. He marveled at my work even in its damaged state and consoled us, saying: "We are pleased with the young man; we see what he is capable of. We shall take the painting to old Morgenstern, who will restore it." Morgenstern was one of the best restorers of his day, but he had to work a long time on my painting; it was not only badly scratched, but the varnish had been laid on too heavily. When this was removed, worm-holes became visible in the old wood and filling them involved much labor. In short, it took a long time for my painting to receive the treatment it badly required.

The patricians of Frankfort came to see me. Moritz von Bethmann (the father), Jean Noé Dufay and others stopped in and commissioned paintings. The Electress of Hesse also honored me with a visit and afterwards wrote me a gracious letter. Such recognition brought me much honor and many orders. I made portraits of the wealthiest Jewish families which were well paid for. I painted beautiful Jewish girls and exhibited the paintings in the Museum salons, out of which have grown the modern art societies, and I was made an honorary member—an honor which had not previously been given to any Jew.

Later I received many commissions from the Rothschild family. The branch which had lived in Naples moved to Frankfort. They and Baron Anselm, whose wife Charlotte was an art lover, maintained elaborate establishments. I was admitted into the finest and most brilliant social circles. When I was presented to the Baroness Charlotte, she asked me whether I would teach her. I replied that I did not make a practice of teaching, but that I was at her service. She recognized the pride in my answer and she said: "Baron Gérard used to be my teacher and I paid him a gold louis for every hour." That irritated me, but I repeated that I was at her service. Actually I never gave her a set time for lessons, but accustomed her to my irregular comings and goings. Nevertheless, she was pleased with her teacher; her frequent visits to my studio and her kind letters written in French were evidence of that. She also engaged me to decorate the ceiling of her home. I drew mythological figures in the eight sections, portraying her as Psyche without telling her, but she noticed it at once. On certain occasions I also wrote poems for her. The fruit of my instruction was her illustration of the Passover Haggada for her uncle Anselm.

I designed the subjects, which she executed in the style of old missals. At considerable expense, she had procured miniatures of manuscripts from the Paris library. The text was written by Messeritz, the best Jewish calligrapher of the time, and the entire manuscript cost the Baroness at least several thousand gulden. I was called the painter of the Rothschilds and Rothschild the painter.

At that time the German Federation was in full swing and all the ambassadors and their staffs met frequently at balls and dinners at the home of Baron Anselm von Rothschild. The furnishings of the house showed a perfect combination of wealth and artistic taste; each room was correctly decorated in period style and was full of rare art objects. Only a suitable number of good paintings was lacking, and I was fortunate enough to acquire the famous collection of Herr de Reus of The Hague for the Baroness. Her husband immediately approved the price of 100,000 florins demanded. In general, despite his scrupulousness, the Baron granted his wife anything she asked. For instance, on one occasion, when she wanted 2,000 florins from the cashier of the House of Rothschild, she accidentally added an extra cipher and made it 20,000. Because the sum was so great the cashier thought it necessary to have the Baron's permission before paying it, but the Baron angrily rebuked him and said: "You need not to ask my permission in such cases. You are to give my wife whatever she asks for at once." A wheelbarrow laden with twenty sacks of gold was delivered to her, which naturally amazed her.

I have particularly pleasant memories of several festive occasions in the Rothschild home. The entire diplomatic corps, and leaders in society and finance were invited to a reception in honor of the famous actress Rachel. Everyone tried to be introduced to her. I remained modestly in the background. This was noted by Baron Anselm, who took my arm and led me to her. I shall never forget the refinement, the nobility and the poetic quality of her appearance and her speech: she read a scene from *Esther*. Another large reception was given in honor of the Duke of Hesse and on still another evening living paintings were presented, with the arrangement of which I was entrusted. Some of the subjects were famous paintings; others I composed especially for the occasion. The handsomest and wealthiest members of the younger set were put at my disposal, a large stage was erected and no less a personage than Minister Blettendorf assisted me at the rehearsals and at the performance. The following day the Baron gave me two hundred forty-thaler notes, which stood me in good stead. My financial affairs were in good order and I was gradually able to repay practically everything that my brother Simon had previously expended for me and advanced to me during my student years. This development could not have been foreseen or expected with any amount of certainty. I must therefore acknowledge his responsiveness all the more gratefully. He was generous by nature; at all times, even when he was not too well off, he was ready to make sacrifices for his family.

In spite of all the honors meted out to me and the material success brought about my art, I retained a very humble opinion of my abilities and achievements. Is this genuine modesty, self-knowledge, uncertainty, or the true recognition of what is great, significant and difficult to achieve in art?

In addition to practising my art, I often had occasion to help gratify the noble passion which ruled all the branches of the Rothschild family equally—the passion to acquire antique art objects. Every member of the family was a zealous collector and knowing and appreciating my capacities in that direction, they made use of my services. I must say that I was able to obtain many wonderful things for them at ridiculously low prices. For instance, there was a set of art treasures in the possession of Count Schönborn, who appreciated them less than did his ancestors and his descendants, and who sold many things to me cheaply, which I brought to the Rothschilds. Such objects instigated a competitive dispute among the ladies and the gentlemen of this family; they were jealous of each other in no other way except in the acquisition of art. Everyone wanted what the other was considering. I was often put in a difficult position, because I wanted to remain on good terms with all of them and to spoil my relationship with none.

VANITIES OF YOUTH

FERDINAND LASSALLE (1825-1864)

The keeping of diaries has been a favorite hobby of sensitive youth, but very few have survived or reached the public eye. One of the rarest and most interesting is the diary of King Edward VI of England (1537-1553), which was kept for a number of years before his death at sixteen. Lassalle's jottings belong to his fifteenth and sixteenth years: in them we can already see those qualities of independence, courage and intelligence that later made him one of the leading public figures of his day. He won the friendship of Heine as a lad in Paris, and was called a "wonderchild" in Berlin intellectual circles. His name became a household word when for almost a decade he defended Countess Hatzfeld in a legal feud with her husband. In 1848 he was sentenced to six months' imprisonment for espousing the Revolution. The last years of his short life—he died of wounds in a duel over an *affaire de coeur*—were devoted to organizing and literary efforts in behalf of the Social Democratic movement of which he was a founder.

❈　❈　❈

Thursday, January 16, 1840

TODAY I again had a hard time of it at school. Dr. Tchirner was giving us a lesson on the Odyssey. He put a question on a very important point of grammar to one of the fellows near me. I knew the answer; he didn't. Tchirner asked one fellow after another. No one seemed to know the answer. I was giddy with happiness; I was sure the question would reach me, when it was answered by the fellow in front of me. Vexed, I looked up from the book, and at that very moment Tchirner put a question to me. Naturally, I was unable to answer, whereupon he sailed into me with a vengeance. The blood rose to my cheeks. Yes, I wept, I wept. To be scolded, mistreated, insulted for such an infinitesimal thing! Patience . . . patience: the time will come.

367

At three in the afternoon I found myself with nothing to do, so I went to Castner's to play billiards.

My father was very gentle with me again. He kissed me and said, over and over again: "If you will only be good!"

And I—I play billiards on weekdays! No, I promise never to play billiards on weekdays and to avoid it as much as possible on Saturdays and Sundays.

Saturday, January 18

My father came home at noon and said: "You know, son, I really think that what you say about not having received a Christmas report card is true. I have just heard that Rabbi Tiktin has complained to Dr. Schönborn that the Jewish pupils were forced to write on the Sabbath."

My emotion at this moment is indescribable. I sincerely thanked God for the coincidence, but realized that I must take advantage of the opportunity. This I did, and I believe successfully.

In the afternoon I visited Isidor, and played six games with him at Castner's, losing three. Then we went to Orlandi's and later to Hesse's, where we met Jacobsohn, Schlesinger and Guttentag. We went bowling. I won the first game; in the second I had only one opponent to worry about. Though I lost, I covered my stakes. Then I played three games with Isidor, after which he went to his dancing class. I stayed on and played Schlesinger for a silver groschen, losing three groschen. When I left I owed six groschen. I had paid out one and a half silver groschen at Castner's and three at Orlandi's. On the other hand I had won a groschen and a half bowling. Summa summarum: out of twelve silver groschen. For nothing.

When I came home I played Ecarté with mother, winning seven silver groschen, then onze-et-demi with Dr. Shiff. I won a lot at first, but lost it afterward. We played for a silver groschen per point. When we quit and I was about to pocket my money, which had not increased, but diminished, Shiff took five groschen from me and said: "For Ecarté—pay your debts." Father didn't seem to like my playing for such high stakes.

Sunday, January 19.

Quarrels again at noon, and mother was to blame. She wept and nagged without end. We talked of the fact that T. had gone to Russia. My mother said: "Well, a lot of other big people will soon go bankrupt here." She said it with obvious intent.

"Perhaps you think it isn't true?" I suggested.

"Who knows?" answered my mother.

Naturally, my father was furious. I reproached my mother, she became angry and didn't want to pay me my allowance of eighteen silver groschen. I said nothing, but calmly took off my coat and stood near the oven.

"Why don't you go out?" asked my mother. I replied that I didn't have a pfennig to my name and therefore couldn't go out. Touched at last, my mother brought me the money herself. I went to Isidor's store, but found it closed. From there I went to Manatschal's and later found Isidor at home. We went to the theater, and saw *Lumpaci Vagabundus*. The place was terribly crowded. I was practically squeezed to a pulp. Afterward I went with Isidor to Glosse's, to play billiards. Today I spent the following: two silver groschen at Manatschal's, ten for the theater ticket, three at Klosse's, and I lost and paid for six out of eleven games of billiards—six groschen. But two and ten and three and six make twenty-one silver groschen. Twenty-one silver groschen in one day. That is a great deal, a very great deal. It is dissoluteness.

Monday, January 20.

When I came home at noon my mother met me with: "Let me tell you how rudely Dr. Shiff behaved yesterday. Just as I was about to leave for the soirée, Shiff arrived, and though he kept on saying 'I don't feel like going to the soirée; I'm not even dressed,' he ended by asking me to let him come along. He said he would stay in the billiard room. When supper time came around, I said to father: 'Don't order too much to eat. I'm not feeling well and haven't any appetite.' Then father told me that Dr. Shiff had come to him and said: 'Mr. Lassalle, please reserve a place for me at supper.' Can you imagine such manners?" Naturally, I saw nothing wrong, but mother was very bitter about it.

In the afternoon mother visited Aunt Burgheim. Dr. Shiff dropped in to see us. When mother returned and discovered that Shiff was there, she refused to come into the room, sat in the back parlor and groused all kinds of nonsense against Shiff. I defended him warmly. Mother was very much put out with me and only after great effort was I able to calm her. Shiff wrote her a letter, but she refused even to glance at it.

Tuesday, January 21.

Shiff visited us again in the evening. Mother was out. When she returned she was not told of his presence and came into the room where we sat. Shiff wanted to vindicate himself and asked mother why she was angry and what he was accused of. Mother, however, was evasive, and only insisted that he had not been slandered. Finally I brought out several points of complaint. Mother went into a rage and called father, who had to make believe he was angry at me. Only with effort was I able to quiet mother.

Wednesday, January 22.

I had a good day at school. For a few days Tchirner hasn't seemed to be persecuting me. Nevertheless, I was guilty of a major error this afternoon. Contrary to the word I had given myself, I played billiards with Samuel today. I was really weak enough to break my word.

Thursday, January 23.

Since I had to go to Dr. Langendorf's wedding at one o'clock, I wrote a note for myself, *invito patre,* saying I must be home at ten. I took it to Tchirner, who sent me to the rector. I got permission and went at once to Orlandi's and then to Dominick's to have my hair trimmed.

We went to the wedding. My father and mother first, then Riekchen and I.

We came into the hall. I left my sister in the main salon and went into an adjoining room. For as long as possible, I put off the painful moment when I would have to kiss the hand of the bride—that angel! But it had to come. I went in. Trumpets sounded and drums rolled. So much the better! At least they drowned out the infinite number of sighs that my agony forced out of me like the roars of an ox. I got a cramp in my legs; they wanted to move backwards. My neighbors must have thought I wanted to do an egg-dance. The truth was, however, that I hoped some other guest would cut in to present his compliments, and I would be spared. But it was not to be. Inexorable fate would not have it so.

I talked courage into myself, gave myself a host of good advice for the trip, entered the circle, and took her hand.

> Then suddenly a shadow held my sense,
> Prudence and consciousness departed hence.
> I know not whether and what I spoke,
> Into which words my misery broke.

When I came to myself, I was among a group of young people and was outwardly cheerful. I met one Naumann Levy, whom I knew from my dancing class. He is a genial, stupid, Jewish store-clerk, endowed with mercantile jokes, arrogant, good-hearted—in short, a malicious fool. Because I have already let him see my opinion of him more than once, he doesn't like me and thinks he can annoy me by calling me Lassalchen or little Lasalle. Jackass! As if he could so much as look at me even if he were three times as tall as he is.

❊ ❊ ❊

Saturday, April 4.

After school, I sat down to read *Kaufmann und Dichter*. Father came into the room. "Reading novels again. You do nothing all day but read novels."

I asked whether I was not supposed to become acquainted with literature and belles-lettres.

"That is a poor excuse. I forbid you to do it."

I went calmly into the next room, took out a volume of Shakespeare and sat down to read that.

"What have you got there?" my father asked.

"Shakespeare," I answered. "That isn't a novel."

"You've read enough poets!" shouted my father. "Do a writing exercise or read a Latin or Greek poet."

"Homer and Shakespeare," I insisted, "are of different genres, but equally great. Shakespeare is as great a genius as Homer."

"There's a big difference," said father. "One is in Greek, the other in German."

It is evidently not for its own sake that one must do this, according to my father. One does not read Homer for a refinement of spirit and heart, or to marvel at the beauties of his poetic genius, or to submit to his moral influence. One reads him only to learn Greek.

Sunday, April 5.

This morning I visited young Borchert and found him and his brother in negligee. We played chess.

In the afternoon Lachs, Orgler, Krämer and I went to Kreinburg, where we met Hahn and Fürstenthal, whom we took along to Klettendorf. Since my resolution not to play billiards or go bowling expired on April 1, I bowled one game. We were gay and I had a very good time.

When I got out in front of my house, I met Isidor and Friedländer, who were going to see the Spanish horsemen. They had come to fetch me and had got permission from my mother for me to come along when I arrived home. I went up. Mother was no longer at home. It was already late, we had to hurry and found no more seats on the upper level, so we had to sit on the lower level, where we had the opportunity to be buried in sand or battered by the horses' heads. I got into an argument with a man who wore a light coat and carried a riding whip; I would have been glad to make him better acquainted with his ears.

When we returned home my mother had not yet come home. Father, I knew, was at a formal dinner. So I went to Hesse's again with Isidor and Friedländer to play billiards. I didn't get home until a quarter after eleven, and only with effort and the display of a great deal of tact was I able to turn away the storm.

Tuesday, April 7

At noon my father came home much disturbed and asked me to show him my diary. Fright gripped me. I brought it and unlocked it. Father looked to see whether I had written in it every day. When he came to last Sunday's entry, he read it. What could I say? Father had heard that I played billiards Sunday evening, and wanted to see whether I had entered it. The scene that followed was terrible. Father turned pale, then red, and sighed so heavily that it broke my heart. In the afternoon I told the story to Isidor, who felt sorry for me. When, in the evening, I found father less sour, I thought I had weathered the affair. But the best is yet to come.

Wednesday, April 8.

It came. Today father asked about my report card. I think that if at that moment all my veins had been pierced, not a drop of blood would have flowed out. Father asked whether, with the holidays commencing, I hadn't yet received a report. I said I hadn't.

"When do you get the Easter report?"

"I don't know."

"Very well. I shall write to the rector. He will tell me. I'll wager you are deceiving me. But I'll find out the truth!"

My torments at that moment can only be felt, not described. I was in the clutches of such anxiety that I didn't know what to do. But what marvelous contradictions arise in the human soul! I, who had forged my father's signature, and was driven further and further into deceiving him—I prayed more devoutly than ever before that God might help me keep this a secret, and that this first fraud of my life might also be the last. I felt calmer after I had prayed, as if I really could believe that God would heed prayers that ask for the concealment of a fraud. Nevertheless, I was at peace about it.

As a precaution, I resolved not to write into my diary for the time being. I was afraid that it might be used against me, as my entry of Sunday night was. I carried out this resolution, and filled these spaces at a later date.

Thursday, April 9.

Today we had our examinations. It is decided that I am to go to the commercial school in Magdeburg. My father has already been in touch with the school authorities.

Friday, April 10.

I am really much more calm about the report card.

Saturday, April 11.

Today is my birthday as well as my sister's. I haven't written any poem for the occasion. When I came down, my mother gave me two ducats, and two pairs of gloves; my father a scarf and vest. He also made peace with me about the billiard affair, but intimated that he still had his doubts about the report card. He also took my two ducats, to keep them for me. My sister got many gifts. Young Urbach gave me Shakespeare's poems, bound uniformly with the *Works* I own, and Isador gave me an autograph album.

In the afternoon I took a walk with young Urbach. On the Ring we met Haber whom I told that I would leave for Magdeburg in about two weeks. He told me he was leaving the next day, to spend three weeks with his parents, after which he would go to Berlin to study for a year, take his examination and then, without visiting his parents, go deep into Russia.

"Dear Ferdinand," he said, "it is likely that we shall never see each other again. It is possible that I will never come back out of Russia. I would remember you anyhow, but I would be happier if you wrote something in my album."

I went with him. He was very sad, and repeated that he would never see me again. I wrote in his album. When we parted, we both wept.

In the evening I discovered that Haber had been arrested at the University for revolutionary activity.

Sunday, April 12

Mother gave me money for the theater. I came home too late and was greatly distressed by it, but it didn't help me any.

Monday, April 13

This morning my father was very much vexed because I asked him for a new coat. Finally he said: "Don't you think I'll catch up with you? Here!" and he showed me a sealed letter to Schönborn. "This afternoon I will know everything. I will see your report, and I'll bet you five to one that you've been lying to me. God help you!"

I could have sunk through the floor and needed all my self-control not to lose everything out of despair. When father went to business, I locked myself in my room, resolved to weep away my despondency. But I saw at once that tears would do no good. I must act. I tried to go to Tchirner, to get my report card and my transfer, and be protected at least to that extent. But I couldn't find out where he lived. Now I was really desperate. At any moment everything might be discovered. I was closer to suicide than ever before. But I did not do it, and in my failure to do it lies incontrovertible proof that I am not an egoist. For whatever my fate is to be, I don't want it to come on me now, when I am miserable, in the grip of despair. I want it to come when I am at the peak of happiness, at a ball or some such place. I shall not be afraid of death when it appears, but invitingly reach my hand out to it. Not my love of life restrained me from acting today, but the thought: "What will my father and mother say? How unspeakably unhappy I shall make them! My father would be devoured with shame at having been the father of a suicide. My mother would die of grief and sorrow. I would make myself happy, but those dearest to me on earth—my father and mother—I would make miserable." No, I could not be such an egoist. I consoled myself and argued that in two years I would have forgotten the whole thing, and if I thought of it at all, it would be with a smile.

When I came home my father sent for me and told me I must either confess or accompany him to the rector. Once more fate smiled on me. I confessed that I had signed the Michaelmas report, because Rudiger had marked me falsely, but that I had received no Christmas report, which was true, but I didn't say that we had received slips instead. Father either knew or guessed more. He went with me to the rector. I staggered rather than walked.

In a few minutes he knew everything. He wept. What I felt cannot be described. A thousand times I cursed the first day when, because I was afraid to show father my report, I signed it myself.

God, I know of so many fathers who let their sons sign their own reports, without examining them. Siegfried Wohleim comes to his father and says:

"Father, I have a report card."

"Is that so? Where is it?"

"Here. Sign it, but don't look at it. It's too bad." He holds his hand over it, leaving his father room for the signature, which the father affixes calmly.

While Isidor was still at school, I often heard his father say: "I haven't seen your reports for a month. I suppose you sign them all yourself. I cam imagine how good they are!" On the other hand, I know many fathers who would have thrashed their sons and then not have thought any more about it. But I know of no one who could take the matter so much to heart as did my father! All the greater the wrong, then, in hurting him.

The next day I had to fetch the report cards from Tchirner and give them to father. I pass over an interval whose results I will only summarize. My father's happiness lasted a week longer. Then we made peace. I promised never to do anything of the kind again, and my departure for Magdeburg was fixed.

MY MOTHER'S MAGIC

BERTHOLD AUERBACH (1812-1882)

The harmonious blending of environment and tradition is present to an extraordinary degree in the life of this man of letters. The beauty of Jewish family life and ceremonies and the wonderful Black Forest country of Germany where he was born—in Nord-settin—and lived as a child left a lasting impression upon him. He was saturated with a passionate love of Nature and Freedom, which dominated his successful career as a novelist, playwright, poet and revolutionary patriot. Incidentally, he was a fervent apostle of the philosophy of Spinoza. When antisemitism swept Europe in the 70's and 80's, Auerbach waged an uncompromising struggle against its perpetrators. Even this brief recollection suggests his warm sympathy for his people as well as his unpretentious gift for narrative.

❋ ❋ ❋

A SON of my mother's brother, who had learned the butcher's trade from his father, had emigrated to America and had not been heard of for many years. One day he suddenly appeared and showed that he was as charitable as he was prosperous. This cousin was a powerful man. He spoke very little, and had the bearing of a distinguished Spainard, for he came from Latin America. He wanted to revisit his home and also to show it to his wife. She was a dark-skinned Creole of slight build. When my cousin said, "Manuela, this man, this woman, is related to me in such and such a way," then Manuela embraced and kissed them; and she wept in order to indicate that she was sorry that she could understand no other language but Spanish.

One day my cousin said to me: "Of course it is a blow not to find my parents alive, but I regret as deeply that your mother is no longer alive, for I have her to thank for my good fortune. My father, you know, was your mother's brother; and when I was making ready to depart, accompanied by my parents and family, we passed by your home. Your mother, wishing to bid me adieu, called me into the house.

376

She placed her hand upon my head and blessed me. Then she gave me something carefully wrapped and sealed and said, 'Take good care of this. Don't open it ever. But wherever you decide to remain, give it to the first poor person you meet who asks for alms. Observe this well, and you'll have luck.'

"On the way, my teacher, who also accompanied me, explained that this gift was an old custom which was as full of wisdom as it was of feeling: for whoever carries a gift that is intended for an act of charity becomes a Messenger of Good, and the Forces of Evil have no power over him.

"Naturally, I soon forgot this, as I did much else. I entered the New World. Things went badly. I joined up in the Mexican Army. But if I should tell you all that I lived through, I could not recount my experiences in days. We seized a canoe and paddled down a river (I don't know the name); but the boat capsized and all of us plunged into the water. What happened to my comrades I don't know. I got myself safely to land, wandered for days through the forest in indescribable misery, fell upon my knees before the huts of savages and clasped my hands, begging for food and water. Finally I reached the ocean and hired myself out as ship's cook. I landed in Buenos Aires, I could find no employment, I wandered through the streets in desperation. Thereupon a beggar asked me for a coin, and then, and then only, I recalled your mother's gift. I found that I still had it and gave it to the beggar. Suddenly, I was in the midst of a great commotion: the beggar was showing the onlookers what I had given him. It was a quarter of a ducat! He tried to return the money, saying that I had surely erred. I denied this. Then, a carriage drawn by two magnificent horses halted directly in front of us. In the carriage sat a man of aristocratic appearance. He stepped out and asked what was going on. I told him the whole story. He considered the fact that I had not used the gift for myself in the face of distress very noble, and when, in answer to his query, I said that I had been looking for employment as a cook, he laughed and replied that I had come to the right man.

"It turned out that he was the owner of a tremendous slaughterhouse. If I were to tell you the number of oxen, cattle and sheep that were slaughtered there each day, you would regard it as boasting. To make a long story short, this man took me into his own home, and Manuela is his daughter. Yes, I became his son-in-law. Now just imagine what your mother's joy would be if I could have related this story to her! Yes, indeed, that my parents are dead is a blow, but not less so than that your mother is not alive."

MUSICAL RECOLLECTIONS

HEYMANN STEINTHAL (1823-1899)

Steinthal, an important anthropologist of the nineteenth century, combined a vast store of general knowledge with an acute grasp of Jewish learning. Born in Gröbzig in Anhalt, Germany, he was educated at the University of Berlin, where he made a brilliant record under the renowned Wilhelm von Humboldt and later occupied a chair in philology. He studied Oriental Languages and Literatures in Paris, and became, with his brother-in-law Moritz Lazarus, a founder of the science of folk-psychology. His interests are reflected in the following memories of the musical atmosphere of his childhood associations. He was remembered as a superb teacher by students who attended his lectures on the Bible and the philosophy of religion at the important Hochschule für die Wissenschaft des Judenthums.

※ ※ ※

NO impression, not even of the eve of the Day of Atonement, was as powerful as that of the eve of the Ninth of Ab. Though it came at the height of summer, the synagogue was already dark when we entered. The chandeliers were not lit, and only one candle burned on the omed—the cantor's lectern—which usually had two candlesticks on it. I saw the hazzan moving slowly and silently toward his place, his head bowed, not wearing the usual prayer-shawl and with felt slippers on his feet, just as all of us were either in felt slippers or in our socks. I had seen him and other members of the community similarly clad during the shiva period—the seven days of mourning after the burial of parents or children. Very softly, voiceless, he began: *Borchu* . . . (Bless ye the Lord Who is to be blessed). And how awe-inspiring it was when the lofty dark room was filled with the hollow response: *Boruch* . . . (Blessed is the Lord Who is to be blessed for ever and ever). And when we had said the customary evening prayer standing, then—as if our dearest had been torn from us—we sat down on the floor or on footstools, and our reading-stands were laid sideways, so that the sideboards served as desks for the reading of Jeremiah's Lamentations. Everything seemed disrupted, a scene of destruction, and we sat as if resting on the road to slavery. We were in small groups, each around a stump of candle that one of us had to support by hand. The tiny flames, shadowed by our bodies, were more terrifying than the darkness; one might have thought the lights would betray us to the pursuing enemy. The most alarming part of the evening, however, was the uncurtained holy ark. Boards, profane boards, instead of the holy of holies—these were the symbol of the destruction of the Temple. Now I really felt that the dearest thing of all had been wrenched away from us—destroyed, degraded. I saw the parable.

The hazzan began the Lamentations softly, in varying, short, mournful tones that trembled with pain. All else was silence, which never happened in the synagogue at any other time. The whole year through, the hazzan shook his body slowly forwards and backwards as he prayed; today, however, he moved sideways—right and left. I had seen many people shake in this way, silently except for occasional sighs, during shiva. With what symbolical force all this impressed itself on my fancy! I heard the daughter of Zion weeping uncontrollably in the night, and saw the tears on her cheek, saw her inconsolable, alone, restless, helpless— she had sinned. And God is just! At the second lament I raised my voice; at the third it already had its normal strength. The lament has a different rhythm, so it is read in a different tempo, in curt outcries of despair. Here the poet does not weep for his people, but for himself, that he must look on all this misery. The *Ach bi* ("Surely against me . . .") of the third verse cut into my heart. Yes, "there was no pain like unto my pain."

But we had a most singular hazzan. How beautiful his voice was I must leave undetermined, but I believe it could compare with those of our famous hazzanim. That alone would not have made him singular. He was that because he was no fool*; he was a scholar. He was not a talmudic giant, but he was well-read, not only in the Talmud and the Midrash, but also in the Bible and medieval books on ethics, insofar as they were available to a man living in a small town. He was a genuine pastor for his community. He never sang songs; he merely prayed aloud, for himself and for us. Often he prayed in tune because his feeling,

---

* He was not spared hearing the proverb—like all proverbs only partly true—that all hazzanim are fools. To this he would reply, smiling quietly: "Yes, but not all fools are hazzanim."

seeking expression, passed from the spoken word to the melodic. He had no thought of showing off or of an audience. And we believed him, thinking: "He is talking to the Lord our God." So he ruled our spirit and our mood in sorrow, in joy, and above all, in sadness. His reading was incomparable and deeply moving, which it could not have been had not every syllable been clearly enunciated. This clarity of speech was worth more to me than all the musical training in the world. Only the man who understands what he is saying and really feels it can do it as he did. But he also sang operatic arias—for instance, the prayer from the *Freischütz* for "Thou sustainest the living with lovingkindness. . . ." It was as well-suited as if the melody had been written for the text. How it emphasized the cry: "Who is like unto Thee, O Lord, among the mighty!" This came from his comprehension of how to adapt his text to melody. But it was not achieved after carefully rehearsed preparation; he prayed, and one cannot rehearse a prayer. In fact, he was reproached for the habit, which also had its bad aspects, but he would not change. He refused to look through the prayer book beforehand. All his chants and readings were inspirations of the moment. He wore no elaborate headgear, but covered his head—on which was only a small black cap—and the rest of his body with a woolen prayershawl, draped in a wide fold on the right shoulder, so that his right arm was free. When he said, "We will celebrate the mighty holiness of this day," or the "May it be Thy will, O Lord. . ." before Mussaf (the supplementary service), he drew his tallith over his head to touch the lectern, so that—like children who build their own small house in the larger one—he might close himself away from the world. Oh, he knew how to pray sententiously, and in dread and trembling. Softly, plaintively, he began his "Poor in deeds am I. . . ," then grew louder, then murmured softly again, and again cried out and once more sobbed softly, always letting his feeling and voice rise and fall with the significance of the words. Then he threw his tallith back and loudly began the Kaddish, which summoned us to prayer more imperiously than bells, and the Amen resounded in chorus from the congregation—a response to his melody and powerfully telling. Yes, we prayed with devotion.

Our hazzan gestured at two points, though those who stood on his left could not see it at all and those on his right probably didn't notice it. My father's pew was just behind the omed, and he had a cupboard instead of a simple stand. On its free side was a leaf that could be raised and lowered to any height. From my perch on this I could see the hazzan very clearly. He made a gesture when he sang: "Man has come out of the dust and returns to dust." Here he pointed his index finger downwards, raised his hand and let it sink again, pointing to the floor. And when he sang of the high priest sprinkling the sacrificial blood, he made the gesture of sprinkling. I was convinced that his gesture had as much weight with God as the gesture of the high priest.

I am afraid that these musical memories, which have unfailingly refreshed, comforted, cheered and encouraged me throughout my life, will not move the reader. Yet one more remarkable piece remains to be mentiond. I know a recitative that no one has ever heard and that no person has ever sung, completely, but which has accumulated in my imagination bit by bit. It concerns the 90th Psalm, which is read by Jews on Saturdays and holidays, together with other psalms. Most people know the usual way in which these psalms are read; they are mumbled by every person for himself, and then suddenly shouted in jubilation. Our hazzan also followed this custom. But he would proclaim one verse and then another, according to his mood, and usually they were verses from the 90th Psalm. He did this without thinking that anyone was listening to him. And no one would have heard him, except for one boy who listened to him carefully—and that was I. Long after the death of the man, when I myself had reached manhood, I realized quite by accident that I could say the whole Psalm as he had done it. I had constructed an ideal whole out of parts I had actually heard. But the man had thought and felt it as a whole.

How did it happen then that this great hazzan settled in a small town while still young and remained there contentedly for the rest of his life? Was he not aware of his abilities? Without a doubt, he was. He had left his native village in Russian Poland about 1812 and come to Germany to seek his fortune, taking a basso and a tenor along with him. The trio passed through many cities that did not please them. Our hazzan was looking for a pious, peaceable community that would appreciate music, and he did not find it. One Saturday and the subsequent weekdays he spent in Bernburg without singing a note, the city displeased him so. On Friday he came to Grötzig. From the gate one could look down the street leading to the market place. He stood there in ill-humor, but he had three people to provide for. One house immediately disclosed itself as belonging to the baker, because girls came out of it carrying the Sabbath loaves and cakes. A charming young girl approached him. He asked her where the *gabbai* (warden) lived. She said: "Come with me. The gabbai is my father." Keep your acclaim and your money! He was done for. Within the year the girl had become his wife. He argued himself into staying: autumn was here, winter was at hand, war was likely, and the community was a pious as he could hope for—what more could he want? He stayed the winter and the following summer, married, let the basso go and got a good job for the tenor in the vicinity. He studied with Reb Tanchum, a splendid scholar, and when his teacher died he refused to touch the piano for a year and had it stored in the attic, from where it was never brought down again. Instead of playing, he studied on alone, and when his first son was born he named him Tanchum. So it was natural for him to stay. Where else would he have received so hearty a *yashar koach* (congratulation) from the congregation after the service? Where else would the men and boys, inspired by his prayer, have wished one another such a joyful "Good Sabbath" and "Good Holiday"?

TORAH IN AMERICA

ISAAC MAYER WISE (1819-1900)

Inspired by the ideal of liberty, Wise left Bohemia and arrived in New York in 1846. "I felt that from now on I was no longer an imperial Schutzjude (court Jew) but that I was breathing a free atmosphere." He was elected Rabbi of the congregation in Albany that year, but soon afterwards, because of his zeal for liberalizing Judaism, organized a new synagogue and initiated certain basic reforms. He was consumed with the idea of adapting religious ideas and ceremonial to American life. Blessed with tremendous energy and glowing eloquence, he became the founder and the spearhead of the Reform movement. Among the institutions he initiated are the Hebrew Union College in Cincinnati and the Union of American Hebrew Congregations. In addition he was a prodigious publicist, and it is due to occasional space in his journal *Die Deborah* that we have his memoirs covering the years 1846 to 1857. Wise wrote vividly, sincerely, unpretentiously. His *Reminiscences* are unique in American autobiographical literature. Who "Mrs. F." is remains a mystery.

❋ ❋ ❋

I HAVE stated that Mrs. F. and some other ladies had come to Albany to be present at the dedication of Temple Anshe Emeth, in September, 1851. Miss Graetz was one of the most prominent of these visitors. She was the sweetheart of the celebrated author, Washington Irving. Since he was not a Jew, and she would not marry a Christian, they both remained unmarried, but carried on an active correspondence with one another to the end their lives. This Miss G. was the original of Walter Scott's Rebecca in *Ivanhoe*. The great novelist pictured her faithfully, although he knew her only from her portrait, her letters, and the oral description by Washington Irving.

These ladies, all of whom were Portuguese Jewesses, importuned me to write a history of the Jews instead of a history of the Middle Ages. I had communicated my purpose to Mrs. F. some time before, and she had requested me to devote myself rather to writing Jewish history. Upon my refusal, she sent her well-instructed agents to convince me. When I persisted in the pursuance of my original plan, she came with this bevy of Portuguese Jewesses to persuade me.

Any one who does not know this particular class of American women may consider this proceeding strange. American women exercise great influence in religious matters. This is also the case often with the native-born Jewesses of Portuguese descent. In addition, they are very proud of their descent. They lay the greatest stress on the genealogical tree. They are Jews and Jewesses from pride of ancestry. Hence Jewish history is of prim importance in their eyes. They like to hear about the Jewish worthies of aforetime. The princes of Judah and the heroes of the olden days are of great interest to them, because their blood flows through the veins of the present generation of Jews. Ancestral pride of birth has been beaten out of the German and the Polish Jews with whip and knout; but it has persisted in these American Portuguese.

Then, as now, there were but few works on Jewish history in the English language, and therefore Mrs. F. desired that I, willy-nilly, should undertake this task. I expressed my doubts as to my powers and protested my inability, but all to no avail; I had to submit. If any man living can succeed in holding his own in the face of the opposition of six women, I can but admire and congratulate him; for I was not able to do so. Mrs. F. and her bodyguard would not desist until I promised to begin my studies in Jewish history at once. Therefore I had to begin with Genesis once again in the winter of 1852. May God forgive this woman all her sins, and also this one! First she made a Jewish editor of me, and then also a Jewish historian. From that hour on I ceased to be free and unconcerned. I had to study and write constantly. I was confined indoors, had to leave the management of the school to the congregation almost entirely, and acquired a new ailment; viz., chronic absent-mindedness, so that frequently I could not distinguish between hat and the hatbox, and put the latter on my head in place of the former. My wife found it necessary to inspect me every time I left the house. If it happened that I escaped without submitting myself to her inspection, I was sure to be laughed at; for there was certain to be something odd about my costume. I disliked to be considered eccentric, hence submitted with childlike humility to the surveillance of my wife. A person as absent-minded and dreamy as I was required a guardian indeed.

After I had quite finished the first volume of the history from Abraham to the destruction of the first temple, had worked myself almost to death, and had fallen head over heels into debt, I wrote the introduction, in which my standpoint is clearly stated, and took the manuscript to New York in the spring of 1853. In spite of letters of recommendation from the most prominent men, such as Horace Greeley and William H. Seward, no publisher was willing to accept the work. I peddled it about for three days, visited every publisher and bookdealer, was received courteously everywhere; but as soon as I had read my introduction, the decision was pronounced as follows: "No one would buy such a godless book." This was the general judgment. After three days I returned home thoroughly humiliated.

During my return journey I felt very despondent. The steamer *Rip Van Winkle* was too small for me. I flitted about restless as a bat until the captain forced me finally to play chess with him. "What in thunder is the matter with you? You have lost your wits," he said to me. I then told him some impossible stories, but not the truth. He opened one bottle of champagne after the other, until he could no longer distinguish the chessmen. We then decided to call it a drawn game. We now retired, but I did not sleep. Morning dawned upon me lying still awake. We arrived in Albany on time. I went home, but I had not the courage to awaken my wife. I was ashamed; for she had seen how steadily and enthusiastically I had worked. She knew how I had entered into the task with my whole heart and soul. "She will take my failure to heart," thought I. "Let me put off for several hours my own shame and her mortification." When she did receive me, I was my old self once again—calm, determined, the jolly companion. I depicted wonderful things. She believed all I said, and I rejoiced in her joy.

The scholars and literati of the library, who had grown into a sort of mutual admiration society, met in solemn council at noon. Whatever any one of us wrote pleased all the others, although we criticized and attacked one another mercilessly. Indignation ran high at the mercenary souls of New York who could not appreciate a soaring spirit, who did everything for money and nothing for literature, etc. Let Boston be tried. Boston had better taste, nobler feeling. Wood suggested that I pass as an American Christian in order to satisfy the stupid mob; but no definite conclusion was reached. Before long I realized that I would have to help myself, or else should have to give up the whole project. I wanted to be sure first of all, whether or not my work had any merit. I read portions of the manuscript to celebrated scholars, and then handed it for examination to impartial literary experts, with the definite understanding that no corrections were to be made. "If it is not good enough

386 MEMOIRS OF MY PEOPLE

as it stands, it had better not be printed at all." After I had been assured by competent judges that the book ought to be printed, and Amos Dean had agreed with this decision, it did not take me long to make up my mind. "Since I have begun to write on Jewish matters, I shall not be dependent on the good will of each and every wretched publisher. I have no money," so my thoughts ran, "but there is money enough in the world. I have written a book, it is true, that will shock the whole world; but they will have to pay for it nevertheless. The free, unhampered thought must out into the world. If Judaism in America must depend on the calculations of a few publishers, it can never amount to anything. Forward, then, in God's name."

The next morning I closed a contract with a printer for two thousand copies of a book of four hundred pages octavo, to be printed on good paper, and to be neatly bound. The contract called for about two thousand dollars more than I possessed. While the book was on press, I told my friends of my rash undertaking. The faithful ones, who had stood manfully and fraternally by me in all my struggles—my old guard—did not fail me now. Within a few days several members of my congregation had subscribed sufficient to cover the whole indebtedness, and had deposited the money for me in bank. Two thousand dollars was an enormous amount of money for Albany at that time, and every one understood that my undertaking was exceedingly risky; but my friends, for all that, did not leave me in the lurch. I may be permitted to say now that there was no one among all the Jews that had emigrated to America who had to fight such a coterie of bitter enemies as I; but, on the other hand, there is none who can boast of having found such a host of true, steadfast, and intimate friends as did I.

In the summer of 1853 I was received into the company of Faust and Gutenberg's magicians. I had never learned witchcraft, it is true, nor was the secret power revealed to me of conjuring the devil; but I was initiated into the mystic brotherhood of the printers and typesetters. I was named a knight of the black art at J. Munsel's, No. 78 State Street, Albany. It cost me much beer and furnished me much sport, but I was an apt pupil and made rapid studies in the lofty art, so that I soon mastered the secrets of the letter case and proofreading. Correcting proof, reading proof, or whatever may be the technical term for this noble business, was my chief occupation that summer. Goethe tells us that he who never ate his bread in tears does not know the heavenly powers. Well, even Goethe did not know everything. Whoever has not read proofs set up by obstinate typesetters, who pay no attention to a correction, though it be made ten times, but trust to Providence that it may turn out all right, he knows you not, ye heavenly powers. Since that time, a quarter of a century ago, I have never succeeded in getting away from the atmosphere of the printing-room. I have often execrated Gutenberg and all his apprentices. Whoever has given himself into the power of magic can never free himself from its bonds. The insane longing to consume printers' ink pursues him like an evil fate.

While I was being initiated into the black art, I did another foolish thing. I had engaged several traveling agents to secure subscribers for the book. In order to facilitate their work, I sent proof-sheets to various newspapers, so that the book was defamed sufficiently before it left the binder. Every scribbler attacked the unfortunate volume. A host of pious souls prodded me with pens and pencils, as though Satan had let loose all the legions of hell against me. They did not criticise the book; they found no mistakes, faults, nor errors in it; but they complained, howled, and lamented in ear-splitting fashion over my godlessness, infidelity, and irreligiosity. They called me a heretic, an un-Jewish Jew, an anti-Christian, a German rationalist, a disciple of Spinoza, of Thomas Paine, and of the devil; in short, they depicted me and my book in so monstrous a manner that I was compelled to laugh often and heartily at the prevailing stupidity. The Christians were even more bitter than the Jews. I was pleased beyond measure that rabid fanaticism could not point out a single mistake nor convict the foreigner of any errors in English style. I laughed at the manner in which my learning was exaggerated. On this account I was pronounced to be a most dangerous person. It appeared to me extremely comical to find among the raging flood of condemnatory newspaper articles a letter from Theodore Parker, who praised the book highly, but regretted that it was too orthodox in tone; while Dr. Illowy, of blessed memory, published in the *Occident* a bill of excommunication in Hebrew against me and my book. Not a soul had the courage to take my part, and I was too proud to do so myself, until finally a physician—Dr. Arnold, of Baltimore—published an article in the *Occident* with the heading:

"The Philistines are upon thee, Samson."

This encouraged me somewhat, and I wrote thereupon several insignificant rejoinders in the *Asmonean*.

But wherefore this hue and cry? I had declared in the introduction that miracles do not belong to history, and I proceeded to explain the miracles as natural events. I described the revelation at Sinai word for word according to the sources, and added that the event was described thus in the Bible, but made no further comment. But this was not my worst sin in the eyes of my opponents. I wrote Jewish history from the democratic point of view. In this I differed from all my predecessors; hence the monarchy was unjustified and contrary to the laws of Moses. If this was true, the Messianic belief of both Jews and Christians was without foundation. Therefore I had no reason to palliate the faults and weaknesses of David, Solomon, and the whole dynasty. I exposed all the intrigues of the court, and pinned my faith to the prophets who had thundered against the kingdom and the kings. The faithful believers could not forgive me this, and yet I do not retract one word even to this day; and I have also lived to see how the twenty-five hundred copies of my book have worked a revolution within Judaism and Christianity. Today the book is orthodox in every truth, as Theodore Parker asserted at that time; but at the time of its appearance it fell into the orthodox camp like a veritable bomb. It frightened the saints out of their wits, and the half-saints wrapped themselves in the mantle of sanctity and cried aloud: "See how holy we are, we who have not only not written such a book, but none at all! We have not only not read this book, but none at all!" The host of sycophants increased from day to day, until all had become canonized and my book had been hounded to death.

But the seriousness of the situation became apparent particularly when the book was placed on sale. It had been defamed, the entire clergy was arrayed against me, and there seemed to be no liberal people. My agents sold scarcely sufficient copies to pay their expenses; the book lay in the bookstores unsold, and I was in dire straits. I had debts like an Austrian staff officer, and no prospect of paying them. What distressed me most was that I could not pay my friends the money they had advanced; and although my creditors were very lenient, and even offered me more money, I could not sleep for many nights, and I began to quarrel with myself and my insensate folly.

The worst feature of the case was that my wife discovered the true state of affairs and understood my misery in spite of all the care I took to hide the newspapers, and in spite also of my assumed jollity. She worried much more than I, because her disposition was milder than mine, and she could not hide her grief from me. She wanted to comfort me, and in doing so she laid bare the wounds of her own heart. This was exceedingly distressing for me. I found her in tears at one time. "What is the matter, dear child?" "You are so good, and the world treats you so shamefully," she answered. It was as though I had received a dagger thrust. I could not overcome her mournful mood either by flattery or kisses. I began to ponder and to consider: Is not the world too wicked to appreciate the truth? Is it not more sensible to look out for myself and to leave everything else to God? Here I thought of my friends, my faithful guard, and I had to acknowledge that the world was not so very wicked after all. Thereupon I had to confess to myself that the people were not at fault; for they had not harmed me, but that it was I who had thrown down the gauntlet to bigotry, orthodoxy, yes, to the whole pious crew. These were only protecting themselves. This is not wicked. Hence I had only myself and my own folly to blame. True, I was incensed at bigotry, but not at the bigots who desired to defeat their opponent.

MY SOUL'S TRUE NATIVE LAND

GEORG BRANDES (1842-1927)

Although born and educated in Denmark, Brandes (né Morris Cohen) became a powerful force in modern European culture. He fought uncompromisingly against conventional thought in the realm of literature, philosophy and social science, persisting in the belief that a fundamental conflict existed between religion and modern science and philosophy. His great work, *Main Currents in Nineteenth Century Literature,* remains a classic of literary criticism. Of a piece with his mental outlook was the choice of Hellenic over what he conceived to be Hebraic values. These recollections indicate some of the psychological impacts that must have influenced his decision. After World War I he publicly affirmed the constructive value of the new-born Jewish homeland in Palestine.

❊　❊　❊

ABOUT this time it dawned upon me in a measure what birth and death were. Birth was something that came quite unexpectedly, and afterwards there was one child more in the house. One day, when I was sitting on the sofa between grandmamma and grandpapa at their dining-table in Klareboderne, having dinner with a fairly large company, the door at the back of the room just opposite to me opened. My father stood in the doorway, and, without a good-morning, said: "You have got a little brother"—and there really was a little one in a cradle when I went home.

Death I had hitherto been chiefly acquainted with from a large, handsome painting on grandfather's wall, the death of the King not having affected me. The picture represented a garden in which Aunt Rosette sat on a white-painted bench, while in front of her stood Uncle Edward with curly hair and a blouse on, holding out a flower to her. But Uncle Edward was dead, had died when he was a little boy, and as he had been such a very good boy, everyone was very sorry that they were not going to see him again. And now they were always talking about death. So and so many dead, so and so many wounded. And all the trouble was caused by the Enemy.

There were other inimical forces, too, besides the police and the Enemy, more uncanny and less palpable forces. When I dragged behind the nursemaid who held my younger brother by the hand, sometimes I heard a shout behind me, and if I turned round would see a grinning boy, making faces and shaking his fist at me. For a long time I took no particular notice, but as time went on I heard the shout oftener and asked the maid what it meant. "Oh, nothing!" she replied. But on my repeatedly asking she simply said: "It is a bad word."

But one day, when I had heard the shout again, I made up my mind that I would know, and when I came home asked my mother: "What does it mean?" "Jew!" said mother. "Jews are people." "Nasty people?" "Yes," said mother, smiling, "sometimes very ugly people, but not always." "Could I see a Jew?" "Yes, very easily," said mother, lifting me up quickly in front of the large oval mirror above the sofa.

I uttered a shriek, so that mother hurriedly put me down again, and my horror was such that she regretted not having prepared me. Later on she occasionally spoke about it.

School is a foretaste of life. A boy in a large Copenhagen school would become acquainted, as it were in miniature, with society in its entirety and with every description of human character. I encountered among my comrades the most varied human traits, from frankness to reserve, from goodness, uprightness and kindness, to brutality and baseness.

In our quarter of an hour's playtime it was easy to see how cowardice and meanness met with their reward in the boy commonwealth. There was a Jewish boy of repulsive appearance, very easy to cow, with a positively slavish disposition. Every single playtime his schoolfellows would make him stand up against a wall and jump about with his feet close together till playtime was over, while the others stood in front of him and laughed at him. He became later a highly respected conservative journalist.

In lesson time it was easy to see that the equality under one discipline, under the hierarchy of merit, which was expressed in the boys' places on the forms, from highest to lowest, was not maintained when opposed to the very different hierarchy of society. On the lowest form sat a boy whose gifts were exceedingly mediocre, and who was ignorant, moreover, from sheer laziness; to him were permitted things forbidden to all the others: he was the heir of a large feudal barony. He always came late to school, and even at that rode in followed by a groom on a second horse. He wore a silk hat and, when he came into the schoolroom, did not hang it up on the peg that belonged to him, where he was afraid it might be interfered with, but in the school cupboard, in which only the master was supposed to keep his things; and the tall hat crowning so noble a head impressed the masters to such an extent that not one of them asked for it to be removed. And they acquiesced like lambs in the young lord's departure halfway through the last lesson, if the groom happened to be there with his horse to fetch him.

It seemed impossible to drive knowledge of any sort into the head of this young peer, and he was taken from school early. To what an extent he must have worked later to make up for lost time was proved by results. For he became nothing less than a minister.

Nothing was ever said at home about any religious creed. Neither of my parents was in any way associated with the Jewish religion, and neither of them ever went to the synagogue. As in my maternal grandmother's house, all the Jewish laws about eating and drinking were observed, and they had different plates and dishes for meat and butter and a special service for Easter. Orthodox Judaism, to me, seemed to be a collection of old, whimsical, superstitious prejudices, which specially applied to food. The poetry of it was a sealed book to me. At school, where I was present at the religious instruction classes as an auditor only, I always heard Judaism alluded to as merely a preliminary stage of Christianity, and the Jews as the remnant of a people who, as a punishment for slaying the Savior of the world, had been scattered all over the earth. The present-day Israelites were represented as people who, urged by a stiff-necked wilfulness and obstinacy and almost incomprehensible callousness, clung to the obsolete religious ideal of the stern God in opposition to the God of Love.

When I attempted to think the matter out for myself, it annoyed me that the Jews had not sided with Jesus, who yet so clearly betokened progress within the religion that he widened and unintentionally overthrew. The supernatural personality of Jesus did not seem credible to me. The demand made by faith, namely, that reason should be fettered, awakened a latent rebellious opposition, and this opposition was fostered by my mother's steady rationalism, her unconditional rejection of every miracle. When the time came for me to be confirmed, in accordance with the Law, I had advanced so far that I looked down on what lay before me as a mere burdensome ceremony. The person of the Rabbi only inspired me with distaste; his German pronunciation of Danish was repulsive and ridiculous to me. The abominable Danish in which the lesson book was couched offended me, as I had naturally a fine ear for Danish. Information about ancient Jewish customs and festivals was of no interest to me, with my modern upbringing. The confirmation, according to my mocking summary of the impression produced by it, consisted mainly in the hiring of a tall silk hat from the hatmaker, and the sending of it back next day, sanctified. The silly custom was at that time prevalent for boys to wear silk hats for the occasion, idiotic though they made them look. With these on their heads, they went, after examination, up the steps to a balustrade where a priest awaited, whispered a few affecting words in their ear about their parents or grandparents, and laid his hand in blessing upon the tall hat. When called upon to make my confession of faith with the others, I certainly joined my first "yes", this touching a belief in God, to theirs, but remained silent on the question as to whether I believed that God had revealed Himself to Moses and spoken by His Prophets. I did not believe it.

I was, for that matter, in a wavering frame of mind unable to arrive at any clear understanding. What confused me was the unveracious manner in which historical instruction, which was wholly theological, was given. The history masters, for instance, told us that when Julian the Apostate wanted to rebuild the Temple at Jerusalem, flames had shot out of the earth, but they interpreted this as a miracle, expressing the Divine will. If this were true—and I was unable to refute it then— God had expressly taken part against Judaism and the Jews as a nation. The nation, in that case, seemed to be really cursed by Him. Still, Christianity fundamentally repelled me by its legends, its dogmatism, and its church rites. The Virgin birth, the three persons in the Trinity, and the Sacrament of the Lord's Supper in particular, seemed to me to be remnants of the basest barbarism of antiquity.

Under these circumstances, my young soul, feeling the need of something it could worship, fled from Asia's to Europe's divinities, from Palestine to Hellas, and clung with vivid enthusiasm to the Greek world of beauty and the legends of its Gods.* From all the learned education

* Brandes elaborates this point in a letter to the *Frankfurter Zeitung* which is quoted in *The Jews* by Maurice Fishberg (pp. 467-468:) "As a rule, writers when speaking of me refer to my Jewish origin. I may remark en passant that there is no danger that I should overlook in which religious community I was born. I confess that if all my life I were not constantly reminded of the fact by others, I should have forgotten it, so little significance has it had for me. . . . As soon as any one puts his pen to paper to write about me, for or against me, invariably the first thing he says is that I am a Jew! How funny! If there is anything I am not, it is this. The whole of Denmark and the whole of Finland are impregnated with Judaism; their God is Jewish; their religion is recon-

I had had, I only extracted this one thing: an enthusiasm for ancient Hellas and her Gods; they were my Gods, as they had been those of Julian. Apollo and Artemis, Athene and Eros and Aphrodite grew to be powers that I believed in and rejoiced over in a very different sense from any God revealed on Sinai or in Emmaus. They were near to me.

And under these circumstances the Antiquities Room at Charlottenburg, where as a boy I had heard Höyen's lectures, grew to be a place that I entered with reverence, and Thorwaldsen's Museum my Temple, imperfectly though it reproduced the religious and heroic life and spirit of the Greeks. But at that time I knew no other, better door to the world of the Gods than the Museum offered, and Thorwaldsen and the Greeks, from fourteen to fifteen, were in my mind merged in one. Thorwaldsen's Museum was to me a brilliant illustration of Homer. There I found my church, my God, my soul's true native land.

structed, developed Judaism, with a few mystic additions. The Old Testament in both lands is a holy book; and the New, which is still holier than the Old, was written by Jews. Half the Danish culture originates from Palestine; half its literature is thence inspired. Even the real Danish names, Petersen, Hansen, Jensen, etc., are Jewish names, Biblical names. If, then, a solitary young man succeeds for a short time in cutting adrift from the prevalent Judaism, he falls back again on all fours; returns, like so many Danes, to one of the many representatives of Jerusalem, to the Pope, or to Grundtvig, or (like Strindberg) to Swedenborg. There was a time when I was about the only man in the whole country who was not a Jew. Nevertheless I might almost say that the sole thing that everybody in the country knows about me, and the sole thing that they communicate to the whole world, is that I am one. They all live and breathe in Jerusalem's atmosphere. All the churches are full of it. It was not long since it was pumped into the universities. And he among the Danes who earliest, most zealously, and most obstinately in his spiritual life strove towards Athens they are never tired of dragging back to Jerusalem, which they can never eliminate from their own minds."

WELLSPRINGS OF MY FAITH

LUIGI LUZZATTI (1841-1927)

Luzzatti was one of the celebrated figures of modern Italy. Born of well-to-do, observant parents in Venice, he made a brilliant record at the University of Padua where he subsequently taught economics. He occupied a seat in Parliament for more than three decades, served as a popular Minister and Prime Minister, and was decorated by King Victor Emmanuel III for his accomplishments in behalf of workers, especially in regard to the development of cooperative associations. Religion was one of the central interests of his life. These personal footnotes reveal the sources of his religious beliefs and at the same time reveal the struggle to discover a modern scientific outlook beyond the confines of conventional Judaism and Christianity.

✳ ✳ ✳

MY family divided its interests between trade and the synagogue; and I grew up in this atmosphere of activity and of faith. We dealt in textiles, hemp, and rice, and we managed a small manufactory for woolen fabrics and a larger one for carding flax. Marco, my father, was an excellent manager, and according to the custom in Jewish families of that period, centered his life around his home and the temple. We lived in peace and accord with our workers, by whom we were loved and respected. Every Sunday we invited them to dinner. I often used to go to our shop, which interested me deeply; and there, from the time I was five years old, I breathed in the dust of labor and learned to know the common people. Because of this, and also because I was strong and simple, the workers came to like me. Imperceptibly a firm bond was established between me and those who toil, a bond that has lasted all my life.

The events of the year 1848 are among the most vivid of my early recollections. I was then seven years old. I was attending a private Jewish school near our house when we heard the news of the outbreak at

Castello. The hatred of the Austrians had been instilled in us with our mother's milk and my family thanked God in their prayers for this outbreak against the detested foreign domination. Everyone was rejoicing. A national guard was formed. My uncle, Giuseppe, who was an expert swordsman and could handle the musket, became an officer. He was the man of arms in our family. My older brother, Davide, joined the ranks of the *guardia della speranza,* a company in which were enrolled boys upwards of nine years of age. I was not old enough to join this corps, but daily I would practice with gun and sword in our garden. And young though I was, I experienced all the emotions of the siege of Venice. When the shells began to shower our house, which faced the Lagoon, we were compelled to move to another house near the Square. It is from this house that one day I saw Daniele Manin passing hurriedly along the street, and my mother stopping him to ask anxiously for some news. There was talk of revolution, but Manin replied that everything was under control. Later, I saw the specter of death stalking through the streets of our city,—death under the triple form of hunger, cholera, and bombardment. The Austrian shells rained in on us even in our new home. One night the booming was continuous and my mother tried to encourage us with the words: *"Non gavè paura, le xe bombe che se stua nel Canal."* (Venetian dialect, meaning: "Don't be afraid, they are only shells which are put out in the Canal.") But I was not afraid. My parents sought out another residence near Castello, and then in order to escape the shells and the spread of the cholera, we were forced to go to live on a barge. Despite these precautions my eldest brother fell ill with the cholera. My mother, a saintly and selfless woman, guarded over us all like an angel; it was at this time that she undoubtedly contracted the heart ailment to which she succumbed much too soon.

But the Austrians soon returned. The failure of the Venetian Revolution was for us all a cause for mourning and tears.

Now the houses of the well-to-do families were commandeered to lodge Austrian officers. We too were compelled to take one of them into our home. I was only eight years of age when Venice fell, but I understood well enough. Never did I allow that officer—at bottom a kindly and well-disposed Bohemian—to caress me. He liked to stroke my curly blond hair, but I railed against him and fumed at the foreign domination. Jokingly he called me the "little rebel".

In my youth my dominating passions were a ferocious hatred of the invaders and an intense love for my country.

At the age of fourteen I went through a serious illness which nearly led me to my grave, and the reaction from this perhaps decided my future course. I refused to take any medicines, but nature and the tender care of my mother soon restored me to health. My intellectual development was very rapid. I read everything; I studied everything. Literature, philosophy, Latin, Greek, mathematics, physics, natural history—everything engrossed me. I began then, at seventeen, to study the history of religions, an interest which has never left me. A group of studious young men used to meet at my house to study together, to converse and discuss. Full of enthusiasm and idealism, our discussions revolved about the aspirations of our Fatherland and of modern science. These were the most beautiful and productive years of my lifetime, and to this day I still draw upon this intellectual accumulation, that intellectual capital. I was reading Schiller, Shakespeare, Petöfi, Mickiewicz, Kant, Spinoza; I learned by heart nearly all of *The Divine Comedy*. I used to alternate my more serious studies with long recitations of *Childe Harold* or of some other favorite Byronic masterpiece. During those years I also learned to play the violin well, I became proficient in Hebrew, and I advanced to first place in my class at the lycee.

The chief influence in my life at that time was probably my contact with Samuele Romanin (celebrated Italian historian of Jewish origin. His most famous work is the monumental *Storia documentata di Venezia*.) I had the good fortune to see him often in his little room meditating or engrossed in his researches and his endless documents. From him I learned that the love of truth lightens even the hardest toil. When he was a young man, an irresistible attraction had drawn him to the marvelous city that was Venice. For one who has a deep love of study, there is an inescapable lure in that fascinating city, which has such an illustrious history extending over fourteen centuries, a city which still preserves intact its republican majesty in the canvases of Bellini, of Titian, of Carpaccio, and possesses such significant mementoes of its past glory in its magnificent palaces which challenge time itself. Romanin was one of those select few who express their love through thought and honest work. It seemed to him that the best way in which he could manifest his affection for the city was to retell her history, and strengthened by admirable patience, he set himself to the task. I used to cherish in him the tranquil mind of a man performing his civic duty and who was aware that his work was a valuable contribution to knowledge. The task before him was a difficult one. He had to fight his way against old prejudices rooted in romance and poetry, because before Romanin there had existed no real history of Venice, but only lore—poetical and romanticized fabrications. Myths consecrated by art are perhaps the most difficult things to uproot, but he never for a moment doubted of the outcome, because he knew that the final triumph belonged to truth. And even when in the most recent works he saw repeated over and over again the same old errors, he never despaired but carried on his work of real historical research, while at the same time in his many public lectures held at the Athenaeum he endeavored to present and popularize the real history of Venice.

In this atmosphere my mind was formed. A proud youth, I passed through the streets of Venice like an Athenian in the Agora of Athens. Up to the age of sixteen I continued to go to the synagogue and to pray with effusion to the God of Israel. Then I began to break the fast (so rigidly observed by Jews), without, however, the knowledge of my parents. To this day I still remember the agonizing qualms of my conscience. It was not so much having broken fast that troubled me as the realization of having hidden the sin from my parents and especially my mother. That was a memorable day in my life. My doubts sprang not so much from any scientific analysis as from a youthful impulsiveness, and they concerned not so much the inner truth as the outer manifestations of religious practice.

With the passage of years, skepticism assumed rational form with ideas derived from the study of philosophy and of history.

But a religious feeling has remained with me always as the center of my spiritual life, and I continued to be a believer in the fundamental and universal aspects of religion. My beliefs changed only in regard to tolerance of other people's beliefs and in regard to the need of outward religious practices.

But my mother was still confident of my ultimate orthodoxy. One day, when she was visited by some Catholic friends who attributed many evils to the Jews, she called me from my studies to answer these charges. I did not wish to appear melodramatic before those people or to provoke a scene in the presence of my mother. I simply returned to my room, took down a volume from which I studied the system of popular banks of Germany as advocated by Schulze-Delitzsch, and showing it to them I said: "Behold how the usurer and the son of usurers are planning to combat usury. There are usurers among Jews as well as among Catholics." And I ended by quoting a pertinent saying of Saint Bernard.

They answered me that it was only an exceptional Jew who was not a usurer. I replied that that might have been the case at the time when the Jews had no occupation other than money-lending, when they could be neither farmers, nor industrialists, nor practice any professions. But today such usurers form a very small minority. Our visitors were silenced. Had I really convinced them? It is far easier to penetrate into minds agitated by political dissensions than to convince those who are consumed by religious passions. It was then that I recall saying to my mother, who had been proud of my rebuttal, that all the great religions must sound in unison like the different strings of a celestial harp.

I no longer had any faith in the old religion, but two main reasons prevented an open break. The first was the profound love I bore my family, especially my mother, who would have been profoundly hurt by a public abjuration. As it was she was silently grieving over my refusal to attend the services at the temple on the Sabbath and on the other Jewish holidays. The other reason was an inner hesitation which has never left me to this day, a fear that in thus breaking away from Judaism I would inadvertently be committing a crime—I would be abandoning the persecuted in favor of the persecutors. In fact, when I did finally abandon Judaism I was for a time an unmitigated agnostic. It seemed to me then that I was in some measure honoring my ancient faith by not exchanging it for some new one. This explains why, notwithstanding the intimate friendship which bound me to Fedele Lampertico, a sincere Catholic (also an outstanding Italian economist of the nineteenth century), there occurred between us those frequent controversies over religious matters which, as so often happens when the disputes have to do with God, usually irritated instead of clarifying the minds of the disputants. Giacomo Zanella, a priest and poet who watched over us like a spiritual father, had learned of these youthful outbursts, and in a letter to me he urged us to show restraint and mutual respect in our disputes concerning Catholicism.

"I have heard that you have exchanged some bitter letters over religious matters. I beseech you both to be tolerant. There are so many other interests that bind you two, so many other grounds on which you can love and respect one another."

How much understanding is revealed in this recommendation, and how much honor does this simple caution shed on the soul of the eminent priest!

The wholly Christian atmosphere which I breathed outside of my paternal home, led me to meditate on the Gospels. Especially stimulating were the solitary trips I used to make across the melancholy Lagoon to the lonely isle of Saint Francis of the Desert, which was still steeped in the memory of the legendary landing there of the Seraphic Saint on his return from Syria. My veneration of this most saintly of saints had its inception during those brief sojourns on that lonely island, and my interest in the Franciscan retreat was perhaps an indication of the sprouting of a seed which later flourished freely, which resulted in further study, and which time deeply imbedded in my soul.

The Gospels then seemed to me superior to the Pentateuch. I expressed these sentiments to my old tutor Mosè Soave before I did so to my mother. He sought out passages from the Psalms and the Prophets, especially in Isaiah, passages which he held to be superior even to the Sermon on the Mount. Despite the deep respect I bore him, I began to confute him, and I dare say that since that day I had ceased to be a follower of my paternal faith. As I have said above, I had already committed some minor infractions in orthodox practice. But now hardly a day passed in which Jehovah and Jesus did not cross in my thoughts.

Aside from the question of conversion, two fundamental Catholic elements fought within me. I remember, among other things, a long discussion, resumed several times, that I had with the venerable Abbé Zanella on our frequent strolls about the streets of Venice. The Abbé maintained this line of reasoning: Christianity could not have come about without the Mosaic religion, but after Jesus this older religion had almost lost its reason of existence. To this thesis I made the following objections, which disturbed him somewhat but to which he never made adequate reply. As soon as Christianity, I would tell him, had survived the pagan persecutions, it undertook to persecute the Jews who had been banished from their native soil and from Jerusalem. This people, dispersed throughout the world, debased and often massacred, always remained faithful to the God of Israel, while the other ancient religions once professed in Europe died out one by one. In order to justify this heroic resistance, the Christians were wont to say that God himself preserved the Jews as a living testimony of the crucifixion of Jesus.

Another factor that in my adolescence drew me to a Christian atmosphere were my visits to the island of San Lazarro, the home of the Mechitharist congregation of Armenian monks. I was a strong rower, and in a boat given to me by my father I made frequent pilgrimages to this retreat. Here my conversations with the monks usually fell on two favorite topics, religion and persecuted peoples. In a period when great masses of peoples were held oppressed by a few dominating states, the stories these Armenian monks told me of the sufferings they had endured, caused me to take this unhappy people to my heart. When many years later I had occasion to mention these people to the great Gladstone, he found in me an Armenian soul whose pity found an echo in his own.

Giorgio Politeo was another teacher who, since 1857, had taught me philosophy, and whom after Abbé Zanella I regarded as one of my spiritual fathers since I derived from him so much divine inspiration.

He seemed a reincarnation of Socrates. In a mild voice he spoke to us like the ancient Greek thinker to his disciples. A liberator of the human reason, he sought to bring forth the latent faculties of our moral essence by tempering his discussions with brilliant interpretations of the Gospels. Talking with him gave us wings to soar from the everyday world to the heavens and back again.

In the years before he was sent into exile, I remember having had a mild controversy with this teacher. I had written a paper on the manner in which the outstanding martyrs of great causes had met their death— men who died for knowledge, for country, for liberty, for religion. In this essay I attempted, as far as was possible, to grade the moral value of the immortality which these great spirits all acquired by dying, whether they sought this immortality outright, or ignored it as some did, or even proudly refused it. To me it seemed that the most sublime example of individual and conscious energy was embodied in the scientist who, almost certain of death, inoculates his own organism with some fatal element in order to study its effects.

To Politeo, on the other hand, the religious martyrs were the most sublime. I would then ask him which of them died with the purest and most disinterested courage? And he would answer me with a sentence of St. John Chrysostom, which frequently appeared in our discussions: "Every man has the special worth of the thing he loves. Do you love the earth? Then you are the earth. Do you love God? Then I must talk with you as though you were God."

And in this we were in perfect agreement because the martyr who dies for the love of God and not for worldly glory looms far superior to those who accompany their sacrifice with hope of fame and the cult of posterity. Politeo even suggested that whoever would undertake to write and explain the last hours of man on earth would be performing a great service to truth; there is no better apology for death than the last hours of the living, no greater apology for truth and the moral ideal than death itself. In those last moments the great falsehood of life is revealed; the mind, in all its sadness, has intuitive flashes of some supernal truth, of something that is different from and contrary to what has been practiced or believed on earth. In the depths of the human soul, in the recesses of the mind which seems already hushed, as if compressed and suppressed by the avalanche of worldly passions, there now rises, especially in cases of great individual and social catastrophe, a simple and authoritative voice, a voice free from rhetorical artifices, a voice which seems to be a protest and an ideal, a call of remorse and of the need of expiation and of pardon. If ordinary men react in this manner when confronted with death, how much more revealing of new moral secrets are the last earthly moments of the great figures who give up life for the sake of their faith! But Politeo hastened to say:

"How different are the martyrs of politics from the martyrs of the first three centuries of Christianity, those martyrs who took Christ as a model for their meditations and their sacrifices! The political martyrs are an expression of supreme worldly energy, of the heroic paroxysm of courage, of magnanimity, of pride; while the others, the Christian martyrs, have by a supreme calm, a sublime resignation, a prayer and a pardon for their torturers; for their dream of a truth that is not of this earth lets them make their sacrifice without calling attention to it with grandiose words."

But I, fortified by my historical studies, would then recount the deeds of the Jewish martyrs during the Middle Ages, and I would ask him, "In what category would you put these martyrs? We know that the Crusaders in their journeys to the Holy Land went out of their way to massacre the Jews, notwithstanding their defence by the great Saint Bernard of Clairvaux. Those Jews who were besieged in the Tower of Spires or at York never wavered when they were confronted with the terrible dilemma of abjuring their faith or being massacred. The oldest man among them would first kill the men, the women, and the children, and finally himself. Joseph Ha-Kohen, the physician of Avignon, in 1575 published a work entitled *The Vale of Tears,* that can truthfully be described as *The Deeds of the Jewish Martyrs.* These unfortunates calmly preferred death to abjuration, without even the consoling thought that their blood might bring about the victory of their faith. Nor did they enjoy the compensation of an apostolate that assured them of approaching triumphs, such as alleviated the sufferings of the Christian martyrs who, with their thoughts fixed on Jesus, were confident that the sacrifice of their earthly existence would cause them to be resurrected in the divine essence. No, the Jewish martyrs fell sadly and alone, without even a comforting belief in the immortality of the soul. These martyrdoms move us so deeply precisely because they were not adorned by any human or divine grandeur, and were without any human or divine rewards."

But at this point Politeo introduced a new note in our discussion, a distinction between those who sacrificed themselves for the truth and those who died for an error. I could only reply that at the last tragic moment of death such sophistry is inconceivable and that every religious conviction sealed with blood is an expression of the highest moral truth. To this, my teacher could not help agreeing.

I shall never forget these discussions. I shall bear them with me to the end of my days. From that day to this, that is from 1857 to 1926, I have remained a Deist. Without being attracted to any particular church, I have defended all religious beliefs and all persecuted peoples with the same fervor, but where the Jews are concerned, my feelings and my eloquence rise even higher. You may ascribe this to my origin or perhaps to a sort of reparation I seek for having abandoned the faith of my fathers. But the central principle of my spiritual life, then and now, is an absolute respect for all forms of worship. Whoever harbors this respect in his soul feels impelled to defend the freedom of worship with all his powers, with his tongue, with his pen, and even at the danger of his own life, just as one would defend one's country. And this applies to all worship, even to that from which we are compelled to dissent on high moral, philosophic, or religious grounds. Without regard for these two fundamentals, the defense of the persecuted has always appeared to me as sheer hypocrisy. With the passage of years I witnessed a period of silence in the matter of religious persecution, because during that time the people were absorbed in achieving their political liberation. It was later, when the political questions seemed to have been resolved, that agitation reverted to the achievement of religious freedom. As if in revenge for the oblivion to which they had been subjected, the religious problems now threaten once more to play an important part in the history of humanity.

A FESTIVAL REVERIE

ISRAEL ABRAHAMS (1858-1925)

Abrahams was one of those rare men who lived and spoke as he wrote and thought. He was learned, modest, charming—an ornament of English Jewry. During his youth he was deeply influenced by Solomon Schechter, a notable scholar whom he succeeded as Reader in Rabbinics in Cambridge. Of his numerous writings, perhaps his portrayal of a great epoch of Jewish history in *Jewish Life in the Middle Ages* will have permanent value. Central to all his achievement, however, was an unflagging concern with religious ideals and institutions. His temperament was too poetic for systematic thought, but his works are charged with living religion, Abrahams' characteristic humanism breathes through this affectionate reminiscence of the succah (booth), one of the most delightful customs of the Feast of Tabernacles.

✳ ✳ ✳

MY earliest succah was my mother's. In those days—how many years ago I do not care to count—my summer holiday lasted exactly nine days a year. We needed no train to take us to our country destination—we just stepped into our little city garden. In brief, our one and only annual outing was spent in our succah, and we young boys and girls enjoyed our change of scene far more than I have relished longer and more distant excursions in recent years. It has been said that the pleasures we make for ourselves are fuller and fairer than the pleasures which are given to us.

Perhaps this is why we loved our succah, for we made it ourselves. We did not employ a professional carpenter to put in a single nail, or plane a single beam. We bought rough logs and boards at the city timber yard, which was never rebuilt after the fire of a quarter of a century ago. We planed the logs and grazed our fingers, but the pain did not count. Though all these preparatory stages occurred a fortnight beforehand, the actual building operations never began until the night when the great Fast was over. Old traditions clung to us, and somehow we knew that it was a special merit to close the Day of Atonement, hammer in hand, putting in the first nail of the succah, passing as the Psalmist has it "from strength to strength".

Our succah was much admired, but no critics were more enthusiastic than we were ourselves. It goes without saying that we had many visitors, for people in those days had a keen eye for a succah. People who neglected us all the year, rubbed up their acquaintanceship as Tabernacles came round. We did not wonder that our succah was popular, for we really believed that our architectural design was an original one, and I retained that notion until only a few days ago, when an old illustrated jargon book, printed in Amsterdam in 1723, was cruelly placed in my hands, and on page 45 I beheld to my chagrin the picture of just such a succah as ours was. We put it together in this fashion. Four upright beams were connected at the top and at the bottom with cross bars of wood, and thus was obtained a hollow shell of substantial strength. Our next step was to put in the flooring. How we wasted our wood by ingeniously cutting the boards just three-quarters of an inch too short! But that difficulty was overcome, after many councils of war, and we then put on the roof, not flat, but sloping. The sloping roof was a great conception. It did away almost entirely with the rain difficulty, for the water glided off the thick leaves at the top and saved us from the necessity of tarpaulins or glass superstructures. Most people make the succah roof flat and then build a sloping wooden or glass frame above the roof. Our plan was not only prettier, but it enabled us to remain in our succah without closing the top in all but very heavy showers. We had a tarpaulin ready in case of exceptional rain, but I can only recollect one or two occasions on which we scaled the garden walls and placed it in position over the greenery. But our master stroke lay in the walls. There were no walls at all! A few lines of stout string made a lattice-work on which we fixed thick layers of fragrant myrtle branches and laurel leaves. The effect was fairy-like, and we did not spoil it by attempting to "paint the lily". The only decorations which we introduced were clusters of grapes, which trailed their luscious path along the very walls, a few citrons in their own early amber yellow, which hung from the bright roof, and an odd chrysanthemum or two still growing in their mould, which added the necessary streaks of color. All this was not so costly as it may sound, for we bought in very cheap markets, and saved much of the wood from one year to the next.

Over the way, our neighbors had their succah too. This was also very pretty, and many preferred it to ours. It belonged to a more conventional and ornate type, for it was really a sort of summerhouse which stood all the year and was dis-roofed when Tabernacles drew nigh. We boys used to like to have a hand in their decorations as well as in our own, though it went to our hearts to see the beautiful apples and pears betinselled with wrappers of gold and silver paper. The gilder in those days was the only "proper" beautifier. Then, reams of colored papers were cut into strips and twined into chains. Finally, out came the samplers which the girls worked with their own fingers. These samplers contained the succah benedictions embroidered and crocheted in the drollest of droll Hebrew letters, but somehow as they were brought out year by year, and were hung in position on the walls with the mizrah facing the west, a silence of mingled gladness and tenderness fell upon them all. It seemed like a stocktaking of past memories, and a renewal of past, forgotten loves. But we loved best our own little bit of nature unadorned.

Sadly lacking in ornament, whether natural or artificial, was a succah which many of my readers will recollect. It belonged to a remarkable man now dead. He had more piety than pence. He occupied three or four rooms on the top floor of a tall house in Bevis Marks, and he had not even a square foot of open space. Must he therefore be robbed of the privilege of sitting in his own succah, nay, of sleeping in it? Perish the thought! A convenient trap door in one of his garrets suggested an ingenious plan. He first raised the trapdoor, removed the skylight— which was very rickety and easily detached—and hung sheets round the hole, the sheets trailing to the ground and beyond, and catching the feet of unwary visitors. Of course, we all would go and see this old gentleman every Tabernacles. He refused admittance to none, whether you could comfortably squeeze yourself in was your business, not his. You plodded your weary way up five or six flights of stairs and stumbled through a hole in the sheetings. If you have never before seen the sight that greets you, prepare for a surprise! You would find no furniture in the room but a simple chair and bedstead. One wall contained nothing but a red handkerchief on which was imprinted a fancy picture of Jerusalem with Moses and Aaron on either side of the Ten Commandments, while olive branches figured in all possible and impossible corners of the picture. The other wall was filled with a huge scroll on which, with his own hand, he had written out at great length the wonders of the Leviathan on which the good shall hereafter feed. But the most amazing thing was the host himself. He would be so seated that his head and shoulders were directly under the very aperture in the roof. He was near-sighted, but when he espied you, eagerly would he seize your arm and push you into the place which he vacated, so that *you* too had your head under the center of the hole while you recited the proper blessing. Of course he slept in his queer succah every night, and equally of course he had an annual cold in the head for at least three months afterwards.

Such humble constructions were almost invariably the result of poverty. One well-known case occurred in which a succah was built on a small balcony outside the first-floor window of a house in Amsterdam, if I remember accurately. The poor owner could not help himself. He could not act like our previous friend, for he did not live at the top of the house. So he just opened the window slightly at the top and slipped into the crevice half a dozen long sticks parallel to one another. (He was a stick-dealer by profession.) Then he opened the lower half of the window, squeezing it up as tight as it would go. This lower part of the window he left open the whole week, for the succah was made by covering the projecting sticks with leaves. The man who lived on the ground floor was not a Jew, and beheld his first-floor neighbor's arrangements with astonishment. He remonstrated in vain, so he went to the magistrate for redress, and a summons was granted. The case came on just the day before Tabernacles, and the decision was a good joke, well remembered by many. "You are robbing this man of his light," said the magistrate, "And I give you just eight days in which to remove the obstruction." The Jew readily promised that he would obey the order of the court, which he did when the festival was over.

But one unsightly succah that I knew, owed its ugliness to the owner's stinginess. He was very rich, but was a thorough miser. He made his succah small to save his hoarded shillings; and he made it unattractive lest too many visitors should present themselves. He constructed the walls out of old packing-cases, and did not take the trouble to erase the inscriptions daubed upon them. As you approached his succah your eyes were greeted with the legend: "This side up with care," "Empty crate, to be returned," and so forth. The inscription that puzzled me most ran thus: "Dog-hooks not to be used." I never knew what a dog-hook was, and it only occurred to me to look while writing these reminiscences. I find from Lloyd's Dictionary that a dog-hook is a kind of iron bar or wrench, for opening iron-bound cases; but a German toy-dealer tells me they are really hooks for cranes that are used chiefly for hoisting barrels but not suitable for slenderly made cases. This miserable man was one of the first I knew to apply to Baron Lionel de Rothschild for laurel branches to cover the roof of his succah. Even in those days the Rothschilds never refused any such application, though the scale on which the branches are supplied is now far more extensive. I believe that special bushes and trees are planted at Gunnersbury to meet the ever-growing demand on Tabernacles. Many a poor East-End Jew, who would otherwise be forced to forego the pleasure, is thus enabled to build his succah. But I do not quite see why some of my West-End friends also avail themselves of Mr. Leopold de Rothschild's princely generosity.

I have mentioned some humble succahs, let me introduce my readers to a very beautiful one which might be seen a few years ago at the Hague.

Mr. D. Polak Daniels, a warden of the Jewish congregation in the Hague, and a member of the Municipality and of the County Council for South Holland, is undoubtedly the owner of one of the handsomest succahs that have ever been built. This notable succah, which stands in the spacious garden in his residence in the Spuistraat, was built nearly forty-five years ago by Mr. Daniels's father-in-law. It is almost square, and constructed of wood and painted glass. The internal decorations are extremely handsome and tasteful, the prevailing color being light blue. The colored glass is very fine. The succah is so constructed that when taken to pieces the panels of two of the sides form a box in which all the other parts are deposited. There is an interesting episode in connection with this succah, the fame of which has spread beyond the confines of the Hague. During the lifetime of the late Queen of Holland this succah was mentioned at her Majesty's dinner table. Queen Sophia was well versed in Jewish history and observances, and she expressed a wish to see Mr. Daniel's succah, it being then the Feast of Tabernacles. The request was of course complied with, and on the following afternoon the Queen paid her visit, which lasted half an hour. In the course of conversation with her host her Majesty displayed her Jewish knowledge. She asked Mr. Daniels, for instance, whether he was a Cohen (Priest), and whether the Cohanim still adhered to the prohibition against touching a corpse. Although contrary to Court etiquette to partake of refreshments, her Majesty made an exception in this case, in order to carry out the custom of eating and drinking in a tabernacle. On taking leave the Queen laughingly said to Mr. Daniels: "I take your word for a great deal, but you cannot make me believe that your ancestors in the desert lived in such splendid booths as this." What a contrast this to one poor fellow I knew who turned his shop-shutters into walls, and a few old flat baskets into roofing, rather than have no succah at all. Indeed, there is room for both kinds of service to God, for the wealthy and the poor. If the service is cheerfully rendered, who knows which finds the more acceptance?

Yet I came out not to preach, but to jot down some memories of succahs I have known. In my youth, the public succah was not yet a popular institution. There was a rather fine one erected in the courtyard of Bevis Marks Synagogue, but of that more anon. It must not be forgotten that if the city synagogues had no succahs, the Rav's was an excellent substitute. When I first remember it, it was already large and substantial, with a fire-stove in it and, if I recollect truly, it was lit by gas. Old Dr. Adler received his guests with patriarchal courtliness, and the flow of learned discussion and of casual gossip on communal affairs was ceaseless. A fine feature in the late Rav's character—which his son inherits—was his cheerfulness. It was at a notable breakfast to the communal magnates given by Dr. Adler in his succah that the idea of the United Synagogue first took practical form. Opposite, on the other side of Finsbury Square, stood Jews' College, with a pretty succah in a small glass conservatory on the stairs. I must have seen it during my father's tenure of the principalship, but only remember it as it was when Dr. Friedländer succeeded him. My experience has proved that succahs are mostly made by those who have least room.

The succah of the Bevis Marks Synagogue is the only one I have ever seen in which a distinction was made between rich and poor. But, after all, those who paid for the mizwah deserved to get something for their money. There was, in fact, a reserved compartment for the wardens and officials and the high-born aristocracy, while the plebeians flocked into a larger and less ornate succah which stood in front of the other. In my days the Sephardim did not build many private succahs, the only ones I remember were those of Mogador and Gibraltar Jews, a stately specimen being that of Dayan Corcos in Bury Street. A fine old gentleman he was. Always dressed in Moorish costume, with a flowing white satin tunic, a crimson or yellow sash, and a red fez or a turban, he cut a splendid figure. He often welcomed me as a boy and gave me Mogador cakes, shaped like rings, the chief ingredient used in their concoction being almonds. But to return to Bevis Marks. The succah was not a permanent brick building as it is with other synagogues nowadays, still less was it used all the year round as the minister's drawing room, a use made of the Tabernacle in a West-End synagogue. The Bevis Marks succah was taken down piece by piece and stored in a shed through the

year, side by side with an old obsolete fire engine. Even in my youth
the memory of the oldest inhabitant failed to recollect a single instance
in which this fire engine had been used. The succah was pieced together
every year; it was very strong, but, as I hinted before, was much more
like a succah than the brick constructions in the West-End synagogues
nowadays, but these last are yearly becoming more beautiful, more
bower-like. Well, the one I am now dealing with was painted green outside, but the inside was not pretty. The smaller reserved compartment
was much more gorgeous, of course. But the larger public section had
no proper greenery on the roof, for the covering was made of wicker-
work. Though this was economical, it was not aesthetic. I believe that it
has been altered in recent years. But the most interesting feature of the
Bevis Marks succah was Mr. Belasco, the beadle. His tall, burly form
recalled the pugilistic heroes which his family had produced in the past
ages of the glorious prize ring. This Mr. Belasco, however, was as
good-humored as he was big. Naturally, as there was no other public
succah in the neighborhood, many Tedescos (German Jews) contrived
to squeeze themselves into the company of the blue-blooded. Mr. Belasco
enjoyed tracking out the intruders. "These Tedescos are welcome to
enter," he said, "but they shall have none of my olives." Let me explain.
Mr. Belasco used to go round with a small keg of Spanish olives—even
the olives were Sephardic—and permitted every hidalgo to insert his
fingers and take one of the tempting morsels. This would go on merrily
till Mr. Belasco came to an questionable Tedesco. "You are not a
Portugee," he would say. "O yes, I am a Portugee," was the response.
Mr. Belasco was not taken in by the insinuating smile of his all-confident
interlocutor. "If you are a Portugee, say *Sheman Yisrael*," came the
crushing rejoinder. The mere *Tedesco* would attempt to repeat the first
line of the *Shema'*, but would almost invariably say Yi*t*rael for Yi*s*rael—
a common mistake of Ashkenazim who try to read in the Portuguese
style. This new shibboleth of Mr. Belasco's always succeeded in weeding
out the interlopers, but much ready wit was displayed, and altogether
every one enjoyed the scene immensely.

For the present I must break off here. I have forgotten to tell many
things: how, for instance, one friend of mine reserved his finest tapestry
for decorating his succah walls and locked it up all the year. "This is
recommended in the Talmud." Another man I knew made an elaborate
crown of leaves and flowers and fruits and suspended it from the ceiling
of his dining room to remind him of the succah which he did *not*
possess. The smallest succah of the pretty type that I ever entered was

Mr. Bernay's. It was one of the daintiest objects on view at the Anglo-Jewish Exhibition. But we must beware lest we allow the succah to find its way exclusively to museums. The succah is an antiquity, but it must not become a mere object of curiosity to antiquarians. It has not yet exhausted its vital possibilities.

PREFACE TO SKEPTICISM

FRITZ MAUTHNER (1849-1923)

It is of his boyhood in Horspitz, a little town in Bohemia, that Mauthner writes in the following chapter of his confessions. His family, like that of the late Justice Louis D. Brandeis, was linked to the followers of Jacob Frank, the leader of a mystical movement that ended in mass conversion to Catholicism. His grandfather, who had served as an officer in the sect, made an enormous impression upon him and, together with the atmosphere at home and in school, was a fact of great psychological importance in his later mental development. After the completion of studies in Berlin, he began a long career as a man of letters. He wrote a number of profound works on semantics and philosophy. In his advocacy of skepticism he was a lineal descendant of the author of Ecclesiastes. "Ecclesiastes," he wrote, "is the Song of Songs of Skepticism."

✳ ✳ ✳

EVEN more important than the fact that I was not to become acquainted with the barracks were the two circumstances which differentiated my school experience from that of other German boys: I was a Jew and I was a German boy living in a Slavic country. It is necessary to expand on both situations.

I was a Jew by descent, a Jew from the northeastern corner of Bohemia who had never learned to know the Jewish religion or Jewish customs; at the most I had heard Jewish words and expressions more frequently than a German child. Jewish manners were foreign to my parents' home. I found myself in the rare and almost singular predicament of having two grandfathers who had practically renounced Judaism at a time when other Jews had barely left the ghetto—one in his mode of life, the other officially. My father's father, contrary to the laws of his time, managed—with the aid of royal consent—to obtain for himself something like a baronial estate and castle, not far from Königgrätz on the Elbe. Here he and his much younger wife lived like Junker landlords, had contact with Jews only on business and maintained their household so aristocratically that after his death the estate had to be auctioned and his two sons were left to fend for themselves like poor devils. As far as I can remember, I never saw my father or my uncle practising any Jewish custom or rite. The Jewish conception is that membership in Judaism is impossible without a knowledge of Hebrew, but my father did not know a syllable of Hebrew. On the high Jewish holidays he used to say to us, with some self-reproach: "You're growing up like heathens." That was the sum total of the Jewish upbringing he gave us. Once, when I wanted to learn something of the traditional ceremonies of Passover, I had to ask for an invitation from an old brother-in-law of my mother's. In this way I managed to be present—only once—at one of the most beautiful and ancient of Jewish customs, and with as much curiosity as an outsider. My uncle said afterward that I sat there like a goy.

My mother's father—that venerable old man who merits a biography of his own—had in his youth, at the end of the eighteenth century, joined the Frankists, who recruited their ranks from kabbalists or apostate Jews, and either believed in or awaited a new Messiah or a consummation of Jesus Christ. My grandfather was said to have been an officer in the sect, which was organized on the military model, in the Frank Castle in Offenbach, and to have retained the painting of the "Queen" in his possession after the dissolution of the movement. Later the sect was severely prosecuted, in Russia as well as in Austria. My grandfather returned to his home and from then on was scornful of religion, though he thought it appropriate to visit the synagogue on important holidays. In the small Jewish community of Horspitz he was considered a scholar, a free thinker and a heretic. When he died in 1876 at a patriarchal age, his coffin was followed by a rabbi, a Catholic priest and a Protestant clergyman.

I should like to draw a comparison between the commonly accepted derogatory presentation of Jacob Frank's adventurous life and my mother's offerings to historical fact. Her memory may have been colored by the reading of historical novels; the stories in which my grandfather, as a Frankist officer, fought real soldiers, may belong to this imagined category; it is not impossible that my mother confused the Frankists with the Sabbatians of an earlier century. Frank lived and died before my mother's time.

But her own memories are certainly admissible unconditionally. I refer to this oft-repeated story: she was a little girl when Frankist emissaries arrived in Horspitz to retrieve from my grandfather certain documents and the picture of the "Queen," Eva-Emunah, Frank's daughter. The fact that my grandfather possessed these papers and the picture lead to the conclusion that he had really held a high post in the "army." Was it under Frank himself, or under his daughter?

I cannot answer these questions definitely. If my grandfather lived only to the age of 101 years, and was born in 1775, he was too young during Frank's lifetime to belong to his bodyguard. But my mother held to a reckoning which gave her father's year of birth as 1766, so that he lived to the age of 110. He would then have been twenty at the time of Frank's own adventures. Another family tradition had it that my grandfather attached himself to the court of Frank's daughter only after Frank's death. He was supposed to have been in Offenbach simultaneously with the son of a rich Jewish family from Prague. This man, Herr von Portheim (before being ennobled, the family was known as Porges), was renowned even during my boyhood as a musical connoisseur. He manifestly did not join the Frankists until after Frank's death and was said to have been sent there by his father, who was a devout follower of the new Messiah and who preferred to have his son play at soldiering than to serve in the Austrian army. As an old man, Herr von Portheim spoke very disparagingly about the "Queen's" court. It is certain that my grandfather had no connections with the upstart cult members of my own time. But if my grandfather lived in Offenbach with Herr von Portheim, he did not know Frank himself and was only a page or an officer for Eva-Emunah. After his death, unfortunately, I did not have the opportunity to search through his papers for the possible existence of documents referring to the Frankist period.

My own home was really devoid of religious affiliations. Only as an adult did I officially leave the Jewish community, without acknowledging any other. I grew tired of irking policemen at every census because I had failed to write in the blank space asking for religion. This step was taken by my old mother as a matter of course. She was somehow proud of the fact that even her father had not been a faithful Jew.

One can better understand now the statement for which my experience used to be inadequate expression: to be a writer, as I felt I was, I lacked not only a German dialect—a genuine mother tongue, but the basis of a childhood faith—a mother religion. To put it curtly and roughly, my father was a-religious, my mother anti-religious. My father had been brought up literally without the knowledge of any catechism whatsoever; he accepted the existence of some God, whose name he did not exactly know, just as he was convinced that children may not receive a second helping without saying: "More, please." (I learned this phrase before I understood it; for a long time I thought it was the Czech name for a dish). Father derived his convictions from his environment; belief in a God was proper, as it is to the English. But since my father never uttered one word or voiced one thought about the Jewish religion, I am inclined to believe that his concept of God—not on the basis of reading— was in accord with the superior forms of Christian Deism. My mother, on the other hand, knew a great deal about Jewish matters; about the ceremonial instructions, the sagacity, the shrewdness and the commercial capacities of the rabbis. She told these stories as if they were legends of long ago; scorn and even blasphemy were integral parts of the telling. She quoted Heine and at sublime moments the tolerance of Lessing's *Nathan the Wise*. I suppose we children had passed on to us the heresies that my grandfather had transmitted to her as religious instruction. Judaism was the one religion with which she was acquainted and she had no respect for it.

Reared among such traditions, I hardly knew until I was eight years old what it meant to be a Jew. Whether or not it was my father's wish I don't know, but religion and Bible-reading were not in our private tutor's curriculum. The State, however, took all religions, including the Jewish, under its protection. So that when I entered public school I had to "make up" religion. This did not mean getting instruction in religion. It meant, according to the old Asiatic custom, acquiring some familiarity with Hebrew and with reading the Bible. When I entered school I was unable to identify a single Hebrew letter; a year later I could recite certain things as well as I could say the Czech oath of allegiance. The extraordinary difficulty of Hebrew and the quite unscientific method of instruction made any headway in the spirit of the language impossible; it was only a question of cramming the memory.

Scientific investigation of the Hebrew language has been most successfully carried on by non-Jewish scholars; Jewish scholars must first desert the Jewish tradition. I am sorry that I lost my too quickly gained knowledge as rapidly as I acquired it. What I needed to know about the structure of Semitic languages for my later work I had to learn from the beginning.

A religious struggle was aggravated in me by this Jewish instruction that fell on me so suddenly. I discovered that I was a Jew, and my passionate spirit induced me to take seriously the rules and regulations which rabbinism has derived from the Bible. I wanted to become a pious Jew in order to save the souls of my father and mother. These childish struggles I tried later to re-create in the diary of the hero of my novel, *Der neue Ahasver*. I wrote the diary for the novel, so that it is in a sense invented, but my own religious struggles are faithfully and realistically incorporated in it. I shall therefore not repeat here how, for months, I tried to observe Jewish ceremonial laws secretly in my irreligious home, how later—through contact with my Catholic schoolmates—I exchanged Jehovah for Jesus and knelt in all the Catholic churches, fervently asking the saints in all the chapels for a miracle; how a teacher, recognizing my predicament, directed me to the brilliant sermons of the Jesuit Klinkow-ström, how this priest led me to study first the fathers of the Church, then its history, and how, after two years of zealous but dilettante Catholicism I emerged—at the age of fifteen—a rabid, atheistic enemy of the Church. This conviction lasted for a longer time. I was old before I realized that our era is too quietly godless to necessitate such intense enmity toward the Church.

I may say that I was thrust into becoming, on my own, a believing Jew, a miracle-seeking Catholic and a youthful freethinker by the manner in which the Jewish religion was taught us at school. The instruction was imparted according to classes but at the same time and by the same teacher to all the Jewish students of the three higher institutions of learning. Religious instruction for the Protestants was administered in much the same way and with quite the same errors. Only the Catholic religion was an organic part of the school system.

Instruction in the Jewish religion was altogether grotesque. The teacher was unquestionably a patient and amiable gentleman who understood Hebrew in a Jewish fashion. But in all matters that comprised education, according to our high school wisdom, he was so glowingly ignorant that he sank lower in our opinion than the worst pietists. The main reason for our disrespect was the fact that though he was a language teacher he did not know Latin, whereas we could already decline *mensa*. As we grew older we discovered that he lacked general culture. The other teachers did not consider him their colleague, they called him Mr. Adler and looked down on him with marked haughtiness; we Jewish students aped them and behaved badly toward him. We loved to annoy him with the name of Jesus. It was either against his conscience or against his belief to utter the name, and instead of saying "after the birth of Christ" in giving dates, he always said "according to the present erroneous calculation." We always managed to say "after the birth of Christ," at

which a painful smile would come over his round face, as if someone
had pinched him surreptitiously. But he did not dare to forbid our saying
the name.

There were two parts to the Jewish instruction: religion and Hebrew.
The course in religion was disgraceful. What a gifted child could learn
in a month—the content was approximately that of Luther's catechism—
we had to masticate for eight years. It was a shame to force the little
manual into the hands of nineteen-year-old young men; even the Catholic
Church does not require a sacrifice of intelligence to such a degree. It
imposes a lot of dogma on beginners, but there is adequate positive
information for them as they progress. Yet even this quite theoretical
religious instruction had no serious aim: it was taught to us as a stale
dilution of a natural religion based on the Ten Commandments. The
Jewish religion never required more, really, than learning the Hebrew
Bible.

Instruction in Hebrew was on a quite different level from any other
course. Among the pupils were many who belonged to orthodox families,
and into whom the Hebrew language had been drilled from their earliest
youth. This discipline was logical from the point of view of Jewish
orthodoxy: a knowledge of the Bible and of the Talmud constitutes the
rudiments of learning. With these boys, who included two of the worst
rascals in the class, the teacher could read the Old Testament to his heart's
content, split grammatical hairs and even enter into a comparison of
rabbinical commentaries.

The rest of us, who studied Hebrew only in school and for school,
sat by in delightful idleness. I stood it for a year, as long as I held to my
secret belief in Jehovah; but when my dilettante Catholicism asserted
itself, hatred for the Old Testament and for the Hebrew language rose
up in me. The information which had been too rapidly injected into me
trickled out and it was over.

Thus our religious instruction consisted of two unrelated halves—a
moralizing course in religion that was too stupid for the most stupid
among us, and practice in semitic philology, which can provide nuts for
scholarly Orientalists to crack. Since we had long considered ourselves
Jewish Germans or German Jews, we participated in the work as little as
possible, becoming virtuosi in playing truant from the lessons as well as
from the Exhorta, a dull Sabbath sermon which was supposed to terrify
us into observance.

I think I may safely say that during the last two years of my schooling
I did not once set eyes on our instructor in religion. My bold resolve to

stay away from the class followed a queer argument between me and Mr. Adler. He tried to handle the older students as a professor does and instituted a kind of seminar. When he offered evidence of the existence of God, he wanted the students to balance their childish objections against this old scholastic structure. It was easy for him to subdue the young people with the sophisms on which the most brilliant students of the Catholic Church have sharpened their wits for centuries. On that day we were discussing the venerable ontological proof. I knew nothing as yet of its history or of its dismissal by Kant. But I raised my hand and tried to present my own arguments against its logic. Mr. Adler countered with opposing statements; I rejected them. Almost in tears, Mr. Adler replied: "He who bears his God in his heart does not doubt the power of these fine old proofs. You have no faith and therefore all this teaching is of no value to you." I didn't need to be told this twice; I never came again. Two of my Jewish fellow-students, seeing that no coercion was used on me, followed my example.

God's mercy hovered over us, unrighteous as we were. Our teacher evidently considered it contrary to his Jewish faith to report a Jewish scholar or to fail him. He made a practice of giving us a mark in religion that corresponded to the average of our other marks, and he usually raised it a bit. He could not bring himself to give a pupil an "unsatisfactory" mark even if the pupil had already been condemned by the other teachers. He was certainly a Talmudist.

This worthy pedagogue's worst worry came with the graduation examination. The supervisor was a man of superior culture; even something of an Orientalist. He could well have permitted himself a question on the subject. And if he did, the system of marking the Jewish students higher than they deserved would have been exposed. The examination, therefore, found my teacher, not me, in a sweat.

In spite of my laziness I was such a good pupil and did so well in the written examinations that, according to custom, I was entitled to the oral examinations. I had counted on this and had not worried about the university entrance examinations. The supervisor used to put especially tricky questions to such students, but he did it only out of kindness, to create the opportunity for honors. This, too, did not seem terrible to me. But the Jewish teacher worried all the more. He suspected what my knowledge of Hebrew was like. In eight years I had made such progress and had forgotten so much that I could not decipher the Hebrew alphabet quickly and easily. The most innocuous question would have condemned the teacher irretrievably, because he had always marked me excellent in religion, that is, Hebrew.

At my examination—it was a hot day in July—the supervisor, who had been friendly with me for eight years, was in fine humor and teased me with all kinds of difficult questions, which I half-answered, earning good marks thereby. I was quite merry, I was enjoying the banter of the supervisor, who may have wanted to ascertain how much I knew but who may also have wanted to display his own comprehensive knowledge. I had to suppress a smile whenever I looked at the miserable teacher of religion, who sat like a criminal before execution. His sweat of anxiety was his salvation. The supervisor thought he was suffering with the heat and ordered him to go home. The two others who were taking the examination with me were Catholics, and he had asked me enough questions. I was quite happy, but what could my happiness have been beside the bliss on the face of Mr. Adler, who now left the room after exchanging a shy glance of understanding with me. The God of Justice never deserts a Jew in danger, he must have thought.

I have tried to present this experience with the pleasure it gave me at the time. Actually the thing was revolting. Let us compare our situation with that of our Catholic fellow students. They received strict religious instruction, not only from the parochial school but also in the secular institution. They had to learn prayers by heart, had to go to mass on Sundays and holidays, had to master difficult courses in religion and church history, knowing it more thoroughly than general history, and above all, they had to swallow the infallibility of these subjects like dumb puppies and dared not assert themselves. The Catholics justifiably felt themselves at a disadvantage beside the Protestants and Jews. Before the final examinations, in particular, we were apt to hear bitter comment on our exceptional status, for religion, like general history, was a real grind to them. The Catholics had to get up at five o'clock in the morning; Protestants and Jews could sleep until seven.

But I must say, nevertheless, that the relationship among the students of the various creeds was extremely cordial. Hatred of the Jew, which has been known as anti-Semitism for more than forty years, was naturally present, since malice or envy invariably seeks an outlet in racial condemnation or some other fashion. But it arose only in passionate discussions between good friends. At the Piarist schools the priest-teachers were often mean and unfair to the Jewish students, but it must not be forgotten that the lower grades contained many Jewish children who were not real Europeans, and who either had to assimilate or leave school.

THE DEATH AND BIRTH OF AN ARTIST

BORIS SCHATZ (1867-1933)

Schatz was a talented artist who will be remembered chiefly for his establishment of the Bezalel Art Society in Palestine and his vigorous effort to inaugurate a native school of Jewish art. The story of his vicissitudes in Tsarist Russia and later in western Europe is characteristic of many of his lesser and greater fellow craftsmen during the middle and second half of the nineteenth century, whose struggle for artistic expression was likened to the quest for intellectual and spiritual loyalties. If Palestine, within a generation after Schatz settled there, can boast of teeming artistic activity, it is considerably due to his pioneering, and that of men stirred by similar dreams. The chapter of his memoirs that follows is a candid dramatic tale of an artist in search of his medium and his soul.

✳ ✳ ✳

IN MY youth, I spent a year in Vilna with the family of General Dimianowitch, whose children I taught drawing. At first they seemed to take an interest in me solely as an artist and their children's art teacher. But as time went on they began to discern a human being in me, and this man of rare personality and his noble wife concerned themselves with my life and thoughts. I was engaged at the time in carving a little statuette out of black wood. The mistress of the house, busy with her everlasting embroidery, would spend all her free time in my quarters. Our hands and eyes were occupied but we kept up a continuous flow of conversation. I should say "she" rather than "we," for I usually listened. These talks drew us closer together; she developed a real maternal feeling for me and my heart was overflowing with gratitude. I would not have hesitated a moment to give my life for this generous, cultivated woman. During one of our intimate chats, she shocked me profoundly by suggesting that I change my faith. I was an unbeliever anyway, she explained, and it did not seem just or reasonable that I should suffer because of my religion. She offered to act as my godmother, the General would be my godfather, and I would receive a scholarship and be admitted to the Academy. I should mention here that I had already been graduated with honor from the local art school, but the Academy refused to admit me because as a Jew I had no legal right of residence.

I was deeply pained by this uncivilized attitude towards our people on the part of thoughtful, kindhearted persons. I was certain that it stemmed from lack of association and thus understanding of Jews. In a voice trembling with emotion, I attempted to make my position clear: I explained that every religion comprised two elements, ethics and ritual; that the latter was essential, in my opinion, only for the uneducated who are incapable of comprehending its essence; that the ethics of all creeds is the same; that only the ignorant clergy create and fan hatred among different peoples; that science and art are warring against this evil and I had faith in their ultimate victory that it was contrary to every ethic to betray one's loyalty to parents and people until such a time as mankind will rise to that level of culture foreseen in the prophecy of Isaiah: ". . . and all men shall become brothers, and there shall be but one language and one God."

My confession and my tone seemed to make a deep impression on the lady and she must have reported the conversation to her husband.

That night, after dinner, he called me into his study for a smoke and in the friendliest manner spoke so glowingly of freedom that I forgot his epaulettes. Before I left, he assured me that had I accepted his wife's suggestion, he would have asked me to leave his house because he would have regarded me as a traitor.

This experience, together with the discovery that these cultivated folks harbored in their minds many of the slanders and myths about Jews, served to convince me that for the common good it is not enough that we learn the language and ways of living of other peoples but that the rule must be reciprocal and understanding must be mutual. I began to supply my hosts with books by modern authors like Bogrov and Levanda. Their effect was immense. These kindly folks who used to complain bitterly about living in "Sheenytown" replaced all their children's tutors, including the teacher of Russian, by Jews! "I want to uproot this hatred from my children's hearts, of which I, with all my good will, find it hard to rid myself," he used to say. And who can tell how many such men there are among our oppressors?

He had an extensive library of Russian and foreign books, which he placed at my disposal. He helped me with the choice of books and my reading opened new worlds and new horizons. When I studied the Bible and the Talmud as a child, I was concerned only with ideas. My teacher was careless in his pronunciation of words and the pupil followed suit. Why, it was even considered good form to slur over the text with half words and half phrases. Later on when I studied Hebrew, German and Russian independently, I never read aloud, never listened to the sound of words or the music of a sentence. I did my best to understand the sense of the author; that was all. Indeed, it happened frequently that soon after I had finished reading a book, I would retain the substance of what I had read but had no idea of the language in which it was written. I would *see* when reading and remember what I had seen, but I would *hear* nothing at all.

To General Dimianowitch I owe my first appreciation of the beauty of words, the resonance and plasticity of diction. When he read aloud to me and the children *The Song of Merchant Kalashnikoff,* a famous ballad by the poet Lermantov, I not only saw but felt with all my being the power and the music of words. I was transported to the atmosphere of Old Russia; I breathed its very air. Who knows, I might have learned to feel the power of the Russian tongue as keenly as I do the plasticity of sculpture, if circumstances had not compelled me to leave the country.

My life with the family was a happy one. The summer I spent with them in the country left me in superb physical condition. Yet, the hopelessness of my admission to the Academy robbed me of my joy. Involuntarily I began to think of countries where art academies make ability rather than the accident of birth the qualification for admission.

It happened at that time that the famous sculptor Mark Antokolski came from Paris to visit his parents in Vilna. I thought of asking him to accept me as a pupil. To be sure, the General had often expressed his disapproval of artists studying abroad, pointing out the irrelevance of contemporary paintings, with their ever-present nymphs and similar subjects so out of harmony with the native spirit. It was his feeling that this was the result of removing the artist from his country and culture during his formative years. Nevertheless, he saw no other way out for me and approved my intention of turning to Antokolski.

It was the custom then to approach those favored of fortune only by means of letter. Accordingly, in collaboration with a friend, I composed a long epistle in which I described the ancient sufferings and present obstacles of our people in Russia and expressed a desire to go abroad in order to become his pupil. This letter, together with several of my works in wood and black marble, I left at his house with the message that I would return the next day for a reply.

In response to my ring, the door opened at once. A small man in a blue jacket whom I took to be the servant ushered me in politely and pointed to the open door of the study. But a second glance told me quickly that he was Antokolski himself. I had never seen him before but one good look was enough to convince you that you were in the presence of an unusual man. He was slight but well proportioned. I noted particularly his small delicate hands. His features were regular, sharply outlined and his lips were energetic, compressed. Only the eyes, though rather severe, reflected suffering—rather, sympathy with suffering, that universal pain that stamps the true genius. He offered me a chair, sat down on the edge of his desk, and, picking up my little carvings, examined them.

"Not so bad, not at all bad," he mused. "What did you make them with?"

I pulled a finely sharpened penknife out of my pocket and showed it to him. I was so nervous that I could not utter a word.

"You want to leave Russia and be my pupil?" he asked.

I managed to breathe "yes," and with my heart beating like a pump I was prepared to hear him say that I could get ready for the trip. Instead, he spoke of the necessity of Jews remaining in Russia and of getting closer to the people, the language, the literature, of sharing the country's joys and sorrows so that we learn to express them in our art and become an organic part of its national spirit. Poor dreamer! He believed that all our misfortunes are temporary, that they were perpetrated by a group of conscienceless men—"Bashibazuzuks" he called them—and that it would not be long before we would both be restored to our rightful place in society and even be rewarded for the injustices we have so long suffered.

The result of our talk was that he granted me a scholarship and promised to secure for me the privilege of matriculating in the Academy. However I again was disappointed. Not that the Academy refused the request of the country's most celebrated sculptor. It was a requirement that no student could live outside a certain area and the governor of the city would not grant me the right of residence. Some kindhearted folks offered to register me as their manservant, consoling me with the fact that even the famous poet Frug lived in the city by virtue of a similar arrangement. However, I refused to consider the suggestion, and in my disgust threw my scholarship to the winds.

The story had leaked out and spread in Vilna and I became something of a celebrity overnight. I was invited everywhere. I received orders for work on all sides, and tutoring jobs poured in. At long last I was enabled to devote myself wholly to art. But soon thereafter I faced another inner crisis: I lost my faith in the usefulness of art, although I continued to love it passionately. My nature protested against the viewpoint which is summed up in Pissareff's remark that a clay pot is more useful than the statue of Apollo Belvedere. Still I could not help but note and bemoan that the high priests of art served merely the pleasure of the rich who in reality respected them as little as their tailors and barbers. Being the son of an underdog, impoverished people and sharing its sufferings, I did not wish to truckle and pander to the rich, and lost my desire to pursue my studies. No wonder that the Russians spoke of "our Antokolski"! One could hardly call him a Jew. On second thought, he belonged to no people; he was the property of the privileged few who utilized his genius for their own pleasure.

My newly awakened doubts were buried deeply within me. I did not have the courage to share them with my friends. I continued to work, but the sacredness of the cause was destroyed.

Then I was drawn to a circle of youths who surrendered all personal interests in order to devote themselves to the education and betterment of the masses. As a consequence, I regarded art only as a means of existence and my studies lagged. I still possessed the technique I had acquired but the driving spirit was gone. The monotony of making portraits to order began to tell on my nerves. Often I would fling my theory to the wind, seize a chunk of clay, and model feverishly. But my fingers would not obey my will. I had used them for lucre too long and now they refused to fashion the beautiful images that haunted my mind. Finally this struggle between reason and feeling became intolerable. I decided to desert my art and seek out another occupation where I could employ my natural abilities.

I chose mechanics. I recalled my boyhood inventions and I now imagined myself a new Edison, improving society through my great inventions. Forthwith I tackled the study of mathematics and physics, actually accomplishing a good deal. But the further I progressed the clearer it became that this new calling would require many years of university studies and other things far beyond my reach. In addition, I noted that most engineers were employed by industrial plants where they necessarily spent their talents and energies for the purpose of producing inferior products and of exploiting the workers; that inventors were few in number and they too were obliged to rack their brain for complicated mechanical devices for the manufacture of useless frills or for destructive war machines. So I burnt my bridges behind me and another dream burst.

The period that followed was perhaps the most miserable in my life. I felt an utter emptiness. I despaired the purposelessness of my sufferings and my existence; even the attempt to reassure myself that my educational work was directed for the good of humanity failed to bring me solace.

I was brought back to art by a simple experience, one of these tricks that life plays on us now and then. It happened in Warsaw. During a drawing lesson that I was giving to the sons of a plutocrat, I suddenly caught the strains of a peculiar chant in the courtyard. The singer wailed in a hoarse, muffled voice like an echo from the grave just three words, "Handele, Handele, pantsvö." The words were repeated with such desperate persistence, with such ghastly monotony that they gave one the creeps. Immediately my pupils were at the windows aping the wretch, roaring with unbridled glee, utterly forgetful of their art and their teacher. I stepped over to the window and witnessed a ghastly scene.

In the blackness of the narrow, chilly yard stood the drooping figure of an old clo' Jew with a white patriarchal head. His spare body was wrapped in mixed rags, his misty gaze was directed toward the garrets inhabited by the poverty-stricken who supplied his wares. He stood in the rain, alone and forlorn. He was noticed only by a barking puppy and the pampered children of luxury who teased and mocked him from the *belle-étage*. Their innocent laughter chilled my blood and I left hastily lest I forget myself.

I modeled him.

That was my first attempt to use art for propaganda purposes. I worked with the passion of a prophet whose soul is filled with a message. I longed to reveal to everyone the soul of that Jewish pauper, tormented by hunger and cold, mortally wounded by human contempt; a man whose comical rags conceal the soul of a being.

I awaited impatiently the opening of the exhibition. I was the first to enter the hall. My ancient rag-man was placed in an obscure corner which fortunately showed him to good advantage. The natural color of the clay with a thin coating of glue in the dim light gave him a peculiar pallor reminiscent of the ancient images of the early Christian martyrs. He was forlorn among the luxuriously gilt-framed pictures, yet by contrast, strong and appealing, demanding attention. It was as though he were crying aloud for the thousands like him that dwell in our midst. I sat down on a bench not far away and waited. A group of priests approached. Without as much as turning toward my old man, they walked straight to a large canvas entitled "The Demon." It portrayed a nude woman half wrapped in a fur coat—the newspapers had advertised that she was the painter's wife—standing near a bathtub. The group stood before the picture a long time, now approaching, now receding to examine it from all angles and discussing it in muffled tones. They left without noticing my "Handele." Others followed suit. Then, to attract attention, I rose and planted myself in front of my work. . . . I felt so sick at heart that I could not remain another minute. I felt as though I must run as far as my feet could carry me. At that moment a group of young folks entered. They headed for "The Demon" like the others, but one of them stopped in front of "Handele." I could see his face clearly, and my heart suddenly stopped when I saw the expression of "Handele" reflected in his face. He felt. He understood.

The next day an account of the exhibition by a brilliant young critic appeared in a newspaper. He fearlessly attacked the painters for the poverty of thought, for their tiresome superficial beauty, for their blindness to the real beauty and degradation of life. He cited "Handele" as an example to be followed. He alluded to the imperfect technique of the young artist but lauded the depth and richness of soul which the established artists might profitably cultivate. I was triumphant. I had found my goal, at last!

I knew my shortcomings. I understood that an artist must first master his medium before he could express his innermost self, and that whatever comes out of the artist's heart will find its way to the heart of the people. I worked like a demon. As my instructor, I chose the greatest of artists—Nature. I spent whole days in the market place, watching trade, poverty, wrangling—the feverish struggle for existence. I watched the faces express laughter and grief, tenderness and greed. I made a number of masks expressing the whole range of emotions and studied painstakingly Darwin's work on the subject.

At an international exhibit I saw some sculpture by famous French artists and I was profoundly impressed by the gracefulness of their execution. Our native sculpture, by comparison, appeared awkward, lumbering, strained. It was like the utterance of an old man, haltingly coughing cumbersome phrases to express thoughts which in themselves were worthwhile; while French sculpture conjured up a light-headed singer who scintillates and fascinates with her silvery voice, singing a trifling composition whose words are not even heard. Had I only that voice, I would sing a different song! Come what may, I decided to go to Paris.

Even though I was weighed down with the responsibility of supporting my wife and aged father in Paris, I persisted in my original program and entered the Academy of Cormon. This choice rested on the conviction that sculpture alone was too restricted for the themes I intended to work out. I was obliged to combine intensive study with occupations that provided living expenses, but, all considered, I managed quite well. I was in good physical trim, my mind saw clearly the road before me, and my heart was at rest.

The need to earn a living took me to various places. A good deal of the time I worked for Antokolski and did models for the famous Dreyfus ceramic factory. The latter led me to study decorative art for which I developed a strong, lifelong interest. During the early years of my stay in Paris I sought in my work the solution of purely technical problems; I lived under the spell of the French masters which robbed me of all individual original effort. Man became an artistic problem which posed itself in the form of paintings, statues or models; no less Nature, which took on the appearance of the neatly trimmed, artificially planted rows of trees and the landscaped lawns of the public parks.

I succeeded admirably at the Academy, becoming within a short time the only student granted free tuition. At the end of the first year I received a high rating for drawing, but I had no luck with my painting. It was colorful; yet it was marred by a hardness of outline characteristic of sculpture and by a dry quality which Cormon used to call "sour." He advised me to go South where an object, illumined by brighter and lyrical colors, would evoke less of abstract texture and more symphonic composition. Accordingly I left for the Mediterranean coast. There, in the little town of Banules on the Spanish border, I worked for six months. To this trip I owe not only my understanding of color but also my artistic personality. If it be true, in the phrase of the critic Marcus Ehrenpreis, that such of my work as "The Shadhan," "Habdalah," "Sabbath Eve," "A Jewish Mother" and the like are characteristic of my childhood reminiscences and reflect the poetry of the Exile, then it is equally true that all of the works conceived in Banules are no longer "wistful smiles through tears" but rather "the mighty song of a brave, liberated Jew who sings of the glorious past and hopes for the future." I conceived these pictures while roaming in the quiet grandeur of the Pyrenees. Halting in the rocky caverns or listening to the murmurs of the sea, my mind was caught in visions: I saw a stately old man with the heroic heart of a Maccabee sounding the trumpet call to battle, gathering about him the surviving handful of liberty-loving Jews who preferred to meet death as free men than survive as slaves. I saw the prophet Jeremiah persecuted by his own people who, incapable of understanding his desire to save them, shut him up in prison. The people who were deaf to his appeals are gone to their doom; he stands alone in the desert, bemoaning the fate of his people and composing the most beautiful elegy ever written, the Book of Lamentations. I saw the great genius whose light illuminated mankind in its cradle and still burns brightly— our teacher Moses. So imposing was his personality and so remarkable his deeds that, when the misty curtain of myth is torn away and the floodlight of science is thrown upon them, they gain rather than lose in greatness. His extraordinary life unwound before me as in a cinema, beginning with the tiny basket afloat on the Nile to his majestic old age in the desert mountains. I modeled several sketches for five groups with numerous bas-reliefs which were to comprise a series on The Life of Moses.

The peaceful grandeur of this retreat brought close to nature again, taught me once more to love, to understand and to feel the ecstacy of her embrace. I recollect clearly a moment when the marvelous view of the sea and the sunset in the mountains made me forget my own existence, melting me into a throbbing part of the surrounding beauty. It happened at the close of day. My wife and I had sailed out to sea in a fishing boat to cast the net for sardines. We were at a considerable distance from the shore; the beach was out of sight; around us and beneath us the limitless sea breathed with a motion that was hardly perceptible. Suddenly, at the very edge of the horizon the crimson outline of a mountain crag appeared like molten iron against a golden yellow background. It glowed deeper and deeper, turned to purple while expanding and at the same time changing to all the colors of the rainbow, from yellowish-purple to bluish-violet. The whole fairy-tale spectacle blended with the soft, swaying surface of the water which appeared purple-red close to the boat. On the opposite side, the sky took on a pale, pearl-like hue, dotted with slightly visible golden spots that made it seem infinitely deep while the scattered stars and the moon were such as I had never yet seen. Sparkling happily, they sent forth an airy soothing light, and the reflection in the sea formed paths splashed with silver and gold. We sat breathlessly holding hands, full of awe in the face of this incomparable grandeur, with a prayer on our lips. Then, from a distant fishing boat there reached our ears the melody of a Parisian street ditty. . . .

In the fervent hours of my youth, when my head was full of rosy dreams of the absolute equality and brotherhood of man, I did not understand these ideals as the property of the leisure class. I knew well that so long as people continued to consume with ease products of huge toil and pain slavery cannot cease. What I dreamed of was a decent, modest humankind which would throw off the false sheen of civilization and build a wholesome natural life. Now I came to feel that only through intimacy with nature could human beings learn the meaninglessness of luxury and thus set themselves free. I dreamed of gathering a group of likeminded comrades who, conscious of all the evils resulting from our false conception of civilization, would settle in such natural surroundings as those of Palestine and would create a kind of nucleus for the mankind of the future in the manner of the early Christians. However, when they had grown mighty, unlike the conquering Christians, they would devote themselves to higher pursuits than the exercise of despotic power and the persecution of men of different faiths. Science would be their sacred hope, art and labor their source of wisdom. Not merely slavery to the machine and brute labor in the factory, but devotion as a conscious free being to work which, in proportion to the effort and imagination poured into its creation, would bring joy and happiness to the creator.

It was out of this vague Utopia that my project of the Bezalel Society for creative arts evolved and was ultimately organized in Palestine.

FROM RUSSIAN PALE TO ARGENTINIAN PAMPAS

MARCOS ALPERSON (1867-)

An overpowering drama was enacted in the steerage of hundreds of vessels that carried the unhappy cargo of migrants of the last decades of the nineteenth century. Driven to the new world by want and persecution, they clustered mainly in the metropolitan centers. However, there were groups who took advantage of the services of the Jewish Colonization Society, organized in 1891 in order to settle East European Jews on the land. Alperson was a member of one of the earliest groups in Argentina. Born in Lanzkron, a small town near Kamenetz-Podolsk, and inspired by the ideal of pioneering, he became a leader in the Mauricio settlement. He corresponded with Hebrew and Yiddish periodicals in Europe, was the editor of a Yiddish weekly at home, and recorded the experiences of the colonists in stories and in a three-volume history of Mauricio. Something of the disenchantment of these brave souls is reflected in his simple, fluent, colorful memoirs.

❊ ❊ ❊

ON Sunday, August 23, 1891, after thirty-two days on the high seas, the steamer *Tioko* approached the port of Buenos Aires. I and my fellow-immigrants anxiously turned our faces toward the distant city, barely visible amidst the palm trees. It loomed before us like a Promised Land, a new Eden which the generous Baron Hirsch had bought for us. At long last we were free men, with soil of our own to cultivate. No more pogroms!

Small boats carried us ashore, and we found ourselves in a rather large, wooden building with countless rooms and cubicles. There we met about two hundred other Jewish immigrants who had arrived a few days earlier. Several dusky natives beckoned to us by the universal gesture language and led us to a long common table where food was served. Suddenly I noticed a thin yellow-bearded fellow hopping from group to group and apparently whispering confidential news of an extraordinary character into everyone's ears. Before I knew what was afoot, he reached my corner and warned us against eating the food.

"It's horsemeat they're serving us, I tell you," he whispered with assurance. "Don't eat it."

The excitement mounted and reached its peak when a young chap from Kiev sprang to his feet and shouted, "Get out of here, you hypocrite! Who asked you to interfere?"

He slapped him so hard that the smack was heard throughout the hall. The meddler, hurt and crestfallen, disappeared. Thereupon the hero and his patriarchal father-in-law went from table to table and reassured us. They asserted that the rumor was utterly false. Certainly there was no reason for serving horsemeat in a rich cattle country like Argentina. They knew that troublemaker in the old country: he was a chronic swindler and beggar. They succeeded in calming us. Some of us resumed the repast, but others, despite all assurances, did not touch meat for the duration of our detention.

After the tables were cleared, an official gave every male person a pass which permitted sightseeing (women were not permitted to leave). However, we had to return to the "immigrant hotel" by five o'clock.

The city was deserted when a small group of us began our tour. I was filled with sadness as I saw the ramshackle houses with iron-gratings on their locked doors and windows. A few tramcars moved sleepily through the principal streets. Here and there a nun, garbed in black robe and white veil, and wearing a large pendant crucifix, walked serenely by. About two hundred meters from our "hotel" we came upon a row of gypsy tents. The children blocked our path, begging for oranges, pennies and even bread. A barefooted policeman, or *vigilante,* clad in a threadbare uniform dozed peacefully at the street corner. We stared at one another. Was this Buenos Aires, the capital of the Argentine Republic? Later we learned that we had arrived soon after the revolution of 1890 which resulted in the removal of Dr. Miguel Juarez Selman. It was his mis-government and politics that was responsible for the impoverishment and drabness of the city. Finally, a vigilante brought us safely back to our quarters.

At the green iron gate of the Immigration House we encountered several flamboyantly dressed ladies and fat-bellied men in evening dress. They shouted and gesticulated to our womenfolk through the iron gratings. They plied our children with candy, and at intervals whispered something to the guard who, as I later learned, refused to admit any of them. Some of them recognized old friends among the immigrants and burst into tears. Whether they were tears of joy or sorrow, I did not know at the time.

Then a representative of Baron Hirsch, carrying official papers under his arm, arrived. The guard opened the gate for him with great deference. He informed us that within a few days we would be on our way to the settlement which the Baron had bought for us. "Your departure awaits only certain routine formalities required by the Government," he confided, "and everything will be ready." In an eloquent address he expressed regret that the committees in Galicia and Germany had sent us abroad somewhat prematurely. He cautioned against having anything to do with the men and women outside the gate. "They are scum," he said pointedly. "You must not allow your wives and daughters on the streets alone. . . ." After conferring briefly with the officials of the Immigration House, the young man departed.

The moment he left the immigrants began to cry, "We were sold out! No land has been bought for us here! We were tricked. The whole plan of colonization is a fraud." "Missionaries, that's what they are," yelled one, "they want to convert us!"

During the hubbub and confusion some of the outsiders slipped into the Immigration House. They mingled with the immigrants and fanned the flames of distrust by painting harrowing pictures of our future in the projected settlement. Most of us resented their presence. Fists began to fly. In the ensuing scuffle a few frightened men packed their belongings and fled with their wives and families into that dark world whence there is no retreat.

On the following day Dr. Leventhal, our appointed administrator, arrived. A tall, handsome person with penetrating black eyes and an aristocratic bearing, he made an indelible impression. We gathered about him and at the mere wave of his hand became tensely quiet.

"Children," he began in the vernacular, "the good Baron sent Sir Coolian and me throughout the world in order to find a place where you and our persecuted brethren could make a decent home. We found the Republic of Argentina to be the most suitable. It is a vast, free, fruitful country that can absorb all the oppressed Jews. We have secured enough land to make all of you happy settlers. Unfortunately, we have had no time to execute our plans for housing and supplies; in fact, we have only the bare land. But nobody is to blame. The governments of Galicia and Lithuania insisted that we take you away or they would drive you out." Casting his searching, magnetic eyes over the whole assemblage, he continued in his mild, reassuring voice: "It will be impossible to house all of you in the city until the houses are built. Your families must be kept from the nets of the wicked. Yesterday a few of your fellow travelers left you and followed a road they will regret. I implore you to be patient and exercise our traditional virtues of endurance and purity in overcoming the first unavoidable difficulties that colonization creates. In the end you will be rewarded with peace and plenty. Believe me when I tell you that you will be happy."

No sooner had he concluded his hortatory remarks than from all sides there arose shouts of joy: "Send us, Doctor, we will gladly go! Hurrah for Baron Hirsch!" The Doctor went away, elated by the response.

Afterwards we discussed his remarks with great earnestness. Enthusiasm ran high. We eagerly anticipated our new life as farmers.

On Saturday morning two men arrived, one of them a well-dressed young man of striking appearance. Both were greeted with high regard by the immigration officials. The young man introduced himself as the Rabbi of the West European community, a congregation of French, English, German and Belgian origin. Through his interpreter, who we learned later was the sexton, he invited us to attend services at his synagogue. About ten of us ventured into a little muddy street, whence we were led into a dark, narrow room graced only by an altar, a pulpit, and a few benches with a dozen prayer books. Such was the synagogue at that time. (Today the immigrants have a well-organized congregation and own a beautiful Temple in which services are magnificently conducted with the aid of an organ and a choir led by a cantor.) Immediately after the services the Rabbi left and the sexton related some disheartening tales. This Rabbi, Henry Joseph, had married a gentile, he said, and the immigrants from Poland were a sorry lot. "The synagogue is deserted all year round," he concluded, "except on the Holy Days. I myself am a survivor of those whom Lazar Kaufmann brought here three years ago."

My heart shrank within me. "You are one of the Kaufmann group?" I asked, trembling. "Perhaps you know the Wiener family?"

"Are you a friend or relative?" he asked.

I explained that Wiener was my wife's uncle, and I mentioned the circumstances under which he had joined Kaufmann. He told me where they now lived and what their fate had been. They had fared badly.

We asked him to give us all the details of Kaufmann's plan of colonization, remarking that, as we were on the eve of embarking on a similar venture, the story would be helpful as well as interesting. After much coaxing, he gave us this account.

"In 1881 when the brutal edicts of Count Ignatiev, Minister of Interior under Czar Alexander III, almost crushed our people, a committee of three prominent Jews was sent to Paris and London to prevail upon influential Jewish leaders to facilitate the emigration of Russian Jews to America, Canada or Palestine. Two members of the committee returned empty-handed after haunting the doorsteps of the Jewish philanthropists. The third, Kaufmann, had the misfortune of meeting an agent who represented himself as a messenger of the Argentine government and promised him great things: land, cattle, and financial subsidies. On that basis Kaufmann was able to gather a hundred families to sail with him to the Argentine, where they found misery. Kaufmann was duped by the agent; between the depots of Palasios and Manigato the families were cast off without food or a roof over their head. Within one month more than three hundred of their children died of cold and starvation. Many of the families continued the journey on foot to Buenos Aires, and many of the young women were trapped in the web of prostitution. Some are still stranded there, suffering unbearable hardships. There is talk of Dr. Leventhal including them in his colonization plan which will bring them salvation," concluded the sexton as he completed the saga of the earlier ill-fated settlement scheme.

We cried a little, and with overburdened hearts returned to the Immigration House. That same afternoon we were all taken to the railroad station to entrain for our land.

From that moment on, our chain of suffering stretched through thirty years of toil, darkness and humiliation. We waged a hard and desperate struggle, and very few of the first pioneers survived it.

When we arrived at the station it was long before traintime. We sat down on the grass facing the station and, as befits happy settlers on their way to their own homesteads, the young burst into singing Eliakum Zunzer's "Plough." The women bought oranges and bananas quite cheaply, exchanging their Russian kopecks for shining new pesos. Everybody was in a mood of elation and anticipation. The sun shone brighter than usual, the air was mild and caressing, and everything was in bloom and dazzling green. Our hearts were overjoyed with the surrounding bountiful beauty that is the Argentine's. At nine in the evening our train began to move and we were on our way.

The train rumbled on. None of us slept that night. We were eagerly planning our new life. We argued and debated and tried to solve, all at once, the many problems, both personal and collective, that we could foresee. Much heated argument was spent over the question of grouping the various families in separate colonies according to section of origin, like those coming from Bessarabia or Podolia, and with whom to pair the Litvaks (Lithuanians) among us. We still had a rather vivid recollection of the party given by the captain of our ship in honor of the baby born aboard to Hayyim Tucker's wife. We were all gay and drinking heavily from the captain's two hundred bottles of Madeira with which he presented us. The Polish hasidim made of the event a gala affair, when a sober Litvak began to reprove them for their exuberance. Forthwith a fight broke loose and empty wine bottles scaled the Litvak's head. One hasid paid for it with a night in the brig. This had created a division between the Polish and Lithuanian families. But now on the train we decided to live in harmony, since we were bound by a common and very uncertain destiny.

At daybreak we arrived at the station of Casarez. By a given sign whose mute language we had already mastered, we were directed to descend and wait for further instructions. Through the tall grass that had completely covered the rails, the light of a pale sun illumined a desolate landscape. Only two huts, one made of boards and the other of tin, with liquor bars installed—that and the puny station comprised the town of Sasarez.

Not a living person was there to receive us: not a single representative of the Baron's colonization office to bid us welcome. Only the lone railway clerk who looked at us with mild curiosity and stole frequent suggestive glances at our women. When he saw that no one paid him any attention, he shook his mane, locked himself in and was seen no more. We ate up every crust of bread we could scrape up from our trunks. Our children became hungry. The two taverns had no bread for sale. Impatiently we looked in all directions in the hope of catching sight of someone coming to lead us unto our land. . . . Hours passed and no one was seen coming. The crowd began to mutter. Our discontent mounted with our despair and reached an angry roar. Curses aimed at the delinquent colonization officials began to fly thick and fast.

This agony of waiting was broken at about two in the afternoon. The crack of a whip ended the suspense. From the gnarled brushwood there suddenly emerged a row of wagons propelled on huge ungainly wheels and drawn by innumerable horses. They lined up along the whole length of the railroad station. A young man riding a magnificent stallion alighted and in Spanish issued an order to the dark-skinned drivers. Thereupon they piled up on the grass heaps of hard dried rolls which were known as "galletas." Soon another gentleman arrived, pale and aristocratic of feature and manner, who welcomed us in German and introduced himself as our administrator, Mr. Gerbl. He urged us to eat the rolls if we were hungry. Our sense of shame which had already been undermined at the German border, the crumbs given to us by our German brethren, and our oppressive hunger no longer left room for hesitation. Without further coaxing we pounced savagely on the galletas. The copper-bronzed faces of the Argentinians contorted at witnessing this scene, and they expressed deep sympathy for the "poor emigrants" and "poor children."

After we had finished eating our rolls soaked in water, little ladders were dropped from the wagons to the ground, and Mr. Gerbl cavalierly invited the women and children to mount the wagons. To the men he turned and said in another tone: "You future colonists will have to make your way on foot." He instructed the first young man, who, as we learned, was the engineer, to hire guides for us, and bade us farewell. He spurred on his horse and quickly disappeared in the thickets of thorns and grass. Like herrings in a barrel, the women and children were jammed onto the wagons. The cracking of the whips soon filled the air, and the wagons were off with our families.

The blond engineer left us men at the station while he went into the inn and seemed to have forgotten all about us. The hours passed, we became impatient, and still there was no sign of him. The sun was setting and darkness fell rapidly. Suddenly out of nowhere four horsemen appeared and greeted us in a friendly manner. Seeing the hasidim among us with their long caftans and flowing beards, they inquired curiously: "Curos? Santos?" (priests, holy men?). The young engineer arrived somewhat intoxicated and impudently commanded us to form a line two abreast. At his command "March!" the caravan of wanderers started to move. Our hearts were heavy-laden. The sun sank deeper into the brush behind us and a red glow lighted up the whole landscape. An old Jew scanned the fringe of clouds on the western sky and prophesied rain.

"Where do you see rain?" asked one, while others laughed, pointing to the cloudless expanse.

"There!" persisted the old man, indicating a ribbon of clouds nestling at the rim of the sun's orb.

"Well, brethren, we have an astronomical genius among us, none other than Hayyim Selig Slonimsky!" ridiculed the schoolteacher of Dinivetz. "What do you think of our village star gazer? Let us march faster, children, before the rain overtakes us!"

We accelerated our pace through the tall grass, the thistles and the shrubbery of the plain.

Night came swiftly. The sky turned ashen gray, then became a spectacle of changing colors, partly green and partly pitch black. Heavy darkness enveloped us in an awesome spell of stillness. Instinctively we pressed closer together, gripped by a nameless terror. Then the pampas grass started to rustle and soon the thundering tempest of the great Argentine plain swung into full fury. "Pampero! Pampero!" the horsemen guides muttered to one another in apprehension. Its meaning hit us with full force when we were caught in one of the great wind storms of the Pampas which hurled at us, rolling clouds of dust and uprooting everything in its wake. We all lay down, seeking protection close to the earth. Momentarily the wind stopped and a painful silence set in. A bolt of lightning streaked the darkened sky and a deafening crash of thunder almost lifted the earth from its foundation. In the weird flash of lightning we saw the guides deserting us and we were left to the mercy of the rolling thunder and slashing lightning. Heavy raindrops, first warm, then ice cold, began to fall, the wind rose to gale force and a terrifying war between the "pampero" and the rain burst overhead. The rain won, pouring down in torrential floods and silencing the storm. We were soaked and drenched to the bone. We took one another by the hand and we pressed forward into the troubled darkness without path or goal beneath ceaseless lightning and clapping thunder. After trudging through the slushy fields for an hour, we came head on against a wired fence and some of us had our faces scratched by the fence poles. As we faced the wall of wire that blocked our tortuous progress, the cry "Russos" was heard and an ear-splitting whistle of the gauchos pierced the night. A flash of lightning revealed two of our lost horsemen on the other side of the fence. Under the assumption that this must be our own ground, we started to climb over to the other side. The thought that we had reached port at last gave us courage to defy the rain and storm.

An hour later the rain subsided to a heavy drizzle. The older men began to show signs of fatigue; the young stalwarts strode onward, straight into the jaws of the darkness. We broke up into small groups and scattered over the soggy steppe until the voices of each band lost contact with the other and were muted.

Suddenly one of my group of four halted; his feet gave way under him, and in a second he was flat on the wet grass. "Leave me behind, brothers," he begged. "My strength is gone." We were unable to move him from an ever swelling pool of rain. What to do? With great difficulty we lifted him up, dragged him for a hundred yards, but the effort quickly tired us. Yet we could not let him die!

"Listen to me, brothers," said the old Jew in a weak voice, "leave me behind. You can't help me. I am a man over fifty. Didn't taste food on the ship; in the Immigration House the food was also unclean. Fasted all day today. . . . Columbus' dried rolls were not for my teeth. Now this tramping through the wastes has finished me. In my breast pocket is my passport, in my left sock I have thirty-five rubles wrapped up in oilcloth. . . . Thought of sending the money home to my wife and four daughters who are starving. . . . Now you will use it for dressing me in a shroud," and the old man burst into tears like a child.

We comforted him, told him he was not yet dying, and that he would soon recover. Together we raised him, wrapped him in a quilt and started to carry him. The rain stopped completely, but we three were wet of perspiration. As we climbed up a hill, one of us gaily shouted: "I see a light in the distance!" At last a settlement, we happily confirmed. Our old man who looked like a corpse quickly began to revive.

"We are saved," he exclaimed and was able to stand on his own feet. After ten minutes of rest we took our invalid under the arm and started toward the light from where we heard voices.

We came upon a camp fire in a forest clearing. "Here, have some hot soup and dry your clothes by the fire!" the campers said, welcoming us with fine sympathy. Isaac Krell, the slaughterer from Lithuania, a young rawboned Jew with a red beard, was standing under a thickly branched tree by the fire and dishing out to us soup and meat. He was one of the forty men whom Dr. Leventhal had sent ahead to prepare quarters for the families. Other straggling bands of our travelers were arriving and they asked that we send out searching parties for the rest. My wife, with our infant in her arms, was soon beside me and was thanking God for seeing me alive. I was wet and had the chills. My wife threw her shawl over me, gave the infant to me to hold, bent over me and whispered in my ear, "Be quiet, now you are a woman. Follow me!"

Thus she cautiously led me into the women's tent, which was guarded by a policeman, and ordered me to lie on the floor beside our little ones. She covered me with all the clothes and rags she could find to warm me up, and I slept till morning. The date was August 31, 1891.

It was our first day in Mauricio, and from that time on we began to feel the heavy hand of the colonization magistrates, directors, administrators, inspectors and their like. The tent was soon flooded with the morning light. I wanted to rise and leave, but my wife restrained me in a hushed voice: "Lie still, the policeman is looking. I will let you out the moment he turns his head!"

The noise of the women and children in the tent was deafening. The stench was hot and oppressive. I wanted to get out of this female's hell in the worst way. But there was the policeman standing sentry like a faithful dog. Perhaps I was punished for stealing into the midst of hundreds of women and allowing myself to be transformed into almost one of them.

Suddenly a sturdy Jew with a thick blond beard appeared at the entrance. The pockmarked policeman gesticulated with his hand, signifying refusal. But the firmly built Jew insisted on entering and shouted in Russian: "My wife, my Masha, my children!" even though the policeman indicated he did not understand a word. Impatiently the Jew pushed him aside and in a second the policeman's saber gleamed over his head. A stream of blood spread over the Jew's face and beard.

"Blood!" the women screamed. "Blood! They are slaughtering and killing!"

The men came running, while the brown-skinned vigilante disappeared. The wound was not serious, but the excitement was fierce.

"Blood!" the Jews shrieked, "we are being bled the first morning in our new home. Let us escape!" The women echoed this cry at the top of their lungs.

A blond young man with glasses mounted an upturned barrel and harangued the excited immigrants as follows: "Black! I see everything black! We were deceived, brothers! . . . This is not the place of refuge to which the Jewish people are aspiring. The officials of Baron Hirsch are not the fit captains to lead our floundering ship through the stormy sea. Have you not noticed how cruelly the various committees dealt with us on the whole journey from Lemberg, Crackow and Hamburg! Have you not felt the contempt and ridicule of our philanthropic providers? How they fingered your muscles like the ancient slaves! That was there, in Europe. Here, on Argentine soil, the committees drove us like cattle through angry weather in blackest night. Many of us lie sick in the woods and on the fields, perhaps in high fever (as really was the case), some are beaten up, and others are still missing. And here already blood! Moses David from Litnivetz lies with a cleaved skull!" He finished this recital of woe with a whimper and, looking at him, the women burst into lamentation.

Yes, despite the arrogance, insensitivity and miscalculations of the various philanthropic committees, hope of a bright future was firmly imbedded in our blood stream and animated our senses, and nothing could dim the dazzling colors with which we pictured our future.

A bell tolled and the commotion and hubbub quieted down.

When the din of the bell died down, two young men emerged from the administration building: one was minus a hand and the empty sleeve of his jacket swayed sleepily; the other by contrast was a robust fellow in patent leather boots. The one without a hand issued the command: "Immigrants, form a line!" We quickly obeyed. Throughout our voyage we were overly trained.

"Galletas!" the other fellow cried out. "One for each person."

After the dried rolls were distributed, I went off by myself to look over the neighborhood. A small sparsely wooded forest. There were some thickset willow trees, a greater number of poplars and very few acacias. In the center a house built of clay with a tile roof, the door and windows painted green. This was the administration office and the living quarters of the manager Gerbl, a German officer and an apostate. In an annex made of tin lived the French Jew, the engineer Tiricini, with his assistants. A hundred and fifty meters away was the tent where the women and children were strewn on quilts and bedding covering the ground and two vigilantes stood guard to keep their men out. It was reeking with filth and therefore dubbed "Matushka." Nearby there was a pigsty covered with straw, inherited from the previous owner who had sold the property to the Baron and who had had no time to remove the pigs. That pigsty was assigned as quarters for the men. The pigs did not seem to mind us, and we nicknamed the hostelry "Hotel Tchancho," in honor of its former owners.

Meanwhile the Spanish gauchos drove in a number of fat steers, lassooed them, hurled them to the ground, and our sturdy red-bearded butcher immediately slaughtered six of them ritually. In no time fires were lighted and the meat was roasted in the open, barbecue style. Some of us wished to have salt for cooking. But Gerbl assured us that salt was here more expensive than meat. The camp became gay and happy. As night fell Gerbl made a roll call to see if all were present. It appeared that three unmarried men of our group had failed to turn up yesterday. Searchers were dispatched and they brought them in half-dead before darkness fell. We gave them the best accommodations at our "Hotel Tchancho" and listened all night to their stories of harrowing experiences. We all fell asleep, snoring in unison with the resigned pigs.

The following morning my wife said to me, "Come, let us look for some dugout in the field where I can sleep with the children. I will not return to the 'Matushka' even if I have to die. The stench and noise are more than I can bear."

After our ration of meat and rolls, we went off with our three children in search of a suitable place in the open where we might camp by ourselves. We were lucky in finding a horse hide softened by the rain. My wife helped me in fitting out a tent as in the time of Adam. We gathered enough soft grass for a floor. We moved our meager belongings to our gypsy tent. The rest we received six months later. Thank God, we had become homeowners on Argentine soil! After a tasty supper we fell soundly asleep under our own roof. We knew little of fear then. Hope enchanted us, weaving rich illusions of the future.

In the morning we were terrified to find a green black spotted snake in our tent. Fearful that it might strike our children, I stepped on the snake's head but failed to kill it because of the soft grassy floor. It wound itself around my boot. Still unalarmed, I reached for a knife, cut off its head, which I hung out as a trophy on the front pole of my tent.

Having recovered from this fright, we were destined quickly for another. Three riders on magnificent chargers surrounded our tent. Two of the horsemen were Gerbl and Tiricini, the third a stranger. They scrutinized our tent, its interior, our sleeping children, and the dead snake which was still throbbing.

Gerbl asked me: "Where did you find the snake and how did you kill it?"

"I found it near my wife," I answered and told him the whole story, which he in turn communicated to the Spainard beside him.

"Were you much frightened?"

"Quite a bit," I answered.

"Well, it is only a kulebra and wholely harmless. Now, where did you obtain the skin and the poles for the tent? You need not feel uneasy, only tell the truth."

Without hesitation I told him the truth, which he again translated to the Spainard whom he addressed as "Señor Comissario". I was becoming panicky as he questioned me closely about my name and that of my wife, about our place of birth, our ages, the number of children we have, and whether I had worked at farming. He noted my answers carefully in a book.

Seeing that I was considerably shaken up by his examination, he said smilingly, "Come to the office in an hour. We will let you have two more skins, wood, poles and rope, and you can make yourself a stronger tent to be able to withstand the gale. Adios!"

And they galloped away. Greatly relieved, I went for our ration of food at the summons of the bell. The food was hot and tasty. A column of smoke billowed to the sky. A big table and benches were devised around which the families seated themselves. The food was served and that time we ate from plates like human beings. After the meal some were writing letters. The younger boys and girls strolled off to the woods singing songs of hope. But they, too, soon succumbed to an overpowering mood of despair and hate toward the officials of Baron Hirsch. They had planted the seed of hate which had flowered in us for thirty years. Every official of the colonization hated us and we him. It was the hate that existed between master and the serf, between the strong and the weak, between a stepmother and children. That day the settlers were writing letters home and they were not happy letters. I, too, on the earthen table prepared an article for Alexander Zederbaum's Hebrew newspaper, *Ha-Melitz*.

Others followed my example and made themselves tents in order to escape from the filthy "Matushka". During the day we spent the time in the company of the rest, and in the evening we retired to our tent.

BIRTH PANGS IN ZION

MOSES SMILANSKI (1874- ?)

When the history of modern pioneering is recorded, the epic of modern Palestine will receive an honorable chapter. Smilanski was among the dreamers who transplanted themselves from European civilization to the oppressed and neglected province of the tottering Turkish Empire in the 80's and 90's of the last century. A successful farmer and an authority on agricultural problems for almost a half century, he has recorded in stories, essays and memoirs the life and adventures of both Jews and Arabs during that significant era. This chapter of his memoirs, written with the biblical simplicity and insight that characterizes his prose, is something more than the narration of uncommon experiences; it is a graphic portrayal of Tiomkin, a leader who just missed becoming the Herzl of East European Jewry.

❋ ❋ ❋

IT WAS during the Feast of Tabernacles in 1891. All three of us sat in the large carriage with its four horses, driven by my good friend Hvedka. Father had his gaze fixed far ahead of us, mother had a tear all but rolling down from the corner of her eyes; while I, the third one, with my mother's milk all but visible on my lips, sat listening to the hammering of my heart. The carriage was taking us from our village to Yelisavetgrad, the district capital; and to Tiomkin.

After a stern war at home for a full year it had been decided to take me to him, to Tiomkin himself, and to ask him whether anyone like me was fit to go to the Land of Israel. Whatever he said would be acted on.

What would he say? That was the problem which busied my mind, worried me and set my heart hammering so.

Tiomkin was the new star rising at that time above the horizon of the Lovers of Zion; the star that dimmed all the others and won all hearts. He was a young engineer of exceptional organizing abilities, a person of influence with a radiant future. While yet a student in the

443

Russian capital he had devoted himself to the new movement and its local activities. At the first general meeting of the Lovers of Zion in Odessa he had appeared and had won all hearts, including that of the old leader, Dr. Pinsker. All eyes were turned on him, expecting great wonders. The post of Chairman of the Jaffa Executive Committee which had just been reconstituted was offered him. He gave up the prospects he already enjoyed in his own profession, in which he had already made a name, and accepted. He was the hero of the day.

What did he look like I asked myself as we crossed the porch of the house in which dwelt the man on whom my future turned; and I answered myself, "Like John of Gischala."

I knew what John of Gischala looked like. To be sure, I had become heretic two years earlier when a Tolstoyan colony had settled in our village, and I had ceased to put on phylacteries. But I believed in the rising of the dead. For how might a Jewish lad stop believing in the dead and go on living? And among the dead whom I hoped to meet some day in the flesh, John of Gischala took one of the first places. Why? Lord knows, and that strange secret which has rendered ineffectual all Josephus' efforts to make us detest the heroes of the Jewish War against the Romans.

And my great desire to see him led me to picture him, tall and upright, with eagle eye and every line of his noble face etched with bravery.

Then how could this contemporary hero look other than that ancient one?

Nor did my youthful imagination deceive me. Before us stood a tall, broad-shouldered man, erect as a cedar. A real hero. His face was fine and delicate, with a square black beard down to his chest. His eyes were large, black and good. He had a peculiar charm, a wonderful grace. A king.

"So this is your son?"

"Yes. Take him. He is yours." The words burst from my father's lips.

His friendly eyes rested on me.

"Should such as he go to the Land of Israel? Why, he's still a boy!" My mother stood in the breach.

The fine, delicate face became grave and earnest at once.

"What are you thinking of doing in the Land of Israel?"

"I want to till the ground."

"Do you know what lies in store for you?"

"I know."

"You are delicately brought up and life is hard there; work that wears out the body in the fields, a hard bed and little food at home. A furious scorching sun. Your strength will fail and you will regret your decision. Your bitter heart will cause you to write bad, discouraging letters home. And you will have done us harm instead of good. . . ."

My mother's face grew bright with satisfaction and hope. My father's face lowered. I cried out, all but weeping for shame:

"I'll write no bad letters home—whatever happens."

A shadow of a smile crossed the grave face; he set his hand on my shoulder, and his pleasing musical voice reached my ears:

"You'll go with me. I shall take you to the Land."

My fate had been decided.

After the Festivals my father accompanied me to the little station on the Yelisavetgrad-Odessa railroad, and handed me over to Tiomkin.

"I've brought him to you—as Hannah brought Samuel to Eli."

The train started. My father vanished with tears in his gray eyes. My heart shrank within me. A hand was set on my shoulder and the pleasant voice whispered in my ear, "Courage!"

I regained control of myself; he was beside me.

On either side of the railway line were scattered forsaken Jewish villages, filled with Jews glum and bowed under the yoke of making a penurious existence which drove them beyond the ken of themselves and their Maker, and who were moaning under the rod of bitter exile. A bird of the heavens had spread the news within these villages that a new redeemer had arisen, one who would pass before them to prepare a way to the Land of Israel; and that this redeemer himself was being borne on the train as he took his way toward the Land of their desire. They crowded into the train in groups at every station, groups of Jews with faces blackened by the worries of making a living, and with eyes sad and frightened by the whip of exile; but now those eyes lit up in the hope of seeing him face to face, this man who bore redemption for them. Little by little the train filled up with a multitude till there was no place left, and all of them pressed round him. One came to listen, and another just to look. He sat captive for hours without ceasing to speak and listen; while the charm on his face, which captured the hearts of all who saw him, never vanished. The crowd was happy and hopeful; for a moment some unseen hand had removed the worry of livelihood and the grief of exile from those faces, and gave them a holiday.

"Rabbi Tiomkin, please excuse me. Could you tell me whether it's true that the soil there, yonder, is white and fit to grow nothing but black pepper and locusts?"

"And Rabbi Tiomkin, won't the earth there, for instance, grow potatoes and beets there?"

"Excuse me, sir. A Jew like me, for instance, would he be able to make a living there? For instance, to buy grain, fruit or fish from the gentiles there and sell them in town?"

"I have four hundred rubles. Could I buy a colony there for myself and my family?"

He answered every question willingly and gracefully, the first first and the last last, without growing tired or annoyed.

The questions about making a living came to an end; and out of the deeps of yearning souls gushed other questions.

"Rabbi Tiomkin, this Palestine of yours, is it near Jerusalem?"

"Is it true . . . as they tell . . . that on the stone of Jerusalem the dried congealed blood of our fathers can be seen to this day?"

Through the crowd of questioners pressed a woman, straightening her kerchief which had been pushed askew so as to show her hair. She stood before him as though she were ashamed, and breathed heavily.

"Please tell me. Have you seen Mother Rachel's grave with your own eyes?" And does it still stand there solitary by the wayside?"

There were tears in her voice.

The day declined. Darkness covered those standing there. It was impossible to see the faces of either questioners or answerers. But the voice went on; telling of the Western Wall, of the Tower of David, of the Cave of Machpelah. And more he told; of the colonies, of the new Jewish farmer who sowed and reaped, and of that farmer's daughter binding the sheaves.

A sigh was heard, and then a moan, and somebody suddenly cried: "Jews, let's say the Evening Prayers with minyan (full quorum)!"

They rose as one man and recited the prayers with fervor, their voices choking with tears, sighs and hopes. And he, who had been reared among gentiles and did not understand the tongue of his people and the tongue of his prayers, returned to his brethren, their troubles, their hopes and their prayers.

Tiomkin's promise was not fulfilled. He was not the one to take me to the Land. One of the Odessa "doctors" who considered himself insulted denounced the Committee to the Government, and a wire was sent to Odessa from the capital that an influential man of good appearance should be sent to handle the matter. Who could they send other than Tiomkin? At the request of Dr. Pinsker he delayed his journey to Jaffa in order to visit St. Petersburg first. I could not wait. What were Odessa and her delights to me? I stood on the threshold of the Promised Land. Could I waste even one hour?

I was still too young to receive a passport for abroad without a guardian, so Tiomkin found me one of the emigrants, and I started out alone. He told me to converse with nobody until my arrival, and not to write home if anything did not seem in order to me. Further, he gave me a verbal message to his friends about his arrival, and a letter to Israel Belkind asking him to keep an eye on me.

When I arrived I found the entire country waiting impatiently for the arrival of the leader. While we were still on board ship off the coast at Jaffa a man with long hair falling to his shoulders approached us and asked, "Which of you has something from Tiomkin with him?"

"That's me, and I have to deliver it to Joshua Hankin and Joshua Eisenstadt."

"I'm Hankin, and here's Eisenstadt as well."

On shore, in the hotel and the street, everybody was asking when Tiomkin would arrive. The camp was awaiting its leader.

Tuesday, Kislev 6, 5652

A bright morning. The sun's rays are laughing across the quiet sea which gleams and sparkles like a polished mirror. The three-master stood in near the coast. A swarm of little boats hovered on the surface and between the rocks, waiting for a sign to make for the ship. On the shore, on the steps descending to the sea, in and around the courtyard of the Customs House, were assembled the fine folk of the Jewish population, all of them come to welcome the leader. Most of them were standing; a few sat on the seawall among the Arabs with their baggy breeches. The officials in their red barbushes sat apart from the crowd on tiny chairs, the mouthpieces of their narghiles between their lips, sipping their black coffee in tiny sips and seeing nobody and nothing around them.

I recognized but few faces among the fine folk. Hankin, Eisenstadt and Belkind set out for the ship in a boat. Olga stood by the wall gazing at the ship. By her stood a tall man in a coat that came to his knees, his hair, his beard and his eyes black, his face very grave and marked with deep thought. "That's Aaron Eisenberg," whispered into my ear my new companion, Cohen of Rishon Lezion, in a voice of respect and esteem. A group of youngsters who never ceased whispering among themselves took a special place. "Those are the youngsters of Wadi Hanin," my companion whispered to me again. On one side stood those who were to become Tiomkin's companions on the Committee, the wise writer Y. M. Pines and Ben Tovim. Beside the former stood some of the men of Gedera. The crowd as a whole was composed of the immigrants and the "representatives" who had arrived on the previous boats.

I was in a good mood. The great crowd excited my imagination. The soldiers of the army were standing awaiting their leader. He stood there among them, standing head and shoulders above those assembled, his fine black eyes sparkling with feeling, his fresh cordial voice ringing with assurance and faith. They all pressed about him stretching out their hands, and he found words for each one separately.

"And here's my pioneer! You have no regrets so far?"

My handshake, into which I put all my strength, was my reply. It said, "I'll follow you, I'll run to your order, I'll never turn away from you."

The large assembly slowly took its way along the shore, Tiomkin at the head, Olga at his right hand. They remembered times in St. Petersburg. I pushed to his left, kept there and would not give place to anybody else. At his side I felt so secure and mighty.

The Arabs stood staring in wonder. Where did these folk come from? And who had brought them thither? The crowd hurrying along the shore was held up and turned aside. In addition a big caravan of donkeys bearing sacks to the shore was held up and the jingling of their bells stopped.

In the main street the crowd broke up. Tiomkin and a small group entered Hankin's house. The large room was filled with people. Tiomkin spoke of the denunciation. He had not gone to St. Petersburg, and matters had been arranged without him. Eisenstadt objected to Pines' warning in the press against too hasty purchases of land. Finally Tiomkin rose and said with an easy smile:

"I have done my duty as friend; it is time for service. There are no more friends. There is only duty and work."

At the Kamenetz Hotel in the German quarter the courtyard was full of people awaiting Tiomkin. He had only just entered his room and folk were already knocking at the door. Ere he removed his traveling clothes he had already assumed the yoke of labor.

It was with great difficulty that I found a few minutes for consulting him on my future, and telling him of my wish to work in Rishon with one of the farmers. He agreed, but warned me against certain individuals in that colony, and advised me to work with one of the Bilu settlers. He also gave me a letter of recommendation to Bloch; for in those days the rule of Bloch was in force, according to which strangers might not enter the colony without a permit.

In the Rishon diligence everybody spoke of Tiomkin.

"He has the face of a king."

"Even Bloch will begin to behave in front of him."

"The Baron has sent an order to honor him as a king is honored."

"The Government officials will also treat him with respect."

"And the Arabs—did you see how they were looking at him?"

"He has brought a check for a million francs with him."

The first Executive Committee had its offices in the narrow winding lane uniting the Customs Street with the town square; they were situated in the second story of an Arab house, up narrow flights of stone stairs which were dark and gloomy even in the daytime. From the steps one passed through a small dark corridor, into a large hall with two windows looking out on the lane. All day long this hall hummed like a beehive with the press of people. These were the "pioneers" who arrived on the Russian ships in hundreds every Tuesday. One of the doors from the hall led direct into the office of the chairman, Tiomkin himself. It was besieged all day long by a multitude, each one of whom awaited his turn. Many of them had business with him; his name had gone before them all the way from the Exile to the Land of Israel. Others desired nothing but to see him. The former entered in turn one at a time, while the rest stood by staring at those happy ones with a mixture of jealousy and satisfaction; they were happy to stand by those who had been with him. Those who came out of his office had their faces bright with light and hope. They had found something good in his office, and this infected all those standing in the hall, producing some spiritual harmony among them.

Sometimes his door would open and he would come out into the hall himself, standing head and shoulders taller than those there. He would look at them with friendly eyes and ask what the matter was. There was nothing the matter, but they would all press round him to bask in the shining of his face. He would gradually be pushed from his place at the door till he stood in their midst. He asked and they answered, they asked and he answered, with his enchanting smile. His voice alone sufficed to promise all that was good.

It did not need to be put into words. He spoke and they would listen, listening to far more than he said. When he left them they would go out of the hall, satisfied and hopeful, each bearing a spark of happiness and good tidings home with him.

Noon would arrive. The Chairman would leave the office and go to his lodging at the Kamenetz Hotel. Part of the crowd would still be found in the hall; it was hard for them to forsake him; some, who came from the colony, would eat their food there and stay the night. Some of them would follow him at a distance, as he walked through the streets surrounded by his assistants and friends, gazing at him with pride and satisfaction: "There's our leader." The Arabs in the streets also made way for him. The elders and men of countenance sitting on their chairs all along the road would rise in his honor and greet him, and whisper:

"Ras el Yehud!" (Chief of the Jews.)

In the German Colony friends, notables, representatives and guests would all be awaiting their turn. During the noon hour and the hours that followed there would be ceaseless meetings.

We had two holidays in the week; they were the Sabbath and Tuesday, when the ship from Russia arrived at the port. While it was still dark we would start out afoot from the colony, and by the time the sun rose we were already seated on the shore at Jaffa awaiting the arrival of the ship. I used to wait for two things: for letters from home and to see what the fresh arrivals looked like. Every ship brought newcomers in hundreds. They were of various kinds. A small section were men of substance. Some of these had come to look for a portion for themselves; others were the representatives of the societies which were springing up in the Exile at the time like mushrooms after rain. A few of these would remain in Jaffa for a week or a fortnight; some of these latter would leave funds for the purchase of land in the hands of the Executive Committee while others returned empty-handed with mocking smiles on their faces. Some would return by the same boat the same night. And some would stay on in the country until they found the tracts they required. These for the greater part fixed the mode of life in Jaffa.

Most of the arrivals were poor folk without anything. Some were typical immigrants who had found their way to Jaffa only by mistake.

Some passed through Jaffa on their way to New York. Those with funds continued their journeys elsewhere or else returned to "blessed Russia"; those who lacked funds remained in Palestine despite themselves and became "workers". These latter fell as a burden on the Executive Committee. The intervention of Tiomkin led to Bloch's orders regarding strangers being revoked, so that permission could be given for the poor arrivals to work in the fields of Rishon Lezion. Hundreds of men filled those fields and hundreds went on to Rehoboth, where fresh work was beginning. Temporary tents were set up in Wadi Hanin by order of the Executive Committee; most of the workers lived there, walking to their labors in Rishon or Rehoboth. In the colonies themselves hundreds were crowding into the cellars, the attics and every available nook and cranny.

Apart from these two varieties there was a third type, for whom my eyes searched among the crowds of arrivals leaving the boats and climbing up along the shore. I recognized them by special signs, and my heart went out to them. These were folk who were attracted to the Land of Israel not for plots of land, not to make a living, not even by reason of the general well-being that sat heavy on their shoulders, but because of—who can tell? Maybe the stories of their teachers, sown as seen in their hearts and now blossoming; maybe the warming rays of the sun of the Love of Zion, the rays of the sun of the fatherland; or the tears they had shed over the pages of Josephus' *Wars of the Jews;* or something tremendous and powerful, some urge without name or description. The "idealists" or the "ne'er-do-wells"—so they were known throughout the neighborhood, with a smile on the lips.

I used to recognize them by the clarity of the fine, youthful faces, the shine of their bright, glistening eyes, the expression of faith, of aspiration and of a search for something hidden that marked their faces, their eyes and their every movement. For the greater part they were youths or very young men. Mostly these did not stay in Jaffa; they would proceed to the offices of the Executive Committee to see *him*. After they had seen him, whether within the walls of the office or in the street, they would leave for the colonies. From the colonies they would return, or would be brought back in wagons to the hospitals or the cemetery or straight to the ship, with bitter despair on their brows.

There were also those who thought of the public weal and who had come to the country just for the purpose of "delivering the motherland". These remained in Jaffa, bothered Tiomkin, called meetings and, with the "representatives" referred to above, determined the form of life of Jaffa and of the country.

I was still too young to take a hand in public affairs, nor did they attract me. Apart from the seashore and the hall of the Executive Committee's offices, there was another place in Jaffa of which I was fond. It was a certain shop, which served as a spiritual center for all the youngsters from the colonies far more than it did for the sale of groceries. The owner of the shop, a man of exalted spiritual character, attracted the youngsters by his fine spirit. He was concerned with communal affairs far more than with his shop and business, and looked after the affairs of each of his numerous friends. There we would sit among the sacks of flour and peas, and would converse of Tiomkin and of communal affairs without entering into the thick web of communal work.

I did not know that Tiomkin's way was not strewn with roses, and that he had met with thorns from the day of his arrival. I found it out very suddenly.

Months had passed. It was evening. After a hard day's work and a scanty supper I lay on my couch in my room, weary and somewhat annoyed and grieved. Why, I did not know. Suddenly there came the rattle of wheels and the voices of men in conversation. A moment later a crowd of acquaintances and friends from Jaffa and the colony burst into the room, all of them in a happy frame of mind and speaking together.

"Michal Halperin has bought a tract of land in Wadi Hanin in order to establish a model colony there on new social foundations. The Workers' Organization of Reheboth will found the colony with the general funds of the organization. The organization will build the houses and plant the vineyards. And so when a worker reaches the age of about sixty and can't work any longer he'll be able to settle in this colony, each man in his own house under his vine and under his fig tree. And besides this colonizing event there's a family event. A son has been born to A.A. and he intends to call his a new name—Ben-Carmi (Son of my vineyard)."

I was excited by my guests and their news and hastened to my landlady to get some loaves and olives; and incidentally I told her of the changes that were going to come about in our world. She did not quite comprehend what I was talking about, but loaded me with the best she had. And the landlord, hearing my words, shook his head.

"A new colony . . . There won't be anything without the Baron. . . . Vanity of vanities . . . They'll be sure to fail. . . ."

In Wadi Hanin there was rejoicing. All the folk from Jaffa and the colonies stood crowded and pushing round the solitary stone house. A fire had already been lit as a beacon in the middle of the open ground. Round the beacon stood the speakers, and as each finished his speech he bounded across the fire to the other side. A guest was speaking, one of the Lovers of Zion from Odessa; his voice was hoarse, his beard unkempt, his eyes burnt like a flame and he adjured those assembled to be faithful to Tiomkin.

And who might be expected to rebel? I wondered in my heart. Then came Halperin himself on a bounding steed, his head bare, his long hair and beard streaming in the air, his eyes gleaming with a strange fire, a sword in one hand; he raised the sword and smote at his hand. The blood did not begin to spurt but those assembled cried out. He raised the sword again and shouted in Russian, "I swear to you with my blood—if I forget thee, O Jerusalem, let my right hand be forgot!"

Tiomkin was among those present, but that evening he did not join the public. There was some important meeting for him and his companions. Only on the following morning, after the circumcision ceremony, did he deliver his speech, which remained engraven on my memory for many years. He stood in the shade of a lofty mulberry tree with all the assembly gathered about him, and he spoke in Russian. For the first time in my life I heard an address given with the divine touch, and I was amazed and entranced. His words poured over me like a tremendous stream, like some waterfall. It seemed as though one of the prophets of old had arisen before us; for in sooth it was a prophetic speech. Those were explosive, enchanting, amazing words of his, such as had power to arouse a multitude and send them through fire and water.

For some reason he had a bitter heart. The meeting of the day before had annoyed him. His words hinted at opposition and underhand work. He spoke with enthusiasm of the work we were engaged in and put heart into the assembly. He raised his voice in rebuke against the men who were obstructing the work and sowing dissension and hatred and jealousy. On them he scattered fire and brimstone. Then once again he spoke words of comfort and called for work, sacrifice and peace.

When he finished his address the entire assembly stood as though petrified. They grieved that his voice had stopped, and only after a few seconds did the hurrahs ascend to the heart of the heavens.

But I stood transfixed. I asked my friend Cohen, the know-all, what the fear was; who was obstructing; who was acting in underhand fashion. And he answered me with a rebuke:

"You have your head so close to the hoe that you know nothing."

The troubles of Tiomkin began from within. In his office there were two aides-de-camp; the scholarly writer Y. M. Pines and A. Ben Tovim. The former had been the representative of the Lovers of Zion for a number of years before the Executive Committee had been officially established.

For many years he had dealt with Petah Tikva and Yesod Hamaala, and it was he who had founded Gedera. The other was a newcomer in the country and had the confidence of the great scholar Rabbi Samuel Mohilever, who feared Tiomkin's "Godlessness". These two aides did not approve of their chief. Pines found himself insulted by being reduced from the first place after so many years of work, and Ben Tovim put his faith in the "wall of Bialystok", where Mohilever acted as rabbi. But that was not the main issue.

In addition to them Tiomkin had unofficial advisors and assistants whose influence upon him was greater than that of his official aides. These were Joshua Eisenstadt and Joshua Hankin. The former was a temperamental person with a rich imagination, who found a messianic movement in the Love of Zion and who, in everyday life, would take hasty steps and also mislead his companions. The second was a man of uncommon energy and activity, but with him too it might happen that his will was greater than his capacity. There were a number of important activities behind him. It was he, together with Eisenberg, who had begun the acquisition of the land of Rehoboth, and likewise brought his beginning to a satisfactory conclusion. He had purchased the soil of Hedera. And it was he who had begun, with the financial assistance of a representative from south Russia named Dolnik, to acquire the land of Wad al Hur, and to weave that dream of the Valley of Jezreel which he and others were to realize thirty years later.

The official aides were jealous of the unofficial advisers and their influence. Pines had even earlier regarded the imaginings of Eisenstadt and activities of Hankin with distrust; and the beginnings of the dissension between Tiomkin and his aides was to be found in the most important work he began.

Tiomkin was an energetic man with considerable will power and a broad view of life. He could not restrict himself to the bounds set by the Odessa Committee. What was the upkeep and support of a few colonies to a man who was meditating a mass movement and the establishment of a foundation for the return of the Jews to their own border?

Tiomkin realized the tremendous movement developing among the

Jewish masses in Russia and also among the comfortably-off, and strove to unite them both by strong and real bonds to the great effort of re-building the Land of Israel. Hence his plan was to purchase the land with the funds of the people and build upon it. His first step was to extend the bounds of land purchase and acquisition, to free it from all suspicion of philanthropy and to approximate it to a national effort. He knew the obstacles in the way of land acquisition in the country; and that everybody who might wish to purchase a portion of land large or small, could not come and buy. So he proposed to acquire large tracts of land in various parts of the country through the Committee, to divide them into plots and sell them to immigrants. To this end it was necessary to keep up extensive propaganda activities among the immigrants, as well as carrying out his project on the land. So he depended upon the above-mentioned two men, Eisenstadt for propaganda and Hankin in the acquisition of land.

With the support of Tiomkin the latter prepared a far-reaching plan for the redemption of land. In this field he was the chief and only worker, for Tiomkin desired to concentrate all activities of land acquisi-tion in the hands of a single individual.

Tiomkin's official aides would not agree to this. They disapproved of Hankin and were dissatisfied at this plan of centralization of land purchase. Further, they feared lest one person should enrich himself at the expense of the public. And it was not without their approval and moral support that certain of the new arrivals and old-established settlers began taking a hand in the redemption of the land, with hopes of making a good thing out of it. There was a certain Epstein in the country with a murky past—not to be confused in any way with the honorable name of Levin-Epstein; there was Aptikman, a lively and diligent man; there was Herzenstein, one of the first arrivals; there was Karlinsky of Reho-both, an enthusiastic young man. Round these and apart from them there grew up a number of agents from Jaffa and Petah Tikva, familiar with the land, its language and customs.

And thus it came about that there were a host of "redeemers" for those lands that could be redeemed, but there was a shortage of farmers to purchase the land and establish colonies. They began to hunt for these latter among the immigrants and "representatives", promising them hills and valleys; and occasionally they succeeded in their efforts. For some of the representatives walked about like great men, seeking "new paths", and refusing to be enslaved by the discipline of the Executive Committee.

Some among them followed the new saviors out of impatience. There was much ado, and the confusion was even greater than the ado.

Hankin, seeing there were competitors, redoubled his efforts, and discovered an active partner among the local Arabs who had influence among the gentry and officials and found him partners with capital. The account of Tiomkin, that is of the Executive Committee, was at his disposal. He started purchasing beyond his means and beyond the scope of the stream of immigration. Sometimes he was not sufficiently careful about details owing to his eagerness to complete matters, and money would be irretrievably lost. Nor did his competitors remain quiet; they raised the price, intrigued one against the other and all together against Hankin, spread false reports, lied and swindled. The whole country hummed like a beehive.

Tiomkin gathered his remaining strength. He tried to act as intermediary, to make peace, to unite, to unify and bring matters into order, but all his efforts were consumed from without by jealousy, enmity and contemptible competition. He did not have sufficient coordinating abilities for the needs of the moment.

The plague spread and stripped the movement of its beauty and sanctity. The holy spirit departed from the hall of the Executive Committee. It became like a market place. Every face was suspicious. Every word was a hint or a secret. Sometimes one might hear shouts and curses there. And if the chairman appeared on the threshold of his room his face was pale, weary and filled with suffering.

Round the Executive Offices, in the street, in the hotel, in the "khan" and at every crossroads stood cliques of agents and shopkeepers, quarreling about the "redemption" of the land. And sometimes words of warning could be heard, threats and evil prophecies.

Every day matters became worse. Folk spoke of cases that were to be brought or already had been brought; lawsuits between one "redeemer" and another; between the redeemers and the redeemed; and between one or other of these and Arabs. The air became filled with slander, denunciation, and the profanation of the honor of Israel.

Sometimes the redeemed, those who had purchased land for working and colonizing, arrived to establish their colonies and found that the land they had purchased did not exist. Sometimes they settled on land which did not belong to them, and the rightful owners drove them off.

Tiomkin began to walk like a shade. Grief had ploughed deep furrows in his brow.

And internal troubles as well as external were now added to the lot of the Committee. Tiomkin was busy twenty hours a day and knew no rest, neither by day nor by night. He forgot the warning of Moses' father-in-law, "Both thou and this people that is with thee shall surely wither, for the thing is too heavy for thee." By reason of his worries he neglected the work. He did not write to the Committee in Odessa nor let it know of all his actions. He did not look after the books and the accounts. He went beyond the budgets of the Committee, for he counted on the payments of those who would purchase plots. The finances became entangled. The boundaries between private money and public money became confused.

The confusion increased from day to day. Many of the purchasers thought better of it and came to demand their money back from the Committee. Money paid to Arabs in advance seemed as though it would be lost for good.

At the end of the winter the three pillars of the Movement, Ahad Ha'am, Mazé and Ussishkin, came to the Land of Israel. It did not take long for Ahad Ha'am to find out what was wrong. Hopes and imagination were of no effect against his logic. He did not agree with Tiomkin and did not support him, and Tiomkin's power declined.

Then came the Summer of 1891.

Jaffa was as noisy as before. Every Tuesday the ships still sent off their new immigrants. Buyers and sellers speaking in hints were still wandering about the streets; but signs of impatience and weariness could be recognized on every face. Within the walls of the Executive Offices, which had now passed to fine quarters in the Christian Ajami district, there was little comfort. The solemnity had vanished. Sometimes it would be whispered from mouth to ear that stringent restrictive Government regulations were on their way. Who spread the news or prophesied so dismally?

The evil came. Heaven and earth began to war against the tender movement headed by the gentle man of merits.

Fever broke out among the immigrants. The hospitals in the towns and colonies were filled to overflowing. The hospitals fed the cemeteries. The sickness was worst among the workers, who labored in hundreds in the colonies, and among the poor immigrants at Jaffa. Nor were the well-to-do delivered. In addition to malaria, typhoid struck down its victims. People began to flee as from the sword. The ships arriving at Jaffa brought the immigrants and those leaving took them back again.

The well-to-do stopped coming. Among those who left were the well-to-do. Poverty increased and so did distress. The situation of the Executive Committee grew worse from day to day. The poor camped at the doors of the offices for days on end, demanding aid. Some threatened to denounce the Committee to the representatives of the Russian Government, since the Committee had deceived them, led them astray to perish in a desert land; and they demanded to be returned to Russia at the Committee's expense.

And the calamity which had been feared did not fail to arrive. One cloudy day the Government decree against Jewish immigration and the purchase of land was published. And as a result all the moneys invested as advance payments on land were lost in a single day. All the immigrants who arrived at the shore were compelled to return. The Turkish officials began to mishandle the immigrants according to their time-honored system.

Tiomkin strove to stand in the breach. All his powers roused in him at this final hour. He strove to wrestle with the evil decrees. And to begin with he seemed to succeed. He arranged a system of "baksheesh" which made it possible to continue the arrival of immigrants at Jaffa in a decent fashion. With the aid of Hankin he also found ways and means of completing various land purchases. But his heroic struggle could not continue for very long. The noose round the neck of the Executive Committee and the youthful movement grew tighter and tighter. The financial confusion at the Committee reached its peak, a period of crisis set in and Tiomkin was summoned back to Odessa. He left the country less than a year after his arrival.

At the end of the summer I arrived from Hedera where I lived then, not having visited Jaffa for a long time. I arrived consumed with fever, broken by doubts and smashed by the persecutions of the officials. Once more I went to the place where I had seen his gracious face and heard his magic words. I found the rooms of the Executive empty. Nobody was there. The assistants of Tiomkin went about mournful and heads downcast.

Through the streets of the town immigrants were being transferred from the ship to the serai (prison) until the next ship left Jaffa. Young Arab scum were running behind, pouring abuse on them and throwing stones.

Tiomkin was not there. The lightning had flashed, illumined the face of the heavens and their fullness and vanished. And now once again all was darkness and heavy gloom.

BIRTH OF A ZIONIST

THEODOR HERZL (1860-1904)

Herzl was the founder of modern political Zionism, and perhaps the most influential force in the life of his people in the last half century. Born into a cultivated, well-to-do family in Budapest, he became a prominent publicist while a young man. How the idea of a Jewish State formed in his mind is told in the following selection from his magnificent *Diaries*. "I wrote as I stood, walked, lay in bed; out in the street, at the table, in the dead of night when sleep was driven from one." The pages burn with passionate thought and activity, and his glowing personality fairly leaps out of every page. The same spirit pervades his famous *The Jewish State* in which he incorporated his firm belief in and a practical plan for the establishment of a state in Palestine. His colossal effort in behalf of his dream broke his body and he died in the prime of life in 1904. The time of writing is Easter, 1895.

❀ ❀ ❀

I HAVE been engaged for some time past upon a work which is of infinite magnitude. As yet I do not know whether I shall carry it to a conclusion. It has the appearance of a mighty dream; but for days and weeks it has been permeating my whole being, down even into the region of subconsciousness, has accompanied me everywhere, hovered above my ordinary conversations, glanced over my shoulder into the absurdly trivial occupations of the journalist, disturbed and intoxicated me.

What it will grow into it is as yet impossible to divine. Only my experience tells me that it is strange, even as a dream, and that I ought to write it down—if not as a memorial for mankind, at least for my own future enjoyment or contemplation. And perhaps as something between these two possibilities: for literature. If out of the romance no deed is born, at least the romance will have been achieved.

Truth to say, I no longer know whether, after all, the romance was not what first came into my mind: though not as "literature" for its own sake, but as a means to an end. And the fact that after so short an interval I should no longer remember this clearly, proves sufficiently how necessary is this written record. Greatly have I regretted that I did not start a diary on the very day of my arrival in Paris, to receive the experiences, observations, and apperceptions for which there is no place in a newspaper, which pass too swiftly and uniquely. In this way much has vanished beyond recovery.

But what are the experiences of a journalist compared to the matter which now preoccupies me? What dreams, thoughts, letters, meetings with men, actions, shall I have to live through—what disappointments if I fail, what grim struggles if I succeed! That deserves to be placed on record.

Stanley interested the world with his little travel book, *How I found Livingstone*. And when, indeed, he traversed the Dark Continent the world was greatly moved—the whole cultured world. And how little are those undertakings compared with mine! (Today I must still say: compared with my dream.)

When did I first, it might be asked, begin to think about the Jewish Question? Probably when it first arose. Most certainly ever since I read Dühring's book. In one of my old scrapbooks, which is now stored away somewhere in Vienna, are to be found my first remarks upon Dühring's book and the Question. At that time I had not yet a journalistic channel for my literary work—that was, I believe, in 1881 or 1882; but this I know, that even today I still occasionally say things which are written there. In the succeeding years the question persistently gnawed and tugged at me, tormented me, and made me very wretched. In fact, I always came back to it whenever my own personal experiences, sufferings, and joys lifted me on to a higher plane of vision.

Naturally each passing year effected a change in my thoughts, a process of which I was fully conscious. In the same way, too, a different man looks out upon me from the mirror than on some earlier day. But the person—in spite of changed features—is still the same. By the signs of aging I recognize my own maturity.

At first the Jewish Question pained me bitterly. There was, perhaps, a time when I should have been glad enough to escape from it, over into Christianity—no matter into what camp. At all events, these were but the indefinite yearnings of youthful weakness. For I say to myself with the candor of this chronicle—which would be utterly valueless if I hoodwinked myself—I say to myself that I never seriously contemplated either baptism or change of name. The latter, indeed, is vouched for by an accident. When, in my raw beginnings, I went with a manuscript to the Vienna *Deutsche Wochenschrift,* Dr. Friedjung (the distinguished author of *Der Kampf um die Vorherrschaft in Deutschland*) advised me to adopt a less Jewish-sounding pen name. This I roundly declined, saying that I intended to continue bearing my father's name, and that I was prepared to withdraw the manuscript. Friedjung ended after all by taking it.

Subsequently I was just an ordinary writer, with small ambition and inconsiderable vanities.

The Jewish Question, of course, lay in wait for me everywhere and upon all occasions. I sighed and scoffed at it, felt wretched, but for all that did not really feel its grip, although I conceived the plan, even before I came to Paris, of writing a novel of Jewry. I had meant to compose it during the journey through Spain upon which I set out in the summer of 1891. It was at that time my most urgent literary plan. The principal figure was my beloved friend Heinrich Kana, who at Berlin, in February, 1891, had blown out his brains. I believe that by the novel I wanted to lay his ghost. The novel, in my first sketch, was called *Samuel Cohn,* and among my loose notes there must be not a few which have reference to it. Above all, I wished to contrast the suffering, despised, and worthy class of poor Jews with their wealthy brethren. The latter are not touched by anti-Semitism, of which they are the real and principal cause. The milieu in which Kana moved was to be contrasted with that of his rich relatives.

The *Neue Freie Presse* summoned me to Paris as its correspondent. I accepted, because I at once foresaw how much of the world I would see and learn in that position; yet felt a pang of regret for the relinquished purpose of the novel.

At Paris I was drawn—at least as onlooker—into politics. I saw the means whereby the world is ruled. Also I stared at the phenomenon of the crowd, long without comprehending it. Likewise my relationship to anti-Semitism here became freer and more detached, as I had not to suffer from it, at any rate directly. In Austria or Germany I constantly have to fear that someone will shout "Hep! Hep!" after me. Here, at least, I pass "unrecognized" through the crowds.

In that "unrecognized" there lies a terrible reproach against the anti-Semites. The cry "Hep! Hep!" I have hitherto heard only twice with my own ears. The first time at Mainz, when passing through the town in 1888. I dropped into a cheap music hall in the evening, drank off my glass of beer, and when I got up and walked through the noise and fumes towards the door a fellow called after me "Hep! Hep!". Around him there burst out guffaws of brutal mirth.

The second time, "dirty Jew" was called after me at Baden, near Vienna, when I was driving home for the Hinterbrühl after visiting Speidel. This insult touched me more keenly as it was the strange sequel to my conversation in the Hinterbrühl, and because it resounded on "home" soil.

In Paris, then, I achieved a freer attitude towards anti-Semitism, which I began to understand historically and to excuse. Above all I recognized the emptiness and futility of the efforts to "combat" anti-Semitism. By declamations upon paper or in closed circles there is gained nothing at all. These even tend to be ridiculous. I grant that by the side of schemers and simpletons very excellent people do also sometimes sit on such "relief committees". These resemble the relief committees after—and before—floods, and achieve pretty much the same results. The noble Bertha von Suttner is mistaken—the mistake, I admit, redounds greatly to her honor—when she believes that such a committee can do anything. It is exactly the same as with the societies to promote peace. A man who invents a terrible explosive does more for peace than a thousand mild apostles.

This, too, was roughly what I replied to Baron Leitenberger when he asked me, three years ago, what I thought of the *Free Journal* for *defence against*. . . . Not much, I thought. Something could, however, be done by journalistic means, and I unfolded to him the plan of a people's paper for combating the hatred against the Jews, a paper which was to be conducted by a true-bred Christian. But the Baron thought my plan too indirect, or else too costly. He wanted to fight only on a small scale. Against anti-Semitism, to be sure!

Today, it is true, I am of the opinion that what then seemed to me adequate would be an impotent, foolish effort.

Anti-Semitism has grown, continues to grow, and so do I.

I now recall two successive conceptions of the Question and its solution which occurred to me during these latter years. About two years ago I wanted to solve the Jewish Question by the help of the Catholic church, at least in Austria. I wished to gain access to the Pope, not without previously securing the support of Austrian princes of the church, and to say to him: Help us against the anti-Semites, and I will initiate a great movement for the free and honorable conversion of Jews to the Christian church. Free and honorable, in that the leaders of this movement, I in particular, would remain Jews and, as Jews, propagate conversion to the majority-faith.

We, the steadfast leaders, would have constituted the frontier generation. We should have still adhered to the faith of our fathers. But of our young sons we would make Christians, before they reached the age of independent choice, when conversion looks like an act of cowardice or of calculation.

As usual, I had thought out the whole process even down to its remotest details, saw myself already conferring with the Archbishop of Vienna, stood in imagination before the Pontiff—who both greatly regretted that I wished to remain but one of the frontier generation—and launched the slogan of the intermingling of races across the world.

At the first opportunity of oral intercourse I meant to win the editors of the *Neue Freie Presse* for this plan. Already earlier I had given them a piece of advice which, to the detriment of the Liberal party in Austria, they ignored. For about a year before the franchise reform movement of the socialists became acute, I recommended, in a leading article of their Christmas number, that they should suddenly demand the universal franchise. By this the liberals could regain the firm ground they had lost among the people and with the intelligent working-class. Subsequently the franchise reform movement challenged them from without, and they did not cut a very happy figure.

It is true, my position with the leader writers was not one of very great authority; they thought me just a *causeur* and feuilletonist. And so Benedikt, too, rejected my Papal idea, when I spoke to him about it here, even as previously Bacher had rejected the universal franchise idea.

But there was something in Benedikt's rejoinder which struck me as true. He said: "Through a hundred generations your tribe has adhered to Judaism. You now propose to set yourself up as the limit of that development. This you cannot; have no right to do. Besides, the Pope would never receive you."

Without my newspaper, of course, I could do nothing. Whence should I have taken the authority? What countervailing service could I have promised? The services of the leading Liberal paper might, perhaps, have induced the shrewd Pope to do something, to make a declaration, or drop a hint. As it happens, I later on heard of a remark made by Leo XIII about the paper: "A pity the *Neue Freie Presse* is so well-done."

After this abandoned conception there ripened in me subconsciously, in that inscrutable way, another, less political, more contemplative. This

I clearly developed for the first time in my conversation with Speidel when I went from Baden where I was staying to see him at the Hinter-brühl, last summer. We walked, philosophizing, across green meadows, and fell to talking about the Jewish Question.

I said: "I understand anti-Semitism. We Jews have maintained our-selves, though by no fault of our own, as alien bodies among the various nations. In the ghetto we have acquired a number of anti-social peculiarities. Pressure from without has broken down our character, and it needs another pressure to restore it. Actually, anti-Semitism is the consequence of Jewish Emancipation. But the general public, lacking an understanding of history, regard us, not as an historical product, not as the victims of earlier, more cruel and even more bigoted times than the present. They do not know that we are what we have been made to be, through torments; through the church making moneylending a dis-honest trade for Christians, and through the rulers impressing us into the money traffic. We cling to money, because on to money we were thrust. Moreover, we had to be ready always for flight, or to save our possessions from rapine. That is how our relation to money started. Also we, *servi camerae,* of the Emperor served as a kind of indirect tax. These sufferings transformed our character which at one time was proud and great. For we were men who could defend the State in time of war and must have been a highly gifted people to have been thus slain during twenty centuries and yet to be alive.

"Now it was an error of the doctrinaire freethinkers to believe that men can be made equal by an ordinance promulgated in the State-Gazette. When first we left the ghetto we still remained, for a time, ghetto Jews. It was necessary that we should be given time in which to get used to our freedom. But the nations, in whose midst we dwelt, had not this generosity or this patience. They see only the bad and conspicuous characteristics of the recently emancipated and have no suspicion that it is to their own injustice that these qualities are due. Add to this the prevailing socialist opposition to movable capital to which the Jews have been compelled to turn exclusively for centuries past.

"But so soon as the Jews leave money alone and turn to the liberal professions, from which they were formerly debarred, they introduce a terrible pressure into the economic life of the middle classes; a pressure, it is true, from which they are the first to suffer.

"That anti-Semitism, however, which is a strong and unconscious force operating among the great masses, will do the Jews no harm. I consider it a movement valuable to the Jewish character. It is the education of a group by the masses and will possibly lead to the group's absorption. Nothing educates so surely as hardship. A form of Darwinian 'mimicry' will ensue. The Jews will adapt themselves. They are as the sea-calves, whom a cosmic accident cast into the water. These assume the form and properties of fishes which in reality they are not. If, now, they return to the firm earth and are permitted to remain there for a few generations, they will re-transform their fins into feet.

"The effects of one pressure can only be cancelled by the other pressure."

Speidel said: "That is a cosmogonic conception."

Afterwards I drove away into the gathering night across to Baden. Just as my cab was speeding through the tunnel behind the cholera chapel, two young fellows, one of whom wore the uniform of cadet, came sauntering by. I believe I sat huddled in a corner, absorbed in my thoughts, when I distinctly heard somebody shouting after the vehicle: "Dirty Jew!"

Anger boiled up in me. I fiercely turned round on the two lads; but already they were far behind. And in a moment, too, my brief desire to scuffle with street Arabs had evaporated. Moreover, it had been no affront to my person, which was unknown to them, but to my Jewish nose and my Jewish beard which they had seen in the half-gloom, behind the lanterns of my cab.

But what a curious echo to my "cosmogonic interpretations". Cosmology in such a case is of little use.

A few months later I sat to the sculptor Beer for my bust. The course of our conversation led us to observe how little it availed the Jew to be an artist, and clean as regards money. The curse persists. We cannot get away from the ghetto. And I talked myself into a great heat and was still all aglow when I went away. With the swiftness of that dream in a water-tub of the Arabian Nights there arose in me the outline of this play (*Das Neue Ghetto*). I believe that I had barely progressed from the Rue Descombes to the Place Péreire before everything stood finished in my mind.

On the following day I sat down at my desk. Three blissful weeks of glow and labor.

I had thought that by this dramaturgic eruption I would have written the matter off my heart. Quite on the contrary. I became ever more deeply immersed in it. The thought grew stronger in me that I must do something for the Jews.

I now paid my first visit to the Synagogue of the Rue de la Victoire*, again found the service solemn and touching. A good deal of it reminded me of my young days, of the temple in the Tabakasse at Pesth. I looked closely at the Paris Jews and found the family-likeness in their faces. Bold, crumpled noses, furtive and crafty eyes.

Was it then, or on an earlier occasion, that I conceived the plan of writing a book upon *Jews As They Are?*

I now remember that it was earlier. I spoke about it already in the autumn, in Vienna. I wanted to visit the localities to which cosmic accident had scattered the Jews in groups, particularly Russia, Galicia, Hungary, Bohemia; later on the Orient, the new Zionist colonies; finally again, Western Europe. From all these realistic accounts there was to emerge a picture of the undeserved misery of the Jews. A demonstration that these are human beings, whom men slander while not knowing them. For here in Paris I have acquired reporter's eyes such as are needed for snapshots of this kind.

I became personally acquainted before Easter with Daudet. On one occasion, among other matters, we got on to the subject of the Jews. He confessed to being an anti-Semite. I explained to him my own standpoint, and once again grew warm (which goes to prove that I am really a man who thinks aloud). When I told him that I wanted to write a book in defence of, and about, the Jews, he asked, "A novel!" "No," I ventured, "preferably a book for men!" To which he said: "The novel carries further. Remember *Uncle Tom's Cabin*."

I then waxed somewhat eloquent and so carried him too along with me, that finally he said: *"Comme c'est beau; comme c'est beau!"*

And that made me uncertain again about *Jews As They Are,* and I once more thought of making it a novel. Only Samuel Cohn—Heinrich Kana—was no longer to be its principal figure. According to the first plan, the final chapter would have dealt with the emotions that preceded Samuel's suicide. He sauntered at eve along the Unter den Linden, and because of his imminent death felt himself superior to all around him. He scornfully eyed guards—officers, with anyone of whom he could now pick a quarrel. Meditating how he should turn his suicide to account, he was a lord of life. Indeed, he walked along with such a proud and imperious gait that everyone instinctively made way for him. And that again made him feel more forgiving, and he went quietly home and blew out his brains.

In its present form, Samuel was the weaker but much beloved friend

* Partly destroyed by Nazis in the winter of 1941.

of the hero, who, through the accidents of his life, is led to discover or, more accurately, to found the Land of Promise.

Aboard the ship which is to take him and his commissioned staff of landseekers to the new shores, and just before weighing anchor, he received Samuel's latter of farewell.

Samuel writes: "My dear, good fellow, when you read this letter I shall be dead."

At this, the hero dashes his fist with the crumpled note to his heart. But the next moment he feels nothing but anger.

He gives the order to clear. Then he stands in the bows of the ship and gazes steadily out into the distance where lies the Promised Land.

And he takes the letter in which there is withal so much touching love and loyalty and shouts into the wind: "Fool, knave, scoundrel! A lost life that belongs to us!"

Already I have lost sight of the stages by which I advanced from the plot of a novel to practical conceptions, though it all lies but a few weeks back. Subconscious processes.

Perhaps, indeed, these are not practical ideas at all, and I shall become a laughingstock in the eyes of those whom I earnestly address. And I am caught fast in the novel? But even then what I have pondered over during this time, and continue to ponder, is worth recording.

Suddenly, one day, I wrote a letter to that Baron Hirsch who has busied himself about the Jews so conspicuously, and with a millionaire's characteristic folly. When this letter was written I put it away and slept on it for fourteen days and nights.

When, even after that interval, the letter did not seem foolish to me, I posted it. This is what I wrote:

Sir,—When may I have the honor of calling on you? I should like to converse with you upon the Jewish Question. This is no case of a newspaper interview, nor yet a veiled or overt affair of money. It would appear that the calls made upon you are so many that one cannot be sufficiently quick in forestalling impure suspicions. I desire only to have a Judacio-political talk with you, the effects of which will perhaps reach forward into a time when you and I will be no longer living. And that is also why I should like you to fix a day for our meeting, when you can devote one or two hours undisturbed to the matter. Owing to my usual occupations, a Sunday would suit me best. It need not be next Sunday. Whenever you like.

My project will interest you. But slight as is the hint I am herewith conveying, I nevertheless will ask you not to show this letter to your entourage—secretaries and others. Be good enough to treat it as confidential.

Possibly you are already acquainted with my name. In any case you know the paper which I here represent.

Yours very faithfully,

Dr. Herzl,

Correspondent of *Die Neue Freie Presse*

That is the text, according to the draft which I have preserved. In copying it I may have changed a word here and there, because I was not yet thinking of keeping all this for remembrance.

My chief fear was lest this letter might be regarded as a journalistic artifice to obtain money. For assuredly I did not wish to meet the man because of his wealth, but only because he is a highly useful force for my purpose.

Several days went by. Then I received his reply from London:

> 82, *Piccadilly, W.,*
> *Londres, le Mai, 1895*

Monsieur le Dr. Herzl,
　　Paris

Je viens de recevoir votre lettre ici où je vais passer deux mois. Je regrette donc, avec la meilleure volonté du monde, de ne pouvoir vous fixer le rendez-vous que vous me demandez. Peut-être pourriez-vous me dire par lettre ce que vous vouliez m'expliquer de vive voix, en mettant "Personnel" sur l'envelope que vous m'adresserez.

Je vous demande pardon de vous répondre par la main de mon secrétaire, et en français, mais les suites d'une ancienne blessure de chasse à la main droite ne me permettent plus de tenir la plume longtemps.

Recevez, Monsieur, l'expression de mes sentiments distingués.

M. de Hirsch

To this letter I replied:

> 37, *Rue Cambon, 24th V. 1895*

Dear Sir,—I very much regret that we were not able to meet here.

To write what I had meant to tell you is not easy. Not to speak of the external accidents which may befall a letter, my intentions which serve a considerable purpose, might be injured by idle curiosity or spoilt by the negligence of persons who by some accident have come to know my plans. Moreover, my letter may reach you at a moment when, owing to some outside distraction, you cannot read it with full and concentrated attention. But if you were to reply to me by the hand of your secretary, with some polite formula of *prise en consideration,* you would henceforward cease to count for me. And that, perhaps, would be regrettable in the interests of all.

Nevertheless, I will write to you. Only—as the old saying goes—I am too busy, just now, to be brief. The fact is, I do not wish to weary you by a long-winded disquisition. As soon as I have time, I shall submit to you the outline of a new Jewish Policy.

What you have hitherto undertaken was as magnanimous as it was mistaken, and as costly as it was useless. Hitherto you have been but a philanthropist, a Peabody. I will show you the way to become something more.

But, please, do not think that I am a fantast or a fool of merely a new variety, though it is true my way of writing to you departs somewhat from the ordinary. I admit from the outset that possibly I am mistaken, and am quite open to correction.

I expect by no means to convince you all at once, for you will have to change fundamentally certain views which you have hitherto held. All I desire, although presumably I am quite unknown to you, is your fullest attention. In conversation I should probably have compelled it; through the medium of a letter that is more difficult. My letter lies among many others upon your desk, and I fancy that you receive enough letters every day from beggars, spongers, imposters, and industrialists of philanthropy. That is why my letter will rest in a separate envelope, bearing the inscription, "Dr. Herzl's letter." This I would ask you to put aside, and only to open when you have an entirely calm and clear head. Just as I had desired it for our conversation, which did not take place.

Yours very faithfully,
Dr. Herzl

In this case also my rough draft is not quite reliable. I now believe that in copying it out I changed several expressions. In short, that was its purport, and again my only fear was lest Hirsch, or some third person glancing over his shoulder, might believe that I was after money.

During the following days I prepared my memorandum. Countless slips of paper became covered with notes. I wrote standing, in the Chamber, in the restaurant, at the play.

The matter blossomed out, under my hand, into a multitude of details. In the middle of these preparations Hirsch surprised me with a second letter:

Londres, 26 Mai

Monsieur Herzl, 37, Rue Cambon, Paris

J'ai reçu votre lettre d'avant-hier. Vous pouvez s'il n'est fait déjà, vous épargner un long exposé. Je me rendrai dans quelques jours à Paris pour 48 heures, et vous me trouverez dimanche prochain (2 Juin) à votre disposition à 10.30 du matin, 2, Rue de l'Elysée.

Recevez, Monsieur, l'expression de mes sentiments distingués.

M. de Hirsch

This letter caused me a certain satisfaction, because I saw that I had gauged the man accurately, caught him at the point of least resistance. Evidently the words that he could become a greater than Peabody had impressed his imagination.

Now I made notes with all the keener zest, and by the Saturday preceding Whitsun they had swelled into a thick bundle. Then I arranged them according to their matter in three sections: Introduction, Improvement of the Jewish Race, Emigration.

I made a clean copy of the notes and found that they covered thirty-two closely-written pages, although I had only used catchwords, to aid my memory during the interview. I was, and am, compelled to reckon with my shyness at the start.

Here, in my intercourse with famous or well-known people, I have often been ridiculous because of my nervousness. Spuller, by no means a luminary (although it was he who invented the *esprit nouveau*) once disconcerted me to the point of imbecility when I called on him during his term of office.

On Whit Sunday morning I dressed myself with discreet care. I had purposely broken in a pair of new gloves the day before, so that they should look little worn but not brand new. Rich folk one must not treat with too much deference.

I drove up to the Rue de l'Elysée. A palace. The monumental courtyard, the noble sidestairs—not to speak of the main staircase—impressed me very much. Wealth affects me only in the guise of Beauty. And here everything was genuinely beautiful. Old pictures, marble, subdued gobelins. Confound it all! Of these effects of wealth men of my kind are not thinking when we speak disparagingly of it. Everything was in truly great style, and so, a trifle dazed, I allowed myself to be handed forward by one footman to another.

Hardly had I reached the billiard room when Hirsch came out of his study, shook hands with me in a hurried and absent-minded way as with an acquaintance, begged me to wait a little, and vanished again.

I sat down and looked at the exquisite Tanagra figures in the glass case. The Baron must have engaged an expert for good taste, I reflected. Now I heard voices in the adjoining room and recognized the tones of one of his philanthropic underlings with whom I had exchanged a few words once in Vienna, and on two occasions here.

I did not like the idea of his seeing me here as he went out. Perhaps, indeed, Hirsch had purposely so arranged matters. That again made me laugh, for I had no intention whatever of becoming his dependent. Either I would bend him to my purpose, or I would go away with my object unachieved. I was even ready with an answer if, during the conversation, he should offer me an appointment with the Jewish Association: "Into your service? No. Into that of the Jews? Yes."

Presently the two officials came out. I shook hands with the one I knew. Then I said to the Baron: "Can you give me an hour? If it is not at least an hour, I would sooner not begin at all. I need that time, merely to indicate how much I have to say."

He smiled: "Go ahead."

I drew out my notes: "In order to make the thing more perspicuous I have prepared one or two points."

I had barely talked for five minutes when the telephone rang. I believed it was prearranged. I had even meant to tell him at the start that he need not have himself called away by a fiction, that he should tell me quite frankly whether he was free. He, however, said into the telephone that he was at home to no one. This showed me that I had gripped him. He was giving me an opening.

So I proceeded:

"In what I am about to say you will find some things too simple, others too fantastic. But by the simple and the fantastic men are led. It is astonishing—and notorious—with how little intellect the world is ruled. Now, it was by no means my original purpose to concern myself with the Jewish Question. You also, I take it, did not at first think of becoming Patron of the Jews. You were a banker, you engaged in big transactions; finally you devote your time and your money to the Jewish cause. In the same way I was, to begin with, a man of letters, a journalist, with no thought of the Jews. But my experiences, my observations, the growing pressure of antisemitism, compelled me to face the issue.

"Very well, those are my credentials."

"Into the history of the Jews, with which I had meant to begin, I will not enter now. It is sufficiently known. Only upon one thing I must lay stress. Through our two thousand years' dispersion we have come to be without a central direction of our policy; and that, I consider, is our chief misfortune. It has done us more harm than all the persecutions. It has destroyed our character, caused us to grow inwardly rotten. For we had no one who would educate us—if only from motives of monarchical unselfishness—to be right good men. On the contrary, we were pushed into every dishonest trade, imprisoned in the ghetto, where we festered alongside of one another; and when at last they let us out they demanded suddenly that we should display at once the qualities of free men.

"Now if we had a unified political leadership, the necessity for which I need not labor, and which need by no means take the form of a secret association—if we had such leadership, then we could proceed to the solution of the Jewish Question—a solution from above, and from below, and from every side.

"And that object, which we shall pursue as soon as we have a center, a head, will determine the means we must employ?

"It can be one of two objects: either to remain where we are or to emigrate.

"Both alike involve certain measures of national education, for even if we emigrate it will be a long time before we reach the Promised Land. It took Moses forty years. We perhaps shall not twenty or thirty. In any case, there will meanwhile arise new generations whom we must educate.

"Now, with regard to education, I propose to lay down, from the very outset, quite different methods from those which you pursue.

"First, there is the principle of philanthropy, which I consider thoroughly mistaken. You breed professional beggars. It is a fact worth noting that in no nation is there to be found so much philanthropy and so much beggary as among the Jews. The conclusion is forced upon one that between the two phenomena there must be a connection, and that philanthropy causes the disintegration of the national character."

He interrupted me: "You are quite right."

I continued:

"Years ago I heard that your experiments with Jews in the Argentine produced either bad results or none."

"Do you wish me to reply as you go along, whenever I have some objection to make?"

"No; I would prefer you to let me develop the whole body of my argument. I know that some things will not be absolutely exact, because hitherto I have not collected figures and dates. Let me just formulate my principles."

After this Hirsch noted his objections on a writing tablet.

I said: "Your Argentinian Jews do not behave very well, so I am told. One detail in particular struck me: that it was a peculiar kind of house which you first built."

Hirsch threw in: "Not true. That house was not built by my colonists."

"Well, let that be; but in any case you did not set about the thing in the right way. You drag these Jewish agriculturists across the sea. They must think that in the future, too, they will have a claim upon your support, and that is conducive least of all to the joy of labor. What such an exported Jew costs you he is not worth. And how many individuals at the most can you transport across? Fifteen or twenty thousand! In one street of the Leopoldstadt (the East End of Vienna) alone there live more than that number. No; direct means are not of any use for propelling masses of men. You can only produce an effect by indirect means.

"In order to draw the Jews on to the land you would have to tell them a fable about the winning of gold. Imaginatively it might be put somewhat like this: Whoever ploughs, sows, and reaps will find gold in the sheaf. Which, indeed, is true; only the Jews are aware that it will be a tiny lump. So you might tell them more rationally that he who manages best will receive a premium, which may be very high.

"Only, I do not believe that it would be practicable to plant the Jews upon the land—that is to say, in those countries where they are now living. The peasants would dispatch them with their flails. One of the strongholds of German anti-Semitism is Hesse, where the Jews are small farmers.

"With twenty thousand of your Argentina Jews you have proved nothing, even if they prosper. But if the experiment fails, then you have furnished a terrible argument against the Jews.

"Enough of criticism. What is to be done?

"Whether the Jews remain or whether they go, the race must first be improved on the spot. They must be made strong for war, joyful in labor, and virtuous. Afterwards let them emigrate—if it be necessary.

"To accomplish this improvement you can use your resources better than you have hitherto done.

"Instead of buying up Jews singly, offer huge prizes in the principal anti-Semitic countries for *actions d'éclat,* for deeds of great moral beauty, for courage, self-devotion, virtuous conduct, great performances in Art and Science, for the physician in times of epidemic, for the soldier, the inventor of a remedy, of some article of public utility, no matter what— in short, for anything great.

"By this prize you achieve two objects: one, the amelioration of all; the second, advertisement. For since the matter is uncommon and dazzling it will be talked about everywhere. And so the knowledge will spread that there are good Jews, and how many of them.

"The first, however, is more important, to wit: the improvement of the race. The individual recipient of the annual prize does not matter to me. I am more concerned with the others, who will all strain upwards, higher, to attain the price. Thereby the moral level is raised—"

Here he interrupted me impatiently:

"No, no, no! It is not my intention to raise the level at all. All our misfortunes spring from the fact that the Jews aim too high. We have too many intellects. My aim is to restrain the Jews from excessive ambition. They must not progress at too great a pace. All the hatred is caused by this fact. As for my plans in the Argentine, there you are also ill-informed. It is true that at first some ne'er-do-wells were sent over to me, whom I should have liked to throw into the sea. But now I have already a good many decent folk over there. And it is my intention, should the colony prosper, to charter a fine English ship, to invite a hundred newspaper correspondents—you are invited herewith and now—and to make a trip across to the Argentine. All, of course, depends on the harvests. After a few prosperous years I could show the world that the Jews are, after all, fitted for agriculture; and that may lead to their being allowed, even in Russia, to work on the land."

I thereupon said: "I did not interrupt you again although I had not finished. It has interested me to hear at what exactly you are aiming. But I realise that it would be useless to tell you the rest of my ideas."

He now remarked half-condescendingly, as though I had asked him for a job in his countinghouse: "I perfectly realize that you are a man of intelligence."

I only smiled inwardly. Things such as my enterprise are above *amour-propre*. I shall have to see and hear a good deal more.

And Hirsch qualified his praise to this effect: "But you have such fantastic notions."

Thereupon I got up. "But did I not tell you from the very first that this will appear to you either as too simple or as too fantastic? You do not know the function of what is termed fantastic, and that only from a height can one survey the great movements of mankind."

He said: "To emigrate would be the only thing. There are enough countries to be bought."

I almost shouted: "Yes, but who tells you that I do not wish to emigrate. Here it is written down in these notes of mine. I shall go to the German Emperor; and he will understand me, for he has been brought up to an understanding of great matters."

At these words Hirsch's eyes flickered once perceptibly. Was he impressed by my brusqueness or by my intention of speaking to the Emperor? Perhaps by both.

I now put the notes away in my pocket, and concluded:

"To the German Emperor I shall say, 'Let us depart. We are strangers. We are not allowed to merge in the people, and, what is more, we cannot. Let us depart. I will indicate to you the ways and means which I shall employ for this exodus, so that we may leave behind no economic disturbance and no void.'"

"The money?" I said laughingly and defiant. "I shall raise a Jewish national loan of ten milliards."

"Fantasy!" smiled the Baron. "The rich Jews will give nothing. The rich are bad; care nothing for the sufferings of the poor."

"I am one. I am perfectly ready to hand over everything, provided the others do likewise."

I did not take this pretty conceit more seriously than it was meant, and turned to go. His final words were:

"This is not our last conversation. As soon as I come over here again from London I shall give you a *signe de vie.*"

"Whenever you like."

I once more passed along the beautiful staircase, the noble courtyard. I was not disappointed, but stimulated. Upon the whole, an agreeable, intelligent, genuine man—vain, *par exemple!*—but I could have worked with him. With all his obstinacy he has the appearance of being reliable.

At home I was propelled at once to my writing table.

Vienna, April 16th, 1896.

This is where, last year, I interrupted my connected narrative, for there followed several weeks of unexampled productivity, during which I no longer had the composure necessary for making an orderly report of the ideas which crowded in upon me. I wrote as I stood, walked, lay in bed; out in the street, at table, in the dead of night when sleep was driven from me. The slips are dated. I no longer have leisure to copy them out. I started a second book, in which to enter each day any occurrence of note; and the slips were put away. I am now asking my good father to copy them for me into this book, in the order in which they were written. I know now, and knew during all that time of vehement production, that much of what I wrote down was wild and fantastic; but I exercised no self-criticism so as not to impede the flight of my imagination. For purging criticism, I thought, there will always be time.

In those notes the Jewish State is pictured now as something real, now as the material for a novel, because at the time I was not yet sure whether I should really dare to publish it all as a serious proposal. This rationally explains the inconsequent appearance of these notes; all I cared about was to let no idea elude my grasp. Even in the second book indeed, I occasionally treat the matter from the novelist's standpoint.

Certainly for myself, but perhaps also for others, even what is fantastic in these disconnected notes will later on have an interest. Today I hand them over to my good father, subject to these common-sense reservations—which certainly are not uncalled for—to be entered here by him.

Third Letter to Baron Hirsch, Paris
Whit-Monday, June 3rd, 1895

Dear Sir,—In order to guard against the *esprit de l'escalier* I made notes before going to see you. On returning home I found that I had stopped at page six; and I had twenty-two pages. Owing to your impatience you learned only the beginnings; where and how the idea begins to blossom, that you no longer heard.

No matter. In the first place, I expect no immediate conversion; secondly, my plan depends by no means upon your two eyes.

It is true I would have gladly made use of you as being an available and known force, for the sake of celerity. But then you would have been merely the force with which I would have begun. There are others. There is, ultimately and above all, the mass of Jews to whom I shall know how to find my way.

This pen is my power, and you will find it out, provided I retain life and health—a reservation which you also are compelled to make with regard to your own work.

You are the great Money-Jew; I am the Jew of Mind. Hence the difference in the means and ways we employ. Be pleased to note that you could not hitherto hear of my experiments, because the first has just been made with you, on you. I am arriving.

Of course, you confronted me with gentle irony. It was what I expected. I told you so in the preamble. That is how new ideas are received. And with it all you had not even patience enough to hear me out. But still I will not be silenced. I hope you will live to witness the glorious growth of my ideas. You will then recall that Whit-Sunday morning—for I believe that with all your irony you are an open-minded man and accessible to new ideas; also you have tried to do much for the Jews—in your way. But will you understand me if I tell you that the whole story of man's evolution gives the lie to your method? You want to maintain a great body of people upon a certain level, nay, even to press them further down? *Allons donc!* We are not ignorant of the stages which our humankind has passed through, from the earliest days to those of culture. The movement is ever upwards, despite obstacles, despite the painful slowness, upwards, ever upwards. There are reactions, true. That is not a mere phrase. Our grandfathers would be astounded if they came back to life; but who would try artificially to produce a reaction, let alone that it is impossible. If it were possible, do you not think Monarchy and Church would accomplish it? And how great are their powers over the bodies and souls of men! What is your power in comparison? No; at the most you may hold progress up for a little while, and then be swept away by the whirlwind.

Are you aware that you pursue a terribly reactionary policy— worse than the most absolute autocracies? Fortunately your strength is insufficient. Your intentions are good, *parbleu, je le sais bien*. Hence my desire to give direction to your will. Do not let yourself be prejudiced by the fact that I am fairly young. At my thirty-five years people are Ministers of State in France and Napoleon was Emperor.

With your polite sarcasm you cut me short. I am still liable to be put out in conversation. I still lack the aplomb which I shall acquire as something indispensable for breaking down opposition, for stirring the indifferent, consoling the distressed, inspiring a craven and demoralized people, and for my inter-course with the masters of the earth.

I mentioned an army, and you already interrupt me when I began to speak of the moral training for the march. I suffered the interruption. And yet I have already thought out also what is to follow. The entire plan. I know how much is necessary. Money, money again, and more money; means of transport, commissariat for a multitude (by which is not to be understood merely food and water, as in Moses' simple times), preservation of discipline, organization of sections, treaties with some Heads of States for permission to emigrate, with others for permission to pass through their countries, treaties of guaranty with all, and the setting up of new and glorious habitations; previously, the mighty propaganda, the popularization of the idea through news-papers, books, pamphlets, traveling lecturers, pictures, songs. Everything directed from one center, with a conscious purpose and spacious vision. But finally I should have had to tell you what flag, and how, I mean to unfurl. And then you would have asked me mockingly: "A flag: what is that? A wooden pole with a rag of cloth?" No, sir, a flag is more than that. With a flag one leads men to any place one chooses, even to the Promised Land.

For a flag they live and they die; it is even the only thing for the sake of which they are ready to die in masses, provided one educates them to this end.

Believe me, the policy of a whole nation—especially when it is so widely scattered over the earth—can only be made by means of imponderables that hover high aloft. Do you know out of what beginnings the German Empire grew? Out of reveries and songs, fantasies, and black, red and golden ribbons—and in a short time. Bismarck did no more than shake the tree which the fantasts planted.

What? You do not understand the Imponderable? And what else is religion? Just consider how much the Jews have suffered during two thousand years for the sake of this "fantasy." Aye, only the fantastic grips men's souls. And whoever does not know how to deal with it may be an excellent, worthy and matter-of-fact person, and even a benefactor in great style, but a leader of men he will never be, and not a trace of him will remain.

And nevertheless, a people's imagination must be rooted in firm realities. How do you know that I have not perfectly prac-tical ideas for the detail? Detail, it is true, which itself is of vast dimensions.

The exodus to the Promised Land presents itself practically as an immense transport undertaking, without parallel in the modern world. Transport, I said? A complex of all human activities which will fit into each other like a system of cogwheels. And this is an undertaking which, even in its first stages, will provide a livelihood for the aspiring mass of our young men: for all those engineers, architects, technologists, chemists, physicians, lawyers, who passed out of the ghetto during the last thirty years and thought that they would find their bread and their little bit of honor outside of Jewish barter, who now have to despair and are beginning to form a terrible proletariat of the educated. But to whom belongs all my love, and whose number I desire to multiply no less than you wish to diminish it. In whom I perceive the future strength, dormant at present, of the Jews. In a word, men like myself.

And out of this educated proletariat I form the general staffs and cadres of the army which is to seek, discover, and conquer the Land. Their mere departure will produce a certain relief among the middle classes of the antisemitic countries, and ease the pressure.

Do you not see that at one blow I gain both capital and labor of Jewry for the purpose? And their enthusiasm as well, once they have realized what is before them?

I admit this is but the barest outline. But how do you know that I have not already thought out the details that complete the picture? Did you so much as let me finish?

It is true, the hour was advanced; you had perhaps an appointment, or were busy; I cannot tell. Only the ventilation of such a question cannot depend upon little accidents of that kind. Have no fear, it does not so depend.

You will have the wish to continue our conversation, and I—without waiting for you—shall always be ready to provide the continuation. If the suggestions I have given you work in your mind, and you wish to speak to me, then write: *"Venez me voir."* That is sufficient, and I shall come to London for a day. And if on that day I shall no more convince you than I did yesterday, then I shall go away as composed and serene as I went away yesterday. Would you like to make a wager? I shall raise a National Loan among the Jews. Will you engage to contribute fifty million marks when I shall have raised the first hundred millions? In return I shall make you Chief.

What are ten thousand million marks to the Jews? They are surely richer than the French were in 1871, and among these how many Jews were there not? As a matter of fact, we could march even with one milliard, if necessary. For that will be working capital, the foundation of our future railways, our emigrant fleet, and our navy. With it we shall build houses, palaces, working-men's dwellings, schools, theaters, musicians, government buildings, prisons, hospitals, asylums—in short, cities —and shall make the new Land so fertile that thereby it becomes the Promised Land.

This loan will itself become the principal form of the emigration of capital. That is the State-financial core of the matter. It is perhaps not superfluous to remark as a politician: *I am no business man, and do not intend ever to become one.*

Jewish money in heavy masses is available for a Chinese loan, for Negro railways in Africa, for the most out-of-the-way undertaking—and for the deepest, most immediate and tormenting need of the Jews themselves there should be some.

Till the middle of July I remain in Paris. Then I shall go abroad for a considerable time. It is in the service of the Cause. I beg you, however, to maintain complete silence on this point, as on all others that I have touched upon. My actions may not appear to you, for the time being, as of any importance; that is precisely why I am pointing out to you that I attach much value to entire secrecy.

For the rest, I assure you in all sincerity that our conversation, incomplete though it was, has been interesting to me, and that you did not disappoint me.

I greet you,

Faithfully yours,
Dr. Herzl

These notes of mine are no labor to me, but merely a relief. I disburden myself of the thoughts which ascend like air bubbles in a retort and would end by bursting the vessel, if they found no escape.

Dear me, Lombroso, after this confession, will perhaps think me mad. And my friend Nordau will be silent about the anxiety which I cause him. But they are wrong; I know that twice two are four.

These notes prevent me from entering in my book what precedes. With the fair copy I have got no further than the conversation with Hirsch.

But the growth of the new ideas is more important. Who knows how soon it will cease?

Withal I have that fear which Heyse describes in that wonderful little poem about the artist. I tremble "lest over night I die, die before this work be done."

Ah, once it is copied out and my loose notes locked up and safely deposited here with the Academy, after I have arranged for a copy of the book, then the treasure is in safe keeping and an imperishable possession of mankind.

Of all, not of the Jews alone.

After these candid words there may be some who will think me a megalomaniac. Others will say or believe that I have an axe to grind, or desire to blow my own trumpet.

But my peers, the artists and philosophers, will understand how genuine it all is, and will protect me.

THE PROPHET'S LANGUAGE—AND THE PEOPLE'S

ELIEZER BEN YEHUDA (1858-1922)

It was the perusal of George Eliot's *Daniel Deronda* that brought the wandering spirit of this extraordinary character to Palestine to fight a titanic battle for the rebirth of the Hebrew tongue. Born in Vilna—he later discarded the family name of Perlman for a Hebrew *nom de guerre*—and educated in the lore of his people, he broke with religious tradition, followed the progressive and revolutionary movements of the day, and finally arrived at the conviction, in 1878, that Jews, like other nationalities, must struggle for political independence and establish a modern Hebrew culture in Palestine. The tale of his persistence, despite want, hostility and even imprisonment, in adapting the Hebrew tongue for everyday usage has an epic quality and makes Ben Yehuda's personality live as a radiating force in the rich annals of Hebrew letters.

✵ ✵ ✵

A S WE steamed along the Syrian coast en route to Jaffa, we began to pick up many Arab passengers, most of them tall and brawny youths arrayed in finest Arabian costumes, laughing and making merry. Beholding them I was seized with the melancholy premonitions of a man returning to his home which is being inhabited by strangers. These gaudy youths were going to Palestine as citizens, while I, I was the foreigner.

At night—our last before docking at Jaffa—I couldn't sleep. I paced the deck, for hours it seemed. But I couldn't rid myself of this gnawing feeling of apprehension. The sky, I recall, was clear, dappled with innumerable stars. Everything seemed asleep, except myself. I went below, only to return a moment later. And then suddenly the darkness began to dissolve, slowly the east became tinged with red and gold. Soon my wife was on deck, in the company of our Russian acquaintance. Now a black streak began to loom on the eastern horizon, gradually increasing in size as we approached it. The port of Jaffa! Small houses began to crop up out of nowhere. By this time the deck was buzzing with people, scurrying about, packing their trunks. A dozen small boats surrounded our ship, and from them scores of sailors leaped on our vessel like so many jackanapes. They pounced upon our valises, and before we knew it we were being rowed towards shore to the hoarse strains of the oarsmen. Fifteen minutes later I was standing on the sacred ground.

A Jew approached me and asked—in what language I don't remember—if I was seeking a Jewish hotel. I nodded and we followed.

I had been in the hotel for ten minutes or so, when I sensed that my feeling of anxiety had vanished. The hotel wasn't different from the usual run of Jewish inns, except that it was impeccably clean. The proprietor, a simple Russian Jew with a blank face, greeted me in Hebrew, but when I replied in the same language he was startled. Upon hearing my name his face broke out into reverence and amiability. He told me that he had read my "Letters from Paris" which were printed in the *Havatseleth*. Upon learning that the publisher of the journal was at his home in Jerusalem, I asked the proprietor to wire him that I would see him the following day.

After breakfast the three of us took a stroll through the city. Jaffa in those days was inhabited almost entirely by Arabs. We did see several Jewish faces, however, peeping out of small tailor shops. Some Jews were seated behind small tables upon which were piled coins and bills of all sizes and shapes. I approached one of them and had my francs exchanged for Palestinian currency. It was my first transaction in that land, and it was carried on in Hebrew.

After lunch we reserved three seats in the coaches that were leaving for Jerusalem that very evening. There were no trains of course, and each evening saw a caravan of horses and wagons filing out of Jaffa for the overnight trek to Jerusalem.

I can well remember the long orange groves that lined both sides of the road, and our driver, Hayyim Jacob, a small lean Jewish youth of about twenty-five. After a short distance he turned around to inform us, in French, that we were coming to the agricultural school. Mikveh Israel. When I asked him how it was that he knew French, he replied that he was a student at Mikveh Israel. Did he know Hebrew? Some, was the reply. We started to converse in Hebrew and, to my extreme delight, he was quite fluent. Since then whenever I had to travel between Jaffa and Jerusalem I always made an effort to ride with him, while he in turn used to pride himself on being my "official chauffeur." And not long ago, when the Jewish Carriers' Club was honoring its oldest member, Hayyim Jacob, I received a special invitation to the festivities.

Upon getting out of the coach at Jerusalem the next morning, I was greeted by two men who had been sent by Israel Dov, the publisher of the *Havatseleth*. We parted with our Russian friend and went along with these two men.

It is very difficult for anyone now to appreciate how deserted and forlorn were the streets of Jerusalem in those days. The streets were lined with small dingy huts, with long-dilapidated structures, or with grimy stores having large holes for doors. Here and there I spotted someone hammering in a nail.

How uninspiring reality can often be in comparison with one's glowing expectations! When our guides informed us that we were passing by the Tower of David I was unmoved. Why? I don't know. It was like walking through any other town.

When my wife and I entered the home of Reb Dov we found him engrossed in morning prayer. Upon seeing us he removed his phylacteries, welcomed us kindly, and immediately invited us to spend the high holidays with him. His wife, however, who put in her appearance with her four children, felt it was her urgent duty to reprove my wife for not having her head covered with a shawl like all married women in Jerusalem. My wife wasn't offended in the least and quickly covered her head.

After breakfast Reb Dov took me aside and offered me four dollars a month to assist him in editing his journal. After the holidays, he said, he was planning an extended trip through Russia and other countries in search of new subscribers and, of course, new subscribers will mean an increase in salary. I accepted readily—the lure of working on a national Hebrew journal was too much for me. And on Friday, October 5, 1881, my first editorial appeared in the *Havatseleth,* and it was directed against the Alliance Israelite Universelle for opposing Russian and Rumanian migrations into Palestine.

On Saturday we called on Jehiel Pines, the representative of the Montefiore Memorial Foundation whose aim it was to establish charitable institutions in Palestine. When Reb Dov got wind of my visit to Pines, he was quite vexed. They had been opponents for some time. Reb Dov claimed that the Englishman was opposed to public education and enlightenment, and so it went. I was aware of the squabble between the two, but I went nevertheless. After all, Pines did represent English Jewry.

The visit was very formal. I recall that Madame Pines expressed her astonishment at "two such young people, and not hasidim at all, leaving Europe for Palestine. What can you do here?" I was speechless. Luckily Reb Jehiel interrupted by extending us an invitation to be his guests the latter days of the holiday season. We accepted gladly.

Sometime afterwards I received an unexpected invitation from the Russian consul to call on him. It seems that our Russian acquaintance had spoken to him about me. He welcomed me graciously and we chatted for an half hour or so. I found him to be scholarly and liberal. He spoke very sympathetically of the Jews, and promised to help me whenever he could. I left him in high spirits.

It took me a week to grow accustomed to the fact that I was actually in Palestine, the land where my fathers had once lived and died. What a wonderful feeling! To tread the same ground, to stare at the same skies, and to breathe the same air.

The Feast of Tabernacles came along, which meant a respite from my work on the *Havatseleth*. Reb Dov, also, was free, and so we spent a good part of the holiday week discussing all sorts of questions. There were thirty thousand Jews in Palestine, we concluded, with over a half of that number living in Jerusalem. They did not speak a common tongue, but each one spoke the language of the country from which he had emigrated. And the strangest thing of all was the fact that the Ashkenazim, the Jews who had come from countries of Eastern Europe, did not work at all, but depended for their livelihood on the good graces of the *halukka,* while they spent their time studying the Talmud. On the other hand the Sephardim, Jews of Spanish origin, were diligent, hard-working souls. In Jerusalem at that time there were three or four large Jewish synagogues and two small hospitals. We chatted about Rachel's Grave on the road to Hebron and about the agricultural school of Mikveh Israel near Jaffa, which the Turkish government had given to the Alliance for a hundred years. And then of course there were Sir Moses Montefiore's orange groves and the Petach Tikva colony which Jews of Jerusalem had bought three years previous.

But Jerusalem was a Jewish city, everything considered. Shops were closed on Saturdays and holidays, though I confess that the sight of closed shops on Saturday never inspired me with exultation.

I don't remember whether we touched upon Arab-Jewish relations. One thing was clear, however: the Mohammedan Arabs were not our enemies, but they did look down upon us as a sorry lot of weaklings who couldn't defend themselves.

The first two days of the Feast of Tabernacles brought many visitors to Reb Dov's, and invariably it was the Sephardim who made the best impression. They were usually well-groomed and conversed in fluent Hebrew, whereas the Ashkenazim were shabbily dressed and spoke in Yiddish. Only the more elderly of the Eastern European Jews seemed to have succeeded in wiping the gloom of the Exile off their faces, and this because they had had occasion to mingle with the Sephardim.

On the third day of the holiday Reb Dov and I paid a visit to Rabbi Raphael Meir Panizil, Chief Rabbi of Palestine, the "First of Zion" as he was referred to by the Jews. Though not the greatest of scholars, he nevertheless impressed me profoundly. He could easily have passed for one of the patriarchs of old. He was tall, erect, with a wrinkled face and a well-trimmed beard. He wore a long glittering robe, a silver necklace, and a resplendent silken hat. Everything in his house seemed to sparkle, including the doorman who stood erect, with a sword hanging at his side. I thought of Jacob's last words to his children: "The scepter shall not depart from Judah."

On the eve of Hoshana Rabba my wife and I called on Reb Jehiel as we had promised, and that evening in 1881 was destined to be one of the most significant that I spent in Palestine. After a lavish dinner Reb Jehiel and I began to discuss the Hebrew language and, in what to me will always remain a sacred moment, we dedicated ourselves to the task of making Hebrew the national tongue. Though afterwards Reb Jehiel didn't adhere to the compact as faithfully as he might have done, nevertheless it can be truthfully said that his house was the cradle of modern living Hebrew.

That same week we rented a small place for ourselves and left our temporary lodgings at Reb Dov's. Ours was a small dark house close by the Temple Mount, and it overlooked the ruins of what no doubt once had been stores and shops. We had two rooms which one reached by a narrow ladder from the yard below. Adjoining our rooms was a single room, occupied by a Sephardic family who, though destitute, managed somehow to keep the room immaculate.

Wanting to look every inch the Palestinian, I grew a beard, shed my European clothes for the long mantle and tarboosh, and walked about the town wrapped in a praying shawl and phylacteries. I kept this up until I was convinced that it was pointless.

In the early days I saw no practical way of furthering the cause of

Hebrew, save by conversing in the language with my wife and friends. But that wouldn't suffice. An entire generation would have to speak it, but what could I do to hasten the coming of a new generation?

There is a saying to the effect that help often comes from unexpected places. Well, it did come, and from an unexpected place. It was a rainy day in December. A man entered the house, introduced himself in Hebrew as Reb Nissim Behar, a representative of the Alliance. He had been empowered to open a school for boys in Jerusalem. He wanted to know if I would accept a post as teacher. I refused blandly, adding that I would consider it only on one condition—if I were permitted to teach in Hebrew.

"Yes," he exclaimed, "that is precisely why I came to you."

I was overjoyed, though the salary was meager—fifty francs a month for six hours of teaching a day. It was small remuneration indeed, but later I discovered that his organization had made no provisions for a Hebrew teacher at all. They had set aside two hundred francs a month for two instructors in religion, but Reb Nissim Behar had secretly expropriated twenty-five francs from each instructor's wage in order to hire a Hebrew teacher. And that is how it all began.

I became a full-fledged citizen of Jerusalem, having adopted the name of Ben Yehuda, son of Judah. This dropping of my European surname— an uncommon deed then—signified for me the severing of all connections with my European existence. I feared, however, that some of my friends would persist in calling me by my old name. They would come in:

"Tell me, sir, what is your surname?"

"Ben Yehuda!" I would reply curtly.

"Yes, Ben Yehuda, but that's the name you invented when you came to Palestine. Like a pen name. What is your real surname?"

But by this time I had my Turkish birth certificate out, and all talk ceased.

The rebirth of Hebrew and of the Jewish people in Palestine—what a beautiful dream! Once in Palestine, I realized that like all dreams this one could not simply be wished into existence. The leaders of the Ashkenazim vehemently opposed all agricultural settlements and any idea of a national revival. It is true that a group of them had once bought a small plot of ground with the express purpose of settling on it and raising crops. But this was an isolated instance and did in no wise shake their leaders' stubborn opposition.

Even Reb Dov and Rev Jehiel weren't as enthusiastic about a national Jewish homeland as I thought they would be. Reb Dov was too much the hasid to become aroused over such vulgarities as hewing rock and tilling soil, while Reb Jehiel Pines was by nature fonder of dabbling in religious and social trivialities than in attaching himself to such a tremendous undertaking as the upbuilding of Palestine.

But there were also many who sided with me. There was Herzberg, for example, author of the popular *Familienpapieren,* who, though ignorant of Hebrew and Hebrew literature, yet concurred with my beliefs. I mustn't forget Reb Nissim Becker, but he was unfortunately often hampered by the wishes of the Alliance whom he represented.

Dire events abroad, pogroms in Russia and Rumania, soon began to bring Jews by the hundreds to the port of Jaffa. And thus was initiated the renascence of the Jewish homeland in Palestine. And as I stand now looking across a gulf of years, I keep marveling at the fact that all of this came to pass during the limited space of one generation.

MY LIFE IN SAN FRANCISCO

REBEKAH KOHUT (1864-   )

A critic has suggested that Rebekah Kohut's memoirs may be regarded as the modern counterpart of those of Glückel of Hameln. Certainly they are lively, candid, feminine; and they portray a chunk of American life that is alive mainly in the memories of old timers. Another extraordinary contemporary, Henrietta Szold, in the preface to the memoirs, wrote as follows: "Not only have we the first American-Jewish autobiography by a woman past her thirtieth year, with experience and achievement to lean upon, but we have mellow influences to deal with instead of the harsh, callous grind of a mechanized life. Mrs. Kohut's American roots reach down through the 1880's and 1870's to the generation that followed the Civil War. The South in which she spent her early American years was not so stricken but that the chivalrous traditions of a more prosperous past softened the asperities of impoverished and frugal households. And her California period palpitated with pioneering memories. The Richmond and the San Francisco of Mrs. Kohut's formative period bear little resemblance to the Boston and the New York of the East European little Jewish girl."

✻ ✻ ✻

MY father entered into a second marriage because he was unable to occupy himself with the cares of the household. Within a few years, however, the new wife, too, became an invalid, and it had to be with the assistance of the "little mother" of the household, my sister Esther, that we were carefully reared until we reached the age of self-help.

Arduous burdens, a small salary, congregational cares, home duties—these might have been enough to weigh heavily and affect my father's fine nature. Yet they didn't. He remained as active and alert as ever. He had amazing energy, a marvelous capacity for diversified interests, a great love of humanity as a whole and individually. And in the family he combined the father's authoritativeness with a mother's tenderness. In the outer world, however, he had no will to advance his personal and material interests.

A scholar, possessing all the potentialities for literary achievement, he left behind brilliant fragments, interesting monographs on medicine, threequarters of a revised American Bible, but no great, complete, unified memorial of scholarship. He had the scholar's mind without the scholar's aloofness. The door to his study room never remained shut for long. There were too many conflicting demands upon his time and energy. Many of them he could have ignored, but he loved human contacts and was happiest when he was helping others.

Such talents as he possessed he could not commercialize. If he wrote for newspapers, as he frequently did, it was because of his interest in the subject, not for the possible remuneration.

It was the same with medicine. His object in studying it was not an eventual prosperous practice, but to make himself like one of the healers of old. He wanted to minister to the poor. His rabbinical charge, he felt, was something more than presiding over ritual and preparing a sermon. But his congregation did not see eye to eye with him on this. They objected to his medical and literary activities, and to his plans for the education of children. Putting through an educational program was always a struggle.

A rabbi's life was no sinecure. To his family it was an especial trial. You never knew when you would be called upon to uproot yourself and move elsewhere. The rabbinate was not so stable as it is today. The trouble lay mostly with the "business" side of congregations, which were largely interested in drawing worshippers from other congregations. In this they expected help from the rabbis. My father could not bring himself to it; it was extremely distasteful to him. Once his flock even met in secret to consider asking for his resignation because of a heinous offense of which he had been guilty. The father of one of his wealthy congregants had belonged to another synagogue. When he died, his son left our congregation to join his father's, and my father approved. A serious matter. Congregants were few, each one counted.

A pall usually settled upon our family in the summer when the renting of congregational pews began and it was learned that some family had decided to worship elsewhere. But my father loved human beings whether they worshipped at his synagogue or not, and he cherished theories which were not conducive to prosperity. Here may be the appropriate place to tell that a well-known artist in Richmond painted my father as Jesus.

Today many rabbis are elected to their posts for life. But in the 1870's the rabbis might have been classified as floating population. It was difficult to keep track of the wanderings of some of them. Only a few Jewish communities were large enough to build temples and offer stable, inviting opportunities for capable men.

The state of California was at its period of greatest romantic appeal, and the glamor of the Golden Gate, radiating over the entire country, touched my father, too. The West allured with the many tales of the land flowing with milk and honey. To be a pioneer, or almost a pioneer, was a pleasing thought. He saw as his own duty in such a world not the hewing of roads and the building of houses for people to dwell in, but the building of a spiritual house in which souls might dwell. His thoughts of California were induced by a venturesome spirit rather than by a restless nature. So, when simultaneous calls came from congregations in Hartford and San Francisco, he chose the latter. After seven years in the dear old city of Richmond, he pulled up stakes and with high hopes turned his face west. He left several months in advance of the rest of the family to prepare our new home for us.

In the early autumn of 1875 we bade farewell to Richmond. At that time it took ten days to cross the continent—ten days in a railroad train! Our party almost filled one coach, as we were accompanied by a bridal couple and two boys whose parent had entrusted them to our custody. There was no dining-car service, so we were obliged to carry along our own food. The members of the congregation had donated huge hampers filled with foodstuffs, and at each stop we hurried off the train for hot coffee. How we ever escaped spells of indigestion is a mystery.

The journey was enlivened by our anticipations and fears. In the imaginations of the boys and girls of that decade the place of the "movies" was taken by harrowing tales of Indian warfare. The tribes were resentful over the many new railway lines that cut through their stamping-grounds. It was a year before the Custer massacre. As our train left the East, my brothers, at each curve of the track, expected to see Indians. As a matter of fact their apprehensions came true; on two different occasions Indians discharged arrows at the train—probably a gesture of resentment rather than a desire to do definite harm. Yet the act had its effect upon us. I was convinced that the Indians were as ferocious as I had been told. Later my notions were upset in a distressing manner. I was left without my perfected design of the universe when we found other Indians peacefully selling beads at Cheyenne and other stations.

The little house on Larkin Street, which had been furnished us by the congregation, seemed palatial. In delight and wonder we began our acquaintance with the city which only a few years before had been El Dorado.

San Francisco afforded the most vivid contrasts. Half of the city was still sandhills; other districts gave all the appearance of a well-built city, conscious of itself and anxious to appear to good advantage. It was the most cosmopolitan city of America. One could see members of almost every nationality on the streets. It presented the curious anomaly of crudity and sophistication, of rough free-handedness and an attempt at culture. Chinatown was squalid and Barbary Coast sinister, but San Franciscans preferred that attention be given their art galleries and libraries, their flourishing social and literary clubs, and their public school system, which ranked third in the United States.

Though only the shadow of the fever of '49 remained, placer mining was still attracting prospectors from the East. The day of the orange grove was beginning. At California seaports the wooden sidewheeler had given way to iron and steel propeller vessels, the *Colima* being the first of the new steamships to be launched by the Pacific Mail Company.

A young city, San Francisco already had tradition. The '49 rush and the period of the Vigilantes had gone into history, and native historians were vying with one another to chronicle those times. The men who had participated in the gold epic and who had emerged triumphant were ensconced in magnificent mansions upon the heights, and engaged in the business of acquiring dignity and tradition. Those who were not as fortunate adjusted themselves to the commercial life of the new city or went under. Such stories as were told!

Amazement and delight were my first reactions to California. Almost everyone carried flowers. Almost every house, however rude and humble, was decorated with flowers. The glory of Richmond was in her magnificent trees and her rosebushes; in San Francisco one's eye met floral beauty in every form, without the wonder of it ever palling. The variety of California flowers, the profusion of them, the people's appreciation of them, colored life gloriously. The calla lilies grew in great hedges around the homes of the humblest, and covered the ugliness of wooden fences. Geraniums and heliotrope, vine-trained, were used to hide the rough walls of huts.

Our home boasted no garden in front. It seemed almost a symbol of poverty that no flowers grew about the place. But there were always plenty inside the house, and always enough to take in bouquets to our teachers.

The diversity of weather in San Francisco made an immediate impression upon our young souls. In the course of one day we experienced not four seasons but six. It was some little time before we grew accustomed to the various motifs; before we took it for granted that winter would express itself through cold winds in the afternoon; that this would be followed by the heavy fogs which rolled in from the bay and made traffic difficult; that these would roll away and give us clear starry nights which made us glad we were alive.

My father immediately became an active member of the community. He wrote for *The San Francisco Call, The Chronicle, The Argonaut;* became identified with prison reform and the anti-vice crusade; organized a society for the study of Hebrew by Christian clergymen. Several times he was asked whether he would serve on the board of education, but he felt his hands were already too full. He was still interested in medicine, and had just taken up service in a new congregation. But above all he was occupied with his Hebrew studies. He was working upon a revised English version of the Bible, and was in regular correspondence with the great scholars of Europe and America.

Our home was the gathering place of an interesting group. All sorts of people came to us, among them many striking personalities. Michael Reese, who had been a resident of Richmond and later left $200,000 for the construction of the Michael Reese Hospital in Chicago, was a frequent visitor, though he had the reputation in his lifetime of being a recluse. Miss Apponyi, a California member of the famous Hungarian family of that name, exchanged memories of Hungary with us. John Swett, superintendent of public schools and one of the original Forty-Niners, became a dear family friend. Toby E. Rosenthal, afterward one of the most distinguished Californian painters, received at our home encouragement which was instrumental in making possible his first trip to the studios of Europe. Adolph Sutro was frequently in the Larkin Street house. Sutro was a name to conjure with in San Francisco in the seventies and eighties. Who did not know of Sutro, of Sutro's Gardens and Sutro's Baths, of "Mount Parnassus" and the famous Cliff House? He collected a magnificent library of rare books and precious manuscripts and decided to donate the library to the city and provide a building to house it. His visits to our home were for the purpose of consulting my father about various Oriental and Semitic manuscripts.

An intimate clerical friend was the Rev. Dr. Guard, whose son, William J. Guard, is the best-loved official of the Metropolitan Opera House.

Shortly after our arrival in San Francisco, Isaac M. Wise came to the city in behalf of the Union of American Hebrew Congregations. He became not only our guest but my father's inseparable companion during his stay, and we children got to adore him. This great man, who so thoroughly imposed his personality upon American Judaism, was a delightful talker and full of fun. Dignity and command were his, but not austerity. He encouraged us to be intimate with him. And our ease in his presence was in delightful contrast with the solemn reverence we had been taught to show our elders. In Richmond he had fascinated us by relating many of the incidents of the war that he had witnessed, and of his various pilgrimages to the great Lincoln. His time and efforts had been spent in behalf of Jewish soldiers, though he had emerged from the civil conflict more American, perhaps, than many of the descendants of the Mayflower passengers. Only a man of his striking personality could have so large a following as his. As almost mere babies, I recall, we responded to the magnetism of the man. We liked to hear him talk, and to look at his wide expanse of brow, and his head which was so huge for his body, and the eternal spectacles perched upon his forehead, and worn under his hat. (Even in photographs the spectacles appear upon his forehead.) His sermons, as we heard them in later years, were given in an almost conversational style and at once drew his hearers into intimate relationship with him.

The remarkable thing about the relation between Isaac M. Wise and my father was that they remained close friends in spite of the differences in their attitude towards Reform and Orthodox Judaism. The conflict between Reform and Orthodoxy concerned itself chiefly with changes in the Jewish liturgy and the ceremonials of the synagogue and the home. The reformer shortened the public service by the excision of the prayers dealing with the ancient sacrificial service and its restoration in a rebuilt Temple on Zion. He favored the use of the vernacular almost to the exclusion of the Hebrew language in public and private worship. He introduced the organ into the synagogue, and abolished the women's gallery and the separation of the sexes during the hours of worship. In general, he showed little mercy to customs and festive and mournful commemoration days based upon the rabbinical tradition in contradistinction to the biblical law. But, repudiating the rabbinical institutions, he came to lay less and less stress on the dietary laws, even though they were rooted in the Mosaic law. The most radical went so far as to advocate the transfer of the seventh-day Sabbath to Sunday. Thus Reform cut deep into the heart of Jewish life, and not rarely caused enmity between brothers and friends. It is therefore noteworthy that the friendship persisted between my father and Dr. Wise, who was one of the extreme Reformers.

During our first days in California we children entertained the fallacy that we were rich. This was because of the currency. The huge silver dollars in which our father's salary was paid, gave to our youthful imagination an impression of correspondingly huge purchasing power. Rattling in his pockets, they sounded like the mint or a declaration of dividends. The mere sight of the mountainous pile lying in the upper bureau drawer was enough to make us enthusiastic about the rabbinate, given such gingerly recognition in Richmond and such liberal recognition in San Francisco.

When the Rabbi's dollars left the house, however; when they careered along under the wooden sidewalks with the market basket, or fell under the assaults of the clothier or bookseller, they seemed to go into some shark's mouth, like minnows, without putting up any sort of a fight, without even first having made an impression.

We were poor. The five girls and two boys in our home insisted upon growing bigger and bigger every day. Dresses passed from larger to smaller children, in the transition acquiring patches and other marks of service. But we were not to be so conscious of our secondhand clothing and patched shoes as of our secondhand school books. Childish pride told us we should be able to purchase new textbooks like other pupils, not used volumes which advertised our poverty. My over-sensitiveness in this regard caused me intense suffering as a young girl.

Almost everybody except ourselves seemed to be enjoying wealth. What was wealth? The power to buy new school books and ride to school instead of trudging blocks and blocks and climbing hills in the rain; the power to own a dress which was not handed down from sister to sister; the power to take lessons and go on picnics. The life story of any dress in our family could be divided into five chapters, each chapter headed with one of the five sisters' names. How often we wanted the story suppressed, or discontinued after the first chapter; but circumstances insisted upon spinning out the tale to its conclusion.

Although our poverty and shabbiness made no difference socially, since we were the Rabbi's children, yet my sisters and I were really unhappy. We blamed the congregation. We felt it stood between us and contentment. There was such a marked contrast between what, to our mind, was a rare human being and the compensation that was granted him. The root of the trouble was that San Francisco had too many congregations, and none of them thrived. This also had a bad spiritual effect. On account of the unhealthy rivalry among the congregations, they were more concerned with membership drives than with higher values. My father, so much a man of warm human contacts, was sickened by the petty competition, and chose lay associates rather than the company of local rabbis.

My brother and I often spoke of the situation, and in our adolescent way we expressed very decided views not only as to Jews and Judaism but as to rabbis as well. We did not see the other side of the picture. These groups were having their own struggles. Only inherent love for the faith kept the congregations alive. We did not realize, either, the common tendency of the heterogeneous groups—among Jews as well as among Christians—to consort with others of their own temperament and identity of origin. Just as in Richmond there were the Polish, Sephardic (Spanish-Jewish) and Ashkenazic (German-Jewish) congregations among the Jews, so in San Francisco, to an even larger extent, people divided themselves into groups according to their European backgrounds.

My younger brother, Felix, was enrolled in the University of California. As between medicine and the rabbinate, he had chosen the former for his future career. His father's wish was that the boy prepare himself to be his successor, but Felix did not feel the spiritual call strongly. His impatience with the congregations was transmuted into antagonism against the ministerial service. To his mind his father was not appreciated. The boy did not realize that this was of less moment to his parent than to himself.

As my brother and I walked the hills of San Francisco to our respective schools, we formulated the platforms for our future, and one of the important planks was: No poverty. We were thus running counter to one of the family's pet obsessions. Its members waxed sentimental about poverty, about its enobling virtues, about the wicked rich and the good poor. It was my habit to argue, in rebuttal, that the rich were not always wicked, nor the poor always good.

For every person who comes unscathed through poverty, there are a dozen others upon whom it places its mark; whose spirit it crushes, and whose outlook it warps, leaving them twisted, unhappy, embittered creatures. And so for myself I decided against poverty. I hate it because it is the most deadly enemy of all—the parent of vice, ignorance, mendacity, crime.

And yet I have been poor a large part of my life.

Father's study was in the basement of the house. On pine shelving from ceiling to floor fitted against each wall stood his books in Hebrew, German, English, Sanskrit, Persian, Arabic, books on all subjects, medical as well, arranged in orderly rows like captains, corporals and privates, standing at attention. The long table was piled with newspapers and open volumes, evidence of the owner's constant association with literary and scientific research. My father did not require the quiet of the cloister for his studies; he could concentrate upon his work with half a dozen of us about, and he allowed us to use his room for our study room also. He encouraged us, in fact, to browse there all we liked, and never labeled certain books as forbidden fruit. Excellent modern psychology that for one of his generation.

We soon learned how to use the reference books, but always supplemented our information by interrogating father, who was glad to help us. His methods of teaching, however, were often at variance with current school methods. Nevertheless our teachers had great respect for us because there was someone at home who took such pains to prepare us for our school work.

And the preparation of our school lessons was a joy, certainly by contrast with our practicing on the piano. For despite our limited means, we were given musical instruction, the belief having then prevailed— does it exist today?—that no young woman could be considered cultivated and refined unless she could play the piano. Tedium, thy name is piano practice. I, for one, absorbed this sort of refinement under protest.

The library became the meeting-place of the family. For me it served the purpose of the drawing room in a mansion. It was the one place to which I brought my friends, as it was the one place where poverty was not in evidence. One might judge from it that we were both rich and wise. I enjoyed the snobbery of it.

It was not long after we were established in San Francisco that I began to broaden my worldly knowledge by eagerly reading the periodicals, dailies, weeklies, monthlies, religious and secular. But my reading had all to be saved up for Saturday and Sunday, the weekdays being taken up with school studies. So how to get the most out of Saturdays and Sundays became a problem. I had to appear at the Temple Saturday mornings; then I was pressed into service to teach religious school, at which pupils were only one or two years younger than myself. And there was so much that I wanted to read, so many things about town that I wanted to see. For instance, there was the sensation of the moment, Dennis Kearney, the sand-lot agitator, the demagogic spouter who sought prominence by, among other things, pronouncing himself the friend of the workingman and inveighing in thunderous tones against the Chinese. Every speech of his closed with "The Chinese must go," a slogan suggested to him by a newspaper acquaintance. My brother and I, having heard of the crowds that packed his tent to cheer his war-cry and curious to know what it was all about, went to his meetings on Saturday mornings before attending the Sabbath services. My father, strongly against such appeals to the baser passions of the mob, would have rebuked us sternly had he learned of our presence at the sand-lot meetings.

It was my dissatisfaction with the congregation and my duties toward it that brought me, by not altogether pleasant ways, more leisure to read and improve my knowledge. During divine service on the Sabbath, instead of following the prayers, I read the Bible, and at Sunday-school instead of teaching catechism, I used what I liked from the Bible as the subject matter for instruction. The catechism was the only teaching manual allowed Sunday-school teachers in those days, and one morning, when the chairman of the school board visited the classroom he was surprised to hear me telling the story of Ruth.

"Why are you not teaching the catechism?" he demanded.

Hotly, disrespectfully, I replied: "I teach what I please."

When he left the room I realized that my father might be an innocent sufferer from my outburst, and went home heavy-hearted. Surely enough, he was called to account for neglect of the Sabbath School, and I was dismissed. Of course, I was fearfully sorry and repentant that my father should have been involved. Yet the bit of leisure was a great joy, and one of the direct results was an enlarged knowledge of American history, in some respects also revised knowledge; for San Francisco's version of the Civil War differed widely from Richmond's. Between the two influences, the Union finally dominated in my receptive mind, despite my mother's continued bitterness. The San Francisco schools and a performance of *Uncle Tom's Cabin* made me an ardent believer in the righteousness of the Union cause.

Imagine, therefore, my excitement when I was selected as the representative of my class to shake hands with General Grant, the Union's military genius, at a reception to him in Mechanic Pavilion, in which the school children participated—the supreme honor. And I hurried home breathless with the news, forgetting for the moment my mother's intense antagonism.

"Go upstairs and wash that hand," the little rebel mother remarked grimly. But—in 1920 my mother cast her vote for the Republican Party, the party of Lincoln and Grant.

Friday nights at home were devoted to singing and story-telling. Forgotten were the little cares of the week. My father would have us be like a guild of singers, with himself as choirmaster. There was nothing he liked better than to direct the chorus and hear the hearty outpouring of our voices. He himself contributed a baritone of considerable volume, and among the girls it was the rich contralto of my sister Minnie that sounded best. After the singing my father's talents as a story-teller were called into play. He never failed to delight us, and we could listen to the same thing over and over again. Several of the tales he told us were published in *The Argonaut* and received high commendation for their interesting subject matter and charming style. Our favorite was the one he called *The Man With The Marble Heart.*

It must not be imagined that we were a closed family circle on Friday evenings and Saturdays. On the contrary. My father, with his big, expansive nature, believed in sociability, and wanted us to broaden our outlook through having many friends. The family's meagre purse did not prevent our entertaining a great many people. My father would have been unhappy had he not been able to act as host. Every year, at the Passover festival, he had us invite our friends and teachers to our home for the first two evenings of celebration, the Seder services, they are called. They were memorable evenings. Usually there were about forty or fifty guests, a great many of whom were Christians.

Once I asked my father why he invited Christians.

"To let people see that we have no secrets," was his reply. "You can be made to believe fantastic things about people when you do not know them. But when you know, you cannot be misled. So many lies are manufactured about us—especially in regard to Passover—and they gain credence among the unthinking and the ignorant. But those who know us will see that these are lies. Throw open the doors and let people view us as we are. In this way we dissolve antipathies and make friendships, and when efforts are made to defame us, we will have friends who will champion the truth."

This was his policy throughout his life. The individual friendships contributed to the general good of his people. But his valuable work along these lines did not always receive appreciation from people of his own religion. Men who preached clannishness and exclusiveness were not wanting in Israel, and they were ever quick in their blind demagoguery to attack him for his friendships with Catholics and Protestants.

Not only was he attacked for the good work he was doing; narrowness went even further. In some mid-western city—Cleveland, I believe—there was a converted clergyman named Bettelheim. By some strange method of reasoning, certain members of the congregation arrived at the conclusion that my father should be held responsible for the religious beliefs of all the world's inhabitants bearing his name. A meeting was called, and the indignant rabbi subjected some of his narrow-minded congregants to a severe flaying which they did not forget for some time, and which cleared the air permanently.

My father and his "Christian" relative became good friends through correspondence and exchange of photographs, and very recently I learned that it has been suggested to establish a memorial to him as the first Protestant missionary to China.

Across the street from the Temple was a bakery. The baker's son, Julius Kahn, was my brother Felix's intimate friend, and visited us frequently. He became one of my father's favorites. Julius Kahn's ambition was to be an actor, and he undertook earnest study for the stage. My father did not discourage him, but said he believed he would advance to a wider stage and do more important work than behind the footlights. In following Julius Kahn's life, we experienced the satisfaction of seeing this prediction come true. The young man was on the stage for several years, then entered political life and was elected to Congress as a representative of California. He became one of the ablest legislators in Washington. His constituency returned him to office again and again, and he was given legislative responsibilities of increased importance. As senior Republican member of the military affairs committee of the House during the Great War, he drafted the bill calling the men of the country to the national service.

Another young San Franciscan of Jewish parentage, destined to become one of the great actors on the American stage and a still greater producer, was beginning a stage career at that time, with the Baldwin Theater Stock Company. My father had known David Belasco's father when David and his brother, who also went in for acting, were mere lads, though the family lived at a distance from us, on Howard Street, in a part of San Francisco which, like New York's East Side, has produced some of the best human material. I recall the furore when the Baldwin players were arrested for giving a performance of Salmi Morse's

Passion Play, which Belasco had staged and acted in. Another player in the cast was James O'Neill, famous for his protrayal of the Count of Monte Cristo. Mr. O'Neill died about ten years ago. Had he lived a few years longer he could have enjoyed the sudden ascendance of his son Eugene to a foremost place among American dramatists.

My first year at high school was a period of torment to me. The junior class of high school was located in a building only two blocks away from Chinatown. The proximity to this quarter, then branded as dangerous for young girls, aroused in me a peculiar spirit. I hated everything that made it necessary for me to go near that morbid part of the city. I hated the school, the teachers, the educational system, the hilly streets I had to trudge, while well-to-do friends rode, the rain, the German professor's accent. Poor Professor Sanger! Had he seen some of the notes I indited about him. Poor professor indeed! He was recognized in after years, at the University of California, as one of the greatest educators on the west coast.

School, once a haven, became a prison to me. Ordered one day in the history class to prepare a composition upon any subject I pleased, I chose, in a spirit of sheer recklessness, to write a sarcastic essay on the unsuitableness of the school building, the unfitness of the teachers, and the incompetence of the board of education. The essay shocked the teachers and was transmitted to the principal of the high school, who happened to be my father's friend, John Swett.

"The style is good," he commented, amusedly. "Which shows that the teaching isn't so bad." Then he disciplined me by expelling me from the history classes for the rest of the term. Father taught me history at home.

It was a critical time for me. I was not naturally rebellious, but everything in the educational scheme seemed especially designed to irritate me. And there was no understanding teacher or friend at school who brought out the best in me, no one to command my respect or reverence.

The second year at high school, however, saw a momentous change. In a different building, located in a different section, I breathed more freely. The teachers seemed better, the subjects more interesting. Fled was the morbidity induced by the nearness of Chinatown with its frowsy white women sitting at the windows of Chinese homes.

What had the greatest effect upon me was my friendship with the class teacher, Caroline Lora Hunt. No teacher before had given me sympathetic understanding. Hers was the influence I needed.

There were two things that had brought us together; on her part interest in Jews and Jewish history, on my part the autograph craze. Miss Hunt directed our after-school reading and formed her pupils into a literary club to which we contributed weekly for the purchase of books. At the end of the term the books were distributed, and as a special mark of personal interest in me, she sent a copy of *The House of the Seven Gables* to Hawthorne, whose cousin she was, with the request that he inscribe it for me. Needless to say, I prize the copy among my most precious possessions.

Miss Hunt was small and stout, with lovely blue eyes. In the days of Montague curls, kept flat on the forehead with bandoline, she wore her mass of hair brushed straight back. Altogether her appearance and manner were simple, and her gentleness, especially, contrasted markedly with the ways of one of my teachers at the other school. She had, too, a sparkling sense of humor and a fund of anecdote about her Puritan ancestors that was both interesting and instructive.

Without any apparent effort, she called out the best that was in me. Her inspiration caused rapid strides in my development. My knowledge and capacities increased, my sympathies broadened and deepened. Altogether, I was transformed from the sarcastic faultfinder of the year before.

When I think of my adolescent adoration of Miss Hunt, I am not inclined to laugh at myself. She was truly a rare human being, worthy of anyone's admiration. Of course, loverlike manifestations are always funny. I used to walk up and down the street in hope of catching a glimpse of her, and saved up pennies to buy her flowers, and often, after sitting up all night making poultices for my sick mother and going to school discouraged and depressed, it needed but a nod of recognition from her to buoy me up and the merry twinkle in her eye to carry me happily through the day.

She was the cousin of another famous writer, Helen Hunt Jackson, author of *Ramona,* and took me along on her visits to her. Like Bret Harte, Helen Hunt Jackson was a venerated name in the west, because of her paeans to the Rockies and her popular novels about California. At that time she was an invalid and had chosen to spend her last days among the hills and wild flowers near the Golden Gate. It was in a spirit of awe and reverence that I accompanied Miss Hunt to the novelist's home, and with joy that I received a copy of *Ramona* with her autograph.

Miss Hunt's interest in me and my family led to her meeting my father and taking up the study of Jewish history under his guidance. She also came to one of our Seder services.

Another fine influence in those days was my friendship with my classmate, Emma Wolf, later a brilliant authoress noted particularly for her story, *Other Things Being Equal*. She and I used to roam the sand-hills together on botany excursions.

Botany was in our curriculum. Is music in the curriculum for larks? How could one live in California and not become a botanist? Saturday afternoons and Sundays we went over the hills of Saucelito and San Rafael, yellow poppies around us, carpets of maidenhair ferns under our feet. The sandhills of California! Who can forget them? Mountain high, uninhabited for blocks and blocks, with little oases of wild flowers breaking up their bare, desolate vistas.

One of eight daughters, Emma Wolf, was handicapped from birth by a useless arm, but there was no defect in her mentality. Her memory was the most remarkable I have ever encountered. She could quote with equal facility the texts of long poems or the fatality statistics of each of the world's great battles.

On our walks we hunted for new specimens of flowers, which we took home and mounted. We vied with each other in trying to get together the largest and best collections. I also sketched flowers, which I had learned to do not from an urge to artistic creativeness, but from mere love of beauty. Those walks, indeed, did a great deal to stimulate our sense of beauty.

But what meant most of all to me, perhaps, in those impressionable days of adolescence, was the exchange of innermost thoughts with my classmate. I had begun to doubt the worthwhileness of all the sacrifices it seemed to me that my father and his family were making for Judaism. What was the use of it all, I questioned. Why make a stand for separate Jewish ideals? Why not choose the easier way and be like all the rest? The struggle was too hard, too bitter.

Emma Wolf was undergoing much the same inner conflict. It meant real suffering to both of us. The spiritual growing pains of adolescence are hard to bear. They cannot be laughed out of existence.

THE ANARCHIST IDEAL

ABRAHAM FRUMKIN (1873-1940)

Frumkin narrates those experiences that lifted him out of a home of traditional atmosphere in Palestine into the feverish anarchist circles of the Jewish labor movement. His father, Israel Dob Frumkin, who had settled in the Holy Land in 1860, was the editor of a number of early Hebrew periodicals. He had incurred the disfavor of the rabbis by criticizing certain philanthropic institutions, and for some time he was placed under a ban. Frumkin's first literary efforts were in the Hebrew tongue. Won over to the labor movement, he became a prominent Yiddish editor and publicist, with activities centering chiefly in Constantinople, London, and finally in New York City. It is a little-known world that he portrays in these absorbing memoirs, a world, however, which left its impress on thousands of immigrants whose children and grandchildren are now influential members of society.

❋ ❋ ❋

BETWEEN the years of 1893 and 1895 my youthful life passed through a tremendous transition. The change was so thorough and fundamental that I could easily designate it as my second birth. I truly felt myself reborn. Whatever the antecedent years had given me—traditional Judaism, national sentiments, personal ambition—all this vanished and made way for new thoughts and emotions. I was transplanted to a new environment. From its vantage point I saw the world in a fresh light and I judged things by different standards. Thus one day in 1895 I decided to devote the rest of my life to the Anarchist idealogy.

There was another interesting circumstance which marked the beginning of my career as a Yiddish journalist. Prior to that time Hebrew had been the medium of my writing. In December 1895, there appeared my first article in Yiddish, in the London *Arbeiter Freind*.

In order to clarify for myself the contributing factors responsible for my embracing the Anarchist philosophy, I shall have to dwell upon several preceding events.

In the spring of 1891 I left my native country, Palestine, where Jewish colonization had begun to take shape, and traveled to Constantinople. There I intended to study law, in order to make myself useful in Palestine as a lawyer. I was young then and an ardent member of the "Lovers of Zion" (Zionism as such was then hardly known). Before long that dream dissolved in disappointment, for the monthly stipend I was to receive in support from the "Lovers of Zion" group in Haifa, failed to arrive.

In Constantinople fate brought me together with Moishe and Nastia Shapiro, who in later years played a dominant rôle in the life of the Jewish Anarchists in London. Moishe Shapiro was then young and had come from a middle-class family of southern Russia where he had graduated from a scientific institute.

Their home was the rendezvous of the Jewish intellectuals of Constantinople. There Jewish and world problems were properly sifted, and the hungry would find a place for appeasing their hunger, although the Shapiros themselves were often in want.

It was at that time that I met the Zionist propagandist and fiery orator, Joseph Zeff. He exercised a magnetic influence upon everyone with whom he came in contact. Together we founded a club, "Research in the Language of Zion," and a Hebrew school—the first of its kind outside of Palestine—where Hebrew was the language of instruction. After nine months, however, it was closed for lack of funds. I left Constantinople for London, and then for New York.

Both in London, where I stayed for a year, and during the first few months in New York, I was still an adherent of the "Lovers of Zion". But gradually I started to fraternize with Socialists and went to their meetings. Their ideas and argumentation impressed me. In New York then (1893) I met two friends from Constantinople: Ablomuntzew (Abel), an Anarchist, and Hillel Shulman, a Social-Democrat. Each of them tried to win me over to his side. In the process they dragged me to their respective powwows and supplied me with illuminating literature.

In the beginning the Social-Democratic movement appealed to me. I found the Anarchists too noisy. The terroristic acts flaring up in France at that time repelled me. On the other hand, anarchistic writings attracted me. By contrast the social-democratic output lacked warmth.

In Ablomuntzew's supply I discovered a bound volume of the

London *Arbeiter Freind,* which, among other things, contained Yanofsky's editorials written under the pseudonym "Bas Kol". I recall reading and rereading them with intense pleasure. Those editorials undoubtedly contributed to my conversion to Anarchism.

At this time I also met Philip Krantz, editor of the Social-Democratic *Arbeiter Zeitung.* I submitted to him my first story in Yiddish, which he rejected. I met him again on the eve of my return to Constantinople. I was taking along all the anarchist periodicals and brochures I could find in New York; my Social-Democratic literature was then incomplete. I appealed to Krantz for additional material. We went to the office of the *Arbeiter Zeitung,* which was situated on the second floor of 93 Delancey Street. He said to an associate: "This comrade is sailing for Turkey. Give him all the reading matter we can spare!" He gave me a number of bound volumes of the *Arbeiter Zeitung* and of the *Zukunft* and additional brochures. Loaded with this material I sailed at the end of 1894. How I smuggled the contraband past the Turkish customs inspectors is a chapter in itself.

Shapiro fell upon the stuff with rare avidity. Both of us carefully analyzed and discussed it with the result that he, too, began to show sympathy for Anarchism. When we had exhausted the collection, we thirsted for more knowledge. Shapiro packed his bags and traveled to Paris and London, whence he brought back trunks full of books and brochures in French, English, and Russian.

Again we plunged into reading. At Shapiro's home nothing was heard except wranglings about Anarchism and Social-Democracy. Even his eleven-year-old son Sanda, the later well-known comrade Alexander Shapiro, ex-secretary of the Anarchist International, was pouring over the books of Kropotkin and Grav.

In London Shapiro established contact with the Russian group of revolutionaries including Felix Wolchowsky, J. Goldberg, and Simon Cahan, who were living in the London suburb of Hammersmith. Every week they would send us their revolutionary bulletin and we would mail it to Russia concealed in letters. Shapiro also learned that the London Jewish anarchist group was preparing to reissue the organ, *Der Arbeiter Freind.* When the first few issues arrived, we nearly wept for joy. The paper was small, only four pages, and filled with material written in a bald, foreign sort of Yiddish. That day I was seized by an impulse to write something for our paper. I sat down and dashed off a sketch entitled *Legal Prostitution.* I read it to Shapiro and sent it off to London. It was my first attempt in Yiddish.

Impatiently I waited for an answer. Finally when the latest number arrived, there was a note for me in the paper's "letter box" which read: "Happy to have read your manuscript; will be published in the next issue." And so it was.

From then on, I contributed every week: stories, articles, correspondence. I was beginning to feel cramped in Constantinople. What on earth was I doing there? Secret powers were drawing me to London, and at the first opportunity I sailed.

Shapiro, too, decided to move his family to London, where he planned to establish a Yiddish publishing house. As I was a typesetter by trade and possessed technical skill, we arranged that I go there first and prepare the ground.

I arrived in London on a Friday morning in April 1896. I paid my first visit to the editor of the *Arbeiter Freind,* William Wess, at his home in Stepney Green. My first impression of him was indeed painful. Before me stood a pale man in his thirties, with shrunken cheeks, strained eyes, looking sleepless and tortured.

Wess was born and educated in Libau, Kurland. He emigrated to London as a young man and started as a factory worker. He mastered the English language and read ravenously. In the 80's he joined the Jewish Socialists. Together with Ruderman, Hillelsohn, and others, he nursed the *Arbeiter Freind,* and its existence depended on him alone.

He received me warmly, but seemed in a hurry.

"Come along, please, to the printing shop. We'll talk on the way," he said.

It was late. The paper was to come out that same day, and he had not yet written the "comments" for that issue. Not only did he write for the paper, but he set it, made up the first page, and closed the plates. He was the editor-compositor.

Poor fellow! He also had to translate the theoretical article for the second page, which was a weekly feature, to write a synthesis of the week's labor and political news, the "letter box," and fillers, besides looking over and correcting proofs and manuscripts. His only staff writer, S. Yanofsky, provided him with a weekly feuilleton and a serial based on Georges Ohnet's novel, *Doctor Ramo,* or *The Life and Ambition of a Heretic.* The day I saw Wess, he had received a letter from Yanofsky advising him that he would not go on with the translation because that French writer had tricked Yanofsky: the hero at the end turns penitent.

Yanofsky suggested that the editor himself finish the serial. What an idea! He was not a writer. He had enough trouble as it was.

We had reached Rumford Street, a dark, narrow thoroughfare where the composing room of the *Arbeiter Freind* was situated. Through a damp cellar we climbed up to an attic, where I left the editor-compositor working till late at night. He had to set the pages, take them to the printing shop, mail the paper to the subscribers, and attend the weekly anarchist lecture in "Sugar Loaf".

"Sugar Loaf", a familiar meeting hall on Henbury Street, in White-chapel, was the center of all the Jewish anarchist conferences and conventions. The Friday night lectures bore an international character. They were delivered in Yiddish, in English, in German, and in Russian. Among the speakers heard were the keen critic of Marxism, W. Tcher-kessoff; the brilliant English orator, John Turner; and, from time to time, our own Rudolf Rocker. Rocker, a native German, had not foreseen at that time what an important part he would come to play in the Jewish labor movement in London. The Yiddish speakers included J. Kaplan, William Wess, H. Sacks, S. Freeman, and J. Friedman.

Verbal propaganda was carried on by the only Jewish anarchist group in London, *Arbeiter Freind*, a small, compact and effective circle. In later years I participated in various group activities in London, Paris, and in New York. But none, as I recall, matched the ardor and devotion shown by the *Arbeiter Freind*. Most of its members were poor workers, ready to give everything for the movement and the paper. Despite their clashing temperaments and frictional views, the body as a whole functioned in exemplary harmony.

Within the *Arbeiter Freind* we had also female workers who rarely missed a meeting. In most cases they excelled with their silence. But when it came to practical assignments and fund drives, they were in the forefront.

The picture would not be complete if I failed to mention some outstanding rank and filers. I have a vivid recollection of the little shoe-maker, Rubinstein, who came to the office directly after work to find out if the paper was ready for distribution among the few Jewish book-stores; he appeared worried lest something might have gone wrong at the printer's. Another interesting comrade was the kindly, illiterate Karkelwitz. He was unable to read the *Arbeiter Freind,* but was ready to go through fire and water for it. He raced through rain squalls and fogs from meeting place to meeting place, peddling the paper and begging to be told what was in it. The poorest of the poor often parted with their last sixpence for the movement. The thought of such unstinted devotion warms the heart.

For his work of editing, setting and mailing the *Arbeiter Freind,* William Wess was paid twenty-two shillings a week (something over five dollars) whenever there was money to pay. The paper was started with a working capital of £12, and deficits began mounting in its third week. I was therefore not surprised when Wess asked to be relieved of his duties and the job was offered to me. Under the conditions, talk of salary was superfluous. Fortunately I had a remunerative trade. Three days a week I worked at my friend Shapiro's printing shop, and the other three I spent on the paper.

The transfer of the paper to my supervision took place without fanfares. Farewell-and-Welcome Dinners were then unfamiliar events. The second week in May 1896, my byline appeared on the second page under the lead article and also my address where "all communications to the editor" were to be sent. Thus it became known that I was the new editor.

I retained the same features: "Notebook" on the first page; the theoretical article, a feuilleton, a short or lengthy story on the second page. Then followed articles of general interest, correspondence, labor reports, etc. A careful reader would have noted a change in style as well as in the selection of content.

In those days we had no original material of a serious nature upon which we might draw, and had to rely on foreign sources. Wess confined himself to English; I had French books and brochures at my disposal, and my friend Shapiro helped. The score of issues under my editorship (May-November, 1896) enclose a rich variety of interpretive articles. Besides the "Notebook", each issue contained propaganda columns, a reading of which today causes one to smile. But who cared if they made an impression or not? Young blood revolted against every form of tyranny and against every kind of social debasement. Faith in the common man's striving for freedom was deep and unwavering. The people are still kept in darkness and in ignorance. . . . The servants of the State and Capitalism benumb the people's mind and befog their spirit. It is imperative that we rouse them unceasingly. . . .

In the *Arbeiter Freind* I published a number of my own short and longer stories. One, *Upon God's Altar,* was a terrifyingly graphic presentation of religious fanaticism. Others, such as *The Will* and *For a Piece of Bread,* dealt with the swampy and spiritually degraded life of the Polish Jews overrunning Constantinople. The play *He and She* took for its background a Jewish colony in Palestine. Friends praised my stories and encouraged me to write. But my output failed to gratify me. My writing was too tendentious; the element of propaganda over-balanced the art of description. I quickly realized that artistic writing was not my forte.

The *Arbeiter Freind* had no permanent quarters, no office. I prepared most of the work at home. I read proofs in the composing room; I also wrote the notices and odds and ends there. The composing room was above a stable on Rumford Street, and it was without a serviceable table. Under such difficult circumstances we brought out the *Arbeiter Freind* week after week.

My home with the Shapiros was in the London suburb of Leighton. It was a spacious, comfortable, peaceful home, surrounded by trees and lawns. It had several rooms. One was used by Shapiro as a small printing shop where we set up Sergei Stepniak's *Underground Russia* in Yiddish. This work appeared in weekly pamphlets. It was pleasant to work there. The house was only ten minutes from Epping Forest, which was used as a picnic ground by Londoners.

Shapiro held open house in Leighton as he had previously done in Constantinople. Guests arrived on Sunday from London, spent a few hours at the house, then made off for the "Forest" singing revolutionary songs or discussing social problems. Shapiro himself was troubled by innumerable questions. What disturbed him most was: Can one be an Anarchist and save money in the bank at the same time? Apparently it troubled him to know whether good anarchists may put away money while other people were starving.

One Sunday afternoon we had distinguished visitors: Kropotkin with his wife and daughter. Before, during, and after lunch, we kept up a banter and discussion. Shapiro was in a seventh heaven of joy. Then he stumbled upon his vexing question about anarchism and bank accounts. That was characteristic of him and of his generous wife, Nastia. Neither of them knew the meaning of savings. They always fed the hungry even when they themselves had little to eat. They pawned valuables and with the proceeds they staged "banquets" consisting of herring, potatoes, and black bread. When they had money they placed it in an open drawer, and whoever needed it just walked over and helped himself.

I do not remember whether or not Kropotkin gave Shapiro the desired "answer" to his "question". In all likelihood he did not take him seriously. What Anarchist ever had enough money to put in a bank?

The following incident will perhaps illustrate Kropotkin's own financial state.

Kropotkin lived exclusively on the honoraria he received quarterly from the English magazine, *Nineteenth Century,* for which he wrote. One day Sergei Stepniak (Krawtchinsky) visited him in Bromley. That evening, as he was about to leave, he discovered he did not have the necessary fare to return to his home in Hammersmith, a three-hour's journey from Bromley. All he needed was a half crown, and Kropotkin did not have a shilling. Mrs. Kropotkin finally obtained the half crown from a neighbor.

Speaking of the *Arbeiter Freind,* I have already mentioned the fact that we had no home, or desk, or table. Fortunately, we had no need of a desk. We had no manuscripts, good or bad, to put away. We lived, as it were, from hand to mouth. Today such poverty is unimaginable. The poorest of magazines has a stack of stuff awaiting turns, and even printed galleys are held in readiness. But all I had inherited from my predecessor was the paper's masthead and the heads of its established features.

The magazine had no contributors to speak of. Therefore, I had to rely on my own resources. Wess was tired out and could not assist. For a time he continued to expedite the paper's distribution, but soon he gave that up in order to devote himself to anarchist propaganda in English, a task which was very dear to him. Contributions from local scribes were crudely written and of no value.

Upon my accession as editor, I obtained contributions from abroad. From Constantinople I received articles written by Dr. Ben Zion under the pseudonym "The Little Man". He was an educated man and a linguist, with a fluent Yiddish at his command which he integrated with erudition, scope, a sense of humor and criticism. Earlier, in Odessa, he had evinced great interest in the Yiddish theater which was blossoming at that time, and he spent a fortune on it. He composed the play, *Esther of En Gedi,* later plagiarized by American Jewish playwrights. As a young man he was said to have embraced Christianity and to have worked as a missionary; but when he joined our intimate circle in Constantinople, it was clear that he had severed all relations with the Christian-religious world; and now he unmasked all forms of clericalism with trenchant sarcasm. He lived in poverty, a circumstance which further convinced us that he was no longer a missionary.

His articles ran in a series under the general heading, *Something about Natural History,* and were written in an allegorical style, very much in the spirit of parables. He wrote of the nature of certain plants and animals, from which inference was clearly directed to the world's evils that sprang from social injustice. Having been born, brought up, and educated under Tsarist despotism, Dr. Ben Zion had grown accustomed to the style of illegal literature, a trait which was responsible for the hidden meaning in his writings. There was no need to write in this fashion for the London *Arbeiter Freind;* but that did not matter. The ingeniously worded articles submitted by "The Little Man" were deeply interesting.

One day in July 1896, the mail from America brought me a pleasant surprise—a lengthy manuscript from the pen of Mr. M. Katz. It was entitled *From the Diary of a Superfluous Man.* I knew the writer from New York's anarchist weekly, *Freie Arbeiter Stimme,* where his sparkling feuilletons, called *The Speculations of a Philosopher,* were appearing regularly. He was then an editor of the anarchist monthly, *Die Freie Gesellschaft,* published in New York. I ran his contribution with pleasure. It enabled me to become the friend, at first by letter and later personally, of the cleanest, gentlest, and noblest soul I was ever privileged to meet.

Simultaneously I received from America some poems signed by one L. Rabotnik, now better known as the work of the elderly bard, A. L. Wolfson. His revolutionary verses in the *Arbeiter Freind* were an inspiration to our readers. He and a certain Albert Levine also sent in news stories concerning the life of Jewish workers in America. Thus our weekly became alive and arresting.

During the period of my conversion to Anarchism there had appeared in New York the monthly, *Freie Gesellschaft.* It served as an invaluable instrument of Anarchist education, and, moreover, it was a literary delight. Discriminating readers found it a rare stimulant to the mind.

This occurred a few years after the suspension of the *Freie Arbeiter Stimme.* For three years that weekly had been the nerve center of the American-Jewish Anarchist movement. Subsequent attempts to revive the paper had failed. As a consequence, Jewish Anarchists took recourse to verbal propaganda and to lecture halls. However, on October 15, 1895 a small group which had been organized in the summer of that year issued the first number of the *Freie Gesellschaft.* This appeared under the joint editorship of M. Leontieff (L. Moisiew) and M. Katz.

It is hard to estimate the influence which that magazine exercised over me. The major portion of the serious articles it featured were adapted from the writings of Kropotkin, Tscherkassoff, and other prominent thinkers, which I had read in the original. But such translations were of singular value to the partisan readers, the bulk of whom read nothing but Yiddish. For them the *Freier Gesselschaft* opened a new world. It revealed to them treasures of scientific knowledge, ideas of culture, and education.

MY ROAD TO HASIDISM

MARTIN BUBER (1878-   )

The literary quality of this personal history is characteristic of Buber's manifold writings. Whether he is interpreting ancient Scripture, unveiling the spirit of folklore, fashioning the concept of nationalism or probing the recesses of the human spirit, his artistry is warmed by an impassioned vision. It is for this reason that he has inspired several generations of thinkers and scholars who regard him as the paladin of contemporary Jewish thought. This autobiographical excursion indicates dramatically how Buber brought into harmony two divergent veins of culture—the mystical heritage of Israel and the tradition of the West. He has combined them in practical life too, for he taught Religion and Ethics at the University of Frankfurt until 1933, and for the past several years has been a member of the faculty of the Hebrew University in Palestine.

* * *

IN MY childhood (I left Vienna, where I was born, for Galicia at an early age, and grew up in my grandparents' home), I spent the summers on an estate in Bukowina. Occasionally my father took me to the neighboring town of Sadagora. Sadagora is the seat of a dynasty of zaddikim (zaddik: a just man, a perfect man), that is, of hasidic rabbis. The initiates talk of miracle-rabbis and consider themselves well-informed. But they are like all initiates—informed only in the realm of external superficialities. The legendary ancestral greatness has waned in the descendants of the zaddikim. They try to retain their power by utilizing all kinds of petty magic, but their manipulations do not dim the hereditary glow on their foreheads, nor distort their innate grandeur. Their involuntary nobility is more telling than all their deliberate activity. Certainly, the soaring faith of the first hasidim is lacking in present-day communities. The supreme devotion of the early believers no longer exists, attended by adoration of the zaddik as the perfect man, in whom immortality has found mortal incarnation. Our contemporaries are rather disposed to look on the zaddik principally as a mediator, through whose intercession they hope to find gratification of their mundane desires. And yet their baser inclinations are deflected; they shudder with fear when the rebbe stands in silent prayer, or, at the third Sabbath meal, holds magic discourse on the secrets of the Torah. Even these degenerates, in the unknown depths of their souls, retain Eleasar's luminous dictum: that the world was created for the sake of the perfect man, for it is said: "And God saw the light, and it was good," but good means only the perfect one (Yoma 38b).

This knowledge I acquired in my childhood, in the dirty little town of Sadagora, from the benighted hasidim. My perceptions were those of a child—not through ideas, but through pictures and emotions. I learned that the world is for the perfect man, and the perfect man is none other than the real savior. These days the zaddik is generally entreated in regard to essentially earthy needs, but is he not still, despite this, what he was once thought and held to be: the savior of the spirit, the teacher of the cosmic, the guide to the divine spark? His power is misinterpreted by the believers, he himself misuses it, but does it not remain, at bottom, the legitimate power of the abundantly overflowing soul over the soul-impoverished? Does it not contain the germ of a future order? Somewhere, in a childlike fashion, these questions dawned in me. And I was able to make comparisons. I compared the zaddik, on the one hand, with the district chief, whose power rested on habitual coercion; on the other hand, with the Rabbi, who was a righteous and God-fearing man, but the employee of a worship-directorate. Here was something incomparable; here—humbled, but uninjured—was the living germ of humanity, true community and true guidance. Something primeval and eternal was in it; something lost, yearned for, returning.

The ornate palace of the Rabbi repelled me. The hasidic house of prayer and its ecstatic congregation were strange to me. But when I watched the Rabbi stride through the rows of supplicants, I understood what a leader was; when I saw the hasidim dance with the Torah, I knew what a community was. Out of this grew the perception that common veneration and common joy are the foundations of real human communion.

During my adolescence this early perception began to slip into the unconscious. I spent my summers elsewhere and was finally on the verge of forgetting the hasidic impressions of my childhood. But after several years I returned to a newly-acquired estate of my father's, near Czortkow, which was the seat of a collateral line of the same dynasty of zaddikim. Even today the traditional memory of the great Rizhiner dominates Sadagora. He was called the great Rizhiner because he fled from the town of Ruzhyn, near Berditschev, when the Russian government suspected him of claiming kingship over the Jews. After much wandering, he settled in Sadagora. The immediate memory of his son David Moshe was alive in Czortkow. Unfortunately, I learned little about him then. My impressions this time were indistinct and fugitive. This may have been due to the fact that in the interim I had been seized by the mental ferment which frequently characterizes the decisive years of youth, awakening the creative functions of the intellect, but bringing to an end the natural vision and perception of childhood. I was intellectually estranged from the hasidim, deprived of a naive communion with their being. Because of my thinking processes, I believed myself removed from their world. I confess that I looked on them no differently from Graetz: I looked down on them from the heights of a rational man. I saw nothing of their life, even when I was directly before it, because I wanted to see nothing.

Nevertheless, though I paid no attention, I first heard, at this time, the name which I later identified with superb revelation—the name of Besht. It is made up of the initial letters of the words Baal Shem Tob (Master of the good name, therefore master of the spiritual forces). The name refers to Rabbi Israel ben Eliezer, the founder of Hasidism. One of the dairy farms of my father's estate was called after Tlust, the market town nearby. The Baal Shem had once been a poor teacher in Tlust. (The town became famous during the War, in Russian army dispatches, for it was fought over a long time.) According to legend, it was here, on the night he completed his thirty-third year, that the Baal Shem had the dream which announced that his time had come.

But during my visit, I was remote not only from Hasidism; all Judaism was strange to me.

Until my fourteenth year, I lived with my grandfather, the midrashic scholar. Salomon Buber's world was the Midrash; he lived in it with a wonderful calm of soul and intensity of labor. He issued text after text derived from the Midrash, that incomparable compilation, overabundantly rich in lore, proverb and magnificent metphor. In it, split into a thousand fragments, lies hidden a second Bible, the Bible of Exile. Without ever having acquired the philological training of the western world, my grandfather labored over the scripts with the thoroughness of a modern scholar, but he possessed, in addition, the mastery of the talmudist. The talmudist has at his command, for every sentence, and every phrase, every possible reference in his literature, not as stuff retained in the memory, but as an organic part of his whole person. The intellectual passion which is evidenced in his stream of work grew out of the untouchable, unerring childishness of an untainted soul combined with an essentially Jewish being. When he spoke Hebrew, as he always did to foreign guests, it sounded like the speech of a sovereign returned from banishment. He did not think about Judaism; he had it in him.

So long as I lived in his home, I was well-rooted, though some queries and doubts disturbed me. On my departure, the turbulence of the period assailed me. Until I was twenty, and to a lesser degree even afterward, my spirit was in constant and multiple flux. Tension and release followed one another, determined by manifold influences, forever assuming new forms, but remaining without a pivot and without cumulative substance. I really lived in the *Olam Ha-Tohu,* the world of confusion, the mythical limbo of lost souls. I experienced mobile spiritual fulfillment, but neither Judaism, nor humanity, nor the presence of the divine was in it.

Zionism provided the first impetus for my release. I can only suggest here what it meant to me: revival of coherence, equilibrium and replacement in the community. No one needs the salvation of a racial bond so much as the youth gripped in spiritual search, and flung by his intellect into the ether. A Jewish youth needs it more than any. The others are protected by thousands of years of inherited unity with a native soil and by traditional national sentiments. The Jew, even if he has a newly-acquired, natural feeling for and a cultural understanding of German natural art and customs, is nevertheless immediately threatened by it and abandoned to it insofar as he does not find his way to his own group. The most dazzling accumulation of intellectual wealth and the most wanton pseudo-productivity (only the well-rooted person can be genuinely productive), are not enough to compensate the unrooted person for his lack of the sacred insignia of humanity, of placement, of communion and unity.

That Zionism influenced me and allowed me to re-appraise Judaism was, as I said, only the first step. National confession alone does not change the Jew; he may remain as impoverished spiritually—if not quite as unsupported—with it as without. For some people, however, national confession is not sufficient unto itself, but a soaring upward. It is not a haven, but a passage to the open sea. Such people are led to transformation, and so it happened with me.

I became acquainted with Judaism before I actually comprehended it. My second step, after considerable groping, was therefore the will to cognizance. By cognizance I do not mean a storing up of anthropological, historical and social data, though these may be important. I mean the immediate recognition, the eye-to-eye recognition, of national character in its creative documentation.

That is how I came to Hasidism.

Hebrew, which was part of my boyhood background, had been neglected in the world of confusion. Now I acquired it anew. I began to take hold of it in its essence, which cannot be transmitted to any other language, least of all to an occidental language. And I read, again and again driven off by crude, awkward, unformed content, but gradually overcoming the unfamiliarity, unveiling the substance, contemplating and essence with growing devotion. One day I came on a booklet, the *Zevaat Ribesh,* the testament of Rabbi Israel Baal Shem, and these words shone before me: "He apprehended the character of ardor in its entirety. He rose from his sleep in a passion, for he was sanctified, he had become a different person, according to the characteristics of the Holy One, blessed be He, when He created the world." It was then that I, suddenly overwhelmed, experienced the hasidic soul. Something indigenously Jewish rose in me, blossoming, in the darkness of exile, to a new conscious expression. I perceived the very resemblance of man to God, as deed, as an act of becoming, as a duty. This indigenously Jewish concept was also indigenously human; it was the content of human religiosity. Judaism as religiosity, as piety, rose in me at that moment. My childhood experience, the memory of the zaddik and his followers, reawoke in me, and lighted my way. I comprehended the idea of the perfect man. And I perceived my responsibility in proclaiming it to the world.

Now came the time for study. At the age of twenty-six, I withdrew from party activity for five years. I refrained from writing and lecturing. I lived in solitude. With great effort, I gathered together what I could of the scattered literature—some of it has disappeared entirely—and sank into it, discovering one secret domain after another.

My first published work came about in a strange way. Among all the books, anthologies of the sayings of zaddikim and collections of legends about their lives, there was one volume which was peculiar and different from the others. Therefore it was the most nationally characteristic of all. It was the *Sippure Maasiyoth,* stories by Rabbi Nahman of Brazlaw, a grandson of the Baal Shem. Nahman had told these tales to his pupils. After Nahman's death, one of the pupils had written them down and published them, in an obviously distorted form. In part, they were pure fairy tales, on the oriental model, in part they were creations of a singular art, symbolic, sometimes vaguely allegorical, woven out of the calm of mystical experience and the gossamer of constructive fantasy. They were not teachable, but they possessed an instructive trait in common. Rabbi Nahman himself called them the garments of his teachings. A comprehensive commentary had been provided by the pupil. But the content was distorted by all kinds of utilitarian and vulgarly rationalistic interpolations; the form was ruined by a confusion of line and opaqueness of color, which—as one could see from certain surprising passages— had been pure to begin with.

Almost involuntarily I began to translate. I began with a few of the stories. I thought of children as my readers. When I finished, I found that what lay before me was more wretched than I had supposed; it was in no way comparable to the similar tales found in the *A Thousand and One Nights*. When I saw my pieces in print, I was utterly disheartened. This could not go on. In translation the distortions were more apparent and the organic form even less distinct. The purity was not even sustained, let alone enhanced. The stories would have to be told out of my own being, just as the painter absorbs the lines of his model in himself and creates the picture out of the formative memory. Modestly and clumsily, I began with the *Tale of the Bull and the Ram;* with added assurance and freedom, I went over to the *Tale of the Wise and the Simple,* then to *About the Son of the King and the Son of the Maid. The Tale of the Rabbi and His Son* was the first one which was born of itself, in my own writing. In the two final stories, *The Tale of the Master of Prayer,* and *The Seven Beggars,* and in the pieces I reconstructed anew, I experienced a sense of union with the spirit of Nahman. I had found real fidelity, more adequately than his immediate disciples. I had conceived and carried out the task of serving as a belated messenger to the kingdom of a strange language.

I felt my innate bond with hasidic truth even more strongly in my second book, *The Legend of the Baal Shem,* which sought to reconstruct the inner events in the life of the master through a selection of traditional sayings. These I drew from popular literature and from the spoken word. A short time after writing the first of the Nahman tales, I had begun to translate for the second book as well. And here, too, I was met by disappointment. The stories I encountered were, for the most part, recorded in a crude and clumsy form, and they failed to acquire winged words in translation. Once again, with increasing independence, I arrived at an individual form. But the more independent I became, the more profound grew my fidelity. Therefore, despite the fact that the greater part of the book consists of my own treatment of traditional motifs, I may honestly maintain that I bear within me the blood and the spirit of those who created the motifs. Through blood and spirit they were re-created in me.

Later, several years after the completion of both books, I evolved a different form of artistic fidelity to popular hasidic tales. But this does not fall within the scope of these memoranda, which tell of my way to Hasidism.

However, a humorous but significant experience I had in 1910 or 1911 does belong here. It also occurred in Bukowina, in Czernowitz, the capital, which is not far from Sadagora.

After a lecture I had given there (it was the third of my *Three Lectures on Judaism*), I went to a café with several members of the organization which had arranged the evening. I always liked to follow a formal speech, which does not permit contradiction, with an informal chat in a small group. Here conflicting views, objections and questions are brought out, and personal influences may be brought into play.

We were in the midst of a moral-philosophical discussion, when a well-built, prosperous-looking, middle-aged Jew approached our table and greeted me. My obviously cool reply brought from him a reproachful: "Doctor, don't you recognize me?" When I was forced to confess that I did not, he introduced himself as M., the brother of one of the farmers on my father's former estate. I invited him to join us. After inquiring after his personal life, I resumed the discussion with my companions. M. listened to the talk, which had taken a turn for the abstract, very intently. It was clear that he did not understand a word of it, but the devotion with which he listened was like that of believers who do not need to know the meaning of the words of a litany, since the combination of sounds gives them all the benefits they need and is more sententious than content. After a while, I asked him whether he wanted to talk to me. I would be glad, I said, to go off with him to discuss his affairs. M. said energetically that he did not. The talk resumed, and with it, M.'s attention. After another half hour had passed, I asked him again whether there was anything I could do for him. No, no, there was nothing, he assured me. The discussion came to an end, and we arose. It was late, but as frequently happens after such an hour of give-and-take, I was not tired. I felt even more refreshed than before, and decided to take a walk. At this moment M. approached me with an unspeakably shy air. "Doctor," he said, "I would like to ask you something." I told the students to wait, and sat down with him. He was silent. "Please go ahead," I said, "I will give you any information I can." "Doctor," he said, "I have a daughter." He stopped, then he continued. "And I also have a young man for my daughter." Again a pause. "He is a lawyer. He passed his examinations with honor." M. was silent again, for a longer time. I looked at him encouragingly. I assumed that he wanted me to do something for his prospective son-in-law. "Doctor," he said, "is he a good person?" I was overwhelmed, but I felt that I must not deny him a reply. "Well, Mr. M.," I explained, "after what you have told me, one may easily assume that he is diligent and capable." But he persisted: "Doctor," he asked, "has he got a good head?" "That is harder to say," I replied, "but he could not have accomplished what he did with industry alone. He must have something inside his head." Again M. was silent; then he put one more question, obviously the last. "Doctor," he said, "should he become a barrister or a solicitor?" "In that I can give no advice," I answered. "I don't know the young man and even if I did, I would hardly be able to make a suggestion on such a point." Now M.'s face assumed an expression of almost dejected resignation, half-plaintive, half-understanding. He spoke in a tone which was an indescribable fusion of grief and humility. "Doctor, you don't want to tell me, but I thank you just the same for what you have told me."

Though this amusing, meaningful incident seems to have nothing to do with Hasidism, it nevertheless gave me new insight. As a child, I had received an impression of the zaddik, and through all the surrounding pollutions of reality, I had sensed the pure idea—the idea of a real leader of a real community. In the interim between youth and manhood, there blossomed out of this perception of hasidic teaching the concept of the perfect man, the realization of God in this world. Now, in an amusing incident, I perceived the function of leadership incarnate in my own person, through my own experience. I, who was not a zaddik, not a man secured in God, but one endangered before God, a man ever wrestling anew with the light of God and ever newly offending before God's abyss—I had the inner experience of a zaddik, I had been asked about trivialities and I had replied in trivialities. The true zaddik is asked about revelation and replies with revelation. But I had experienced the fundamental conduct of his soul before the world; I knew his responsibility.

Every person has an infinite sphere of responsibility—responsibility before the infinite. He moves, he talks, he observes, and every movement, every word, very glance stirs waves in world events. How strong and how far-reaching they are he cannot know. Every man affects the fate of the world through his whole being and all his acts, to a degree unknown both to him and to others. Such unreality as we can perceive is only a tiny segment of the inconceivable, manifold, invisible influence of all on all. Every human act is a vessel of infinite responsibility. But there are some people in whom this infinite responsibility exists perpetually, in a special, unusually active form. I am not referring to rulers and statesmen, who wield power over the external destiny of large commonwealths. The sphere of their influence may be delimited, but in order to be effective, they turn from individual, enormously-menaced existences, which look on them with a thousand questions, to the abstract, which appears unseeing. I refer to those who hold their ground against the thousandfold querying glance of individual lives, who give faithful response to the trembling lips of every questioning creature that comes to ask an opinion. I mean the zaddikim, the real zaddik. He is the person who continually compounds the depths of responsibility with the lead of his words. He speaks, and knows that what he says is fate. He does not decide the destiny of countries and nations, but always and again the petty and the great paths of individual, finite and yet boundless lives. People come to him, and each one demands his verdict, his help. Though the needs they bring to him are corporal, in his discernment there is nothing corporal which does not undergo transfiguration; there is nothing material which cannot transcend into spirit. This is what he does for them all: he elevates their needs before gratifying them. So he becomes the savior in spirit, the teacher of the cosmic, the guide to the divine spark. Around him, around the perfect man and the real savior, the world revolves. It weighs against him, forever and ever.

IN THE WAKE OF THE RUSSIAN REVOLUTION

JACOB MASÉ (1860-1924)

The tense atmosphere that pervaded Russia after the seizure of power by the Bolsheviki is reflected in Masé's revealing account of his meeting with Lunacharsky, one of the intellectual leaders of the Party. The writer saw the upheaval from a unique vantage point, for he spent all his adult years, from 1893 to his death in 1924, as the Crown Rabbi of Moscow. And he was something more than a government official. Deeply learned and devoted to progressive education and the Zionist movement, he kept abreast of the changing times and inspired a group of younger intellectuals with his ideas. His four-volume autobiography is one of the best in modern letters.

❊ ❊ ❊

IN THE summer of 1919 the government suddenly stopped supporting the Tarbuth Hebrew schools. After some reflection on our part we decided to take up the matter directly with the Minister of Education, Lunacharsky; consequently, I sought out Dolgorokov who, only the year before, had asked me on the Minister's behalf to sign a petition requesting President Wilson for food and medicine for Russian children. Besides myself, the petition was also signed by Patriarch Tikon and Rabbi David Tevil of St. Petersburg. The President responded generously.

After listening to my bitter complaints against the commissariat's hostility towards Hebrew cultural institutions, Dolgorokov assured me that he would speak to Lunacharsky on my behalf. A short time later I received a telegram from Yaroslavl: "Comrade Dolgorokov has informed me of your desire to see me. I shall be pleased to see you if you come to Yaroslavl. Lunacharsky, Minister of Education." I promptly turned over the telegram to Rudnitsky so that he could procure the necessary permits and railroad tickets for himself, my secretary and me. Rudnitsky was in possession of papers from the Tarbuth directors that would substantiate our claims before the ministry. My secretary, Zusmanovich, I took along because of my poor health. The three of us, then, left Moscow on a Thursday evening and arrived in Yaroslavl the following morning.

This city had been an aversion of mine since the days of Alexander III when it was a hideout for the "Black Hundreds". That same same year also the Whites had instigated an uprising against the Tsar who, once the rebels were crushed, burned down a goodly portion of the city.

Leaving the station for the main street, we couldn't sight a coachman anywhere. And so we trudged along wearily, our valises in hand. We searched about for an hotel or a tea parlor, but there was none to be found. Finally, after getting well into town, we spied a house, which was really a tavern masquerading behind a tea front. We stepped in and beheld the proprietor, a ferocious-looking, potbellied Russian, seated at a table. As soon as his eye caught my face, he became enraged; but his strong business instinct would not allow him to affront me. He asked us what we wanted. Having been informed by my two companions that we would like to have some tea, he exclaimed:

"Go into the other room!"

We went in, but it was reeking with smoke. I returned and asked him if he happened to have a room without smoke—to which he retorted:

"Yes, in Berdichev!"

We were resolved to leave immediately, but by this time fatigue got the better of us and we had to sit down for a spell. Just then someone brought in tea, without our asking for it. You cannot imagine how insipid that tea was! We rested a while longer and paid the bill. "This is what I call paying for insult and repose on one check," I thought to myself.

We left the house and stepped out into the street. At last we found a coachman. Rudnitsky, who always knew his way around, had him take us to the house of a Jewish widow. Only after much knocking did she open the door—and then she vanished; apparently we had awakened her. She showed the three of us to a room, already crowded with beds and sleeping men and women, and suggested that we grab a couple of beds and make ourselves at home. Seeing, however, that I shrank in disgust, she showed us discourteously to a sofa in the dining room, forewarning us meanwhile that in another hour or so the guests would be up for tea. Naturally, I didn't undress, but lay down on the sofa, trying in vain to relax. I sent off Rudnitsky to learn where Lunacharsky resided and when he would receive us.

In the meantime word got around—how, is beyond me—that I was in Yaroslavl. Hosts of Jews began filing into the house, curious as to my business with Lunacharsky. In good Jewish fashion they kept bombarding me with elaborate schemes and proposals. I insisted that I was in town merely to visit relatives. Now, of course, it was the relatives' turn to get wind of my presence—information that I had wanted to conceal from them at all costs—and thus my nephew made his appearance and whisked me away from the hotel to his home. After a bite to eat, I stepped out for a stroll. Wanting to make most of my time I entered a barber shop. The barber was a Lithuanian Jew, one of the many who had been exiled by Nikolai Nikolaievich, commander-in-chief under Tsar Nicholas. To my amazement he called me by name.

"How did you know who I was?" I asked him.

"By your picture," he replied. "You're Jacob Isaievich Masé, and you're here of course to get a trim for the Sabbath and for the minister, Lunacharsky, whom you've come to see."

I was dumbfounded, and in that instant I was reminded of something that I read in Sholem Aleichem, and what he himself had once told me—that the Jews have an uncanny sense of smell, and can scent the arrival of a stranger a thousand miles off. After the haircut I proceeded to Lunacharsky's quarters, but via crooked alleys and lanes, so as to throw off the "bloodhounds". I was about to congratulate myself upon my success when I perceived a crowd of Jews stationed at the entrance to his quarters. They greeted me as I entered. *These* "bloodhounds", I reasoned, have brains too; they didn't go around trailing me step by step.

"Friends," I remarked to them, "I wouldn't congregate like this in front of the hotel if I were you."

I entered the room of the Minister—a title indiscriminately employed by Jews when referring to any and all government officials. The room was prettily decorated—but, of course, it boasted its share of beds. At one end stood a long desk around which girls were sitting and typing. One of them, a very pretty Armenian, with dazzling eyes, approached me smilingly and said:

"I presume you've come to see Anatoly Vasilievich. He's busy just now, but he'll be out shortly."

She bade me sit down and handed me a copy of the local newspaper. By chance I came across a speech which Lunacharsky had delivered to a large assembly on the previous day. He quoted from the prophet, Amos, and referred to him as a communist. All the prophets were communists, so ran the argument, since no decent person can be other-wise. He then proceeded to expound this theory simply and lucidly for popular consumption. I hadn't yet concluded the article when the author himself entered, welcomed me kindly and bade me sit down beside him. I handed him the sealed envelope which Dolgorokov had given me for him. He tore it open, read the contents and began speaking:

"Moscow—" here he recited a list of strange names, "—it isn't ad-visable at present."

Not until a little later did I perceive that he was dictating a reply to the letter that I had just brought him. Finally, he turned to me: "Yes?"

I felt very uneasy. I just couldn't discuss a subject so close and dear to me in this room full of beds and typists. I was at a loss, and in-stead of saying something I kept glancing about the room. Undoubtedly, the Armenian sensed my discomfort, for she turned to Lunacharsky and said, "Wouldn't it be better if we'd step into the other room? It's empty, you know, and we won't be disturbing the girls."

He consented and we followed her in. Immediately I felt relieved. He sat down behind his desk, I in front of him, and the Armenian girl beside a typewriter on his left. Her presence seemed to inspire me to speak.

I took from my pocket a telegram that I had received from my friend, Gisin, who happened to be in Humel then. He deplored at length the closing of the admirable Hebrew school in that town, and for no reason other than that Hebrew was the prevailing tongue in the school. It ended thus: "Parents, teachers and pupils—all have authorized you to speak to the commissariat on their behalf." Lunacharsky read the telegram, returned it to me, and began dictating again:

"Moscow. Narkompros. Wire immediately by whom, when, and upon what grounds were such repressive measures taken against the Hebrew school at Humel. . . . Send it off promptly."

Soon I began explaining to him fully my views on the matter:

"As people's commissar of public instruction you certainly know, sir, the important position that the Hebrew language occupies in the civilized world. Every major university has a chair dedicated to research into its history, grammar or philosophy. Its literature is one of the oldest and richest—a veritable treasury of human knowledge and achievement. Can you then demand of its people that they cease transmitting their language to their children? From earliest times it was the sacred duty of every parent to teach his child Hebrew. A town that did not maintain schools for the poor and fatherless was excommunicated. No government, save perhaps that of the Emperor Hadrian, has ever attempted to proscribe its study—and what did the people do in that instance? They stowed away with their Bibles in subterranean caves or pits, there to continue the study of that ancient tongue.

"You quoted Amos in your speech—what would you say to an entire generation arising who shall never have heard his name? Yes, it is true that during the past twenty-five years or so the Jews had begun to forsake their language, but that period is now closed. Look, an overwhelming desire is growing within the people to speak this language and to employ it at all times and occasions. And this desire, let me add, is not the caprice of a small sect, nor is it limited to the Zionists alone, but it is the will of an entire people.

"Now that the new law explicitly states that any group consisting of no less than twenty-five people may found a school of their own, draw up their own curriculum, and will withal be aided by the government—why should Hebrew fare worse than other tongues? Even prior to the revolution our teachers were enunciating and disseminating the doctrines of liberty and freedom. If you shut down these schools, sir, you will be doing to death those very principles which we fought and died for."

Lunacharsky: "I don't know of anyone who is disputing the value of Hebrew except your own brothers—the Yiddishists. They maintain that since Hebrew is the language of the bourgeois and not of the masses, it can have no rightful place in public schools. And am I not forced to agree with them?"

I: "I assure you, sir, that I am intimately acquainted with Jewish life, and I know that when a father speaks of sending his son to school he is referring to his learning Hebrew, and never Yiddish. As for Hebrew being the bourgeois tongue, it is precisely the bourgeois who makes certain that his children are taught every language under the sun except Hebrew. Our greatest authors, poets, and scholars have sprung from the poor and from the masses. And now what will be the end of it all? Yiddish is being forgotten, Hebrew is not being taught, and the Jewish people will be left without a language."

Lunacharsky: "Such a contingency doesn't trouble me much. However, I am interested in your assertion that Hebrew is the language of the proletariat. That is new to me. You do have a poet, Bialik, I recall now—did he arise from poor stock?"

I: "From the very poorest, sir. And the same thing is true for almost every important Hebrew writer."

Lunarcharsky: "And Sholem Aleichem?"

I: "Well, his people were probably regarded by fellow villagers as being prosperous. But the average bourgeois, I believe, would faint if he were identified with them. The prosperity of people such as they, as Maxim Gorky will verify for you, consisted in their having a piece of white bread once a week, namely on the Sabbath."

THE WORLD IS MY FATHERLAND

ERNST TOLLER (1893-1939)

The hand of the dramatist and the voice of the revolutionist are always present in these vivid memoirs. A strong element of courage and tragedy too. For Toller belonged to the generation that spent its best energies fruitlessly in the first World War and suffered the disillusion of the postwar years and of the upsurge of Fascism. He had soldiered in the war, was imprisoned for his participation in the short-lived Bavarian Soviet Republic (1919), and spent his latter years as an exile in Europe and America. It was during the five years of his imprisonment that he wrote plays like *Masse Mensch* and *Hinkeman,* setting a new note in modern drama. To that period belong also the sensitive verse of his *Swallow Book*. During the civil war in Spain, he made an heroic effort to win the sympathy and aid of the American public for the Republican forces. On the day that his books were burned by the Nazis he wrote: "Beneath the yoke of barbarism one must not keep silence; one must fight. Whoever is silent at such a time is a traitor to humanity." A fitting epitaph, despite his suicide.

❀ ❀ ❀

MY maternal great-grandfather received permission from Frederick the Great to settle as the only Jew in Samotschin, a little town in the Netzebruch near the Polish border. My great-grandfather paid for this privilege with money. It was a thing of which the great-grandson was very proud; I used to brag about it to my schoolfellows, and dreamed of advancement and ennoblement.

My paternal great-grandfather, who was of Spanish extraction, had an estate in West Prussia, and an aunt of mine used to relate that he ate off golden dishes while his horse fed from a silver manger; but with his sons the manger had become copper and the dishes mere silver. As a boy I used to dream of these legendary riches; in my dreams the old man was devoured by his horse, while I looked on placidly and unsympathetically; indeed, rather with an unaccountable feeling of satisfaction.

In my grandparents' house the loft was full of huge, dusty old folios, heavily gilt. My grandfather used to read them all day and sometimes even all night, while my grandmother ran the shop, served the customers, and did the housekeeping. This was the business that my father inherited after a brilliant career at the University and some time as a chemist.

Samotschin was an intensely German town, and both Protestants and Jews were proud of the fact. They spoke with scorn of the other towns in Posen, where no distinction was made between Catholics and Poles. Ostmark had first come into Prussia's hands with the second Partition; but the Germans regarded themselves as hereditary rulers, merely tolerating the Poles. These little villages of the plain, invaded by German colonists, acted as outposts, as buffer territory between Germany proper and the Polish estates and farmland. Poles and Germans fought relentlessly over every foot of land; and any German who sold land to a Pole was regarded as a traitor.

We children called the Poles "Polacks" and firmly believed that they were descendants of Cain, who slew Abel and was branded by God.

Against the Poles, Jews and Germans showed a united front. The Jews looked upon themselves as the pioneers of German culture, and their houses in these little towns became cultural centers where German literature, philosophy and art were cultivated with a pride and an assiduousness which bordered on the ridiculous. The Poles were declared to be no patriots—the poor Poles whose children at school were forbidden their mother tongue, whose lands had been confiscated by the German State. But on the Kaiser's birthday the Jews sat at the same table as the Reserve officers, the War League, and the Home Defense Corps, and drank beer and schnapps and raised their glasses to the Kaiser's health.

I was born on the first of December, 1893. Looking back on my childhood days I find myself remembering disconnected and fragmentary incidents.

I see myself wearing a little short dress, standing outside our house looking at a cart. It is big, bigger than Marie, as big as a house. Marie is the nurse, and she wears a red coral necklace—round, red corals. She is sitting on one of the shafts, rocking to and fro. Then Ilse comes out with her nurse. She runs up to me and we hold hands; for some time we stand hand in hand and look at each other curiously. Ilse's nurse is gossiping with Marie, but suddenly she calls out:

"Come away, Ilse! He's a Jew!"

Ilse drops my hand and runs away. I can't understand what the nurse means, but I begin to cry bitterly. At last the other nurse departs with Ilse, and Marie tries to comfort me, taking me in her arms and showing me her corals; but I don't want the corals, and I break her necklace.

I am friends with the night watchman's son. When the others cry "Polack" I cry "Polack" with them; but he is my friend for all that. His name is Stanislaus, and he tells me how the Polacks hate the Germans.

In the market place they have been taking up the pavement and digging trenches. It is Saturday night, and the workmen have left their spades and pickaxes in a little hut made of rough boards while they go to the public house. Stanislaus and I sit in one of the trenches, a narrow ditch covered with planks. Stanislaus spits.

"Tonight one of the workmen will die as a punishment for digging here. They've no right to dig here; it's Polish earth. The Germans stole it from us. But let 'em go on digging just here where they've begun, let 'em go on digging another hundred yards down, and they'll come upon the King of Poland. He has a white horse in his stable, so beautiful that the Captain's horse would look like a billy goat beside it. When the time comes, the King of Poland will mount his horse and ride up from below the earth and drive them all away. All of them. You as well."

I ask Stanislaus when that time will come. Stanislaus knows more than I do, for his father is the night watchman. But he presses his lips together and sets his mouth obstinately.

"Spit then, and give me a marble as pledge."

I spit and he takes the marble but says nothing. All night I dream that Stanislaus is standing in the market place blowing on his father's horn. And suddenly a white horse comes galloping out of our ditch, its brown saddle covered with Kaiser-pictures.

I collect Kaiser-pictures. In my father's shop there are lots of fascinating things, string, bonbons, lemonade and raisins, little nails and big nails; but best of all are the Kaiser-pictures. And they are the hardest to steal. There is one in every packet of chocolate; but the chocolate cupboard is kept locked, and the key is on a bunch which Mother carries in her blue checked apron. Mother is always working; she is working when I wake up in the morning. She works in the shop, in the granary, she does the housekeeping, she gives food to the poor and invites beggars in to the midday meal, and when the farm hand goes to the fields to plow and sow it is to her he comes for supplies. Every evening she sits reading, deep into the night, often falling asleep over her book. And if I wake her up she says:

"Do let me be, child, reading is the only pleasure I have."

"Why are you always working, Mother?"

"Because you must eat, my dear."

If Mother isn't careful I steal the key, and then the pictures out of the packets of chocolate. The chocolate itself is only incidental. They are beautiful pictures of ancient Germans, dressed in skins and leaning on huge clubs; their woman squat beside them polishing their shields. Stanislaus thinks they used their blond hair to polish the shields with, hair which looks like straw bed hangings. In most of the packets there are pictures of our own Kaiser wearing a red velvet cloak over his shoulders and holding a ball in one hand and a gold poker in the other.

I am lying in bed one morning, looking at my Kaiser-pictures, and I ask myself if the Kaiser ever has to go to the bathroom like me. The question worries me, and I run to mother.

"You will finish up in prison," says mother.

So the Kaiser does *not* go to the bathroom.

The street between the church and the market place is called the Totenstrasse, the Street of the Dead; but the people who live there don't see any particular sense in the name. They stand at their doors and gossip, grumbling at the burgomaster because the pavement (of which everybody in the town is very proud) stops halfway up the street. "As if it had been cut off with a knife," says Herr Fischer the dealer. I am glad I don't live in the Totenstrasse. I have never seen a dead man, only once a skull and some bones that the workmen dug up when they were making a well near the mill. Stanislaus and I played ball with the skull, using the bones as bats; and Stanislaus gave the skull a kick.

"Why did you kick it?"

"Grandmother said he was a wicked man. Good people don't stay in their graves. Angels come and fly away with them to heaven."

"Well, they don't eat potatoes in their skins."

I like potatoes baked in their skins, not at home but with Stanislaus. His grandmother, his mother and father, his three sisters and four brothers all live in the Dorfstrasse in a little house made of mud with a thatched roof. They all sleep in one room, which gets very hot. There is no pavement in the Dorfstrasse, but nobody thinks of complaining to the burgomaster about it. When I go and see Stanislaus at dinner time I find them all eating baked potatoes and groats or baked potatoes and pickled herring. I stand in a corner watching them with my mouth watering.

At last Stanislaus' mother tells me to help myself. "If there's enough for eleven, one more won't make much difference."

Stanislaus digs me in the ribs.

"You can imagine it's roast meat."

"We don't have roast meat every day."

"You could if you wanted to."

I take my cap and run home.

"You oughtn't to go there for dinner," mother says to me, "eating their food when they have so little."

"Why haven't they got more?"

"Because it's God's will."

The Totenstrasse is very long—I suppose to give the dead on their way to the churchyard a chance to decide whether they would rather stay in their graves or fly up to heaven.

Uncle M. has just died. I wonder very much if he was a good man. I go to the churchyard, break off a branch of yew, whittle it, and sharpen the end. Then I climb the wall and bore down into uncle's grave to see if he is still there. But the sexton surprises me, and I run away.

On the way home I ask myself, What is a good man?

I hear doors slamming outside. It ought to be dark in the room. Father sleeps there, and mother over there. But it isn't dark now, and their beds are empty. Have they been kidnaped? There is a red glare outside. Somebody is blowing a horn, on and on, a wailing note. I jump out of bed, wrench open the door and run out into the street; and there on the other side of the market place is a house on fire, all red and green and black. Firemen with shining helmets are running about wildly, and a gaping crowd stands watching it all. Julie, our cook, catches sight of me and drives me back to bed.

"Why is that house on fire, Julie?"

"Because God always punishes people."

"But why does He want to?"

"Because little children ask too many questions."

I am frightened, and I can't get to sleep again—the night smells of smoke and burning; it smells of God.

In the morning I stand looking at the charred wood and blackened stone, still hot.

"They haven't found so much as a button; the poor thing must have been burned to ashes in her bed."

I turn round quickly, but the man who was speaking has gone on.

I run home and sit down in a corner, still clasping the stick I was poking the ashes with.

Herr Levi comes and laughs at me.

"A nice thing you've done."

I don't move.

"The whole town knows it was you who set fire to Eichstädt's house."

Herr Levi lights a cigar and goes away. First Julie said I was to blame, and now Herr Levi.

I crawl under the table and stay there till evening. What did I do wrong yesterday? I undressed, I washed myself, went to bed and fell asleep; but I didn't really wash, only promised mother I would, which was a lie. Is that what caused the fire? Is that the reason for this terrible punishment? Is God so strict? I think of baked potatoes and of Frau Eichstädt burned to death.

It is dark in the room, and I lie there listening. On the right of the door there is a thin circular glass tube, which I am forbidden to touch. Marie, the maid, crosses herself before she dusts it.

"That's where your Jewish God lives," she grumbles; and my heart thumps. I daren't touch it. What if He were to jump out of the tube and cry: "I am the Lord God! I have come to punish you for lying. . . ."

But I won't let myself be frightened any longer by the Lord God in the tube nor by the thought of baked potatoes; with one leap I am at the door, and climbing onto the chest of drawers I tear the Lord God down. I break the glass tube into bits. He does not appear. I throw it onto the floor. Still He does not appear. I spit on it and stamp on it. The Lord God does nothing. Perhaps He is dead. He surely must be. I gather up the broken glass and paper and stick them down the crack of the sofa: tomorrow I will bury the Lord God.

Back in bed again I feel very happy. Everybody shall hear how I have killed the Lord God dead.

I had always thought that boys and girls all went to the same school. But Paul and Isle go to the Evangelical school, I go to the Jewish school, and Stanislaus to the Catholic school. But they all learn to read and write just like me and the schoolrooms all look just the same. Our teacher is called Herr Senger. When he comes in to take the class we all cry: "Good morning, Herr Senger." He sits down at his desk and puts his pointer in front of him. If you have not done your homework you must hold out your hand, and Herr Senger canes you with his pointer. "That's to punish you." If you have done your homework well Herr Senger takes you on his knee and rubs his prickly cheek against yours. "As a reward," he says.

In recess we compare our sandwiches.

"I've got meat."

"I've got cheese."

"What have you got in yours?"

"He hasn't got anything in his."

Kurt tries to hide his poor sandwich, but we won't let him. We laugh at him, and Kurt cries: "I'll tell my mother on you," and we call back: "Sneak!" Then Kurt throws down his bread and begins crying.

Going home from school, Max says: "My people won't let me play with Kurt; his mother does our washing. Poor people are dirty and have fleas."

I am playing with Stanislaus. I have had a train as a present and now I am the engine driver and Stanislaus is the signalman. In the middle of the journey I whistle.

"Right away," cries Stanislaus, and whistles shrilly with two fingers in his mouth.

"Have you got fleas?"

"Right away!"

"Are you dirty?"

Stanislaus kicks the train over, reducing my lovely present to twisted metal.

"Max said all poor people are dirty and have fleas. And now you've broken my train. Do you call yourself my friend?"

"I'm not your friend. I hate you."

In the streets the children cry: "Yah to you, dirty Jew!" I have never heard this before. Stanislaus is the only one who doesn't say it, and I ask him what it means.

"In Konitz the Jews killed a Christian baby and made Passion-cakes with its blood."

"That's not true."

"Well, is it true that we are dirty and have fleas?"

Herr Senger, the teacher, is crossing the market place when a boy runs after him and sings:

> "Jiddchen, Jiddchen, schillemachei,
> Reisst dem Juden sein Rock entzwei,
> Der Rock ist zerrisen,
> Der Jud hat geschissen."

Herr Senger goes on without turning his head, and the boy calls out: "Konitz, yah, yah! Konitz, yah, yah!"

"Do you really believe that the Jews killed a Christian baby in Konitz?" I ask Stanislaus. "I'll never eat Passion-cake again."

"Idiot! You can give it to me then."

"Why do they shout, 'Yah, yah, dirty Jew'?"

"Don't you shout 'Polack' after us?"

"That's different."

"Different, hell! If you want to know, grandmother says it was the Jews killed our Savior on the cross."

I run into the barn and crawl into the straw, feeling miserable. I know the Savior. He hangs in Stanislaus' room; red tears run down his cheeks, and he carries his heart open in his breast and it is all bleeding. Underneath it says: "Suffer little children to come unto me." When I am there and nobody can see me I pray to the Savior.

"Please, dear Savior, forgive me for letting the Jews kill you dead."

When I am in bed I ask mother: "Why are we Jews?"

"Go to sleep, you naughty boy, and don't ask silly questions."

But I can't go to sleep. I don't want to be a Jew. I don't want the other children to run after me shouting "Dirty Jew!"

In the carpenter's yard there is a hut where the "True Christians" meet. They blow trombones and sing Hallelujah and kneel on the ground and shout, "Thy Kingdom is at hand, O Zion!" Then they embrace one another, and blow their trombones again. I want to be a "True Christian" too, so I follow the others into the hut. The preacher pats me on the head and gives me a lump of sugar and says that I am on the "right path".

"We will all celebrate Christmas together in love and good will," he says, and I say, "Yes".

"And you, my boy, shall have this little Christmas verse to recite."

I am blissfully happy. I am not a Jew any more, and I have a Christmas verse to learn; nobody will ever be able to call "Dirty Jew!" after me again. I take up a trumpet and blow it when the preacher blows his trombone; and then in a clear solemn voice I recite my Christmas verse. But next day the preacher says he is very sorry, but the Savior would rather Franz recited the verse.

I thought of my own childhood, of my misery when the other children shouted "Dirty Jew!" at me, of my childish appeal to the picture of Christ; of my terrible joy when I realized that nobody would recognize me for a Jew; of the first day of the war and my passionate longing to prove that I was a real German by offering my life to my country; of my writing from the Front to the authorities to say that they could strike my name from the list of the Jewish community. Had it all been for nothing? Had it all been wrong? Did I not love Germany with all my heart? Had I not stood in the rich beauty of the Mediterranean landscape and longed for the austere pinewoods, for the beauty of the still, secret lakes of North Germany? And was not the German language my language, the language in which I felt and thought and spoke, a part of my very being?

But was I not also a Jew? A member of that great race that for centuries had been persecuted, harried, martyrized and slain; whose prophets had called the world to righteousness, had exalted the wretched and the oppressed, then and for all time, a race who have never bowed their heads to their persecutors, who had preferred death and dishonor. I had denied my own mother, and I was ashamed. It is an indictment of society at large that a child should have thus been driven to deception.

But was I an alien because of all this? Is blood to be the only test? Does nothing else count at all? I was born and brought up in Germany; I had breathed the air of Germany and its spirit had molded mine; as a German writer I had helped to preserve the purity of the German language. How much of me was German, how much Jewish? I could not have said.

All over Europe an infatuated nationalism and ridiculous pride was raging—must I too participate in the madness of this epoch? Wasn't it just this madness that had made me turn Socialist?—my belief that Socialism would eliminate not only class hatreds but also national hatreds?

The words. "I am proud to be a German" or "I am proud to be a

Jew," sounded ineffably stupid to me. As well say, "I am proud to have brown eyes."

Must I then join the ranks of the bigoted and glorify my Jewish blood now, not my German? Pride and love are not the same thing, and if I were asked where I belonged I should answer that a Jewish mother had borne me, that Germany had nourished me, Europe had formed me, my home was the earth, and the world my fatherland.

ON THE MOUNT OF OLIVES

JESSIE E. SAMPTER (1883-1940)

Zion became the lodestar of this poet's life in her youth. A native of New York City, she became active in the small but burning Zionist movement there. The first World War gave her verse and her devotion to Zionism a new verve, and in 1919 she went to Palestine, making her permanent home in Rehoboth. She was devoted to the work of Hadassah, the American Women's Zionist Organization and continued her literary efforts in behalf of Palestine, believing that its future "lies not in the hands of fate but in our own hands".

❋ ❋ ❋

IT WAS a Hadassah party. And instead of giving it in the Hotel de France where most of the physicians and nurses of the American Zionist Medical Unit (Hadassah) dwell, we chose an even better place. We went for a moonlight picnic—it happened to be full moon— to the site of the Hebrew University on Mount Scopus. It was a farewell party to two of the nurses, Miss Malin and Miss Kaplin. Miss Aaronson, our dietitian, had charge of the sandwiches and tea and goodies, and she packed them, not forgetting the samovar, in the motor lorry. Some of us climbed in with the food; others drove up in an automobile and a couple of carriages; but most of the party of about fifty persons walked up the three miles or so. I drove up in a carriage with Miss Szold.

It was the loveliest hour of all the day in Jerusalem, just before sunset, a breeze stirring, a soft light over the city. We wound out of the town and up the hill, past the tomb of Simon the Just and the other cave tombs, winding through the gray valley with its scattered gray-green olive trees. It was already the end of May, and only the watered gardens were green and bright with flowers. The treeless hillside, as we wound up it, was already gray, and the road white with blowing dust. Thistles grew on each side of the road, thistles with many kinds and colors of gay blossoms, yellow, purple, red and white. We passed the military grave-yard that is some day to be made into a garden spot. Now it is row upon row of white wooden crosses, with a little patch planted with white wooden magen davids (Stars of David). Here lie those who fell in the fighting around Jerusalem.

The sun set in streaks of crimson behind Jerusalem. The domes and minarets within the walls of the Old City shone with pale rose reflections. On the other side, as we rose on the shoulder of the hill, there were revealed before us the step descent of the wilderness of Judaea, strange yellow hills streaked with patches of many colors, weird in outline, a desert of mountains; and far, far below, the turquoise blue sheet of the Dead Sea with the blue Jordan winding into it, and the purple-blue dream hills of Moab in a long straight line beyond. No other land is like this land. So soft are the colors and yet so vivid, so immense are the distances, the heights and depths, and yet so near seems the farthest point that can be seen. Again I realized my land; again I thrilled with the wonder of being in it; I can never become accustomed to the fact that I am here. Our beautiful city, beautiful in the distance, in the setting sunlight! I was oppressed with our vast task, with our weaknesses, our mistakes. I said to Miss Szold: "Will we ever deserve our Land?" And Miss Szold answered: "If we can ever overcome our arrogance."

A cold wind greeted us on the hilltop. The home of Lady Grayhill, which has been bought with the surrounding land as the site of the Hebrew University, stands to the east of the road. This house is not yet at our disposal, so long as Lady Grayhill is alive, since she herself may still wish to use it. And no wonder! Our first University buildings are to go up across the road. It was now fairly dark, and we had only the gray light of gloaming to see by. An Arab by the roadside was piping a soft monotonous melody on a shepherd's pipe. We entered the lodge, and passed through into the garden and around the white stone house. The house is simple and has good lines, the sort of building we should be glad to use, and the garden is beautiful, neglected and yet cultivated. We passed among the shadows of the trees, down rough stone steps, through air heavy with the fragrance of pines. We passed through a colonnade of white pillars and climbed down to a large stone platform with a low stone wall about it, which covers a cistern. Here we made our headquarters.

The party straggled in by twos and threes; almost all the American Jews were there, and their friends. The supper was stacked up on the stone wall, which also made convenient seats, and the brisk wind heightened our appetite. It was now so dark that we could not see the depth below us that fell away to the east, nor the waters of the Dead Sea. At about half past nine a streak of rose appeared in the east, and deepened and brightened, and out of it bulged the great white moon. Gradually it rose, making clear-cut and deep shadows on the whitening hillside. And by the light of the rising moon our American Palestinian friends formed a ring on the platform and sang and danced a rondo. The wallflowers literally sat on the wall, and joined the dancers in the singing of Hebrew songs that made rhythmic dance music. In and out in many involved figures, in true Palestinian fashion, moved the rapid dancers, their motions graceful and spiritlike in the light of the broad white moon, their shadows dancing beside them. Not all of them were really graceful and spiritlike; old and young, fat and thin, all joined in the merriment.

And as the moon rose higher and higher, the Dead Sea reappeared, a sheet of silver. A few of us left the platform, for we wished to sing songs together. We climbed a little farther down the hillside towards the east, where is the foundation stone of the University, a large square white block with two smaller blocks arranged in a pyramid upon it. We meant to sit there, but the wind was so strong and cold that it drove us back, and we found a more sheltered nook on the hillside with stones to sit upon. And there we sang the songs of exile in our own land. Before our eyes passed visions of the Russian ghetto, of the little heder of the rebbele. And behold, below us lay the Dead Sea, near-seeming as if one could touch it, and the wilderness of Judaea.

So great are the heights and depths of my land, so near to one another the tears and the laughter. In my land that is beautiful above all other lands! It is not merely my love, it is not a forcing of sentiment to say that the dust and thistles of Palestine are beautiful. White dust, and gold and purple thistles. And how much more its roses!

A few days later I drove again to the University site, in the daytime, this time with Patrick Geddes, the Scotch professor who is making the plans for our University. A non-Jew, he has seen the vision of Israel redeemed as many Jews have not seen it. Sometimes, as I listen to his inspired words, I foolishly wish he were one of us. For he is one of us in a wider than the narrow national sense. A little way from the Grayhill house we left our automobile, and Professor Geddes went with others of the party to explore the stony hillside. I stayed at the side of the road waiting for them, and I found a seat on the loose white stones of the wall. As I sat there in the sunshine and the wild wind that caught my skirts and my veil, I happened to look down at a stone beside me, and I saw that the top of it was covered with fossil shells. One of them was clearly outlined in the stone, and several others had left their inverted imprint upon it. That white sandstone, more than two thousand feet above sea level, that mountain top of which it is a fragment, was once at the bottom of the sea. And so my mind wandered to times even more remote than the ancient days of our people. Below me to the east rolled away the wilderness of Judea, parched yellow in the sunshine, and in the hollow lay the bright blue of the Dead Sea. Beyond that the Mountains of Moab, now gray as a strip of cloud. As many times as I have seen that long straight upland—for one can see it from many parts of Jerusalem itself—I have never seen it twice the same. Every shadow, every light claims it for its own and repaints it in new colors.

Again I noted the many kinds and colors of thistles, flowers of many families but all with thorns or burr-covered leaves. These, like the camel, carry their water a long time.

But within the garden of Lady Grayhill's house, within the University grounds, there was a riot of other flowers, cultivated yet seeming wild. The trees, too, crowded each other to the stone wall. Birds were singing among the pines, and a broom tree, covered with fragrant yellow flowers, had been bent low over one of the paths and blocked our way. There were pomegranate trees with burning crimson blossoms, there were roses of Sharon—they are called hollyhocks in America, but the name and the flower have a fresher beauty here—there was a vine of passion flowers creeping over the ground, with its odd and exquisite blossoms of purple and white. How different seemed the hillside in the brightness of day! Only the fragrance was the same.

Again I walked through the white colonnade and looked out over the wonderful and terrible valley below. Here I found shells too, but not sea shells; I found war shells, fragments of them, from the fighting of recent years. Professor Geddes found an old rusty iron helmet. We gathered flowers also—a strange medley of treasures. A young man met us there with blueprints and photographs of the University plans. There were pictures of the great dome that is to be, designed by Professor Geddes, with the magen david woven into glorious patterns. That dome is to rise across the road from the Grayhill house. As we came out on the road again and looked over the thorny, rocky fields, I pictured to myself the great dome that is to rise. I looked at my companion, a lean tall Scotchman with a long gray beard that made one think of tropic mosses and strange adventures. I looked into his blue gray eyes, the eyes of a child or a poet, and I felt a deep gratitude for all that may come to us from the visions of that heart and mind. We gazed down over Jerusalem, beautiful in its stoniness, and Professor Geddes told me more of his plans, of the trees that are to be planted, cypress and olive trees, a whole forest of olives in the valley between Jerusalem and Mount Scopus. In vision I saw Jerusalem rebuilt.

And as I thought of Jerusalem rebuilt, I thought also of the Temple. And it was not standing on the old Temple site above the Wailing Wall where the blue dome of the Mosque of Omar rose far below us. It was not standing in the city.

"That dome of the University," I asked, "is one going to be able to climb up into it?"

"There will be a gallery around it," answered Professor Geddes, "and there young men and women will go together, chanting the one hundred and forty-eighth psalm."

Our new Temple shall arise on a mountain, on the crown of beauty of Jerusalem, and look down into the deepest valley of the whole world.

ISRAEL, LOST AND REGAINED

EDMOND FLEG (1874-   )

It was inevitable that the generation which lived through the Dreyfus case should find a renewed interest in the cultural tradition of the Jews. Of that small but important circle of writers who undertook to rehabilitate the Jewish literary tradition in French, Fleg (though he was born in Geneva) was a central figure and his significance transcends the boundaries of his adopted country. All of his writings—verse, plays and stories—breathe the spirit which he records in these memoirs. The quest for meaning and spiritual sanctions as a Jew will strike a familiar note to those bred in the culture of the Western world. Fleg is known to American readers chiefly through an abridged version of his admirable *Anthologie Juive* and his poetic biographies of Moses, Solomon, and Jesus.

❊ ❊ ❊

IN MY childhood I saw things that no doubt you, my unborn grandchild, will never see. My father was a zaddik, a devout, saintly man, following the Scriptures, and my mother the joyous priestess in her home. At that time religion was mingled with every act of life, but in so simple a way that I saw no religion in it.

I found it quite natural that in the morning my father enveloped himself in a white shawl with black stripes, and wound bands of leather about his forehead and his left arm, while murmuring words which were not mere words. The blessing after meals seemed as much of a necessity to me as the meal itself, and on Friday night there seemed nothing unusual in seeing my mother extend her hands, which had become transparent, over the wicks flickering in the oil.

All that governed the kitchen was hierarchically regulated. One must not eat butter after meat, nor use a knife to cut the chicken which was to be used for cheese; two vessels were used, one for meat and the other for milk foods, and to confuse them were a sin.

544

When a goose arrived from Strasburg it bore around its neck, upon a red seal, signs which fomented archaeological controversies around the kitchen sink, because it was important to my mother and to Lisette the cook, to establish by careful scrutiny at what hour of which day the animal had been bled, and if it were lawful to metamorphose it into delicious food.

Ham, oysters, crabs, game, had but a nominal existence; their taste was unknown to me, as were the color and form of these forbidden foods.

To have entered a tramcar on a Saturday would have seemed as venturesome as to ascend to the moon, and to blow out a candle on that day as unthinkable as to blow out the sun.

Certain rites—but what a ceremonious word for these familiar acts—returned each year as normally as did the seasons which they accompanied; there was the waving of the palm with a perfumed citron, or a row of lights on a board, arranged in decreasing sizes, which were lighted from the smallest to the tallest.

Once every year I ate alone at noon, and my brothers, who were old enough to fast, returned from the synagogue with wan faces whose pride I admired.

At other times my mother and old Lisette went on a hunt into all the corners of our home, and into all the pockets of our clothes searching for crumbs. The round loaf on the table ceded its place to thin cakes without leaven. At dinner my father, his hat upon his head, chanted Hebrew melodies. Bitter herbs and mortar were passed from hand to hand, four cups of wine were drunk, and the door was left open for someone who did not enter.

I did not understand what all this meant nor did I ask about it of others or of myself. I only felt one thing—that the faces of my parents had at these times a radiant joy and serenity that I have not seen since, except in the pictures of the greatest of the saints.

It was not only impure foods that were forbidden; other inhibitions forbade lying, laziness, gluttony, coarseness, spitefulness, every manner of evil; and the spirit of unity, of kindness, and of love as obviously held sway as did the customary domestic acts. Morals were not discussed, rarely mentioned. They were practised. They were as much a part of life as were our daily habits. I never heard a word that was not tender and gentle between my parents. To lie before them, to use an ill-sounding or querulous expression, would have been unthinkable. A gentle but firm justice punished our faults and rewarded our will to do well. The example of toil and of thrift taught us every hour of the day. Pleasure had its place but was not an end in itself. Charity was practised as a natural function. My father was frequently consulted, disputes were submitted to him, and so much of peace emanated from him that adversaries who came to consult him left our home reconciled. Perfect manners, goodness of heart and high-mindedness illumined our very humble home to which one climbed by ascending a somber staircase.

Then there was God; we lived with God, but His presence was subconscious, never spoken of. I did not hear the mention of His name; I only uttered it during the evening prayer which my mother, or even Lisette, bade me repeat before tucking me into bed. It was a very brief prayer; a few words in Hebrew which I repeated without understanding their meaning, and then a single sentence: "God protect Father, Mother, and all those I love." Yes, it was a short prayer, and yet this it was which caused the undoing of my respect for the family-worship.

The light having been put out, I remained alone with the God to whom I had just recited a lesson. Then I spoke to Him. In what terms? In what language? How can I repeat it to you, my unborn grandson? If you in turn know these impulses toward the invisible, if you feel as I felt, this thrill from beyond, if you silently respond to this call from within, you too will find the words which came to me.

I knew God was present, very far away and yet quite close, all around me and in my heart. I told Him all my faults and I besought His forgiveness. I wanted to be better; I could not be without Him. I promised Him to do better, I implored Him to help me. And He did help me, I am sure of it. I rose to Him. He enveloped me. He held me. I fell asleep in His arms.

Who taught me to pray in this way? No one. But what were all the incomprehensible litanies and inexplicable gestures worth compared with this voiceless and formless prayer? I will try to write words which will lend my stammering thought the clarity it needs. I began to feel a contrast between my prayer when alone, which was close to me, and the prayer of my father which I did not comprehend. Or rather, mine only seemed to me to be a prayer, the other a habit that God did not notice.

My critical sense too began to grow. I did not write on Saturday at school. That was forbidden. But at college my elder brothers wrote on that day just as on other days; their studies made it necessary. My father went to his office on Saturday after synagogue services. He also wrote, his business made it necessary. Was therefore the rest on the Sabbath day only important for very little boys?

Once I was taken on a journey, and at the hotel where we dined the fat and the lean were mixed, and cheese was served after meat, and even ham appeared on the table. My parents ate and permitted me to eat of this forbidden dish. Then the food forbidden at home was no longer forbidden when one was away from home? The law was law no longer?

Thus like all children of all time, I began despite myself to scrutinize my parents, and drawing conclusions from their inconsistencies I very slowly began to break their idols.

Others unconsciously became my accomplices. The first of these was my teacher of religion, the cantor of the synagogue. He had a beautiful voice, a beautiful beard, a beautiful soul. But as a teacher he puzzled me. I was at this time attending college, and was proud of my Latin. Now this man taught that the Hebrew had no grammar, which caused me to feel dubious about that language and what it inculcated. Then too, his method alone would have discouraged the most inquisitive of minds. I mumbled prayers which he declared untranslatable. The catechism began with a sentence which amused me: "Who are you, my child? I am a young Jew of Jewess." As for the sacred history and the Psalter chanted by my illiterate cantor, how badly it sounded after my Greek or Roman history.

My father, who read Hebrew in the evenings, would say to me occasionally: "It is a very beautiful language." I did not think it was. How could I? Jewish values were poorly presented to me—knowledge gained at college alone counted.

And that which was begun by the ignorance of the cantor was continued by the cynicism of the Rabbi. Occasionally he came to visit us in the evening after dinner, and we took our seats again around the table, a glass of claret was poured for him, and we listened as he talked.

He had a shaven lip between his magisterial whiskers, and he was an enchanting conversationalist. The whole town doted upon his wit. Could I divine that his skepticism concealed his faith, and that he truly found joy in proclaiming the divine unity. To judge by the God who spoke to me at night, the caustic humor of his earthly representative seemed altogether too human.

Professor of Comparative Philology at the University, he scoffed disdainfully at the small traders of his community, whom, however, upon every possible occasion he heartily served. If one were to believe

him, the Jewish tailor, when he passed by his shop, felt of the cloth
at the back of his rabbinic coat because he had bought it of the Christian
tailor, and the cattle dealer, who sought a good match for his daughter,
declared: "I am not a cattle dealer; I am a manufacturer of meat."
There were some Jewish tales—amusing Jewish tales, over which I
laughed but also blushed a little: the story of the two Jews who had
dined at a restaurant and left the door open as they went out on a
stormy night, and who muttered on hearing themselves abused from
within: "Listen to the antisemites," or of Moses, playing *écarté* with
God in Paradise, saying: "Above all, God, no miracles."

This gallery of portraits and this collection of stories, pleasant as
they were, marred Israel to my too sensitive soul. And I could not
forget these grotesque pictures when I betook myself against my will
to the synagogue.

I was taken to the synagogue for the first time according to custom
when I was a very small boy, to roll up one of the sacred scrolls with
a long linen band covered with colored letters. I wore my velvet suit
with pearl buttons, and was in a state of elation, for from the height
of the gallery my mother was watching me, and the gold stars painted
in the blue ceiling seemed to me real stars in a real heaven.

But I had come to know the cantor and the Rabbi too well. They
robbed the place of its illusions. And excepting for the rare moments
which the music transformed, or when the hidden splendor of the
ceremony suddenly burst forth in its manifest beauty, what boredom
I felt in those dull hours, weighed down the more by the meticulous
phrases of an unknown tongue!

What physical irritation I felt against those persons without breed-
ing who read their newspapers or conversed aloud; what disgust when
I heard the only words spoken in French, and these, in order to stimulate generosity, announcing under the eye of the Holy Law the amount
given for charity by each donor.

At the age of thirteen years, when I "made my first Jewish communion", I could chant very well before the ark, without sounding
a false note in the biblical text of which I understood not one word,
and in the evening after the festival I could recite in one breath the
benediction which had remained Hebrew to me. But when I was
alone at night in my bed, face to face with the God who came to me,
I asked myself quite mystified if indeed He was the God of Israel.

He was, my child. All those prayers the meaning of which escaped
me, magnificently revealed Him, all those ceremonies the emptiness of

which gave me a sense of loneliness, emanated from His presence. But I knew it not—it was badly explained to me, and I was to wander a long time among men and thoughts before arriving at the truth.

Ah, you will say, this is a strange way of explaining to you why I am a Jew. But you will not understand why I am a Jew unless you first understand why I ceased to be a Jew.

In those early years of my adolescence the break was not yet conscious. But my spirit unconsciously turned away from the spirit of my people. And I was soon to discover another world.

In my fourteenth year I had overtaxed my strength. My best friend and classmate at that time, now a pastor and professor of theology, lived in the country. I was in need of fresh air; his mother desired to have me visit him. I played the piano and because of my love of music I was invited to a neighboring home, where I became a daily guest.

An old lady lived there with her daughter and three sons, two of whom were already grown men. Widow of a famous writer, she had known "Monsieur Taine", "Monsieur Renan", "Monsieur Got", and had traveled much in Italy. Her conversation was replete with memories. In my home there was great respect for intellectual culture; here one enjoyed familiarity with it.

The quite rustic dwelling faced a large meadow, which commanded a cliff where the Rhône turns in a rocky circle. My elderly friend helped me to see in nature that which had never been pointed out to me. The play of clouds and the drama of light were events for her; they became events for me.

I did not quite understand just what seemed new to me in this home, but harmony reigned therein in a very different way from that I had known. Strange and tiresome though the religious customs (which chimed with the days, months, and years for us) had seemed to me, I never conceived of existence without them. But here were no dietary laws, no imperious rites, no oppressive prohibitions. One went to services on Sunday; that was all. And yet not quite all. Work, charity, the kindness which were merely practiced in our home, were here consciously lived, and helped one to achieve a clear conscience. The moral instinct was enriched and clarified by all the light that the living word could bring to it.

Then the mother, the brothers, the sister, were so detached from one another in their own definite interests! If there were a question concerning a walk, or blame or praise of any act, of a decision to be taken, however important, each one of them expressed his ideas as though it were permissible to have individual ideas. The ancestral community spirit which in our home imposed itself upon us would have hindered such divergencies. And dimly I felt myself rebelling against it.

I have since understood what was happening to me then. In Geneva, where I was born, the sects were strictly separated. I had no life other than the Jewish life. Our ghetto was not shut in by chains, but none the less it was a ghetto. I had come out of it for the first time. I looked upon free air and a free sky, and my spirit liberated itself not only from the rites of the Jewish family but from the family itself.

The following winter a book took me still further away from Israel —the Gospel. It was not my friends who placed this formidable discovery before my eyes. Their sense of delicacy would not have permitted them to do this. But I, whom no one had known how to interest in the Old Testament, I wanted to know this Jesus who was preached to them on Sundays. I still see beneath the trees of the old square, the stand of the secondhand bookshop, where for a few centimes I bought all this revelation of suffering. I still hear my heart cry out at the furtive reading of those eternal pages. I was the shepherd close to the cradle; I was the fisherman of Tiberias; I walked with the paralytic; I again saw the light with the blind; I again came to life with Lazarus; "Our Father" was my prayer, the Sermon on the Mount was my sermon; the agony on the cross my agony. But at the end of my Passion, I did not murmur as did the Christ: "Forgive them, they know not what they do." No, I remember that, crucified by horror and shame for my race, quite small and alone in my room, I cried out "Dirty Jews, dirty Jews!"

I have told of my anguish at that time in my book, *L'Enfant Prophète*. I do not wish to go over it again. But to show you that that story was not merely a romance and to make clear to you what I dared to call in those far-off days "my religious thought", I will copy here, without any changes in its poor style, that which I then wrote in my diary and found last night among some old papers:

"I am not a believer; it is my old religion that is at fault, my poor religion, the ruins of an unfinished building. What care for forms, what absurd customs! Alas, laws against eating ham, against tearing paper on Saturday, the custom of eating bread without leaven for seven days, have long since caused my soul to rebel though I dared not confess it. The reading of the New

Testament has finally detached me from all this. I have wept real tears while reading about the tortures of Jesus, and I have felt ashamed of my fathers who sullied themselves with the blood of this just man whom they so treacherously crucified. Yes, I am ashamed of my people. I have heard it said that a Jew and a Christian can never live in peace together. I am not a Jew, oh no!

"It may be a despicable thing thus to put the faith of one's ancestors out of one's heart, but I do not feel that I must imitate their errors. My opinions are my own, no one has inculcated them within me. I have read no books concerning them. I have heard it said that Christians alone can understand their religion, because their religion is the life of Jesus. It is also my religion because this life so radiant is the life that shall be my example; his charity, his mercy, are the objects of my admiration; these are what my soul loves and what it finds truly great.

"I understand Jesus, but do not look upon him as a supernatural being; that is beyond my comprehension, and I cannot think him divine by closing my eyes; that were unworthy of my intelligence. But I can better understand Jesus than I can understand a God, absolute master and judge of all things. It is not that I am an atheist, oh no! I say my prayers every night, but I pray to God within me who is not a ruler. I have been told that God is a spirit. Why should he not be the thought that makes its voice heard in the conscience of each one of us? Perfect faith, I admire it, I envy its possession but, alas, I have it not. I cannot be a Jew. I can be a Christian. And if I can follow him I have chosen as my model, if I look upon the good as God, and if I think he may be the revelation of an omnipotent God, am I so very blameworthy? May I be pardoned if I err, may I find mercy above if I have doubted. God, let Thy light enter within me, reveal Thyself to me if Thou art."

Since that time I have reviewed the process of the trial of Jesus and I hope that you, my child, more correctly informed, will never know the sorrow of accusing your whole race—which was my first sorrow.

Yet this God of my prayers, the one gift and the most precious which was left to me of Israel, this God whom I already so coldly called the Good but who so vitally dwelt within me that I still addressed myself to him as to a living person, even this God was to forsake me.

It happened a year later and in the most trivial way. I was eager to become a philosopher, and there being no class in philosophy at

Geneva I trusted myself without a guide to the thousand pages of a popular history of philosophy. At last I was to know. In haste I opened the big volume. First of all, religion—How was it that there were such varying ideas about God, and so many that were contradictory?

Of the God of Israel not one word; is He then unimportant? But I learn that a certain Protagoras wills to ignore whether there are Gods or not, and that a certain Critias maintains they were invented by a legislator as cautious as he was crafty. Socrates, I am told, revealed the moral God, the God of "civilized nations". Plato placed him in the "realm of ideas". Aristotle identified him as "the pure act", the Stoics confounded his unity with that of the universe, and Plotinus made of him a trinity. What was I to believe? Whom was I to follow? I was perplexed.

In the Middle Ages, the same disputations were translated into scholastic jargon: St. Augustine does not agree with St. Thomas, Averroes is not in accord with Scotus. In modern times the warfare continues; Malebranche against Descartes, Liebnitz against Spinoza!

Of course, there were many evidences offered, the familiar evidences of the existence of God. But I had read too much; the evidences proved nothing to me. And how triumphant I felt when Kant arrived with his heavy club and pulverized all these affirmations. Oh, how well he spoke! How right he was! Yes, we impose upon things the laws of our own being, we cannot conceive of them in and of themselves; we know not the Being nor the Substance nor the Absolute, nor God.

Then Herbert Spencer came forward like a prestidigitator holding the doctrine of evolution in his hands. Three turns of his cuffs and I saw the One producing the Many, and the Simple producing the Complex, from the humblest atom of matter to the loftiest creation of the spirit. Twice presto chango, and by enchantment the vegetable emerged from the mineral and man from the animal! A little shove, and from Heredity and the Association of Ideas, suddenly these ancient illusions escape, Good, Evil, Freedom, God!

Finally Auguste Comte and his Positivism brought certitude to me. Humanity had evidently passed through three successive stages: in the theological period it explained natural phenomena by supernatural causes; wonders, miracles, were the acts of God. In the metaphysical period mankind has recourse to abstractions converted into realities, faculties, essence and accident; in the third period, the period that still obtains, we happily limit ourselves to knowledge through observation and experimentation in the relationship of phenomena. This last method, the only one that is of value, has created modern science and has forever supplanted metaphysics and theology; there is no other religion than the Religion of Humanity; the problem is settled.

Upon this discovery of the great void an entire wall of my inner life collapsed. I should have perished but nothing happened. I was too proud of being a philosopher to complain of the errors that encompassed me. My nightly conversations with God changed in tone. The words, *Reveal thyself if thou art,* which I formerly repeated in my agony, were no longer a prayer; they were a summons. I defied this God, I blasphemed against Him. Then, giving up the effort to obtain speech from the nonexistent, I abandoned Him and His silence.

Far distant as I was at this time from Israel, I was to take myself still further away. I went to Paris and entered the higher class of rhetoric, attended the Sorbonne and was admitted to the Normal School. Here was material to help me to come to my senses, but the contrary happened. I wanted to combine for myself some austerity with much self-indulgence, but I must confess to you that toward my twentieth year I was soaring to a height of pretentiousness from which in the face of certain facts I was compelled to descend later on. Seeming to be under the spell of what I chose to call my charm, some of my comrades amused themselves by forming a small circle about me, whose loyalty was tempered by raillery. We were called the "Aesthetes", and I have a notion that this was not a misnomer. I leaned upon Anatole France and Renan, and had drawn from the pure strings of these two masters the sophisticated waters of my dilettantism, for we were dilettantes.

One must not take the world too seriously; one did not even know if it existed, for one left crass certitudes to the common people. Society was not worth the trouble of mingling with it. Of what importance to subtle spirits were eternal principles, the Rights of the Man and the Citizen, the battle of parties or the form of the state? Ethics also seemed very dull; Good and Evil were dumbbells that one need not trouble to handle. Art alone counted, not only the art of words, sounds, forms and colors, accessible after all to inferior bipeds who could read a book, listen to a concert or walk through a museum, but the art of creating from moments taken from one's own life an opus worthy of contemplation.

My chief function then was to admire myself, and as in the fluid mobility of my self-scrutiny it would have seemed a poor thing to admire but one person within myself, I distinguished at least five, each of which corresponded to one of my friends; there was Des Grieux who was bored by Tiberge, the Pylades of an ever bitter Orestes, the Agathon of a modern Socrates, the satirist who juggled with the shadow of things, and the romanticist whose piano endured in turn frenzies and ecstasies.

Could so complex a being inhabit this lowly earth without peril? Would not life in simplifying him cause him to perish? It was decided that such a misfortune must be prevented. My Socrates was not terrified by one more hemlock story. He brought me a vial of seeming poison which however he had filled with pure water; otherwise you would never had had a grandfather.

Do not think, my child, that I illuminate the past for the unique satisfaction of evoking flittering memories. If there be one quality—or one defect—commonly attributed to Israel, it is too great concern for this earthly existence. Idealist or materialist he clings to life, be it to exploit or to ennoble it. To turn away from it, to abdicate before his time, either in contemplation, in inaction or in death, is not the habit of the Jew. I had forsaken the rites and the laws of my people. I had rejected their God; and the inmost voice of my people had grown silent within me.

I was in this state of mind when the tidings came that Captain Dreyfus, banished to Devil's Island as a traitor in 1894, had been unjustly condemned for the one and only reason that he was a Jew. At first the whole matter did not interest me. It was a news item which could not disturb my contemplative life, and with the little thought that I consented to give it, I believed it unlikely that seven army officers, because of mere *prejudice* could have sent an innocent man to hopeless imprisonment. It was incredible to me.

However, the agitation increased throughout the country in favor of the condemned man. Several of our teachers interested themselves in his case; soon he had defenders among my comrades in the school, even among the Aesthetes, and detached as I might be from worldly affairs, I in my turn was obliged to descend from my empyrean for him.

I had one close friend who was not a student of the Normal Institute. We had come to know one another in the last year of college, and were soon bound together by an affection that still endures. The deep tenderness which united us was the attraction of an altogether intellectual sympathy. Our greatest joy was our mutual understanding, and the formulating of our ideas in unison. I felt a certain pride in maintaining this aspect of our friendship. I did not want it to consist of mutual acts of service which seemed to me the current money of sentiment, nor of that cheap confidence which expresses itself in the exchange of secrets. In fact, a sort of shyness separated our souls that were really so close to one another. The Dreyfus affair was to reveal the cause to me.

He was brought up in an environment foreign to every reactionary or even conservative tendence; very sensitive, but of a sensitiveness without any romanticism, and saturated with the destructive indifference which was that of Maurice Barrès in his early years. He was highly intelligent and much more endowed than was I with the force of logic, (we will call him the "Logician") and had accepted all the conclusions of our common nihilism.

If ever there was a loyal and a free spirit, it was his; he had liberated himself from all philosophical illusions; he had broken all social idols; even the love of fatherland had given way under his analytical keenness.

His overwhelming skepticism, contrary to mine, admitted from the beginning that the innocence of Dreyfus was eminently possible, but in the measure that the successive disclosures drew me closer to this hypothesis, to my great astonishment I saw his opinion develop in the contrary direction.

It was soon declared that, in violation of the rights of the defense, a secret document had been submitted to the military judges of Dreyfus; that it had determined their verdict, and that neither the accused nor his lawyer were in a position to disprove it. This act seemed to me to create a presumption in favor of the Captain; what need of new secret proofs if previous ones sufficed? This method of reasoning did not affect my Logician, except in the domain of pure abstraction, and one could not tell if it were applicable to the case in point.

The illegality which was shocking to me, seemed in itself to justify a revision of the trial. He contended that this illegality might spring from interests higher than those of the defense, and that a revision should not be suffered except for more peremptory reasons.

It was known that Dreyfus had been condemned through the examination of a memorandum written, it was claimed, by his hand, and stating the number of documents delivered to a foreign power. When this memorandum was published in the press, it was found that the handwriting was strangely like that of another officer, Commandant Esterhazy. A large number of experts affirmed that the handwritings were identical. The Logician replied: "What do they know about it? They only worked on facsimiles."

It seemed to me that the motives had never been clearly set forth, which would have explained the crime of Dreyfus; on the other hand, Esterhazy was a gamester, and letters written by him were known to have expressed the wish that France might meet a new Sedan. My friend replied that Esterhazy might be a scoundrel and Dreyfus be none the less guilty. And then were those much discussed letters authentic?

If Colonel Picquart was to be incriminated in a forgery or in the use of forgery which showed that the General Staff shielded Esterhazy, this accusation presented nothing very strange; but if it could be proven that Commandant Henry had committed a forgery in order to prevent revision, this forgery became the patriotic act of a devoted soldier, who, knowing of documents which could not be seen without danger, had no other aim than to produce an equivalent.

What gave me pause in this reasoning was that it was irrefutable if one admitted the inherent premise which was nothing else than a tacit vote of confidence in the military tribunal and the officers of the staff. But this confidence, so far as my friend was concerned, had in it nothing of superstition; it was, he said, confidence in the only men who were informed. On the one side he saw specialists who know; on the other side, amateurs who guessed. Between the two he did not hesitate in making his choice.

For a long time I was hesitant in my choice; then I was so no longer. For those, whom my Logician called amateurs, those who, according to his point of view were guessing, according to my point of view—*knew*. We discussed every new incident of the affair (every day brought forth new incidents) and we tried to convince each other. We did not succeed and I was greatly troubled. I could neither doubt his intelligence nor his good faith nor his heart. How was it that he saw error where I saw truth? In his confidence in certain officers, which could be but a tentative attitude of the critical mind, did there not enter, without his being conscious of it, something instinctive and mysterious? And I myself, when my faith went out to those other, could I maintain that nothing within me stood between my judgment and the facts? What were these subconscious forces which caused us to oppose each other? Why did I dread them without defining them? Were they to destroy our beautiful friendship?

We might well fear it, for all about us old bonds were being loosened. You may read the story of the "Affair" in your history books. That which you will not find therein is the accent of passion to which it gave expression. At the Sorbonne the classes resolved themselves into meetings, and in the salons the evenings ended in fist fights.

Streets were frequently guarded. Long lines of civilians or of soldiers kept the crowd in check which in turn spat upon the villains or the heroes. These civil discords destroyed happy friendships, and even the peace of the simplest homes. Whether one were for Dreyfus or against him, one was always the enemy of someone, it might be of one who had been a friend for fifty years; it might be of a brother or even of a father. For underneath the drama of the "Affair", secret and long drawnout, another drama was being enacted which combined in hatred two conceptions of society, of life, and of the world.

The most clearly visible aspect of this hidden conflict was the battle waged against Israel. Dreyfus being a Jew, certain anti-Dreyfusards held all Jews responsible for his crime, and for the disorders in the country which their determination to exculpate him provoked. Even if his innocence could be proved, the Jews were blameworthy in desiring to exonerate him. The honor of a Jew was as nothing compared to the safety of a nation. If thoughtful men without religious affiliation, if some Christians, some Catholics, even priests (and some could be named) enrolled among his defenders, they were undoubtedly corrupted by Jewish gold or by the Jewish mind.

It was said that an enormous syndicate had been formed, the Syndicate of Treason, the funds of which were contributed by Jews throughout the world, to aid those who plotted to disarm France in order to deliver her to her enemies. And this was said not to be unique in the world's history. Wherever the Jew had appeared, he had brought about ruin. He had undermined the Roman Empire and was in league with the barbarians at the time of the great invasions. Because of him, Spain of the Visigoths had yielded to the Arabs. Because of him, the Poland of Poniatowsky was dismembered. In the Middle Ages, he had extorted all the gold of earth through usury, and then made use of it in 1789 to finance a profitable Revolution which camouflaged him into a citizen everywhere, and permitted him to realize his dream of villainous domination throughout a debased century, over the dirty rubbish heap of a vanished order. Greedy, sensual, a thief and forger, the Jew was a traitor by choice and by his very nature, and if Dreyfus needed a motive for his crime the one fact that he was a Jew explained his treason.

This philosophy of history in the invective vein could not affect me. In vain did I search through the most secret recesses of my subconscious being. I did not recognize myself in this portrait of the Jew. I was quite sure I was not planning any sinister project by which the world since the first crisis revealed the survival of their solidarity and their narrow conception of nationality.

Thus wishing to show confidence in those who were appointed to the administration of his country, and to find in them interest in and sympathy for his country, my dear Logician had not found it illogical in himself to believe that, without absolutely excluding Jews from every public function, they were only to be allowed a voice in the State proportionate to their numbers in the nation.

I was stupefied. Did Jews really govern France? Was it indeed necessary to deprive them of the rights they now had—the rights they had won? Was it because of their solidarity that Jews believed Dreyfus to be innocent?

How could a lucid and passionless intelligence conceive or accept such hideous conclusions? I could find no answer and could not divert my mind from seeking one.

It was a sad night on which I suddenly realized that accord between my friend and myself was no longer possible, that our misunderstanding had not its origin in facts, nor in their interpretation, nor in the conclusions more or less cogent, which we had drawn from them, but in a reality which had escaped us, more real than we ourselves and very very ancient. Interested at closer range now in the Dreyfus battles, I had signed a protest in favor of Picquart which appeared in the daily press. In his tender consideration, my friend has made me feel that as a stranger or semi stranger I should have abstained from taking part in this protest. From the viewpoint of pure logic he was not wrong, but I tried to persuade him through a letter to the contrary.

Admit—I wrote him—for an instant that all those who signed the protest had excellent reasons and that those same reasons were my reasons. Did I in signing arrogate to myself a right that was not mine? Do I violate any French law in expressing my opinion, my personal feeling, my pain and my indignation? There is no question here of a political matter but of a judicial matter. I claim that there is an abuse of power and tyranny in the application of the law. Strangers who live in France are liable to suffer under such conditions as well as the French themselves. Will you reply that they can go away? Yes, if it were the legislation itself which annoyed them; but, on the contrary, they may remain and protest in the presence of an illegal act which plunges them and with them a large number of the French people into consternation.

Having the right to protest, I added, I made of it a duty, believing myself obliged to express an opinion publicly that I had not concealed from my comrades. That the attitude of the ministry was hostile toward the school was well-known, and if disciplinary measures were to be taken against the protestants, it would have been painful to me to be omitted.

Thus I reasoned after the event, but I did not reason about it while signing the protest. I became a social being; for the first time I took action, and I believe that action does not only result from clear reasoning intellectually developed, but often from a strange impulse the origin of which may be obscure. I felt that my dilettantism was only superficial, that I had need of justice, that those humanitarian interests that I had derided were my very own, that life would never give me sufficient proofs to the contrary to cause me to doubt certain age-old theories, though seemingly childish and overstressed and even voiced by imbeciles.

Was there then mingled with this human solidarity a Jewish solidarity which made the drama I was living through more tragic? I could no longer doubt it. But what difference did that made to me? I could neither resist the call of the one nor of the other; both took possession of me as part of my very being.

And I looked upon my friend who seemed so different, so distant! Had we not been in agreement so long because I had been ignorant of myself so long? Did the constraint that I so often felt in his presence reveal a chasm that could never be bridged over? Must that which had united us be renounced? Gentle as was his friendly reproof, did it not shut me out from his country and from his friendship at the same time?

And, while I was weighing and measuring these unhappy thoughts, the "Affair" was becoming a personal challenge to me. My transcendent egotism was fast disappearing. I awaited the morning papers in agony. I read them as though the fate of this man were bound up with my fate, with the fate of his entire race, in which, little by little, I discovered my own place. His letters were published. Beneath the poor declamatory style I heard the cry of tortured innocence. And reaching me across the sea, this cry clutched at my throat and tore at my heart. At night on my bed I thought of the prisoner. I saw him alone on that tropic rock encompassed by the malign silence of his guards. He too was abed in the night fettered to a straw pallet by two iron clamps. And without moving he cried out—he cried out. And his cry reawakened other cries I had if I were to give myself to other studies, if later in life I were to have a family without being able to leave my children the legacy of an ideal that had been handed down to me from my ancestors, I should always feel a dim remorse, the consciousness of having been faithless to a trust. And I thought of my father no longer living, and I reproached myself for not having appreciated that Jewish wisdom which he commended to me, and which lived in him. I reproached myself for my failure to find any bond between Israel's past and my own empty soul.

It was then that I heard Zionism mentioned for the first time. You cannot imagine, my child, what a beacon light that was. Consider that at the time of which I write to you, the word Zionism was never mentioned in my presence. The antisemites accused the Jews of constituting a nation within the nations; but the Jews, at least those whom I met, denied this. And now behold, the Jews were declaring: We are a people as others are; we have a country as others have. Our country must be given back to us.

I now learned that the Zionist idea had its remote origin in ancient prophecies; the Bible promised their return to the Holy Land to the dispersed Jews; thruout the Middle Ages they lived but by their faith in this promise; in the eighteenth and nineteenth centuries great souls, Maurice of Saxony, the Prince de Ligne, Napoleon, had foreseen the significance from the philanthropic, political, economic, religious and moral points of view, that a Jewish re-gathering in Palestine would have. Since 1873 colonies had been established and developed there and finally a new apostle, Theodor Herzl, summoned the Jews of the whole world to create the Jewish state there. Was this the solution I sought? It explained many things. If truly the Jews were only a nation, one could understand why they were looked upon as Jews even when they ceased to observe their religion, and one could only understand why the nations that had sheltered them might accuse them of not sharing their national interests.

The Zionist ideal thrilled me by its loftiness. I admired in these Jews, and wished I could have admired in myself, this fidelity to the ancestral soil which had endured two thousand years; and I was thrilled by the vision of the exodus which would take many of them back from their various places of exile to their regained unity.

My Logician on his part approved of my enthusiasm. He saw clearly that my Zionism would, in the end, be in accord with his growing nationalism, accepting certain consequences that would be antisemitic. Thus our two minds had in a way traveled in parallel lines, both of us leaving behind us the vision of humanity for that of country —country for me being the Jewish land. But from the beginning I again felt confusedly that my logic was less precise than his, and that if I wished to be, according to my custom, honest with myself, it would not be possible for me to accept his entire process of reasoning in all its harshness.

The third Zionist Congress was about to open at Basle. I decided to attend it. My knowledge of the German language made it possible for me to follow the debates rather closely. Theodor Herzl told of his efforts to obtain a charter from the Sultan. The Executive Council reported that one hundred thousand Jews were already enrolled in the movement and inferred that at least five hundred thousand Jews throughout the world were already Zionists. A plan for Jewish colonization in the Island of Cyprus was rejected as opposed to the plan of colonization in Palestine. The thesis of certain opponents of Zionism who saw in the movement a danger to non-Zionist Jews was refuted.

I heard many gifted men endowed with eloquence and faith, but I was chiefly an observer. What different types of Jews there were all about me: this pale Polish Jew with his prominent cheekbones, that German with spectacles, this Russian with the angelic expression, that bearded Persian, the clean-shaven American, the Egyptian with his fez, and that dark phantom, enormous in his great caftan, with his fur cap, and the blond curls falling from his temples. And in the midst of all these strange faces, something happened to me that was bound to happen; I felt that I was a Jew, essentially a Jew, but I also felt myself French, a Frenchman of Geneva, but French.

It was now certain that the Zionist program in no way implied the return of all Jews to Palestine—a thing numerically impossible, for the Jewish country only offers itself to those Jews who feel that they have no other country. French on my mother's side, my soul and mind were turned towards France, at first when very young through the gratitude of my parents as Jews towards that country. Later through my own literary aspirations, and through my prolonged life in Paris in the midst of college youths and students at the Sorbonne and at the Normal Institute whose friendship and affection had helped me to be myself; and finally through the anguish that the Dreyfus drama caused me because of France which was lacerated and torn over it.

In my thoughts I could not separate the place of my birth, Geneva, from the great Fatherland of the spirit to which Geneva itself in so many ways belonged. When then, abandoning the egotism of the dilettante, I searched, as did my Logician, for a tradition in the depths of my own being, I found there, more powerful and more vital than my Jewish instincts as yet barely awakened, the French tradition mingled with that of Israel.

What then was Zionism to me? It could arouse me, as it still does, this great miracle of Israel which affects all Israel; three million Jews will speak Hebrew, will live on the soil of the Hebrews. But for the twelve million Jews who will continue to be dispersed throughout the world, for all of these and for me, the question, the tragic question remains: What is Judaism? What ought the Jew to do? How be a Jew? Why be a Jew?

The reply was slow in coming. I could not invent it. It must be searched for, searched for throughout the history of Israel, from the mythical days of the Bible up to the latest hours of the present time. This task would demand years, perhaps a lifetime. I was like Taine when, face to face with the necessity of voting, he found himself constrained to write his book, *The Origins of Contemporary France,* in order to arrive at his own conclusions. But I was not Taine. I lacked courage. I was dominated by other ambitions which demanded less austerity. Literature and the theater attracted me. I could not resist their appeal. But the unanswered question came back to me ceaselessly. How be a Jew? Why be a Jew? And ceaselessly together with it came the reproach of my conscience to my indolence which had not made reply. Some years passed. I saw my dear Logician frequently. Passing from nationalism to royalism, his way of thinking had developed harmoniously, and comparing it with my own disordered way, I suffered. Every morning I read two articles in a daily paper which still appears; the one set forth the doctrine of integral nationalism in clear terms and perfect language; the other translated this doctrine with prodigious inventiveness into silly insults accompanied by coarse epithets. These insults, almost all of them, were leveled at Jews, and being leveled at Jews, they were leveled at me. Each morning I read this paper; each morning, as on the day before I read it again. And the reading of it each morning left me in a state of wrath and distress.

I married. My son was born to me, he whose son you are to be, my child. And then a strange thing happened. On the morning which this son was born, by chance I did not read that paper. And since that day I have never read it. Why did the birth of my son liberate me from this nightmare? I did not know. But when he was one year old, something else occurred that was not less surprising. One of my plays had just been produced with some success, and there were many reasons for me to persevere in my work. I abandoned it all and without cessation for three years I studied Judaism. I believe that I now understand the power that spurred me on, and the hour chosen for its exercise. Even then without a doubt, I was obeying the instinct which today dictates this book for you. I may not teach my children the religious practises of my fathers, nevertheless, I would transmit to them something of Israel.

Is there an ancestral memory? I can no longer doubt it, because that which I then learned seems to me not to have been learned at all but to have been remembered. To begin with—Hebrew. I will never know it as I should wish to know it! But I know enough of it already to be convinced that one cannot understand Israel without understanding Hebrew. Those words which I so often heard pronounced in my childhood, those strange syllables the meaning of which remained a mystery, suddenly opened out to me as doors to a treasure house. And it was not alone their significance which brought me light but the soul that emanated from them. This soul reflected a whole world, the world of my father, my own world, in the evident relation of derivatives from the same root; in the rudimentary structure of the phrase, in the illogical incoherence of images; in the lack of power to express pure abstraction, the uncertain contours of the verb hardly distinguishing past, present and future, but which seems to move in the realm of eternity.

SOURCES AND LITERATURE

There is no intention of providing here a full bibliography of Jewish autobiographical literature. Rather, the aim is to indicate the scope of the field and offer examples that will aid those who may desire to plough the field further. The following divisions give, (I) collections of literature that include autobiographical excerpts, (II) articles and books that treat of the subject interpretatively and bibliographically, and (III) sources of the selections in this book together with relevant autobiographical literature. It should be added that while periodical literature has been utilized in the preparation of this work, the items are so copious, especially during the last seventy-five years, that a description of all the references would require a little book; consequently only some of the most vital of these memoirs are included in the notes under III.

I

Anonymous ("Editors" unnamed), *Youth Amidst the Ruins,* published by Hashomer Hatzair Organization, New York, 1941. Excerpts from diaries of European pioneers-in-training during the Blitz years 1939-1940.

Appel, Judah, Editor, *Betokh Reshith ha-Tehiah,* Tel Aviv, 1936. Memoirs of members of the Hovevi Zion movement in Tsarist Russia.

Bach, Hans, Editor, *Jüdische Memoiren aus drei Jahrhunderten,* Berlin, 1936. Excerpts from the memoirs and diaries of thirteen German Jews.

Basuk, Moses, Editor, *Sefer he-Haluz,* Jerusalem, 1941. An anthology of the writings and recollections of members of the Haluz movement.

Ben Zwi, Isaac, Hashin, A., and Zerubbabel, Editors, *Yizkor, Zum Andenken fun die fallene Wachter un Arbeiter in Erez Yisrael,* New York, 1916.

———, Editor, *Kobez ha-Shomer,* Tel Aviv, 1937. Reminiscences and letters of the Shomer organization in Palestine.

Bernfeld, Simon, *Sefer ha-Demaoth,* Berlin, 1923-1926, 3 vols. Exclusively martyriological excerpts.

Broides, Isaac, Editor, *Vilna ha-Zionith we-Asakneha,* Tel Aviv, 1930. Some memoirs of Vilna Zionists, 1881-1924.

Citron, S. L., Editor, *Sefer Zikkaron,* Vilna, 1925. Friends' recollections of a remarkable woman, Esther Rubenstein.

Dinabourg, Ben-Zion, Editor, *Toledoth Yisrael,* Tel Aviv, 1926-31, vols. V, VI (each 2 parts). Occasional brief excerpts.

Eisenstein, J. D., Editor, *Ozar Masaoth,* New York, 1926. 24 texts of Jewish travelers from the 9th to the 18th centuries, a large part of which has been Englished in E. N. Adler's *Jewish Travellers,* London and New York, 1931.

Gaon, Moses David, *Yehude ha-Mizrah be-Erez Yisrael,* Jerusalem, 1928, 2 vols. Short excerpts in vol. I.

Goitein, S. D. F., Editor, *Von den Juden Jemens,* Berlin, 1934. Several interesting fragments.

Habas, Berahah, Editor, *Aliyath ha-Noar,* Jerusalem, 1941. Memoirs of youth settlers and pioneers in Palestine.

Höxter, Julius, *Quellenbuch zur jüdischen Geschichte und Literatur,* Frankfort a.M., 1922-1930, 5 vols. A one-volume abridged version in English, translated by Moses Jung, London, 1938. A number of excerpts.

Kahana, Abraham, Editor, *Sifruth ha-Historia ha-Yisraelith,* Warsaw, 1922-1923, 2 vols. Excerpts presented as historical sources.

Katzenelson-Rubashow, Rachel, Editor, *The Plough Woman,* New York, 1932. English translation from the Hebrew by Maurice Samuel. Reminiscences of pioneer women in Palestine.

Marcus, Jacob R., Editor, *The Jew in the Medieval World* (315-1791), Cincinnati, 1938. Brief excerpts as historical sources.

Schwarz, Leo W., Editor, *A Golden Treasury of Jewish Literature,* New York, 1937. Some modern literary autobiographies.

Sokolow, Nahum, Editor, *Sefer Zikkaron,* Warsaw, 1889. Brief memoirs of Hebrew writers, pp. 117-194.

Winter, J. and Wünsche, A., Editors, *Die jüdische Literatur seit Abschluss des Canons,* Trier, 1896, 3 vols. Some excerpts in vol. III.

II

Baron, Salo Wittmayer, "Biography," pp. 324-348, and supplement, pp. 214-218 in *Bibliography of Jewish Social Studies,* 1938-39, New York, 1941. Lists autobiographies published during 1938-1939.

Grunwald, Max, "Memoirenliteratur" in the *Jüdisches Lexicon,* vol. IV, pp. 71-82. Especially valuable for modern European items.

Letteris, Meir Halevi, *Zikkaron ba-Sefer,* Vienna, 1868. Opens his memoirs with a brief discussion of general and Jewish autobiography.

Marx, Alexander, "Glimpses of the Life of an Italian Rabbi of the First Half of the Sixteenth Century (David Ibn Yahya)," in *Hebrew Union College Annual,* vol. I, pp. 605-639, Cincinnati, 1924.

Roth, Cecil, Editor, "Biography," pp. 114-156 in *Magna Bibliotheca Anglo-Judaica,* London, 1937. A number of English-Jewish memoirs.

———, "The Memoirs of a Sienese Jew" in the *Hebrew Union College Annual,* vol. V, pp. 353-402. Illuminating comment and bibliography.

Schechter, Frank, "An Unfamiliar Aspect of Anglo-Jewish History" in *Publications of the American-Jewish Historical Society,* vol. XXV, pp. 63-74, Phila., 1917.

Schechter, Solomon, "A Jewish Boswell" in *Studies in Judaism,* First series, Phila., 1915, pp. 142-146.

Spiegel, Shalom, *Hebrew Reborn,* New York, 1930. Considerable reference to modern Hebrew autobiographical literature, with valuable bibliography.

Waxman, Meyer, *A History of Jewish Literature from the Close of the Bible to Our Own Days*, New York, 1932-1941, 4 vols. Discussion of memoir literature in vol. II, pp. 506-516; vol. IV, pp. 842-866, 1044-1047.
Zinberg, Israel, *Die Geschichte fun der Literatur bei Yiden*, Vilna, 1929-1935, 6 vols., 8 pts. Occasional discussion of memoirs.

III

BOOK ONE

FAMILY ALBUM: The manscript of Ahimaaz' memoirs—he modestly calls it *Sepher Yuhasin*—was discovered by Adolph Neubauer in the Cathedral Library of Toledo in 1895, after being buried more than 800 years, and reproduced in his *Anecdota Oxoniensia*, vol. II, pp. 111-132 (Oxford, 1895). The present translation by Leo W. Schwarz is abridged and the order of the original somewhat rearranged. Kahana has edited the text, with notes in *Sifruth ha-Historia ha-Yisraelith*, vol. I, pp. 113-140 (Warsaw, 1922), and M. Salzmann has edited a critical edition with a rather literal translation in *The Chronicle of Ahimaaz* (New York, 1924). There is also a brief self-portrait of the famous physician Sabbatai ben Abraham Donnolo (913-982), a relative of Shephatiah ben Amittai, in the Preface to his commentary on *Sefer Yezira*, p. 123 ff. (Warsaw edition). Another personality in the 9th century of whom we have a bit of autobiography is Eldad the Danite. See the English version in L. W. Schwarz' *The Jewish Caravan* (New York, 1935), pp. 193-196, and the critical edition of D. H. Müller, *Die Recensionen und Versionen des Eldad Had-dani* (Vienna, 1892). For the contemporary Arabic account of Ibn Yaaqûb, a Jewish ambassador to the court of Otto the Great, see G. Jacob, *Ein Arabischer Berichterstatter aus dem 10. Jahrhundert* (Berlin, 1896).

LOGBOOK OF A PHYSICIAN: Five of these excerpts are from the personal correspondence of Maimonides, collected in A. Lichtenberg's *Kobez Teshuboth ha-Rambam* (Leipzig, 1859). The first jotting is quoted by a 16th century writer, Eliezer Askari, from an old manuscript in his *Sefer Haredim* (Sedilikow, 1836). It fittingly opens the account, despite the doubt that has been cast upon its authenticity (v. Simon Eppenstein, "Moses ben Maimon, ein Lebens- und Charakterbild" in *Moses Ben Maimon, Sein Leben, Seine Werke und Sein Einfluss*, edited by J. Guttmann, vol. II, p. 24, Leipzig, 1914). The account under "1172" is excerpted from the noteworthy *Epistle to Yemen*. The whole letter has been rendered freely from a Hebrew translation of the original Arabic, by Sabato Morais, in *The Jewish Quarterly Review*, vol. XXV, no. 4, pp. 330-369 (April, 1935). See also in the same issue, published in commemoration of the 800th anniversary of the birth of M., "Texts By And About Maimonides" by Alexander Marx, which contains the text from another manuscript of the absorbing letter to Samuel ibn Tibbon, included here under '1199' and reprinted from *Maimonides* by Yellin and Abrahams, pp. 202-203 (Phila., 1903), a handy, delightful biography. An illuminating comparative study could be made of M. and the autobiographies of his Islamic contemporaries. Consult, e.g., Heinrich Frick, *Ghazālis Selbstbiographie* (Leipzig, 1926); the first considerable autobiographic Arabic work of the military leader, Usāma ibn Munqidh (1095-1188) in *Souvenirs historiques,* edited by H. Derenbourg (Paris, 1895); and the travel-journal of the poet Ibn Jubyr of Valencia (1145-1217) in *Ibn Gúbayr, Viaggio,* edited by C. Schiaparelli (Rome, 1906). There are also autobiographic passages in the poetry of Judah Halevi (c. 1085-1140) and in the *Tahḳemoni* of Judah Alharizi (1170-1230) particularly the travel-diaries in "Gates" 35 (pp. 289-296) and 45 (pp. 348-369) in the edition of A. Kaminka (Warsaw, 1899) which may be compared with the literary reminiscences of the Arabic editor Yāqūt in his *Geographical and Literary Dictionary,* edited by C. Barbier de Meynard (Paris, 1861).

EVERY MAN HIS OWN MESSIAH: Slightly abridged from "Ozar Eden Ganuz" published in A. Jellinek's *Bet ha-Midrash,* vol. III, pp. xl-xlii (Leipzig, 1855), translated by I. M. Lask. The paragraph relating to the attempted conversion of the Pope is from part of the ms. of "Sefer Eduth" which was reproduced in the *Monatschrift für Geschichte und Wissenschaft des Judentums,* vol. XXXVI, p. 558 (Krotoschin, 1887). The memoir of A.'s pupil is reprinted from G. Sholem's *Major Trends in Jewish Mysticism,* pp. 145-150 (Jerusalem, 1941) where the life and thought of A. are brilliantly elaborated. The following was composed by an otherwise unknown Abraham ben Samuel whom scholars such as Jacob Reifman and Israel Davidson have identified with A. The character of the writer and his individual approach have a great deal in common with that of our subject, and the following translation of what is a spiritual autobiography of a high order is therefore appended here:

> To what avenger of blood shall I cry
> When my eyes are the hands that have shed my blood?
> I have tested the hearts of haters amany
> None can hate me as hates me my heart.
> Many were wounds of foes and their blows.
> None did smite and wound like my soul.
> Wanton misleaders led me to do ill.
> Nothing hath led me astray like mine eyes.
> From fire unto fire I went wandering wide.
> Flame burnt me not like my scorching desires.
> In nets and in traps I was snared, I was caught.
> Never a trap snared me like my soul.
> Scorpion and serpent have stung me and bitten.
> My flesh has been bitten more deep by my teeth.
> Princes gave chase, they pursued me for naught.
> None gave chase as chase gave me my feet.
> Yea my pains grew too mighty, too heavy for me.
> No pain so great as my obduracy.
> Aye, my grief and my sufferings at heart are increased.
> My sins even more, even more.

To whom and of whom can I make my wail
When all my destroyers come forth out of me?
Therefore I know nothing so good as to shelter in Thy hidden mercies.
Make Thy mercies plain unto those who cannot even moan
O God, O King seated on Thy Mercy Throne.

Incidentally, A.'s contemporary, Nahmanides, has recorded his experience at the religious disputation at Barcelona in 1263 in his *Sefer Vikuah ha-Ramban;* v. J. D. Eisenstein's *Ozar Vikuhim,* pp. 86-94 (New York, 1926) which contains extant texts of the most important Jewish-Christian disputations.

BY THE WATERS OF THE TAGUS; Abridged from Asheri's testament in Israel Abrahams' *Hebrew Ethical Wills,* vol. II, pp. 163-200, a testamentary collection that contains occasional autobiographical excursions. Five vivid accounts of the suffering during the Crusades by contemporaries are available in *Hebräische Berichte über die Judenverfolgungen während der Kreuzzüge,* edited by A. Neubauer and M. Stern (Berlin, 1892).

CASTILIAN VIGNETTE: From the Preface of the author's *Tsedah la-Derekh we-Zavdin le-Orha,* translated by Leo W. Schwarz. The text used is that of Kahana, *op. cit.,* vol. II, p. 33 ff. For the brief experiences of Esthori Pharhi, see the preface of *Caftor wa-Pherah,* p. 1 ff. in Edelman edition (Berlin, 1852). Incidentally, until modern times the preface was widely utilized as the literary form in Hebrew literature for autobiography. Mr. Abraham Yaari of the Library of the Hebrew University of Palestine has prepared a bibliography of about 200 examples, which is in manuscript awaiting publication. One of the best sources for memoirs in later Hebrew literature is *Kiryath Sepher* (Jerusalem, 1923—), a quarterly bibliographical review issued by the Library of the Hebrew University.

ADVENTURE IN THE HOLY LAND: A copy of the Florentine manuscript of Meshullam's letter was made by D. Kapsal and A. Berliner and sent to A. M. Luncz who published it in *Yerushalayim,* vol. I, pp. 166-219 (Vienna, 1882). It is reproduced, somewhat massaged, in Eisenstein's *Ozar Masaoth,* pp. 86-106 (New York, 1926) which was used as the text for the translation of E. Adler, *op. cit.,* pp. 156-208. The above-mentioned books contain the texts as well as references to other pilgrims in the Holy land from medieval times to the 18th century. V. also the valuable descriptive bibliography by Luncz, "Sifruth Yisrael be-Madah Erez Yisrael" in *Yerushalayim,* vol. XI-XII, pp. 1-50 (1916), and vol. XIII, pp. 18-40 (1919). An interesting parallel of an Arab historian-traveler will be found in the autobiography of Abdar-Rahman ibn Khaldun (1332-1406) edited in *Prolégomènes* by MacGuckin de Slane (Paris, 1863-68).

TWILIGHT OF SPANISH GLORY: This self-portrait has been pieced together from passages in the Prefaces to A.'s commentaries on the books of Joshua, Kings and Deuteronomy, and translated by Leo W. Schwarz from the texts in Kahana, *op. cit.,* pp. 59-64. V. the autobiographical poem of A.'s son Judah, "Telunah al ha-Zeman" in his *Vikuah al ha-Ahabah,* pp. 6-11 (Lyck, 1871). The expulsion of Jews from Spain is writ large in contemporary records: v. the account of Abraham ben Solomon of Torrutiel who brought up to date the *Sefer ha-Kabbalah* of Abraham ibn Daud and who was a lad of ten when the catastrophe occurred (in Kahana, *op. cit.,* vol. I, pp. 202-205). Among the distinguished refugees was Abraham Zacuto, historian and court astronomer to Emanuel I of Portugal, who frequently alluded to his experiences in his *Sefer Yuhasin* (v. e.g., pp. 57a, 222a-223a, 228a in Freimann edition, Frankfurt a. M., 1924) and the Preface to his astronomical work, *Der Almanach perpetuum des Abraham Zacuto,* edited by B. Cohn, with Hebrew and German texts (Strasburg, 1918). Rabbi Elijah Capsali recorded the tales of the refugees in Candia, thus presenting a vivid eye-witness account in his historical work. V. Moses Lattes, *Likkutim Shonim me-Sefer debei Eliyahu* (Padua, 1870). Similar accounts may be found in the Ibn Vergas' *Shebet Yehuda,* Gedaliah ibn Yahiah's *Shelsheleth ha-Kabbalah,* Joseph Ha-Cohen's *Emek ha-Bakha,* and Joseph ibn Yahia's *Torah Or* (Bologna, 1537-38). There are also tales by refugees in A. Marx' "The Expulsion of the Jews from Spain" in *The Jewish Quarterly Review,* Old Series, vol. XX (1908), pp. 240-271, and addenda in the New Series, vol. II (1911-12), pp. 257-258; also Jacob Moses Toledano, "Mi-Kitbe Yad" in *Hebrew Union College Annual,* vol. V (1928), pp. 403-409. A good account of the decades immediately following the expulsion can be found in S. P. Rabinowitz' *Mosaei Golah* (Warsaw, 1894).

THE ROAD TO ROME: Only a facsimile of the original ms. of the Diary remains in the Bodleian Library in Oxford. It was published by Neubauer, *op. cit.,* vol. II, pp. 133-223 and abridged in Eisenstein, *op. cit.,* from which E. Adler made an English version, *op. cit.,* pp. 251-328. The excerpt here included is the first part of the story, and it is rounded out in the following Molko selection. A handy edition of the original edited by A. Kahana was published in Warsaw, 1922. For a description of R. by Abraham Farissol, a contemporary, v. Kahana, *op. cit.,* vol. II, p. 55 ff.

POPE, EMPEROR, AND THE INQUISITION: from J. Ha-Cohen's *Dibre ha-Yamim le-Malke Sarpath ule-Malke Beth Ottoman Ha-Tugar,* vol. II pp. 91, 94-96 (Amsterdam, 1733), translated by L. W. Schwarz. V. also for additions to the omitted visions *Hayath Kaneh* (17th cent.?). Of the extraordinary circle of mystics in Palestine during this period, M. Probably met Joseph Karo who mentions him in his curious spiritual diary, *Maggid Mesharim* (in which a voice speaking in the first person, quite parallel to Socrates' *daimon,* acts as his mentor). V. also the autobiography of Hayyim Vital, the disciple and successor to Isaac Luria, *Shibhe R. Hayyim Vital* (named also *Sefer ha-Hezyonoth*) which was published from the autograph ms. by a descendant (Jerusalem, 1866).

THE STORY OF MY IMPRISONMENT: The selection is an abridged version of *Megillat Ebah* ("Ebah" comprises the first letters of the opening words of Lamentations, "How doth the city sit solitary!"), translated by I. M. Lask. A text based upon an old ms. in Kahana, *op. cit.,* vol. II, pp. 277-290. David Gans, a contemporary (1541-1613), of Prague chronicled important events in his history, *Zemah David*. There are a goodly number of autobiographical writings of this time, occasioned particularly by the brutalities of the Chmielnicki massacres: *Yaven Mezula* (a phrase from Psalms 69:3, "I am sunk *in deep mire* . . .") by Nathan Nata ben Moses Hanover, in Kahana, *op. cit.,* vol. II, pp. 298-318; the great talmudic scholar Sabbatai Cohen who fled from Vilna to Moravia wrote, in addition to elegaic poems, *Megillat Efah*. V. the Wiener edition of *Shebet Yehuda,* pp. 134-139 (Hanover, 1885). Of the same circle was Aaron Kaidanover who fled to Fürth and tells his story in the Preface to *Birkat ha-Zebah,* edited by his son-in-law Nahum (Amsterdam, 1669). Experiences of those living in Central Europe during the 15th and 16th centuries are recorded in the following: a Hebrew diary edited by M. Ginsburger, *Die Memoiren des Ascher Levy aus Reichshofen im Elsass (1598-1635),* (Berlin, 1913); the diary of the great *shtadlan,* Josselman of Rosheim, edited by Kracauer in *Revue des études juives,* vol. XVI, pp. 85-101; Judah Loeb of Prague described the capture of the city by the Swedes in 1648 in his *Milhama ba-Shalom:* v. Hebrew text and Latin translation by J. C. Wagenseil in *Exercitationes Sex Varii Argumenti,* pp. 103-159 (Altdorf, 1687); another fascinating figure was Joseph Solomon Delmedigo (1591-1657), physician, scholar and traveler whose personality may be glimpsed in the Prefaces to a number of his works by Samuel bar Judah Leib, v. Kahana, *op. cit.,* vol. II, p. 165 ff. Of incomparable interest is a batch of letters written by Jews in Prague on the afternoon of Friday, November 22, 1619, to relatives and friends in Vienna and impounded by the Imperial forces. They were discovered in the Imperial Archives in recent years and published by A. Landau and B. Wachstein in *Jüdische Privatbriefe aus dem Jahre 1619* (Vienna, 1911).

LIFE IN LOMBARDY: The selection is from M.'s *Haye Yehuda,* edited by A. Kahana, p. 13 ff. (Kiev, 1911) and translated by I. M. Lask. Additional personal glimpses can be found in his letters: L. Blau, *Leo Modena's Briefe und Schriftstücke* (Budapest, 1905-06). The earthquake referred to by M. is described in the first part, "Kol Elohim," of *Meor Enayim,* pp. 6-22 (Vilna, 1864) and partly translated by the Editor in the Introduction. The memoir of M.'s grandson, Isaac Ha-Levi, "Medabber Tahpukot," edited by L. Blau in *Ha-zofeh me-Erez ha-Ger,* II-III Budapest, 1912); Joseph ibn Yahia, *op. cit.,* and David ibn Yahia in A.

Marx' *"Glimpses of the Life of an Italian Rabbi . . ."* (listed above under II). In addition to the document from which "Trouble in the Siena Ghetto" is excerpted, there are a number of Italian memoirs of the following centuries: an earthquake in Livorno in 1743 is recorded by a Yedidiah ben Nahman Michael Nahmani in "Megillath Yedidiah mi-Liborno," edited by Isaac Rivkind from a ms. in the Mortimer Schiff Collection of the Jewish Theological Seminary, *Reshumoth,* V, p. 405 ff. (Tel Aviv, 1927); there are flashes of self-revelation in the letters of M. H. Luzzatto; a diary of a medical student in Rome, one Judah Gonzago (the Editor was unsuccessful in his attempts to locate this ms.), is described and quoted from by A. Berliner, "Aus den Memoiren eines römischen Ghetto-jünglings" in *Jahrbuch für jüdische Geschichte und Literatur,* vol. VII, pp. 110-132 (1904); also S. D. Luzzatto's which exists in Italian and German translations, the original having been lost. (*Autobiografia di S. D. Luzzatto* (Padua, 1878), and some recollections of his childhood were published serially between 1858 and 1862 in the earliest Hebrew weekly, *Ha-Maggid* (Lyck).

MY DOUBLE LIFE AND EXCOMMUNICATION: The Latin original may be found in *Uriel Acosta's Selbstbiographie, lateinisch und deutsch* (Leipzig, 1847). The present translation is a revision of the rare Limborch version, *The Remarkable Life of Uriel Acosta* (London, 1740). V. Gebhardt's *Die Schriften des Uriel da Costa* . . . (Amsterdam, 1922); I. Sonne, "Da Costa Studies" in *The Jewish Quarterly Review,* vol. XXII, pp. 247-293. For the picturesque contemporary, Rabbi Manasseh ben Israel, v. the prefatory memoir of *De Termino Vitae,* translated into English by T. Pocock (London, 1709). Manasseh was acquainted with Joseph Delmedigo (v. note on Heller). The luminary of those times, Spinoza, gives occasional personal glimpses in his letters, A. Wolf, *The Correspondence of Spinoza* (London, 1928) and in the first part of the unfinished essay, *On the Improvement of the Understanding.*

TROUBLE IN THE SIENA GHETTO: Pp. 391-399, "The Memoirs of a Siennese Jew (1625-1633)" edited with an admirable Preface and Notes by Cecil Roth in *The Hebrew Union College Annual,* vol. V (Cincinnati, 1928). For other Italian memoirs v. note on Modena.

MEMORIES OF AN UNHAPPY CHILDHOOD: The ms. together with an English version which is used here, slightly revised, was published by Alexander Marx, "A Seventeenth-Century Autobiography," in *The Jewish Quarterly Review,* New Series, vol. VIII, pp. 276-283 (1917-1918).

MY JOYS AND SORROWS: This selection comprises three passages: pp. 146-153, 180-194, 197-208, out of the fifth book of Marvin Lowenthal's *The Memoirs of Glückel of Hameln* (New York, 1932), translated from the original Judeo-German. There are also a number of German and Hebrew versions. Of G.'s notable descendants, two autobiographers, Simon de Geldern and Heinrich Heine, are included in this volume.

DEFEAT OF SATAN: The extraordinary full-length autobiography of E. in which he includes a biography of his illustrious father was published by D. Kahana, *Megillat Sefer* (Warsaw, 1896), the part included here p. 54 ff. A stimulating psychological study of E. has been made in M. J. Cohen's *Jacob Emden: A Man of Controversy* (Phila., 1937). Among contemporaries who crossed swords with E. v. Preface to E. Landau's *Noda bi-Yehudah* (Prague, 1811), and the apologia of J. Eybeschütz *Luhot Eduth* (Altona, 1855). A. Cardoso's autobiography from a ms. in the E. N. Adler collection was published by C. Bernheimer in *The Jewish Quarterly Review*, vol. XVIII, pp. 112-127 (1927-28).

I WAS A SLAVE: From an undated booklet, probably printed in England soon after H.'s death, entitled *An Authentic Narrative of the Life and Conversion of J. C. Lebrecht, a Jew, who died in the Faith of the Son of God, November 13, 1776, at Königsberg in Prussia*. Autobiographies of converts are extensive in and after the 18th century; a reading of the literature is a fascinating excursion into psychology and indicates that the tendency to regard converts as charlatans is unjust. E.g., v. P. Cassel's *Aus guten Stunden* (Berlin, 1874), A. Capadoce, *Conversion du docteur Capadoce, Israélite portugais* (Paris, 1848); *Conversion de Marie-Alphonse Ratisbonne* edited by T. R. de Bussières (Lille, 1894); a Rabbi who became a Protestant minister, C. Freshman's *Autobiography* (Toronto, 1868); of the 3 autobiographical vols. of E. A. Steiner, v. *From Alien to Citizen: the Story of my Life in America* (New York, 1914); R. F. Schwob's *Moi. Juif* (Paris, 1928); two Jews who became converts and returned to the Jewish faith, D. Harnsohn's *Zichroines fun a Baal Teshuvah*, 2 vols. (Jerusalem, 1934), and S. Freuder's *My Return to Judaism* (New York, 1922); and a Catholic convert to Judaism, A. Pallière's *The Unknown Sanctuary*, translated from the French by Mrs. Stephen S. Wise (New York, 1928); the wife of the eminent Catholic philosopher, R. Maritain's *We Have Been Friends Together* (New York, 1942). An extraordinary amount of material has been assembled in the works of S. L. Citron, *Meshumadim* (Warsaw, 1921) and *Me-Ahare ha-Pargod*, 2 vols. (Vilna, 1923).

KING FOR A NIGHT: All the family documents relevant to Saul Wahl were published in H. Edelman's Gedulat Shaul (London, 1854). The translation of the selection by Leo W. Schwarz is from pp. 1-6, based upon a unique ms. in the Bodleian Library, Oxford. For biographical data on K. v. *Shem ha-Gedolim he-Hadosh*, pp. 114-115 (3rd ed. Warsaw, 1882). An historical appraisal in G. Karpeles, *Jewish Literature and Other Essays*, pp. 272-292 (Phila., 1895).

DAYBOOK OF AN ADVENTURER: This travel-diary, together with a documentary study of the Von Geldern family, was first published in D. Kaufmann's *Aus Heinrich Heines Ahnensaal*, pp. 283-296 (Breslau, 1896) and edited in German by H. Rubin in *Archiv für jüdische Familien-*

forschung, vol. I, pp. 18-22, 33-42 (Vienna, 1913) from which the present translation was made by Libby Benedict. The continuation of the diary appears to be in possession of Prof. N. H. Torczyner of the Hebrew University in Jerusalem: v. "Mi-Miktabe Shimeon de Geldern Al Nesioto be-Erez Yisroel" in the Luncz memorial issue of *Yerushalayim,* pp. 106-110 (Jerusalem, 1928) which includes three letters written by G. during his stay in Palestine. The most recent sketch of G. is the first essay in F. Heymann's *Der Chevalier von Geldern* (Amsterdam, 1937).

VICTORY FOR JUSTICE: B.'s memoirs were brought out simultaneously in Hebrew (*Zikronot R. Dob mi-Bolehov,* Berlin, 1922) and English (*The Memoirs of Ber of Bolechow,* London, 1922) by M. Vishnitzer. From the latter the selection here comprises pp. 60-67. For contemporary portraits v. M. Wasserzug's *Memoiren eines polnischen Juden,* edited by H. Loewe (Berlin, 1911), and Isaac Berens'—related to David Oppenheimer—"Eine Familien-Megillah" edited by I. M. Jost in *Jahrbuch für die Geschichte der Juden und des Judenthums,* vol. II, pp. 39-82 (Leipzig, 1861).

PIONEER IN SWEDEN: The ms. written in Judeo-German was first brought out by the Israelitiska Litteratur-Sällkapet edited by J. Seligmann, with a reproduction of a fine oil portrait which hung in the Stockholm Public Gallery: *Aron Isaks Sjelfbiografi* (Stockholm, 1897), the selection here comprising substantially pp. 9-39, translated by Leo W. Schwarz. There are two German versions, *Aaron Isaacs Minnen,* edited by A. Brody and H. Valentin (Stockholm, 1932) and *Denkwürdigkeiten des Aron Isak,* edited by Z. Holm, pseud. (Berlin, 1930); and a Yiddish version edited by N. Shtif, *Aaron Isaacs Autobiografia* (Berlin, 1922). An informative account of seal-engravers is given in "The Jewish Artist before the Time of Emancipation" by F. Landsberger in *The Hebrew Union College Annual,* vol. XVI, pp. 321-414 (1941). Very few memoirs of Scandinavian Jews have been published: v. the lively recollections of M. A. Goldschmidt in the last vol. of his *Collected Works* (Copenhagen, 1887), and the note on the reminiscences of G. Brandes below.

A KABBALIST IN PARIS: The autograph ms. of A.'s diary is in the Library of the Jewish Theological Seminary of New York and has been reproduced in full in *Sefer Maagal Tob ha-Shalem,* edited by A. Freimann, 2 vols. (Jerusalem, 1934): part of it was published by the same editor in the publications of the Mekize Nirdamim (Berlin, 1921) and extracts from 1755-1778 published in E. Adler, *op. cit.,* pp. 345-368 from which the selection here is reprinted. Other contemporary accounts have been made available in J. D. Eisenstein, *op. cit.* The material from the diaries of Ezra Stiles, the first president of Yale University, relating to that picturesque traveler Rabbi Isaac Karrigal is assembled in G. A. Kohut's *Ezra Stiles and the Jews* (New York, 1902). The diary of another observant traveler a generation earlier, one Abraham Levy, written in

Judeo-German, has been preserved: v. *Israelitische Letterbode,* p. 148 ff. (Amsterdam, 1884-1885). As for the Baalshem of London known as Dr. Falk (1708-1782), a ms. diary is preserved in the Beth ha-Midrash of the United Synagogue of London as well as of his valet, Zwi Hirsch of Kalisch. For the latter v. E. N. Adler's *Hebrew Manuscripts,* p. 46, ms. no. 2441 (Cambridge, 1921).

A TRIP WITH ISRAEL BAALSHEM: While hasidic literature is rich in more or less legendary biographical materials, memoirs of the zaddikim are rare. M.'s reminiscences from the text in A. Kahana's *Sefer ha-Hasiduth,* p. 62 (Warsaw, 1922) translated by Leo W. Schwarz. M.'s father, Zwi Hirsch, apparently also knew the Baalshem: v. "Beth Zaddikim" in *Sefer Niflaoth ha-Yehudi* (Warsaw, n.d.) p. 84 ff. Unique in hasidic literature is the autobiography of Nahman of Brazlav's amanuensis, Nathan of Nemerow: *Sefer Yeme Maharnath* (Lublin, 1919) and his volume of correspondence *Sefer Alim li-Terufah* (Berditchev, 1896), and an enlarged edition (Warsaw, 1900). The best sources for personal experiences are the thousands of letters, many of them still in manuscript, written by the zaddikim. Kahana's anthology gives a fair sampling, but even since the publication of his book a batch of the Baalshem's letters have been brought to light.

MY STRUGGLE WITH AMAZONS: M.'s work was first published in 3 vols. (Berlin, 1792-93) and was translated into English by J. C. Murray, *Solomon Maimon: An Autobiography* (Boston, 1888) from which the selection was revised. It is high time that this masterpiece was again made available to the English-reading public. Sidelights on M.'s character in S. J. Wolff *Maimoniana; oder Rhapsodien zur Characteristik Solomon Maimon's* (Berlin, 1813). For M.'s Berlin contemporaries of the Enlightenment, v. L. Bendavid, *Selbstbiographie* (Berlin, 1804) who appears with others in *Bildnisse jetzt-lebende Berliner Gelehrten mit ihren Selbstbiographien* (Berlin, 1805-06) with portraits by J. M. S. Lowe. Of Moses Mendelssohn, who left no memoirs but appears in almost all contemporary memoirs, there is a batch of letters exchanged with Fromet M., largely written in Judeo-German, together with other correspondence in the Jubilee edition of his writings, *Gesammelte Schriften,* vol. XVI (Berlin, 1929) and vol. XI (Berlin, 1932) where the above-mentioned batch is printed in German script; v. also Moses Mendelssohn, *Brautbriefe,* edited by I. Elbogen in the Schocken series (Berlin, 1936). A descendant has gathered the traditions in *The Mendelssohn Family* by S. Hensel (English edition, New York, 1882). V. notes on Heine, Zunz, Herz, below.

WEDDED TO THE MUSE: Some of the latter portions of M.'s self-portrait, which are of especial interest to the literary historian, have been omitted here. The text was printed in *Sefer Zikkaron,* pp. 117-126, edited by N. Sokolow (Warsaw, 1889). V. also M.'s *Mein Leben* (Warsaw, 192?). A batch of ten letters of M.'s were edited by I. Rivkind, "Iggaroth" in

Reshumoth, vol. V, pp. 408-434 (Tel Aviv, 1927). Life in the Russian and Polish villages and cities of that period is recorded in numerous memoirs: e.g., A. Cahan's *Blätter fun mein Leben,* vol. I (New York, 1926); P. Wengeroff's *Memoiren einer Grossmutter; Bilder aus der Kulturgeschichte der Juden Russlands im 19. Jahrhundert* (Berlin, 1908); I. Kopeloff's *Amol is Geven,* with a Preface by H. Zhitlovsky (New York, 1926); G. Lewin's *Das Buch fun mein Leben* (Warsaw, 1937); Shmarya Levin's *Childhood in Exile,* the first of 3 vols. also in Yiddish and Hebrew, translated by Maurice Samuel (New York, 1929); M. Berlin's *Fun Volozhin bis Yerushalyim; Episoden,* 2 vols. (New York, 1933; Hebrew ed. Tel Aviv, 1939); H. Zhitlovsky's *Zichroines fun mein Leben,* 3 vols. (especially II and III) (New York, 1935, 1940); S. Dubnow's *Sefer ha-Hayyim,* vol. I (Tel Aviv, 1936); Dob Stock's (real name: Berl Stock-Sperber) *Mi-Mahoz ha-Yalduth* (Tel Aviv, 1938); A. A. Friedman's *Sefer ha-Zikronoth* (1858-1926) (Tel Aviv, 1926).

HOW I WROTE MY SONGS: Appearing first serially in the *Morgen Journal,* the complete Yiddish text together with an English rendering by S. Hirsdansky and a foreword by M. Rosenfeld was published by the Zunzer Jubilee Committee (New York, 1905). Reprinted here, somewhat revised, are substantially pp. 10-41. V. also M. S. Zunzer's *Yesterday* (New York, 1939). Memoirs of *badhanim, hazzanim, meshorrerim,* etc. are rare, even for our own times. There are some personal notes in Solomon Lifschütz' *Teudath Shlomo* (Offenbach, 1718), a book about cantorial music by a relative of the famed Josef Süss Oppenheimer; v. also the reminiscences of Elkan Cohen in *Oesterreichisch-ungarische Cantoren-Zeitung,* vol. III, nos. 6-8 (Vienna, 1882) and M. Rosenfeld, a cantor in Pisek, *ibid.,* vols. XI-XII (1891-92); A. J. Paperna's *Meine Erinnerungen an A. Goldfaden* (Warsaw, 1923); G. Levin's *Das Buch fun mein Leben; Frülings-johren in Lublin* is replete with musical recollections; P. Minkowsky's "Mi-Sefer Hayyai" in *Reshumoth,* vols. I-V; and A. Friedman's *Fünfzig Yahre in Berlin* (Berlin, 1929).

LOVE FOUND A WAY: Most of the memoirs out of Eastern Europe during the past 75 years mention experiences with hasidism. None are more graphic than K.'s *Meine Zichroines* (2 vols., Berlin, 1922) from which the selection, translated by Samuel Kreiter, comprises substantially vol. I, pp. 185-305.

LIFE OF A HUMORIST: The translation of this fragment is by Tamara Berkowitz Kahana: v. *Das Sholem-Aleichem Buch,* edited by I. D. Berkowitz (New York, 1926). Recollections of S. A. by his son-in-law in *Ha-Rishonim de-Bene Adam,* 2 vols. (Tel Aviv, 1938), and by his brother, W. Rabinovitch, *Mein Bruder Sholem Aleichem* (Kiev, 1939). Of the memoirs of the Yiddish writers, v. those of J. L. Perez, first published in *Die Jüdische Welt* (Vilna) and a Hebrew rendering by M. Z. Wolfobsky, *Zikronotai* (Tel Aviv, 1928), and Sholem Asch's

"Rückblick" in *Menorah: jüdisches Familienblatt für Wissenschaft-Kunst und Literatur,* vol. VIII, pp. 511-538 (Vienna-Berlin, 1930).

MEMORIES OF CHILDHOOD: This selection from "Pirke Zikronoth," which was published in pp. 86-144, vol. V of *Reshumoth,* and translated by I. M. Lask. A. H.'s voluminous correspondence is also revealing: *Iggaroth A. H.,* 6 vols. (Jerusalem, 1923-25). Another recollection of South Russian hasidism by a contemporary writer, A. B. Gottlober, *Zikronoth mi-Me Yalduti,* 3 vols. (Warsaw, 1880-1881).

BEFORE THIRTY: From a posthumously published ms. "Ketaim Autobio-grafiim," pp. 6-17, edited by J. Cohen and F. Lahower in vol. VI *Keneseth* (Tel Aviv, 1941). "Sapiah" was published in vol. II, pp. 129-167 of *Kitbe H. N. Bialik* (Berlin, 1923), and translated into English by I. M. Lask, pp. 39-140 in *Aftergrowth and Other Stories* by H. N. Bialik (Phila., 1939). B.'s letters are published in *Iggaroth,* edited by F. Lahower in 4 vols. (Tel Aviv, 1938). The agony of spiritual read-justment, stimulated by the Enlightenment, runs like a red thread through the memoirs of creative spirits: v. J. L. Gordon's *Kitabe J. L. Gordon,* vol. I (Tel Aviv, 1928); P. Smolenskin's *Ha-Toeh be-Darche ha-Hayyim,* with an introduction by R. Brainin, 4 vols. (Warsaw, 1905), R. Brainin's *Kol Kitbe R. B.,* vol. III (New York, 1940), and M. Ben-Ami, a writer's recollections of S. "Perez Smolenskin" pp. 447-458, 556-573, vol. XLIV (Jerusalem, 1925); M. L. Lilienblum's *Hatot Neurim* (Vienna, 1876); S. Tchernichowsky's brief "Autobiographia" in *Ha-Shiloah,* vol. XXXV, pp. 97-103 (Odessa, 1918).

CHILDHOOD IN LITHUANIA: The ms. is still in progress, and the selec-tion was Englished by the writer's son, Louis Berg. A fascinating portrait of childhood in Lithuania will be found in I. A. Kasovich's *Sechsig Johr Leben* (New York, 1924) which has been rendered into English by Maximilian Hurwitz, *The Days of Our Years* (New York, 1929). V. also E. S. Brudno's *The Fugitive* (New York, 1917).

BOOK TWO

WHEN THE BRITISH CAPTURED SAVANNAH: Unfortunately only this fragment was preserved in White's *Historical Collections of Georgia* (New York, 1855). S.'s father also kept a diary out of which portions are quoted in *The Occident,* vol. I, pp. 381-384, 486-489 (Phila., 1844). V. G. A. Kohut's "Early Jewish Literature in America" in *Publications of the American Jewish Historical Society,* vol. III, p. 115 ff. Autobio-graphical literature of Jews in the Colonial and Revolutionary epoch is sparse, although there is reason to believe that memoirs and bundles of letters are still extant in family papers and official archives. V. note on Noah below and a few brief specimens of Benjamin Franks who sailed on a "brigantine" with Captain Kidd, "Benjamin Franks, Merchant, and Captain Kidd, Pirate" in *Publications of the American Jewish Historical Society,* vol. 31, p. 229 ff. (1928); David S. Franks, an associate of Franklin and Jefferson, in "New Light on the Career of Colonel David S. Franks," by O. S. Straus, *idem,* vol. X, pp. 101-108 (1902), Isaac Gomez, Jr., a New Yorker of the fourth generation then, *idem,* vol. XI, pp. 139-144 (1903); and for letters of the Hendricks, Gratz and Lopez families, v. W. V. Byars, *B. and M. Gratz, Merchants in Philadelphia, 1754-1798* (Jefferson City, 1916); from the family papers of Henry S. Hendricks of New York, C. Roth's *Anglo-Jewish Letters,* pp. 141, 221-228 (London, 1938). Roth also reprints several letters to Lopez on pp. 161-164, 168-170, 177-179. S.'s role as commissary recalls Jews of his age and even earlier who served British and Continental armies: v. D. M. da Costa's diary and letters (Ms. 2227, Catalogue of ms. in the British Museum), several letters published in C. Roth's *Anglo-Jewish Letters,* pp. 136-140; M. Grunwald's *Die Feldzüge Napoleons nach Aufzeichnungen jüdische Teilnehmer und Augenzeugen* (Vienna-Leipzig, 1913); and the *Autobiography of Godfrey Zimmerman, formerly in the Commissariat Dept. of the Army under Napoleon* (London, 1852). As for memoirs of soldiers, with the exception of the *Life* of Josephus, the literature is sparse until modern times when the Jews entered military life either as conscripts or professionals: v. Meno Burg's *Geschichte meines Dienstlebens* (Berlin, 1854); experiences in the Russo-Jap War, G. Levin's *Iberlebenissen* (Vilna, 1931); in enemy armies of World War I, J. Mistal, *Milhomo Notizen fun a Jüdische Officier,* 2 vols. (Warsaw, 1924); S. Eisenberg's *Milhomo-Shtoib* (Klerksdorp, South Africa, 1935); edited by M. Spanier from letters from the front Lieutenant Sender, *Blätter der Erinnerung für seine Freunde* (Hamburg, 1915); H. Bloch's *Kriegstagebuch eines Juden* (Vienna, 1924); and the great Australian commander's letters, edited by F. M. Cutlack, *War Letters of General Monash;* the story of the Jewish Legion in V. Jobotinsky, *op. cit.* (Berlin, 1930); F. Molnar's *Erinnerungen eines Kriegsberichterstatters* (Vienna, 1925).

I PROTECTED OLD GLORY: Pp. 303-307, punctuation and spelling somewhat revised, of *Travels in England, France, Spain and the Barbary States in the Years 1813-14 and 15* (New York, 1819). V. I. Goldberg's biography with full bibliography *Major Noah: American-Jewish Pioneer* (Phila., 1937), and D. Philipson's *The Letters of Rebecca Gratz* (Phila., 1929), L. Hühner's *Rebecca Franks, an American-Jewish Belle of the Revolution* (New York, 1894), and the early chapters of *Reminiscences,* by Isaac M. Wise (Cincinnati, 1901).

MENDOZA, THE FAMOUS PUGILIST: It is curious that in an age when memoirs spawned from the presses and London could boast of many colorful Jews the most interesting work should be that of a pugilist. The Editor is indebted to Mr. Joseph Wheeler, Librarian of the Pratt

Free Library in Baltimore for making available a copy of this rare book, *The Memoirs of Daniel Mendoza* (London, 1826). There are some interesting autobiographical passages by an itinerant Russian savant, Solomon Bennett, in a polemical leaflet against Chief Rabbi Hirschel, *The Present Reign of the Synogogue of Duke's Place Displayed in a Series of Critical Theological and Rabbinical Discussions* . . . (London, 1818); the eccentric acquaintance of Lord Byron, I. Nathan's *Fugitive Pieces and Reminiscences of Lord Byron* (London, 1815); of the popular cantor and singer, with some reference to his competitor, John Braham, in Jacob De Castro's *Memoirs* (London, 1824); some dramatic anecdotes and tales of immigrant life in M. Lissacks *Jewish Perseverance* . . . *An Autobiography* (London, 1851) and Philip Abraham's *Autobiography of a Jewish Gentleman* (London, 1860). On a higher plane are the diaries of the Montefiores compiled by L. Loewe from "five journals by Lady M., besides many valuable papers and letters, including documents of great importance, as well as of no less than eighty-five diaries of Sir Moses M., dating from 1814-1883, all in his own handwriting": *Diaries of Sir Moses and Lady Montefiore* (2 vols.) (London and Chicago, 1890). There are also two volumes of an early daybook of Lady M. published privately both in English and Hebrew (London, 1877), part of the latter being reproduced in Eisenstein, *op. cit.,* pp. 299-330.

SCHOOLDAYS: These diary jottings are combined from *Das Buch Zunz,* pp. 12-18, edited by F. Bamberger (Berlin, 1931) and "Mein erster Unterricht in Wolfenbüttel" in *Jahrbuch für Geschichte und Literatur,* vol. XXX, pp. 131-138 (1937), and translated by Libby Benedict. An excellent study of Z. by S. Baruch (A. S. Oko) "Leopold Zunz—Humanist" in *The Menorah Journal,* vol. IX (1923), pp. 1-9, 128-136, 216-229 (New York). There are some memoirs of a number of great contemporary scholars: I. M. Jost in Pascheles' *Sippurim,* 2 vols. (Prague, 1855); H. Graetz' *Tagebuch,* edited by M. Brann "Aus H. Graetzens Lehr- und Wanderjahren" in *Monatschrift für Geschichte und Wissenschaft des Judenthums,* vols. LX-LXIII (1917-1919); I. H. Weiss' *Zikronotai* (Warsaw, 1895) and an abridged German version by Moritz Zobel, *Meine Lehrjahre* (Berlin, 1936). A vivid account of a meeting with Z. in the summer of 1876 by the poet J. L. Gordon "Shaah Ahath shel Korath Ruah" in *Reshumoth,* vol. V, p. 77 ff. (1927). A brief sketch of a contemporary pedagogue, *Eine Autobiographie,* Heymann Arnheim's in *Israel Lewy Festschrift,* pp. 382-391, edited by M. Grunwald (Breslau, 1911).

THE STAMP OF MY BEING: The selection is abridged from the version of T. W. Evans' *The Memoirs of Heinrich Heine* (London, 1884). G. Karpeles has pieced together autobiographic passages from H.'s other writings in *H. Heines Memoiren* (Berlin, 1909); v. also H. Bieber, *Heinrich Heine: Confessio Judaica* (Berlin, 1925). V. A. Meissner's *Geschichte meines Lebens* (Zurich, 1881), and L. Börne's *Briefe aus Paris 1830-33* (Hamburg, 1832-34).

ROTHSCHILD OF ARTISTS: Out of O.'s *Erinnerungen* edited by A. Oppenheim (Frankfort a.M., 1924) and translated by Libby Benedict. Quite a number of artists of the 19th and 20th centuries have written memoirs, e.g., T. A. Rosenthal's *Erinnerungen eines Malers* (Munich, 1927); I. Ruhumowsky's *Mein Leben und Mein Arbeit* (Paris, 1928); J. Epstein's *Mein Weg von Ost nach West* (Vienna, 1929); T. R. Riess' *Die Sprache des Steines* (Vienna, 1925); Max Liebermann's *Gesammelte Schriften* (Berlin, 1924); L. Pasternak's "Mi-Zikronotai al Tolstoi" in *Ha-Tekufah*, vol. XXV, pp. 554-561; W. Rothenstein's *Men and Memories*, 2 vols. (London, 1931-32); J. Epstein's *Let There Be Sculpture* (New York, 1940); M. Chagall's *Ma Vie* from the Russian by B. Chagall (Paris, 1931) and now being done into Judeo-German. V. note on Schatz below.

A SALONIST REMEMBERS: The reminiscences were dictated to a friend and edited by J. Fürst, *Henriette Herz, ihr Leben und ihre Erinnerungen* (Berlin, 1850), the present selection being translated by Libby Benedict from the excerpt in H. Bach, *op. cit.* Of H.'s contemporaries, v. R. (Lewin) Varnhagen, *Ein Buch des Andenkens,* 3 vols. (Berlin, 1834), and the studies of the latter and Dorothea Mendelssohn in M. Sussman's *Frauen der Romantik* (Jena, 1931). Women memoirists are numerous in the 19th century; e.g., Therese Devrient, *Jugenderinnerungen* (Stuttgart, 1905); for Dorothea M. and the Veits, *Briefwechsel* edited by S. M. Raich, 2 vols. (Mainz, 1881); F. Lewald's *Meine Lebensgeschichte* (1861-1863), 6 vols. (Berlin, 1888); Sarah Bernhardt *Memoiren* edited by A. Kohut (Leipzig, 1908) and *Ma Double Vie* (Paris, 1907); P. Wengeroff, *op. cit.*

VANITIES OF YOUTH: The diary was first published, massaged here and there, by P. Lindau, *Ferdinand Lassalles Tagebuch,* and a faithful edition of the original, edited by F. Hertneck in a book of the same title (Berlin, 1927) from which the selection here was rendered by Libby Benedict. V. E. Bernstein's edition of *Intime Briefe Ferdinand Lassalles an Eltern und Schwestern* (Berlin, 1905). Also the autobiographical passages in Moses Hess' *Rom und Jerusalem* (Vienna, 1919); E. Bernstein's *Kindheit und Jugendjahre, 1850-1872* (Berlin, 1926).

MY MOTHER'S MAGIC: From Anton Bettelheim's *Berthold Auerbach* (Berlin, 1907) translated by L. W. Schwarz. V. A.'s *Tagebuch aus Wien* (Breslau, 1848); Berthold Auerbach's *Briefe an seinen Freund Jacob Auerbach,* 2 vols. (Frankfort a.M., 1884); L. Bamberger's *Erinnerungen* (Berlin, 1899); E. Lasker's *Erlebnisse einer Manneseele* ed. by A. (Stuttgart, 1873); F. Lewald's *Erinnerungen aus dem Jahre 48* (Berlin, 1850).

MUSICAL RECOLLECTIONS: S.'s recollections are incorporated in *Über Juden und Judentum* edited by G. Karpeles (Berlin, 1925) and the selec-

(
tion, reprinted in H. Bach, *op. cit.*, pp. 140-147, was Englished by Libby
Benedict. The immense participation of Jews in the musical world in
the 19th and 20th centuries produced many shelves of memoirs: e.g.,
T. Devrient, *op. cit.* and those of her husband Eduard D., a famous
actor, *Meine Erinnerungen an Felix Mendelssohn-Bartholdy und seine
Briefe an mich* (Leipzig, 1872); Felix Moscheles' *Briefe von Felix Mendelssohn-Bartholdy und Ignaz und Charlotte Moscheles* (Leipzig, 1888),
and of the same notable family, related to Heine, I. Moscheles, *Aus M.'s
Leben* (Leipzig, 1872, and Englished, 1873) and F. Moscheles' *Fragments
of an Autobiography,* in which he mentions a ms. of his mother's
memoirs (New York and London, 1899); F. Hiller's *Erinnerungsblätter,*
with interesting episodes anent Meyerbeer and Men.—Bartholdy (Berlin,
1884); the popular composer Goldfaben is vividly portrayed in A. J.
Paperna's *Meine Erinnerungen an A. Goldfaden* (Warsaw, 1923); the
violin virtuoso and organizer of the Palestine symphony B. Huberman's
Vaterland Europa (Berlin, 1923); significant reflections on a group of
East European singing-actor troupes in F. Kafka's "Aufzeichnungen über
eine jüdische Wandertruppe" in *Almanach des Schocken Verlags* for
1934-35 (Berlin).

TORAH IN AMERICA: The selection is from W.'s Reminiscences, rendered
from the German by D. Philipson, p. 215 ff. (1901). Dr. Jonah B. Wise,
W.'s son, has informed the Editor that W. did not intend to compose
a literary *vita,* but wrote his reminiscences piecemeal when copy was
lacking for *Die Deborah* which he edited. He discontinued in 1857
because "so many of the actors in the stirring scenes of his life were
still living, and he did not wish to present some of these in an unpleasant light, as would have been necessary in describing the motives which
actuated them in their opposition to his plans for union among the
Jewish congregations of the country". American memoirs in the 19th
century are rare, but a large number have been preserved in manuscript
and a dozen or more have been privately published in the last decades.
E.g., v. the reminiscences of a pioneer settler of Ohio, Joseph Jonas, in
the *Occident and American-Jewish Advocate,* vol. I, pp. 547-550; vol. II,
pp. 29-31, 143-147, 244-247; Morris Lasker's "The Story of a Texas
Pioneer" in *The Menorah Journal,* vol. XXIV, no. 2, pp. 194-203 (1936);
the memoirs of a Southern merchant, *Autobiography of Julius Weis*
(privately printed, New Orleans, 1909); interesting Civil War documents,
S. M. Collis' *A Woman's War Record* (New York, 1889) and a Con-
federate Major, Mayer's Diaries, 1862-65 (ms.); the autobiographical
poems of the actress Adah Isaacs Menken, *Infelicia* (Phila., 1869); extracts of "Records of My Family" by Israel Solomon in "An Unfamiliar
Aspect of Anglo-Jewish History", in *Publications of the American Jewish Historical Society,* no. 25 (1917); and for the West "Letters of a
California Pioneer", *ibid.,* no. 31, p. 135 ff. (1928); J. B. Levison's
Memories for My Family (privately printed, San Francisco, 1933) with
some graphic episodes about Virginia City, Nevada in the Wild West
days, and R. Kohut's *My Portion* (New York, 1925). Also D. Philipson's

My Life as an American Jew (Cincinnati, 1941) and C. Adler's *I Have Considered the Days* (Phila., 1941).

MY SOUL'S TRUE NATIVE LAND: The selection comprises pp. 17-18, 40-41, 53-54 of B.'s *Reminiscences of My Childhood and Youth* (New York, 1906). V. the revealing letters to his family *Breve til hjemmet 1870-71* edited by A. Hjorth-Moritzsen (Copenhagen, 1938). V. note on A. Isak above and F. Mauthner below.

WELLSPRINGS OF MY FAITH: The selection is from L.'s *Memoire autobiografiche e carteggi,* 2 vols. (Bologna, 1931, 1935) translated by Marcel Grilli. Available in English is L.'s *God in Freedom,* translated by A. Arbib-Costa, with a biographical memoir by D. Askowith (New York, 1930). For other spiritual odysseys, v. notes on Brandes, Mauthner, Toller, and Buber below. V. G. Levi's *Autobiografia di un padre di famiglia* (Rome, 1868).

A FESTIVAL REVERIE: Pp. 63-75 of *Festival Studies* (London, 1906). A.'s essay, *The Glory of God,* published shortly before his death, is a fitting epitaph; a good biographical appreciation by C. G. Montefiore in *Transactions of the Jewish Historical Society of England,* vol. XI, pp. 239-246 (1926); Lucy Cohen's *Recollections of Claude Goldsmid Montefiore* (London, 1940); also, for the upper strata, *Reminiscences* of Lady Constance Battersea in whom the Rothschild and Montefiore streams meet (London, 1922) and L. Cohen, *Lady de Rothschild and Her Daughters* (London, 1935); unusually vivid is M. Oyved's (Edward Good, famous London cameo dealer) *Visions and Jewels* (London, 1925); a picture of Jewish anarchist circles in London in A. Frumkin's *In Frühling fun Yiddischen Socialism* (New York, 1940); V. Jabotinsky's *Die Geschichte fun Jüdischen Legion* (Warsaw, 1929) contains lively recollections of the experience of the Jewish Legion during World War I. For notations on the memoirs of English Jews who attained distinction in the artistic, literary, political and scientific world, v. C. A. Stonehill's catalogue, *The Jewish Contribution to Civilization,* with a preface by Stefan Zweig (London, 1940). For South Africa, especially the memoirs of the pioneer settler of Natal, N. Isaacs' *Travels and Adventures in Eastern Africa,* 2 vols. reprinted from a rare earlier edition (London, 1936); L. Cohen's *Reminiscences of Kimberly* (Johannesburg, 1911) and *Reminiscences of Johannesburg and London* (London, 1924); and Ferdinand de Rothschild's *Three Weeks in South Africa: A Diary* (London, 1895.)

PREFACE TO SKEPTICISM: Pp. 110-122, of M.'s *Erinnerungen* (Munich, 1918), the note on pp. 306-307 being incorporated in the text. Of extreme interest is M.'s only discussion of the Jewish spirit, "Skepticism and the Jews", in *The Menorah Journal,* vol. X, no. 1, pp. 1-14 (1924). The varieties of spiritual experiences of German-writing intellectuals make a fascinating chapter of modern culture: v. T. Lessing who turned from Christianity to Zionism and was murdered by the Nazis in 1933, *Einmal und Nie Wieder: Erinnerungen,* especially the short testament "Gerichtstag über mich Selbst", pp. 315-332 (Prague, 1935); F. Oppenheimer, important political thinker and leader of the cooperative movement, *Erlebtes, Erstrebtes, Erreichtes: Erinnerungen* (Berlin, 1931); Gustav Landauer, leader of the short-lived Bavarian Soviet who fell with its downfall, *Ein Lebensgang in Briefen,* edited by Martin Buber, 2 vols. (Frankfort a.M., 1929); the great novelist, Jakob Wasserman's *Mein Weg als Deutscher und Jude* (1921), Englished by S. N. Brainin, *My Life as German and Jew* (New York, 1933); F. Kafka's *Tagebücher und Briefe* (Berlin, 1937), and autobiographical fragments in *A Franz Kafka Miscellany* (New York, 1940); the psychologist M. Lazarus' *Aus meiner Jugend, Autobiographie* (Frankfurt a.M., 1913).

THE DEATH AND BIRTH OF AN ARTIST: S.'s memoir was written in 1905 but was first published privately in 1925 (Jerusalem), abridged and revised by the Editor. Antokolski looms large in contemporary memoirs; for his own story, "Autobiografia", *Viestnik Evropy,* 1887. The poet S. S. Frug also wrote his memoirs in the Zionist weekly *Yevreiskaya Shizn,* nos. 39-40 (1916). Considerable relevant material out of contemporary correspondence will be found in F. Kobler's *Jüdische Geschichte in Briefen aus Ost und West* (Vienna, 1938).

FROM RUSSIAN PALE TO ARGENTINIAN PAMPAS: Substantially pp. 13-59, vol. I of *30 Yohr in Argentina: Memoiren fun a Colonist,* 3 vols. (Buenos Aires, 1922-1928) translated by Samuel Kreiter. An abridged version appeared serially in vols. VII-VIII of *Menorah* (Vienna-Berlin, 1929-1930). The Editor has not been able to locate any other Latin-American memoirs of Jews, and those of agriculturalists in all countries are rare. There is a literary description of the Jewish colonies in the Entre Rios in Alberto Gerchunoff's *Los Gauchos Judíos* (Buenos Aires, 1926). On the Woodbine Colony in New Jersey, v. K. Sabsovich's *Adventures in Idealism* (privately printed, New York, 1922).

BIRTH PANGS IN ZION: From S.'s *Zikronoth,* vol. I, p. 64 ff., 3 vols. (Tel Aviv, 1928-1929). Life of the early settlers, native and immigrant, in Palestine is described in numerous memoirs: v. J. D. Yellin's *Zikronoth le-Ben Yerushalayim* (Jerusalem, 1924) and his daughter-in-law, I. Yellin's *Le-Zeazae: Zikronotai,* 2 vols. (Jerusalem, 1938, 1941); the latter's father, Y. M. Pines' *Kitbe,* vol. I (Jerusalem, 1935); I. Nussenbaum's *Ale Heldi,* p. 203 ff. (Warsaw, 1929); A. Frumkin, *op. cit.* old Jerusalem and the early Hebrew press in chapter I; Ahad Ha'am, *op. cit.,* p. 95 ff., daybook of visit to Palestine in 1891; E. C. Reiss, *Me-Zikronot Ish Yemshalayim* (Jerusalem, 1934); the years 1907-1919 of a noted Hebraist, N. Touroff in *Sefer Touroff,* pp. 25-39 (Boston, 1938); M. Diezengoff, the popular mayor of Tel Aviv, *Pirke Zikronoth min ha-Eber ha-Karob* (Tel Aviv, 1931) and E. Ben-Yehudah below.

BIRTH OF A ZIONIST: The selection comprises the early jottings in H.'s magnificent *Tagebücher*, 3 vols. (Berlin, 1922-1923) of which an abridged version was rendered serially in the *New Judea* v. III-IV (1926-1927)—reprinted here are excerpts in Oct. 15, 29, and Dec. 24th, 1926—as well as in the memorial issue of the *New Palestine*, pp. 129-180 (1929), the latter translated by Maurice Samuel. A brief memoir "Selbstbiographie" opens *Theodor Herzls Zionistische Schriften* edited by L. Kellner (Berlin, 1920). H.'s letters from 1896-1904 *Miktabim* (Tel Aviv, 1938). H.'s collaborator Max Nordau's brief "Meine Selbstbiographie" in *Zionistische Schriften* (Berlin, 1923); Shmarya Levin's *Be-Maaraka* (English translation *The Arena*, New York, 1932), vol. III of *Me-Zikronoth Hayai* (Tel Aviv, 1939); the beginnings of socialist-Zionism are related in *Kitbe Nahman Syrkin*, vol. I, pp. 281-305 (Tel Aviv, 1939) and Zerubbabel (real name, J. Witkin) *In Anfang*, vol. I (Tel Aviv, 1938); the leader of the Misrahi party, M. Berlin's *Zikronoth*, 2 vols. (Tel Aviv, 1939-1940); the leader of the Revisionist party, V. Jabotinsky's "Sippur Yamai" in *Golah ve-Hithboleluth*, vol. I, pp. 17-96 (Tel Aviv, 1936).

THE PROPHET'S LANGUAGE—AND THE PEOPLE'S: Abridged from B-Y.'s memoirs *Ha-Halom we-Shibro* which was published serially from 1917-1918 in *Ha-Toren*, vols. IV-V (New York) and translated by Maurice T. Galpert. V. 60th Anniversary Volume *Sefer Zikkaron*, especially recollections of B-Y.'s son, Ben Avi, p. 31 ff. (New York, 1918) V. previous note for memoirs of contemporaries.

MY LIFE IN SAN FRANCISCO: Pp. 35-62 from K.'s *My Portion* (New York, 1925). American Jews have produced a vast array—about 175—of memoirs in the last three generations. About 35 are listed in J. Mersand's "American Literature on and by Jews", in the *Universal Jewish Encyclopaedia*, vol. I, p. 269. Among the best are those in Yiddish: A. Cahan's *Blätter fun Mein Leben*, 5 vols. (New York, 1926-1931), I. Kopeloff's *Amol in America: Zikroines fun dem Yiddischen Leben in America in die Yohren 1883-1904;* Z. H. Masliansky's *Zichroines: Finfzig Yohr Leben un Kämpfen* (New York, 1924), and I. Kasovich, *op. cit.;* outstanding for literary quality are L. Lewisohn's *Upstream* (New York, 1922), *Israel* (New York, 1925), and *Mid-Channel* (New York, 1929); M. Hindus' *Green Worlds* (New York, 1938); M. Samuel's *I, The Jew* (New York, 1927); J. Cournos' *Autobiography* (New York, 1935); H. Woodward's *Through Many Windows* (New York, 1926) and *Three Flights Up* (New York, 1935); M. Gold's *Jews Without Money* (New York, 1930); E. Ferber's *A Peculiar Treasure* (New York, 1939); L. Untermeyer's *From Another World* (New York, 1939); among those in high places: O. S. Straus' *Under Four Administrations: From Cleveland to Taft* (New York, 1922); H. Morgenthau's (father of Henry Morgenthau, Jr.) *All in a Lifetime* (New York, 1923); A. Flexner's *I Remember* (New York, 1940); and L. D. Wald's *Windows on Henry Street* (New York, 1934). Of the large World War I vintage dealing with immigrant adjustment: M. E. Ravage's *An American in the Making* (New York, 1917); E. Hasanovitz' *One of Them* (Boston, 1918); R. Cohen's *Out of the Shadow* (New York, 1918); and M. Antin's *The Promised Land*.

THE ANARCHIST IDEAL: Pp. 57-84 of F.'s *In Frühling fun Yiddischen Socialism*, translated by Samuel Kreiter. Apart from those who synthesized the radical ideologies with Judaism mentioned above, Jews who participated in the great social and labor movements have recorded their experiences in numerous memoirs: the activities of a Russian revolutionary between 1893-1906, who finally settled in Palestine, M. M. Rosenbaum's *Mi-Zikronotaiv shel Socialist-Revoluzonär* (Tel Aviv, 1935); for the Bund, H. L. Posnanski's *Memoiren fun a Bundist*, 2 vols. (Warsaw, 1938), and H. K. Blum's *Zichroines fun a Bundist: Blätter fun Unterirdischen Leben in Zarischen Russland* (New York, 1940); a fascinating account of Siberian exile by the father of the Palestine labor leader and archeologist, Ben-Zwi, Z. *Shimshi* (Jerusalem, 1938); the lives of two famous anarchist collaborators, A. Berkman's *Prison Memoirs of an Anarchist* (New York, 1912) and later experiences in *Now and After* (New York, 1929), and E. Goldman's *Living My Life*, 2 vols. (New York, 1931); L. Trotsky's (real name, Leo Davidovich Bronstein) *My Life* (New York, 1930); among the communist memoirs of Russia, Germany and America, E. Mühsam's *Selbstbiographie* (Berlin, 1928), R. Luxemburg, *Briefe aus dem Gefängnis* (Berlin, 1922), I. Steinberg, *Als Ich Volkscommissar War* (Munich, 1929); J. Freeman's *An American Testament: A Narrative of Rebels and Romantics* (New York, 1936); among the socialists: G. Dobrogeanu's *Amintisi din trecutul in-departat* (Bucharest, 1908); E. Bernstein's *Entwicklungsgang eines Sozialisten* (Berlin, 1930); A. Cahan, *op. cit.*; M. Hillquit's *Loose Leaves from a Busy Life* (New York, 1934); among labor leaders, V. Medem's *Fun mein Leben*, 2 vols. (New York, 1923); S. Gompers, *Seventy Years of Life and Labor*, 2 vols. (New York, 1925); A. Rosenberg's *Die Clockmacher un zehre Unions: Erinnerungen* (New York, 1920); and an unusual account of a worker in C. Reznikoff's *Early History of a Sewing-Machine Worker* (New York, 1936).

MY ROAD TO HASIDISM: From "Mein Weg zum Chassidismus", pp. 659-672 in *Die Chassidischen Bücher*, translated by Libby Benedict (Hellerau, 1928). H. Kohn has written a full biography, *Martin Buber, sein Werk und seine Zeit* (Hellerau, 1930). Cp. B.'s preeminent collaborator F. Rosenzweig's *Briefe* (Berlin, 1935).

IN THE WAKE OF THE RUSSIAN REVOLUTION: The selection is from *Zikronoth*, vol. IV, pp. 7-14 (Tel Aviv, 1936) translated by Maurice T. Galpern. Jewish memoirs of this period are sparse, although it is probable that many have been preserved in manuscript for posthumous publication. V. the jottings from March to November, 1917 in S. M.

Dubnow's "Aus Meinem Tagebuch" in *Menorah,* vol. V, no. 1, pp. 14-15 (Jan. 1927); A. Rosowsky's *Zikronoth Krim* (Tel Aviv, 1940); B-Z. Alfas' *Toledah ve-Zikronoth,* p. 81 ff. (Jerusalem, 1941); I. Babel's semi-autobiographical tales in *Red Cavalry* (New York, 1929).

THE WORLD IS MY FATHERLAND: T.'s autobiography was first published as *Eine Jugend in Deutschland* (Amsterdam, 1933) and brought out in English under the title, *I Was a German* (New York, 1934) of which the selection comprises pp. 11-24, 284-286. V. notes on Mauthner.

ON THE MOUNT OF OLIVES: Vol. VIII, no. 1, pp. 36-40 in *The Menorah Journal* (1922). For Henrietta Szold, mentioned by S.—unfortunately she kept no diary—v. *Henrietta Szold: Life and Letters,* edited by Marvin Lowenthal (New York, 1942). The postwar (I) period in Palestine has yielded a little library of memoirs, some of which are mentioned in previous notes and in the collections in I of Sources and Literature. V. also: *Me-Haye Joseph Trumpeldor,* from his letters and diary (Tel Aviv, 1922); A. Ben-Shalom's *Deep Furrows: Pioneer Life in the Collective in Palestine,* translated by F. Burnce (Boston, 1937), a German emigré; E. Hathern's *Going Home* (New York, 1938); the artist Rubin's "I Find Myself" in *The Menorah Journal,* vol. XII, no. 5 (1926); a Zionist official, F. Kisch's *Palestine Diary* (London, 1938); and many in the volumes of *Keneseth, Davar* and listings in *Kiryat Sefer* (Jerusalem).

ISRAEL: LOST AND REGAINED: From "Pourquoi Je Suis Juif" in F.'s *Isräel et Moi* (Paris, 1936) and published in English, *Why I Am a Jew* (New York, 1929) in a translation by Mrs. Stephen S. Wise, the selection comprising pp. 1-48. A volume of extracts from the letters of F.'s son who was killed at the front; D. Fleg, *Carnets* (Avignon, 1941). For the Dreyfus affair v. A. Dreyfus, *Cinq Années de Ma Vie* (Paris, 1901), translated into English, *Five Years of My Life* (New York, 1901, and *The Dreyfus Case, by the Man, Alfred Dreyfus and his Son Pierre Dreyfus,* edited by C. McKing (New Haven, 1937). For similar cases, v. J. S. Bloch's *Erinnerungen aus Mein Leben* (Vienna-Leipzig, 1922) translated into English, *My Reminiscences* (New York); the Beilis case in Russia (1911-1913), M. Beilis' *Die Geschichte fun Meine Leiden* (New York, 1931); the Frank case in Atlanta, "Die Frank Drama" in A. Cahan's *Bilder fun Mein Leben* (vol. V of the memoirs), pp. 347-593. Other French memoirs: M. Hartmann's *Tagebuch aus Languedoc und Provence* (Strasburg, 1874); A. Weil's *Ma Jeunesse* (Paris, 1888); E. Blum's *Les Mémoires d'un Vieux Beau* (Paris, 1896).

INDEX

Abarbanel, Don Samuel, 39
Aboulafia, Abraham, xi, 21-29
  disciples of, 22-23
  kabbalistic studies, 24-29
  plans to convert Pope, 21, 24-25
Abrahams, Israel, xi, 404-411
Abramowitz, Sholom Jacob (*see* Mendele Mocher Seforim)
Abravanel, Don Isaac (grandson of Don Isaac Abravanel, diplomat and financier), xxi
Abravanel, Don Isaac (diplomat and financier), 43-47
  escape from Portugal, 44-45
  exile in Naples, 47
  expulsion of Jews, attempt to avert, 46
  finance minister in Spain, 45-46
Abravanel, Samuel (*see* Abarbanel, Don Samuel)
Ahad Ha'am (*see* Ha'am, Ahad)
Ahimaaz ben Paltiel, x, 3-14
Aleichem, Sholem, xi, 243-247, 525, 528
Alliance Israélite Universelle, 484
Almohades, Moorish sect, 15
Alperson, Marcos, 430-442
American Revolutionary War, Savannah Jews in, 283-286
American Women's Zionist Organization (*see* Hadassah)
Amittai, Rabbi, scholar and poet (grandfather of Rabbi Amittai), 4
Amittai, Rabbi, son of Rabbi Shephatiah, 9-10
Anarchists, Jewish (*see* Frumkin, Abraham)
Anthologie Juive, Edmond Fleg, 544
Antisemitism, 390-393, 462, 464-465, 529-539, 558

Antokolsky, Mark, 422, 424, 427
Arbeiter Freind, Yiddish periodical (London), 505-512
Arbeiter Zeitung, Yiddish periodical (New York), 506
Argentine, Jewish settlement in, 430-442, 473
Arnold, Matthew, xxvi
Arnstein, Fanny von, 313
Asher ben Yehiel (father of Judah Asheri), 30, 36
Asheri, Judah (*see* Judah Asheri)
Auerbach, Berthold, 376-377
Azariah dei Rossi, xix-xx, 76
  in Ferrara (Italy) earthquake, xix-xx
Azulai, Hayyim David, 182-189

Baalshem Tob, Israel, 190-191, 264, 518
Barbary States, Jewish U. S. consul in, 287-291
Belasco, David, 500
Ben Yehuda, Eliezer, 482-488
  adopts Hebrew name, 487
  entry into Palestine, 482-483
  Hebrew as national tongue, 486
Ber Birkenthal, wine-merchant, 161-165
Berg, Rebecca Himber, 269-280
Besht (*see* Baalshem Tob, Israel)
Bezalel Art Society, The, 420, 429
Bialik, Hayyim Nahman, 254-268, 527
Book of Creation, The, early Kabbalist work, 23, 29
Brandes, Georg, xxii, 390-394
  enthusiasm for ancient Hellas, 394
  schooldays in Copenhagen, 391
  Orthodox Judaism, views on, 392

591

Buber, Martin, xi, xvi, 233, 514-522
  childhood in Galicia, 514-515
  first published work, 518
  hasidic lore, translations from, 518-519
  retirement from world, 518
  Zionism, first contact with, 517
Buber, Salomon (grandfather of Martin Buber), 516

Cardozo, Abraham, 128
Caspi, Joseph ibn, 186
Chapter of Song, A, Mendele Mocher Seforim, 220
Childhood, Memories of an Unhappy, Anonymous, xi, 103-114
Cohen, Morris (see Brandes, Georg)
Columbus, diary of, 43
Confessions of Heinrich Heine, 337
Costa, Gabriel da (see Costa, Uriel da)
Costa, Uriel da, 91-95
  conversion to Judaism, 85
  controversies with rabbis, 86-89
  education as Roman Catholic, 85
  excommunication of, 90
  execution of sentence, 91
  immortality, views on, 87
  Marrano ancestors of, 84
  Portugal home abandoned, 86
  repudiation of Catholicism, 85
  submission to rabbis, 90
Criticus (see Dubnow, S. M.)

Diaries, Theodor Herzl, 459
Die Deborah, American periodical (German section), 383
Disraeli, Benjamin, Viscount Beaconsfield, xxii
Dov, Israel, 484
Dreyfus Affair, 554-558
Dubnow, S. M., xv, 247
  Jewish emancipation, in Russia, xix
  Turkish Rule in Palestine, xix

Earthquake in Ferrara (Italy), 75
  (see also Azariah dei Rossi)
Ehrenpreis, Marcus, 427

Eisenstadt, Joshua, 454-455
Eldad the Danite, ninth century globe-trotter, 22
Eleazar (son of Rabbi Amittai), 4
Eliezer, Israel ben (see Baalshem Tob, Israel)
Eliot, George, 482
  opinion of Solomon Maimon, 192
Emden, Jacob, 128-139
Esthori Pharhi, 37
Etzel Andergast, Jakob Wassermann, xxii
Excommunication (see Costa, Uriel da)
Expulsion of Jews from Spain, 46-47

Ferrara (Italy) earthquake, Jewish survivors of, xix, xx, xxi
Feuchtwanger, Lion, xxv
Fleg, Edmond, xi, 544-567
  antisemitism, attitude toward, 558
  attracted to the Gospel, 550
  Dreyfus Affair, reaction to, 554-558, 562
  Orthodox Jewish background, 544
  revolt against Judaism, 548
  turns to philosophy, 553
  Zionism, approach to, 564
Folksblatt, Yiddish periodical, 246
Frankfurter Zeitung, German newspaper, 393
Frank, Jacob, 412-414
Frumkin, Abraham, 504-513
Frumkin, Israel Dob (father of Abraham Frumkin), 504

Geddes, Patrick, 541-542
Geldern, Simon de (granduncle of Heinrich Heine), 334-336
  (see also Geldern, Simon von)
Geldern, Simon de (uncle of Heinrich Heine), 330-332
Geldern, Simon von (granduncle of Heinrich Heine), 149-160
  (see also Geldern, Simon de)
Gikitila, Joseph, 23
Ginzberg, Asher (see Ha'am, Ahad)

Glückel of Hameln, xix, 115-127
  death of husband, 115-119
  outwits her son's teacher, 119-120
  records a neighbor's murder, 122-
    127
  visits Copenhagen, 126-127
Goethe, Wolfgang, 338
Golden Treasury of Jewish Literature,
    A, Leo W. Schwarz, xviii
Golding, Louis, 40
Gorky, Maxim, 528
Graetz, Rebecca, 383
Guide to the Perplexed, Moses Mai-
    monides, 22, 25

Ha'am, Ahad, xvi, 248-253, 265, 457
  hasidic education, 249-251
  influence on Bialik, 266
  marriage of, 252
  opposition to hasidism, 249
  visit to wonder-rabbi, 252
Habima Company of Moscow, xvi
Ha-Carmel, Hebrew periodical, 216
Ha-Cohen, Joseph, 62
  (see also Ha-Kohen, Joseph)
Hadassah, 539
Ha-Kohen, Joseph, 402
Ha-Melitz, Hebrew periodical, 216,
    246, 266, 442
Hameln, Hayyim, first husband of
    Glückel, 115
Hananel, Rabbi (son of Rabbi Amit-
    tai), 4, 8, 9, 14
Hankin, Joshua, 454-456, 458
Harvard Menorah Society, xv
Hashomer Hatzair, xvi, xvii
Hasidism, xv-xvii, 190, 233, 249, 256,
    516, 521
Havatseleth, Hebrew periodical, 483-
    485
Hebrew Ethical Wills, Israel Abra-
    hams, xi
Hebrew Union College, xi, 383
Hebrew University in Palestine, xi,
    xvi, 514, 539-544
Heden, Sven, descendant of Aron
    Isak, 166

Heine, Heinrich, 149, 325-355, 367,
    415
  devotion to father, 341-348
  father's relatives, 338
  mother's influence on, 327-329
  mother's religious beliefs, 329
  opinion of French verse, 326
  schooldays of, 350-351
Heine, Maximilian (brother of Hein-
    rich Heine), 325, 341
Heller, Yomtob Lipmann, 68-74
  accused of defaming Christianity,
    71
  books condemned, 72
  ransom of, 73-75
Hemelitz (see Ha-Melitz)
Hertz, Abraham, 139-142
  conversion to Christianity, 140
  ransomed by Jews, 141
  slavery of, 140
Herz, Henriette, 313-318
Herz, Hofrat Markus, first husband
    of Henriette Herz, 313
Herzl, Theodor, xix, 48, 459-481
  antisemitism, his explanation of,
    462, 464-465
  at Third Zionist Congress, 565
  correspondence with Baron Hirsch,
    467-471
  experience with antisemitism, 461-
    462
  first thoughts on Jewish Question,
    460
  further correspondence with Baron
    Hirsch, 476-481
  Jewish novel, his, 461
  Jewish Question and Catholic
    Church, 462-463
  Paris correspondent of Neue Freie
    Presse, 461
  plan for Jewish emigration, 479-481
  proposal to Baron Hirsch, 471-476
Hinkeman, Ernst Toller, 529
Hirsch, Baron Maurice de, 430, 432-
    433, 467-471, 476-481
Humboldt, Alexander von, 313, 317
  friendship with Henriette Herz,
    317

Humboldt, Wilhelm von, 378
Hurwitz, Henry, ix
Hurwitz, Ruth Sapin, xvii

Ibn Tibbon, Samuel, x
Intercollegiate Zionist Society, xv
Isak, Aron, 166-181
Israel Baalshem Tob (see Baalshem Tob, Israel)
Israeli, Isaac, 186

Jabotinsky, Vladimir, 48
Jackson, Helen Hunt, 502
Jehudái Gaon, Rab, 186
Jewish Caravan, The, Leo W. Schwarz, xviii
Jewish King of Poland (see Katzenellenbogen, Pinhas)
Jewish Life in the Middle Ages, Israel Abrahams, 404
Jewish Lives (see Josephus)
Jewish Publication Society of America, xi
Jewish Robinson Crusoe, The, Sholem Aleichem, 245
Jewish State, The, Theodor Herzl, 460
Jews of Zirndorf, The, Jakob Wassermann, xxii
Jews, The, Maurice Fishberg, 393
Josephus, xxv, 451
Judah Asheri, 30-36
    contract with Toledo (Spain) congregation, 31-32
    German ancestors of, 34-35
Jüdische Selbsthass, Der, Theodor Lessing, xxii

Kabbalah, 21, 24-26, 62-63, 183, 185-186, 189, 335
Kabbalistic lore, 189
Kahana, Abraham, xiv
Kant, Immanuel, opinion of Solomon Maimon, 192
Karrigal, Hayyim Isaac, 182
Katzenellenbogen, Pinhas, x, 143-148
    great-grandfather's crowning, 144-5
Kimchi, David, 186

Kohut, Rebekah, xxv, 489-503
    in California, 490-493
    rabbinical life in Virginia, 490
    San Francisco in 1875, 492
    visits Helen Hunt Jackson, 502
Kol Mevasser, Yiddish periodical, 219
Kotick, Ezekiel, 233-242
    hasidic betrothal, 234
    hasidic wedding of, 234-236
    revolt against hasidism, 236-242

Lassalle, Ferdinand, 367-375
    friendship with Heinrich Heine, 367
Lazarus, Moritz, 378
Leberecht, John C. (see Hertz, Abraham)
Legend of the Baal Shem, The, Martin Buber, 519
L'Enfant Prophète, Edmond Fleg, 550
Lessing, Gotthold Ephraim, 267, 316, 415
Lessing, Theodor, ix, xxii
Levi, Cerf (second husband of Glückel of Hameln), 115
Life, Josephus, xxv
Light of the Eyes, Azariah dei Rossi, 76
Lilienblum, Moses L., 267
Lovers of Zion, 444, 453, 505
Luzzatti, Luigi, 395-403
    as agnostic, 399
    as Deist, 403
    relations with Catholics, 400-3
    skepticism toward Judaism, 398
Luzzatto, Moses Hayyim, 214

Maimon, Solomon, 192-207, 313
    second bride, negotiations for, 195-199
    strenuous wedding day, 199
    struggles with mother-in-law, 200-201
Maimonides, Moses, x, xiii, 15-20
    false messiahs, views on, 17-18
    in Palestine, 15
    physician to Vizir al Fadhel, 18
    sanctuary in Cairo, 16
    typical day in life of, 19

Maimon, Moses ben (*see* Maimonides, Moses)

Main Currents in Nineteenth Century Literature, Georg Brandes, 390

Major Trends in Jewish Mysticism, Gershom Sholem, xi

Marx, Alexander, xi

Masé, Jacob Isaievich, 523-529

Masse Mensch, Ernst Toller, 529

Master of the Good Name (*see* Baalshem Tob)

Mauthner, Fritz, 412-419
  believing Jew, 416
  family relations with Frankists, 413-414
  introduction to Hebrew, 415
  miracle-seeking Catholic, 416
  religious instruction of, 417-420
  youthful freethinker, 416

Medigo, Judah Leo, 43

Mein Weg zum Chassidismus, Martin Buber, xi

Meir, Rabbi of Rothenburg, 34-35

Meir Margolis, disciple of Israel Baalshem Tob, 190-191

Meissner, Alfred, 352

Menahem ben Zerah, 37-39
  escape to Toledo (Spain), 38
  experiences Spanish pogrom, 38-39
  expulsion from France, 37-38
  opinion of Samuel Abarbanel, 39

Mendele Mocher Seforim, xix, 208-220, 246

Mendele Mocher Seforim, Dubnow's opinion of, xix

Mendele the Bookseller (*see* Mendele Mocher Seforim)

Mendelssohn, Moses, 192, 315, 317

Mendoza, Daniel, 292-312

Menorah Journal, The, American periodical, xi, xv, xvii

Menorah Movement, The, xv

Meshullam ben Menahem, 40-42

Mishpat Shatom, Mendele Mocher Seforim, 217

Modena, Joseph da, secondhand clothes-dealer, 95-102

Modena, Leone de, xix, 75-83
  twenty-six occupations of, 83
  two brides of, 81-82

Molko, Solomon, 48, 62-67
  boasts of Pope's friendship, 64-65
  condemned by Inquisition, 66-67
  disciple of David Reubeni, 62
  return to Judaism, 62

Montefiore Memorial Foundation, 484

Montefiore, Sir Moses, 485

Morgenstern, Julian, xi

My Life as a German and a Jew, Jakob Wassermann, xxii

Nahman of Brazlaw (grandson of Baalshem Tob), xvi, xvii, 518

Nathan the Wise, Gotthold Ephraim Lessing, 415

Nazimova, Alla, xxii

Neue Freie Presse, Vienna newspaper, 461, 463

Noah, Mordecai Manuel, 287-291

Noah's Ark, Israel Zangwill, 287
  (*see also* Noah, Mordecai Manuel)

Nordau, Max, 480

Oppenheim, Moritz, 356-366
  in Roman ghetto, 360-363
  Rothschilds, relations with, 364-365
  studies art in Italy, 359

Of Service to Life, Jakob Wassermann, xxii

Paltiel, Ahimaaz ben (*see* Ahimaaz ben Paltiel)

Paltiel, Rabbi, master astrologer, xiv, 10-14

Parker, Theodore, 387-388
  praise of Isaac Mayer Wise, 388

Penknife, Sholem Aleichem, 247

Perlman, Eliezer (*see* Ben Yehuda, Eliezer)

Physician to Saladin's vizir (*see* Maimonides, Moses)

Pines, Jehiel, 484, 486-488

Pines, Y. M., 448
  (*see also* Pines, Jehiel)

Pinsker, Lev Seminovich, 444, 447

Piomanes, forced recruitment of Russian Jews, 223-228

Plague in Bohemia, 107-111

Pogrom in Toledo (Spain), 38-39

Pourquoi Je Suis Juif, Edmond Fleg, xi

Rabinovitch, Sholom (*see* Aleichem, Sholem)

Rabotnik, L. (*see* Wolfson, A. L.)

Rashi, 186

Ravinitski, V. H., 243

Recruitment, forced, in Russia, 223-228

Reese, Michael, 493

Reminiscences of Heinrich Heine, Alfred Meissner, 352

Reminiscences, Isaac Mayer Wise, 383

Responsa, Jacob Emden, 138

Reubeni, David, 48-62

  arrival in Rome, 61

  claim to royal blood, 48

  in Cave of Machpelah, 54-55

  in Ethiopia, 49-51

  prisoner of Inquisition, 67

  Solomon Molko disciple of, 63

Rosh (*see* Asher ben Yehiel)

Rossi, Azariah dei (*see* Azariah dei Rossi)

Rothschild, Baron Anselm von, 364-365

Rothschild, Baroness Charlotte von, 364

Rothschild, Leopold de, 408

Rothschild, Baron Lionel de, 408

Sabbatai Zevi, 128, 131-132, 134

Sambatyon River, 22, 211

Sampter, Jessie E., 539-544

Samuel (son of Paltiel), minister of finance in Capua, 14

Schatz, Boris, 420-429

  relations with Mark Antolkolski, 422-423

Schechter, Solomon, influence on Israel Abrahams, 404

Scholem, Gershom (*see* Sholem, Gershom)

Sholem Aleichem (*see* Aleichem, Sholem)

Sheftall, Mordecai, 283-286

Schleiermacher, Friedrich (second husband of Henriette Herz), 313

Shephatiah, Rabbi (son of Rabbi Amittai), 4-8

Sholem, Gershom, xi, 21

Silva, Samuel da, 87

Sippure Maasiyoth, Nahman of Brazlaw, 518

Slavery, Jews sold into, 139-142

Smilanski, Moses, 443-458

Spinoza, Benedictus, 84, 376

Steinthal, Heymann, 378-382

Stepniak, Sergei, 510-511

Stiles, Ezra (first president of Yale), relations with Rabbi Karrigal, 182

Story of Sholem Aleichem's Life, The, Sholem Aleichem, 243

Succahs, English, 404-411

Sutro, Adolph, 493

Swallow Book, Ernst Toller, 529

Swedish Jews, first settlement of, 166-181

Szold, Henrietta, xxv, 540

Three Lectures on Judaism, Martin Buber, 520

Tiomkin, Zev, 443-458

Toller, Ernst, 529-538

To the Bird, Hayyim Nahman Bialik, 267

Tub Taam, Mendele Mocher Seforim, 220

Union of American Hebrew Congregations, 383, 494

Uriel da Costa (*see* Costa, Uriel da)

Vale of Tears, The, Joseph Ha-Kohen, 402

  (*see also* Vale of Weeping)

Vale of Weeping, The, Joseph Ha-Cohen, 62

  (*see also* Vale of Tears)

Vambery, Arminius, 40

Veit, Dorothea, daughter of Moses Mendelssohn, 315-316

Wahl, Saul, 143
Wars of the Jews, Josephus, 451
Wassermann, Jakob, xxii
Wise, Isaac Mayer, 383-390
  Albany supporters of, 386
  Jewish history, his, 344
  life in Albany (New York), 383-384
  opposition to his history, 384, 388
  Rebekah Kohut's memories of, 494-495
Wolf, Emma, 503
Wolfson, A. L., 512
Wolfson, Harry A., xiii

Yiddish literature, rise of, 214-219

Zangwill, Israel, xxvi, 287
Zederbaum, Alexander, 246, 442
Zemiroth Israel, Mendele Mocher Seforim, 219
Zevaat Ribesh, testament of Israel Baalshem Tob, 518
Zevi, Sabbatai (*see* Sabbatai Zevi)
Zion, Ben, 511-512
Zionism, xv, xvi, 248, 443-488, 517, 539-543, 566
Zuccalmaglio, Franz von (friend of Heinrich Heine), 351
Zunser, Eliakum, 221-232, 434
Zunz, Leopold, 319-324
  childhood studies of, 320-323
Zunzer, Eliakum (*see* Zunser, Eliakum)